Disciplining Reproduction

Disciplining Reproduction

*Modernity, American Life Sciences,
and "the Problems of Sex"*

Adele E. Clarke

UNIVERSITY OF CALIFORNIA PRESS
Berkeley   Los Angeles   London

University of California Press
Berkeley and Los Angeles, California

University of California Press, Ltd.
London, England

Library of Congress Cataloging-in-Publication Data

Clarke, Adele E.
    Disciplining reproduction : modernity, American life sciences, and "the problems
of sex" / Adele E. Clarke.
        p.   cm.
    Includes bibliographic references and index
    ISBN 0-520-20720-3 (alk. paper)
    1. Reproduction—Research—United States—History—20th century.
2. Reproductive technology—Social aspects. 3. Sex (Biology)—Research—United
States—History—20th century. 4. Life sciences—Research—United States—
History—20th century. 5. Women—Health and hygiene. 6. Animal breeding.
I. Title.
QP251.C56   1998
612.6'07'2073—dc 21   97-1114

Printed in the United States of America

9   8   7   6   5   4   3   2   1

The paper used in this publication meets the minimum requirements of American
National Standard for Information Sciences—Permanence of Paper for Printed Library
Materials, ANSI Z39.48-1984.

For Allan, without whom . . .

CONTENTS

FIGURES AND TABLES

FIGURES

TABLES

PREFACE AND ACKNOWLEDGMENTS

In the course of most long projects, there are key moments that inform the rest of the work. In 1987 I was invited to give a talk at the Woods Hole Marine Biological Laboratories on Cape Cod, once the summer home of several major American reproductive scientists. Some renowned contemporary reproductive scientists were in the audience, along with historians of science and assorted others. I spoke on how and why the scientific study of reproductive phenomena has been controversial for well over a century and remains so today. I also discussed some of the negative consequences of its being construed as "illegitimate science," for those who do it and for the development of reproductive technologies. Through this talk, I came to realize that most people, including most historians of the life sciences, had not recognized this illegitimacy. The reproductive scientists at the talk and others have subsequently told me they were validated by this recognition of a major ongoing problematic of their work—and private—lives.

The article that grew out of this talk (Clarke 1990a, and included in this volume in revised form as chapter 8) also became standard reading in courses on women's health and women's/feminist studies (worlds I have long been part of), where understanding reproductive issues and the reproductive sciences is seen as important to improving the situations of women. The same paper has also been cited by conservative, often religious groups who are strongly opposed in principle to the reproductive sciences and who have sought to bolster their arguments that such science is dangerous and exploitative. Finally, scholars in history and social studies of science assign the paper because it illustrates so vividly how science is part and parcel of everyday social life and not separate from it.

Thus my work, like the reproductive sciences themselves, stands in several ongoing contested arenas and has multiple audiences who attend to it for divergent and even conflicting reasons. Because of this and recent rapid social changes regarding reproductive issues and technologies, the saga of this particular project is more than usually a chronicle of transformations, including my own transformation into a different kind of scholar writing a book quite different from the one I originally conceived.

The project began in the early 1980s, when one of my professors in graduate school, Sheryl Burt Ruzek, asked, "Why can't a scientist build a career on diaphragm research?" This question riveted me and led my work in a radically new direction, straight into the twentieth-century American life sciences. This book is the long version of my answer. It has ended up telling the story of the formation and coalescence of the American reproductive sciences in biology, medicine, and animal agriculture, ca. 1910–1963, and their relations with other key players in the reproductive arena—philanthropic funding sources and a wide array of birth control advocates.

Sheryl's question about building a career in the reproductive sciences intrigued me because it sat at the intersection of most of my scholarly interests and commitments. I had been teaching in sociology and in the emerging area of women's health and women's studies since 1970. I had also been learning about the practices and politics of contraception not only as a scholar but also as a heterosexual woman of the "boomer" generation who, along with others, assiduously sought the very kinds of control over reproduction I write about in this book. We brought these concerns with us into the women's health movement, connecting quite directly to Margaret Sanger, who wrote in 1919: "To fulfill her duty to herself, a woman must know her own body, its cares and its needs . . . her sexual nature. . . . [A] woman possessing an adequate knowledge of her reproductive functions is the best judge of the time and conditions under which her child should be brought into this world. We further maintain that it is her right . . . to determine whether she shall bear children or not" (p. 11). We became activists on behalf of and against different, and sometimes competing, kinds of reproductive control, understanding that, especially for women, the costs of reproductive control were historically high, and often remain so.

Once back in graduate school, I became increasingly interested in the politics of contraception and thought I would study women's perspectives on different means of birth control. When Sheryl posed her deceptively simple question about science and diaphragm research, I realized that what had barely been studied was the development of the sciences in and through which such technologies were created—what I later came to call the reproductive sciences and which I also later discovered had professional "homes" not only in medicine but also in biology and animal agriculture. I did realize that any adequate answer would be very complicated. It was by then clear to me that the problems with women's health care, including contraceptive inadequacies, were certainly not only due to the relative absence of women providers or even the misogyny of some male providers and scientists—though these exist and are consequential.

Through my studies in the history of medicine, I anticipated that a fuller answer would concern the ways in which the life sciences and biomedicine more broadly had themselves been organized and supported historically, especially those sciences directly and indirectly related to sexuality and reproduction. As I moved into this project that became a love of my life, I was also moving into an emergent specialty then called social studies of science and technology. As core assumptions of scientific methods and theories, institutions, and practices were increasingly interrogated, I joined the exciting fray. At the same time, a distinctively feminist science and technology studies was also being forged, linking women's and women's health movements to new sites in the academy. My project on the reproductive sciences allowed me to integrate my knowledge of women's health with these new approaches, today framed even more broadly as cultural studies of science, technology, and medicine. These approaches deepened my analyses of scientific work and practices, including the organization of research materials. They also legitimated my pursuit of the reproductive sciences across the three professional sites where they developed—biology, medicine, and agriculture—as requisite to understanding both the heterogeneities within these sciences and the multiple (and sometimes gendered) interests and cross-fertilizations involved in developing reproductive technologies. Further, in technology studies, examining the early moments in the development of new technologies, called the design stage, was just becoming a focus of investigation. In computer sciences and elsewhere, developers sought to integrate the concerns of users/consumers before making the major investments involved in mass production and distribution, a process now called democratization of participation at the design stage. My project both fit well with and benefited from such new directions.

During the course of this project I have matured intellectually—and so have feminist and cultural studies of sciences. Early hard-edged critiques of science and medicine have been tempered and complicated through grappling over the years with research that revealed the diversity of both the lived experiences of women and of scientists' practices and commitments. Constraints and contradictions—material and symbolic—abound. Our early analyses have also been extended through wonderful and difficult conversations, first within feminisms and then additionally in cultural studies of science, technology, and medicine, in the various sciences themselves, and increasingly *across* all these disciplinary boundaries. Transgressing such boundaries has become something between a hobby and a life's work for many of us. Translating—both within groups and disciplines (themselves often quite heterogeneous) and across such boundaries—is an ongoing challenge.

While I was right about the complications I would find in the history of the reproductive sciences, the deeply controversial nature of those sciences remains the pivotal point. They are controversial because reproduction itself is controversial. When I presented these materials in the late 1980s, I had to convince people inside the academy and beyond of this all-mediating social fact. As this book goes to press, ongoing U.S. domestic terrorism over abortion, very public debate about new reproductive technologies including cloning, and transnational debate about population size and the availability of contraception are routinely in the news. Such media coverage has made most Americans understand that most things concerned with reproduction, tacitly if not explicitly including the reproductive sciences, are routinely positioned close to some center of controversy. And such controversies will likely intensify. But so too will our desires for enhanced control over reproduction.

Significantly, the deep cultural tensions that have permeated reproductive topics historically and in the present have, I would argue, polarized if not balkanized the reproductive arena so that its diverse participants often can neither see nor hear others clearly, much less appreciate either the diversities of position *within* different groups or the sometimes quite dramatic changes of position taking place. These tensions and blindnesses make it increasingly difficult to create, produce, and distribute reproductive technologies that are safe, effective, desired by consumers, and "work" well not only technically in the bodies of users but also in the incredibly differing social and cultural lives of their users and their radically divergent health care situations across the globe. It is against the historical tensions in the reproductive arena portrayed in this book that efforts are now being mounted to genuinely democratize participation at the technological design stage, democratize access and distribution, and develop improved means of fully assessing the safety and efficacy of contraceptives and other reproductive technologies, including infertility services and innovations in animal agriculture, that are major long-term products of the reproductive sciences.

What will be the future of reproduction? This book is written in part in the belief that good scholarship informs social change. It is intended to intervene in contemporary debates and politics by offering an enhanced understanding of the past and through translations and bridging efforts in the present. Representing *is* intervening; representation is itself, in the end, a politics. The book is aimed simultaneously, therefore, at all the multiple and divergent audiences who care about reproduction, including reproductive scientists (in biology, medicine, and agriculture), feminists and women's health activists, my colleagues in cultural studies of science, technology, and medicine, demographers and sexologists (disciplinary neighbors whose histories have also been shaped by events discussed here), historians, social scientists, policy makers, and others interested for policy or personal or other reasons. History matters.

ACKNOWLEDGMENTS

This project has benefited over the years from the generosity of insightful and stimulating communities of scholars. It began as a dissertation at the University of California, San Francisco, and my deepest gratitude is to my thesis adviser, the late Anselm L. Strauss. Anselm's version of symbolic interactionism and his long-term support of my historical sociological research provided me with the intellectual home I had long been seeking. In my pursuit of the reproductive sciences, I was also following his injunction to study the unstudied—which certainly served me well. Ans was a deeply provocative yet gentle and intellectually empowering adviser, and I shall miss him always. My committee—Howard Becker, Sheryl Ruzek, and Leonard Schatzman—was a delight. Howie's grasp of the problem of the illegitimacy of reproductive research aided my extending that analysis. Sheryl asked the question that triggered it all. Lenny's passion for sociology carried me over many rough spots when I returned to graduate school. Virginia Olesen and Carroll Estes were and still are faculty members and colleagues extraordinaire.

A number of historians have also been key to my progress. Gert Brieger and Dan Todes were both gracious and generous in training me in the history of medicine at UCSF. Jane Maienschein, Charles Rosenberg, Gerald Geison, Gregg Mitman, John Farley, Barbara Rosencrantz, and others validated and supported my work in myriad ways, especially during its early stages. Guenter Risse generously provided me with a joint appointment in the Department of the History of Health Sciences at UCSF and teaching responsibilities that certainly enhanced my confidence as a historian.

My deepest thanks go to the stunningly generous scholarly community that has grown up around the history of reproductive sciences: Merriley Borell, who welcomed me first in 1982, Diana Long (Hall), Susan Bell, Nelly Oudshoorn, and more recently Monica Casper, Naomi Pfeffer, Anni Dugdale, Marcia Meldrum, Renee Courey, Lisa Moore, Julia Rector, and others. Sociologist Rue Bucher's early confirmation of the intersectional nature of the reproductive sciences enterprise was deeply affirming. Her intellectual enthusiasm for this project was matched only by her practical assistance. The work and I have both suffered from her untimely death.

I also participated in three extraordinarily helpful groups during the early years of this project. My dissertation group included Leigh Star, Joan Fujimura, Nan Chico, Rachel Volberg, and Kathy Gregory. My writing group included Leigh Star, Kathy Charmaz, Marilyn Little, and Anna Hazan, who is now deceased and sorely missed. My "cohort" in the graduate sociology program at UCSF—Katarin Jurich, Steve Wallace, Nan Chico, Petra Liljestrand, and Gilly West—succored and sustained me.

A number of other scholars have, over the years, provided further insights and assistance on this and other projects: Donna Haraway, Bruno Latour, Ruth Mahaney, Val Hartouni, Evelyn Keller, Peter Taylor, Jane Jordan, Gail Hornstein, and Susan Greenhalgh. My life and this book were both considerably enhanced by participating in a Residential Research Group in Spring, 1996, at the University of California Systemwide Humanities Research Institute based at UC Irvine. Titled "Postdisciplinary Approaches to the Technosciences," the group was convened by Roddey Reid and Sharon Traweek, and included Joan Fujimura, Val Hartouni, Emily Martin, Jackie Orr, and Molly Rhodes. Chapters were kindly read and commented upon by this group, by the Bay Area Technology Studies Group organized by Gabrielle Hecht of Stanford (and including scholars from Stanford and UC Berkeley, UC San Francisco, and UC Santa Cruz) and by Lily Kay, Lynn Nyhart, Hans H. Simmer, Nelly Oudshoorn, Philip Pauly, and Carol McCann. Scrupulous final reading of the entire manuscript was lovingly provided by Monica Casper and Brian Powers. All mistakes are still mine!

A number of very senior reproductive scientists and people associated with such work were kind enough to grant me interviews. Only the very oldest had had careers spanning the period I was examining, of course, so I used these interviews to explore and confirm my analysis of the historical record. My respondents were, thank goodness, deeply validating, drawing on their experiences as students and telling me stories their own advisers had told them. Respondents willing to be cited for the record included Andrew Nalbandov (University of Illinois), Neena Schwartz (Northwestern University), the late Larry Ewing (Johns Hopkins Medical Institutions), the late Roy O. Greep (Harvard University), George Stabenfelt, Reuben Albaugh, Perry T. Cupps, and Hubert Heitman (all of UC Davis), and John Biggers (Harvard University Medical School). In addition to giving me a wonderful interview, M. C. Shelesnyak (Weizmann Institute, Israel), has most generously commented on papers and provided some historical materials and an exceptional bouillabaisse. Michael Wade at the University of Chicago arranged for me to interview the ecologist Thomas Parkes, now deceased, who had worked down the hall from Frank Lillie and his group in the 1930s. I will never forget the stories, kind assistance, and affirmations they all provided. Several sociologists were exceptionally generous and shared their unpublished materials on the history of the reproductive sciences with me: Carl Backman, Daryl Chubin, and Kenneth E. Studer. I thank them especially.

I was given the opportunity to work full-time on this project, a very special gift, by several Regents and Graduate Opportunity Fellowships from the University of California, San Francisco. The always considerate support of the Graduate Division also included awards of Patent Funds for archival esearch in Chicago and Baltimore. I was able to examine crucial archival materials at the Rockefeller Archive Center thanks to a generous grant from the Rockefeller University. The Century Club of the School of Nursing provided a sorely needed grant to support transcription of my interviews. The Sierra Pacific Region of Soroptomists International, Inc., provided a fellowship and friendly support. Elihu and M. Sue Gerson and Tremont Research Institute provided photocopying and library privileges, as well as initial entrée into the history of biology.

Special thanks for kind assistance are also due to the staffs of several libraries and archives. Nancy Zinn, then UCSF university librarian, consistently provided answers and warm support of the project, as did her assistants. Nancy McCall, assistant archivist, and her associates, Gerald Shorb and Harold Kanarek of the Chesney Archives at Johns Hopkins Medical Institutions, were extraordinarily helpful. Permission to examine the then uncatalogued papers of the Carnegie Institution of Washington's Department of Embryology at Hopkins was invaluable, dust and all. Sioban Harlow provided housing and warm hospitality during my visit. Daniel Meyer, assistant university archivist of special collections at the University of Chicago, was most thoughtful in his assistance. Susan Vasquez of the Carnegie Institution of Washington was more than hospitable in providing access to their records and a photocopying machine. June Bente, manager of the Hartman Library, Ortho Pharmaceutical Corporation, kindly provided an extremely helpful bibliography of pre-1940 works on contraception. Don Kunitz, university archivist, and John Skarstad, special collections archivist, at the University of California, Davis, graciously provided access to their recently acquired papers of the Animal Sciences Department as well as sorely needed historical background. Ruth Davis, former archivist at the Woods Hole Marine Biological Laboratories, was also most helpful.

Last but far from least, I want to thank family and friends for loving and sustained support of many kinds over the years: Allan Regenstreif, the late Agatha McCallum, Nat and Vivian Regensreif, Pam Mendelsohn, Arlene Reiss, Jenny Ross, Dan Doyle, Leigh Star, Geof Bowker, and Fran Strauss. This book has been part of my relationship with my husband, Allan, for more than half of our twenty-five years together. So this book is, finally, for Allan, without whom I have no idea *what* would have happened.

PART ONE

Social Worlds in the Reproductive Arena

CHAPTER ONE

Framing the American Reproductive Sciences

One day in 1914, embryologist Frank R. Lillie, chairman of the Department of Zoology at the University of Chicago, received from the manager of his farm a pair of twin calf fetuses with their placentas intact, still wrapped in the excised womb. The genitalia of one of the fetuses looked rather strange. Thus began Lillie's research on the freemartin, which led to the radical conclusion that embryonic sex differentiation is dependent on blood-borne hormones (Lillie 1917a,b). Freemartins were deemed to be sterile female co-twins to males, fetuses that developed from separate eggs but whose placentas had merged in utero, allowing the crossing of blood systems. Hormones, Lillie concluded, were clearly implicated in the production of sex.[1]

In 1917, George Papanicolaou, a zoologist in the Anatomy Department at Cornell University Medical School, was engaged in sex determination research. One day he decided to see whether cells scraped from the vaginal walls of the guinea pigs he was using could indicate at what stage of the estrus cycle the guinea pigs were (Carmichael 1973:47–49). The technique worked wonderfully. With it, researchers could infer the activity of internal organs, and thus analyze the biological activity of hormones on a routine basis. They could even do so over time, and the process was quick and cheap, and did not require sacrificing the animals (Stockard and Papanicolaou 1917a,b). The fundamental biological assay technique of modern reproductive endocrinological research had been constructed.[2]

During 1917, Margaret Sanger, perhaps the most prominent birth control activist of the twentieth century, was deeply involved in framing the project of achieving women's access to effective means of contraception to enhance women's autonomy. She stated the following goals: "For though the subject is largely *social* and *economic* yet it is in the main *physical* and *medical,* and the object of those advancing the cause is to open the doors of the medical profession, who in turn will force open the doors of the laboratories where our chemists will give the women of the twentieth century reliable and scientific means of contraception hitherto unknown" (Chesler 1992:146).

On a cold Christmas morning in 1921, George Washington Corner, a physician and fledgling reproductive scientist, awoke in Baltimore to discover that it was snowing. He was in the midst of a series of experiments on the monkey *Macaca rhesus* at Johns Hopkins Medical School to determine the parameters of the menstrual cycle, a project that required catching each monkey every day to check the vaginal washings for red blood cells. With public transport halted by the snow, Corner walked five miles to the lab, fed the monkeys, and did his monitoring tasks (Corner 1981:164). By 1929 Corner had mapped out the hormonal action of progesterone, an essential actor in the menstrual cycle and subsequently an actor in birth control pills.[3]

One day in 1928, Harold H. Cole was hired as an assistant professor of animal husbandry at the Davis agricultural college farm of the University of California, Berkeley. He had earlier done research on the estrus cycle in the dog and cow, and for his first new project began to seek a hormone test for pregnancy in the cow and horse, based on Ascheim and Zondek's discovery of a gonadotropin in the urine of pregnant women. Using the immature rat for the assay, he and G. H. Hart soon discovered a new reproductive hormone that came to be known as pregnant mare serum gonadotropin (PMSG). PMSG then led reproductive scientists to a much broader understanding of the complex flows of reproductive hormones. The patent on PMSG funded Cole's and others' reproductive research at Davis for many years (Cole and Hart 1930; Cole 1977).

On Valentine's Day in 1934, Warren Weaver, the new director of the Natural Sciences Division of the newly reorganized Rockefeller Foundation, was developing his own agenda for research support. He framed the problematics before the foundation as follows:

Can man gain an intelligent control of his own power? Can we develop so sound and extensive a genetics that we can hope to breed, in the future, superior men? Can we obtain enough knowledge of the physiology and the psychobiology of sex so that man can bring this pervasive, highly important, and dangerous aspect of life under rational control? Can we unravel the tangled problem of the endocrine glands, and develop, before it is too late, a therapy for the whole hideous range of mental and physical disorders which result from glandular disturbances? Can we solve the mysteries of the various vitamins so that we can nurture a race sufficiently healthy and resistant? Can we release psychology from its present confusion and ineffectiveness and shape it into a tool which every man can use every day? Can man acquire enough knowledge of his own vital processes so that we can hope to rationalize human behavior? Can we, in short, create a new science of man?[4]

The Rockefeller Foundation Board answered in the affirmative.

One day in June 1953, Gregory Pincus opened the door of the fledgling Worcester Institute of Experimental Biology to welcome two women. One was Margaret Sanger, and the other was Katherine McCormack, widow of the International Harvester scion and a benefactor of many of Sanger's projects. Pincus, son of an agricultural scientist from New Jersey, had a Ph.D. in genetics and physiology from Harvard, and his reproductive research included experiments in artificial parthenogenesis. Pincus and his colleague Hudson Hoagland, both unwilling refugees from academia, had founded the Worcester Institute in 1944 and were trying to establish it as a freestanding research shop, doing various kinds of experimental work on contract for pharmaceutical companies and others. The hormone research that Sanger and McCormack discussed with Pincus that day in 1953 ultimately led to the birth control pill of which Pincus is a commonly designated "father." McCormack gave him a check for $10,000 on the spot and several million subsequently.[5]

―――――――――

Each of the individuals just introduced represents one of the major social worlds involved in the disciplining of reproduction in the twentieth century: reproductive scientists in biology, medicine, and agriculture; philanthropic foundations; and birth control advocates. This book offers a wide-angle view of each of these worlds and of their interrelations as, through their often uneasy collaborations, the reproductive sciences emerged and coalesced as scientific disciplines in a world often hostile to their development.

Significantly, in part due to the illegitimacy of pursuing the reproductive sciences, this disciplinary endeavor formed later than the study of other major organ systems such as circulation or respiration, though once established it grew rapidly. For example, not a single English-language book on the reproductive sciences was published until agricultural scientist F. H. A. Marshall's *Physiology of Reproduction* appeared in Britain in 1910. Yet by 1940, investigators in the United States had both developed and coalesced the study of reproductive phenomena into a scientific discipline in biology, medicine, and agriculture. Numerous major research centers together formed an established and growing scientific enterprise. Reproductive scientists had garnered close to $2 million in external research support from major mainstream science sponsors such as the Rockefeller Foundation. And the prestigious National Research Council Committee for Research in Problems of Sex, founded in 1921, had funded basic research on reproduction generously for two decades. The committee provided legitimacy and prestige to the reproductive sciences during their formative years. By 1940, preeminence in the reproductive sciences had clearly passed from British and other European centers to the United States. In what became known as "the American century," American reproductive scientists would retain global leadership until its end.

By the 1960s, some of the major technoscientific products of the reproductive sciences had been developed and tested: estrogen "replacement" therapy for treatment of menopausal women, diethylstilbestrol (DES) to prevent premature labor in pregnant women and as a feed additive for beef cattle, the birth control pill, and the intrauterine contraceptive device (IUD). Moreover, these reproductive technologies were being distributed widely both in what was then known as the Third World, particularly former colonies, and in the industrialized United States through newly inaugurated federal family planning programs intended for every county (Davis 1991).

By the 1960s, then, reproduction was disciplined. The modern American reproductive sciences as a disciplinary formation were successfully entrenched and had established resources and enduring relationships with key audiences, sponsors, and consumers of their technoscientific products. This book tells what I believe are the major stories of the making of the discipline. From 1910 to 1963 there were profound changes in the orientations not only of reproductive scientists but also of their key sponsors and markets—the social worlds of birth control, population control, and eugenics movements, and of private philanthropies. All reconstructed their identities, goals, and work in relation to each other within the wider arena focused on reproduction. They mutually articulated new positions and commitments that were transformed into quid pro quos, and those relationships persist today.

This book attempts to answer the questions: How was this disciplinary project accomplished, by what actors, under what conditions, in whose interests, and with what historical and contemporary consequences? The formation and coalescence of the American reproductive sciences involved complex intersections of a stunning array of actors—human and nonhuman.[6] Scientists of impeccable background and others who were marginalized—Bohemian free lovers, major foundations, rats, guinea pigs, birth control advocates and opponents, cows, opossums, eugenicists, women's and men's bodies (both dead and alive), schools of medicine and agriculture, freemartins, stallion urine, primates, plastics, vaginal cells, sexologists—each and all and many others were involved. From the outset, the intersections among them formed an arena in which many social worlds were in contestation. This arena was a site of considerable and sustained controversy that shaped the disciplinary project itself. The controversy continues to this day.

In the remainder of this chapter, I frame some keywords used throughout the book, discuss five crosscutting themes, and provide a brief overview and user's guide to the book.

KEYWORDS

Keywords dwell on the boundaries between ordinary and technical discourse. They are often "bedeviled by semantic shadows" (Keller and Lloyd 1992:2). For Raymond Williams (1976) they refer to commonly used terms plagued in their usage by multiple current and historically varying meanings. Because the keywords of this project are laden with particular and dense meanings, they are best clarified in advance. They include *disciplining, reproduction, modernity, "the problems of sex," basic research,* and *technoscience.*

Disciplining

I argue that reproduction was *disciplined* in several senses between 1910 and 1963. First, in the sense of disciplinary formation, a scholarly specialty in reproduction was essentially initiated after 1910. A nucleus of reproductive (in contrast with evolutionary, developmental, and/or genetic) problems was then increasingly addressed by researchers in sufficient mutual communication and interaction for reproductive science to be identified as a distinctive social world.[7] By 1940, recognizable collective lines of work by identifiable workers were pursued in disciplinary centers of research in each of the three professional contexts of biology, medicine, and agriculture.

But disciplines are complicated sites. They are often rife with conflict as well as cooperation, marked by competing paradigms of concern and competing hierarchies of power. Different constituents often have different agendas and even different overall projects in mind. Here the term *disciplining* becomes inflected with connotations of exercising *control over* participating individuals and groups both within the discipline and related to it—sharing its wider arena of concern. Disciplining thus can involve policing and enforcing particular perspectives. It can operate not only from the top down but also from the bottom up, sideways, and orthogonally. It can be directed at "allies" and "enemies" as well as at implicated strangers and the nonhuman. Disciplines mark territories and usually seek to do so vividly. They are simultaneously constitutive and controlling.[8]

In modernity, the focus of the collective disciplinary project of the reproductive sciences was also disciplining in another and more specific sense: as exercising control over reproduction itself. The fundamental goal was the development of modern technoscientific means and mechanisms through which human beings could exercise increasing control over their own and other species' reproduction. Control over the timing, means ("artificial" or "natural"), and frequency of conception, and especially its prevention, was at the heart of the modernist reproductive project. This assertion, of course, raises issues of who "controls" or "disciplines" whose reproduction, evoking Foucault's (1975, 1977) analysis of biopower. He argues that the two key sites of modern biopower are the body and population. There has been considerable scholarly attention to the former in the late twentieth century. As we move into the twenty-first, I suspect this volume will be part of a refocusing of attention on the latter (e.g., Haraway 1995; Greenhalgh 1996; Ginsberg and Rapp 1995).

Reproduction

Reproduction here refers to the sexual reproduction of predominantly mammalian species. Both nonmammalian and plant reproduction were also studied assiduously during the early twentieth century, but I do not discuss them.[9] But the term *reproduction,* like *sexuality* (Foucault 1978), is itself a historical conception, though not included in Williams's (1976) *Keywords.* Here I provide only a brief glimpse of these instructive complications.

In 1782, John Wesley commented on Buffon's natural history that Buffon "substitutes for the plain word *Generation,* a quaint word of his own, *Reproduction,* in order to level man not only with the beasts that perish, but with nettles or onions" (Jordanova 1995:372). This is the earliest mention of the changing terminology. The processes of creation of new life that had linked humans to God were thereby shifted linguistically to abstract biological processes that marginalize human agency. Jordanova further notes that "having children" then becomes conceptually linked to copying, as in reproduction furniture. She argues that the concept was in transition over the eighteenth century, moving from home and nonprofessional domains to public and professional ones. Much of the symbolic import of generation was then hidden behind the new scientific and rationalized discourse.[10] Strathern (1992:23) sustains this point, noting that we end up with a cultural discourse that leads us to "imagine the very reproduction of persons in a non-relational way." I agree that the symbolic and relational aspects of reproduction do not remain quiescent but continue to burst forth in controversies over reproductive sciences, technologies, and interventions.

Duden (1991:28) links this terminological shift to other disciplines, arguing that "it was medicine, demography and political science which replaced the expressions of *generatio*—whether Latin or vernacular—with 'reproduction.' Prior to this new definition, there simply was no term in which insemination, conception, pregnancy and birth could have been subsumed." This new definition separated the older scientific nomenclature of the nineteenth century, where the inner landscape was imprinted with the names of its anatomist discoverers, from the new functional terminology of demography and political economy. Conceptually, Duden argues, *reproduction* emerged and was linked to the context of *production* as that term moved into the center of political economy around 1850. Thus even the term *reproduction* itself is modern and inflected by economics.

One of the recurrent problems of the twentieth-century reproductive scientists I studied was their own lack of clarity in terminology, leading to misunderstandings that persisted for years (and, some would argue, that still persist intentionally) (e.g., Lillie 1932; Allen 1932). For present purposes, I have used the following terms as carefully as possible:

sex	biological attributes of male and female
gender	social, cultural, and psychological practices associated with males and females
sexuality	human sexual/erotic concerns, identities, and interactions, including but far from limited to intercourse (animal sexuality is ignored)
reproductive system/ reproduction	the bodily systems of males and females allowing conception, gestation, and birth of new members of mammalian species

All of these, of course, are complex, multiple, ultimately interactive, and meaningful boundaries among them are blurred.[11]

I have used *reproductive sciences* as a generic term to include, umbrella-like, all of the following: reproductive physiology, reproductive endocrinology, nonpathological gynecologic and obstetric research, urologic and andrologic research, and animal science and veterinary science addressing reproductive phenomena. That is, a core argument of this book is that reproduction was disciplined simultaneously in three professional domains: biology, medicine, and agriculture. I needed an overarching term to refer to the enterprise in its broadest senses, as the specificities not only can be narrower but also were historically politicized. For example, when George Corner, with whom I started the book, was quite senior, he said, "I never did and still do not see any reason to call myself anything more than an anatomist" (Raacke 1983:931), despite being known for his reproductive physiology of the female cycle and endocrinological work. Today many (but not all) in the field, broadly conceived, use the term *reproductive sciences*.

Modernity

The reproductive sciences between 1910 and 1963 constituted a modernist enterprise par excellence.[12] Modern approaches sought universal laws of reproduction toward achieving and/or enhancing *control over* reproduction. During the modern era, the reproductive processes focused on most intently by reproductive scientists and clinicians included menstruation, contraception, abortion, birth, and menopause; agricultural reproductive scientists also focused on artificial insemination. Control over reproduction was and still is accomplished by means of Fordist mass production–oriented emphases on the rationalization of reproductive processes, including the production and (re)distribution of new goods, technologies, and health care services that facilitate such control. The engineering of new technologies to enhance control over reproduction, to be mass-produced and distributed, was and remains the modernist goal, ever widening and deepening the global consumer pool.

In sharp contrast, postmodern approaches to reproduction are centered on *transformation of* reproductive bodies and processes, seeking to flexibly redesign those very bodies and processes to achieve a variety of goals. The reproductive processes focused on since the 1960s are conception and (in)fertility, pregnancy, heredity and clinical genetics, and male reproduction. In vitro fertilization and embryo transfer are the central postmodern reproductive technologies in both clinical and agricultural settings. Redesign of bodies is achieved through strategies of flexible accumulation (Harvey 1989) of reproductive capacities. These include fertility and sex preselection services, genetic and fetal screening, counseling, and treatment. The economic aim is to create new market niches for elaborated reproductive services.

In short, the common distinction embodied in the phrase "the *new* reproductive technologies," which began to appear in scholarly as well as popular media in the 1970s, constituted a significant boundary, starting a new era. The "new" reproductive technologies are the postmodern transformative ones (including artificial insemination, even though it was developed earlier). George Corner (1981:165) reflected in his autobiography: "The world is agog with the news of the first 'test-tube' baby. I hardly need to point out that the success of that procedure and similar methods such as artificial insemination *in corpore mulieris* depends basically upon knowledge of the primate cycle that has been worked out since the beginning of the century by a few embryologists and gynecologists in Europe and America, of whom I am one." The test-tube baby moment can be viewed as the beginning of postmodern reproduction. As Franklin (1995:326) notes, there have been "significant shifts in the cultural grounding of assumptions about 'the facts of life.'"

While the modernist reproductive body is Taylored, the postmodern body is tailored. However, there is considerable traffic across the varyingly constructed boundaries. In fact, I argue strongly for the simultaneity of even premodern (primarily herbal) approaches to controlling reproduction with modern and postmodern approaches. Modern modes of control over reproduction are requisite (and usually presumed available) for the implementation of postmodern approaches. There is a historically dynamic and cumulative, *not* an exclusive, relation.[13]

Both modern and postmodern approaches to reproduction are achieved through technoscientific reconfigurations of "nature" that intervene by going "beyond the natural body" (Oudshoorn 1994). Over the past century, the desire for control over reproduction expanded the legitimacy of the scientific study of reproductive processes, which, essentially in tandem, supported the legitimacy of human intervention in reproductive processes—of both other species and our own. Here representation in the lab is followed almost immediately by intervention (Hacking 1983) in the field, coop, sty, pasture, operating room, and bedroom. The legitimacy of both representing and intervening in reproductive processes remains contested. However, technoscientific capacities for intervening have expanded from modernist "control over" reproductive processes in both humans and animals to postmodernist "manipulation of" both processes and products (e.g., Austin and Short 1972/1986). In fact, the human/nonhuman distinction is of *decreasing* relevance to reproductive and genetic scientists as reproduction is more fully rationalized. Only as the century-plus–long visions of collaborative scientific creations via genetic screening and therapies used *conjointly* with reproductive technologies are enacted now and in the future will the dreams of Warren Weaver and many others for "a new science of man" come to full fruition.

This study begins in modernity in 1910, the year in which Marshall published his *Physiology of Reproduction,* signaling the formation of an explicit field of endeavor or line of work in the reproductive sciences in Western Europe and the United States. I am not arguing that scientific problems of reproduction were ignored prior to 1910 (see, e.g., Gasking 1967; Farley 1982), and I discuss turn-of-the-century work and approaches at some length in chapter 2. But it was after 1910, especially in the United States, that research on reproduction became focused on an organized, coherent set of problems with both a clearer scope and clearer boundaries with other disciplines.

I end my examination of the formation and coalescence of the American reproductive research enterprise around 1963. For many sciences in the American context (e.g., physics, chemistry), World War II was a boundary line between historic eras, but this was true only in a very limited sense for the reproductive sciences. Because of their highly controversial status, the reproductive sciences did not benefit until the 1960s from the federal largesse that began immediately after the war through the National Institutes of Health and the National Science Foundation (Greep, Koblinsky, and Jaffe 1976:372–85). I end my story when the new, modern, scientific methods of contraception, developed with private rather than federal support, were first distributed under U.S. government sponsorship both in the United States and internationally. At about this time, significant new federal and private funding began to flow directly to the reproductive sciences and contraceptive development; then, arguably, the modern era began to segue into postmodernity, and a different set of stories about the reproductive sciences began to be enacted.

"The Problems of Sex"

Three lines of scientific research were developing and expanding simultaneously in the early twentieth century, all of which were blurrily associated with the term "the problems of sex": (1) *sexology,* or sexuality research, which focused on behavioral activities and aspects including gender, primarily in humans but also in nonhuman primates and other animals;[14] (2) *the reproductive sciences,* which focused on the biological, medical, and agricultural aspects of sex and reproductive systems; and (3) *contraceptive and fertility research,* which focused on directly developing enhanced control over human reproduction through prevention and/or enhancement of conception by means of technoscientific interventions.[15]

Constructing strong boundaries among these three lines of research was itself a major effort of reproductive scientists during this period. Points of intersection and boundary construction with the other two lines of work are therefore addressed at some length. Chapter 4 examines how reproductive scientists from biology and medicine diverted the founding mission of the Committee for Research in Problems of Sex from its initial focus on studies of human sexuality—sexology—to a new emphasis on basic reproductive biology, especially reproductive endocrinology. In chapter 6 I take up the ferocious construction of the boundary between what was to be legitimate academic reproductive science versus explicitly applied contraceptive research. The latter was almost completely exiled from the academy until after 1963.

Basic Research and Technosciences

I have largely limited my scope to what has been traditionally termed "basic" research work undertaken by investigators in biology, medicine, and agriculture on aspects of mammalian reproduction, as well as work viewed by such individuals as directly contributing to fundamental knowledge of mammalian reproduction. These modern investigators sought knowledge of basic reproductive laws and functions.

By "basic" research, I mean investigations toward understanding "normal" reproductive form and function through morphological, anatomical, physiological, endocrinological and other biochemical approaches. For such research on humans, Fletcher and colleagues (1981:286) use the interesting term "normality studies," referring to investigations of the biology of nondiseased humans. Such a term would also be appropriate for agricultural investigations of basic mammalian reproductive functions in domestic species.

Thus my focus on "basic" research largely excludes investigations of disease, pathology, and treatment interventions. In reproduction as elsewhere, the "normal" is constituted in distinction from the "pathological" (Canguilhem 1978; Foucault 1978). And certainly many reproductive scientists in fact focused on diseases and other pathologies and/or hoped their work would contribute to effective interventions (e.g., Pratt 1932). But for reasons of scope, I generally exclude such work. However, in chapter 6 I do address research on contraception, assuredly considered "applied" research by reproductive scientists and assuredly sought as a technoscientific intervention into normal processes.

But the meanings of the term *technosciences* here are more complicated than mere reference to applied research. First, the term challenges traditional notions that basic research produces technologies in a unidirectional fashion. Instead, the two are loosely viewed as co-constitutive, as hybrid (Latour 1987). Second, it challenges the notion that there is in fact some pure form of research that is totally distinguishable from its application (e.g., Kline 1995). Most life sciences research undertaken in the twentieth century has at least been informed by applied concerns, if not guided by them. The term *technoscience* thus signals these complications. Pickstone (1993b:438) also argues that the term has a "specific historical meaning for fields where knowledge, and practice and the economy were intimately related, where knowledge was saleable," where science involved "the creation and sale of knowledge products."

Considerably greater cultural authority generally accrues to basic scientists than to applied scientists or the developers of new technologies. On the other hand, the latter may glean greater fiscal rewards, especially through ties to industry, which have tended to become more direct across the century.

THEMES

This book tells multiple stories about the reproductive sciences. I center my investigation on the theme of disciplinary formation, examining relations among the heterogeneous social worlds involved and implicated in the wider reproductive arena. Other crosscutting themes include illegitimacy, controversy, and boundaries; gender and the technosciences; and the control of life through the rationalization of reproduction in modernity.

Disciplinary Formation

Recent approaches to examining disciplinary formation and the production of new knowledge in science and technology studies and beyond have challenged earlier assumptions that science and scientific knowledge were somehow different and better (truer) than other kinds of knowledge, somehow asocial in terms of the actual contents of science, and somehow less politically and economically driven in their constitution, institutionalization, and practices than the social sciences, the arts and humanities, or, for that matter, business. These newer studies often assumed that adequate accounts of disciplinary formation require addressing both what were called "internalist" and "externalist" dimensions, including theories, ideas, people, research materials, instruments, institutions, research funding, and contiguous fields. They were concerned with concrete practices, constructed boundaries, and constitutive contextual elements of any and all kinds that appeared empirically salient.[16] Rosenberg (1979b) has termed these more inclusive approaches studies of "the ecology of knowledge" and its production.[17]

A crucial orthogonal angle of vision has focused intently over the past decade or so on private funding sources such as patrons and foundations as central organizing and intervening agencies in the formation and development of disciplines and specialties, especially before World War II. Some of these scholars view foundations as the visible hand of capitalism intervening to control the production of knowledge for their own good. Others foreground foundations' commitments to solving social problems through the application of science.[18] Foundations and philanthropists are certainly central actors followed about in the stories told here. While they undoubtedly had agendas, their actions and commitments were heterogeneous and complicated, open to multiple readings and resistances, a point to which I return in conclusion.

Most recently, additional inflections have been added to understandings of disciplinary formation by "new knowledge studies" critically inquiring into processes of knowledge construction. These approaches study both concrete practices and institutions. In addition, they place greater emphasis on the circulation and consumption of both academic and nonacademic (official/unofficial, approved/subjugated) knowledges. Concern centers on the institutionalization and professionalization of official knowledge production, including articulations among universities, governments, foundations, and interest groups. There also has been special interest in boundary transgressions (e.g., Klein 1996; Gieryn 1995). Drawing extensively on Foucault, the new knowledge studies additionally seek to specify what goes unstudied—what Evelynn Hammonds (1994) calls "black (w)holes"—sites of particular tensions of omission. What goes unstudied may not be seen or perceived, or it may be refused—worthy of note regardless. The new knowledge studies have a radically heterogeneous character: "Disciplinarity is about the coherence of a set of otherwise disparate elements: objects of study, methods of analysis, scholars, students, journals, and grants to name a few. . . . [D]isciplinarity is the means by which ensembles of diverse parts are brought into particular types of knowledge relations with each other" (Messer-Davidow, Shumway, and Sylvan 1993:3).[19] Those *relations* are, then, the objects of study.

Issues of "internal" and "external" approaches to the histories of science and technology have, over the years, been moved alternately between foreground and background. Shapin (1992:351) asserts, and I agree, that it does not suffice merely to wave a wand and state that neither extreme is worthy; instead, we still need "systematic exploration of the complex situated practices historical actors have used to construct *their* internal and *their* external domains." But, with Pickstone (1993b), I would add that ways of knowing are themselves cultural formations, and that we also need to examine how *others* construct sciences and their productions. That is, most sciences and technologies implicate other actors who also should be taken into account.

In the historiography of disciplinary formation, Abir-Am (1985) takes up the basic problem of whether any representation of a science is intrinsically hagiographic, as any advertising can be deemed good advertising. She also asserts that in many scientists' "insider history" accounts, differences and conflicts are papered over (rather than focused on) to further empower the historical disciplinary claims that are being made. Abir-Am calls for a more elaborated analysis of power, conflict, and hierarchy within histories of sciences as ways of opening those histories to the important questions of how things might have been otherwise.

The social worlds and arenas approach, discussed next, allows for precisely such questions. It takes a nondeterminative, empirical approach to disciplinary formation and technology development.

Social Worlds and Arenas

I view the reproductive sciences as social worlds—communities of practice and discourse. My goal is to provide historical sociological portraits of these worlds and of the other major social worlds with which they related in the broader American reproductive arena—philanthropic and birth/population control worlds. I seek to capture the fundamental identities of these worlds and to specify their relationships in Park's (1952) tradition of relating the "Big News." I do not map the reproductive sciences as a self-contained discipline, for that would be partial at best. Rather, I view the reproductive sciences as "situated knowledges" (Haraway 1991), appropriately examined within the broader arena in which they were formed and where they "matter" most.

The roots of social worlds theory lie within the Chicago school of sociology and its symbolic interactionist concerns with the making of communities and organizations and with studying their ecologies in particular ways.[20] The commitments of individual actors to collective action, to group work of some kind (be it state building, social movement organizing, or doing reproductive science), structurally situate those individuals. Social groups (such as disciplines and skilled occupations) are then conceived as "social wholes" (Thomas 1914) that make meaning together and act together locally on the basis of those meanings. Social worlds are, for Mead, Strauss, and myself, "universes of mutual discourse."[21]

Social worlds form fundamental "building blocks" of collective action and are the principal affiliative mechanisms through which people organize social life. Society as a whole can be conceptualized as consisting of a shifting mosaic of social worlds that both touch and interpenetrate.[22] Participation usually remains highly fluid. Some participants cluster around the core of the world and mobilize those around them (Hughes 1971:54). These "entrepreneurs" (Becker 1963) typically remain at the core over time. Social worlds and subworlds themselves become units of analysis in the study of collective action.

The concept of an *arena* of concern and action, composed of multiple social worlds, is central to my view of the reproductive sciences. In arenas, all the social worlds that focus on a given issue meet and interact. The collective actors/social worlds involved in an arena can be stunningly heterogeneous. In arenas, "various issues are debated, negotiated, fought out, forced and manipulated by representatives" of the participating worlds and subworlds (Strauss 1978:124). The analyst needs to elucidate which worlds and subworlds come together in a particular arena and why, what their perspectives are, and what they hope to achieve through collective action.[23]

In arenas, establishing and maintaining *boundaries* between worlds—including gaining social legitimation for the worlds themselves and a variety of claims-making activities—are key activities (Aronson 1984). Indeed, the very history of a social world is commonly constructed in the boundary-making process (Strauss 1982).[24] We can also ask whether there are *implicated actors*—individuals and/or groups or nonhuman entities—who, while they do not participate actively (for whatever reasons), are the targets of or will likely be affected by actions taken within the social world or arena (Clarke and Montini 1993). For example, women as the primary users/consumers of the technoscientific products of the reproductive sciences are usually implicated actors in this arena—not present but clearly targeted.

I use the term *enterprise* (Estes 1979) here to capture and emphasize several particular aspects of the overall reproductive sciences endeavor. The reproductive sciences can be constructed as a set of "going concerns" (Hughes, 1971:53), commodities in a marketplace with producers, audiences, sponsors, and consumers. To some, using such business terms will seem inappropriate. But lines of scientific work resemble other lines of work and owe their continued existence to organized markets and funding for that work. Latour's (1983, 1988) interpretation of Louis Pasteur's transformation of the countryside into his "laboratory" can be viewed as an analysis of the organization of markets for bacteriological research. Sapp's (1983) analysis of competition for control of the field of heredity is similar. Social movements within professions and disciplines, commonly framed as scientific reform movements, are often efforts to organize new markets for the work (Bucher 1988). In short, there is a political economy of disciplinary formation, which market analyses can illuminate. Recent studies of disciplinarity and knowledge production, discussed previously, also echo such concerns (Becher 1989:129–49).

Three features of the social worlds and arenas approach are particularly salient to the study of disciplinary formation. First, the approach includes *all* the key actors in the arena, analyzing their properties and perspectives along with the key issues confronting the arena as a whole. This approach not only follows the scientists (Latour 1987) but also attempts to follow everyone and everything else (human and nonhuman) in the situation or arena.[25] Second, the arenas approach is deeply situational and contingent, with contexts and conditions empirically fleshed out, close to the anthropological tradition of thick description. Interactionists assume that things could have been otherwise and try to examine especially consequential moments, turning points, trajectories and careers (of concepts, people, technologies). Histories matter.

Third, in social worlds analysis there is movement to and fro among what have been termed "internal" (scientific, theoretical, methodological) and "external" (social, cultural, economic, institutional) elements. It is the relations among all these elements, typically heterogeneous, that are most intriguing. For it is here in the complexities of dense situations that disciplinary coherence is constructed. It is these ongoing relations that I attempt to portray in this book, taking up the contents and practices of the reproductive sciences from the practical value of "golden hands" in performing intricate lab surgeries such as rat hypophysectomy (removal of the anterior pituitary gland) to the negotiations between reproductive scientists and birth control advocates over decades. The social worlds/arenas approach enables me to elaborate for the reproductive sciences what Rosenberg (1979b) called an "ecology of knowledge" and the conditions of its production.

Illegitimacy, Controversy, and Boundaries

A third theme of this volume concerns the enduring illegitimacy, marginality, and controversial status of the reproductive sciences as a discipline. I underscore the consequences of controversy for the construction of the boundaries of the discipline, for its practitioners, and for women as the major consumers of its technoscientific products. I use the term *illegitimate* to feature both playfully and seriously the construction of reproductive sciences as "bastard science" and to show how its sustained practice generates sustained controversy. The reproductive sciences are marked on the one hand by great potency in the world and on the other hand by shame.

I both contradict and complicate Foucault's analysis of the relations between the reproductive sciences and sexology. I quote him for clarity's sake below (Foucault 1978:54–55, emphasis added). The two claims that I complicate are italicized:

> When we compare these discourses on human sexuality with what was known at the time about the physiology of animal and plant reproduction, we are struck by the incongruity. Their feeble content from the standpoint of elementary rationality, not to mention scientificity, earns them a place apart in the history of knowledge. They form a strangely muddled zone. Throughout the nineteenth century, sex seems to have been incorporated into two very distinct orders of knowledge: *a biology of reproduction, which developed continuously according to a general scientific normativity,* and a medicine of sex conforming to quite different rules of formation. *From one to the other, there was no real exchange, no reciprocal structuration* . . . [W]e would have to see something more than uneven scientific development . . . the one would partake of that immense will to knowledge which has sustained the establishment of scientific discourse in the West, whereas the other would derive from a stubborn will to nonknowledge.

In contrast to Foucault, I argue that the reproductive sciences were quite late to develop in a modern fashion compared with disciplines centered on other major organ systems. Further, the reproductive sciences were and remain illegitimate science precisely because of their historical and specific relations to sexuality and sexology. The "immense will to knowledge" of Western science in terms of investigating reproduction was actually relatively quiescent until well into the twentieth century.

Moreover, for the "will to knowledge" to express itself, not only did there need to be explicit support for the formation of the reproductive sciences, specifically the birth control, eugenics and neo-Malthusian movements. The very boundaries between what would count as studies of sex (sexology) and studies of reproduction (the reproductive sciences) also needed to be negotiated and constructed. What this ultimately involved was what could be considered a division of labor between these two disciplines emerging in the early decades of the twentieth century. This division of labor concerns what Foucault (1978:103–5) discussed as:

> four great strategic unities which, beginning in the eighteenth century, formed specific mechanisms of knowledge and power centering on sex. . . .
>
> 1. *A hystericization of women's bodies* . . .
> 2. *A pedagogization of children's sex* . . .
> 3. *A socialization of procreative behavior* . . .
> 4. *A psychiatrization of perverse pleasure* . . .
>
> Four figures emerged from this preoccupation with sex, which mounted throughout the nineteenth century—four privileged objects of knowledge, which were also targets and anchorage points for the ventures of knowledge: the hysterical woman, the masturbating child, the Malthusian [contracepting] couple, and the perverse adult.

I argue that the division of labor ultimately negotiated allocated to sexology and psychiatry some aspects of the hysterical woman, children's sexuality, and perverse pleasures. The Malthusian couple and the project of the socialization of procreative behavior fell to the reproductive sciences, along with those aspects of the hysterical woman deemed related to the menstrual/reproductive cycle. (Foucault planned later volumes that would have taken up each of those four topics/objects of knowledge.) This division of scientific labor largely persists.

The study of reproduction was, and for many remains, transgressive. Throughout their disciplinary efforts, reproductive scientists regularly and routinely confronted the fundamental problem of the illegitimacy of reproduction as a focus of scientific work. Because the entire field was deemed at least problematic and at worst reprehensible by various constituencies, its very institutionalization was marked by surprising and shifting alliances, episodic organizational efforts, a constant vigilance, and strong desires for enhanced legitimacy. Rather than follow the more common patterns of emergent disciplines of establishing a freshly and explicitly focused society, journal, and routine funding sources, relations with other social worlds from professional organizations to funding sources have been negotiated and renegotiated over time as circumstances of legitimacy shifted. Much has been indirect, tentative, and temporary that, for other emergent scientific disciplines, was direct, explicit, and fairly permanent.

How reproductive scientists negotiated the challenging social opposition to the construction of an autonomous scientific enterprise is a core theme of this book.[26] Some of the major actors chose to address the illegitimacy of their science directly. In 1921, for example, they chose to name the most prestigious institution in the interwar American reproductive arena the National Research Council Committee for Research in Problems of Sex. And they chose to talk and write explicitly about "the problems of sex." Yet the legitimacy problems of the reproductive sciences have not abated. If anything, "the problems of sex" are now even more hotly, openly, and explicitly contested. The public debate about abortion in the United States over the past decade, coupled with terrorist acts and murders of abortion providers, has brought home again and again how contested these topics are. Abortion is but the tip of the iceberg.

What then is the iceberg? The cultural primacy of sex and reproduction in most human beings' lives on the planet in terms of manhood, womanhood and adulthood places the concerns of sexology and the reproductive sciences at the heart of social life. Further, the embeddedness of reproductive phenomena in family and kinship systems, commonly fundamental to the very ordering of life itself, maintains its cultural centrality (Strathern 1992). But these are not easy issues, and in modernity anxieties about sexuality, reproduction, and families abound. Parenting, like sexuality, can be construed as both sacred and obscene. Issues so central to life itself tend to be contested with a stunning extremity. Franklin (1993) points out that the new reproductive technologies have been used not to challenge but rather to reinforce traditional familial and kinship formations. These conceptive technologies are often made inaccessible to homosexuals, inserting homophobia where it had not dwelt. The center requires the margins.

Boundaries are core elements in the analysis of disciplinary formation and knowledge production. But in controversial, marginalized, outlier disciplines, things are more complicated, and transgressions and gerrymandering are rife. Further, the reproductive sciences exhibit multiple boundaries of concern, *all* of which are somehow problematic. First is the boundary between science and society, usually claimed by science.[27] Second are the boundaries delimiting one scientific discipline from another, typically most important during disciplinary emergence (e.g., Keating, Cambrosio, and McKenzie 1992). Third are the boundaries constructed within a discipline between what is to count as "basic" versus "applied." Fourth, especially in modernity, are the boundaries between the "normal" and the "pathological" (Canguilhem 1978; Fletcher, Fletcher, and Greganti 1981). Fifth are the boundaries of hierarchy, prestige, and cultural authority within a discipline, which typically are highly consequential for individual careers. Last are the boundaries of hierarchy, prestige, and cultural authority among scientific disciplines so consequential for both individual and disciplinary careers—the rank ordering of the sciences themselves (e.g., Whitley 1982).

We enter the historical story of the reproductive sciences as *all* of these boundaries are about to be constructed or reconstructed within the cultural terrain of the sciences established in the late nineteenth century. The boundary between the embryonic reproductive sciences and society is faint and shifting. It is transparent and hence easily transgressed and vulnerable to gerrymandering by political groups. Getting contraceptive research into the laboratories was, after all, Sanger's transgressive goal. The boundaries between scientific disciplines are central to the story because the establishment of the boundaries around genetics and developmental embryology also clarified the parameters of the reproductive sciences. Another boundary between disciplines was contested—that between the reproductive sciences and sexology—which we will watch reproductive scientists assiduously construct in the National Research Council Committee for Research in Problems of Sex. The basic-versus-applied distinction was also problematic for disciplinary formation, as illustrated by the fact that the boundary between the reproductive sciences and contraceptive research remains contested and liminal.

The issues of marginality have been studied extensively in cultural, artistic, and social practices (e.g., Ferguson et al. 1990). Transferring this project to the sciences, looking at a marginal science and the kinds of boundary work involved in establishing and maintaining such an enterprise, tells us much about boundaries themselves and the construction of legitimacy. A core theme of this book, then, is the marginality of the reproductive sciences as they have been ignored, overshadowed, and otherwise made invisible by other sciences during the twentieth century. Such invisibling, especially by other life sciences like genetics, has been a strategy to prevent these other sciences from becoming contaminated by clear association and thereby risking marginalization.

Further, due in part to this marginalization, the formation of the reproductive sciences has been among the most ignored by scholars, despite the discipline's importance to and intervention in millions of human lives throughout the world in even its most remote corners (e.g., Tsing 1993). Although investment in reproductive research has been limited, it is likely that the technoscientific products produced downstream, such as contraceptives, have affected more individuals per dollar invested than any other technologies, with the possible exception of large technological systems such as electricity, telecommunications, and transportation. Gender is implicated.

Gender and the Technosciences of Reproduction

Intensive research on sex, gender, and the technosciences, one of the social worlds in which I participate, has been under way since the 1970s. A core project here has been examination of the construction of sex/gender differences both within and across disciplines from the social sciences to the natural sciences and from classical times to the present. Such studies are intrinsically comparative, both within and across sexes and genders (Jordanova 1993). We have learned much about gender and sex from dissecting classical anatomy, physiology, gynecology, neuroendocrinology, neurology, genetics, space biology, and the rhetorical, material, and other practices of many sciences.[28]

It is difficult to conceive of a more sex- and gender-constructing and maintaining discipline and set of practices and discourses than those of the reproductive sciences, and this is another theme of the book. Through studies of these sciences, feminists have begun to address the socially constructed character of the concept of sex as used within the life sciences. That is, the earlier distinction feminists made between sex as biological/natural and gender as cultural/social/political/economic has itself been exploded. Today *both* concepts, sex and gender, are understood as social constructions. The constructions of nature done by scientists can and do, of course, take material concerns—"real bodies"—into account, as constructions of cultural and social phenomena can do as well. It is the meanings attributed to both nature and culture that are indelibly social, cultural, and deeply historical as well. The attributions are, after all, done by humans. In the case of gender, social scientists have been the primary researchers, while in the case of sex, life scientists have done the bulk of the construction work. But these are matters of emphasis and not exclusion. The concepts of sex and gender deeply implicate each other (Oudshoorn 1996c; see also Oudshoorn 1994, 1995, 1996a,b).

Focusing on the modern reproductive sciences, Borell's groundbreaking work demonstrated the centrality of both sex and gender to early British endocrinology, as the "male" and "female" hormones were being identified and birth control came to the forefront of concern. Oudshoorn has focused on the consequences of the organizational relations of the clinic, the laboratory, and pharmaceutical companies for the development of sex hormones and a new conceptualization of "the gendered hormonal body" in the Netherlands and Europe. Her work demonstrates how enhanced access to women as patients was central to both the production of knowledge and the subsequent distribution of technoscientific treatments that go "beyond the natural body." Hall focused on the construction of American reproductive endocrinology, while Rechter examines early clinical applications of the "male" and "female" hormones and their representation in popular media.[29] Long (1997) has examined how medicine produced what it calls a "controlled vocabulary" for the category "woman" in the early twentieth century. She asks how medicine established a linguistic hegemony over gendered subjects and objects, noting that the *Index Catalogue of America's National Library of Medicine* had no entry for "Male" or "Man" until

1955, while "Women" are constant subjects of attention. Martin's (1987, 1988, 1989, 1990, 1992) work attends to the use of metaphor in these vocabularies past and present. The production of sex itself has also been an especially rich topic.[30] Further, U.S. and transnational women's health movements have been increasingly influential concerning the biomedical inscription of bodies, (re)creations of gender, and dynamics of male dominance through science, technology, and medicine.[31]

We are now able to grasp analytically how sex and gender not only are constructed and produced within disciplines but also are made robust by simultaneous alignments across multiple disciplines. That is, we can see how one discipline can rely on another's "conclusions" as foundational in the production of its own knowledge.[32] This has been a pattern of considerable import in the sciences, especially in relation to gender. Yet disciplinary axes of sexing and gendering are intrinsically unstable and changing, and require regular rearticulation and reframing to maintain their cutting (i.e., classificatory) edges. Hence much work *in* the sciences as well as *on* the sciences remains focused on sex and gender. Problems of sex and gender, like race, do not resolve.

Evelyn Fox Keller argues that we need a new taxonomy for this area of study. She suggests (1995:32) it be schematized as "those studies examining the history of (1) women in science; (2) scientific constructions of sexual difference; and (3) the uses of scientific constructions of subjects and objects that lie both beneath and beyond the human skin (or skeleton)." In the first two, the focus is on women, sex, and gender in science. In the last, currently of considerable concern, the focus is on "gender in science," trading "between historical studies of gender, language and culture in the production of science." My emphasis in this book on the organizational culture of the reproductive sciences during their formation and coalescence addresses this very point.

Keller (1995:33) goes on: "Metaphors of gender can be seen to work, as social images in science invariably do, in two directions: they import social expectations into our [scientific] representations of nature, and by so doing they serve to reify (or naturalize) cultural beliefs or practices." Most feminist studies of the technosciences have focused on the latter, emphasizing the negative effects of such reifications on women. Some other feminist studies, and my project is included here, instead take up the influence of social expectations of gender on the course of scientific knowledge per se.[33] In particular, I discuss the effects on the reproductive sciences of the insistence on retaining the "male" and "female" hormone designations, and the related, broader struggles between a reductionist endocrinological and a more physiologically oriented biology of sex (see chapter 5).

Much feminist research on the technosciences, as elsewhere, places women or gender at the analytic center as the objects and/or subjects of inquiry, in attempting to compensate for prior omissions. I have chosen instead to examine sciences and technologies of particular relevance to women, those that often have profound consequences for women's lives. That is, I have sought here to understand the social and technical implications of the organization of the American reproductive sciences per se for women during the twentieth century. Rather than study downstream effects on women, I study the upstream production of knowledges and technologies. These implications are discussed most explicitly in chapter 6 on the development of means of contraception in negotiations with heterogeneous groups concerned with birth control. As Fausto-Sterling (1990:14) has stated: "We don't understand all that much about how science functions as a social activity, one in which ideology plays a part in the creation of the science and the science, thus created, feeds back upon the ideology." The historical moment of disciplinary formation is, of course, especially significant in terms of the very frameworks of conceptualization established. What kinds of knowledge will be produced, and how will it be distributed and used in terms of sex and gender?[34]

Controlling Life

The last major theme of the book seeks to situate the rationalizing of reproduction in modernity, which I see as one strategy within a larger modernist movement toward enhanced control over life itself. Modernity consists of many efforts to rationalize and industrialize a variety of life processes.[35] The phrase "controlling life" is from Philip Pauly's (1987) important book on Jacques Loeb and his disciples in the early and mid–twentieth century, for whom an "engineering ideal of biology" was central. Loeb is an almost mythic character in the history of the life sciences, symbolizing scientific beliefs that biological processes can be fully reduced to physics and chemistry and then reengineered by humans for the good of mankind. Interestingly, one of his disciples was Gregory Pincus, a "father" of the birth control pill. Pincus was a reproductive scientist extraordinaire and a key actor as scientific statesman in the formation of the transnational reproductive arena that has come to maturity over the last several decades of the twentieth century.

But while this book is properly situated within ongoing conversations about rationalization, social control, and biological engineering in studies of twentieth-century life sciences, the term *control* must be problematized. Control is complex and multiple, unstable and difficult. Where did the modernist framework for "controlling life" come from? How did it come to be applied to a model of biology in general and to heredity, evolution, and reproduction in particular? The concept of control through knowledge in the life sciences has a long history to which I will return.

Foucault (1975, 1978) queried most earlier notions of social control by asserting that power is fluid and everywhere, with "positive" and "negative" potentialities of resistance and liberation as well as repression and domination. The title of this book plays on Foucault's use of the term *disciplining* to connote not only formation of a scientific discipline but also the possibilities of containment and control through knowledge—for liberatory, repressive, unanticipated, and unknown other purposes. Many individuals and groups were seeking to control life at the beginning of the twentieth century, and I would venture that even more do so at its end. Because reproduction is socially, culturally, and economically central to the very shape of individual lives, as well as a serious focus of national, corporate, and other global interests, it is a particular site where the desire to control life is vividly manifest. All of the social worlds examined in this book sought to enhance control of life in general and of reproduction in particular. They had varied goals, and power was far from equally distributed among them. But these are complicated stories of negotiations and trade-offs rather than simpler sagas of repression and denial.

In the life sciences, Pauly (1987:4) has argued that "there is a real history to the idea of scientific control of life" distinctive from more general ideas. While well into the nineteenth century, "the limits on biological manipulation were more notable than the achievements," this has been reversed by the end of the twentieth. Humans now have the capacity to create life itself through recombinant DNA biotechnologies. Indeed, what is life—nature— is now negotiated, and the boundaries between nature and culture are blurring and shifting.[36] But Pauly is concerned, as I am in this book, with the beginnings of disciplinarities of biological—including biomedical—control over life itself. He traces a shift in biology from concern with evolution, the organization of organisms, and other "metaphysical" topics to new concerns with experimental control of organisms toward enhancing the capacity to "manipulate" them—to control life itself. The utility of science and technology in achieving liberatory social engineering was an ideal often articulated romantically and idealistically by both left and right, progressives and conservatives, at the turn of and well into the twentieth century.[37] Regardless of political agendas, however, the reins of control usually remain in the hands of scientists, engineers, and related elites, although the politics can be very complicated.

I will argue that the reproductive sciences provide yet another instance of such arguments for control by a variety of elites. First, for reproductive scientists, disciplined knowledge yields the power for successful intervention in life itself. In her early study of the Committee for Research in Problems of Sex, Hall (1978:14) found "implicit models of human society managed by scientists in the interests of human fulfillment." The capacity for scientific management is at the heart of rationalizing and industrializing processes. Indeed, Austin and Short (1972/1986) titled their major reproductive sciences text *Manipulating Reproduction,* describing in the same volume the means of such manipulation in both humans and farm animals. The human/nonhuman distinction has, in fact, become decreasingly relevant to the sciences and technologies of reproduction. However, the issues of *whose* control over *whose* reproduction, under what conditions, and so on, are especially salient to understanding twentieth-century reproductive sciences.

In some important senses, this book can also be read as a case study of elite philanthropic endowment of an emergent discipline—a discipline requisite for the sequence of core projects of twentieth-century life sciences of controlling race, population, heredity, and evolution (Haraway 1995).[38] It frames Rockefeller concerns with the biochemical/endocrinological vision of life, known in the 1920s as "sex and internal secretions," which both preceded and then ran in tandem with the molecular vision of life. Kay (1993b:17) argues that the Rockefeller Foundation, influenced by Jacques Loeb's project of developing an engineering standpoint toward the control of life, sought to develop a "mechanistic biology as the central element of a new science of man whose goal was social engineering." This was very much the "new science of man" articulated by Warren Weaver with which I began the book—the reproductive sciences, genetics, and what Weaver himself later dubbed "molecular biology."[39] What Weaver managed for the Rockefeller Foundation was investment in the middle phase in a broader twentieth-century shift described by Keller (1993:56) as "a change in aim from representation to intervention (or from description to control) . . . to the particular conception of intervention or control that promises mastery over the making and remaking of life. . . . [T]he project of 'refashioning life,' of redirecting the future course of evolution, is recast as a manageable and doable project." The reproductive sciences are requisite for that project.

But it was not only scientific, corporate, and foundation commitments to rationalization, social control, and engineering that aided and abetted the development of the American reproductive sciences. The control of nature is also the control of self (Keller 1992a). Historically, lay people too have avidly sought enhanced control over their own reproduction.[40] Lay people—both women and men—have applied means of (social) control of many kinds, including biomedicalized means of control over reproduction. They have constructed social movements such as the birth control movement, a key actor in the formation of the American reproductive sciences. Instrumental rationalities of control and intervention were the goals in modernity for many people—elites and others. In the heterogeneous materialities of ordering and controlling life, there are no simple means of control—and certainly no innocent ones. Who gets to decide about the design and distribution of the means of control remains the central question.

OVERVIEW AND USER'S GUIDE

This book is a prism, offering many stories of the reproductive sciences, which will be read through many lenses with varied individual's and groups' concerns and agendas in mind. It is a story of the construction of a new line of scientific research in the United States between 1910 and 1963—the American reproductive sciences. My focus is on how certain scientists in specific locales came to envision a set of problems of reproductive research, how they organized themselves to work on those problems, and how they interacted among themselves and with their audiences, sponsors, and consumers to sustain this research and develop it into a recognized discipline—an enterprise. In short, I am interested in their processes of coherence. How and why did these social worlds connect and remain interactive, coherent, and viable across a fairly long time and dramatically changing circumstances, including considerable cultural hostility?

The turn-of-the-century era was one of fundamental changes in the organization of the professions, academia, and the life sciences. In chapter 2 I describe the situations in professional biology, medicine, and agriculture into which the reproductive sciences would soon enter. New approaches to the production of knowledge both in the life sciences and in the institutions in which scientific research increasingly took place—academia—are framed. I also introduce the birth control, eugenics, and neo-Malthusian movements, all of which helped to counter the illegitimacy of pursuing problems of reproduction in science.

Chapter 3 frames the emergence of the American reproductive sciences, particularly their early emphasis on physiological problems—largely the estrus and menstrual cycles of mammals. The American reproductive sciences gained initial impetus from British initiatives such as the naming of internal secretions as blood-borne messengers paralleling the nervous system and the first monograph of the discipline, Marshall's (1910) *The Physiology of Reproduction*. Soon distinctively American aspects of the reproductive sciences emerged in embryological work, very much at the heart of early-twentieth-century American biology. Two key sets of experiments on which much subsequent work was based are described in detail: Lillie's freemartin research and Papanicolaou's vaginal smear.

Chapter 4 focuses on the other major social world in the reproductive arena during the formative era—the National Research Council Committee for Research in Problems of Sex. Supported by Rockefeller funds, this committee was the major funding source of the emergent discipline for several decades. Here reproductive biologists actively seized the means of studying reproduction from sexology. They redirected the mission of the committee from its initial goals of sponsoring social science–based human sexuality studies intended to ameliorate social problems to the investigation of biological and biomedical topics in reproduction. And they did so for over twenty years during which much of the foundational biological and medical research on reproduction was accomplished. The key strategy used by reproductive scientists here and elsewhere in their efforts to build a legitimate and autonomous discipline was arguing for basic research on reproductive phenomena.

Chapter 5 describes how between ca. 1925 and 1940 the reproductive sciences coalesced as a line of work focused on a biochemical endocrinological problem structure. I examine how reproductive endocrinology became the "model research" of the enterprise, providing it with much sought after legitimacy through direct links to nascent biochemical approaches in the life sciences and to the widely advertised scientific "promise" of general endocrinology. During this period, international preeminence in the reproductive sciences passed to investigators in the United States. The signal event of this transfer was publication by American researchers of the second "Bible" of the reproductive sciences, *Sex and Internal Secretions* (Allen, ed., 1932, 1939). The nature of the reproductive sciences enterprise as an active intersection of efforts in biology, medicine, and agriculture is also discussed, as are the benefits provided by the new discipline to each profession.

Chapter 6 analyzes reproductive scientists' use of strategic arguments for basic research with a wide variety of birth control advocates from about 1915 to 1963. During this period, a quid pro quo was negotiated between reproductive scientists and birth control advocates. There were major shifts in the kinds of contraceptives birth control advocates sought vis-à-vis the kinds that reproductive scientists in the United States would actually investigate. Almost all of the key actors in the reproductive arena changed their positions on contraception dramatically during this period. Due to reproductive scientists' strategies in these negotiations, scientific means of contraception eventually won the day. This work paved the way for reproductive scientists to become integral parts of family planning, population control, and infertility research worlds, where they remain today.

One of the most remarkable aspects of the development of the reproductive sciences enterprise was its success at garnering significant amounts of external research funding during the years prior to federal government sponsorship of basic research and despite its taint of social and scientific illegitimacy. In chapter 7 I examine the often surprisingly prestigious funding sources committed to the quite socially risky business of supporting reproductive research from ca. 1910 to 1963, along with some of the sources of research support that usually remain invisible, such as industrial sponsorship. I also note recent funding patterns.

Chapter 8 could have been titled "One Hundred Years of Illegitimacy." It examines the sustained illegitimacy of the scientific pursuit of reproductive phenomena that has confronted individual researchers and the enterprise as a whole throughout the twentieth century. Here I discuss some of the key causes and particular consequences, along with some scientists' strategies for managing their often compromised positions. Readers to whom the impropriety of the reproductive sciences seems particularly important might want to begin with this chapter.

The final chapter offers a detailed summary of the book and a concluding examination of the themes. At heart, *Disciplining Reproduction* is about efforts to control life—human and nonhuman—by rationalizing reproduction. This has been partially, and only partially, accomplished through the shared commitments of multiple worlds and individuals to the production of new knowledge and the consumption of new technoscientific products and interventions.

CHAPTER TWO

Situating the Reproductive Sciences

All scientific work is situated in professional, technical, and institutional social worlds. This chapter offers snapshots of the key social worlds at the turn of the twentieth century that were salient to the subsequent formation of the modern reproductive sciences. Three quite different professional worlds became "homes" for the American reproductive sciences: academic biology, medicine, and agriculture. As the new century unfolded, all of these worlds drew deeply from new physiological approaches to life sciences research called the "new biology," and these scientific professional worlds were themselves located in dramatically changing universities. In the portraits offered here we see the spread of rationalized and industrialized approaches to life in all these sites.

Foucault (1975) has argued that in our studies of the production of knowledge we should examine both what does and does not take place. Another focus of this chapter, thus, is why the reproductive sciences did not appear earlier, along with studies of other major organ systems. A core argument of this book is that reproductive topics were so illegitimate to pursue scientifically and socially that the reproductive sciences emerged "late" compared with disciplines focused on other major organ systems, most of which were "disciplined" by the late nineteenth century. The illegitimacy of reproductive topics was challenged by multifaceted birth control, eugenics, and neo-Malthusian movements in the early decades of the twentieth century, key social worlds in the American reproduction arena also introduced in this chapter. The lay and medical birth control movements brazenly placed women's needs and desires for contraception on the public agenda ca. 1915. Eugenics and demography (the scientific study of populations) then began to establish the propriety of such topics both in the academy (especially among life scientists) and more broadly. Thus by

World War I, several powerful sectors of society sought and supported enhanced control over nature—and women—in many forms, from control over populations and reproduction to improved agricultural production.

These portraits situate the embryonic American reproductive sciences in the first two decades of the twentieth century in professional (biological, medical, agricultural), scientific (the "new biology"), institutional (university), and activist (birth control, eugenic, neo-Malthusian) social worlds. Even in the brief introductions performed in this chapter, we can begin to see the mutual disciplining, reciprocal relations, and negotiations among these worlds as they continually repositioned themselves to take advantage of changing conditions.

PROFESSIONAL WORLDS:
BIOLOGY, MEDICINE, AND AGRICULTURE

At the turn of the century, higher education was expanding and the professions were proliferating, building on earlier efforts. Graduate education took on its modern form from ca. 1890 to 1920. Soon scientists were able to construct recognizably modern professional careers in academic science, in research, and in clinical and applied practice settings in these emerging institutions. The professions were also consolidating as market-based occupations. Universities were being transformed into knowledge production industries, or what Servos (1976) has called "knowledge corporations." The sciences themselves were becoming professionalized and industrialized. That is, the sciences qua institutions resembled less the hobby-like worlds they had been and were becoming more akin to industries with specialized markets, a trend that has continued throughout the twentieth century.[1]

A fundamental feature of the professionalization of a science lies in the field's capacity to exert control and authority over a research domain (Freidson 1968, 1970). This includes scientists' own development of the boundaries or parameters of an area of scientific study, claims to authority or jurisdiction over it, and recognition of those claims by significant others (home institutions, sponsors, audiences, and consumers of the research). Professionalization processes are integral to and overlap with specialization processes.[2]

An important point regarding relations to markets is that the scientific disciplines moved into professional stature both within and outside ivy-covered university walls.[3] After receiving university-based training, researchers could construct careers and consultancies in academia, private industry, and/or government. But both the most esteemed positions and control of the profession remain largely within universities and professional associations. As is also true of law and medicine, ongoing tensions exist among the multiple segments of scientific professions, and the reproductive sciences have been no exception.[4] In the specific case of the reproductive sciences examined here, there were extensive consumer market demands for scientists' professional services as well.[5]

Consolidating the professional positions of biology, medicine, and agriculture proved problematic well into this century.[6] Professional scientific associations, which grew dramatically in numbers and in specialization, helped consolidate positions in the university and beyond (Kiger 1963). These disciplinary and specialty organizations both multiplied and divided the allegiances of academic scientists. As Herbst (1983:203) has remarked: "As service and research rather than teaching became the professors' chief occupations, their loyalties turned from their college and students to their specialty and their colleagues. As they shaped for themselves a new professional identity as scientific investigators, they came to compare themselves to army officers who loved their branch of the service but felt little or no attachment to the post on which they served." The "field" was generally embodied in the professional associations in which scientists were active. Such associations situated scholars more deeply in their professional worlds, and, then as now, one's "real" colleagues could be scattered thousands of miles away without losing their disciplinary effects.

A number of patterns of professionalization in biology, medicine, and agriculture at the beginning of the twentieth century had significance for reproductive scientists. In each professional domain, the reproductive system had been relatively unexplored and therefore constituted a new territory, a new frontier for research. By 1910, few organ systems remained unclaimed as research territories, since tremendous advantages accrued to pioneers. Visible career lines are necessary for scientists to regard a new research area as worthy of their investment and commitment (Coleman 1985:63), and the openness of reproductive research was irresistibly appealing to the curious, ambitious, and daring.

Biology

At the turn of the century, professional biology was an emergent discipline well on its way to becoming a "new fundamental unit of American academic culture" (Pauly 1984:369).[7] Important spokesmen described biology as a fundamental intellectual focus around which many related fields could be arrayed.[8] The framework it offered included, first, an emphasis on basic concepts such as protoplasm, the cell, and evolution, with research problems ranked in order of feasibility and importance (with embryology, cytology, and physiology of invertebrates at the forefront with evolution). A second emphasis was on the development of instruments, techniques, and approaches that relied on the technology of the microscope and controlled experimentation. This biological framework was not rigid but offered an emergent core of concerns with distinctive American (and particularly East Coast) inflections. This core was aided and abetted by a biologists' "summer camp" at the Woods Hole Marine Biological Laboratory on Cape Cod, which many contemporary biologists—and later foundation executives—visited at least occasionally.[9]

A few key scientists actively forged the biological discipline, including such Johns Hopkins graduates of the 1880s and 1890s as E. B. Wilson, E. G. Conklin, and T. H. Morgan.[10] Though from a different background, Charles Otis Whitman shared these scientists' vision of biology and sought to ground it in the university, calling for expanded graduate work in biology in 1887. Frank Rattray Lillie, later to become a leading American reproductive scientist, was Whitman's premier student. Whitman's model zoology department is outlined below:

Morphology	*Physiology*
zoology	human physiology
anatomy	general physiology
histology	physiological chemistry
neurology	hygiene
paleontology	psychology
pathology[11]	

Whitman extensively incorporated newer physiological approaches, and he further noted, "I must mention one of the most inviting fields, . . . namely Experimental Biology."[12] Pauly (1984:371–72) has argued that this new biology was constructed as basic to other lines of research work in two ways: "Biologists convinced their university constituencies that their research problems were the most advanced and far-reaching of the life sciences, and that their concepts and techniques were the best introduction to a large number of areas of more sophisticated study" for graduate and medical schools alike. Within the academy, graduate programs were established in biology first at the private or independent universities, with the public land-grant schools mostly following suit after the turn of the century (Cravens 1978:20). Between 1870 and 1900, biology departments began at Harvard, Johns Hopkins, Clark, Chicago, Columbia, the University of Pennsylvania, Cornell, Yale, Michigan, Wisconsin, California, and Princeton.[13]

But there were also tensions, first between biology and medicine. This "new biology" was independent of medicine, conceived to achieve a fresh integration of physiological and morphological (cytological) concerns (Pauly 1984). Yet the professional goals that medical educators then defined for themselves were key to the establishment of these new departments. Medical reformers in the late nineteenth and early twentieth centuries in fact promoted independent biology departments as part of their efforts to raise scientific standards of professional medical education. Ironically, then, these independent departments prospered in institutions where they were established in anticipation of scientifically based medical schools but where those schools subsequently did not fully develop, largely because of insufficient financial support prior to ca. 1900. Such flourishing biology departments included those at Johns Hopkins, Chicago, and Columbia. In contrast, where medicine prevailed over biology (for example, at the University of Pennsylvania), biology became "ephemeral" (Pauly 1984:370, 392). Biology thus arose as a professional discipline in part because there was an ideal of "biomedical" science that foundered where universities were persistently unable to transform that ideal into the reality of scientifically based medical schools. As it turned out, the science that biologists developed—a biology independent of medicine—was quite different from what medical reformers initially envisioned.

The extension of biological sciences into the new agriculturally oriented land-grant colleges and their development in such "applied" settings gave the "new biology" a uniquely American character. Undergraduate courses in general biology became the institutional norm and then became the basis of support for graduate programs at both private and public institutions. And, central to the subsequent development of reproductive research, this new biology, especially at the land-grant schools, provided a fully scientific biological training base for the later development of animal agricultural science.[14]

This early era was one of major institution building outside the academy as well, and biologists created several types of institutions to support their work. First were the marine and lake biological laboratories such as the Woods Hole Marine Biological Laboratory on Cape Cod and the Station for Experimental Evolution at Cold Spring Harbor, New York (sponsored by the new Carnegie Institution of Washington).[15] Second was the establishment of a wide array of new professional biological associations and journals, listed below:[16]

MAJOR ASSOCIATIONS

American Society of Naturalists (1883)
American Society of Zoologists (1890)
Botanical Society of America, Inc. (1893)
American Society for Microbiology (1899)
Society for Experimental Biology and Medicine (1904)
Entomological Society of America (1906)

American Society of Biological Chemists (1906)
Federation of American Societies for Experimental Biology (1912)

MAJOR JOURNALS

Journal of Morphology (1887)
Journal of Comparative Neurology and Zoology (1891)
Biological Bulletin (Woods Hole) (1899)
Journal of Experimental Zoology (1902)
Genetics (1916)

The scientific identities and contents of these societies and journals changed over the years as various strands of the "new biology" took hold among different groups. Rather than reflecting strictly bounded worlds, these associations and journals also overlapped considerably with those in medicine and agriculture. As Churchill (1981:188) has noted: "A tight parallel cannot be guaranteed. These institutions reflect the revolts and evolutionary developments of the past as well as the present: they may be the offspring of fads, crusades, or individual needs, but once raised to maturity and independence, they lead their own peculiar lives." Indeed, new biological research possibilities developed within a broad and diverse base of institutions that proved crucial for both diffusing the ideas of the "new biology" and supporting those doing biological work.

Medicine

Two intimately linked processes characterized American professional medicine at the turn of the twentieth century: the establishment of medical monopoly over health care and a shift to "scientific medicine." Here I briefly examine these processes in general medicine, then discuss their particular expression in obstetrics and gynecology as the sites of reproductive medicine.

The professionalization of American medicine in the early twentieth century focused on upgrading allopathic, or "regular," medical education toward the goal of creating what Abraham Flexner called "better and fewer doctors" (Larson 1977:163). Sponsored by the Carnegie Foundation for the Advancement of Teaching, the Flexner Report of 1910 recommended upgrading medical schools by expanding the scientific basis of medical training for practitioners. It urged developing full-time medical school faculty members and supporting laboratory-based medical research by that faculty and by outstanding students. Medical specialization would allow further medicalization of new bodily parts and processes.[17]

Institutionally, medical professional associations exploded at the turn of the century. Most also had journals focused on clinical medical science.[18] Major professional medical associations are listed below:

American Medical Association (1847)
American Physiological Society (1887)
American Association of Anatomists (1888)
American Association of Pathologists and Bacteriologists (1901)
American Society for Pharmacology and Experimental Therapeutics
    (1908)
American Society for Clinical Investigation (1909)
American Society for Experimental Pathology (1913)

Hospitals were also built and medical school expanded to encompass new research disciplines and laboratories. Major autonomous medical research institutions were founded, notably the Rockefeller Institute (1901) and the Carnegie Institution of Washington's Department of Embryology at the Johns Hopkins Medical School (1913).[19]

The shift to scientific medicine, then, represented a move from heroic therapeutics and individual case studies to experimental approaches to medical problems and, subsequently, to controlled clinical trials to assess safety and efficacy across multiple individuals.[20] In two particular areas, professional medicine had radically improved its services by the late nineteenth century: bacteriology and immunology had enhanced the control of communicable diseases, while the practice of anesthesia and asepsis had tremendously improved surgical success rates. Anesthesia was initially used around 1846, and asepsis had become largely routine by ca. 1890.[21]

From both within and outside medicine, then, a strong rhetoric developed in support of scientific medicine. The Flexner Report of 1910 called for the reform of medical education, and the foundations, especially the Carnegie and Rockefeller philanthropies, played a major role in promoting and supporting these reforms.[22] The shift to scientific medicine "provided a socially legitimate means of limiting access to the medical profession and regulating competition from poorly trained physicians and medical sects" (Kohler 1979).

During the early decades of this century, a further differentiation began between medicine as clinical practice and as medical science or academic medicine. This generated a "two-track" medical education system based on Flexner's push for full-time medical faculty who both taught and undertook original research.[23] The Rockefeller Institute, for example, had been founded on the principle of linking the delivery of care to the ill with basic and clinical research in a single institutional setting. As Florence Sabin (1934:273) put it, there the patient was "a real part of the material of the research." In a variety of ways, basic medical science during this period was biology in medically sponsored niches. This activity has become known as academic medicine practiced by medical scientists. In fact, George Corner, with whom I began this book, called himself not a doctor or a physician but a medical scientist—a status that scarcely existed in the United States when he was a medical student.[24]

Over the past decade or so there has been considerable debate about the actual scientific bases of "scientific medicine."[25] Regardless, medicine used pro-science rhetoric in the early twentieth century much like the American Medical Association had used antiabortion rhetoric in the second half of the nineteenth century (Mohr 1978)—to gain legitimacy and cultural authority. It was a most successful strategy.

Medical efforts to gain jurisdictional monopoly over the reproductive realm during the late nineteenth and early twentieth centuries were extensive, as an array of alternative providers, especially lay midwives, needed to be displaced to achieve such a monopoly.[26] But the reproductive realm offered sufficient new possibilities for medical research and practice to make the effort worthwhile. The specialty of gynecology was formally organized into the prestigious American Gynecological Society in 1876; the American Association of Obstetricians and Gynecologists formed in 1888; and a combined AMA Section on Obstetrics and Gynecology was established in 1911.[27] Gynecologic practice of the early 1880s had been limited largely to the speculum. In the 1890s, anesthesia and asepsis led to the "opening of the abdomen," and "gynecology rapidly became a surgical specialty. So rapid was the development that there were fears that gynecology would disappear as a separate field and be merged into general surgery; it was claimed in 1905 that 'the specialty is so well advanced that there is not very much more progress to be made in it'" (Stevens 1971:79, 201).

Thus by the turn of the twentieth century, reproductive anatomy and surgery formed the core of gynecologic theory and practice.[28] Then, between ca. 1890 and 1940, obstetrics and gynecology medicalized childbirth, pregnancy, menopause, and (to a lesser extent) menstruation, rendering them as disease processes and thus the legitimate territory of specialist physicians (Oakley 1984; Wertz and Wertz 1977). This medicalization initially centered on hospitalizing childbirth, at the same moment when hospitals were expanding (Starr 1982). The development of the teaching hospital during and after World War I furthered these processes, as did the introduction of anesthesia for labor. Over the next half century, lay midwives as pregnancy and childbirth care providers were eliminated in the United States.[29]

During the 1920s, one key concern of newly enfranchised women of the feminist movement centered on maternal health, and they pushed for the provision of federally funded health care for women and children. The Sheppard Towner Act briefly provided "well baby" care. While opposed by the AMA and terminated in 1929, this act simultaneously raised women's

reproductive health issues in a major public forum and enhanced the specialty status of gynecology, obstetrics, and pediatrics.[30] Asepsis in childbirth
remained highly problematic until well into the 1930s. While infant mortality rates had been reduced, in 1930 the United States ranked twenty-fifth
in the world in maternal mortality rates, behind even Uruguay. This led
to major medical organizing efforts around maternal health issues in the
1930s, including a White House conference in 1933, at the same time that
reproductive research was coalescing. Medical interest in maternal health,
initially relatively slow to develop, reflected the broader effort to expand
medical jurisdictions and reproductive specialties. A number of physician-
led organizations emerged to address these issues including, in 1923, the
National Committee on Maternal Health, which sought to enhance medical control over maternal health generally and over contraception particularly.[31]

During the 1930s, obstetrics and gynecology merged more thoroughly,
fusing women's reproductive health care under one specialty and further segmenting that specialty from both general practice and general surgery. The establishment of the American Board of Obstetrics and Gynecology in 1930 consolidated the medical monopoly over female reproductive
health, instituting needed reforms but also instituting medical care based
on medical intervention in nonpathological processes.[32] In the United
States in 1923, there were 696 full-time obstetrics/gynecology specialists;
by 1949 there were 5,074 (Stevens 1971:162).

The shift to scientific medicine in gynecology and obstetrics was largely
from surgical anatomy to reproductive physiology. It involved the development of functional (physiological) understandings of reproductive systems
and processes to increase potential nonsurgical therapeutics.[33] Ironically,
these alternatives were developed largely by anatomists and physiologists
(Long 1987).

Medical reformers wanted science to reign in all segments of the profession (Sabin 1934). One of the major reformers in obstetrics and gynecology
was J. Whitridge Williams, head of the Johns Hopkins School of Medicine's
Department of Obstetrics, who started campaigning for more anatomical
and pathological studies of the female generative tract in the 1890s.[34] In his
1914 presidential address to the American Gynecological Society, Williams
delivered a "scathing reproach" to his colleagues because, in reviewing articles in the society's *Transactions,* he had failed to find a single "fundamental" contribution to obstetrics. There was "an entire absence of reference to
the biochemical aspects of pregnancy," while obstetricians and gynecologists placed "technical virtuosity"—largely in surgery—above serious attempts "to extend the limits of knowledge."[35] Williams's students, among
others, remained less than enthusiastic about basic research on both educational and economic grounds; they were ill prepared for it, and it did not

pay well.[36] In 1925, Williams lamented that in obstetrics and gynecology, most American medical schools remained a half century behind those in Germany (Longo 1980:223).

The call to research on reproduction was amplified by Williams's colleague at Johns Hopkins, Franklin Paine Mall, head of the anatomy department. In 1913, Mall offered his student George W. Corner an assistantship for teaching and research in anatomy at the same time that Corner was offered a prestigious internship in gynecology under Howard Kelly at the Johns Hopkins University Hospital. To convince Corner to come to the anatomy department, Mall argued for a "sounder scientific base in the clinical branches of medicine," telling Corner that he could "do more for the future of gynecology by basic research on embryology and the physiology of the reproductive system than I could if I merely followed . . . the static program of the distinguished gynecologists." Corner became a convert.[37] One year later, after his initial anatomic research, Corner (1958a:30) recalled:

> I had a much better idea of the normal female reproductive cycle and the concomitant changes in the ovaries and cervix than did the average intern; indeed I may say that I knew more about the physiology of the reproductive organs than did the chiefs of the service, Howard Kelly and Thomas S. Cullen, world renown leaders as they were in pelvic surgery and pathology. Gynecologists' . . . efforts to treat the functional disorders of menstruation and sterility were mere puttering, scarcely advanced beyond the procedures of the Hippocratic era. How could we hope for anything better when we simply did not understand the human cycle?

While developments in surgery had allowed obstetric and gynecologic interventions of form, the new reproductive physiology would allow medical interventions of function—a new medical specialty territory far more ambitious than "mere puttering." Anatomists and physiologists, largely but not always located in medical schools, were the medical reproductive research pioneers (Long 1987). The years from 1920 to 1945 saw the gradual diffusion and acceptance of improved gynecologic and obstetric training (Longo 1980:223; 1981). By the 1930s, clinicians increasingly demanded reproductive physiological research results (e.g., Ehrenfest 1937) and were especially interested in organotherapeutic agents based on reproductive endocrinological research. By this time scientific medicine was also more clearly segmented into basic and clinical lines of research around reproduction.[38] Considerable clinical payoff would derive from basic reproductive research in medicine—on women.

In sharp contrast, however, if we attempt to "chercher l'homme" in early twentieth century medicine, we come up empty-handed. Moscucci's (1990) history of British gynecology accounts for the absence of a male reproductive specialty as reflecting, first, the thorough articulation of a distinctive and medically problematic "female nature" and embodiment culturally available to practitioners by the eighteenth century. No parallel framing of a medicalizable male then existed. Second, she argues that radical intervention in women's bodies was already common practice, from childbirth to "unsexing" via ovariotomies for cysts. In contrast, tampering with men's bodies was less radical: testicles were not removed for hydrocele but were palliatively drained (Moscucci 1990:134). The term *andrology* as the parallel to *gynecology* was used as early as 1891 in reference to a Section of Andrology of the Congress of American Physicians and Surgeons but it quickly disappeared (Niemi 1987:201). Male penile and related reproductive problems long fell within the jurisdiction of urology. Not until 1975 was the American Association for Andrology founded, with its *Journal of Andrology* beginning in 1980. In many sites, however, urology remains the male reproductive medical specialty.

Agriculture

Anticipating that readers may be unfamiliar with the history of agriculture, I provide here a general orientation, paying specific attention to animal agricultural research. By the end of the nineteenth century, economic conditions were becoming favorable for research, leading to increased food production for growing urban, industrial populations (Rossiter 1979). The fundamental goal was to improve farm and ranch production so that fewer workers could supply food to workers in other sectors of the economy (Busch and Lacey 1983). The processes of rationalization, industrialization, and professionalization characteristic of turn-of-the-century biology and medicine also began to affect agriculture, as did the creation of monopolies. Throughout this era, but especially after World War I, American farming was transformed from a subsistence to a commercial enterprise, firmly focused on increasing production (Fitzgerald in progress). Marcus (1988) asserts that there was a shift from a belief that "good character" built good farms to a belief that special knowledge about agriculture needed to be produced, transmitted, and systematically applied. The very organization of agriculture changed from a relatively homogeneous occupational group to one stratified by region, by farm size, and especially by product.

In medicine and agriculture, both applied fields, science provided a rhetorically "neutral" basis for the elimination of certain practitioners as these fields modernized and professionalized. The fields were left to those who would apply the fruits of science in their ever more specialized work. In medicine, institutional forces squeezed out "irregular" or alternative practitioners, including midwives and homeopaths, while in agriculture, smaller, poorer, less mechanized farmers succumbed to competition and market forces (then as now).[39] Large-scale farmers who specialized around specific commodities such as dairy products or corn also most actively promoted and accepted the contributions of agricultural sciences. These sciences in turn accepted such farmers as sponsors, audiences, and consumers—ready markets for their research (Busch and Lacey 1983:26–27; Rosenberg 1976). The advantages of specialization are vividly captured in the following excerpt from a homegrown poem read to the North Dakota State Dairymen's Association in 1910 (Danbom 1989:175):

PULLIN' TITTS
Ay ban a yust gude farmer,
For more an saxteen year;
Av raise some wheat and corn
An ay fat some hog and steer.
An ay watch dat farmer business close,
for whare de money gits,
An ay find it comin' quickest
Van you ban pullin' titts.

Though fraught with problems and conflicts, professionalization and institutionalization began early in American agriculture. Agricultural research in the United States started largely at the initiative of American chemists trained in Germany. They had direct experience with German agricultural experiment stations and understood the benefits of institution building in their own fields. They committed themselves to both agricultural colleges and experiment stations as research sites.[40] In 1862, Congress formed the United States Department of Agriculture (USDA); in 1875, Connecticut established the first state agricultural experiment station, and others soon followed (Rosenberg 1976:148).[41] In 1884, the Bureau of Animal Industry was founded, focusing initially on control of contagious diseases (Wiser 1987). And in 1887, through the Hatch Act, the federal government provided each state with $15,000 per year for support of an agricultural experiment station, thus entering into the research business. This act changed the USDA from a centralized agency into a network of semiautonomous research institutions with nodes in every state.[42] The establishment of federally funded, local and state agricultural extension agents in 1914 added a further layer of middlemen to these arrangements. Federal funding for agricultural research quadrupled during the 1880–1920 period (Rossiter 1979; True 1937), though it was cut during the Great Depression era (1933–40) (Pursell 1968).[43] The ability of agricultural scientists and their "imperious" large-scale farmer constituencies to gain federal support for their research represents a highly successful early example of the socialization of the costs of research to improve production; similar efforts in other emerging professional fields did not fare as well.[44] Agricultural chemistry was a major focus of work at the agricultural experiment stations during the late nineteenth century—especially fertilizer and soils analysis in response to widespread instances of fertilizer fraud.[45]

Chronic tensions in the American agricultural research world around the turn of the century resulted from competing demands—from the practical needs of producers and breeders, to the organizational demands of the agricultural colleges and experiment stations, to the scientific and professional expectations of emergent disciplinary groups, to scientists' own research and career goals and needs.[46] Specialization entered agriculture and agricultural sciences early. Rossiter (1979:212) calls this "force-fed" specialization, achieved through the combined activities of agriculture, science, and government. It was commodity-oriented or commodity-specific research. A fundamental bifurcation thereby occurred along plant-versus-animal lines, with further divisions by type of crop or animal as the specialty areas. The predilections of scientists, along with pressures from specialized client/producers (e.g., corn growers, cattle ranchers, chicken farmers) and their specialty associations, all contributed to these segmentations (Busch and Lacey 1983:27–28).

Animal agricultural science (hereafter animal science) was then unsurprisingly organized by type of animal (swine, poultry, sheep, beef and dairy cattle), with researchers typically specializing in only one.[47] Subdivisions within the Bureau of Animal Industry, whose primary research facilities were established in Beltsville, Maryland, around 1910, also reflected these segmentations (Byerly 1986).

Below is a list of major American organizations and the associated journals in both general agricultural research and animal agriculture.[48]

United States Department of Agriculture (1862); *Journal of Agricultural
    Science* (1905)
American Veterinary Medical Association (1863)
Society for Promotion of Agricultural Science (1880)
Association of Official Agricultural Chemists (1880)
Bureau of Animal Industry of the USDA (1884)
American Association of Agricultural Colleges and Experiment Stations
    (1887)
Association and Experiment Station Veterinarians (1897)
American Breeders' Association (1903–13); *American Breeders' Magazine*
    (1910–13)
National Association of Dairy Instructors and Investigators (1906), later
    American Dairy Science Association (1917); *Journal of Dairy Science*
    (1917)
International Association of Instructors and Investigators in Poultry Hus-
    bandry (1908), later American Poultry Science Association; *Poultry
    Science* (1921)

American Society of Animal Nutrition (1908–12), later American Society of Animal Production (1912); *Journal of Animal Science* (1942)

American Genetics Association (1913); *Journal of Heredity* (1913)
Genetics (1916)

Agricultural Committee, National Research Council (Division of Biology and Agriculture) (1917)

Section on Genetics, American Society of Zoologists (1921–31)

Genetics Society of America (1931)

American Breeders' Service (artificial insemination) (1941)

Society for the Study of Reproduction (1967); *Biology of Reproduction* (1968)

Compared with biology and medicine, animal science generally lagged behind in developing agriculturally based "new biological" research. That is, the "new biology" was imported into agriculture rather than being "homegrown" (Rosenberg 1967). Cravens (1978:20–21) notes that experimental approaches in biology developed far more rapidly in private graduate universities than in public or land-grant universities largely because the private institutions did not have to curry favor with special interest groups, including agriculturalists seeking immediate results. Private universities also had stronger financial support. But, "The state universities and land grant colleges provided full time appointments for the graduates of the private doctoral programs and enrolled far more undergraduate students. . . . [S]ome of the state universities soon rivaled the private universities for prestige" (Rosenberg 1967:38–40). In the decade before World War I, rapid expansion and the lack of trained personnel led to frequent faculty vacancies in agricultural colleges (Rossiter 1986:44). Thus although American animal agriculture professionalized earlier, it initiated *experimental* research later than biology or medicine, especially in the area of reproduction. This was in sharp contrast to the situation in Great Britain, where agriculturally based scientists pioneered in reproductive physiology and endocrinology during the decades before World War I (e.g., Hogben 1974). There it was much more scientifically legitimate and prestigious to do research in agriculture—on both applied and basic topics—because the nobility and the landed gentry had long been involved in agricultural research and innovation (e.g., Borell 1985; Medvei 1982). As we shall see in chapter 3, there lay the origins of modern reproductive sciences, to be elaborated subsequently by Americans.

Animal science in the United States focused on three lines of research work during the turn-of-the-century era: disease, nutrition, and breeding. Bacteriologists and veterinarians undertook disease research, including work on tuberculosis (Rosencrantz 1985), hog cholera (Stalheim 1988), and other specific economically harmful conditions, and remained clustered around the USDA (Rossiter 1979:230–33). The American Society of Animal Nutrition encouraged research and attempted to standardize methods and share information (e.g., Benedict 1910; Aronson 1979, 1982; Marcus 1988). Despite changing its name to the American Society of Animal Production in 1912, "its goals and the content of its meetings remained stagnant and the field became a scientific backwater" (Rossiter 1979:229).

Animal nutrition and husbandry, the predecessors of animal science, then splintered and regrouped in almost contradictory ways. On the one hand, what had been "animal nutrition" (the study of foodstuffs and animal metabolism) was absorbed shortly after 1900 into the more medically oriented science of biochemistry. But it was then conducted with laboratory animals and in university and medical school settings (Rossiter 1979:228). Such studies were also integral to zoological anatomy and physiology (e.g., Evans 1939). On the other hand, the two very clearly applied fields of poultry husbandry and dairy husbandry began to flourish. These gave rise to a cluster of subsciences focused on egg and milk production and were organized ambitiously at agricultural experiment stations and colleges (Rossiter 1979:228; Bugos 1992; Cooke 1997).

This segmentation left the rest of animal husbandry (focused largely on beef cattle, sheep, and swine) to nonscientifically trained husbandmen who worked on improved breeding practices through record keeping (Rossiter 1979:228). Husbandmen (and they were men) more commonly were employed at agricultural experiment stations than zoologists or biologists.[49] In 1903, academic scientists joined with practical breeders to form the American Breeders' Association, which ultimately was taken over by eugenicists and transformed itself into the American Genetic Association in 1913, losing considerable scientific support and membership (Kimmelman 1983; Rossiter 1979). Breeding the best to the best was long the focus of breeding efforts, with a strong emphasis (promoted by the USDA and widespread eugenic thinking) on purebred stock. Mendelian genetics began to be applied after ca. 1920, based largely on Sewall Wright's (1921, 1922) work with guinea pigs and Jay Lush's elaboration of this work for agriculture.[50] The value of the "unseen carriers of heredity" was considered by some breeders ca. 1910 to be "far above that of gold" (Sapp 1983:318). At this point, reproduction per se was not problematized beyond assessing fertility. Rather, focus was on deciding which animals should reproduce and controlling who could reproduce with whom. For example, discovery of the high heritability of feedlot weight gain in cattle made the use of large bulls important in beef production (Byerly 1986:75).

The focus of animal agriculture is on improved animal production. This involves the industrialization of domestic animal reproduction, which requires diverse activities, including, according to the Bureau of Animal Industry, breeding, nutrition, improved means of handling and transportation, prevention of cruelty, improved means of utilizing animal products, promotion of export trade in both animals and products, disease prevention and treatment, promotion of veterinary education, and collection of statistical and economic data. The bureau also sponsored boys' pig clubs and girls' canning and poultry clubs, encouraging the division of animal farm labor on the basis of gender.[51]

Gradually during the 1910–40 era, but mostly after 1925, animal science began to include reproductive research and its applications in breeding livestock. A host of reproductive problems were addressed, including the fertility cycle, pregnancy diagnosis, the role of nutrition in fertility, spermatogenesis, fertilization, and problems of infertility. This knowledge quickly was applied toward the development of artificial insemination and other reproductive technologies that could improve both quality and quantity of breeding and production. There were early attempts at sex preselection and studies of the heritability of twinning, both of which are desirable in cattle production.[52] There was also a shift from "all-purpose" cows to cows bred specifically for beef or dairy production, offering "mouthwatering heaviness or full-uddered promise" (Kimmelman 1987:250) to serve national interests and to enhance exports, especially of cheese. But it is important to remember that in animal agriculture, routine practice was and remains the prompt culling for meat of specific animals performing inadequately at dairying or studding. Thus while improvements in breeding and reproduction were highly desirable, they also needed to be highly and immediately cost-effective.

The first book-length treatment of reproduction including domestic animals published in the United States was *Patterns of Mammalian Reproduction* (1946) by S. A. Asdell, professor of animal physiology at the New York State College of Agriculture at Cornell. Works fully focused on reproduction in domestic animals came somewhat later in the United States (e.g., Nalbandov 1958; Cole and Cupps 1959) than their British counterparts (e.g., Hammond 1925, 1927). A. V. Nalbandov, a reproductive scientist trained in agricultural institutions in the 1930s, has argued that in the American context, the potential for "direct practical applications" of reproductive research in human contraception and in artificial insemination and pregnancy for domestic animals provided considerable impetus for the reproductive research effort.[53] Increased federal funding of agricultural research led to improved production at this time, which gradually included reproductive science (Busch and Lacey 1983; Rossiter 1979).

In conclusion, it is important to emphasize that the boundaries between basic and applied research were blurred within agricultural sciences, as well as among agricultural, biological, and medical research. Rossiter (1979:240) notes that "applied" is not an accurate description of agricultural research at this time, since agricultural scientists "dealt with practical problems that arose in certain economic contexts, but they were not really 'applying well-established theoretical principles to practical problems.'" Kimmelman (1983:174) echoes Rossiter's analysis, arguing that agricultural scientists' understanding of practical applications encouraged early acceptance of scientific theories such as Mendelism and scientific methods such as biometry. In sum, animal agriculture created considerable legitimacy for the emergence of reproductive research because breeding more and better food animals was a clearly articulated and essentially noncontroversial national goal. In return, as one agricultural researcher said, the "scientist is a better Santa Claus for the farmer than the politician" (Finlay 1990:45).

THE "NEW BIOLOGY"

Rationalizing and industrializing processes also affected approaches to scientific work. At the turn of the century, boundaries between various specialties within the life sciences were so blurred as to seem almost invisible. The intensive specialization or rationalization characteristic of modern knowledge in industrialized societies was just beginning (e.g., Oleson and Voss 1979). This specialization involved segmentation, intersection, and realignment of lines of scientific work and of approaches taken in that work. These processes were manifested in overlapping shifts of emphasis that can be summarized as follows:

from naturalist field and laboratory observational approaches to experimentation as the common modus operandi of research work;
from research design based on case and field studies to controlled and quantitative experimentation;
from morphological to physiological approaches (from problems of form to those of function);
from comparative morphological dissection with gross anatomy and histological analysis to physiological experiments with cytological and biochemical analyses;
from an organism- or species-based problem structure to an analytic, problem-based problem structure.

These shifts thus involved realignments of both substantive foci and analytic approaches in multiple lines of research work in biological, medical, and agricultural sciences, though the specifics varied from one science to another. All of these shifts were vital to the construction of an ambitious reproductive research enterprise over the next decades.

One of the most interesting phenomena of early-twentieth-century life sciences is that the highly permeable boundaries among these sciences allowed researchers to move through a variety of problem areas, adopting and adapting various approaches for use in their own work. There were no institutional gatekeepers delineating boundaries. Scientists' moves were thus not necessarily viewed as interdisciplinary.[54] As Whitman, a key articulator of the "new biology," noted: "It is hardly necessary to point out that science has long since ceased to respect territorial stakes as a means of defining its sphere of activity. On a territory no larger than a bacterium a dozen sciences may work in perfect harmony and find no occasion for envying or claiming one another's work. Chemistry is not Botany when it looks at a plant, or Zoology when it enters the animal domain."[55] Researchers constructed the "new biology" out of this flux.

Physiology has its origins in mid-nineteenth-century medicine, especially in the French laboratory of Claude Bernard (1865/1957; Lesch 1984). By the mid–nineteenth century, European physiologists had won their independence from medical anatomy, largely through adoption of an experimental approach to the study of vital processes (Geison 1979:67; Coleman 1985). Physiology developed very slowly in Britain and the United States, and research physiologists "remained essentially parasitic on the larger medical enterprise from which they had emerged" (Geison 1979:68; 1978). However, their experimental approaches were adopted and adapted broadly by other lines of work in late-nineteenth-century life sciences (e.g., Geison 1987; Fye 1987). As Coleman (1971:162) has summarized: "Function displaced form as the goal of biological inquiry. . . . Ideals long the valued possessions of physiology—precise, meaning quantitative, delineation of organic phenomena; experimental control over those phenomena; aspirations toward prediction of those phenomena—were extended to most and perhaps all domains of biology."

How these broad shifts in research approaches occurred has been debated; specifically, was there a "revolutionary change" in the ways scientists worked? Never a unilinear set of changes, these clear shifts of emphasis did not exclude other approaches.[56] Farber (1982b:152), for example, objects to the notion of a *shift from* natural history to physiology; since the roots of physiology lay more in medicine and chemistry, they should be viewed as "parallel traditions," which, at the turn of this century, "partly were hybridized, partly were transformed independently, and partly were synthesized."

The parade toward the "new biology" was led by developmental mechanical *(Entwicklungsmechaniker)* approaches applied in the embryological work of Roux and Dreich in Europe. These ideas and experimental physiological approaches quickly were imported into the United States, becoming the focus of considerable work at the Woods Hole Marine Biological Laboratory and elsewhere. It is important to the development of the American reproductive sciences that embryology was the locus of initial physiological work in biology in both Europe and the United States as it was embryologists who pioneered in the physiology of reproduction in the United States.[57]

The shift within biology from morphological to physiological approaches was accompanied by another shift from histological (tissue-level) to cytological (cellular-level) frameworks. A later shift introduced cell biological (biochemical) and, beginning in the 1930s, molecular biological approaches. If the first set of shifts was from problems of biological form to those of function, the second set concerned levels of action of function— examination of changes in the structure of tissues, cells, and cellular contents. Beginning in the late 1890s, a large number of American biologists, already trained in the techniques of cytology and embryology, began to move into new and transparently applicable domains as they sought to expand their constituencies. Their first area of interest was heredity and breeding, which by 1915 they transformed into the field of genetics.[58]

Almost in tandem with physiology, by the late nineteenth century biochemistry was ascendant. As physiological approaches were integrated into biology and medicine in the United States, biochemical approaches were also, if slightly later. Biochemistry became established in both biology and medicine at this time, and physiological approaches increasingly included biochemistry far more than they had previously.[59] There appear to have been two converging lines of work drawing biology and physiology toward biochemical approaches. One line, developed particularly in Britain, was the study of internal secretions (later termed *hormones* and *endocrinology*). The eminent British endocrinologist Sir Edward Sharpey-Shafer used the phrase "the new physiology" to emphasize the tremendous significance of internal secretions, which rapidly changed the perception of the central problems of physiology (Borell 1978:282). The fundamental shift was from seeing the nervous system as the primary regulator of bodily processes to seeing blood-borne chemicals as sharing such bodily roles (Borell 1976a,b,c). The second line of work consisted of chemical studies of the function of the living cell and its contents. The leading advocate of cellular biochemical and biophysical approaches in the United States at the turn of the century was Jacques Loeb, who sought to fully explain vital processes solely through chemistry and physics (Pauly 1987). Fundamental tensions then emerged in both biology and medicine between those who shared Loeb's mechanist reductionism and advocates of what were called broader "biological" explanations of phenomena. These tensions were rehearsed in the reproductive sciences as well.

INSTITUTIONAL SITES: UNIVERSITIES AND LABORATORIES

Perhaps the most notable feature of the early industrialization of knowledge production was that universities became the primary loci of basic research.[60] Prior to the late nineteenth century, scientific research was minimal and was done largely on an ad hoc basis by amateurs and some quasi professionals, with minimal fiscal support. The newness of research within university settings was captured vividly in a report of the Ogden Graduate School of Science to the president of the University of Chicago in 1902: "The idea that investigative work is one of the great functions of a university is one which has but recently come to due recognition in America; but it has been widely adopted during the last decade, and promises to be a controlling factor in the future development of universities."[61] This was the beginning of what has been called the "American century," and research, especially in universities but also in institutes and industry, was to be its heart.

Intellectual history is rife with studies relating the emergence of American graduate education in science to German and other models of education and inquiry.[62] The combination of more effective laboratory techniques and broad claims that science could improve the human condition set powerful economic and intellectual efforts toward empirical inquiry in motion. A research boom occurred by the turn of the century, accompanied by what Vesey (1965:264–66) called "the academic boom of the early nineties." Clark, Stanford, and the University of Chicago all opened between 1889 and 1892. With Johns Hopkins, founded in 1876, these universities reflected the full-scale entry of industrialists and mercantilists into the business of education, as all were funded by individual wealth (DeVane 1965). Broader philanthropic support grew steadily: in 1920, the total endowment of higher education was about $570 million; by 1940, it was nearly $2 billion (DeVane 1965:75). Business and industry were routinely investing in higher education to support their own research needs.

Undergraduate and graduate education became increasingly desirable for the upwardly mobile middle classes (Coben 1979:230). There was growing demand for professional training for an expanding number of occupations (Beer and Lewis 1974). University enrollment in the United States was about 22,500 in 1860, about 100,000 in 1900, and about 489,500 in 1930.[63] Enrollments in graduate schools also increased dramatically. In 1861, only 3 Ph.D.'s were granted; by 1920, this number grew to 615; in 1934, seventy-four institutions granted 2,024 Ph.D.'s; and in 1940, a total of 3,290 Ph.D.'s were granted.[64] This upsurge in enrollments, especially in the sciences at the graduate level, occurred in part as a response to increased opportunities for professional scientists and highly trained scientific technologists in industrial research and development laboratories (Birr 1979; Coben 1979:229), as well as in applied areas such as agriculture (Rossiter 1986).

The shared, if tacit, model of organization to which university administrators turned during this growth era was that of American business. Many universities rapidly acquired a highly bureaucratic form, with departments headed by chairmen, schools headed by deans, carefully ranked faculty, and so on.[65] Powerful, nonfaculty administrations came to resemble the upper levels of corporate management, and were deeply concerned with educational markets (Vesey 1965:305–6).

The development of laboratories was crucial in the industrialization of basic science research and its location in universities. Universities as institutions gained a monopoly on basic research production by providing these physical plants—the requisite infrastructure for the production of modern scientific research. Organizationally, laboratories provide centralized, organized, and rationalized access to the research instruments and materials necessary to the production of scientific knowledge (Borell 1989). For example, Latour (1983) called a key article on Pasteur's work in nineteenth-century France "Give Me a Laboratory and I Will Raise the World," signaling the requisite infrastructure for global transformation. Similar sentiments were articulated routinely by scientists at the turn of the century. Universities thus became "factories" for the production of knowledge based on scientific research.[66] At the same time, applied research and product development were taken up in a wide variety of academic and industrial laboratories and agricultural settings.[67] Research itself was increasingly rationalized on the basis of market-oriented principles. Sources of research support shifted dramatically from the individual/private means of scientists themselves to collective/public means or foundations more closely tied to specific extrascientific goals. But financial arrangements typically remained ad hoc for many years.[68]

The industrialization of research brought about new institutional forms, new divisions of labor, and new careers in science. While industrialization usually has connoted the proletarianization of a labor force, in the sciences we see both professionalization at the upper end of the hierarchy and the emergence of new classes of workers (graduate student–researchers and technicians) lower in the hierarchy. Such a division of scientific labor occurred in both academic and nonacademic scientific research settings. The majority of technicians' work focused initially on organizing and maintaining instruments, equipment, and materials used in the research. All these, and especially in vivo materials, required extensive and increasingly specialized labor for their maintenance as new standards for research were elaborated.[69]

As scientists began to raise funds for research on their own behalf and began to build their own institutions, they needed to articulate that work and its value to wider, less technical, audiences. This led to the emergence of "scientific entrepreneurs," scientists who promoted their own research groups both on their own campuses and in appeals to external funding sources (Rosenberg 1976; Rossiter 1979). Many of these individuals became key figures in establishing, shaping, and maintaining the extra-academic science institutions that proliferated at the turn of the century, from marine biological stations to the National Research Council. Research groups represented by particular entrepreneurs were often transformed by sponsoring organizations into "centers" of research—clearly demarcated funding entities with the entrepreneurs as recognized leaders. The Rockefeller and Carnegie Foundations, primary funding sources for research in the life sciences at this time, strongly promoted the development of such scientific entrepreneurs and such a "team" or "center" approach, in the reproductive sciences as elsewhere.[70]

Physiological and biochemical approaches brought radical changes to local and national research laboratories. Physiological approaches led to a number of changes in the biomedical research infrastructure (Clarke 1987):

increased demand for in vivo and fresh materials;
increased demand for quantities of same species materials rather than single specimens of multiple species;
development of colonies for on-site access to desired research materials;
increased demand for elaborated scientific instruments;
development of biological supplies and equipment industries;
development of personnel—technicians of several varieties—to manage the labs.

It is in the laboratory itself that the industrialization of science is clearly manifest in the social and infrastructural organization of scientific practices (e.g., Clarke and Fujimura 1992).

Nationally, the newer approach to biomedical research was incorporated in the funding philosophies of the major foundations. Warren Weaver's description of his program in "vital processes" at the Rockefeller Foundation in the 1930s serves as an excellent summary: "Modern physiology is often concerned with cells, single nerve fibers, and tissues rather than with whole organs. The refined modern techniques are permitting a breaking up of impossibly complicated problems into simpler component parts."[71] Given this programmatic agenda, Weaver also explained: "To indicate inclusion rather than exclusion, we will interest ourselves particularly in work in genetics; in hormones, enzymes and vitamins; in cell physiology; in nerve physiology; in psychobiology; and in the whole range of problems specifically and fundamentally involved in the biology of reproduction."[72] Thus the "new biology" had generated considerable institutional support by the 1930s.

MARKETS AND CONTROVERSIES

Two distinct yet related features of the reproductive sciences predated and shaped the era of their emergence. Qua science, reproductive research was both "late" and "improper." I argue here that certain countervailing and legitimating conditions, specifically explicit markets for reproductive research, were requisite before the field could emerge.

The "Lateness" and "Illegitimacy" of the Reproductive Sciences

Modern reproductive research emerged later than research on other major organ systems such as circulation or respiration. Endocrinologist and medical historian Medvei (1982:360) states that there had been little progress in reproductive anatomy, morphology, or physiology from the seventeenth to the nineteenth century. Alan Gregg of the Rockefeller Foundation noted of his Harvard Medical School days, "I remember in 1914 in our class on physiology that I asked Doctor Cannon why there was so little attention given to the physiology of reproduction."[73] The most common explanation for this later emergence is the social illegitimacy of the topic of reproduction. Other explanations stress the retarding effects of technical or conceptual problems within the reproductive sciences themselves.[74]

The "illegitimacy argument" suggests that reproduction, largely because of its association with sexuality, was not a proper subject to pursue in polite society and that scientists therefore avoided explicitly reproductive problems in their work. Judicial efforts to understand the social mechanisms of racial and sex discrimination in the United States have utilized a concept that effectively captures such interactive processes—the notion of "chilling effects." The illegitimacy of the reproductive sciences demonstrates that similar effects may be experienced by natural and social science researchers in their problem selection processes. "Inappropriate" selections may have negative consequences throughout an individual's career, such as loss of status, funding problems, ridicule, and ostracism. "Chilling effects" can also surround whole disciplines such as the reproductive sciences.

In 1928, Vernon Kellogg of the National Research Council explicitly connected the lateness of reproductive science to its illegitimacy: "Systematic scientific study of the fundamental problems of sex and reproduction has not kept pace with medical, education and social needs. This has been due in part to the social taboos which have surrounded the subject and in part to its complexity."[75] Further, many early scientists who did select reproductive problems felt they were placing themselves somehow "beyond the pale" of propriety; others who were more peripherally associated with reproductive research projects feared censure even for that limited involvement.[76] The uproar caused by Alfred Kinsey's research in the 1950s demonstrates the persistent opprobrium adhering to sexual topics (Pomeroy 1982). That a career in the reproductive sciences is still subject to sexual comment and innuendo was brought home to me by the routine preemptive joking of contemporary reproductive scientists. For example, a bumper sticker on the office door of a researcher whom I interviewed read "Reproductive Physiologists Do It for a Living," and the softball team of one reproductive sciences lab is named the "Nads" so that their supporters shout "Go, Nads!" from the bleachers.

In contrast to these illegitimacy arguments, Asdell (1977:x) focuses on technical and scientific reasons to explain the lateness of reproductive research. For mammals, the nonexistence of eggs that could be seen without the aid of a microscope and the time gap between mating and the ability to recognize the products of conception in the uterus were obstacles that could be surmounted only by the invention of suitable visual aids and the formulation of the cell theory. Yet the cell theory was developed in the 1840s, and adequate improvements in microscopy had occurred by the 1870s (Coleman 1971). The point remains—much of the reproductive histology and cytology of the early twentieth century could have been done in the late nineteenth century. Asdell (1977:x) continues his technical argument by noting that the method of reproductive control by hormones was itself so late a discovery that the delay of reproductive research is not surprising on this account alone. However, there were earlier discoveries of the effects of blood-borne tissue extracts such as Berthold's work in the mid–nineteenth century, which he quickly abandoned (e.g., Medvei 1982) and, to our knowledge, no one else took up. Part of this issue (as described in detail in the following) was the social and intellectual sway of reigning neurological theories of the control of physiological processes. Moreover, many physiological, if not biochemical, aspects of reproduction could have been examined—yet they were not. The technical arguments may be necessary, but they are not sufficient to explain the "lateness" phenomenon.[77]

Another set of reasons for the "lateness" of reproductive research, I would argue, was the weakness of organized markets for that research. Specifically, at the turn of the century reproductive medicine was focused on, if not obsessed by, gynecologic and obstetric surgery, and was quite successful with it. For the nonce, problems of function and nonsurgical therapeutics were not "interesting" and could be comfortably ignored. Moreover, biologists, agricultural scientists, and animal breeders were focused on, if not preoccupied with, problems of heredity (and, for biologists, evolution as well). Until they clarified mechanisms of heredity, problems of reproduction were not viewed as pressing. In fact, what turned out to be some key reproductive investigations, such as those of Frank Lillie, originally were conceived as explorations of problems of heredity through embryology. Further, Pauly (1984) argues that up to ca. 1900, biologists were busy entrenching their discipline in academia and only later sought to expand their constituencies by way of genetics. But reproduction was and remains significant to lay people, and a new set of markets for reproductive research soon emerged—the birth control, eugenics, and neo-Malthusian movements.

Birth Control, Eugenics, and Demography/Population Control Movements

In 1905, President Theodore Roosevelt attacked birth control, arguing that the tendency toward smaller families was decadent, an indicator of moral disease, and a practice that would lead to (white) "race suicide" (Gordon 1976:136). The weight and publicity given to Roosevelt's views immediately made birth control a matter of national public controversy. At least reproduction was "out of the closet" of social impropriety—a matter of public discussion and debate. While Roosevelt's comments were particularly remarkable because he was president, British and American birth control, neo-Malthusian, and eugenics advocates were also becoming increasingly organized and vocal on reproductive issues during the early years of the century (Gordon 1976; Reed 1984–85). In addition, strong moral reform movements focused on vice, venereal diseases, and alcoholism also raised sexual issues in social discourse (e.g., Bullough 1994).

All of these activities, but especially the birth control, neo-Malthusian, and eugenics movements, challenged the view of reproduction as an improper social and scientific topic by introducing a more public forum on human reproductive issues. Moreover, the social stature of many of the advocates—elite groups of scientists, physicians, and the educated middle classes from other professions—further legitimated reproductive topics, eventually including the reproductive sciences. As we shall see, by 1963, birth control advocates, neo-Malthusians, and eugenicists established a quid pro quo with each other and with reproductive scientists under the banner of "family planning and population control." But earlier in the century they helped pave the way for reproductive research with their own distinctive and often conflicting activities. Because each of these movements is an actor in this story of the reproductive sciences and the broader reproductive policy arena, I introduce them here.

Birth Control Movements.   Briefly, birth control advocacy was spearheaded by neo-Malthusians at the turn of the century as one solution to problems of overpopulation, though this movement was much stronger in Great Britain than in the United States (Ledbetter 1976). Contraception was even called "neo-Malthusianism" (Sanger 1971:108). The initially separate American feminist lay birth control movements of the first half of this century were in part a response to the difficulties and dangers of abortion, which, though illegal, was a common form of "birth control" in the absence of contraception. After 1915, feminist efforts generated a nationally organized movement composed of many local and a few national organizations. During the years 1915–18, birth control as a topic regularly captured a level of national attention not again achieved until the 1930s due to Margaret Sanger's and others' imprisonments, hunger strikes, clinic raids, and political and religious organizational responses (Chesler 1992:130). Between 1915 and 1920, Margaret Sanger transformed herself from a radical socialist feminist to a liberal humanist advocate of contraception as a woman's right and became the major leader of this movement. Her organization, the American Birth Control League, was founded in 1921. Subsequently birth control became an increasingly liberal and centralized cause (Gordon 1976; Reed 1983; Chesler 1992).

During the 1920s, lay birth control advocates were joined by a medically led birth control movement under the aegis of the National Committee for Maternal Health. Their specific goal was medical control over contraceptive practices, and members eventually included many reproductive scientists (Reed 1983). Many of the arguments put forward by such individuals and groups in both lay and medical movements were essentially economic—calls for reductions in the numbers and improvements in the "quality" of lower-class persons to reduce drains on government (there were significant pushes for socialized medicine, workers' compensation, and the like at this point) and to improve industrial production (e.g., Sanger 1920). Birth control was deemed a necessity of modern life.

Eugenics Movements. Defined by Sir Francis Galton in Britain in 1883, the "science" of eugenics transposes agricultural perspectives on the breeding of plants and animals to humans.[78] In extending stock improvement strategies to the highest reaches of the "Great Chain of Being," Galton stated: "We greatly want a brief word to express the science of improving stock, which is by no means confined to judicious mating, but which, especially in the case of man, takes cognizance of all the influences that tend in however remote a degree to give to the more suitable races or strains of blood a better chance of prevailing speedily over the less suitable than they otherwise would have had" (Bajema 1976:76). It was not until 1906 that William Bateson supplied the name "genetics" (Gardner 1972:406), and most concerns about human breeding and heredity went under the name "eugenics" until at least that time (Ludmerer 1972).

While not explicitly eugenic, research on reproduction fell within the domain of the scientific concerns of eugenicists because it was conceptually contiguous. That is, it was in part through understanding and controlling reproduction that eugenic goals could be achieved. The "promise" of eugenic science lay in public policy arenas on social problems such as immigration, insanity, retardation, alcoholism, reproduction, and population. Here eugenic science offered biologically based solutions that could compete in policy arenas against the environmentalist or "nurturist" solutions offered by progressive and socialist reformers. The goal of "better people through better breeding" had existed within eugenics for some time before 1900. The movement allowed this sentiment to be mobilized, especially among natural scientists: "Most were interested in eugenics because it offered a 'scientific' solution compatible with the world view of the naturalistic mind" (Ludmerer, 1972:14). In both Great Britain and the United States, most leading scientists, including reproductive scientists, were members of the eugenics societies. In the United States, the officers and membership of the organizations read like a Who's Who of American science at the time, especially the biological and agricultural sciences.[79]

Within the eugenics framework, individuals were categorized as either *aristogenic* (having "good" genes) or *cacogenic* (having "bad" genes) based on criteria that varied among eugenicists.[80] Eugenic science offered two major directions for action based on these assessments. Positive eugenic programs called for more children from the "fit," or aristogenic, who essentially were so defined by their membership in a higher social class and the white/Caucasian "race." Negative eugenic programs focused on reducing the numbers of the "unfit," or cacogenic. At the turn of the century, such programs included the compulsory sterilization of the "unfit" and limits on immigration to prevent more "unfit" people from entering the country (Haller, 1963). While scientific eugenics focused on *hereditary* traits (essentially genetic questions), popular eugenics often glossed over this fine point in its designations of who was "fit" or "unfit" to reproduce. There was much confusion and contention—both scientific and popular—about what kinds of traits could be inherited, an area of scientific debate that remains heated (e.g., Kevles 1985).

One of the most debated issues in the eugenics movement during the first decades of the twentieth century was whether birth control was potentially eugenic (e.g., McLaren 1978). Not all eugenicists favored contraception as a means of negative eugenic programming to limit the reproduction of the "unfit," although some, like the British Malthusian League, did (Ledbetter, 1976). Others, however, feared that contraception would also be used by "selfish" women of the "fit" category who should bear more, not fewer, children, and they opposed it on this principle (Gordon 1976). In both Britain and the United States, segments of the eugenics movement favored compulsory sterilization by the state and/or voluntary sterilization (e.g., Blacker 1961; Landman 1932). It was not until the 1920s that American eugenicists began to accept birth control as a potentially eugenic activity. Their acceptance was due in no small part to their having been seriously courted by leaders of the birth control movement, including Margaret Sanger.[81] It was at this juncture that research on reproduction moved to the center of eugenicists' scientific concerns. At the same time, birth control advocates, eugenicists, and public health activists concerned about issues of contraception and population became serious and organized audiences and consumers of the reproductive sciences. Ironically, as chapter 6 documents in detail, the majority of reproductive scientists eschewed most contraceptive research as inappropriate work until well after World War II.

Demography/Population Studies and Movements. Around the turn of the century, analyses of evolutionary, hereditary, and an array of socioeconomic issues began to lead to analyses of whole populations rather than individuals.[82] The eugenics movement was especially important in developments sited at the intersection of the social and natural sciences. Eugenic societies and organizations provided important professional scientific and interdisciplinary meeting grounds where population issues, including reproduction, were addressed. The neo-Malthusian movement was also central, given its claims about problems of overpopulation. Many of the quantitative and statistical methods developed by eugenicists such as Karl Pearson became integral to demography and population studies spawned by neo-Malthusians and population experts.[83] The ambitious institutional infrastructure the new field of population studies developed largely in academia and privately funded institutes. The key population events and institutions are documented by the following list.[84]

International Neo-Malthusian and Birth Control Conferences (1900–25; six conferences)
[Kellogg] Race Betterment Foundation (1913)
Scripps Foundation for Research in Population Problems (1922)
National Research Council Committee on Scientific Problems of Human Migration (1922)
U.S. Immigration Restriction Act (1924)
World Population Conference (1927)
International Union for the Scientific Investigation of Population (1927)
[Population] Research Division of the Milbank Memorial Fund (1928)
Population Reference Bureau, New York University (1930)
Population Association of America (1931)
Office of Population Research, Princeton University (1936)
International Planned Parenthood Federation (1948)

Population Council (1952)
Department of Demography and Human Ecology, and Center for Population Studies, Harvard School of Public Health (1962)

Population studies addressed a variety of reproductive issues, ranging from birth and death rates to maternal and infant mortality studies. Both implicitly and explicitly, many population researchers sought control over population growth through control over reproductive processes. Reproductive biology and medicine were viewed as major sources of such control. For example, at the organizing meeting of the Population Association for the United States, Dr. Henry Pratt Fairchild summed up its mission: "We are all convinced of the importance of having an association to consolidate the population interests of this country. . . . [T]here is . . . a lack of coordination in this field. . . . [W]e are in a position to take up the phenomenon of population as one of the great factors of human welfare to be rationally manipulated, just as we manipulate the other factors in human relations."[85] By about 1940, family planning/population control research and advocacy became the banner for an amalgam of birth control, eugenics, neo-Malthusian, and population/demographic movements (Gordon 1976:391) in their long-term relations with reproductive scientists.

SUMMARY

In the two decades after the turn of the century, the stage was set for segmentation of a new area of scientific specialization—the reproductive sciences. Personnel were trained, and institutional bases and laboratories were established in the three professional settings where the reproductive sciences would form—biology, medicine, and agriculture. Table 1 summarizes the changing situations in these professional worlds. The fantastic growth of graduate education and of both private and public universities provided support for the specialization inherent in the development of the reproductive sciences enterprise. Agricultural scientists apparently were less tarred by the brush of studying reproductive phenomena because manipulating food animals was widely accepted. The growing social movements of birth control, eugenics, and neo-Malthusianism served as emergent and organizing markets—audiences, sponsors, and consumers for reproductive science—for further biological and medical endeavors. Moreover, by raising reproductive topics as appropriate to open public forum, prestigious movement activists also countered the illegitimacy that had slowed the study of reproduction throughout the Great Chain of Being—including humans.

TABLE 1   Professional Worlds of American Reproductive Sciences

	1900	*1940*
Biology	academic biology as an emerging field	established and entrenched academic biology
	few specialties	many specialties
Medicine	beginnings of scientific medicine	fully developed approaches to scientific medicine
	emerging but still fluid professional specialization	established and enhanced specialization
	obstetrics/gynecology based on surgery	obstetrics/gynecology with functional therapeutics
Agriculture	bare beginnings of science (other than chemistry) in agricultural research	established, scientifically based departments with many lines of research
	animal-based research on nutrition and breeding for improved production	animal-based research on reproduction to improve breeding and production
Scientific worlds	morphological/anatomical emphasis with some physiology	biochemical physiological emphasis with some early molecular biology
	biochemistry and cytology as nascent approaches	molecular biology as nascent approach

PART TWO

The Making of the Reproductive Sciences

CHAPTER THREE

Forming the Discipline

Physiological Approaches, 1910–25

The making of the American reproductive sciences took place largely between 1910 and 1940. It is a story of the formation of a newly bounded line
of scientific work—new problem structures and the research that addressed
them—advanced within the broader arena of concern with reproduction
composed of multiple social worlds. My main focus here is not on specific
scientific discoveries,[1] although I do recount several. Rather, my goal is to
paint with broad strokes the basic social processes of this emergence and
coalescence, the formation of social worlds concerned with reproductive
research that would soon cohere into disciplines, audiences, sponsors, and
consumers in a vital and stabilizing arena. The cross-professional connections and porous boundaries between the lines of research are visible
from the outset. There is even evidence of what could be called disciplinary
and/or professional gerrymandering—explicit interventions to transgress
boundaries to achieve desired goals and transform disciplines and professions. Many of the actors involved in the making of the reproductive sciences were also aggressive in developing the new experimental biology of
which the reproductive sciences were an integral—if often ignored—part.

In this chapter, I frame the boundaries of the new problem structure and
the scope of the reproductive sciences in the United States during their
formative years as a scientific social world. From 1910 to 1925, the focus of
reproductive scientists' work began to move from a physiological orientation to an endocrinological one that still predominates today. In the next
chapter, I focus on the other key social world in the reproductive arena of
this era, the National Research Council Committee for Research in Problems of Sex, funding source and legitimation device extraordinaire. This
committee and the reproductive sciences became inextricable worlds, en-

meshed with each other and both situated within the broader reproductive arena.

I begin by delineating specific conditions that made reproductive research ripe for development after ca. 1910. It is easier to move along a "paved" road, or at least a slashed path, than through virgin jungle. At the turn of the century, the "discovery" of hormones as chemical messengers clarified long-standing problems in reproductive sciences. Also a relatively undifferentiated problem structure of "evolution/heredity/development/reproduction" was realigned, and scientists established newly bounded disciplinary formations in genetics, developmental embryology, and reproduction.

Next I discuss key British initiatives in reproductive research at the turn of the century that culminated with the 1910 publication of Marshall's *Physiology of Reproduction*. This was the very first monograph on reproductive physiology—ways to investigate active physiological functioning of the reproductive systems. The book both laid out the parameters of the new line of work and recruited an array of participants. I then turn to foci of reproductive research in the United States between 1910 and 1925. Here research initiatives in biology, medicine, and agriculture are analyzed in terms of the organization of their problem structures, specific problems addressed, and their professional and disciplinary sponsorship. Finally, I detail the shift from physiological to endocrinological approaches, which became and remain the reigning paradigm.

BOUNDING THE REPRODUCTIVE SCIENCES

The reproductive sciences were formed at the turn of the twentieth century in the context of the broader development of the "new biology," with its innovative physiological and biochemical approaches. Two specific developments in the life sciences of this era promoted reproductive research as a distinctive line of scientific work: the "discovery" or construction of hormones as chemical messengers regulating bodily processes, and the segmentation of new disciplines within the biological sciences.

The Emergence of Endocrinology

The emergence of a modern endocrinology between 1890 and 1905 was, in Borell's (1985:1) terms, "part of the general pattern of success experienced at that time by investigators attempting to extract potent chemical products from animal tissues." The scientific import of the discoveries of hormones lay in the shift from neurological theories and explanations as triggers of physiological processes (nervous stimuli) to chemical explanations (chemical stimuli) for such processes (Borell 1985:11). While modern endocrinology began with the study of gonadal extracts, its focus quickly shifted to nonreproductive hormones.[2] But turn-of-the-century confirmation of reproductive endocrinological processes eventually promoted the broad development of the reproductive sciences.[3] Modern endocrinology emerged largely in Britain through the efforts of medical and agricultural scientists, with significant contributions also made by French scientists, by German gynecologists, and, later, by American researchers.[4]

The list below summarizes major turn-of-the-century developments.

1849: Transplantation of fowl testes prevents atrophy of cockscomb after castration (A. A. Berthold)

1889: Rejuvenating effects of testicular extracts (C. E. Brown-Séquard and A. D'Arsonval)

1891: Remission of myxedema after doses of thyroid extract (George Murray)

1894: Vasopressive effects of adrenal extract (Edward Sharpey-Schafer and George Oliver)

1902: Pancreatic extract (secretin) (William Bayliss and Ernest Starling)

1905: The term *hormone* introduced for chemical effectors (Ernest Starling)

1922: Preparation of insulin (Frederick Banting and Charles Best)

1923: Active ovarian follicular extract (first isolation of a reproductive hormone) (Edgar Allen and Edward Doisy)[5]

Several of these now classic researches demonstrate that the roots of modern endocrinology lay in part in clinical medicine (Borell 1976a,b,c). And clinicians certainly applied the fruits of endocrinological research in clinical practice as quickly as they could. Some biologists and medical researchers later blamed clinicians for moving too quickly, thereby creating clinical and media disasters that had negative consequences for the legitimacy of basic research.

For example, endocrinologist Herbert McLean Evans stated that "endocrinology suffered obstetric deformity in its very birth," referring to Charles Edouard Brown-Séquard's work with animal testicular extracts of ca. 1889 (Borell 1978:283). Brown-Séquard had made highly disputed claims that such extracts had rejuvenating effects when ingested by older adult human males (Borell 1985:1). Years of monkey and goat gland and other male animal testicular transplants into men and other animals (stallions and rams) followed (Hamilton 1986; Rechter 1997). So, too, did accusations of clinical quackery.

Endocrinology was especially vulnerable to controversy at the time because there was virtually no purification of extracts or regulation of their clinical use. Clinical applications—collectively termed *organotherapy*—were made of many kinds of unspecified organ extracts, including gonadal extracts. The popular press reported hotly debated claims of the effectiveness of such treatments for a wide variety of problems. According to Borell, the resulting "tension between the clinic and the laboratory became a major feature of the early years of endocrinological research," especially regarding gonadal extracts.[6] Shortly after Brown-Séquard's work, the discovery that thyroid extracts alleviated myxedema (1891) and the identification of adrenaline (1894) and secretin (1902) fueled the organotherapy debate between clinicians and laboratory scientists. The "use of organ extracts by practitioners . . . quickly outstripped study of these same preparations by experimentalists" (Borell 1985:3). This intense use was also related to the rise of serotherapy (immunology) at about the same time (Borell 1976a). Both were viewed as new miracles of scientific medicine.

In 1895 Edward Schafer (later Sir Edward Sharpey-Shafer), a British physiologist and endocrinologist, became a laboratory-based champion of and spokesman for the theory of internal secretion. To counteract the sensationalism of organotherapeutic claims, he "was stern in his demeanor and terse in his accounts of progress" (Borell 1976a:314). Borell also credits him with salvaging endocrinology from morally based scientific exclusion through his editorship of the *Quarterly Journal of Experimental Physiology* and his own research. Saved from expulsion from physiology, endocrinology became what he termed the "New [Chemical] Physiology." Thyroid extract, adrenaline, and secretin, with their concrete, respectable, and nonsexual applications, helped to legitimate and promote endocrinology. The term *hormone* was introduced in 1905 by Ernest Starling, another British investigator, to specify blood-borne chemicals serving physiological functions. Starling noted that although chemical substances were as important to physiological regulation as nervous stimuli, their study had been previously overlooked.[7] Gradually, endocrinology itself became a specialty, segmenting off from general physiology.[8] In general endocrinology before World War I, the main contributors were British and German scientists. Because of the war itself and the increased prestige and funding of American scientific and medical research after the war, initiative then shifted to the United States, although British, French, Dutch, and German researchers continued to make contributions.[9]

The Three-Way Split: Genetics, Developmental Embryology, and Reproductive Sciences

As endocrinology was emerging during the late nineteenth and early twentieth centuries, other areas of the life sciences were also reorganizing. For decades there had been a densely interwoven nexus of problems in the life sciences grouped around "evolution/heredity/development/reproduction." The differentiation of this nexus into separate problem structures began with the clarification of a sex-related chromosome and the "rediscovery" of Mendel's work in 1900. These new problem structures became the bases of emergent and realigned disciplines: genetics, developmental embryology, and the reproductive sciences—the three-way split. One of the major literatures in the history of the life sciences is focused on these issues, especially the formation of genetics.[10] But this ambitious literature has ignored reproductive processes.[11]

I turn next to a rather internalist account of this three-way split. I demonstrate how certain problems of reproduction were clarified and isolated—in a somewhat sideways fashion—as genetics and developmental embryology set their own disciplinary agendas. Briefly, two intensive approaches during the late nineteenth century—cytology and *entwicklungsmechaniker* (developmental-mechanical) approaches applied in embryology—began to yield important discoveries at the turn of the century.[12] Researchers from a variety of fields and with different skills addressed these problems, working against a shared backdrop of debates about the inheritance of acquired characteristics, Darwinism, and the Haeckelian assertion that ontogeny recapitulates phylogeny. They also shared research materials: cytologists worked predominantly with fertilized eggs; the experimental embryologists applying *entwicklungsmechaniker* approaches worked with both fertilized and unfertilized eggs and embryos.[13] A series of discoveries from both lines of work between about 1880 and 1910 asserted that hereditary information was borne by chromosomes, that there was a sex chromosome related to sex determination, that chromosomes were composed of many genes, and that in sexual reproduction fertilization with meiosis was the means by which hereditary material from both parents was joined in offspring. These discoveries, along with many other intellectual and social changes, allowed researchers in 1900 to grasp the implications of Mendel's work of 1866.[14]

From 1900 to 1910, the nexus of problems surrounding heredity, evolution, reproduction, and development began to be segmented by researchers into newly bounded disciplinary formations. The field of genetics in the United States emerged as a particular set of problems focused largely on genes and chromosomes. The definition of heredity advanced by the new geneticists was largely restricted to the sexual transmission of heritable factors from one generation to the next (e.g., Oppenheimer 1967, Sapp 1983). As Churchill notes (1979:140), classic American genetics traces its roots to these early understandings of "sex and the single organism": "Related but significantly different, all three processes [of fertilization, development, and gamete production analyzed at the turn of the century] added up to a complete ontogenic cycle. . . . Classical geneticists described the first and third of these processes as . . . essential to the understanding of inheritance. . . . [T]he cytological side of classical genetics stands out foremost as the study of sexual events, namely gametogenesis and zygote production." As cytology joined with Mendelism, attention was focused almost exclusively on hybridization experiments and concern over the factorial constitution of the gametes—genes. Sapp (1983:342) notes that this conceptualization eliminated from the core activities of such a genetics problems of importance to both naturalists and biometricians. Genetics in turn segmented into organism genetics and population genetics. The former studies heredity at the individual level of transmission, and the latter addresses evolutionary problems associated with heredity and variation in populations as groups rather than in individuals.[15]

This conceptualization of genetics excluded considerations of the chain of mechanisms leading to cellular differentiation—the traditional embryological problem of development.[16] In Churchill's (1979:140) words, the new geneticists "were restrained enough to leave the further elucidation of the . . . process, or complex of processes, of growth and generation to the embryologist."[17] This still complex web of problems, usually focused through organ systems, remained within the jurisdiction of the new developmental embryology and was pursued experimentally. This new embryology also set up further boundaries for itself, essentially ignoring evolutionary and regenerative problems that had been traditional concerns (Hamburger 1980). New problem areas had been clarified, as Maienschein argues (1984:480), in that embryologists had a clearer task in delineating epigenetic development from the organized egg while cytologists could explore subchromosomal morphological "factors." Pauly (1984) sees these changes as the efforts of biologists to move into new areas as part of their broader attempts to expand constituencies and markets.

Through these developments, researchers interested in reproduction also acquired a clearer agenda and potential new constituencies for what would become the reproductive sciences. Crucial for reproductive research was that problems of heredity and evolution had become scientifically distinct from those of both embryology and reproduction. The delineation of reproduction as a bounded and clarified research area was then accomplished by F. H. A. Marshall (1878–1949), who made precisely such intellectual distinctions in *The Physiology of Reproduction* (1910). He stated that the scope of the physiology of reproduction sufficed as a more than adequate set of scientific problems without heredity, variation (evolution), and cytology. Marshall thus astutely grasped the segmentation processes that were under way at the time. I am not asserting that the reproductive sciences took up "leftover" problems or became a discipline by default; I am asserting instead that what happened to the problems of reproduction at the turn of the century has been largely ignored by historians of twentieth-century life sciences as they carefully traced the origins of modern genetics and developmental embryology.

The embryologist Frank R. Lillie, who turned to reproductive research after 1917, offered a further delineation of the three-way split in his 1919 text, *Problems of Fertilization:* "It is commonly said that there are *two* main problems in the physiology of fertilization, viz.: the initiation of development, or activation, and biparental inheritance. Indeed, so long as we regard fertilization primarily as a problem of *prospective* significance in the life of the organism, *we shall miss the more specific aspects of the process.* Once fertilization is accomplished, development and inheritance may be left to look after themselves."[18] I see Lillie's call for a *retrospective* view of fertilization as asserting a third set of problems in the physiology of fertilization: the sexual reproductive systems as a third line of work, a new discipline. How were the products joined in fertilization themselves produced? What other processes are involved in fertilization per se? What happens in the involved organs *before* fertilization? The "borderline" nature of these research problems is evident (e.g., Maienschein 1985d:161). Initially, the boundaries between and among several of these lines of work were unclear. Regardless, drawing on their own varied backgrounds, researchers pursued problems that might fall within two or more emergent lines of work or shape a new line in its own right.[19]

In sum, several distinctive new lines of scientific work—new social worlds—were delineated and clarified during the first decades of the twentieth century as problems of evolution were segmented. Evolutionary theory was preserved, and new disciplines of genetics (both organism- and population-based), developmental embryology, and the reproductive sciences were added to the biological crown. Historical and social studies of the American life sciences have not usually considered the reproductive sciences as one of the lines of work emerging largely from embryological efforts within the interlocked web of problems of evolution, heredity, development, and reproduction. They were.

BRITISH INITIATIVES IN REPRODUCTIVE RESEARCH

While research on reproduction was conducted in many places, the strongest contributions in the early twentieth century were made first in Great Britain.[20] Between the 1890s and 1910, British scientists synthesized a new reproductive physiology through their research and writings.[21] They collectively offered a fresh vision of an enterprise, explicitly inviting scientists and practitioners from biology, medicine, and agriculture to join in the work.

Walter Heape, sometimes affiliate of the Department of Zoology of Cambridge University,[22] initiated a scientific social world around reproductive research in Great Britain at the turn of the twentieth century. He did so through his own research and through his writings, which articulated a broad conception of a problem structure for reproductive research that has persisted throughout the century. In 1890, Heape began "those researches on the comparative morphology and physiology of the reproductive processes for which he made his name famous" (Marshall 1929:588). Heape's (1894, 1897, 1898) first work in this vein addressed the menstrual cycle in monkeys, describing the histology of the uterine cycle and including an account of ovarian changes. Later he studied the menstrual processes of women as well.[23] Heape's 1900 paper, "On the 'Sexual Season' of Mammals and the Relation of the Pro-oestrum to Menstruation," reframed many issues in mammalian reproductive physiology, especially regarding the estrus cycle.[24] F. H. A. Marshall (1929:588) asserted that this "paper will always stand as the first important contribution to the comparative physiology of breeding in the higher animals." Heape's second key paper (1905) showed that ovulation in the rabbit depended on the act of mating and occurred about ten hours afterward. In this work, Heape asserted that ovarian activity was conditioned by some unspecified extragonadal substance, which he called "generative ferment" (Parkes 1962a). Recent writers regard this article as the initial research on the hypophysiotropic hormones (e.g., Velardo and Kasprow 1972:1–2). Heape's later papers focused on sex determination, a central problem in both early British and American reproductive sciences.

Sociologically, it is the breadth of Heape's conceptualization of reproduction that is most significant. Heape, who had an eye not only for comparison but also for practical application, clearly envisioned the work of the reproductive sciences as directly pertinent to agriculture and medicine. Around the turn of the century, he published on artificial insemination, ovum transplantation with rabbits, and fertility, barrenness, and abortion in sheep. In 1906 he wrote *The Breeding Industry*, which emphasized the economic importance of that industry in Great Britain, encouraging better record-keeping and broader application of scientific methods.[25] His interest in human fertility was addressed in his *Sex Antagonism* (1913) and *Preparation for Marriage* (1914), which prescribed a very narrow role indeed for women—largely procreative and preferably silent.[26]

F. H. A. Marshall was not a student of Heape, who taught only briefly. However, Marshall met with him (Parkes 1962b:71–2) and then trod firmly in Heape's footsteps in constructing the first full physiology of mammalian reproduction. In fact, Marshall's *Physiology of Reproduction* (1910) was dedicated to Heape. After graduating in natural sciences from Christ's College,

Cambridge, Marshall obtained his doctoral degree at the University of Edinburgh, working with Cossar Ewart on problems of heredity and reproduction. Marshall worked with Ewart on prolonged interspecies breeding experiments—telegony.[27] At the same time, he undertook work on the problem of the estrus cycle, first in sheep (at Ewart's own farm), then in the ferret and dog (Parkes 1952–66:ix). Like other researchers in agricultural settings, Marshall had the advantage of access to plentiful mundane materials in terms of established herds and farm animals (Clarke 1987).

Marshall was also working under the encouragement of Edward Schafer (1850–1935). Later Sir Edward Sharpey-Shafer, he was a professor of physiology at the University of Edinburgh from 1899 to 1933 (Borell 1978:282). It is thus not surprising that in a paper on the dog, published with W. A. Jolly in 1905, Marshall claimed that the ovary was an organ of internal secretion, relating secretion patterns to the estrus cycle, the development of corpora lutea of the ovary, and the role of the corpora lutea in the maintenance of pregnancy (Parkes 1962a:72). Marshall also distinguished two types of ovarian internal secretion (follicular and luteal hormones), relating them to their respective roles in the reproductive cycle. It was not until the 1920s that his assertions were fully demonstrated as accurate (Parkes 1952–66:x). Marshall later became Carnegie Fellow and Lecturer on the physiology of reproduction at Edinburgh, returning to Cambridge in 1908 as a lecturer and then a reader in physiology in the School of Agriculture, and editor of the *Journal of Agricultural Science*.[28]

Heape thus began a synthetic and intersectional tradition in reproductive physiology, which Marshall then refined and articulated. A central argument of this book is that three lines of work—in biology, medicine, and animal agriculture—were drawn together in the first decades of this century to form a larger scientific research enterprise around mammalian reproduction. This was Marshall's (1910:1, emphasis added) own vision of the problem structure of reproduction: "Yet generative physiology forms the basis of gynaecological science, and must ever bear a close relation to the study of animal breeding. In writing this volume . . . I have attempted, however inadequately, to co-ordinate or give a connected account of various groups of ascertained facts which *hitherto have not been brought into relation*." Marshall drew together research from zoology and anatomy, obstetrics and gynecology, physiology and agriculture, anthropology and statistics.

Marshall (1910:2) had in mind several explicit audiences for his work, addressing it "primarily to the trained biologist, but it is hoped that it may be of interest also to medical men engaged in gynaecological practice, as well as to veterinarians and breeders of animals." In a preface to *The Physiology of Reproduction,* Schafer noted the expanding audiences and markets for reproductive research and information: "The importance of such knowledge to the community in general is now becoming recognized, and the interest which the subject awakens is no longer confined to the medical profession and to breeders of animals. . . . [T]he multiplicity of facts which are set forth, and the manner in which questions of difficulty are discussed, will have the effect at once of satisfying and of stimulating inquiry in a most important, if hitherto somewhat neglected, branch of Physiology" (in Marshall 1910:vii). Marshall's own introduction echoed Schafer's theme of the prior neglect of the field.

How was this work received? A review in the *American Journal of Obstetrics and Diseases of Women and Children* (E. M. 1911) stated:

> There is hardly any doubt that among physicians interest in generative physiology has increased in recent years. . . . As far as we are aware, this is the first comprehensive treatise dealing exclusively with the physiology of reproduction and as such, the work fills a definite need. The titles of the chapters indicate the wide and catholic scope of this book. . . . It may be said without hesitation . . . that we have seen few books in recent years which afford a better sense of satisfaction. The author reveals a masterly grasp of his subject; the presentation is clear and judicious, and every study of any importance upon generative physiology receives proper consideration. In fact, the references alone should render the book of great value.

It is no wonder, then, that Marshall's work became the classic of the field for over two decades.[29] After Marshall's death, reproductive scientist Alan S. Parkes edited later editions, then called *Marshall's Physiology of Reproduction*. Parkes's (1952–66) preface to the third edition noted: "The appearance of *The Physiology of Reproduction* in 1910 was an event in the history of biological literature. Here, for the first time, was a book containing virtually everything known about the physiological processes involved in reproduction, a book which mapped the present and pointed the way to the future. The work was immediately acclaimed as a masterpiece and placed Marshall in the front rank of British biologists."

Marshall (1910:2) began *The Physiology of Reproduction* by distinguishing problems of heredity from those of reproduction: "The all-important questions of heredity and variation, although intimately connected with the study of reproduction, are not here touched upon, excepting for the merest reference, since these subjects have been dealt with in various recent works, and any attempt to include them would have involved the writing of a far larger book. Similarly, the subject matter of cytology, as treated in such works as Professor Wilson's volume on the cell, is also for the most part excluded." Marshall thus asserted that the scope of the physiology of reproduction per se provided a more than adequate problem structure for the reproductive research endeavor without including problems of heredity and cytology. He organized the scope and parameters of reproductive physiology into the following sixteen areas:

1. the breeding season
2. the estrus cycle in mammals
3. changes in the nonpregnant uterus over the estrus cycle
4. changes in the ovary over the estrus cycle
5. spermatogenesis and insemination
6. fertilization
7. accessory male reproductive organs and insemination
8. biochemistry of the sexual organs
9. the testicle and ovary as organs of internal secretion
10. fetal nutrition: the placenta
11. changes in the maternal organism during pregnancy
12. innervation of the female generative organs, uterine contraction, parturition, and the puerperal state
13. lactation
14. fertility
15. factors determining sex
16. phases in the life of the individual/life cycle

Thus Marshall conceived the endeavor broadly, and he kept the same organization of the scope and problems of the field in the second edition as well (Marshall 1922).[30] Parkes (1952:v) lamented that Marshall's second edition "missed the very rapid expansion of the subject, especially on the endocrinological side, which took place during the 1920s."[31] Reproductive endocrinological research undertaken by American investigators composed the bulk of this expansion, signaling the shift of the center of gravity of the reproductive sciences enterprise from Great Britain to the United States. The shift is clear from the next major standard work in the reproductive sciences: *Sex and Internal Secretions: A Survey of Recent Research.* Edited by Edgar Allen in 1932, this work largely presented U.S. research undertaken after 1921 with the Rockefeller-sponsored support of the National Research Council Committee for Research in Problems of Sex, and is discussed in later chapters.

Several lines of work in the reproductive sciences were addressed by later British investigators. F. A. E. Crew, one of Marshall's students, worked for many years on the problems of sex determination. Crew's *Genetics of Sexuality in Animals* (1927) follows in Marshall's tradition of focus on the relations of morphology to physiology, forging a link between genetics and physiology. Crew (1927:vii) noted that "genetic phenomena must be accepted as evidence of the action of a long chain of physiological processes during development and differentiation."[32] His book *Sex-Determination*

(1933), emphasizing its physiology, went through four editions.[33] John Hammond, based at the Institute of Animal Nutrition of the School of Agriculture at Cambridge with Marshall, was another British pioneer in the reproductive sciences enterprise. In 1925 he published *Reproduction in the Rabbit,* with an introduction and an essay on the formation of the corpus luteum by Marshall. This work, along with his *Physiology of Reproduction in the Cow* (1927), broke new ground in agricultural reproductive science.[34]

As Sir Edward Sharpey-Shafer sponsored and encouraged linkages of British agricultural reproductive research to the medical sciences, so too did Alan S. Parkes, Guy Marrian, and Solly Zuckerman. Sir Alan Parkes earned one of the first undergraduate degrees in agriculture at Cambridge in 1921, where Marshall was his tutor. He completed his Ph.D. in zoology at Manchester University on factors governing the sex ratio. In 1923 Parkes moved to the physiology department of the Medical Sciences Faculty, University College, London (Parkes 1966b:Chapter 1), the site of some of the most advanced nonreproductive physiological and endocrinological research of the day (Borell 1978). And it was this tradition that Parkes took up and directed toward reproductive problems. Guy Marrian, a biochemist at University College, collaborated with Parkes on a variety of reproductive endocrinological studies (Marrian 1967). Sir Solly Zuckerman, based first at the London Zoological Society and later in the anatomy department at Oxford, became one of the leading British investigators of reproductive phenomena, especially in primates. His primary foci were the ovary and oogenesis, hormones of the reproductive cycle, and the prostate; some of this work was collaborative with Parkes (Zuckerman 1930, 1970, 1978). In 1930 the (British) Medical Research Council, in response to numerous applications for hormone research, established a Committee on Sex Hormones with Marshall as chair and Parkes as secretary. Though this committee was short-lived, it seems to have improved the status and recognition of this research area: in 1932 Parkes was called to the National Institute for Medical Research at Hampstead to work on a wide variety of problems in reproductive endocrinology.[35]

Within fifteen years of the publication of Marshall's text, there were three major centers of reproductive research in Great Britain: at Cambridge, Edinburgh, and University College, London. Research on reproduction in Britain was ambitiously conducted under biological, agricultural, and medical auspices. Moreover, the medical and agricultural research efforts, sponsored respectively by the government's Medical and Agricultural Research Councils, were formally brought together by consultative arrangements between the two councils and by grants from both for common biological problems.[36] A rather different pattern characterized American developments.

FORMING THE AMERICAN REPRODUCTIVE SCIENCES, 1910–25

During the years after 1910, reproductive research in the United States began to develop in biology and medicine. Research initiatives on reproductive problems in agriculture lagged some years behind, and early investigators based in American agricultural institutions were themselves generally trained in biology (usually zoology).[37] My selection of the year 1910 as the beginning of modern American reproductive research is based first on Marshall's establishment of the scope and parameters of a modern reproductive science, second on the clarification through the three-way split of distinctive lines of work in genetics, developmental embryology, and the reproductive sciences, and third on certain specific events in American reproductive research. Of course researchers in the United States were pursuing problems that fell within Marshall's parameters before 1910. But subsequent developments in the United States echoed Marshall's articulation of reproduction as a line of scientific work. Such specific events included, for example, studies of the physiological processes of fertilization begun in 1910 by Frank Lillie at Chicago and his students, especially E. E. Just, which lasted to about 1921, and Leo Loeb's (1911) demonstration of the fact that the presence of a corpus luteum in the ovary inhibits spontaneous ovulation in mammals.[38]

The porousness of disciplinary and professional boundaries is salient here. At the turn of the century, neither biologists nor medical scientists could limit their research to established lines of work because many of these lines of specialization had not yet fully emerged. It was a focus on the physiology of particular reproductive processes, such as fertilization or the estrus cycle, that organized the problem structures of research after ca. 1910— as framed by the researchers themselves. And fertilization as a scientific problem, for example, could be claimed by embryologists and reproductive physiologists alike. Thus my selection of 1910 as the moment of formation of the modern American reproductive sciences is sociological as well as founded in specific discoveries of the reproductive sciences.

There was no parallel articulation of Marshall's parameters of the physiology of reproduction in the United States until Frank Rattray Lillie presented "A Classification of Subjects in the Biology of Sex" to the National Research Council Committee for Research in Problems of Sex in 1922. Below is an overview of his classification:

I. The Genetics of Sex
    1. The inheritance of sex and of sex-linked characters
    2. Cytological (sex chromosomes)
II. Determination of Sex
    1. Genetic or zygotic factors in determination of sex

    2. Environmental factors in the determination of sex

    3. Interpretation of sex ratios with reference to sex-determining factors

III. Sex Development; Differentiation of Sex

    1. Descriptive, normal (including hermaphroditism)

    2. The problem of sex hormones

       a. Histological

       b. Experimental

       c. Chemical

    3. The study of other [internal secretions]

IV. The Problem of Sex Inter-Relations [sexuality]

V. Sex Functions

    1. Variations of sex glands under experimental conditions: (transplantation, vasectomy, X-rays and other radiations, antibody injections, vital staining, general physiology of the sex glands)

    2. Sterility (incompatibility of gametes, other causes, experimentally produced sterility)

VI. Systematics of Sex in Animals and Plants

        (Aberle and Corner 1953:102–4)

Aimed directly at a major funding source, Lillie's articulation was much broader than Marshall's and included explicitly genetic aspects.[39] Although Lillie made no explicit mention (at least not in this version of his classification) of reproductive research as an intersection of efforts in biology, medicine, and agriculture, his listing certainly included topics of concern to investigators in all these fields.

Table 2 details the major contributors by profession, the major problem structures by profession, central foci of their work, and their primary research materials in the United States from ca. 1910 to 1925. The researchers noted here compose what I have called the first generation of American reproductive scientists.[40]

One fundamental feature of reproductive research in the United States is the difference in approaches across the three professions that addressed it: biology, medicine, and agriculture. Problems in the life sciences can be conceived in various ways: analytically, by organism, by organ system, by location (e.g., biogeography), by environment (e.g., ecology), and so on. In addressing reproductive problems, biologists tended to focus on analytic problems (sex determination, sex differentiation, fertilization); medical scientists focused on the organ system (reproductive system); and agricultural scientists focused on reproductive phenomena in particular domestic animals (sheep, dairy and beef cattle, swine, and poultry). This pattern reflected the different audiences, sponsors, and consumers of the research produced by each profession. Biologists' focus on analytic problems re-

TABLE 2 The American Reproductive Sciences ca.1910–1925: Professions and Major Problem Structures

	Biology	Medicine	Agriculture
Focus of Problem Structure	analytic problems	reproductive organ system and analytic problems	domestic organisms and analytic problems
Unit of Analysis	species	humans (individual)	populations of selected species
Problems Addressed	Sex determination/differentiation: Lillie 1916, 1917a, b Reproductive endocrinology: Lillie 1917a, b Reproductive cycle: Hartman 1920, 1921 (opossum) Fertilization: Lillie 1916a, 1919 Just 1919 Testicular function: Moore 1919, 1923 Painter 1922, 1923 van Wagenen 1924	Ovary: L. Loeb 1911 Acai 1920 Mammary gland: Myers 1917 Estrus cycle: Stockard and Papanicolaou 1917 (guinea pig) Evans and Long 1920 (rat) E. Allen 1922 (mouse) Corner 1923 (monkey) Papanicolaou 1926 Corpus luteum: Corner 1915, 1921b Papanicolaou and Stockard 1920 Papanicolaou 1926 Long and Evans 1922 Loeb 1923 Reproductive endocrinology: Allen and Doisy 1923 Evans and Long 1921, 1922 Hypophysectomy: Crowe 1910 Smith 1917 Fertility: Hartman 1924	Sex determination/differentiation, twinning: Lactation: Gaines 1915 Brody et al. 1924 L. J. Cole 1916 Estrus cycle: McKenzie 1926 (sow) Artificial insemination: Lush 1922

flected their commitments to developing and moving through "basic" scientific problem structures; their unit of analysis was the species. Physicians' focus on organ systems reflected the established division of labor in medicine and its patterns of specialization by organ system for delivery of clinical services; their units of analysis were both individual humans and human populations. Agricultural scientists' focus was also based on the extant division of labor in animal agriculture, which was by type of organism; their unit of analysis was populations of those organisms.[41] Despite these differences, an intensive mutuality of concerns prevailed across these professional situations. Their differences were in emphasis rather than substance, and often these reproductive scientists had more in common with each other, at least intellectually, than with colleagues within their own professions.

As table 2 shows, the major problems addressed during the 1910–25 era lay in basic reproductive physiology, from fertilization to sex differentiation to the estrus cycle in females, with both medical and agricultural scientists focusing on the latter problem. Reproductive endocrinology was emerging as well (e.g., Allen and Doisy 1923).[42] Between 1900 and 1925, considerable work, both in the United States and abroad, addressed the functioning of reproductive organs such as the corpus luteum and relationships between these organs and the growth of cancerous tumors.[43] Despite its focus on cancer, this work also contributed to the reproductive research endeavor.

EMBRYOLOGICAL ORIGINS

As we have seen, British initiatives in the reproductive sciences came largely from researchers in medical and agricultural institutions (both physiologists and anatomists) and were encouraged by developments in physiology and endocrinology. In contrast, U.S. initiatives in biology, medicine, and agriculture derived much more from work in embryology. Embryological origins were characteristic of initiatives in all three professional situations of biology, medicine, and agriculture.

The vast majority of early American reproductive scientists pursued embryological problems prior to or simultaneously with their reproductive work. Below is a list by profession of reproductive scientists who did embryological investigations, noting the materials on which they pursued this work.

BIOLOGICAL RESEARCHERS

1. Frank R. Lillie (1908, 1917a,b): chick and freemartin calf
2. E. E. Just (Manning 1983): marine invertebrates
3. Carl Hartman (Vollman 1965): opossum and primates

MEDICAL RESEARCHERS

1. Charles Stockard & George Papanicolaou (1917): guinea pig
2. Edgar Allen (1922): mouse
3. George W. Corner (1981): pig, human and primates
4. Herbert Evans (Amoroso & Corner 1975): humans, birds, vertebrates
5. George Bartelmez (Bodian 1973): humans, birds and primates
6. Phillip E. Smith (1917): frog and rat

AGRICULTURAL RESEARCHERS

1. Leon J. Cole (1917): freemartin (calf)
2. Frederick F. McKenzie (1926): pig
3. Emil Witschi (1932): amphibia

Even some of the latecomers to the field began from explicitly embryological work, including Gregory Pincus, a reproductive endocrinologist and key developer of the birth control pill (Ingle 1971). Several investigators were led to reproductive problems in the course of pursuing explicitly embryological problems. Here I focus on two classic researches: Lillie's work on the freemartin calf and Papanicolaou's on the estrus cycle of the guinea pig.

Lillie's Freemartin Research

Lillie's research on the freemartin, described earlier, was perhaps the most famous piece of reproductive science to come out of the Department of Zoology at the University of Chicago. According to Lillie, the bovine freemartin was a "natural experiment." Lillie's research (1916b, 1917a,b) ultimately revealed that a freemartin is a sterile female co-twin to a male, from a separate egg, but whose chorionic vessels (placentas) have merged with the male's in utero, allowing crossing of blood systems. That blood-borne chemicals—hormones—were consequential in embryological development was the major finding of this work.

The research began in 1914 when the manager of Lillie's private farm sent him a pair of twin calf fetuses with their membranes intact.[44] Leon J. Cole, of the Department of Experimental Breeding in the College of Agriculture, University of Wisconsin, heard of Lillie's work on this problem and contacted him in hopes of correlating their efforts. Cole's department was working on multiple births in cattle: twins, double monsters, and freemartins.[45] There was considerable sharing of materials between the two emerging centers of reproductive science because the freemartin problem was important to both.[46] Lillie and his group relied primarily on the Chicago stockyards for freemartin material, acquired through a foreman at a Swift and Company abattoir and through the special efforts of the department's collector. Lillie noted that "every uterus containing twins below a certain size from a certain slaughter house is sent to me for examination without being opened."[47]

Lillie first investigated whether the twins came from the same or separate eggs. Prior research had argued for male twins from the same egg, largely because the twins were monochorial (attached to a single placenta), a phenomenon usually associated with one-egg twins. However, it did not make sense to Lillie that only one of a pair of male twins would be affected in utero. Lillie, who began to examine corpora lutea (sites of recently released eggs) in the ovaries, wrote Cole: "I am faced with the irritating difficulty that most of the uteri are received with one or both ovaries missing," making it impossible to determine whether one or two eggs had been released.[48] Sufficient material gradually was amassed to demonstrate that there had consistently been two corpora lutea (one in each ovary), and two originally separate chorionic vessels (placentas) had fused in utero. Since the freemartin usually possessed mammary glands and both female and male external genitalia, and since if it were male, sex ratios would be strangely skewed, Lillie (1917a,b) concluded that it began as a female.

In 1916 both Cole and Lillie published early abstracts of their work in *Science*. Cole, reflecting his more genetic concerns, focused on sex ratios. Lillie (1916b:612, emphasis added) focused on sex differentiation through the exchange of blood between fetuses: "If one is male and the other female, the reproductive system of the female is largely suppressed, and certain male organs even develop in the female. This is unquestionably to be interpreted as a case of hormone action. It is not yet determined whether the invariable result of sterilization of the female at the expense of the male is due to more precocious development of the male hormones, or to *a certain natural dominance of male over female hormones*." In his classic paper, published in 1917, Lillie emphasized that a vascular connection between the fetuses is requisite for development of a freemartin, and that influences of blood-borne hormones were acting on extant rudiments in the bisexual embryo stage. He concluded (1917a:415): "The course of embryonic sex-differentiation is largely determined by sex-hormones circulating in the blood." Figure 1 is one of the images that appeared in Lillie's article.

Such research continued at Chicago for some years.[49] Lillie noted that the work had "wider application than we expected . . . embryonic and astomoses blood vessels may have quite different results in different animals."[50] Lillie also found that intersexes in goats and swine may be genetic rather than hormonal in origin.[51] In 1917 he had thought that sex hormones were intensifiers of gene action, but by 1932 subsequent research had demonstrated the complete absence of sex differentiation in the absence of sex hormones (Lillie 1932:1–11, esp. 6; Danforth 1932). The freemartin work generated considerable interest in agricultural, popular sci-

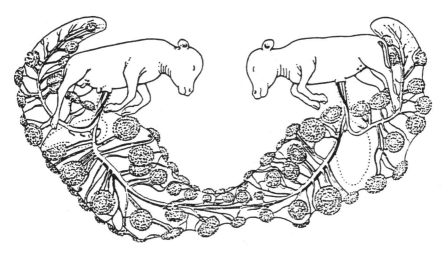

Figure 1. Lillie's freemartin research materials. Lillie (1917a).

ence, and medical circles. One popular article noted: "Twins in cattle may be about two percent of all births in some breeds and the two sexed twins form about half of all the twin births, making the matter of sterile cows that produce no milk of economic importance to the dairy industry."[52] This work deepened connections among Lillie's group and agriculturally oriented centers of reproductive science headed by Cole at Wisconsin and by F. A. E. Crew at Edinburgh.[53] Lillie's work is also cited as pathbreaking in terms of developing theories of immunological tolerance important in medicine (Billingham and Beer 1984). Such concerns were indicated by a popular science service's request to Lillie for a simple account of it in 1922: "There is a wide public interest just now in the subject of endocrinology. In fact the public seems . . . to take it up as a fad in succession to the Freudian complexes now going out of fashion."[54]

The importance of the freemartin work was multifold. First, the work clearly demonstrated hormonal influence on sex differentiation in utero. Thus the production of sex, a classic turn-of-the-century biological problem, involved not only genetic but also physiological processes. Second, the freemartin research "introduced biologists to the problems of the nature, origin, and action of sex hormones at a time when almost nothing was known about the subject" (Willier 1957:219). One might even say that Lillie imported endocrinology into the embryology of his day.[55] Third, problems of sexual differentiation that the work posed were central to several other major reproductive investigations, including work by Emil Witschi, Carl Moore, and Dorothy Price.[56]

The thorny problems of what "determines" sex versus what "differentiates" organisms by sex during development that so absorbed Frank Lillie are classic examples of "boundary line" research. Star and Griesemer (1989) have found that such problems often become "borderline sink-holes," unresolved and commonly ignored. In fact, some years after his original work, Lillie (1932:5) reasserted that "we must make a radical distinction between" the two, with sex determination as chromosomal (genetic) and sex differentiation, in higher animals, as hormonal. That distinction has not held. Over seventy years after the freemartin research, many aspects of these problem have yet to be clarified and remain quite challenging.[57] The biologist Anne Fausto-Sterling (1989, 1993, 1998) asserts that these problems may be particularly complicated by the sustained view among scientists that sex is dimorphic (divisible into two categories) rather than continuous, despite much empirical evidence to the contrary. The confounding of sex and gender by many reproductive scientists, and their commitments to dimorphic sex and to gender differences, may be contributing to the *scientific* problem.

Papanicolaou's Vaginal Smear

The second classic embryological investigation leading to important, explicitly reproductive research was that of George Papanicolaou at Cornell Medical College in New York City (Stockard and Papanicolaou 1917a,b). Charles Stockard was a zoologist by training who had been sponsored for the position of chair of anatomy at Cornell by Franklin Paine Mall, chair of anatomy at Johns Hopkins. Mall felt that the future of experimental anatomy lay in recruiting from the ranks of more experimental zoology, thereby promoting border crossings (Corner 1960:181). Stockard began working in teratology while a student of Thomas Hunt Morgan at Columbia (Oppenheimer 1984) and was interested in the influence of chemicals upon developing embryos. He began studying effects of alcohol on guinea pig embryos in 1909 (Pauly 1996).

Through sponsorship by Morgan, Papanicolaou joined Stockard in these efforts as an assistant in anatomy at Cornell in 1914. Papanicolaou held a Greek medical degree and a German doctorate in zoology. He had worked on sex determination in Munich, a project he resumed at Cornell using guinea pigs from the same colony that supplied Stockard's research. While historical accounts vary, it seems most likely that Papanicolaou initiated the use of vaginal examination and vaginal cell smears on slides to ascertain the estrus cycle stage in order to obtain ova at precise stages of development for his own work on the problem of sex determination.[58] He studied cells from the guinea pig vagina throughout the estrus cycle to determine whether stages of estrus could be indicated by the changing composition of those cells over the cycle.

The answer was a clear yes. But the implications of this research for reproductive investigations went far beyond Papanicolaou's initial modest goals. The stages of the estrus cycle could be determined by microscopically examining smears of easily accessible cells, a procedure that could be done on a routine basis without surgery or sacrificing the animal. Moreover, such cells could serve as indicators of changes from normal phasing due to ablation (removal) of hypothesized hormone-producing organs, and/or transplantation of hormone-producing organs, and/or injection of hypothesized hormone extracts into the animal. And the indicator was not expensive to obtain, nor were the animals! Cheap, fast, and accurate are technical research goals rarely achieved simultaneously.

Each of these dimensions of the smear technique—speed, accuracy, and low cost—gave investigators latitude and flexibility. They could "infer what was happening in the internal reproductive organs without inspecting them directly," an extraordinarily powerful advance (Zuckerman 1970:22). Because so little was known about the sequence of events of the estrus and menstrual cycles, not until these events were more precisely determined and cataloged could experimenters gauge the alterations effected by ablation or transplantation or injection. Intervention for clinical or other reasons was dependent on histologists then painstakingly determining these gradual changes. The significance of earlier contributions of German and Austrian gynecologists lay precisely on this point. In the 1870s, they had cataloged the effects of female castration during the period when oophorectomy (removal of the ovaries) was a popular treatment for dysmenorrhea and certain neuroses. Later, Emil Knauer (in 1896) and Josef Halban (in 1900) noted that the ovary probably produced some special substance that normally maintained the uterus (Borell 1985:12, Corner 1965). The vaginal smear technique permitted systematic examination of the biological activity of different organs imputed to produce such hormones.

Ironically, having such accurate, cheap, and accessible indicators in laboratory animals was initially viewed as important to the production of laboratory animals in colonies, especially but not exclusively for embryological research![59] The other implications of the technique were appreciated quickly, and it became central to many reproductive endocrinological investigations. For example, while developing a colony of mice for a course in embryology, some of the implications of his morphological work drew Edgar Allen into pioneering investigations in reproductive endocrinology. He and Edward Doisy, a biochemist, soon achieved the first isolation of a reproductive hormone, active ovarian follicular extract (Allen and Doisy 1923; Doisy 1932).

The smear method also became a primary means of studying the estrus and menstrual cycles in different animals. Here Papanicolaou's work was followed quickly by Long and Evans's parallel efforts on the rat (1920,

1922), Edgar Allen's on the mouse (1922), Corner's on the monkey and sow (1921b, 1923), Hartman's on the opossum (1923), and Evans and Cole's work on the dog (1931). Agricultural animals studied included the cow, ewe, mare, and sow.[60] As Evans (1959:vii) later noted, "It appeared, indeed, for a time that the application of the vaginal smear method would be all that was required to segment the stages of the estrous cycle in all animals . . . [but] the beautifully distinct changes in the vaginal lochia of small rodents were peculiar for the smaller forms." Only in the dog was the estrogen level high enough to show pronounced vaginal changes. But Papanicolaou, deeply committed to cytology (1933), pursued the vaginal cytological smear as a potential indicator of something in women. He ultimately found that a vaginal smear could indicate potential and actual pathological changes in the cervix and uterus useful for diagnosis of cancerous, precancerous, and other abnormal conditions. The "Pap smear" is now the most widely used cancer screening technology in the world.[61] Papanicolaou also attempted early pregnancy detection through smears, but the Ascheim-Zondek urine-based test proved more successful (Carmichael 1973).

In addition to the two classic investigations of Lillie and Papanicolaou, , the importance of embryological work for the development of reproductive sciences was reflected in the inclusion of a major chapter on embryology in *Sex and Internal Secretions* (Willier 1932:94–159), the American "bible" of reproductive sciences, first published in 1932.[62] George Corner, (1961:ix–xii), in his foreword to the third edition, stated: "To the embryologists of Europe and America we owe in large part also the successful analysis of the mammalian reproductive cycle that has been achieved during this half century." That is, like the gene theory and genetics in the United States (Gilbert 1978, 1987, 1991), the American reproductive sciences also have embryological origins, however long ignored.

It can seem surprising or counterintuitive that problems of reproductive physiology and endocrinology were pursued in America in the early twentieth century predominantly not by physiologists but by zoologists and anatomists, most with backgrounds in embryology. Addressing this historical problem, Diana Long (1987) undertook a statistical analysis of the disciplinary affiliations and identities of "sex researchers" publishing in the *American Journal of Physiology* from 1923 to 1947. While only about one-third identified themselves primarily as physiologists, two-thirds were members of the American Physiological Society. Long argues that sex researchers, regardless of discipline, gained many benefits through associating with the prestigious physiological society and journal. Prestige and legitimacy were important cultural resources and goals for early reproductive scientists whether they considered themselves anatomists, zoologists, physiologists, or endocrinologists.

The freemartin work supported the endocrinological direction of American reproductive sciences. Then, because of its incredible value as an indicator and its ease of use, the vaginal smear led many investigators from different disciplines and professions into this new domain of reproductive research. By 1925 the reproductive sciences were fully initiated as integrated lines of modern scientific work, with emphasis shifting from classical physiological work to an explicit biochemical endocrinological focus.

DOABILITY AND THE RISE OF REPRODUCTIVE SCIENCES

Reproductive research had long been viewed as controversial by some constituencies because of its association with sexuality and clinical quackery, and because of its potential capacity to alter "natural" patterns of reproduction and create "brave new worlds" (Clarke 1990a). Why would so many investigators of considerable stature and renown nevertheless pursue reproductive research between the two world wars? I argue here that they did so because, after 1917, reproductive research was highly "doable" research, especially when compared with embryology at the time.

Fujimura (1987, 1988) put forward the concept of the "doability" of research: assessing whether a specific line of work (a set of investigations focused on a particular set of problems) is feasible and worthwhile to undertake at a specific time and place. To construct doable problems, investigators must assess their particular needs for doing the actual experiments or other aspects of investigation, the work organization and commitments of the laboratory or other research site, and the support of various kinds available in wider scientific and related worlds for doing that work. Doability thus requires investigators to fit or align their research problems simultaneously across experimental capacities, laboratory organization and direction, and the broader worlds of fiscal, scientific, and extrascientific support. Before beginning the work, scientists must both pull together and articulate a wide array of requisite elements to make as sure as possible, given the circumstances, that results recognized as worthwhile will emerge downstream. The concept of doability provides a framework for examining the rise of American reproductive sciences after the three-way split. The question is whether the emergent and newly bounded disciplines (genetics, developmental embryology, and reproductive sciences) all offered researchers equally attractive lines of highly "doable" research after 1910. The question must be answered at the levels of the experiment, the laboratory, and wider social worlds.

Doable research in genetics preceded that in reproductive physiology. Key to increased genetics research at the experiment level after 1910 was the use of *Drosophila*, corn, guinea pigs, and chickens as major research materials—the "right tools for the job."[63] As Ross Harrison

(1937:370), a noted embryologist from Yale, commented, "Much progress has depended upon the fortunate findings of organisms that illustrate this or that principle clearly or such as submit to the most ruthless experimentation." In terms of laboratory personnel, histories of genetics fully document the adequacy of staffing (Rosenberg 1967; Mayr and Provine 1980).

Doability must also be assessed at the level of the social world, which is more complicated. It includes the likelihood of research payoffs from pursuit of the line of work, the wider scientific legitimacy of pursuit of those problems, and fiscal and other kinds of support for research. It also includes, with varying degrees of salience, the social legitimacy of those problems. In genetics, the initial investigations that triggered the three-way split were immediate proof of the doability and probable high payoffs of genetics research. The scientific legitimacy of problems of heredity and evolution had been well established for centuries and intensified after Darwin (e.g., Cravens 1978). Because genetics research was cheap at the time, fiscal support was initially not a serious issue. Wider scientific support was extensive among both agricultural breeders and biologists. Through enhanced control over hereditary processes in plants and animals, genetics promised tremendous profitability. Moreover, the eugenics movement provided broad social legitimacy for pursuing enhanced control over heredity in humans. By 1915, *The Mechanism of Mendelian Heredity*, by T. H. Morgan and his associates, had fully established this line of work.

Highly "doable" research on reproduction began with Papanicolaou's work in 1917. The vaginal smear technique for obtaining an indicator of estrus stage was as potent for the development of reproductive sciences as the visible chromosomal structure of *Drosophila* was for genetics. Taking speedy advantage of applicable results such as the smear technique is important in constructing doable problems. The freemartin investigations of Lillie and his associates immediately linked this work to cutting-edge endocrinological problems. Both studies triggered the flood of reproductive investigations in biology, medicine, and agriculture noted earlier. The development by P. E. Smith (1916, 1927, 1932) after 1916 of hypophysectomy techniques (the surgical removal of the anterior pituitary without brain or other damage) permitted finer-grained assessments of the biological activities of hormones, and such techniques were often used in conjunction with vaginal smears. Having "golden hands" in doing hypophysectomies could also be a major factor in career advancement (Greep, personal communication).

In the laboratory, the biochemical nature of the endocrinological thrust of reproductive sciences quickly led investigators into collaboration with biochemists.[64] These collaborations took different forms at various research centers, although the reproductive scientists rather than the biochemists seem to have established the research agendas, as Kohler (1979, 1982) has argued. For example, George Corner at Rochester hired biochemist Willard Allen. Similarly, H. L. Fevold served as a research chemist in the laboratory of Frederick Hisaw, first at Wisconsin and later at Harvard. In Herbert Evans's Institute at Berkeley the chemist was Choh Hao Li. Lillie and his colleagues at Chicago worked closely with Fred Koch of the Department of Physiological Chemistry. And Edgar Allen at Washington University in St. Louis worked closely with Edward A. Doisy, a professor of biochemistry in the School of Medicine.[65]

However, the greatest change occurred with regard to scientific and social legitimacy and support at the wider social world level. Beginning in the 1910s and increasing after World War I, the birth control, eugenics, and neo-Malthusian movements raised reproductive topics as appropriate to public forums. Prestigious activists from these movements, including many scientists, also countered the illegitimacy that had slowed the development of reproductive research. Another upsurge of fiscal and social support for reproductive research during the interwar years came through the National Research Council Committee for Research in Problems of Sex. This committee, which existed from 1921 to 1962 (National Academy of Sciences 1979:v), was funded by prestigious Rockefeller and other philanthropies. By establishing a "clear and present" boundary between the reproductive sciences and sexology, and by capturing the committee for basic reproductive research (as described in the next chapter), these scientists simultaneously gained legitimation, funding, and a strong basic research identity. Powerful sectors in American society sought and supported enhanced scientific control over nature in many forms. Doability must also be assessed in this broader context of expanding the production of scientific research and its downstream applications.

But doability is a relative phenomenon and must be assessed comparatively. This is particularly true of research at the turn of the century because of the highly porous nature of disciplinary and professional boundaries that permitted investigators to move relatively easily in new directions. I have noted that research in both genetics and reproductive sciences was very doable during this era. In contrast, it can be argued, after the exciting flood of experimental work between 1890 and 1910, embryology experienced a slump between 1910 and 1925. Ross Harrison (1937:370) of Yale, a leading American embryologist, lamented in print that embryology had been doing poorly from 1910 to 1925, the very years that saw the formation of American reproductive sciences and dramatic growth in genetics: "The fertility of the soil [in embryology] seemed to have suddenly run out and tillage no longer worth while. What more human, then, than the gold rush to genetics and general physiology. . . . Later came another gold rush to endocrinology, now perhaps at its height."

Willier and Oppenheimer's (1964) collection of classic papers in the history of embryology also illustrates this slump. The volume includes six articles from 1888 to 1908, nothing between 1908 and 1913, only four articles between 1913 and 1924, and nothing else until 1939. Moreover, two of the articles published between 1913 and 1924 were by Lillie, one on fertilization and another on the freemartin. Both can be viewed as works in the physiology of reproduction rather than in embryology. Of the other two articles, one was written by Charles M. Child on susceptibility gradients, and the other was by Hans Spemann and Hilda Mangold on the organizer concept; neither line of work was highly productive in the long run, although Spemann was awarded the Nobel Prize in 1935 (Hamburger 1980). During this period, doable lines of work in embryology failed to produce advances and the field was viewed as comparatively dull: "Embryology . . . appeared increasingly to be in some disarray" (Horder, Witkowski, and Wylie 1986:111–12; Gilbert 1991).

Thus while embryology was exerting less attraction, genetics and the reproductive sciences began to exert more, and both younger and more established scientists were drawn into these emergent lines of work. For example, Allen (1979:123) stresses that "the agricultural climate around the turn of the century . . . emphasized genetic transmission rather than embryonic differentiation as the crucial problem to be understood." Like genetics, then, the reproductive sciences were an "open territory" drawing investigators into a new field as American biology expanded. Investigators in either field could construct doable problems. They could meet immediate research needs, produce good scientific work with relative ease, obtain funding and other kinds of legitimacy, develop their individual careers, build laboratories as centers of focused research, and help found new disciplines and subdisciplines. Clearly, both genetics and the reproductive sciences profited greatly from embryology's loss.

CONCLUSIONS

The late development of reproductive physiology is explained largely by its illegitimacy and by the preoccupation of biologists at the turn of the century with problems of heredity and evolution. Once the basic mechanisms of heredity had been identified and placed within the new discipline of genetics, problems of reproduction and developmental embryology could cohere. The determination that hormones regulate many general physiological phenomena in addition to nervous system regulation gave impetus to all of endocrinology. Core research problems pursued to 1925 included mechanisms of sex differentiation, fertilization, the estrus cycle, and the isolation and synthesis of gonadal hormones.

Much early American reproductive research had its origins in embryological efforts. A slump in developmental embryology between about 1910 and 1925 appears to have led many workers to abandon that field for highly "doable" work on explicitly reproductive and genetic problems. I would extend Fujimura's definition to assert that doability generally implies some kind of profitability, for almost all research done in twentieth-century America has been pursued or at least justified on such practical grounds—regardless of profession. The practicality of the split between developmental embryology and genetics was not merely a matter of efficient research organization or competition for resources but also a reorganization that clarified the productive capacity of a new line of work—genetics—that would rapidly prove itself in terms of profitability in plant and food animal (re)production. Nor did the reproductive sciences hide behind the skirts (or more accurately the trousers) of embryology but, despite moral opprobrium, initially claimed its identity boldly as "the biology of sex" for similar practical payoffs. "What counts" in the American life sciences may itself be distinctive. As Horder and his associates (1986:111) have noted, "All the more intriguing then is the question of why it was in the United States that the 'split' between embryology and genetics occurred so prominently." The splitting off of reproductive sciences was also prominent in the United States, despite its general lack of recognition in the history of biology and medicine. Indeed, if we seek an "ecology of knowledge" (Rosenberg 1979b) and the conditions of its production, we must also ask, "What science counts to whom and under what conditions?"

By 1925, reproductive research was fully initiated as a modern line of scientific work in American biology, medicine, and agriculture. But, despite its broad applicability, it remained a relatively minor endeavor involving only a handful of researchers. In the next fifteen years, the scientific world of reproductive research would coalesce around endocrinology and become a full-fledged enterprise. It did so largely through the fiscal sponsorship and legitimacy bestowed upon it by the National Research Council Committee for Research in Problems of Sex, which was formed in 1921. This highly prestigious, Rockefeller-funded entity was fundamental to the making of not only the national but ultimately the international reproductive arena for the rest of the century. We turn next to the story of this committee, which involved the construction of yet another set of disciplinary boundaries, this time with sexology.

CHAPTER FOUR

Seizing the Means of
Studying Reproduction

The NRC Committee on Problems of Sex

Between 1921 and 1941, American reproductive scientists led by Frank R. Lillie successfully seized the means of studying reproduction by redirecting the mission of the National Research Council Committee for Research in Problems of Sex (NRC/CRPS). In short, they captured the sponsor. They did so through strategic use of arguments for basic research, and they redirected the mission from what we would now term sexology to basic reproductive science with a major emphasis on the enterprise's emergent core activity of reproductive endocrinology. By 1931, this redirection of research effort was recognized by a shift of ultimate sponsor funding from a social action agency (the Bureau of Social Hygiene) to a biomedical research agency (the Natural Sciences Division of the Rockefeller Foundation). Scientists were seeking funding, legitimacy, and autonomy for the reproductive sciences during their vulnerable years of formation and coalescence as a scientific enterprise. They were stunningly successful, simultaneously achieving several goals: broad legitimation for reproductive research through association with the National Research Council (NRC); significant funding; direct relationships between major centers of the reproductive sciences enterprise and a major biomedical research sponsor, the Rockefeller Foundation; and a "basic" research identity for the reproductive sciences.

The coup of achieving major sponsorship for two decades fundamentally shaped the organizational context and infrastructure of the reproductive sciences in ways that are manifest even today. It was here, in the NRC/ CRPS, that the American version of the division of labor between sexology and the reproductive sciences was forged. It was here that key aspects of the research agendas of each discipline were articulated. And it is here that I challenge Foucault's (1978:54–55) assertion that sexology and the reproductive sciences were not mutually constitutive. I argue instead that many aspects of what would count as sexology and as reproductive science, at least in the American context, were hashed out in the committee between 1921 and 1941. Ongoing negotiations among a heterogeneous cast of characters with divergent commitments to knowledge production yielded competing agendas for funding. The basic reproductive sciences seized the day.

In forming their enterprise, reproductive scientists frequently confronted powerful demands from various audiences, including funding sources. These scientists felt they were being asked to engage in work they saw as either unscientific, beyond the scope of their envisioned enterprise, and/or threatening to their autonomy over their work. This conflict arose in part because actual and potential clinical and applied uses of the reproductive sciences were manifold and comparatively transparent even to lay audiences, and because the boundaries of the reproductive sciences were permeable at this time, especially but not only with sexology. To retain their autonomy and control, the main strategy reproductive scientists developed to manage such "external" audience demands was the making of arguments for basic research. They would assert that "basic" research should have priority over clinical and applied efforts—that it should be done first and foremost. Such research could, of course, safely take place under biological, medical, or agricultural institutional auspices—far removed from the taint of human sexual interaction. Reproductive scientists further argued that through basic research all of the diverse, conflicting clinical and applied needs and desires of their various audiences, sponsors, and consumers could ultimately be met.

In constructing "basic" reproductive sciences in the 1920s, these investigators quickly became embroiled yet again in the problematics of boundaries. In the last chapter we saw how scientists pursuing reproductive problems benefited from new boundaries constructed around *other* disciplines (e.g., genetics and developmental embryology), which also served to demarcate their own. In this chapter we examine the construction of a boundary between the emergent reproductive sciences and the discipline that has come to be called *sexology*—studies of sexuality mostly in humans. Here it was reproductive scientists themselves who crafted many of the boundary markers, since many individuals and groups seeking scientific studies of sexuality would have been more than pleased to have their work included under the rubric "the problems of sex" supported by the Committee. Havelock Ellis, Magnus Hirschfeld, Richard Krafft-Ebbing, Sigmund Freud, and many others were constructing new conceptualizations of sexuality and seeking scientific legitimacy for their endeavors as well.[1] Among other research, they sought a biology of erotics, an anatomy and physiology of sexuality, pursued as the "scientific study of sex." Gradually they and others began to frame human sexuality as falling within an emergent social sci-

ence of "sexology." In this chapter we see how reproductive scientists constructed such work as separate from the natural sciences' biological studies
of mammalian reproductive system phenomena, or even from most animal
sexual behavior. What would ultimately distinguish sexology was its (almost) exclusive focus on humans as objects of study. This emphasis allowed
such research to be framed as social science and hence beyond the scope
of NRC sponsorship.

The strategic arguments for basic research made vociferously and effectively by reproductive scientists were part of their broader effort to construct a legitimate, autonomous, authoritative, and well-funded reproductive sciences enterprise. Such arguments were used both within and by the
NRC/CRPS to educate, persuade, trade off, manipulate, and coerce (Strauss
1991) support of basic reproductive science. While such arguments are now
considered classic rhetoric for the legitimation of scientific research, between 1920 and 1940 they were relatively new. They were also being used
in innovative science planning and policy development schemes, especially
within and by the NRC (Kargon and Hodes 1985:305; Bugos 1989).

Given the chronic problem of social and scientific illegitimacy confronted by reproductive scientists, arguments for basic research were especially apt. The aura of supposed neutrality and objectivity associated with
basic research was invoked, providing scientists with the proverbial ten-foot
pole with which they could touch reproductive organs with propriety. Basic
biological research arguments also deleted sexuality from the research
agenda. Such arguments were used successfully to develop long-term institutional arrangements to benefit the larger enterprise. Analytically, they
were arguments regarding the core activity of the enterprise—basic research first and foremost, and largely in reproductive endocrinology. Such
activities may be particularly characteristic of the early stages of construction of a scientific enterprise (Coleman 1985).

Reproductive scientists used arguments for basic research in a variety of
settings and with a variety of other significant social worlds within the larger
arena of human reproduction. In this chapter, I examine one particular interactive setting that included a research-sponsoring agency (the NRC/
CRPS) and its funding sources (the Bureau of Social Hygiene and the
Rockefeller Foundation). The chapter is thus an analysis of the interactions
between an emergent scientific discipline (the reproductive sciences) and
key related social worlds (sponsors and funding sources).[2] In chapter 6, I
examine strategic arguments for basic research as they were used in relation
to a much more amorphous and diverse set of social worlds, those of birth
control, eugenics, and neo-Malthusian population control advocates.

The story I tell here of the NRC/CRPS is only one among many that
have been and will be narrated. One of the key topics that engaged the
Committee for decades was the (largely) biological construction of gender,

especially via reproductive endocrinology. The work of a number of other scholars analyzes these and related issues.[3] The struggles within the Committee, at least those preserved in its records, obviously conflate sex and gender but also seek to rationalize and naturalize gender. Hall (1974, 1978) has argued that in fact the language of psychobiology was aimed at bridging the natural sciences/social sciences divide to create what we might now call a hybrid or transdisciplinary scientific approach to sex. Haraway (1989:22) echoes this in discussing the "tying of technical and mythic strands that weave the scientific objects of knowledge we call race and sex." In contrast to these approaches, my analysis emphasizes the seizing of the means of studying reproduction through the natural science lenses of biology and medicine. Of course this is not the only work the Committee supported (see Aberle and Corner 1953). However, it is the story most important to reproductive scientists, for whom separating sexuality from reproduction became paramount to the formation of the reproductive sciences as a discipline—for disciplining reproduction.

I begin with a brief account of the initial funding of the NRC/CRPS by the Bureau of Social Hygiene, its founding, and its initial mission.[4] I then offer an analysis of specific uses of strategic arguments for basic research by reproductive scientists within the NRC/CRPS. Next I turn to a major consequence of the success of these arguments—the shift of sponsorship from the Bureau of Social Hygiene to the Rockefeller Foundation's Division of Medical Research. One of the ironies or contradictions in the development of the NRC/CRPS program between 1921 and 1940 is that toward the end of this period, *after* sponsorship had shifted to the Rockefeller Foundation, there was a serious shift of research support back toward human sexuality research. This culminated in the 1940s with the NRC/CRPS providing extensive sponsorship for Alfred Kinsey's pathbreaking research on human sexuality (Aberle and Corner 1953; Pomeroy 1982). The chapter concludes with an analysis of this shift in its wider contexts of the development of alternative funding sources for "basic" reproductive science and its enhanced social and scientific legitimacy. The linkages of the Committee to Warren Weaver's vision of "a new science of man," including molecular biology, are also examined. Throughout I discuss proposals for Committee action that did not succeed as well as those that did in order to better track the full range of choices and opportunities, fleshing out what might have been as well as what was.[5]

THE BUREAU OF SOCIAL HYGIENE AND THE NRC/CRPS

The Bureau of Social Hygiene (BSH), located in New York City, derived from the commitments of John D. Rockefeller Jr. and others to creating an organization for "the study, amelioration and prevention of social conditions, crimes and diseases which adversely affect the well-being of society."[6] Rockefeller's initial interest was triggered through his appointment in 1910 to a grand jury to investigate white slavery in New York City. He took his membership considerably more seriously than expected and founded the BSH to continue these activities.[7] The BSH was incorporated in 1913 and terminated in 1940. Its goals were amelioration of the practices of prostitution, vice, venereal diseases, and narcotics addiction, and support of criminal rehabilitation, criminology, eugenics, birth control, and sexuality research. The work was undertaken through grants to a wide variety of individuals and organizations. While the BSH was essentially a Rockefeller funding agency, funds were also channeled through the BSH from other philanthropies, including Paul Warberg, the New York Foundation, and the Spelman Fund.[8] John D. Rockefeller, Jr. was, however, the primary donor, contributing $5.8 million during the bureau's existence (Aberle and Corner 1953:4). Precisely because of the controversial nature of many of its activities, the BSH was established and maintained separately from other such agencies, including the Rockefeller Foundation.[9] In the BSH as well as the foundation, concern with the application and use of science was a strong tradition rather than fundamental academic research for its own sake (Kohler 1978:490).

One organization supported through grants from the BSH was the American Social Hygiene Association, whose primary concern was sex education.[10] Earl F. Zinn, a graduate student in psychology, was in charge of research promotion for this group (Zinn 1923). Sophie Aberle and George Corner (1953:9–13)'s biography of this committee, on which both served as members, takes up this point. They attribute the initial idea for NRC sponsorship of a program of sex research to Zinn in a 1920 meeting with a human sexuality scientist and educator from the YMCA. The BSH was then under the leadership of Katherine Bement Davis, who was its general secretary until 1928 and was herself an early human sexuality researcher.[11] Davis had come to the BSH after a long career in social work and penology focused on the rehabilitation of prostitutes. She held a doctorate in political economy from Chicago, where she had studied with Thorstein Veblen, taking a minor in sociology with such faculty as George Vincent, later president of the Rockefeller Foundation (Lewis 1971:439).

Through the actions of Davis, Earl Zinn was able to present the idea for a sex research group directly to John D. Rockefeller, Jr., who gave his approval. Zinn then became an employee of the BSH, focusing on sex research development plans (Aberle and Corner 1953:9–13). Zinn next sought the assistance of Robert M. Yerkes, chairman of the Research Information Bureau of the NRC, to develop and present the proposal for sex research to the NRC.[12] After its organization, Zinn was appointed executive secretary of the committee, while Yerkes served as chairman.[13] It was thus the BSH that initiated and sponsored the proposal for a committee for research in problems of sex to the NRC.

There are varied accounts of the initiation of the CRPS within the NRC. Most of these "origin stories" are "insider histories" and as such must be viewed as political reconstructions of events for varied purposes, especially legitimacy (e.g., Strauss 1982). My analysis in this chapter draws on the tensions and contradictions in these insider histories, both published and unpublished. The account offered in the First Annual Report of the NRC/ CRPS, written by Zinn, stated:

> On July 1st 1921 the Bureau of Social Hygiene made an appropriation of $10,000 for one year for the promotion of *a plan* for systematic research on sex problems designed to provide a better scientific foundation for an understanding of *sex in man.* According to this plan it was proposed to secure the endorsement of an accredited scientific agency, preferably the NRC, and to have the agency in question assume the responsibility for the development and administration of the plan. In November 1921 the NRC endorsed the proposal. . . . It was proposed that a special committee composed of representatives of the related biological sciences attached to the Division of Medical Sciences . . . be appointed to administer this project.[14]

An account by Rockefeller Foundation administrator Max Mason, written after interviews with two committee members, notes that in 1920, when the "palliative" work of the BSH "was not getting anywhere," Zinn formally presented a plan to the NRC for the scientific study of sex.[15] The proposal for a committee was initially brought to the Division of Anthropology and Psychology of the NRC, which decided to turn it over to the Division of Medical Sciences. Aberle and Corner (1953:10) attribute the Anthropology and Psychology Division's "unresponsiveness" to the fact that it was itself a new division, "and there seems to have been a feeling that these subjects [anthropology and psychology] still had to win justification as natural sciences." Sponsorship of a program of research on sex promoted by an outside group was not viewed as likely to be particularly helpful toward that end. Aberle and Corner (1953:11) stress that the social illegitimacy of sexuality and sexology explained this division's avoidance of association with sex research: "Even the scientific profession [was] very sensitive."

Nor was the initial response of the Division of Medical Sciences positive. Aberle and Corner (1953:11) noted unease at the NRC from the outset regarding whether the potential social science aspects of the research fell within the more natural sciences–oriented mission of the NRC. Only when Victor Vaughn, a physician and hygienist familiar with venereal disease, succeeded to the chairmanship of this division did the proposal receive positive review. Vaughn, lending clinical legitimacy to social aspects

of sex research, called a conference of investigators and physicians considered qualified to pass upon the merits of the project.[16] The BSH gave the
NRC $10,000 to cover the costs of the conference and, anticipating ap-
proval, for research to be subsequently generated by it.[17] The conference
adopted the following resolution:

> The impulses and activities associated with sex behavior and reproduction
> are fundamentally important for the welfare of the individual, the family, the
> community and the race. Nevertheless, the reports of personal experience
> are lacking and the relatively few data of observation have not been collected
> in serviceable form. Under circumstances where we should have knowledge
> and intelligence, we are ignorant. To a large degree our ignorance is due to
> the enshrouding of sex relations in a fog of mystery, reticence and shame.
> Attitudes toward the subject have been fixed by moral teaching, religious
> instruction, and social propaganda, all based on only a slight foundation of
> well-established fact. In the presence of this secrecy and prejudice, scientific
> investigation would be difficult. The committee is convinced, however, that
> with the use of methods employed in physiology, psychology, anthropology,
> and related sciences, problems of sex behavior can be subjected to scientific
> examination. In order to eliminate any suggestion that such inquiry is un-
> dertaken for purposes of propaganda, it should be sponsored by a body of
> investigators whose disinterested devotion to science is well recognized. For
> these various reasons the committee recommends that the National Research
> Council be advised to organize and foster an investigation into the problems
> of sex.[18]

Significantly, both Zinn's account and this resolution of the NRC conference explicitly discuss the problems of sex to be studied as human problems
and the research work as falling within what would now be called sexology.

The NRC then proceeded to establish the CRPS. Its initial members
were Walter B. Cannon (professor of physiology, Harvard Medical School),
Edwin G. Conklin (professor of biology at Princeton), and Yerkes. Conklin
served only a few months and was replaced by Frank R. Lillie (professor of
zoology at Chicago). Two more members were soon added: Thomas W.
Salmon (professor of psychiatry at Columbia University's College of Physicians and Surgeons, and a former member of the Rockefeller Foundation
staff) and Katherine B. Davis (executive secretary of the BSH).[19]

The multidisciplinary composition of the committee reflected its initial
mission: "More rapid progress toward an understanding of sex in its many
phases will result if, in addition to the work now being done, *a systematic
attack from the angles of all related sciences is made,* with knowledge of sex as
the central objective. This is the main purpose of the Committee" (Aberle
and Corner 1953:15, emphasis added). The multidisciplinary nature of the
initial mission of the NRC/CRPS is clear. Its own founding statement was
also well publicized, as in this account in the *Journal of the American Medical*

Association: "This committee was organized in November 1921, for the purpose of promoting, coordinating and systematizing research on sex problems to the end that conclusions now held might be evaluated and a better understanding of human sexuality obtained" (Zinn 1923).

REDIRECTING THE MISSION: ARGUING FOR BASIC RESEARCH

The mission of the NRC/CRPS was redirected from its initial broad multidisciplinary focus on problems of human sexuality through reproductive scientists' arguments and their agenda for *basic biological research* on reproduction. This capture was accomplished through the following:

avoidance of developing the BSH-required overall plan for multidisciplinary research;
full articulation of a plan for basic biological research;
designation of research on humans as inadequately scientific;
token funding of research on humans;
major funding of "fundamental" biological research.

The initial project of the committee, as specified by the first BSH grant, was to be a survey of extant research and a plan for future work.[20] Despite multiple meetings and efforts, no plan was ever formulated. Further, the committee's deliberations on this plan were not formally recorded: "Many of these orientation surveys and discussions were placed on file, so to speak, only in the heads of the committeemen" (Aberle and Corner (1953:15–17). Zinn compiled some bibliographies, but no survey was put to paper (that has been archived). Sociologically speaking, in the absence of a general multidisciplinary plan, *any* plans put forward would have considerable weight. Committee members were then invited to prepare or procure outlines from their own fields of competence. Two were prepared at this time:[21] a program for research on sex neurobiology and psychobiology commissioned by Chairman Yerkes from K. S. Lashley, then at the University of Minnesota, and Frank Lillie's plan arguing for basic research on the biology of sex. Lillie's agenda succeeded in capturing and redirecting the mission of the NRC/CRPS.[22]

Thus while at its outset the committee did what might be termed "outreach work" toward the development of multidisciplinary research on "the problems of sex," systematic organization of such research was not undertaken, despite superficial bureaucratic statements of such commitments.[23] Aberle and Corner's (1953:15–17) comment on the absence of such a plan reads like an apologia: "In retrospect it is clear that the body of knowledge upon which plans for research had to be based was so diffuse and inchoate that it could not readily be reduced to form suitable for publication." The

First Annual Report of the NRC/CRPS, prepared by Zinn, similarly lamented:

> The condition specified by the Bureau of Social Hygiene in making the original grant for the promotion of this project included the formulation of a comprehensive and detailed research program. The scope and complexity of the problem, the uncertain outcome of research together with the obvious necessity of considering in relation to a research program such factors as presence and availability of interested investigators, adequate research facilities and a carefully considered administrative plan, indicated clearly the impracticability of attempting to fulfill this condition within the time specified. Such a program as was originally contemplated should develop gradually and in the directions indicated by the results of the researches.[24]

Chairman Yerkes summed up these deliberations more candidly: "Our committee was appointed primarily to prepare a program of research on problems of sex and to formulate plans and recommendations for the conduct of fruitful investigations in this field. Thus far it has seemed wiser to proceed somewhat opportunistically with special lines of investigation than to attempt the formulation and support of a general plan."[25]

In sharp contrast to the absent general plan, Frank Lillie's proposed agenda for basic biological research was most ambitious. It classified a very rich set of subjects in the biology of sex (see Appendix 2). This agenda became the heart of the committee's program between 1921 and 1940, and served as the basic problem structure of the American reproductive sciences for decades.[26] Fundamental to my argument, it specifically *excluded* humans as research materials for biological research.

In explaining the redirection of the committee's mission, Aberle and Corner (1953:18) assert that Lillie, as an involved scientist, was in a better position than other committee members to propose a plan and that "biological questions were fundamental to the other problems; furthermore, the biology of reproduction was much more advanced in 1922 than the physiology and psychology of sex behavior." This analysis ignores the fact that other members were also scientists in salient areas, and that the explicitly avowed purpose of the committee was to stimulate underdeveloped research areas. Aberle and Corner's (1953:18) description of the committee at its outset is not only apologetic but lacks any analysis of power: "The reader must remember the situation in which the Committee found itself in 1922. A little group of earnest people was facing a vast realm of ignorance and half-knowledge, scarcely knowing even where or how to begin. By planning of the sort Lillie had done so well *something could be done* to pick out feasible problems with which to begin investigation" (emphasis added).

Another decision of the NRC/CRPS at this time, to fund only a limited number of reproductive sciences centers each led by a major investigator rather than broader funding of individual investigators (Aberle and Corner 1953:22–23), even further curtailed support for the "human side" of sex research. In his study of the formation of sexology, Bullough (1994:121) talks of an "old boy network" of biological researchers; he and others have commented on the fact that actual members of the committee were among the major recipients of its funding for the first twenty years, including Yerkes, Lillie, and Lashley. Such a pattern would be frowned upon today as a serious conflict of interest, if not expressly prohibited in funding policy. Lillie and his plan for "fundamental" research unequivocally succeeded in "seizing the day."

As the NRC/CRPS developed as a working committee, it created its own vocabulary for the categories of research it sponsored. Some was to be considered on the "biological side," while other projects that had greater application to people or that used human subjects were to be considered on the "human side."[27] As research on the biological side came to predominate, various rationales for this approach were expressed. First, research using human subjects was deemed less scientific than investigations using laboratory animal materials:

> In the more fundamental biological, physiological and psycho-biological investigations where lower organisms are used, experimental conditions can be maintained. Fortunately many of the underlying problems can be worked out initially here. Unfortunately the results are not always directly applicable to human needs. If a contribution to the alleviation of human sex problems is not to await the slow progress of fundamental research it is necessary to study directly the higher forms including man, even though the accuracy of the experimentalist must be sacrificed in some instances for the less acceptable methods, scientifically considered, of the clinician. When this is done, however, the results should be accepted but tentatively and every effort made to check and supplement them by specific investigations under experimental conditions.[28]

Ironically, these comments were supposedly prepared by Earl Zinn, a psychologist, though I suspect Yerkes's pen was involved.

Second, those who studied human sexuality were portrayed as quacks or cranks by Yerkes, as he ceremoniously and contradictorily tipped his hat to the ultimate value of sexuality research: "Is there any species of social situation in which biological research can flounder more helplessly, hopelessly, and uselessly than in that of sex? It is at once curiosity breeding and satisfying. Our committee has not yet been bombarded by those hundreds of curious and more or less ill-balanced persons who, if they could obtain financial support, would like to study one or other seemingly interesting and perhaps important aspect of sex life."[29]

Third, clinicians and others were specifically portrayed as unscientific:

"With reference to the study of human problems the situation is not so favorable. Therapeutic, educational and social considerations insistently demand a better understanding of sex phenomena. But because of the complexity of the problems, trained investigators have for the most part turned to problems where complicating factors can be eliminated, leaving the field to the clinician, the educator and the social worker. This has resulted in a large amount of sporadic research, much of it of doubtful value."[30]

An NRC/CRPS report then gets to the heart of the matter—a critique of social science methodologies: "As a further step in defining the nature and scope of the project it [the NRC/CRPS] determined to promote and support important investigations in which human subjects are used; but that these investigations would be selected on the basis of the degree to which methods employed conformed to the requirements of science. It further determined to encourage and support at every opportunity methodological research applicable to the study of human sex problems."[31] This First Annual Report explicitly stated that while the committee would fund "human investigations," these would be "primarily investigations in method. . . . The introduction of better methods and the coordination of research in this field offer a splendid opportunity for Committee initiative." Scorn on the part of natural scientists toward the social sciences on methodological grounds was particularly strong during this period (Vesey 1965:135). After all, "the new biology" was introducing new rigor to the life sciences. Ultimately, very little research using human subjects was undertaken during the first two decades of NRC/CRPS research support despite committee membership representing psychiatry, sociology, anthropology, and sexology.

Reflecting the redirection, the committee quickly reframed and restated its own mission. In his statement in the First Annual Report, Yerkes first tipped his hat to the importance of keeping "close to human needs" and then proposed a strongly basic research–oriented agenda to avoid wasting energy and scattering resources:

> I am convinced that we should not ignore the practical social need which brought our committee into existence. Instead, we should, I believe, recognize the need of knowledge for the wise conduct of sex education and should formulate our program and plans with a view to supplementing existing knowledge and of this providing an adequate scientific basis for individual and social direction of sex life. . . . [This] does not necessarily mean narrowness of view, the search for the immediately practical, or the neglect of problems whose educational or other sociological bearings are difficult to foresee. . . . [Research in this field] will gain greatly if we wisely take account of the logic of events and keep close to human needs.

[T]he well-nigh endless extent and variety of research on problems of sex makes imperative an order of preference with respect to materials and methods of work. Whatever our general program, we should . . . concentrate endeavor in a certain few carefully selected special fields. Although it is bound to seem invidious, I beg to suggest the following order of preference for the principal pertinent divisions of scientific method.

1. Physiological and chemical—including all functional studies of the sex life of the organism or of organic groups except those of 2 and 3.
2. The psychological, psycho-pathological, educational and sociological.
3. The general biological, including the genetical and such morphological modes of inquiry as are intimately related to physiological needs.
4. The morphological, in the sense of structural analyses and detailed studies of structure not manifestly essential to effective work under 1, 2 and 3. . . .

That as objects of research, organisms be preferred in general as follows:

(a) the primates
(b) other mammals
(c) other vertebrates
(d) plants.

Yerkes outlined a nonhuman primate research plan in the same report. Nonhuman primate research development was one of his lifelong foci, and by 1923 he had already initiated his own primate researches at Yale.[32]

The same pattern of hat tipping to human needs while clearly framing a strongly biological research agenda appeared in an article by Zinn (1923:1811–12) announcing the NRC/CRPS to the American Medical Association:

Though this project was motivated originally by the need for a better understanding of sex in its human aspect, this was not interpreted by the National Research Council or the committee to mean that investigations were to be limited to those of a technological nature determined by the needs of medicine, education and hygiene. The pressing need for useful knowledge was realized; and while it was agreed that these problems should be given all possible consideration, it was the opinion of those responsible for the project that its objective should be more inclusive; that in addition to contributing to the alleviation of current individual and social sex problems, it should aim at a better understanding of the underlying factors—biologic, physiologic and psychologic—which are basic to any real understanding of human sexuality. This conception markedly extended the scope of the project and brought the realization that its systematic development would be a matter of years. . . .

[M]ajor lines of investigation must be marked out if the project were not to flounder hopelessly in this complex field. The following subdivisions were selected . . .

1. Biology of sex (systematic and genetic aspects)
2. Physiology of sex and reproduction
3. Psychobiology of sex (infrahuman)
4. Psychobiology of sex (human, including individual, anthropologic, ethnologic, sociopsychologic aspects).

Sexology was ranked lowest in priority. In the First Annual Report of the NRC/CRPS in 1923, Zinn again performed the hat-tipping ritual, noting that research in biology and physiology was quite well organized: "motivated primarily however, by the desire to contribute to the systematic development of the respective sciences rather than by consideration of human need. . . . As a first step, therefore, in the organization of this field the Committee has set up as a guiding principle the following: *That it shall promote and support those researches which give the most promise of contributing to an understanding of the human aspects of sex.*"[33] Yet at this time the committee chose to narrow its agenda still further, explicitly eliminating studies of sex pathology and venereal disease from its purview.[34]

In sum, these "mission" documents reflect considerable distancing from the BSH's initial goals in funding the committee. "Human aspects of sex" were very broadly conceived, sexuality or sexology studies per se were all but eliminated from investigation, and few studies using human subjects or materials were sponsored. In 1932, a decade after the committee's inception, Yerkes offered an apt and succinct reconstruction of its history: "Historical statement. Instigated by Mr. Earl F. Zinn, representative of the Bureau of Social Hygiene, in the autumn of 1921, the Division of Medical Sciences, National Research Council, organized a conference to consider the practicability of attempts to further study of fundamental biological problems of sex."[35] Apparently accepting Yerkes's reconstruction at face value, Aberle and Corner (1953:15) noted: "It should be emphasized that the Committee never aimed at a limited study of human social problems of a sexual nature, but rather at the scientific study of sex as a biological phenomenon." The committee's funding source, Rockefeller's BSH, certainly had.

LOST ARGUMENTS AND FAILED
STRATEGIES FOR THE "HUMAN SIDE"

The redirection of the mission of the NRC/CRPS was resisted by some members, and the issue of funding the "human side" of sex research became a thorn in the side of the committee. After the initial redirection and reframing of its mission to the "biological side," "human side" advocates on the committee pushed their alternative positions quite strongly several times between 1924 and 1931. There were several quite heterogeneous "human side" positions. The first included (relatively) simple advocacy of social science approaches to "the problem of sex," *human* sex psychology and behavior. Ironically, the founding of the Social Science Research Council (SSRC) in 1923 added to the committee's difficulties in sponsoring *both* natural and social science research.[36] That is, the existence of the SSRC allowed the NRC to make its focus on the natural sciences more exclusionary, demarcating, policing, and enforcing even more profoundly the border between "the social" and "the natural" in classic Enlightenment fashion.

During the first decade of the committee's work, psychiatrically and anthropologically oriented members and fundees apparently failed to mount and publish more than a few social science studies using speaking humans as research subjects (Clarke forthcoming). One failed attempt provides a useful exemplar. In 1924, the committee wanted to fund an investigation by George V. Hamilton, a psychiatrist, on marriage, including sexuality within marriage. Hamilton, a physician who had also done extensive studies on primates, had strong sponsorship from Yerkes, who had worked with him. However, the NRC, which had to authorize the actions of the CRPS, refused to approve Hamilton's research. Vernon Kellogg, chairman of the Division of Medical Sciences of the NRC, later stated they had refused "because they considered it primarily sociological, and because quite frankly they were not sure that it was a scientific undertaking, although Yerkes . . . felt it was."[37] The NRC/CRPS then went to the BSH with the matter (likely via committee member Katherine Davis, who was also directing the BSH). The BSH agreed to act as sponsor of the project if the NRC/CRPS would serve in an advisory capacity. NRC/CRPS member Adolph Meyer, a psychiatrist at Johns Hopkins who had also had a grant but failed to publish, acted as primary adviser.[38] Here the committee, likely led by Yerkes, persisted, successfully arranging funding for research on the "human side" despite a serious challenge by the NRC.[39] Hamilton conducted in-depth survey interviews of couples about what we would now call their sexual practices, which led to a controversial publication. Later his findings were generally confirmed by Kinsey's research. The public controversy over his research was such, however, that many who had wanted the committee to sponsor the work were relieved that it had not.[40]

A second position, or complex of "human side" positions, seems to have constellated around what Hall (1978) has termed "hybrids," research areas and topics that seemed to stand at the intersection of the natural and social sciences and/or necessitate both social and natural science approaches to be fully understood. According to Aberle and Corner (1953:93–97), one classic hybrid area was called "sex psychology and behavior" prior to 1932 and "the psychobiology of sex" afterward, reflecting the outcome of certain negotiations. While elusive, the term *psychobiology* has been understood to mean "attempts to find the model of human behavior and social organization in animal studies" (Hall 1978:3). It has roots in both Edwin Embree's program of human biology at the Rockefeller Foundation and Yerkes's developing program for psychobiology more broadly. The "psychobiology of sex" is a subfield focused on topics in *both* sexuality and reproduction.

Another possible reading of the committee's negotiations here concerns the NRC/CRPS as one site among many where what would count as natural and social sciences was being constructed along with the boundaries between them (Hall 1978; Haraway 1989). In this reading, a form of "legitimate Western science" was being constructed, amid considerable contestation. What kinds of natural science could be done using humans? To whom would social science count? For what purposes? What kinds of natural science could be done using nonhumans while successfully transposing the results onto humans? This final question became the guiding one for the committee (Clarke forthcoming).

Struggles over work such as the Hamilton study and the uncertainty of future support for the kinds of social science research it wanted to fund led the committee to develop a proposal for its own future as an independent agency. This proposal included terminating its affiliation with the NRC, sponsoring research on both the "human and biological sides," and planning for a new national institute, with smaller local institutes at various university centers of reproductive sciences.[41] This proposal was then approved by the Executive Committee of the Division of Medical Sciences of the NRC, which perhaps hoped to rid itself of this embarrassing millstone. However, the proposal was not received favorably by the Rockefeller funding source, the BSH, which provided the committee's support. Forcing the matter, the board of the BSH (likely with input from Rockefeller Foundation staff) preferred to have the work continue under the auspices of the NRC. The board then voted a major appropriation to the committee of $325,000 over the five years 1928–1933, "for the support of those phases of the work which lie *within the scope* of the [National Research] Council."[42]

This plan for an independent and hybrid sex research agency seems to have been the primary response of "human side" advocates within the committee to the redirection of its mission toward the "biological side" over the first five years.[43] However, the timing of this proposal (1927–28) was unfortunate. Because the foundation was in the midst of upheaval and reorganization, major new endeavors received short shrift.[44] Moreover, their proposal for a new institute was presented in the same year that Executive Secretary Zinn told L. B. Dunham (the new director of the BSH) that the committee wanted a renewable grant of $750,000 over five years, which Dunham and others thought exorbitant.[45] Further, the issue of whether to fund individuals, universities, or institutes was under hot debate in the Rockefeller Foundation itself (Kohler 1991). Finally, Young Turk "philan-thropoids" who had their own agendas for the management of science were conducting a palace revolution inside the foundation (Wheatley 1989).

Thus the committee's proposal for autonomy trod on tender toes in terms of *both* its fiscal scope and its quasi-autonomous organizational frame-work, and had multiple negative consequences. President Fosdick of the Rockefeller Foundation wrote to Dunham: "I frankly think the Committee on Sex Research has gone stark mad. To talk in terms of $750,000 is just sheer idiocy, and if I were you I would call Vernon Kellogg on the telephone and tell him frankly that the project as developed is far too scopy and com-prehensive for serious consideration. . . . [T]his sounds like the work of a lot of college professors who have assumed that millions are at their dis-posal."[46] Further, these events seem to have led directly to the ouster of Earl Zinn as executive secretary,[47] which in turn led to the termination of the committee's "promotional work," defined as educational outreach work on sex research for the lay public, which had essentially been left to Zinn to do.[48] Yerkes, at least, was disturbed by its termination.[49] Zinn went on with his career in psychology, finished his doctorate at Columbia, and was hired by the Yale University Institute of Human Relations in 1936, shortly after it had hired Erik Erikson. Ironically, this institute then received $4.5 mil-lion from the Rockefeller Foundation for its first decade of efforts, (1929–1939), at integrating scientific knowledge of human behavior, with rational control of behavior as the ultimate goal (Morawski 1986:237, 219).

The NRC Division of Medical Sciences itself then noted its own success in limiting the committee to natural science research: "In regard to the gen-eral policy of the committee, it may be said that owing to the administrative change [Zinn's departure?] but mainly to the growth of agencies for the promotion of research in the social sciences, it seems evident that hence-forth the main attention of the committee will be concentrated on the sup-port of the main projects now in hand rather than on expansion by the development of new projects."[50] Thus the initial redirection of the mission of the NRC/CRPS had extensive long-term consequences.

Committee members were not willing to give up easily. The obvious al-ternative of pursuit of the "human side" of sex research through the SSRC was raised, and Zinn had taken some initiatives in 1928 before his ouster.[51] These initiatives appear to have lapsed on his departure and were not in-voked again until 1929, when Lillie suggested a division of sponsorship of research on "the problems of sex" between the NRC and the SSRC to Max Mason of the foundation. Mason noted: "Lillie feels that the committee, while willing to try to combine the whole range of sex research in one un-dertaking, has found great difficulties in the psychiatric end and does not feel it has succeeded at all well there. The suggestion has been made that a separate grant be made to the SSRC to administer on the human side."[52] However, no such move was made. Lillie's conceptual limitation of the social sciences to psychiatry may illustrate the difficulties social scientists may have confronted when serving on the committee or making proposals to it. It certainly clarifies the position of this key reproductive scientist on the study of sexuality: it belonged elsewhere, far from the work of reproductive scientists.

The failure of the NRC/CRPS to seriously address the "human side" and the successful redirection of its mission to the "biological side" during its first decade were summed up by Yerkes in 1932, again with clear notation of the proper types of research materials and subjects:

> It was planned and hoped at the outset to advance knowledge of general biological, physiological and psychological aspects of sex with equal effectiveness. It now appears that things have happened quite differently. Review of the titles of the five hundred and more publications which give credit to this body for assistance reveals some interesting facts. Of morphological papers there are only a few; of studies in the psychobiology and psychopathology of sex in man barely more; of contributions to the psychobiology of sex in animals other than man there are several, while the titles classifiable under the general biology and physiology of sex in other organisms than man overwhelmingly predominate. Probably no member of the group would have predicted the degree of this disproportionality. The inference is obvious that scientific progress cannot be forced. The committee far from fretting over its mistakes of prediction, has rejoiced in progress, wherever achieved, and sought for the reasons for backwardness in certain fields of inquiry.[53]

Yerkes's interesting use of the passive voice here denies the actions and agency of both "human side" and "biological side" advocates.

THE SHIFT TO ROCKEFELLER FOUNDATION SPONSORSHIP

In 1931, sponsorship of the NRC/CRPS was transferred from the BSH, a private social action agency, to the Natural Sciences Division of the Rockefeller Foundation, a basic research funding agency. In my analysis, this move powerfully acknowledged the redirected mission of the Committee, as the events preceding it also confirm.

How far the committee had departed from its original mission became clear when L. B. Dunham became director of the BSH after Katherine B. Davis's retirement in 1928. Dunham reviewed all BSH-supported programs, including the NRC/CRPS, and reported to the Rockefeller Foundation: "There can be no doubt as to the outstanding eminence of this committee. . . . I find myself totally unable to estimate the value and significance of this work, nor is there anyone on my staff of the Bureau of Social Hygiene who is competent to do so. Dr. Pierce of the Rockefeller Foundation in his report on this matter says in part, 'I do not see the immediate practical application of the results of this work, though practical application may emerge in the course of time.' He [Pierce] then goes on to say, 'I can recommend most strongly that aid for this work be continued as research of the highest type.'"[54]

Dunham concluded that the committee was not an appropriate program for the BSH to administer. He believed that since the committee fell within the field of medical research, and since the research was basic and "may not be of great public benefit," it should be sponsored directly by a Rockefeller program specializing in basic research while remaining under the auspices of the NRC or those of a medical center.[55] Dunham also discussed alternative Rockefeller agency sponsorship with Dr. Kellogg of the NRC, who said the NRC had no objections to continuing to sponsor the committee "if it led over into the field of what he termed human biology. On the other hand, if it seems to be turning primarily into the field of social sciences, it is not within their jurisdiction."[56] Alternatively, Dunham wrote, the committee could be refocused by having the BSH push for more research on the human side and selectively funding projects the NRC/CRPS proposed.[57] However, both Woods and Fosdick of the Rockefeller Foundation eschewed such an interventionist stance.[58] Instead, feelers were sent out to the Board of Directors of the BSH regarding the possible transfer of the NRC/CRPS to another Rockefeller agency.[59]

Behind the scenes several other possible scenarios for the future of the committee were constructed and scrutinized. One possibility, articulated between about 1924 and 1928, was for the NRC/CRPS to join the Human Biology Program administered by Edwin Embree of the Rockefeller Foundation. "Human biology," as described by Kohler (1991:126), is "probably best understood as one of many attempts, in the wake of the medical reform movement, to capture the biological and behavioral side of medicine for university science departments." Embree was attempting to build a coherent program in "human evolution" out of scattered elements from human heredity and eugenics to the remnants of a mental hygiene agenda (Abrams 1993; Jonas 1989:130–31). One possibility for development through Embree's program lay in a dream of Frank Lillie's to establish an ambitious interdisciplinary "Institute of Racial Biology" at the University of Chicago (discussed below). But this did not cohere at the time, and neither did Embree's program. He left the foundation in 1928.

Instead, by 1931 a modus vivendi between the BSH and the foundation had been worked out regarding the transfer of the NRC/CRPS. Dunham found the foundation staff quite responsive to his suggestion that where the scientific work in biology indicated the desirability of having supplementary work carried on in other fields, such as sociology, the Rockefeller Foundation would bring these matters to the attention of the BSH. Dunham further noted that the BSH would happily act as a liaison between the committee and those in the birth control field who sought advice from scientists doing basic research in the biology of sex.[60] In 1931, the transfer of the committee to the Natural Sciences Division of the Rockefeller Foundation was completed. The foundation's resolution stated that the transfer was undertaken because the work of the NRC/CRPS was "more clearly in the field of the present research programs of the Rockefeller Foundation than in the program of the Bureau of Social Hygiene."[61] The "biological side" had been validated by one of the most prestigious scientific funding sources in the Western world.

RENAISSANCE OF THE HUMAN SIDE OF NRC/CRPS RESEARCH

In one more surprising turn of events, shortly after the transfer of the committee to the foundation, a gradual shift toward the inclusion of research on the "human side" began. This shift, of course, runs against the grain in that the committee was now fiscally sponsored by a basic science research agency (the Rockefeller Foundation) rather than one specializing in social science and social action (the BSH), and was also still under the auspices of a natural science research agency (the NRC). A number of factors contributed to this second redirection of the mission of the Committee which had multiple repercussions for the reproductive sciences:

the desire of the NRC/CRPS to sponsor new lines of work;
the emergence of alternative funding sources for "basic" research in the
        biology and endocrinology/biochemistry of reproduction;
changes in Rockefeller Foundation funding priorities and organization;
the shift of the NRC/CRPS from the Natural Sciences Division to the
        Medical Sciences; and
the fading glamour of reproductive endocrinological research

I discuss each of these issues in the remainder of this chapter.
    In the annual report of the committee submitted in 1932, the gentle push for funding in new directions including the "human side" began: "*Survey of situation and forecast.* The foregoing indicates gratifying progress in extension of knowledge of the general biology and physiology of sex in infrahuman animals, much of which probably is applicable to man, coupled with relatively slight and slow advance in knowledge by the study of man himself. . . . Without thought of ceasing to promote lines of research which have proved their importance, it is pertinent to inquire whether conditions are now sufficiently favorable to developments in some of the more backward fields of inquiry to justify renewed effort by the committee to promote research in new directions."[62]

To allow development in new directions, especially psychobiology, which was Yerkes's pet area, the committee urged the foundation to fund directly some of the major reproductive research centers it had helped to develop.[63] By the end of 1932, such a program had been articulated with the foundation: "The Committee judges that one period of its activity is now drawing to a close, and recommends that the future interest of the Committee be directed more particularly towards the biology and physiology of sex in man, and to the psycho-biology, including psychopathology, of sex."[64]

The committee anticipated three new lines of research: the neural basis of sexual behavior; the comparative study of psychobiology of sex in man and lower animals; and the comparative physiology and psychobiology of sex in primates.[65] Over the decade, this list expanded to include primate and human psychosexual development and sexuality. It culminated in the 1940s with extensive support of Alfred Kinsey's research.[66] The thrust of much of this work was the construction of systematic sex/gender and race differences.[67] The continuance of research in sex and race differences, in reproductive sciences as elsewhere, has sustained particular constructions of difference that are invidious to many. The emphasis on group difference also distracts attention from the range of variation *within* particular groups.

"Human side" research sponsored by the committee continued to emphasize the methodological development of means of studying sex behavior experimentally and quantitatively.[68] Adolph Meyer, a committee member, was given grants totaling $14,000 for human sex behavior studies, ultimately unpublished. According to Aberle and Corner (1953:46), this was due to his aversion to quantification of human action. In sharp contrast, Alfred Kinsey, a biologist trained by William Morton Wheeler, formerly had specialized in the study of gall wasps (Evans and Evans 1970; Pomeroy 1982:35). Certainly his training in the natural sciences rather than the social sciences and his systematic efforts at quantification fit well with the preferences of the committee, despite his choice of humans as research materials (Aberle and Corner 1953:49–50). Kinsey's biological background was also appreciated by the foundation.[69] I discovered no objections to his research as "social science" by the NRC.[70] The challenges subsequently posed by some social scientists to Kinsey's statistical work (e.g., Geddes 1954) are thus especially ironic.

A second condition contributing to the shift to the "human side" of sex research by the NRC/CRPS was the fact that by the early 1930s a number of new external funding sources for "basic" reproductive research were emerging as alternatives to funding by the committee. Some programs formerly supported by the committee were now funded directly by the Rockefeller Foundation, including Evans's center at the University of California at Berkeley; the Biological Sciences Division of the University of Chicago, including Lillie's reproductive research center; Smith and Engle's center at Columbia; and Stockard's and Papanicolaou's at Cornell Medical Center.[71] The foundation also provided direct funding to other reproductive scientists.

Additional new external funding sources by the 1930s included the National Committee on Maternal Health (f. 1923), the NRC Committee on Endocrinology (f. 1936), the USDA (for support of animal husbandry research, including reproductive endocrinology), and pharmaceutical companies (Greep, Koblinsky, and Jaffe 1976:370–74).[72] The NRC Committee on Endocrinology was funded primarily by the Markle Foundation; after 1940, Rockefeller Foundation support of the NRC/CRPS was reduced explicitly because of the availability of these other funds for aspects of reproductive endocrinological research.[73] (A more elaborate discussion of this funding is offered in chapter 7.)

The strong association of reproductive research or sex research (to use the committee's terminology) with endocrinology was extremely helpful in gaining external funds during the formation and coalescence eras of the reproductive sciences. Endocrinology and biochemistry were both viewed as at the "cutting edge" of research—basic, clinical, and applied—at this time (Abir-Am 1982; Allen 1975; Kohler 1976). Research related to the development of contraception was also attractive for sponsorship by select organizations.

Third, changes at the Rockefeller Foundation between 1928 and 1937 also made a shift toward the "human side" of the committee's mission more feasible. In fact, there seems to have been a strong push from within the foundation toward such a shift. In brief, while the direction of the foundation shifted from health and social problems to the support of basic research in 1928, the long-established Rockefeller tradition of concern with concrete applications and uses of science was sustained (Kohler 1978:490). The stated mission of the Rockefeller Foundation, after all, was "to promote the well-being of mankind throughout the world" (Howe 1982:34). According to Kohler (1976:289), the foundation's perspective was that all science should ultimately be applied, and a distinction was made only between science that was already applicable and that which was not yet so. The goal was to obtain high "social returns" on its scientific investments (Abir-Am 1982:342). In terms of the NRC/CRPS and the reproductive sciences, applicability was judged to be close at hand. The recommendation of the foundation for NRC/CRPS funding in 1932 stated: "A large proportion of the work thus far done is classifiable as general biology and physiology of sex in organisms other than man. In this field, the activity of the Committee has been highly significant. It was essential that this fundamental work on infra-man anticipate and pave the way for that on man."[74]

The foundation itself was also reorganized in 1928. Biology became part of the basic research–oriented Natural Sciences Division, while Medical Sciences and Medical Education became two separate divisions (Kohler 1978:511). Initially the committee was placed in the Natural Sciences Division during this period of reorganizational and economic uncertainty. The Natural Sciences Division had four different directors between 1928 and 1932, at which time Warren Weaver, with whom I began this book, was hired (Kohler 1976:286). At the same time, Alan Gregg became director of the Medical Research Division and began an intensive new program in neurology and psychiatry (Pressman 1997). Initially, Weaver's and Gregg's programs were closely affiliated and their boundaries blurred; they included psychobiology (psychiatry, neurophysiology), internal secretions (hormones and enzymes), nutrition (vitamins), radiation effects, sex biology, experimental and chemical embryology, genetics, biophysics, and biochemistry (Kohler 1976:289).

By 1938, however, Weaver's position had shifted dramatically, and his program both substantively changed and was renamed "molecular biology" (Abir-Am 1982:347). The trajectory of his decisions is instructive. In the past, comparatively little attention had been paid by the foundation itself to the committee, since the funds were administered by the NRC, which had its own boards (Abir-Am 1982:348).[75] Weaver changed this as it was his policy to take a firm hand in the "management of science" under his division, and he did not hesitate to express his opinion. Research to be funded by the Rockefeller Foundation was increasingly subjected to careful scrutiny and analysis in relation to the foundation's own goals.[76]

Weaver, who thought biological truth relevant to individual conduct, statecraft, and social policy (Abir-Am 1982:349), was juggling several possible directions as he assumed the directorship in 1932. Initially he embraced the NRC/CRPS as part of his own independent program, which he first called "psychobiology" or "vital processes." The quote from Weaver to the trustees of the Rockefeller Foundation about "the new sciences of man," with which I began this book, gives the flavor of this moment. Further, in 1933, Weaver had met with Lillie to discuss the advisability of a considerable shift in emphasis in the work of the committee away from the underlying biological problems to the behavior problems. Weaver said he was frankly enthusiastic about the older program, which produced quantitative factual evidence basic to the later applied problems. And he questioned whether those "human side" fields now warranted development.[77]

Another possible direction Weaver was also considering centered on the importation of the methods of physics and chemistry into biology—what ultimately became his molecular biology program. In fact, two analysts assert that the "psychobiology" program served initially to buy Weaver time and protect his plans for molecular biology while he prepared the ground for such a major shift in direction (Fuerst 1982:255; Kohler 1976:289). But Weaver was juggling yet a third possible commitment: Lillie's proposal for an "Institute of Race Biology" at Chicago. While it ultimately failed, the saga of this proposal illuminates the situation at the Rockefeller Foundation at this time.

At the University of Chicago, eugenic concerns had been widely reflected both in the curriculum and in faculty activities. In 1920, faculty member H. H. Newman (1948:235) began teaching a course called "Evolution, Genetics and Eugenics"; he published a book of readings with the same title in 1921. The 1922 budget recommendation for zoology prepared by Lillie sought a geneticist capable of teaching eugenics and social development.[78] As a member of the executive committee of the NRC's Division of Biology and Agriculture, Lillie had approved in 1920 the establishment of a Eugenics Committee within the division. Members, who included Robert M. Yerkes (Yale) and Lewellys F. Barker, Adolf Meyer, and Raymond Pearl (all of Johns Hopkins), organized the Second International Eugenics Congress in 1921.[79] Pushing toward a more scientific eugenics, Lillie presented a paper on sex hormones at the congress.[80] In 1922, Lillie agreed to serve on the Advisory Council of the Eugenics Committee of the U.S.A. of the International Committee on Eugenics, which had specialty subcommittees on research, eugenic birth control, mental and physical measurements, and cooperation with physicians.[81] Thus Lillie was more than familiar with the eugenics movement.

Responding in part to his dean's suggestion that interdisciplinary projects be organized in institutes, in 1924 Lillie began formal development of a plan for an "Institute of Racial Biology" at the University of Chicago.[82] This was likely discussed in the NRC/CRPS context as one of the possible centers to be sponsored by the (proposed and failed) independent (non-NRC) sex research agency discussed earlier (Hall 1978). Lillie had already written to Wycliffe Rose of the Rockefeller General Education Board about his proposal: "The future of human society depends on the preservation of the individual and its extension into the field of public health; but it depends no less on social health, that is the biological composition of the population. . . . The era of universal [racial] contact and amalgamation has come. Moreover, the populations press on their borders everywhere, and also, unfortunately, the best stock biologically is not everywhere the most rapidly breeding stock. The political and social problems involved are fundamentally problems of genetic biology."[83]

Lillie saw eugenics and genetics as extending the study of development (his lifelong research interest) from the individual to the population level. Lillie was far from alone in his shift of rhetoric from race to population at this time, a shift reflected in the life sciences more broadly (Haraway

1995) and in the social sciences, including demography (Gordon 1976/1990; Greenhalgh 1995, 1996). Subjects included by Lillie in his framework for the institute were genetics, cytology, embryology, biology of sex, ecology, and the environment. Interdisciplinary research programs would include racial biology, psychology, sociology, and what might be called social medicine.[84] Lillie later addressed the nomenclature problem, noting that in a discussion he had with foundation staff, the name "Institute of Racial Biology" was viewed as misleading: "(Parenthetically I may say that I borrowed it from the German 'Rassenbiologie'.) I believe, however, that the term 'Institute of Genetic Biology (and Evolution?)' would not be open to misunderstanding."[85] Lillie then further noted the practical applications potential of such an institute "in animal and plant breeding, improvement of inborn qualities of human stock, the congenital basis of disease, population problems, etc."[86]

An entry in Weaver's diary from early 1934 reflects very positively on the proposal. It even appears that race biology could have been a banner program of Weaver's tenure, integrated with molecular biology: "If the plans for development come up to WW's [Weaver's] expectations, it would seem to offer a major if not the major opportunity for advancing the new [Foundation] program."[87] In 1934, Lillie submitted a formal proposal to the Rockefeller Foundation, carefully noting the institute's scientific merit:

> Nor on the side of current human evolution would it have any direct connection with eugenic or birth control propaganda, but would be concerned exclusively with the scientific foundations. There is no gainsaying the conviction that social improvement represents a political ideal of the future. If we are to avoid hasty and socially dangerous political action scientific foundations must be securely laid. . . . Responsibility for scientifically sound genetic prophylaxis rests on the biological sciences. . . . [T]here is an almost total lack of organization for genetic social therapy, except for non-professional propaganda. . . . Indications multiply in this country and abroad, especially in Germany, in England and in Russia, that people are wide awake as to the necessity of a better planned society if our civilization is to endure and develop. They are thinking . . . of control of composition of their populations.[88]

Lillie argued that "human betterment" could be served scientifically through an Institute of Genetic Biology at Chicago.[89] The cover letter from President Hutchins of the University of Chicago asked for a gift of $3 million from the foundation in several stages.[90] Lillie saw the institute as strongly interdisciplinary, with work to be done on a "project" basis, drawing on physical and medical sciences, as well as social sciences (in terms of child development, education, social service, and population problems), and new interdisciplinary foci (such as psychogenetics and psychophysiology of sex and experimental population genetics).[91] Negotiations continued throughout 1934, as Lillie himself planned his retirement.[92]

In a sense, Lillie's proposed institute was an attempt to create a new population biology of genetics that included the "biology of sex," as the reproductive sciences or reproductive biology at Chicago (and elsewhere) by then were known. Simultaneously, there was a well-articulated fit with the recent shift in the eugenics movement to a more population-based, neo-Malthusian ideology that eventually would be termed "population control," reflecting its new inclusion of birth control as a legitimate strategy in the struggle to control both quality and quantity of reproduction. This shift was led in part by Raymond Pearl, with whom Lillie had worked on the eugenics conference noted earlier (Allen 1991). Perhaps Lillie's proposal most cogently frames what Hall (1978) called hybrids, combining both social and natural sciences, with the latter designated to lead the explanatory dance.

In 1935, however, Lillie's proposal dropped out of sight, to be replaced by discussions of a Rockefeller endowment of the Biological Sciences Division at Chicago, which, along with several other established committee centers, was eventually funded directly by the foundation.[93] Had Lillie's proposal been pursued more ardently ten years earlier, when he first framed it, it might have become a reality. There were likely several factors that contributed to its demise in 1934. Certainly the rise of Nazism and its association with extreme eugenic actions thrust all eugenics into disrepute.[94] The Nazi Eugenical Sterilization Law had been passed in 1933, based directly on the "Model Eugenical Sterilization Law" formulated by Harry Laughlin of the Eugenics Record Office based at Cold Spring Harbor.[95] The American Neurological Association was about to publish a scientific repudiation of eugenic sterilization, raising serious scientific questions about eugenics.[96] Geneticists and other scientists had also become disgruntled and impatient with the lack of incorporation of modern genetic knowledge into eugenics.[97] At Chicago, Lillie was retiring, and without him such an institute probably was considerably less attractive to the foundation, if not viewed as a de facto loose cannon. Further, the biological sciences at Chicago conceived more broadly were eminently (and more controllably) supportable and in need of stabilized assistance (Clarke 1993).

And, of course, Weaver had his own ambitious plans for new Rockefeller Foundation research investments. By 1935, he was breaking away from psychobiology and moving strongly and explicitly toward the integration of physical science approaches and skills into biology (Abir-Am 1982:352, 1988; Kohler 1976:291). His revised "molecular biology" agenda clearly did not include the research areas of the NRC/CRPS.[98] In fact, the committee was almost terminated by the foundation in 1935.[99] Instead, Weaver dumped the committee elsewhere in the foundation: in 1937, both the endocrinology and the sex biology/psychobiology programs (including the NRC/CRPS) were shifted to Alan Gregg's Medical Sciences Division. "The assignment of 'psychobiology' to Gregg clarified the internal division of labor within the Foundation between applied and basic programmes" (Kohler 1976:298–300). This spoke more of the future of the reproductive sciences than any other move.

While Weaver's Natural Sciences Division would sponsor basic research more exclusively, Gregg's Medical Sciences Division supposedly required a judicious combination of basic research and application. The latter now better suited the shifting program of the NRC/CRPS. Gregg would also clearly see and be receptive to the implications of the reproductive sciences for addressing human fertility. Gregg wrote in *Science* in 1955, "I suggest, as a way of looking at the population problem, that there are some interesting analogies between the growth of the human population of the world and the increase of cells observable in neoplasms. To say that the world has cancer, and that the cancer cell is man, has neither experimental proof nor the validation of predictive accuracy; but I see no reason that instantly forbids such a speculation." Gregg's argument would have fit well with those of Frank Lillie in terms of the population-level goals of biological understanding and the ability to manipulate individuals (e.g., Mitman 1992:96–109). Social control, here of population, could be achieved through Rockefeller-sponsored biomedicine (Kay 1993a).

A key question, of course, is why Weaver was prepared to abandon the reproductive sciences at this time. Fashion in research funding is not a recent phenomenon.[100] By the mid-1930s, in a number of ways the reproductive sciences had become old hat. Many of the social taboos around sex had eased, and the legitimacy of the reproductive sciences was more established, especially in elite circles. It may well be that Warren Weaver both pushed for a shift to the "human side" and a shift of the committee to the Medical Sciences Division because he preferred to manage only basic research at the cutting edge. Kohler (1976:299) states: "Weaver was relieved of endocrinology, nutrition and sex biology, rather to his relief, for they had lost their fashionable appeal." In 1941, when the foundation trimmed its funding of the committee, its resolution noted that continued funding "at the previous level would . . . give an undue emphasis to an area of research that in any case is no longer in a pioneer or entirely dependent stage."[101]

This loss of appeal may also have been the result of false hopes and promises for clinical applications. The isolation of sex hormones in the early 1930s had engendered enthusiasm for hormone therapies, and the pharmaceutical industry rushed to develop them commercially. After an initial wave of publicity and claims of miraculous cures,[102] by the mid-1930s skepticism had begun to set in.[103] The "odor of quackery" that had wafted over reproductive endocrinology from Brown-Séquard's rejuvenation work in the 1890s persisted, and persists to this day (Borell 1976a; Rechter 1997).

While the "human side" of "the problems of sex" had received greater emphasis by the committee after its transfer to the foundation in 1931, it was not until after 1940 that the balance of support fully shifted to it. Correspondence and documentation concerning the future of the NRC/CRPS from around 1940 strongly suggest that if this shift had not occurred, the committee would have been terminated by the end of World War II. Rockefeller Foundation staff articulated several times that support for the committee had gone on too long.[104] In response to these threats, the NRC/CRPS itself promoted a strong "new" program on the "human side," emphasizing psychological aspects of sex.[105] And by 1944, the NRC/CRPS had won the foundation over to its new program. The foundation then gave the committee $135,000 over three years, stating that as long as standards remained high, "the nature of the field, i.e., problems of sex in human beings, would clearly justify renewal of research grants."[106] The Rockefeller Foundation clearly desired that a more ambitious program of human sexuality research be undertaken, and it called upon the NRC/CRPS to lend its now high stature and legitimacy to this endeavor.

The major funding recipient under the new "human side" program was Alfred Kinsey's scientific approach to human sexuality at his Institute for Sex Research at Indiana University. "The cultural idealization of science in American society was Kinsey's inspiration as well as his validation" (Irvine 1990:36). In 1937 George W. Corner, the new chairman of the committee, strongly supported the "human side" of the work and Kinsey's scientific approach. By 1947, Kinsey was receiving about half the committee's annual allocation, and this level of support continued until the heart of the McCarthy era. Then, in 1954, a federal congressional investigating committee targeted the Rockefeller Foundation for investigation as a dangerous liberal organization. Among the casualties was foundation support for Kinsey's research, which completely ceased.

Meanwhile, sexology gleaned at least a few benefits from the NRC/CRPS. George Corner not only served as a research subject for Kinsey (Corner 1981) but also was a major supporter of William Masters, whom he had trained in gynecology. "As Corner had advised, Masters waited until he was thirty-eight and an established gynecologist before beginning sex research at Washington University." Ironically, the organizational entity he and Virginia Johnson created there was named the Reproductive Biology Research Foundation (Irvine 1990:79–80). Thus in some bizarrely transgressive moves, sexology was pursued under the name of reproductive biology, while reproductive biology was done as "research on problems of sex." Struggles for legitimacy can take many turns.

CONCLUSIONS

My thesis in this chapter has been that basic reproductive scientists and their supporters redirected the initial mission of the NRC/CRPS toward basic reproductive research within natural science approaches. They did so through arguments asserting the value and necessity of fundamental research in providing building blocks toward clinical and applied uses. They thereby succeeded in capturing the bulk of the committee's funds between 1921 and 1940, the vulnerable period of formation and coalescence for the reproductive sciences enterprise. During this period, a total of $1,227,000 was provided to the NRC/CRPS by the BSH and the Rockefeller Foundation.[107]

The major effort of "human side" advocates—to create an independent agency to handle both human and biological aspects of sex research—failed dismally. In 1931, the "basic" research orientation of the NRC/CRPS was confirmed by its transfer from the BSH to the Rockefeller Foundation. The power to fund is the power to direct research, and foundation officers became de facto makers of national science policy (Kohler 1976:284). By the mid-1930s, even Lillie's proposal for an Institute of Race Biology did not gleam as seductively as molecular biology, although the Rockefeller Foundation then directly funded a number of reproductive research centers.

The redirection of the mission of the NRC/CRPS gave both the committee and the reproductive sciences a "basic" research identity, distinguishing them vividly from sexology and from applied contraceptive research. Most of all, the NRC/CRPS gave momentum to the reproductive sciences enterprise itself, sponsoring three editions of *Sex and Internal Secretions* (Allen, ed., 1932, 1939; Young 1961), which served as the bibles of the reproductive sciences for over forty years. The committee was finally completely discontinued in 1962 (National Academy of Sciences 1979:v).

Yoxen (1982:125–34) has argued that one of the reasons British science lagged behind after World War I was the lack of interest of British elites in science and technology development, certainly compared to Carnegie and Rockefeller efforts in the United States, with their "managed biology" based on "a kind of corporatist rationalism." Morawski (1986:220) views the goal of related Rockefeller projects in psychobiology and psychology as aiming at "the rational control of human behavior." Clearly there were also very deep Rockefeller commitments to sex research at historical moments when it was highly controversial and understudied. The capacities to control the biology of sex and human sex behavior were both pursued assiduously through Rockefeller sponsorship.

Sexology or sexuality studies and reproductive biology were also "disentangled" qua disciplines through the work—some might argue the politics—of the committee. The distinctive problematics of human sexuality began to be framed as falling within an emergent discipline of "sexology" with very strong social science elements along with the biomedical. This framing was especially strong among reproductive scientists, who sought to relegate such studies to "the human side" and alienate them from committee funding. However, the boundary between sexology and reproductive sciences moves, depending on who is drawing it and under what conditions. For example, animal behavior studies that take up sexuality were often viewed as closer to reproductive science by biologists (e.g., Beach 1981; Mitman and Burkhardt 1991), but are also claimed by some sexologists (Porter and Hall 1995). It was also no accident that, when committee funding reverted to its initial focus, the individual funded was Alfred Kinsey, a biologist who had studied the gall wasp. His status on the boundary line between the natural and social sciences, with a foot in both worlds, certainly served him well.

The strategic arguments for basic research that were used to redirect the mission of the NRC/CRPS away from sexological research were part of the effort to construct a legitimate and autonomous reproductive sciences enterprise. The redirection succeeded in cloaking that enterprise in a mantle of unquestionable scientific legitimacy. That basic reproductive scientists had their own scientific agenda and followed it with clear and sustaining NRC/CRPS support gave them considerable autonomy in relation to the multiple audiences and sponsors of their work, including other scientists. Such legitimacy and autonomy are in a sense cumulative. They adhere to an enterprise over time. In the next chapter I turn to what reproductive scientists actually did with all this carefully negotiated funding between 1925 and 1940. Then, in chapter 6, I analyze how the legitimacy and autonomy gained by the reproductive sciences enterprise through association with the NRC/CRPS served them well in relation to their other major audiences between and after the world wars—birth control advocates.

PART THREE

Coalescing the Enterprise

CHAPTER FIVE

Coalescing the Discipline
Endocrinological Approaches, 1925–40

Following a formative era focused on a physiological problem structure from about 1910 to 1925, the American reproductive sciences coalesced around reproductive endocrinological problems manifest in all three professional worlds—biology, medicine, and agriculture—from about 1925 to 1940. Whereas the period of disciplinary formation period was one of articulation of a set of problems for the reproductive sciences and the beginnings of careers in the field, the later period was one of deepening investments and consolidation as an enterprise of social worlds within a broader arena centered on reproduction. This is a saga of the coalescence of a scientific social world that the required both legitimacy and autonomy from other sciences and powerful funding sources to survive, much less flourish. Ultimately, during this period, global supremacy in the reproductive sciences shifted to the United States, indelibly marking their success.

I first describe the rise of reproductive endocrinology as model research and the "heroic age of reproductive endocrinology" (Marrian in Parkes 1966a:xx), including the major foci of the reproductive sciences between 1925 and 1940. One of the key factors shaping this era was the discovery of the production of reproductive hormones in the anterior pituitary gland. This became the site of the intersection of reproductive and general endocrinology. I next analyze this intersection as the core physiological and sociological juncture of the coalescence of the reproductive sciences around endocrinological problems. Ties to general endocrinology provided the reproductive sciences enterprise with scientific and social legitimacy and considerable cultural authority; endocrinology has continued to dominate the field.

One of the major landmarks in the history of the modern reproductive sciences in the United States was publication of *Sex and Internal Secretions:*

A Survey of Recent Research (Allen, ed., 1932). Both the book and most of the research on which it was based were sponsored by the National Research Council Committee for Research in Problems of Sex. After discussing the importance of this book and aspects of its reception, I review the disciplinary professionalization of the reproductive sciences in biology, medicine, and agriculture, including the establishment of societies and journals. Interactions across professional boundaries are noted and the mutual benefits of efforts in each professional area to the enterprise as a whole are evaluated. Yet tensions existed, and I also discuss schisms along organismic versus physicochemical lines. Last I delineate what the reproductive sciences did for biology, medicine, and agriculture, including the consequences for each professional field in terms of enhanced basic, clinical, and applied offerings. All five themes of this volume are evident in this chapter: the reproductive sciences as intersecting social worlds, disciplinary development, boundary crossings, gender issues, and the control of (human and nonhuman) life through disciplining reproduction.

THE HEROIC AGE OF REPRODUCTIVE ENDOCRINOLOGY

Guy Marrian called the years 1926–40 the "heroic age of reproductive endocrinology" (Parkes 1966a:xx), while Alan Parkes (1962b:72) described the period as an "endocrinological gold rush." During this period, the chief naturally occurring estrogens, androgens, and progesterone were isolated and characterized, and the hypophyseal (anterior pituitary), placental, and endometrial gonadotrophins were also discovered.[1] Parkes (1966a:xx) has argued that we will never again see another such period in reproductive endocrinology. It was also a most competitive time, "a period of keen rivalry and of fierce competition for priority: and everyone concerned was guilty of publishing too much and too frequently" (Marrian 1967).

Table 3 provides an overview of the foci of the reproductive sciences from 1925 to 1940. Some problems from the formation era continued to be pursued, such as the estrus and menstrual cycles, fertilization, and sex differentiation, but with increased emphasis on endocrinological aspects rather than physiological processes. Newer topics included testicular function and artificial insemination, fertility and sterility, and the properties and biological activity of all of the sex hormones. Most important, the simple one-gland, one-hormone, two-sex segregated construction of the internal secretions of sex (with the testis producing the male hormone and the ovaries the female hormone) was disproved. A much more complex feedback theory, predicated on a diversity of hormones common to both males and females, took its place (see Price 1975). I will comment on only a limited number of the research areas listed in Figure 2, as others have recently

TABLE 3 The American Reproductive Sciences ca. 1925–1940: Professions and Major Problem Structures

Profession	Biology	Medicine	Agriculture
Focus of problem structure	Analytic problems	Reproductive organ system and analytic problems	Domestic organisms and analytic problems
Unit of analysis	Species	Humans (individual)	Populations of selected species
Problems addressed	Sex differentiation: Moore 1930 Witschi 1932 Testicular function: Moore, 1926, 1932 Embryology of sex: Witschi 1932 Willier 1932 Fertilization: Chang and Pincus 1931	Menstrual cycle: Corner 1923 (monkey), 1933 (human) Allen 1926 Hartman 1932 (monkey), 1936 (human) Placentation: Bartelmez 1935 Uterine function: Bartelmez 1933, 1937 Reynolds 1939 Markee 1940 Lactation: Corner 1930 Fertility and sterility: Young 1929, 1931 Hartman 1932, 1936 Rock and Bartlett 1937 Makepeace et al. 1937 Artificial insemination: Young 1929 Guttmacher 1938	Estrus Cycle: H. H. Cole 1930 (cow) Cole and Hart 1930 (mare) Evans and Cole 1931 (dog) Griffiths and Amoroso 1939 (dog) Infectious abortion: Bowman 1935 Mammary glands: Turner 1932 Artificial insemination: Perry 1945

(continued)

TABLE 3 (continued)

Profession	Biology	Medicine	Agriculture
		Reproductive Endocrinological Researches	
	Androgens: McGee 1927 Funk and Harrow 1929 Moore et al. 1929 Moore 1932, 1938 Koch 1932	Estrogens: Allen and Doisy 1923 Frank et al. 1926	
	Prolactin: Riddle et al. 1932 Estrogens: Hisaw and Meyer 1929 Levin et al. 1931	Hypophyseal gonadotropins: Smith 1927, 1930, 1932 Evans and Simpson 1928 Engle 1932 Severinghaus 1932 Li et al. 1940	PMSG: Cole and Hart 1930 Cole et al. 1932 Hart and Cole 1934
	Hypophyseal gonadotropins: Fevold et al. 1931, 1936 Moore and Price 1932 Progesterone: Hisaw et al. 1930	Genetic/endocrinological factors: Danforth 1932 Progesterone: Corner and Allen 1929a, b	Superfecundity: Cole 1937
	Hormone antagonism: Moore 1930	DES: Engle and Crafts 1939	DES: Burroughs 1954

framed the concepts and priorities of discovery (Greep and Koblinsky 1977; Gruhn and Kazer 1989).

First, table 3 demonstrates that not all the research done on reproductive topics was endocrinological in nature. For example, research on the menstrual cycle, begun prior to 1925 and continuing throughout the coalescence period, was only partially endocrinologic. Scientists continued to pursue what came to be called biological or physiological (as opposed to "purely" endocrinological) problems. Corner (1923, 1927, 1933), Hartman (1930, 1931, 1932a,b, 1933, 1936, 1939), Bartelmez (1933, 1937), Hertig and Rock (McLaughlin 1982), and others studied a variety of menstrual cycle questions.[2] These more physiological researches led to sterility and infertility problems as a strong line of postwar research (American Foundation 1955 II:135–98) and became the basis upon which fertility control by hormonal contraception (the Pill) could later be built.[3]

Second, in the scientific discourse on reproductive hormones that began this century, there was (and remains) a startling reification of "male" and "female" hormones. That is, despite consistent research findings that both types of hormones are characteristically found in both males and females, monolithic hormonal attribution by sex has been intentionally sustained, largely by simplification strategies (Star 1983). Specifically, beginning during this period, the estrogenic hormones were constructed as "female," while the androgenic were "male."

Part of this reification of gonadal hormones as sexed was a theory developed in the more social writings of the British reproductive scientist Walter Heape. His theory, asserting that the two supposed "female" and "male" hormones were "antagonistic" to one another, was imported into reproductive endocrinology. In fact, the term "sex antagonism" was then in fairly common cultural usage (Chesler 1992:169), pointing to social phenomena that today are encompassed by the phrase "the battle between the sexes." Heape wrote a book called *Sex Antagonism*, in 1913, which "dealt with male/female conflicts such as the women's suffrage movement, which was of great concern to men raised in a Victorian society. In 1914 he published *Preparation for Marriage*, one of a series of books on human reproduction and the family, sponsored by the Church of England" (Biggers 1991:174). Heape was one of many scientists who published on topics beyond the pale of science, and who sought through such border crossings to use the cultural authority of science to keep women "in their place" (e.g., Russett 1989).

Within the theory of sex antagonism as it was later framed in reproductive endocrinology, some dysfunction (physiological and/or behavioral) was presumed to result if both male and female hormones were found in the same individual (Hall 1974). The most common dysfunction supposed to result was, not surprisingly, homosexuality. The strongest advocate of antagonism theory during the coalescence era was Eugen Steinach

(1861–1944) in Austria. Steinach focused mainly on hormones of the testis; in addition to studies of their biological activity, he pursued research on rejuvenation reminiscent of Brown-Séquard's ingestion of ground testicular materials. But what became known as "Steinach's operation" involved resecting the spermatic duct between ligatures instead of introducing external materials. The operation was quite popular during the 1920s and 1930s, being performed on patients such as W. B. Yeats and Sigmund Freud.[4]

Carl R. Moore and Dorothy Price at the University of Chicago, working with both types of hormones, did research that contradicted the antagonism theory in the 1930s and rendered the processes in considerably greater complexity, as part of the effort to clarify the processes of sex differentiation. Their work, which posited a complex feedback loop, broke new conceptual and substantive ground in the life sciences.[5]

Bernhard Zondek of Berlin entered this saga during the early 1930s as well. Seeking easily accessible sources of female hormones, he turned to the horse as research material. Cole and Hart (1930) in California had earlier prepared follicle-stimulating hormone (FSH) from pregnant mare serum. Zondek thought horse urine might be a useful source and found that it "contained huge amounts of oestrogen." Pregnant mares then became the usual source of estrogen for pharmaceutical companies. (This confounded farmers, who were shocked both at the requests for horse urine and at being paid for it!) An interview with Zondek provides a retrospective account of the next installment:

> F. But you have found that the richest source of oestrogen is stallion urine, haven't you? Z. Yes, I was really astonished when Haussler and I found that stallion's urine contains even more oestrogen than that of pregnant mares. And I was even more astonished to find a high concentration of oestrogen in the testicles of stallions. F. Did you consider it strange to find oestrogen in a male animal? Z. I concluded that oestrgen in stallions had to be a metabolite of the androgenic hormones. Many years later you biochemists substantiated this conclusion by showing through more elaborate methods that testosterone is convertible to oestrogen. But to this day I don't understand how it is that the high concentration of oestrogen in stallion testes and blood does not exert an emasculating effect. F. It is fortunate for the stallion that he has no chance of knowing your trouble. (Finkelstein 1966:11)

Zondek published his work in 1934, and the story seems to have circulated rapidly as a result of the ongoing intercontinental debate about sex hormone antagonism. However, despite citing Zondek's work on estrogen in stallions and that of his Chicago colleagues Moore and Price, Frank Lillie (1939:6, 11) deliberately furthered the reification of sex and gender by not renaming, or at least destabilizing the gendering of, gonadal hormones in his "Biological Introduction" to the major handbook of the reproductive sciences, *Sex and Internal Secretions.*[6] He begins by lauding the "the great advances that have been made and consolidated, especially in the chemistry . . . of the male and female hormones . . . " which have now "served to complicate rather than to simplify our conceptions of the mechanisms of control of sex characters" which have emphasized work in different species. But, Lillie intoned, "Under these circumstances it seems inadvisable to include in a biological introduction the newer chemical terminology. The old terms male and female sex hormones carry the implication of control of sex characteristics and represent conceptions that would still be valid whatever the outcome of further chemical and physiological analysis. . . . As there are two sets of sex characters, so there are two sets of sex hormones, the male hormone controlling the 'dependent' male characters, and the female determining the 'dependent' female characters." Here Lillie eliminates the possibility that science could change its mind over time. And for the most part it did not. Many subsequent discussions of gonadal hormones have been *socially* gendered in this way (Hall 1974). Major lines of "sex differences" research have been based upon it as well.[7]

Other reproductive scientists have objected both at the time and subsequently. For example, Oudshoorn (1994:47) reports that at the First International Congress on the Standardization of Sex Hormones held in London in 1932 (discussed later in this chapter), Dutch reproductive endocrinologists were critical of what they called "the unitary school of sex endocrinology." They objected to the definition of the biological actions of the female hormones as categorically *only* actions in the estrus cycle, specifically because their capacities to stunt growth, produce fatty deposits, decrease kidney weight, and so on, were all ignored by such a narrow definition.

Years later, Amoroso (1963), not referring to sex hormones specifically, complained that "outdated" and "misleading" rhetoric was characteristic of endocrinology quite broadly. For example, he felt the continued phraseology of gonadotropins as parts of one-to-one "feedback" loops when the interactions were already understood to be much more complex misled even scientists. The endocrinologist and historian Medvei (1982:408) has noted that certain supposed "female" and "male" hormones may in fact be identical, a rather "delayed" finding. Whalen (1984) provides a searing critique of scientific language around gonadal hormones, reminding us that "all hormones and their antagonists have multiple effects." That is, what have been called sex hormones are not *only* sex hormones but have other biological actions as well. Even for scientists, this sustained nomenclature is obscurantist.

Questions that Lillie, Amoroso, and Medvei fail to ask, which feminists do,[8] include why such social constructions are made, why do they persist, and who benefits? Such problems of misconstruction of concepts of sex and gender *in* science have negative consequences for the science itself (Keller 1995). The sustained reification of hormones as "male" and "female" in this century can be viewed as a social phenomenon parallel to one discussed by Farley (1982:110–28), who found a "sexless age of reproductive research" in the nineteenth century when sex was denied both socially and biologically. Farley concludes that these biologists' scientific work was shaped by their social assumptions. He further found that when nineteenth-century biologists did discuss a sexual means of *biological* reproduction in a particular species, such as humans, they deemed it the basis of a proper and "natural" *social* division of labor between the sexes, wherein women were assigned to a lifetime of raising children, while men were to be employed outside the home for wages and salaries. Similar social designations have been based on the gendered reification of gonadal hormones (e.g., Harding and O'Barr 1987; Schwartz 1984).

Biologist Fausto-Sterling (1989, 1992:85–88, 1993, 1998) has recently taken up these problems. She argues that there are multiple sexes or, alternatively, that what we call sex is a continuous set of properties and, for most purposes, a classification system of five sexes is fairly accurate, inclusive, and serviceable. This perspective takes the complexities of biology extremely seriously, including the gonadal hormones. We certainly know from the work of Money and his colleagues (e.g., Money and Ehrhardt 1972) on "fixing" humans who apparently do not fit into the binary sex classificatory system, that such phenomena are common enough to have prompted development of routine treatments. The simplified, dimorphic construction of sex has also been challenged by those who study its medical enforcement (e.g., Hirschauer 1991, 1992, 1998; Kessler 1990), and most recently by those who do not fit within the dimorphic classification system. Here we can see today the emergence of a new social movement for change in the medical treatment of hermaphrodites, mounted by hermaphrodites themselves (Chase 1997; ISNA 1995–96).

As this book was going to press, a brand-new second kind of estrogen receptor site was "found." While the already known alpha receptors predominate in the uterus and the mammary gland, the new beta receptor was initially found in rodent prostate tissue, and predominates in the ovaries, testes, and cells that give rise to sperm! The *New York Times* article concluded that "it is time to put to rest—and cremate—the shibboleth of estrogen as a 'female hormone.' . . . Scientists have found evidence of the beta receptor in organs that display little or no evidence of alpha and that nobody had thought of as being under estrogen's dominion, including the lungs, kidneys, intestines, bladder and colon" (Angier 1997). Based on nearly a century of such complications to sex hormone theory, Fausto-Sterling (1998) asks the still radical question "Do sex hormones really exist?" One wonders what the reproductive sciences and biomedicine more generally would have been like had Lillie been as scientific in his nomenclature.

MAKING THE RIGHT (GLANDULAR) CONNECTIONS

Endocrinology became the core activity of reproductive scientists between 1925 and 1940 not solely because these major hormones were implicated in reproductive phenomena, and therefore pursued and discovered; its rises was also a social phenomenon that deserves a sociological explanation.[9] Placing endocrinology at the center of the reproductive sciences enterprise reflected a series of choices and commitments made by scientists from many countries. Developments could have been otherwise, or emphases could have been different. As the centerpiece of the reproductive sciences, endocrinology provided with several structural and strategic advantages. These included the following:

a core, widely recognizable research activity for the social worlds of reproductive sciences;

a core research activity that appeared very distant from the social issues of human sexuality and reproduction;

scientific legitimacy and fashionableness by association with general endocrinology, one of the most promising new areas of research in the life sciences;

a biochemical instead of a "merely" physiological thrust, and strong working alliances with sophisticated biochemists;

established conventions and approaches to biochemical research problems;

a common denominator and a common language across biology, medicine, and agriculture; and

the promise of a host of valuable technoscientific interventions into reproductive phenomena.

Endocrinology was a powerful contender for "most outstanding line of work" in the life sciences at this juncture, to some degree because it was part of a more general trend in medicine. In the 1920s, there was a shift of focus in explanations of disease, from exogenous factors such as germs to endogenous factors such as deficiencies, which could result in disease directly or through impaired resistance (Sinding 1990:200). Biochemical approaches, of which endocrinology was one, were also the methodological and paradigmatic "high ground" in the life sciences during this era (e.g., Kohler 1982). Thus reproductive scientists' work along biochemical endocrinological lines brought scientific legitimacy to the enterprise in relation to the *scientific* audiences, consumers, and sponsors of the reproductive sciences. Scientific audiences existed, of course, in biology, medicine, and agriculture.

During this era, the important pattern was established of biochemists working with reproductive scientists on endocrinological problems. Early reproductive scientists often lacked the sophisticated chemistry requisite for isolation of pure hormones. Corner (1981:233), in recounting his work toward the discovery and isolation of progesterone, states that once he had a practical test for a potent extract, "The stage was now set for the biochemist . . . Willard Allen." Edward A. Doisy, a professor of biochemistry at the Washington University School of Medicine, did key early work on estrogens with Edgar Allan (Allen and Doisy 1923).[10] A third example of this pattern is provided by Frederick C. Koch, chairman of the Department of Physiological Chemistry and Pharmacology at the University of Chicago, who became an integral part of the reproductive sciences center established by Lillie. Koch worked in tandem with Carl R. Moore, Lillie's successor as chairman of the Department of Zoology, on the testis as an endocrine gland and the androgenic hormones. Koch and his associates developed new methods of separation and distillation of male hormones, discovered multiple male hormones in urine through fractionalization, developed a rapid method of distilling estrogenic hormones from stallion urine, studied normal ranges of variation of hormone content in human urine of both males and females (relating nutrition to hormone production), distinguished and isolated urinary and testis tissue hormones, and began synthesis of androsterone.[11] Moore and his group simultaneously worked on the biological activity of male hormones (e.g., Moore 1932, 1938, 1947).

Eventually reproductive scientists became more adept biochemists, although biochemical specialists continued to be included in research teams and centers. Some of these centers became involved in serious rivalries. Long (1990) offers a close reading of the debate about the construction of the anterior pituitary gland. It pitted the Hisaw group at Wisconsin against the Engle group at Columbia (see Greep 1967).

The most significant outcome of the endocrinological focus, however, was the drawing together of scientists from biology, medicine, and agriculture around a shared problem structure. A *core activity* is necessary for the development of an enterprise as a recognizable social world (Strauss 1982). Reproductive endocrinology provided such a core activity. It allowed the reproductive sciences enterprise to cohere quickly as a cross-professional intersectional scientific enterprise. The evidence for this intersectionality is that, quite significantly, major breakthroughs in reproductive endocrinology were made in all three professional situations.[12]

The distance that the reproductive endocrinological focus provided between reproductive sciences and matters of sexuality and reproduction and birth control as social issues was also central to the development of a legitimate scientific enterprise. Biochemistry is usually "sexy" only to scientists. Thus social legitimacy and cultural authority could also accrue to the enterprise as it eschewed, through focus on reproductive endocrinology, direct involvement in the more controversial aspects of reproduction and sexuality.[13]

Of course, much of modern reproductive research initially in Britain (Borell 1985; Marshall 1910) and later in the United States (e.g., Asdell 1977; Corner 1981; Loeb 1911, 1958) had implicated hormonal control of the reproductive cycle. More internalist historians thus have reasonable grounds from which to state that scientists were led to endocrinological problems through their research. My argument does not contest this point. Rather, I am elucidating the social structural advantages that *also* contributed to the institutionalization of reproductive endocrinology as the core activity of the developing enterprise. By institutionalization I mean the centrality of reproductive endocrinology to the reproductive sciences in laboratories, departments, publications, professional associations, and so on. Other problems had been framed and were later de-emphasized or ignored in favor of endocrine problems. It is the shifting balance of the problem structure as a whole, rather than specific problems, that concerns me here.

Intersecting with General Endocrinology: The Anterior Pituitary

A key event in the rise of reproductive endocrinology as model research was the intersection during the 1920s of general endocrinology with reproductive endocrinology. This took place with the discovery that the anterior pituitary gland simultaneously produces both reproductive and nonreproductive hormones, providing a physiological link between reproductive and general endocrinology and between the reproductive system and the rest of the organism. Agate (1975:474) notes that during this era, "probably the greatest obstacle blocking the progress of endocrinology was the confusion and controversy about the function of the hypophysis" (the anterior pituitary gland).

The major investigator associated with clarification of hypophyseal activity was Philip Edward Smith (1884–1970), who began this work at the University of California, continued it briefly at Stanford, and completed it at Columbia's College of Physicians and Surgeons as head of the Department of Anatomy.[14] After initial work in the frog (Smith 1916), he turned to the rat and developed a surgical approach to removal of the anterior pituitary—hypophysectomy. Unlike previous methods, Smith's did not involve contact with the brain. Smith then showed (1927, 1930) that uncomplicated hypophysectomy in mammals resulted in cessation of growth, loss of weight, and atrophy of the reproductive system, the thyroid gland, and the cortex of the adrenal gland, along with other effects. Smith continued hypophyseal research with the assistance of the anatomist Earl T. Engle and the biochemist Goodwin L. Foster with work on the rhesus monkey at Co-

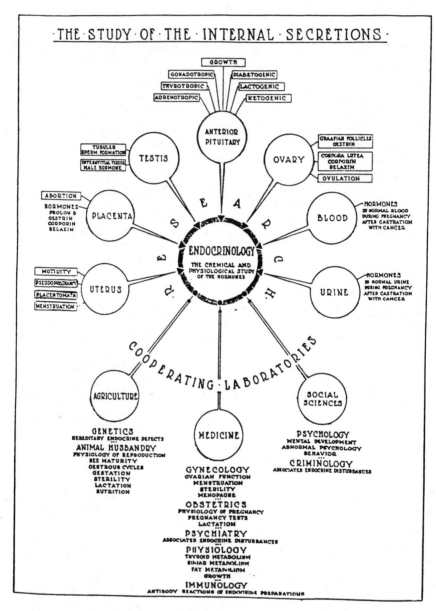

Figure 2. "The Study of the Internal Secretions," by Hisaw, Severinghaus, and Cole (by permission of the Rockefeller Archives Center).

lumbia.[15] Hypophysectomy became the key technology of the coalescence era, as the Pap smear had been during disciplinary formation. It was not, however, an easy surgery to perform. Roy Greep turned out to have "golden hands" for doing this surgery, which, he said, won him a job at Harvard when he finished his degree at Wisconsin during the Great Depression.[16]

The hormones produced by the anterior pituitary upon stimulation by the hypothalmus include adrenocorticotropic hormone (ACTH), which acts on the adrenal glands; thyroid-stimulating hormone (TSH); leutinizing hormone (LH) and follicle-stimulating hormone (FSH), which act on the ovaries or testes; growth hormone (GH), which acts on bones; prolactin (PL), which acts on breasts; and melanocyte-stimulating hormone (MSH) (Wade 1981:13–14). Following Smith, a number of scientists then focused their work on hormones of the anterior pituitary—the point (or gland) of intersection of reproductive and general endocrinology.[17] That is, the problem structure was revised to focus on the gland producing the hormones rather than on the reproductive or nonreproductive hormones and their effects.

A most interesting representation of this disciplinary intersection was created by Frederick L. Hisaw (a biologist), E. L. Severinghaus (a physician), and L. J. Cole (an agricultural scientist), all based at the University of Wisconsin in 1934. See Figure 2.[18] The heart of this representation of "The Study of the Internal Secretions" is endocrinology as "the chemical and physiological study of the hormones." Five hormone-producing sites are listed: the uterus, placenta, testis, ovary, and anterior pituitary. The last ranked foremost in the diagram, placed top and center! I would argue that this status was conferred upon the anterior pituitary by reproductive scientists for both physiological and entrepreneurial reasons. Not only do anterior pituitary hormones interact with many other hormone-production processes, but also the pituitary is the organ of intersection of the reproductive with other bodily systems and of the reproductive sciences with general endocrinology.[19] Research on the anterior pituitary allowed the reproductive sciences to climb aboard the prestigious bandwagon (Fujimura 1988) of general endocrinology research.

One important sociological question concerns the proportion of reproductive as compared with other kinds of endocrinological research undertaken during the coalescence era. Two studies by reproductive scientists of that era directly address this point. Table 4 shows Gregory's (1935:213) bibliographic tabulation from the Index Medicus and Chemical Abstracts. Table 5 shows Evans and Cowles's (1940:908) articles count. Gregory's (1935) assessment, mostly for the years 1927–33, sought to determine the percentage of articles on the corpus luteum (ovarian hormones) among the total publications in endocrinology (note that she did not ask about all reproductive hormones). Papers on gonadotropic hormones of the anterior

TABLE 4   Gregory's Bibliographical Tabulation from Indexes (1935)

A. Interrelationship of the Endocrine Glands from Index Medicus, 1933–1927	75 references
B. Adrenal Cortex Preparations from Chemical Abstracts, 1933–1924; from Index Medicus, 1933–1927	97 references
C. Kidney Extracts, from Index Medicus, 1933–1900	64 references
D. Corpus Luteum, from Index Medicus, 1933–1927	189 references
E. Diuresis and Diuretics (hormonal influence on), from Index Medicus, 1933–1927	333 references
F. Thyroid, from Index Medicus, 1930–1934; from Chemical Abstracts. 1933–1934	282 references
Total number of references	1040

SOURCE: Gregory 1935:213.

pituitary were excluded, as were those on placental, mammary, and testicular hormones. Regardless, she found that fully 18 percent of endocrinological publications dealt with hormones of the corpus luteum. Evans and Cowles (1940) made a direct count from over two hundred journals to analyze interest in the individual hormone-producing glands for the year 1939; they found that 37 percent of articles dealt with the gonads.[20] Thus, in 1939, reproductive endocrinology constituted a significant proportion—almost two-fifths—of all endocrinological publications. From a sociological perspective, it is significant that these authors undertook such tasks of tabulation to demonstrate the centrality of reproductive endocrinology to general endocrinology.

The modern reproductive sciences emerged during approximately the same historical period as modern endocrinology. For intellectual, political, disciplinary, and entrepreneurial reasons, the reproductive sciences enterprise coalesced around reproductive endocrinology. Although both fields had historical associations with medical quackery (Borell 1985), general endocrinology as a research area possessed greater legitimacy and prestige simply because it did not deal with sex or reproduction. Because of this, reproductive scientists attached their enterprise tightly to that of endocrinology through World War II and beyond.

It was both through direct association with broader endocrinological research and through downplaying its own nonendocrinological and more broadly reproductive problem structure that the reproductive sciences enterprise achieved greater legitimacy and autonomy during the coalescence period. To avoid the confusion of reproductive research with sexology and/or with contraceptive research multiple strategies were developed, even though researchers simultaneously drew upon (some would say plun-

TABLE 5   Evans and Cowles's Endocrinology Articles Count (1940)

	No. of endocrine papers published by kind and "interest" value (221 journals)		Relation of papers abtracted in 1939 to those published in 221 journals	
	Total papers published in 1939	Interest value, in percentage	Papers abstracted in 1939	Percentage abstracted
Adrenals	249	8.9	142	57
Gonads				
Female reproductive system	635	22.7	274	43
Male reproductive system	239	8.6	274	43
Mammary glands	61	2.1	17	28
General and/or mixed papers	99	3.5	60	66
Pancreas	339	12.1	150	44
Parathyroid	40	1.3	23	57
Pineal	8	0.3	5	62
Pituitary				
Anterior	216	7.8	125	57
Posterior	56	2.0	37	66
General	51	1.8	24	47
Spleen	17	0.6	6	35
Thymus	26	0.9	5	19
Thyroid	201	7.1	78	38
General	88	3.1	32	35
Glandular interrelationships	378	13.5	221	58
Metabolic interrelationships	79	2.8	45	57
Vitamin-endocrine interrelationships	25	0.9	16	64
Total	2807	100%	1362	48%

SOURCE: Evans and Cowles 1940:908.

dered) resources committed to these other lines of work (as demonstrated in chapters 4 and 6). And, as I will show later, it was precisely because reproductive scientists wanted to continue their deep identification and association with the more prestigious field of endocrinology that no professional organization focused explicitly on the reproductive sciences was begun until 1967. It thus seems apt that many years later the reproductive scientist Neena Schwartz (1984) titled her presidential address to the Endocrine Society, "Endocrinology as Paradigm, Endocrinology as Authority."

SEX AND INTERNAL SECRETIONS: THE AMERICAN BIBLE OF REPRODUCTIVE ENDOCRINOLOGY

During the coalescence era, preeminence in the reproductive sciences shifted from European to American research centers. The marker event in this process was the appearance of *Sex and Internal Secretions* (Allen, ed., 1932). Both its publication and much of the research on which it was based were supported by the National Research Council Committee for Research in Problems of Sex (National Academy of Sciences 1979:v). The committee's "major undertaking for diffusion of knowledge . . . was the preparation of [this] book that became exceedingly influential" (Aberle and Corner 1953:25). The first American book focused on the reproductive sciences, it emphasized even in its title the core activity of reproductive endocrinology, further demonstrating coalescence of the enterprise around it. In his introduction as chairman of the NRC/CRPS, Robert Yerkes noted:

> As its tenth birthday approached, the Committee for Research in Problems of Sex, on suggestion of Dr. E. V. Cowdry, member *ex officio* as Chairman of the Division of Medical Sciences of the National Research Council, voted to celebrate the event by taking stock of knowledge and opportunity within its field of interest. As a major step toward the realization of this purpose, Dr. Edgar Allen was invited to organize a cooperative survey of recent advances in research on internal secretion in relation to sex, with special attention to phases of the subject upon which committee interest and resources have tended to concentrate. The results of this carefully-planned survey of research achievements, whose timeliness will be recognized, are presented herewith to our colleagues in biology and to others who may find them relevant to their needs. Meantime, the Committee proposes to use the findings of the survey as partial basis for decision concerning its present and prospective serviceableness, and in formulation of a new plan and program of activity should it appear that the organization merits continued support. (Allen, ed., 1932:xvii)

Thus the book was intended both as a research handbook with directions for future work and as a promotional device to garner continued support for the NRC/CRPS from the NRC and the Rockefeller Foundation, which was itself undergoing reorganization at the time.[21]

The editor, Edgar Allen (1932:xix), also envisioned the book as a device through which to recruit more scientists to reproductive endocrinology and to expand the enterprise: "This whole field has recently undergone such rapid growth that many new questions have arisen to challenge the investigator's curiosity. An attempt will be made to indicate productive approaches to some of these unsolved or only partially solved problems." All of the contributors to this edited volume were from the United States, signaling the shift to American preeminence in the reproductive sciences. A combination of the negative effects of World War I on European work and the infusion of external fiscal support in the United States through the NRC/CRPS contributed to this shift.[22] Warren Weaver of the Rockefeller Foundation was impressed by the effort, as a 1934 memo reveals: "One gets a vivid picture of the great advance which has been made under the committee. In 1900–1910, there were perhaps six investigators in all making any progress on such problems. There are now well over six investigators at each of a considerable number of institutions. The undoubted leadership of the U.S. in endocrinology can be credited, directly and indirectly, to the committee's activity. In spite of this progress, one is equally impressed by the range, multitude and importance of the specific problems which now present themselves."[23]

The contents of the book reflect Frank Lillie's agenda for biological reproductive research, which he presented to the NRC/CRPS in 1922 (see appendix 2). While the book includes genetic and embryological aspects of reproduction, it is focused primarily on reproductive endocrinology. Thus it also testifies to the import of biochemistry into research in the reproductive sciences. As Aberle and Corner (1953:27) later asserted, "The growth of research in sex gland biochemistry was greatly promoted by the excellent chapters on that subject by the pioneers Doisy and Koch." Both were among of the first generation of biochemists to work with reproductive scientists on endocrinological problems.

As Marshall had done in his *Physiology of Reproduction* (1910), Allen (ed., 1932:xix) specified his intended audiences: "This book is intended for the reader with a moderate biological background. . . . It is not our intent that it should be a 'popular book on sex.' Instead, it is designed for those interested in the progress of research in problems of sex. . . . Physicians who are interested in fundamentals will find much valuable recent material. In supplying a biological foundation for education in matters of sex, it should also attract the interest of serious students of sex functions in man." What distinguishes Allen's remarks from Marshall's is Allen's omission (and Yerkes's as well) of any direct reference to agricultural scientists as a likely audience, despite the fact that several such men had achieved renown for their reproductive endocrinological work in the United States.[24] Further subtle derogation of the applied side of the reproductive sciences is found in Allen's limits on physician audiences to "physicians who are interested in fundamentals." Like many reproductive scientists of the era, Allen was articulating a strong "basic research" stance regardless of institutional or professional sponsorship to distinguish the enterprise from both sexology and contraceptive research. Aberle and Corner's (1953:27) assessment of the impact of the book echoes similar themes: "The book had an immense success. It was read and used everywhere, abroad as well as at home, serving notice to the world that America had a corps of investigators who were making great advances in the whole field of sex biology. For graduate students in departments of zoology, and for the more scientifically minded young physicians with embryological, obstetrical, and gynecological interests, it became a reference book."

Sex and Internal Secretions became the second bible of the reproductive sciences, following Marshall's monograph, which had held sway for nearly a quarter of a century. It is also notable that this NRC/CRPS volume was an edited work rather than a single-authored monograph, as Marshall's had been. The impossibility of any single author mastering the field was clear in the reproductive sciences by 1932, as Maienschein (1991a) found to be true for cytology in the same era.

Sex and Internal Secretions went through three editions (Allen, ed., 1932, 1939; Young 1961), with the final edition also marking the official end of the NRC/CRPS. Some of the changes across the three editions are worthy of attention here. The first edition comprised 912 pages with nineteen chapters. The second edition comprised 1,346 pages with twenty-four chapters organized into five major sections as follows:

A. Biological Basis of Sex
B. Physiology of the Sex Glands, Germ Cells and Accessory Organs
C. Biochemistry and Assay of Gonadal Hormones
D. The Hypophysis and Gonadotropic Hormones of Blood and Urine in Relation to the Reproductive System
E. Additional Factors in Sex Functions and Endocrine Applications in Man

The last section included chapters on the thymus and pineal glands, the vitamins and sex glands, sex drive, and sex functions in man. The two-volume third edition was larger still, with 24 chapters and over 1500 pages. It was divided into six sections:

A. Biologic Basis of Sex
B. The Hypophysis and the Gonadotrophic Hormones in Relation to Reproduction
C. Physiology of the Gonads and Accessory Organs
D. Biology of Sperm and Ova, Fertilization, Implantation, the Placenta, and Pregnancy
E. Physiology of Reproduction in Submammalian Vertebrates
F. Hormonal Regulation of Reproductive Behavior

The last section on behavior was much expanded from the one chapter allocated to this topic in each of the earlier editions. The psychobiology of sex that Yerkes had advocated in the 1920s and 1930s had come to fruition. The papers here covered topics ranging from birds to humans, and the authors ranged from John Money to Margaret Mead.[25] The last printing of *Sex and Internal Secretions* was in 1973.

The next bibles of the reproductive sciences were not published until 1976 and 1977, this time sponsored by the Ford Foundation.[26] Their titles tell of a repositioning of the reproductive sciences enterprise much closer to contraceptive research. Roy O. Greep, Marjorie A. Koblinsky, and Frederick S. Jaffe produced *Reproduction and Human Welfare: A Challenge to Research* in 1976, as a primer on the application of the reproductive sciences to contraceptive research, including a valuable short history of the field. Its main focus was framing future directions for worldwide efforts at contraceptive development. The companion volume edited by Greep and Koblinsky, *Frontiers in Reproduction and Fertility Control: A Review of the Reproductive Sciences and Contraceptive Development,* appeared the following year and more closely paralleled *Sex and Internal Secretions.* Of forty chapters, about half were on hormones and other "basic" research topics, while the other half centered on clinical topics from abortion and sterilization to artificial insemination, and appendices contained ambitious literature reviews. These two volumes marked the end of the modern era of the reproductive sciences and the beginnings of the postmodern. They contained a much stronger emphasis on male reproductive phenomena and presaged the "new reproductive technologies" that were about to explode onto the scene with the birth of the first "test-tube baby" via in vitro fertilization in England in 1978. With their transnational orientation, these volumes reflected the (re)distribution of reproductive and contraceptive research around the world, of which the Ford Foundation was the major sponsor (Hertz 1984). They also reflected the beginning of the end of American dominance of the field.

PROFESSIONALIZING THE REPRODUCTIVE SCIENCES

Table 6 lists the major professional associations and journals addressing reproductive topics in the United States in biology, medicine, and agriculture between 1910 and 1969.[27] All these journals published research on reproductive topics. There is also information available on the relative publication of articles on reproductive endocrinology in these journals prior to 1934. Mengert (1934) analyzed all of the articles referenced in *Sex and Internal Secretions* (Allen, ed., 1932) and offered the listing shown in figure 3.[28] The journals with the highest publication counts within the repro-

TABLE 6   Major Professional Associations and
Journals Publishing Reproductive Research

Association	Journals
Biology	
Association of Morphologists (1890), later American Zoological Society (1902)	*Journal of Morphology* (1887) *American Zoologist* (1961)
American Society of Biological Chemists (1906)	*Journal of Biological Chemistry* (1904)
Woods Hole Marine Biological Laboratory (1887)	*Biological Bulletin* (1902)
Nonsociety journal	*Journal of Experimental Zoology* (1902)
Medicine	
American Gynecological Society (1876); American Association of Obstetricians and Gynecologists (1888)	*American Journal of Obstetrics and Diseases of Women and Children* (1868–1919), later *American Journal of Obstetrics and Gynecology* (1920)
American Physiological Society (1887)	*American Journal of Physiology* (1898) *Physiological Reviews* (1921) *Annual Review of Physiology* (1939)
American Association of Anatomists (1888)	*American Journal of Anatomy* (1901) *Anatomical Record* (1906)
American Medical Association (1847)	*Journal of the American Medical Association* (1883)
Nonsociety journals	*American Journal of the Medical Sciences* (1841) *Journal of Physiology* (1878) *Johns Hopkins Hospital Bulletin* (1889) *Journal of Laboratory and Clinical Medicine* (1915)
Association for the Study of Internal Secretions (1917), later Endocrine Society (1962)	*Endocrinology* (1917) *Journal of Clinical Endocrinology* (1941)
International Fertility Association (1951)	*International Journal of Fertility* (1955) *Journal of Reproductive Medicine: Lying-In* (1968)
Agriculture	
American Veterinary Medical Association (1863)	*Journal of American Veterinary Medical Association* (ca. 1877)

TABLE 6   *(continued)*

Association	Journals
American Society of Animal Nutrition (1908), later American Society of Animal Production (1912)	*Journal of Animal Science* (1942)
National Association of Dairy Instructors and Investigators (1906), later American Dairy Science Association (1917)	*Journal of Dairy Science* (1921)
Nonsociety journal	*Animal Reproduction Science* [international] (1978)

Cross-disciplinary/Cross-professional

Society for Experimental Biology and Medicine (1903)	*Proceedings of the Society . . .* (1903/4)
Carnegie Institution's Department of Embryology (1913)	*Carnegie Contributions to Embryology* (1915)
American Society for the Study of Sterility (1944)	*Fertility and Sterility* (1950)
Society for the Study of Fertility [British] (1949)	*Journal of Reproduction and Fertility* [international] (1960)
Nonsociety journal	*Bibliography of Reproduction* (1963)
Society for the Study of Reproduction (1967)	*Biology of Reproduction* (1969)
Nonsociety journal	*Journal of Reproductive Immunology* [international] (1979)

Contraception-focused

American Birth Control League (1921), later Birth Control Federation of America (1939), later Planned Parenthood Federation of America (1942)	*Birth Control Review* (1917–1940), *Journal of Contraception* (1935–1939), later *Human Fertility* (1940)
International Planned Parenthood Federation (1948)	*Research in Reproduction* (1969)
Nonsociety journal	*Advances in Fertility Control* (1966–1969)

ductive physiology of nonhuman primates were the *Anatomical Record, Endocrinology,* and *Proceedings of the Society for Experimental Biology and Medicine.* Yet similar works were published in such a range of journals that these top three account for only 25 percent of the articles written before 1950 (Studer and Chubin 1976). Long (1987) describes the heterogeneous dis-

PERIODICALS ON ENDOCRINOLOGY OF SEX

WILLIAM F. MENGERT, M.D.

Gynecean Hospital Institute of Gynecologic Research, School of Medicine, University of Pennsylvania

PHILADELPHIA

TABLE 1

JOURNALS PUBLISHING THE MAJORITY OF THE ARTICLES
REFFERED TO IN "SEX AND INTERNAL SECRETIONS"

Journal	Number of References to Each Journal	Cumulative Total of References	
		Number	Per Cent
1. American Journal of Physiology	169	169	6.8
2. Comptes rendus des séances et mémoires de la Sociéte de Biologie	142	311	12.6
3. Proceedings of the Society of Experimental Biology and Medicine	125	436	17.6
4. Anatomical Record	116	552	22.3
5. American Journal of Anatomy	106	658	26.6
6. Journal of Experimental Zoology	99	757	30.6
7. Archiv für Gynäkologie	75	832	33.6
8. Endocrinology	61	893	36.1
9. Klinische Wochenschrift	54	947	38.3
10. Proceedings of the Royal Society of London	52	999	40.4
11. Zentralblatt für Gynäkologi	51	1050	42.5
12. Journal of the American Medical Association	49	1099	44.5
13. Journal of Physiology	41	1140	46.1
14. Biological Bulletin of the Marine Biological Laboratory	38	1178	47.6
15. Johns Hopkins Hospital Bulletin	35	1213	49.0
16. British Journal of Experimental Biology	33	1246	50.4
17. Carnegie Institute of Washington Publications	33	1279	51.7
18. Archiv für die gesamte Physiologie des Menschen und der Tiere (Pflüger's)	32	1311	53.1
19. Archiv für Entwickelungsmechanik der Organismen	32	1343	54.3
20. American Naturalist	28	1371	55.5
315 other journals	1103	2474	100.0

The table shows the 20 journals most frequently cited, the number of references to each and cumulative totals and percentages. For example: The first 10 journals listed published 999 articles, or 40.4 per cent of the total of the 2474 references appearing in "Sex and Internal Secretions."

Figure 3. Mengert's analysis of *Sex and Internal Secretions* (Mengert 1934: 421).

ciplinary commitments of reproductive "physiologists," which partially accounts for the wide range of publication venues.

It is, however, intriguing that the Society for the Study of Internal Secretions, founded in 1917 and later known as the Endocrine Society, was not the major professional base for reproductive scientists during the coalescence period. Several factors seem to have contributed to this. First, biological and medical reproductive scientists had professional and disciplinary commitments to other associations and publications, such as those in anatomy and physiology (see, e.g., Corner 1981). Second, most reproductive scientists were deeply committed to basic research over and against clinical and applied work, while the Endocrine Society was then medical in nature and membership and committed to clinical as well as basic research. As Lisser notes (1967:5–6): "Clinical endocrinology at that time was in disrepute. Conditions were such that any younger clinician, not yet firmly established and despite an unblemished reputation, who dared to embark upon a career in this field was looked upon askance, considered naive and gullible or—perhaps worse—suspected of straying into the realm of quackery, and heading for the 'endocrine gold fields.'" That is, general *clinical* endocrinology, like reproductive endocrinology, was associated with quackery of an especially lucrative type.[29] Basic endocrinological research was not viewed so dubiously. For example, the American Medical Association gave a gold medal to Herbert M. Evans in 1923 for his "discovery" of growth hormone and his creation of gigantism in rats through use of these anterior pituitary hormones (Lisser 1967:7). However, it is also possible that the Endocrine Society, not wanting to add sexual insult to clinical injury, was initially less receptive to studies of reproductive endocrinology for presentation or publication because of its own professional vulnerability. The discovery of insulin in 1922 (Bliss 1982) promoted further general endocrinological work and gave the Endocrine Society further legitimacy. After about 1932, the society became essentially a national organization, no longer continuing its efforts at international representation (Lisser 1967:14).[30] It continues today as a major professional association.

During the coalescence period there were several major international meetings on sex research/reproductive sciences. At the First International Congress on Sex Research, held in Berlin in 1926, which emphasized sexology, few English-speaking basic reproductive scientists were in attendance; two papers published by British workers (one by F. A. E. Crew and the other by Arthur Walton, John Hammond, and S. A. Asdell) on the scrotum and sperm were presented (Marcuse 1928). At the Second International Congress, held in London in 1930, there was considerably greater focus on the physiology of sex, including reproductive endocrinology; basic research was extensive and clearly distinguished from clinical "therapy," contraception, and "sociology of sex" (Greenwood 1931). The United States was represented by Oscar Riddle, C. H. Danforth, F. C. Koch, R. T. Frank, and others. Carl R. Moore, representing the NRC Committee for Research in Problems of Sex, reported:

> Registration of 250–300 . . . from 30 countries of which United States representation was third in numbers (British, 63; Germany, 48; United States, 32; France, 16, Italy, 9; etc.). . . . Biological, chemical, sociological, psychiatric and clinical aspects of sex were represented. From approximately 100 papers presented some 20 per cent dealt with the male gonad. . . . 20 per cent dealt with the female gonad. . . . 10 per cent dealt with interrelations of the

gonads and their hormones and other organs of internal secretion . . . 7 per cent . . . secondary sex characters; smaller numbers were devoted to studies of dietary influences upon reproduction, sex reversals, germ cell biology, senility, sociological influences, contraceptives and psychoanalysis.[31]

Thus, by the 1930s scientists from many disciplines were increasingly focused on international activities, from standardization to technical innovations. Abir-Am (1993) discusses such activities as the construction of transnational objectivity in international space, and such patterns of internationalization were clearly characteristic of the reproductive sciences at this time. Because the broad agendas of the earlier congresses on sex research included sexology, eugenic, and contraceptive concerns, which most American basic reproductive scientists eschewed, there was a move in the early 1930s to have international gatherings only on sex hormones. Two special conferences sponsored by the Health Organization of the League of Nations were then held—one in Hampstead in 1932 focused on estrogenic hormones, and a second in London in 1935 focused on androgenic and luteal hormones. Both sought to establish international standards of biological activity for these sex hormones.[32]

Subsequently, more general international conferences focused on sex hormones began. The Singer-Polignac Colloque, or the First International Conference on Sex Hormones, was held in Paris in 1937 (Brouha 1938). Attending from the United States were Edgar Allen of Yale, P. E. Smith of Columbia, Carl G. Hartman of the Carnegie Institution, F. L. Hisaw of Wisconsin and Harvard, and Aura E. Severinghaus of Columbia (Brouha 1938; Zuckerman 1978). This conference, restricted to "basic" research on reproductive endocrinology, also included scientists from Canada, Great Britain, France, and Germany. Another standardization conference was held in 1938 in Geneva.[33]

The outbreak of World War II curtailed international conferences, and for a few years nationally based organizations and gatherings became the conventional meeting grounds for reproductive scientists. One such conference, sponsored by the American Association for the Advancement of Science, met at a private club in Maryland in 1943. When an African-American scientist was refused entry for several days because of his race, the group determined to find a more hospitable site for future meetings. In 1944, the (now international) Laurentian Hormone Conferences were duly begun in Canada, of which Gregory Pincus served as permanent chairman for many years. In 1945 they began publishing an annual volume of papers, *Recent Progress in Hormone Research,* which continues to this day. These conferences "set new standards in a field previously dominated by physicians who were strangers to the laboratory by bringing together from all over the world outstanding medical and nonmedical scientists from universities, institutes, research hospitals, and from industry" (Ingle 1971:234).

Organizational development of the reproductive sciences was parallel in Britain and the United States. General endocrinological and other professional associations and their journals provided vehicles for publication of reproductive research for many years. The (British) Society for the Study of Fertility began in 1944, although its *Journal of Reproduction and Fertility* was not established until 1960.[34] In the United States, the American Society for the Study of Sterility, formed in 1944, began publishing its journal, *Fertility and Sterility*, in 1950. No organization focused on the full panoply of reproductive phenomena until the founding of the Society for the Study of Reproduction in 1967, whose journal, *Biology of Reproduction,* was inaugurated in 1969. An attempt initiated by the Society for the Study of Reproduction to link up with the (British) Society for the Study of Fertility and jointly produce the *Journal of Reproduction and Fertility* was rebuffed (Cook 1994).

Those associations formed immediately after World War II, the (British) Society for the Study of Fertility (1949/50) and the American Society for the Study of Sterility, captured in both their names and their foci the post-1940s rhetoric of birth control activists. This new rhetoric carefully downplayed earlier themes of sex, birth control, and women's rights in favor of "family planning" and "planned parenthood" (discussed in the next chapter). The clinics of the birth control movement also began to offer sterility and infertility services along with contraception (American Foundation 1955). The growth of the reproductive sciences after World War II (see, e.g., Greep, Koblinsky, and Jaffe 1976; Greep and Koblinsky 1977), which created a flood of publishable papers, also contributed to the viability of new professional organizations and journals.

THE ENTERPRISE AS CULTURAL INTERSECTION

An intersection in the sciences, where two or more worlds or communities of practice come together, can have much to offer both, but it also can pose risks to each participating community. I have argued elsewhere (Clarke 1985, 1990b) that separate and relatively secure institutional and professional situations can allow very heterogeneous scientific (or, for that matter, other intellectual) participation. Fundamental resources are not at risk here. This social phenomenon has become increasingly interesting to scholars in science studies. Star and Griesemer (1989) discuss "boundary objects," which are robust enough to travel across multiple worlds but simultaneously plastic enough to carry local or community-specific meanings.

Such objects help scientists address their needs for cooperation despite their own diverse means and goals. Galison argues that distinct scientific subcultures may interact through development of "trading zones," viewed as "social and intellectual mortar binding together" disunified traditions.[35] Lowy (1992) takes off from these concepts and discusses "pidgin zones" where pidgin is a marginal language native to *neither* side. She argues that pidgin boundary concepts can be very important and the strength of loose concepts can be similar to the (sometimes surprising or counterintuitive) strength of loose organizational ties (Granovetter 1973). That is, a loose concept could allow the development of stable "zones of interaction," even federative experimental strategies, without obliging the participants to give up the advantages of their respective identities (Baszanger 1995).

The American reproductive sciences are exemplary of these patterns of border cultures. The enterprise quickly became a triangulated effort among scientists in biology, medicine, and agriculture. This intersection arose through a problem structure focused on the reproductive cycle and coalesced through one focused on reproductive endocrinology. The enterprise may be construed as an intersection with biochemists as well, but the problem structure remained centered on reproduction. The structure of the intersection is presented as Figure 4. The primary lines of interaction are between reproductive scientists in biology, medicine, and agriculture. Secondary (dotted) lines of interaction are shown as well. Biochemistry is attached to each professional field independently, by and large reflecting the actual organization of the work. All three fields had a tradition of research focused on reproductive phenomena. Each had adequate resources of its own to further the shared enterprise. All had been and continued to be audiences and consumers of each others' research in the larger enterprise of the reproductive sciences.

Such an intersection was neither new nor uniquely American, although emphases were different elsewhere.[36] Corner (1961:ix) carefully notes the contributions of German and Austrian gynecologists to understanding both the human menstrual cycle and the estrus cycles of other mammals, and the contributions of animal breeders and naturalists as well: "Thus at the beginning of the twentieth century and during the next decades investigation in this field became more intense. Naturalists, animal breeders, histologists, embryologists and gynecologists gradually came to understand each others' problems, and began a period of rapid advance not yet ended or even slowed down." Britain had a long tradition of biomedical and agricultural science cooperation. The British Agricultural Research Council and the Medical Research Council were even jointly funded to pursue reproductive research (American Foundation 1955 2:140). Corner (1961:ix) also noted the significance of the impetus provided by psychology, anthropology, and the women's rights movement to the development of the reproductive sciences.

The reproductive sciences intersection was a division of research labor both by the type of research materials typically used and by the "in principle" intent or mission of the work. Reproductive scientists in biology sought to pursue "pure" reproductive science as part of a general effort to grasp biological processes through work largely with laboratory animals. Reproductive scientists in medicine sought to understand normal and pathological reproductive function and to develop diagnostics and therapeutics to ameliorate reproductive pathology through work with humans and with animals as close to humans as possible (especially nonhuman primates). Reproductive scientists in agriculture sought to improve animal production in terms of quantity, quality, and controllability of reproduction, with some development of diagnostics and treatments of pathology, largely through work with domestic animals used for food or other human consumption.

The division of labor by use of very different materials was important to the development of a robust intersection specifically and the reproductive sciences generally, although workers in each field used other fields' special materials on occasion. The intersection thus not only allowed but facilitated communication about reproductive phenomena across very different species. This was of considerable heuristic value, making it easier for scientists to make comparisons and to transpose findings from one species to others. These comparisons and transpositions, which encouraged the linkages among biological, medical, and agricultural research, became the foundation of the reproductive sciences enterprise.[37] And the linkages themselves legitimated the very study of reproductive phenomena that was so problematically illegitimate. Corner (1961:ix) noted that researchers from different lines of work came to "understand each others' problems." Such understandings contributed to their solution in many ways.

The mechanisms and processes of this intersection were multifold. Developments and methods in each area were picked up and used by the others. Research materials were shared (Clarke 1987, 1995b). Joint projects were initiated. The major integrative mechanism was the shared reproductive problem structure. The first shared focus was on the estrus and menstrual cycles, with biologists concentrating on laboratory animals, medical scientists concentrating on nonhuman and human primates, and agricultural scientists concentrating on farm animals. Endocrinology deepened the intersection by providing: (1) a unifying approach; (2) shared methods and techniques; (3) sharing of materials conventions (what to use, how to use it, and how to maintain it); (4) a mutually recognized mode and unit of production; and (5) a common terminology. Not only could researchers use and benefit directly from each others' work, but all benefited through participation in a shared biochemical endeavor increasingly recognized not only by scientific worlds but also by funding sources. Each profession had joined the bandwagon early, and all gained authority and authenticity through the breadth of the endeavor.

Networks developed both within the three professional areas and across them. For example, in 1915–17, a strong line of communication on the problem of sexual differentiation in the freemartin was developed between Frank R. Lillie of the Department of Zoology at Chicago and Leon J. Cole in animal genetics at the University of Wisconsin. They shared research materials, ideas, and strategies.[38] The vaginal smear quickly became a unifying technique for reproductive cycle studies in biology, medicine, and agriculture. In one classic example, Herbert M. Evans, a professor of anatomy at the University of California, worked on the estrus cycle of the dog with Harold H. Cole, publishing their paper (Evans and Cole 1931) shortly after Cole joined the animal husbandry faculty at the University of California School of Agriculture at Davis. Cole (1930, 1977) had done research on the estrus cycle in the cow and later became an agricultural pioneer in reproductive endocrinology. Another major intersectional working group at Wisconsin, discussed earlier, centered around zoologist Frederick L. Hisaw, medical scientist Aura Severinghaus, and animal geneticist Leon J. Cole. A number of other workers, such as chemist Harry L. Fevold (Fulton and Wilson 1966:403–6) and "second-generation" endocrinologist Roy Greep (1967, 1973), were also at this center early in their careers. This intersection in the 1930s was strongly focused on reproductive endocrinology.[39] Figure 4 demonstrates their cooperative work in a grant application diagram.

Research materials were common foci of cross-professional networks. Although nonhuman primates (mostly *Macaca rhesus*) were largely the research materials of choice of medical reproductive scientists, some biologically trained workers such as Hartman also developed such colonies.[40] This intersectional group cooperated so extensively that it was known as "the monkey fraternity" at the Rockefeller Foundation.[41] Another materials intersection centered on pregnant mare serum gonadotropin (PMSG). Harold H. Cole and George H. Hart (1930) of the Department of Animal Husbandry of the University of California School of Agriculture at Davis discovered that the blood of pregnant mares (readily available to agricultural scientists) contained a substance similar to an anterior pituitary hormone known as follicle-stimulating hormone (FSH). Aschheim and Zondek (1927) in Germany had found another anterior pituitary hormone, leutinizing hormone (LH), in the urine of pregnant women. Asdell (1977:xi) notes: "Both discoveries were useful as they provided abundant sources for these hormones. It was no longer necessary to rely on the limited supply of pituitaries for hormones with gonadotropic activity. They were also useful in providing a test for pregnancy in these two species." Pregnancy tests were early and important technoscientific products of the reproductive sciences in both medicine and agriculture (Hartman 1962). Cole and Hart's research greatly benefited from patent royalties for processing PMSG.[42] Andrew Nalbandov has described the difficult and unpleasant aspects of urine collection and distillation. Urine sources were prolific, but distillation processes were arduous and highly scented for many years. Blood sources, such as PMSG, were preferred, and blood could be drawn routinely without harm to the mares. Thus agricultural scientists provided key materials for biologists and medical scientists.[43]

A key sociological question here is what made such an intimate intersection possible. Several factors contributed. Each field was sufficiently established and had its own special audiences, sponsors, and consumer markets bound to it by tradition and interest. They could intersect to create a broader, stronger, and more legitimate endeavor while retaining their institutional and professional independence, autonomy, and resources. For each group, the social structure of the intersection made the other groups helpmates rather than threatening competitors. In the language of social worlds, the intersection formed a wider social world of the reproductive sciences with distinctive subworlds in biology, medicine, and agriculture. Sociologically, the intersectional nature of the reproductive sciences articulated reproductive research with three distinctive professional contexts. In each, and across them all, there was a coalescence of professional interests in and potential markets for reproductive research, which simultaneously created and reinforced the intersection and the broader enterprise. Market demands upon workers in each field varied tremendously. Clinical and commercial applications were constantly sought by practical medical and agricultural interests, and biologists were certainly not immune to such demands. But each subworld had full rights and responsibilities for managing its own distinctive markets and resources.

At the most fundamental level, participants in the reproductive research enterprise were allies in forging a new line of scientific work—both individually and across professions. Initially a frontier ethos prevailed in reproductive research—because so little had been done, there was room for all. Gradually workers in each line of work focused more intently on their own audiences, sponsors, markets, and consumers, while maintaining strong cross-professional ties, linked but autonomous endeavors around reproductive problems. Essentially, these were relations among equals (Lowy 1992), rather than those in a network with a single major actor such as Pasteur (Latour 1983, 1988).

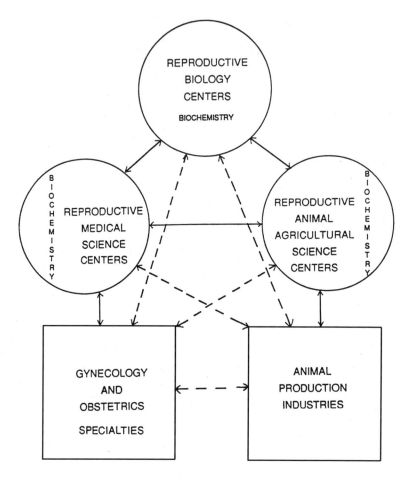

Figure 4. Structure of the reproductive sciences intersection with key applied markets.

Major American centers of reproductive science in
biology, medicine and agriculture, 1910–1945.
Biological centers:

1. University of Chicago, Departments of Zoology, Physiological Chemistry and Anatomy, ca. 1910 (Frank R. Lillie, Ernest E. Just, Carl Moore, Dorothy Price, Frederick Koch, L. V. Domm, R. G. Gustavson, George Bartelmez, J. Eldridge Markee, C. Huggins, Mary Juhn, Karl S. Lashley)
2. Carnegie Institution of Washington's Station for Experimental Evolution at Cold Spring Harbor, N.Y., ca. 1925 (Oscar Riddle, R. W. Bates, Charles W. Metz, A. F. Blakeslee)
3. Harvard University, Biological Laboratories and Medical School, ca. 1926 (Walter B. Cannon, Gregory Pincus, Frederick L. Hisaw, George B. Wislocki, Roy Greep, P. W. Whiting, Karl S. Lashley, M. W. Peck, G. F. Parker)
4. Iowa State University, Department of Zoology, ca. 1922 (B. T. Baldwin, Emil Witschi, W. W. Swingle)
5. Stanford University, Departments of Anatomy, Obstetrics and Gynecology, ca. 1922 (Philip E. Smith, C. P. Stone, John R. Slonaker, Joseph E. Markee, Lewis M. Terman, C. Frederick Fluhmann)

6. University of Wisconsin, Departments of Zoology, Medicine and Agricultural Genetics, ca. 1916 (Frederick L. Hisaw, Roy Greep, A. Severinghaus, Leon J. Cole, T. Painter, Lester E. Casida)
7. Worcester Institute of Experimental Biology, ca. 1944 (Gregory Pincus, M. C. Chang)

Medical Centers:

1. University of California, Berkeley, Departments of Anatomy, Zoology, and Institute for Experimental Biology, ca. 1916 (Herbert M. Evans, Phillip E. Smith, Joseph A. Long, Miriam Simpson, Ruth Okey, Katherine S. Bishop)
2. Carnegie Institution's Department of Embryology at Johns Hopkins Medical School, ca. 1913 (Franklin P. Mall, George Streeter, Adolph Meyer, Carl Hartman, Charles W. Metz, George Corner, Samuel R. M. Reynolds, Phillip Bard, F. F. Snyder, D. R. Hooker)
3. Columbia University College of Physicians and Surgeons, Department of Anatomy, ca. 1927 (Philip E. Smith, Earl T. Engle, Howard Taylor)
4. Cornell University Medical School, Department of Anatomy, ca. 1917 (Charles R. Stockard, George Papanicolaou)
5. Rochester University School of Medicine, Dept. Anatomy, ca. 1923 (George Corner, Willard Allen, Alan Guttmacher)
6. Washington University, St. Louis, Department of Anatomy, ca. 1921 (Edgar Allen, Edward A. Doisy, Willard Allen)
7. Yale University, Departments of Anatomy, Zoology, Obstetrics and Gynecology, Anthropology and Psychobiology, ca. 1921–25 (Robert M. Yerkes, C. Wissler, Sophie Aberle, William C. Young, Edgar Allen, Gertrude van Wagenen, W. W. Greulich)

Agricultural Centers:

1. University of California, Davis, Department of Animal Science, ca. 1928 (Harold H. Cole, Harold Goss, George H. Hart)
2. Cornell University, School of Agriculture, ca. 1930 (S. A. Asdell, William A. Wimsatt)
3. University of Illinois, Urbana/Champaign, Departments of Zoology and Animal Husbandry, ca. 1935 (A. V. Nalbandov, Carl Hartman)
4. Iowa State University, Dept. of Animal Breeding, 1930 (Jay L. Lush)
5. University of Minnesota, Department of Animal Husbandry, ca. 1928 (W. W. Green, L. M. Winters, C. L. Cole)
6. University of Missouri, Departments of Anatomy, Animal Husbandry, and Dairy Husbandry, ca. 1925 (L. E. Casida, Fred F. McKenzie, C. W. Turner, L. J. Wells, Fred N. Andrews, Harry A. Herman)

Hybrid Centers:

Several centers at the above institutions were distinctively hybrid, crossing professional divides for a sustained period, including:

1. University of Wisconsin, Departments of Zoology, Medicine and Agricultural Genetics, ca. 1916
2. Yale University, Departments of Anatomy, Zoology, Obstetrics and Gynecology, Anthropology and Psychobiology, ca. 1921–25
3. University of Missouri, Departments of Anatomy, Animal Husbandry, and Dairy Husbandry, ca. 1925

This figure provides an overview of professional organization. Some individuals, both faculty and students, may have been involved in more than one center. Data based largely on Aberle and Corner's (1953: Appendices 7–8) listing of centers funded by NRC/CRPS. Most scientists published 10+ papers listed by Aberle and Corner. Agricultural centers were usually funded through the state or the USDA.

TENSIONS IN THE FIELD

All was not always smooth in the reproductive sciences, however. One site of contention was the continued significance of morphology and anatomy to (many in) the reproductive sciences when nationally, at least, physico-chemical and molecular approaches were in ascendance. In Marshall's introduction to his *Physiology of Reproduction* (1910:2), he makes an important point about the development of the reproductive sciences: "It may be objected that, for a book on physiology, too much space is devoted to the morphological side of the subject. This has been done purposely, since it seemed impossible to deal adequately with the physiological significance of the various sexual processes without describing the anatomical changes which these processes involve." Marshall obviously thought it was necessary to defend himself in advance, arguing that there was no way to represent physiological processes without examining their concrete manifestations in anatomy/morphology. A key example of the intimate linkages to which Marshall referred in 1910 was Papanicolaou's development, in 1917, of the vaginal smear as a *morphological* indicator of reproductive *physiological* processes. That is, within the reproductive system, many physiological changes (natural or experimental) can be traced through histological and cytological examination of tissue and cells affected by those changes. Soon other tissues and organs such as the ovaries and uterus were seen to have the capacity to serve as indicators of changes in reproductive processes.[44] Reproductive research itself, in terms of both physiological and endocrinological problems, then proceeded via complicated zigzag paths from physiological or endocrinological "triggers" (natural or experimental) to observation and examination of histological and cytological specimens, and back again.[45]

Philip E. Smith's (1927, 1930) development of the technique of hypophysectomy (discussed earlier) considerably accelerated this zigzag development in anterior pituitary endocrinology. The hypophysectomized rat was "one of the most widely used tools of investigation in endocrinology and reproductive physiology today."[46] In short, the rat as technology revolutionized the field. The indicators of hypophysis were both histological and cytological. It is not surprising, then, that Smith was to edit the key text in the field, *Bailey's Textbook of Histology*, from 1932 to 1958 (Christy 1972:1415).

Marc Klein (1963:293) described the logic of endocrine research as follows: "Once morphological exploration is complete, we have to turn to experimental investigation to clear up a problem. The simplest way is to remove an organ and observe the effects on the body as a whole. Then come attempts to replace the missing gland, first by grafting the whole organ or parts of it, followed by extracting active products, first in crude and later in purified form. At that stage the exploration has already passed into the hands of chemists and physicists, who in the end specify the chemical formula and succeed in synthesizing the active principle."[47] Deletion or ablation of its pituitary turned the rat into the equivalent of a blank canvas, an excellent technology through which to study the gonadotropic hormones.

Figure 5 represents another of the classic tools of the reproductive sciences: the caponized cock. As with the rat, the cock was used for experiments of ablation followed by implantation. Here Moore and Price first castrated the cock (shown before and after); they then added hormonal substances or organs, in the mode described by Klein, and studied their effects. These cockscomb experiments and other work with fowl whose feather patterns were affected by hormones were key technologies of early reproductive endocrinology.[48] Thus morphology through histological and cytological work promoted both reproductive physiology and endocrinology. Historian of biology Frederick Churchill (1981:185–86) has suggested that "a closer examination of the interplay between organic form and life's functions deserves the attention of modern as well as nineteenth century historians." In this section I have demonstrated the centrality of that relation in reproductive physiology.

In the reproductive sciences, however, tensions developed during the 1910–40 period between a broadly conceived reproductive physiology and a more narrowly construed reproductive endocrinology. Fissures emerged between those who consistently valued the contributions of morphology (through histology and cytology) to the reproductive sciences and those committed to a purer biochemical endocrinological agenda.[49] The initial evidence concerning the value of morphology is Marshall's (1910) comment quoted earlier that morphology has a distinctive role in the reproductive sciences. Echoing Marshall, in 1925, F. A. E. Crew and his British agricultural science associates came down on the side of a broader physiological program in their introduction to Hammond's *Reproduction in the Rabbit* (1925:v–vi): "The present generation is witnessing 'a return to the practice of older days when animal physiology was not yet divorced from morphology.' Conspicuous progress is now being seen in the field of general physiology, of experimental biology, and in the application of biological principles to economic problems." In 1953, agricultural researcher H. H. Cole (1953:138) of the University of California, who himself pioneered reproductive endocrinology in domestic animals, stated in a review of the field: "It is my impression that there is still much to be learned by a more detailed study of the morphology of the reproductive organs and of the glands controlling them in normal and abnormal animals."

More recently, a number of scientists have commented on the increased value placed on *comparative* efforts, formerly a minority position. For example, in 1963, E. C. Amoroso, a British veterinary surgeon and endocrinolo-

FIG. 13. Bilaterally ovariotomized poulard showing typical capon characters. The bird retained these characters until its death well over two years following the operation. Postmortem revealed no gonad tissue on either right or left gonad sites. (Cf. figures 14 and 15; also figure 24, Chapter VII.)

FIG. 22. Bilaterally ovariotomized poulard with active testicular implant. Photograph was taken approximately 3 years following the operation during which the bird retained the masculine characters shown. It never revealed any indication reversion to the female type of plumage. (Cf. figures 31, 14, 15 and 21.)

54. Effects of castration. Compare the cockerel, or young male, of a White Leghorn chicken at right to the capon, or castrated male, at far right. Castration has altered the comb, wattles, and ear lobes. Observation of the changes wrought by castration in birds and other animals has traditionally been an important technique for analyzing the function of the sex glands and their hormones. Male hormones were first isolated and synthesized in the 1930s.

Figure 5. Key indicator of biological activity: the cockscomb (Domm, Juhn, and Gustavson 1932: 606–7; Borell 1989: 41).

gist, was pleased to look at the future prospects of endocrinology and see that "comparative endocrinology is once more coming to the forefront of biological interest, and its future becomes of immediate concern not only to biology, but to medicine and agriculture as well" (Klein 1963:297). R. V. Short (1977:34) concludes his insider history by noting: "This brief account of the history of our knowledge of the ovaries outlines the value of a broad comparative approach to the subject. By our increasing tendency to specialize we have lost the breadth of interest which our predecessors had. Many of their observations were close to what we now believe to be the truth, but they could not be developed in the prevailing scientific climate." Andrew Nalbandov, professor emeritus of the Department of Animal Science at the University of Illinois, for many years emphasized the diversity of reproductive physiologies across species, especially heterogeneous compared with other physiological systems such as digestion, respiration, and circulation.[50] Nalbandov (1976:2) goes so far as to state, "Some scientists resist accepting diversity, insisting instead on finding a unified scheme that would fit all mammals." He further noted that, during the 1930s and 1940s, some papers demonstrating diversity were refused for publication and presentation on the grounds that the findings must be "wrong."[51] In short, diversity among nonhumans was greeted with about as much glee as multiculturalism has been by conservatives. Further, such "multibodyism," or the diversity of reproductive physiologies, was actively resisted within the sciences because it ran against the grain of the modernist goal of constructing universal scientific laws.

In a number of ways, comparative perspectives have been linked with broader biological viewpoints rather than with narrower endocrinological ones, in the past as well as more recently. For example, at the turn of the century, Frank Lillie pioneered a distinctively broad biological perspective in his comparative embryological and reproductive researches specifically in opposition to the biochemical reductionist perspective held by Jacques Loeb.[52] Emil Witschi provides an example of an agricultural scientist with a comparative eye. Initially trained as a morphologist, Witschi spent most of his academic life at Iowa studying reproductive endocrinology and the problem of sex differentiation. In 1960 he established the Division of Comparative Endocrinology of the American Society of Zoologists during his presidency (Gorbman 1979:1264).

Another example from the first generation of American reproductive scientists is Carl Hartman (1879–1967), who initially taught biology in Texas and spent most of his career at the medically oriented Carnegie Institution of Washington's Department of Embryology. Hartman insisted on being called a reproductive *physiologist* to reflect his commitment to a broader biological view of reproductive phenomena throughout his career (Biggers 1970; Vollman 1965). A final example is provided by third-generation reproductive scientist T. J. Robinson (1978:189–90, emphasis added), who stated in a review of Cohen's *Reproduction:* "This is a refreshingly different book because it deals with reproduction from a classical, biological point of view and is *a healthy reminder that reproductive biology is not all endocrinology.* It is a textbook . . . on comparative animal reproduction. . . . To the reviewer who, like all aging reproductive biologists, has grown up with this relatively new science and so is largely self-taught, this book has opened up areas of comparative reproductive biology which were either unknown or but vaguely remembered."[53]

Many but far from all of the "biology versus endocrinology" tensions in the reproductive sciences seem to be clustered around what I would term "the rat debate"—whether or not scientists view rats as adequate research materials for investigating the full range of reproductive phenomena. In arguing for comparative work to fully grasp reproductive phenomena, Nalbandov complained (1958:i): "Some [graduate students] . . . profess interest only in the aspects of the field that apply to the human animal; others want to concern themselves only with the reproduction of the rat; and still others are content to learn all there is to know about the cow. This attitude is frequently carried over into their professional careers: at scientific meetings, gynecologists walk out when papers on the reproduction of sheep are read, 'sheep men' retaliate by walking out when 'rat men' are reading, and 'rat men' are content to listen only to one another."

Thus we can hear the reverberations of chronic tensions in the field over fifty years focused on the value of morphology, the value of comparative work, and the centrality of endocrinology versus a broader biological perspective. Some of these tensions may well have been and continue to be oblique manifestations of status differences among biological, medical, and agricultural scientists, but this explanation seems necessary yet not sufficient. These biological versus reductionist tensions have pervaded much of twentieth-century biology (Benson 1989), and in this, at least, the reproductive sciences are no different from other specialty areas in the life sciences.

In her study of the disciplinary formation of pain medicine, Baszanger (1995, 1998a,b) also addresses tensions in the field. She too argues that a dual vision is necessary for us to see *simultaneously* the robustness of the new discipline when viewed from without and the differences perceptible when viewed from within. She further argues that such differences occur at the heart of the work of internal legitimation—the efforts of scientists themselves to make sense of their shared work. Moreover, such strained situations may last for a long time and are a normal modus vivendi. In short, difference is usually present if one seeks it out.

Finally, these tensions may reflect a particular genre of debates in the life sciences, and perhaps beyond, which Keller (1995:35–36) frames as "a preference for interactionist, contextual, or global models over linear, causal, or 'master molecule' theories." Both models have been linked to gender, and both have implications for how we attempt to bridge the gulf between representing and intervening and how research trajectories are defined and organized. Those of us concerned with gender *in* science are concerned about how the gendered ordering of the world may be *re*represented in science with negative consequences for science and for women. This may be one such site.

WHAT THE REPRODUCTIVE SCIENCES DID FOR BIOLOGY, MEDICINE, AND AGRICULTURE

The benefits the reproductive sciences conferred upon investigators and their professions varied considerably, and the discipline proved quite flexible during the period of coalescence. As a new line of work within American academic biology, the reproductive sciences provided several clear benefits to this growing academic profession and discipline. The reproductive sciences emerged as biologists were seeking to expand the boundaries of their discipline (Pauly 1984). By about 1910, biologists had secured their academic niches but still needed to incorporate popular new lines of work within the field. The reproductive sciences filled the bill. First and foremost, the reproductive sciences offered both experimental and biochemical avenues of research—the nascent paradigms or approaches in biological work. It thus could link biology with important and highly fundable research directions in medicine yet remain under biological auspices. Both biology and medicine could autonomously pursue the reproductive sciences yet benefit from the exchanges across professions. For biology this meant that biochemical approaches—including reproductive endocrinology—could be established as biological work (e.g., Kohler 1982). Moreover, because of socially motivated funding and the activities of biologists within funding forums, the reproductive sciences became a fundable line of work in biology between the two world wars, when nonmedical research was not often externally sponsored (Dupree 1957).

The benefits of the reproductive sciences to medical scientists and to medicine lay in two distinctive areas. First, they offered to medicine a highly scientific line of work as scientific medicine struggled to become the reigning medical paradigm. Second, it offered an extensive array of information and therapeutics for obstetricians, gynecologists, and urologists (who addressed male reproductive phenomena) regarding the diagnosis and treatment of functional (physiological) reproductive problems. These were among the first real therapeutic alternatives to surgery in these specialties. As in biology, the reproductive sciences offered an experimental and biochemical line of work to reformist medical scientists who sought to establish scientific medicine both within the profession and *as* the profession. It offered strong links with the nascent field of general endocrinology, which, despite accusations of quackery, provided highly successful functional therapeutic interventions in diseases that had plagued medicine for centuries, such as diabetes and myxedema.

The reproductive sciences in medicine were also fundable, sharing sponsorship with biology, for example, in the NRC Committee for Research in Problems of Sex, and developing their own funding sources, such as the Carnegie Institution of Washington's Department of Embryology at Johns Hopkins Medical School. Particularly attractive for medical reproductive scientists were the direct linkages of their work to extant specialties of obstetrics and gynecology. The reproductive sciences in medicine could be both basic *and* clinical, doubly furthering the mission of scientific medicine.

Leonardo (1944:374–76) offered a list of twenty-one advances that reproductive endocrinology provided, including an early pregnancy test, a test for hydatid moles (a serious complication of pregnancy), a hormone treatment for gonorrheal vulvovaginitis in children, a method of determining whether ovulation has occurred (endometrial biopsy), an understanding of anovular menstruation, potential hormonal treatments for lactation, prevention of miscarriage, absence of menstruation and postpartum hemorrhage, treatments for dysmenorrhea, and an understanding of mittelschmertz (intermenstrual pain) as due to ovulation.[54] Corner (1981) also established that miscarriages are commonly the result of problems of the fetus rather than maternal pathology, which had typically been blamed. Papanicolaou did extensive work toward the use of the vaginal smear in the diagnosis of cervical and uterine malignancy.[55] Evans clarified the role of vitamins in reproductive processes, including pregnancy (Amoroso and Corner 1975). Hartman (1933, 1936, 1937) determined the timing of ovulation and fertility in women, publishing his findings as "Catholic Advice on the Safe Period." Fertility and sterility diagnostics and therapeutics became important medical offerings (e.g., Reynolds and Macomber 1924; McLaughlin 1982).

This list of marketable products and services is most impressive. It also answers the question of what the reproductive sciences did for women and men, because neither clinicians nor medical researchers consulted in any organized fashion with patients of either sex about their wants and needs. Not all of these treatments proved efficacious or even safe in the long run; some were clearly carcinogenic, such as DES (administered to women and beef cattle), which was also teratogenic for male and female offspring (e.g., Bell 1995; Marcus 1995). Male hormones such as Hombreol did not last long on the mass market (Oudshoorn 1994). Even today, extensive efforts are made to protect men against unnecessary exposure to hormones (Rosenblatt 1997). No such preemptive concerns are focused on women's exposure, and the safety of estrogen therapy in menopause and the risks of contraceptive hormones are still actively contested (see chapter 8).

In agriculture as in medicine, reformers sought to make agricultural research and practice more scientific. In animal agriculture in particular, reproductive scientists spearheaded that reform movement. Here again the benefits of the reproductive sciences had two basic thrusts: to make animal agricultural research more scientific, and to provide means of improving animal production. In animal agriculture, however, scientific approaches had yielded fewer prior benefits, with the exception of some control over diseases.[56] By and large, practitioners of animal agriculture had been practical husbandmen focused on particular animals and were not themselves scientifically trained. Nor did their audiences or markets for new knowledge—ranchers, herders, and breeders—see animal science as particularly promising. Thus the new animal agricultural scientists had to simultaneously build a foundation for their science within the agricultural academies and develop audiences, sponsors, and consumers for their work in the wider food animal industry (cf. Rosenberg 1976). Reproductive animal science helped them to do both.[57]

The benefits of reproductive science in herd animal agricultural practice included diagnostics, therapeutics, and, most significant, new technologies that drastically improved animal production. Diagnostics included pregnancy tests, sperm potency tests, and means of assessing time of ovulation and fertility. Because fine animals do not necessarily produce fine sperm, sperm evaluation is extremely important for both natural and artificial insemination (Greep and Koblinsky 1977; Herman 1981). Therapeutics included improved understandings of nutritional and vitamin needs for reproduction in domestic species (e.g., Cole and Cupps 1959) and a National Research Council program of research on infectious abortion in cattle (Bowman 1935).

Two key interventions led to improved animal production. First, chicken ranching was transformed from a cottage industry to a factory-based industry, "turning each hen into a mechanical oviduct" by electric light and heating in hen houses that extended circadian rhythms and "kept 'the girls' working well into the night and through their seasonal 'winter pause.'" Hens were also stripped of their maternal functions through the use of kerosene and electric brooders to keep chicks warm. The artificial incubator also allowed flock manipulations so that both chickens and eggs could be standardized (Bugos 1992:133–34). In terms of productivity, these were very successful external manipulations of reproductive processes.

Second, technoscience innovations, notably artificial insemination, also improved production of herd animals and animal science itself (Phillips 1947; Reingold 1982; Brackett, Seidel, and Seidel 1981).[58] Successful application of the technique required means of obtaining, evaluating, preserving, and delivering sperm in a timely fashion, along with assessing fertility in the female (Herman 1981). A bull can "cover," or fertilize, thirty to fifty cows per year under average "natural" conditions. By 1947, using artificial insemination, one bull could impregnate five hundred to a thousand cows per year (Phillips 1947:113). By 1979, the potential number of calves per bull per year was fifty thousand (Reingold 1982:153). While artificial insemination was begun before World War II, large-scale practice did not occur until afterward (Herman 1981; Phillips 1947). It benefited especially from the wartime cryogenics research of Parkes and others in Britain, which dramatically facilitated the transportation of semen (Parkes 1985; Polge 1994).

Improvements in genetics, especially principles for selecting "good" sperm donors and receptors, were fundamentally connected with artificial insemination after about 1925. Sewell Wright's early 1920s statistical work on guinea pig genetics was central to these developments, and it was applied to animal agriculture most notably by Jay Lush.[59] Applied genetics elaborated on the variation of continuously distributed traits in a population, carrying over what was known about rapidly reproducing laboratory species such as fruit flies, guinea pigs, and rats to the much slower reproduction of large food and farm animals. New statistical techniques made it possible to predict breeding values or merit and analyze breeding programs. These have now, of course, been extensively computerized, and genetic fantasies include a "Bovine Nirvana" of optimal genotypes for different environments.[60] Agricultural scientists' work on reproduction prior to World War II also included preliminary investigations of hormonal treatments for superovulation (for twinning or multiple embryo production) and for synchronizing estrus in herds for efficient artificial insemination, embryo transfer, sex determination of sperm and embryos, and multiple embryo implantation.

Figure 6 shows the interrelation of these technologies based on the reproductive sciences in animal agriculture, vividly demonstrating rationalization of the means of (re)production.[61] Intense controversy emerged in agriculture in the 1970s regarding the use of reproductive hormone DES as a food additive for beef cattle. Despite being declared carcinogenic and recalled by the FDA, the hormone continued to be used, leading to a major national scandal (Marcus 1995). The consequences for humans of ingesting hormone-laced meats, such as increased rates of breast cancer and precocious development of breasts in very young prepubescent girls, remain highly contested.

The benefits of the reproductive sciences in agriculture, especially artificial insemination and the "new" reproductive technologies, paralleled the

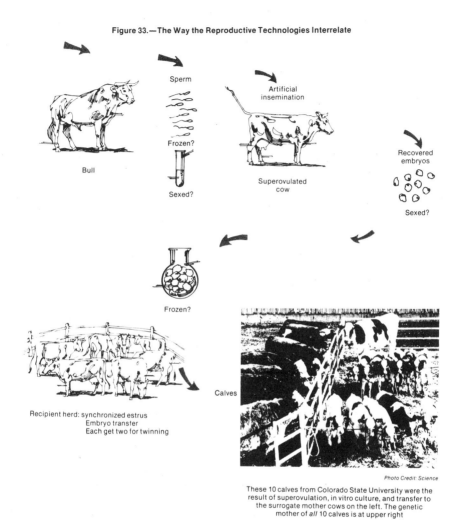

Figure 33.—The Way the Reproductive Technologies Interrelate

Photo Credit: Science

These 10 calves from Colorado State University were the
result of superovulation, in vitro culture, and transfer to
the surrogate mother cows on the left. The genetic
mother of *all* 10 calves is at upper right

Figure 6. Reproductive technologies in animal agriculture (Reingold 1982:
152). Photograph by permission of the Rockefeller Archives Center.

development of safe and effective surgery in medicine—the first significant
improvements over folk practices. The reproductive sciences so improved
the capacity for animal production that they simultaneously established animal science qua science in agriculture and organized audiences, sponsors,
markets, and consumers of scientific research. Practical husbandmen in agricultural academies gave way to scientists who had practical offerings for
their audiences. One stockman assessing animal agriculture concluded,

"Paramount to remaining in a competitive position will be research and more research. . . . The land-grant [agricultural university] system becomes more important than ever before" (Pope 1980:70).

CONCLUSIONS

During the period 1925–40, the reproductive sciences enterprise coalesced around reproductive endocrinology. This was manifest throughout the discipline in biology, medicine, and agriculture as reproductive endocrinology became the "model work" and core activity of the enterprise. Researchers in the United States achieved supremacy, largely through reproductive endocrinological investigations collected in what became the bible of reproductive endocrinology during the mid–twentieth century, *Sex and Internal Secretions* (Allen, ed., 1932, 1939; Young 1961).

The intersection of investigators from biology, medicine, and provided many advantages to participants because each was sufficiently established with their own audiences, sponsors, markets, and consumers bound to them by tradition and interest. These were relations of relative equals, bound together through their boundary crossings. The reproductive sciences provided biologists with a new line of research as they sought to expand their discipline. They provided medicine with a wide array of nonsurgical diagnostics and therapeutics for functional reproductive problems, especially pharmaceutical hormonal products. They provided agriculture with revolutionary reproductive technologies that dramatically rationalized and industrialized animal production.

Such enhanced control over human and nonhuman life through rationalizing and industrializing processes is the mark of modernity. For reproductive scientists, the salience of the human/nonhuman distinction ebbs as the technoscientific products and services they have created are applied to both. However, feedback loops are not limited to hormones. Some of these technoscientific products pioneered during the coalescence period have, in effect, boomeranged. For example, DES, which reached the marketplace in 1940, caused serious problems in women, their male and female offspring, and beef cattle through its carcinogenicity and teratogenicity. These and related controversies have shaped the development of the reproductive sciences ever since and are discussed at length in chapter 8. The desire for enhanced rational control and improvement of social life through the reproductive sciences was also central to the negotiations between reproductive scientists and birth control advocates, as is discussed next.

CHAPTER SIX

Negotiating the Contraceptive Quid pro Quo

Birth Control Advocates and Reproductive Scientists, 1910–63

In the arena of reproduction in the United States throughout the twentieth century, the social worlds that have mattered most to the development of the reproductive sciences have been those of birth control advocates. These included divergent groups such as feminists, physicians, eugenicists, and demographers. From 1910 to 1963, relations *between* reproductive scientists and various birth control advocates were exceptionally complex and changing, while at the same time extraordinary reconfigurations were also occurring *within* each grouping. In what became an intimate dance of realignment, these once distinctive and often oppositional social worlds were reconstituted, transformed, and ultimately integrated, if not fused, through a quid pro quo that met each group's revised needs and goals. The story of these changes is complicated and rife with contradictions and conflicts. None of these multiple worlds was monolithic, nor were they ever fully segregated since their boundaries were permeable. This chapter offers a classic story of the development of "scientific solutions" to the major "problem of sex" in modernity: unwanted pregnancy.

In 1915, in a "frenzy of renown" provoked by feminist activists, the birth control cause hit the major American newspapers and magazines with a force not again equaled for twenty years. Later in the decade, advocates began speaking out, organizing, setting up clinics, distributing illegal birth control information and devices, and seeking improved means of contraception.[1] Then, between roughly 1920 and 1945, the very nature of *modern* contraception was negotiated between reproductive scientists and several varieties of birth control advocates. The reproductive scientists ultimately captured definitional authority over what would constitute modern contraception. After endless petitioning by birth control advocates to produce and test improved, simple contraceptives, reproductive scientists finally agreed to play the contraceptive research game, but only on their own "basic" research terms. That is, to recruit reproductive scientists into the birth control arena, the means of contraception had to be made scientific. Here the process of professional transformation of lay problems to meet professional requirements is fundamental. As Latour (1987) notes, scientists "should be" seen as the driving force even when they are enlisted by others. Who was enlisting whom in this instance is, contra Latour, problematic. Regardless, the power of the culture of science is vivid here. Ultimately it pervaded the worlds of birth control, eugenics, and population control.

It is crucial to remember how very radical birth control was early in this century in the United States. Women were not full citizens with voting rights until five years after Margaret Sanger's first arrest in 1915 for distribution of contraceptives. Distribution to unmarried people was not legal in all of the states until 1972, the year before the Supreme Court decision legalizing abortion. For most of the twentieth century, birth control has been at least as charged and controversial an issue as abortion is now. In many ways the moral propriety of contraception remains the underlying and contested issue: Does using contraception mark women and girls as immoral? What is "natural" for the heterosexual couple? Certainly it is here we see the struggles concerning what Foucault (1978:103–5) described as the "socialization of procreative behavior" and the construction of "the Malthusian couple" as a target and anchor point "for the ventures of knowledge."

From 1920 to 1945, reproductive scientists used several strategies to assert their legitimacy, autonomy, and authority to their often insistent market audience of birth control advocates. First, they carefully distinguished reproductive research from contraceptive research and refused to participate in studies of "simple" contraceptives (such as spermicides, douches, and diaphragms), marginalizing any reproductive scientists who did so.[2] Second, they argued for basic research as the ultimate source of modern contraception and made token offerings from their "basic" research work (such as accurate information on the timing of ovulation). Third, they redirected contraceptive research toward "scientific" methods that would utilize basic reproductive science (hormonal contraception, spermatoxins, IUDs, and sterilization by radiation).

In short, reproductive scientists were successful in insisting upon the culture of science, which operated as what Bijker (1987) has recently called a "technological frame." Such a "frame of meaning" can come to be associated with technologies (such as contraception) positioned among multiple social groups/social worlds. A technological frame—in this instance the primacy of the culture of science within the contraceptive research world—then further guides and shapes the development of those technologies.

Through deployment of the culture of science, reproductive scientists sought to protect and promote the legitimacy, autonomy, and "basic" nature of their work and to simultaneously gain considerable funding and support. By about 1945, a quid pro quo between the reproductive sciences and birth control worlds was established. Through the relations and negotiations among and about birth control advocates, reproductive scientists, hormones, foundations, laboratories, the National Research Council, primates, and others between about 1925 and 1945, a congruence of interests was arrived at that adequately "fit" the changed and changing needs of the major actors in the arena. In the 1950s and 1960s, the quid pro quo began to consolidate as reproductive scientists (largely outside the academy) produced the major modern scientific means of contraception—birth control pills, IUDs, injectable hormones, and improved means of sterilization. The working out of this quid pro quo, prior to and fundamental for the actual development of modern scientific contraception, is the focus of this chapter.

In addition to social worlds and arenas analysis through which it was generated, this chapter also illustrates other recent developments in the social construction of technology.[3] Several emphases are especially important: (1) examining the earliest moments in the making of the technology; (2) analyzing the interests and commitments built into the actual design of the technology by analyzing all the engaged social worlds, their perspectives and commitments, including their interpretations of the technology itself (interpretive flexibility); (3) taking the technology itself to include the eventual institutional distribution, regulatory, and other related systems or networks; and (4) attending to processes of closure when interpretive flexibility supposedly vanishes. Both Woolgar's (1991) key point that we can examine how technologies configure their users and Latour's (1991) notion that technology is society made durable have long histories in feminist technoscience studies (e.g., Cockburn 1985; Wajcman 1995). They resound here as well. Configuring women as the primary users of contraceptive technologies was, in fact, a core goal of population control groups. Callon's (1991) darker point that these are often techno-economic networks and often close to irreversible also pertains. Contraceptives are, after all, what Foucault termed "disciplinary technologies" (Rabinow 1984:17). The reproductive arena was full of conflict from the beginning. Over the decades, further conflicts have been generated as the implicated actors— women users of scientific contraception—have organized resistance and set new agendas.[4] The arena remains conflictful today (Clarke 1997), and closure is not necessarily permanent where controversy lurks (e.g., Hard 1993).

I begin with a brief historical orientation to various technologies of contraception, followed by an overview of the key birth control movements: lay, medical, and social/academic groups, including changes in the kinds of contraceptives these groups advocated from 1925 to 1945. Third is an extended analysis of the responses of reproductive scientists to the ongoing demands of these birth control advocates that scientists do contraceptive research. Here I focus on the specific strategies reproductive scientists used to manage these recalcitrant markets. Finally I examine the quid pro quo that fused the reproductive sciences and birth control and population control advocates into a shared arena where most still dwell today.

CONTRACEPTIVE TECHNOLOGIES: A HISTORICAL OVERVIEW

The following list documents the major means of contraception, with the year of first development; the dates refer to the introduction of these means, not their general availability.

?	Herbal Approaches
?	Abortion
?	Celibacy
?	Castration of men
?	Coitus interruptus
?	Noncoital sex
?	Earliest barrier methods
1600s	Condoms
ca. 1820	Vaginal sponge
ca. 1830	Vaginal douche
ca. 1850	Early intrauterine devices (IUDs)
1840	Vulcanization of rubber
ca. 1860	Rubber condoms
ca. 1870	Trall's rhythm method
ca. 1882	Rubber diaphragm
ca. 1890	Surgical sterilization of women
ca. 1899	Vasectomy
ca. 1925	Hot water sperm incapacitation
ca. 1930s	Improved spermicides, diaphragms, cervical caps, douches, and IUDs
ca. 1930s	Improved rhythm methods
ca. 1950s	Improved condoms
ca. 1950s	Improved sterilization of women and men
ca. 1960	Birth control pill (hormonal)

ca. 1965	Long-acting injectibles and implants (hormonal)
1970s	Improved rhythm methods: "natural birth control"
ca. 1985	Spermicidal sponge (disposable barrier)
ca. 1986	RU486 abortion and morning-after pill
1990s	Injectable immunological contraceptives for women
1990s	Polyurethane and other polymer condoms
1990s	Removable hormone-releasing vaginal ring
1990s	Improved hormonal implants
ca. 2000s	Improved (monoclonal) vaginal prophylactic spermicides
ca. 2000s	Male hormonal contraceptives
ca. 2000s	Male injectable immunological contraceptives
ca. 2000s	Vaginal sperm incapacitation methods
ca. 2000s	Additional female hormonal means (pills, injectables, implants, rings, long-acting IUDs)
ca. 2000s	Improved emergency post-coital contraceptives
ca. 2000s	Injectable sperm incapacitation methods
ca. 2000s	One-a-month hormonal pills

In premodern and early modern times (and in places where similar conditions still obtain today), there was often fairly extensive knowledge of contraceptives and abortifacients, mostly of plant origins. This knowledge was communicated through both oral traditions and printed texts (e.g., herbals).[5] In the seventeenth and eighteenth centuries, the distribution of information about these means of reproductive control was curtailed; the topics were deleted from physicians' texts and given less coverage in herbalist works. The early nineteenth century saw even further limitations on access to such knowledge (Riddle 1992:160). But in the United States by the 1830s and 1840s, linked in part to the popular health movement of the Jacksonian era, this knowledge began traveling again. It often did so through newspaper advertisements and printed brochures that hawked both older approaches and newer devices such as douches, "womb veils," and "female protectors" (probably vaginal sponges). Abortionists and abortifacients were also advertised and increasingly utilized. The late nineteenth century also saw a minor transformation of contraception due to both the vulcanization of rubber (used in condoms and diaphragms) and the development of surgical sterilization (thanks to anesthesia and asepsis).[6] The social "fact" that most powerfully demonstrates the effectiveness of these and other methods such as coitus interruptus is that the average birth rate among white native-born married women dropped by almost half over the nineteenth century, from 7.04 in 1800 to 3.56 in 1900 (Brodie 1994:2). In the past as well as the present, most means of contraception listed above were intended for female users.

However, the last decades of the nineteenth century also saw the rise of a number of "social purity" movements aimed at criminalizing reproductive control and disempowering women, whether or not by direct intent. Many of the means of reproductive control had been commercialized, and opponents could point to increased rates of vice, prostitution, and other "social ills," claiming that these were promoted by women's recent access to means of contraception. Campaigns against both abortion and contraception were led largely by white, middle-class, professional men, many of them physicians. Federal and state legislation and judicial decisions criminalized both abortion (which had been legal before "quickening" for over two centuries) and marked contraception as "obscene" (Brodie 1994; Mohr 1978).

Despite the dates on the chart, in the United States birth control was essentially illegal from about 1873 until 1936, and much later in some states. A federal law, the Comstock Act of 1873, made it illegal to put through the mails any contraceptive advice, device, or information, and the subject was then omitted from new editions of books in which it had appeared. The Comstock Act, aimed largely at controlling vice and prostitution, explicitly defined "the prevention of conception" as obscene, and the law prohibited the mailing of obscene matter. The mails had been (and may well have continued to be) the primary means of distribution of birth control (including abortifacients) for some decades. A variety of state and local statutes also prohibited distribution of contraceptive devices and information.

Twentieth-century birth control advocates mounted many challenges to such laws. Margaret Sanger was especially active, drawing on her leftist roots and allies to mount direct actions against Comstockery. Her arrest with her sister, their related trials and those of other activists, their imprisonment, their forced feeding, but especially their powerful arguments for birth control became part of the "daily news" in 1915 and remained visible for years. The most important early decision on the legality of contraception was made in New York in 1919 when a state court permitted physicians to provide contraceptive advice, but only "to cure or prevent disease" (McCann 1994). The roots of *Roe v. Wade,* the Supreme Court decision of 1973 that made the choice of abortion a matter between a woman and her physician, go back to this earlier decision. The next major legal change did not occur until 1936, when Judge Augustus Hand of a federal appeals court gave doctors the right to advise and prescribe contraception under federal law. This case dealt with seized imported diaphragms destined for a birth control clinic. Judge Hand ruled that while the language of the Comstock Act was uncompromising with regard to contraceptive devices and information, if in 1873 Congress had had available the clinical data on the dangers of pregnancy and the safety of contraceptive practice that were available in 1936, birth control would not have been classified as an obscenity. But state and local statutes remained, impairing physicians' prescription of diaphragms and other means of contraception well into the 1960s. The final two Supreme Court cases focused on legalizing the distribution of contraceptives were *Griswold v. Connecticut* (1965), which stated that the private use of contraception by married Americans is an inherent constitutional right, and *Eisenstadt v. Baird* (1972), which extended the right of contraceptive practice to the unmarried (Dienes 1972; Chesler 1992:376). Not until 1977 did the Supreme Court rule that advertisement and display of contraceptives could not be prohibited. Only since the advent of AIDS, however, have such ads, especially for condoms, appeared in popular magazines. Television networks still refuse to broadcast them (Gamson 1990:271–75).

Despite the increase of birth control activism in the early years of the century, the next round of development and improvement of contraceptives did not begin until the 1920s and 1930s, when better diaphragms, spermicides, douches, cervical caps, and IUDs became available. Importantly, these were the results of birth control advocates' efforts and were not technoscientific products of the modern reproductive sciences that only became available decades later during what became known as the "contraceptive revolution" of the 1960s and 1970s. Then the Pill, new plastic IUDs, and injectable hormonal contraception became available. Continued efforts at technical improvement in the 1980s and 1990s produced implantable hormonal contraceptives such as Norplant, a new over-the-counter spermicidal sponge, the abortion pill RU486 (variants of which are also used as "morning after" hormonal interventions to prevent implantation), and a variety of immunological "vaccines" now in development (Mastroianni, Donaldson, and Kane 1990).

My focus in this chapter is especially on the years 1925–63, which saw the shift from what I call "simple" to "scientific" means of contraception (see Table 7). While this classification is not perfect, it is reasonably easy to divide all the available means of contraception into these two main groups. *Simple* means include spermicides (jellies, creams, foams), barrier methods (condoms, diaphragms, cervical caps, vaginal pessaries, vaginal sponges), douches, the rhythm or "safe period" methods, testicular "heat" methods, and herbal treatments (Langley 1973). These are low-technology means of contraception, though many did require some science to formulate, test, and produce.[7] Simple means are indeed relatively simple to use. Control lies in the hands of the user; use can be discontinued at any time; they can usually be used or not at the time of a given intercourse; the effects are localized to the reproductive system; and most are considered safe enough

TABLE 7   Simple versus Scientific Contraceptive Technologies

Simple Means	*Scientific Means*
Herbals	IUDs
Rhythm	Sterilization
Douches	Hormonal methods (pills, injectables, implants, rings)
Barriers (condoms, diaphragms, cervical caps)	RU486
Spermicides	Immunological vaccines
"Natural" birth control	Monoclonal vaginal methods
Testicular heat methods	
Low-Technology Approaches	*High-Technology Approaches*
Simple to use	Complex to use safely
Control in hands of user	Control in hands of provider
Localized effects	Systemic effects
Can be safely distributed over the counter	Require medical technique for use and/or monitoring
Derived largely from "applied" research (according to scientists)	Derived largely from "basic" research (according to scientists)

to be distributed over the counter.[8] Although virtually all of these simple methods existed by 1915–20, their availability was quite limited until after World War II, and even later in some regions (Gordon 1976). Scientists typically view them as nonscientific, derived instead from clinical practice and "applied" research. And scientists' perspectives are of special concern in the negotiations.

Modern *scientific* means of contraception include birth control pills, plastic IUDs, surgical sterilization, immunological means (vaccines), and injectable and implantable hormonal contraceptives (e.g., Depo-Provera and Norplant). These are high-technology methods. Hormonal methods (pills, injectables, and implantables) are systemic; sterilization was then and must still be considered permanent and involves major surgery (under general anesthesia) for the female; IUDs must be inserted by specially trained personnel. All require medical intervention for initiation, monitoring for safety, or removal. All derive from extensive "basic" research. According to the FDA, none can be distributed safely over the counter.[9] Of these high-technology "scientific" methods, only sterilization, spermatoxins, and IUDs were available prior to 1960, and then only on a very limited basis (Langley 1973). This chapter is concerned with the cumulative shift from advocacy and production of simple means of contraception to complex, scientific means and the divergent ways the heterogeneous social worlds concerned with contraception were involved in this shift.

BIRTH CONTROL MOVEMENTS

This section offers a substantial discussion of the three major birth control advocacy groups or social worlds in the United States during the first half of the twentieth century: lay, medical, and social/academic (eugenicist and neo-Malthusian) groups. I emphasize each group's specific patterns of contraceptive advocacy (Berkman 1980), referring to its preferred means of contraception and the rationales offered for those choices. I examine both contraceptive advocacy of extant methods and contraceptive research advocacy of new and/or improved methods. Different constituencies within birth control and reproductive research worlds preferred different means of contraception, at different times, for different categories of users, and for a wide variety of reasons.

Lay Birth Control Movements

The lay birth control movements of the first half of this century became organized phenomena composed of many divergent groups ca. 1915.[10] Initially, decentralized groups appeared on the grassroots level in many areas of the country, mostly deriving from progressive labor and socialist groups, and including such personages as Margaret Sanger and Emma Goldman. Sanger, herself a nurse, had come to advocate what she ultimately named "birth control" through treating women who were sick and dying after undergoing abortions to prevent unwanted children. Many women turned to her as a nurse for birth control information when they did not dare ask their physicians (Sanger 1938/1971). Through the work of her birth control clinic, her arrests, and her speaking tours between 1915 and 1917, Sanger became the leader of the lay (nonphysician and nonscientist) movement and remained a key actor for many decades (Chesler 1992). World War I gave birth control a boost through massive distribution of contraceptive information and condoms to stem the tide of venereal disease among soldiers. In a Baltimore study, prewar sales of condoms were estimated at 2 to 3 million per year; postwar (mid-1920s) annual sales were about 6.5 million (Gordon 1976:206).

During the 1920s, just after women obtained the vote, birth control could have become the next central feminist issue. However, the decade following World War I was largely one of conservatism and antifeminism. The major women's groups were (re)focusing on two streams of feminist work. One group sought to sustain women's citizenship and seek equal rights via the League of Women Voters and the National Women's Party. A second focused on women's work and maternal and infant health via the Children's and Women's Bureaus of the Department of Labor and the federal Sheppard-Towner Act, which provided, between 1922 and 1929, what we now would call "well baby clinic care" at little or no cost. Women active in these latter efforts have become known in recent scholarship as "welfare feminists." They were mostly white, middle-class women who sought state sponsorship and protection for all women, especially (but not only) in their capacities as mothers (e.g., Fildes, Marks, and Marland 1992). The lay birth control movement became the third stream of feminist work, but the birth control cause was still considered so radical in the 1920s that neither the civil rights nor the welfare feminist groups would publicly support it (McCann 1994).

In 1921 Margaret Sanger and colleagues founded the American Birth Control League (hereafter the ABC League). By 1926 it claimed thirty-seven thousand members, mostly women (Cott 1987:91). Their main strategy was to open local birth control clinics and provide, under medical guidance, contraception to all women who sought it. Sanger's ultimately successful strategy enrolled both physicians and academic scientists, who were among the first eugenicists to support contraception. Sanger explicitly deployed the academic biological scientists (including Raymond Pearl, Edward M. East, and Clarence C. Little) to limit the authority of physicians in the merging and expanding birth control movements. Her rhetoric for contraceptive advocacy simultaneously shifted from enhancing women's bodily autonomy to producing better babies (McCann 1994:120–21). Through such alliances, the birth control movement became a more liberal and centralized cause, increasingly shorn of its feminist roots (Gordon 1976:238).

The other major, and competing, lay birth control movement organization and strategy was the National Birth Control League, founded in 1917. Led by Mary Ware Dennett, this group focused on legal reform, seeking both federal and state-by-state repeal of the prohibitions on contraception as obscene. They explicitly rejected Sanger's direct-action strategy of providing birth control and opening clinics. Yet despite their more general conservatism, they opposed physician authority over diaphragm and other contraceptive use, arguing instead for women's autonomy in a more fully feminist fashion. However, it was the Sangerists' clinic-founding strategy that ultimately won the day for birth control. This strategy has endured under multiple names up to the present, but with considerable medical rather than feminist authority.[11]

An ideology that families should have only as many children as they could afford started to emerge by the beginning of the twentieth century.

The Great Depression seems to have consolidated this "economic ethic of fertility" into the ultimate cultural arbiter of parenting decisions (McCann 1994). Ironically, the depression also challenged traditional economic (and eugenic) theory, since even many individuals of "good stock" found themselves thrust into poverty. Lay birth control theory then shifted emphasis from reducing the population of the inferior to helping the poor (including the "new" poor) to plan their families, using birth control, so that they could "afford" their children. This shift fit well with medical, clerical, and social work ideologies. The ABC League began to argue that birth control provided a flexible tool offering greater choice for all. Most women agreed: a survey conducted by Gallup in 1938 for the *Ladies' Home Journal* found that 79 percent of women favored birth control and 76 percent thought that family income was the most important consideration in decisions about having children (Ray and Gosling 1984–85:401).

In the 1930s, birth control clinics began offering infertility therapy as well as contraception, although efforts to include birth control clinics as part of the New Deal failed. Clinic rhetoric changed to "child spacing" or "family planning" rather than "birth control," seeking to include men in the project. Reflecting these changes, advocates who had founded the Birth Control Federation of America in 1939 as the new central organization for the movement changed its name in 1942 to Planned Parenthood Federation of America. Eugenicists in the birth control movement were strong advocates of this new name (Gordon 1976:344). Sanger hated it and resented the euphemism. She also specifically rejected encouraging the middle and upper classes to have more children (positive eugenics). However, by 1942 Sanger was sixty-three years old and tiring. Her influence was beginning to wane in her own organization, and she had also failed to cultivate a successor who shared her vision, much less a core bloc within the organization (Reed 1983:122; Chesler 1992:391–92). The radical-to-liberal tack of the birth control movement after the 1920s was reflected in the shrinking importance advocates placed on female reproductive autonomy (Gordon 1976). The lay female and often feminist birth control advocates who had been so active and outspoken in the 1910s and 1920s had gradually been replaced by professional men, including physicians, who were much more organizationally minded and quickly grasped the reins of leadership of the family planning/population–oriented infrastructure composed of over 350 clinics and advocacy groups in the United States and abroad (McCann 1994:175). World War II made birth control important to even more people than before.

By about 1945, the ideology and rhetoric of birth control, emphasizing women's rights and freedom for all to enjoy sexuality without fear of pregnancy, had changed to one promoting family planning that directly addressed family economics, including men in its appeal. This new rhetoric of "planned parenthood" offered the possibility of bringing Taylorist approaches of "scientific planning" and "scientific management," drawn from the factory and marketplace, into the "private" sphere of the family (Banta 1993). If in business Taylorist rationalizations and efficiency allowed greater control over production processes, in the family they allowed greater control over reproductive processes—not only conception but also child spacing and family size. Sexuality, like the uncertainties of the marketplace, could be tamed and controlled to some degree. This kind of social engineering with the help of biology had actually been the ideal of Jacques Loeb, whose tradition and experiments Gregory Pincus (soon to be father of the Pill) chose to emulate (Pauly 1987).

The expansion of "family planning" services to include problems of infertility and sterility was also strategic. These services were designed to provide something for everyone—even the infertile and Roman Catholics—within the broader planned-parenthood frame (e.g., McLaughlin 1982). Consumer demand among the infertile was starting to develop (Pfeffer 1993). For the movement to progress, it also had somehow to address the tremendous Catholic opposition to contraception at the time. Obviously, such expansion widened social legitimacy. This aura of social beneficence clung to the "family planning" movement through its next shift to a "population control" rhetoric from 1945 to 1965 and beyond. The focus and rhetoric of controlling fertility and treating infertility thus served as a segue between two radically different movements.

Lay birth control proponents initially sought woman-controlled rather than male methods explicitly to enhance women's bodily autonomy. They cited "sex experts" who had condemned coitus interruptus and periodic abstinence as unhealthy and sexually repressive (Gordon 1976:xiv). Lay women's contraceptive advocacy initially focused on the doctor-fitted diaphragm with spermicides as the most effective means of contraception. The Sanger-led birth control movement introduced this method through hundreds of local clinics spread across the United States. But the safety and efficacy of these methods had not been studied in the United States. In 1923, Sanger therefore founded the Birth Control Clinical Research Bureau as a department of the ABC League to serve as the research arm of the lay birth control movement. Several prominent scientists, most with eugenic goals, served on the advisory board.[12]

Women physicians working in movement-sponsored clinics then did pioneering (and illegal) American research on diaphragms and other contraceptives (Kopp 1933; Reed 1983:106,114–15,124–26). The bureau began publishing its own *Journal of Contraception* in 1936. Since the diaphragm was more effective when used with spermicides, research and testing of spermicides were then sought from reproductive scientists. Since there then was no consumer guarantee of product contents, efficacy, or safety, birth control advocates also sought government regulation of spermicidal products (Borell 1987a). Ironically, the contraceptive advocacy strategy of Margaret Sanger's ABC League gave the power to prescribe birth control to physicians, not to women. Another feminist organization, the Voluntary Parenthood League led by Mary Ware Dennett within the lay birth control movement, objected strongly, if unsuccessfully, to both the diaphragm-only and the prescription-only/"doctors-only" contraceptive advocacy of Sanger and her associates (Gordon 1976:292). However, Sanger had calculated that the price of acceptance of contraception by the medical world would be a medical monopoly on the new service. She also thought nothing could bring greater prestige to contraception than to have it associated with the magic of medical science (Reed 1983:101). On this point remember that Sanger was a credentialed public health nurse.

Through the 1930s, lay birth control advocates began to seek contraception that was cheaper and easier to use for the masses of women who had no access to a physician or clinic for diaphragm fitting and prescription. Considerable debate ensued about the best means of contraception for the "uneducated," "poor," "indigent," or "lower social types." Sanger's ABC League ferociously held out for the diaphragm. There were two other alternatives: new and improved "simple" methods (such as better spermicides that might also prevent sexually transmitted diseases) or new "scientific" methods (hormonal or immunological). Sanger's industrialist husband, Noah Slee, ended up producing spermicides to assure quality and availability for the ABC League clinics. A Canadian industrialist, Alvin Kaufman, also began working to produce improved simple contraceptives, as did American industrialist Clarence Gamble (Reed 1983:114, 221).

Birth control advocates ultimately looked to reproductive scientists for scientific solutions (Borell 1987a), seeking a "magic bullet" (Vaughn 1970) or a "technological fix" (Reed 1983). By 1940, lay birth control advocates were actively seeking more sophisticated and scientific means of contraception specifically for "the masses" both nationally and abroad: "The future of Birth Control necessitates the discovery of a method which is simple and effective and which does not require the cooperation of the individual" (Baskin 1934:94). A major strategy used by lay birth control advocates to recruit biomedical scientists and others to their cause was organizing both national and international conferences on birth control, neo-Malthusianism, eugenics, and population issues and inviting leading scientists to present their work. For example, Sanger chaired the World Population Conference of 1927 held in Geneva, one of the earliest moments when population control discourse began to supplant that of birth control (Horn

1994:50). Birth control advocates and sexologists also attended the International Congress for Sex Research in 1930, focused primarily on reproductive biological research.[13] These were lively sites of intersection for all.

Medical Birth Control Movements

Physicians also had their "own" birth control movement and organizations, primarily the National Committee on Maternal Health (NCMH), which included clinicians as well as both medical and biological reproductive scientists. The goal of this organization was professional medical control over contraceptive practice as preventive medical work.[14] But the NCMH represented only some physicians' positions. Prior to 1940, many if not most physicians opposed birth control. In 1924, Robert Latou Dickinson, founder of the NCMH, published "Contraception: A Medical Review of the Situation," which marked the beginning of informed, open discussion of birth control as *clinical* technique in the leading medical journals. This article was read to the American Gynecological Society and mailed to three thousand physicians in defiance of the Comstock Act. Dickinson sought to establish the subject as "susceptible of handling as clean science, with dignity, decency and directness" (Reed 1983:183–4).

Dickinson's other major strategy was to "wrest birth control from the hands of agitators"—essentially to take over the Sanger-led ABC League and its clinics and place them under "proper medical guidance." The physicians who worked in the many ABC League clinics around the country, mostly women, were somehow not "proper" enough or not "guiding" enough. However, Dickinson's and others' efforts in this direction were confronted directly by Clarence C. Little, geneticist, eugenicist, president of the University of Michigan, and member of the ABC League advisory board. Little stated: "The medical profession has not lived up to its obligations or opportunities in this particular matter . . . [and] has not earned the right to take over the work in a field which others have tilled for them" (McCann 1994:83–84). Sanger drew deeply on the support of such "progressive eugenicists" as Little, East, and Pearl in her confrontations with organized medicine. She sought to maintain both as allies, playing them off against each other while she retained the key leadership role.[15]

During the 1920s, the contraceptive advocacy of the NCMH was mixed. The committee sponsored two lines of research: basic studies of reproductive problems that might lead to improved contraception, and studies of simple chemical contraception—spermicides. Hoping to sponsor joint research, the NCMH approached the main sponsoring agency of the reproductive scientists, the National Research Council Committee for Research in Problems of Sex (NRC/CRPS). Its queries were summarily rejected. Because of the Comstock laws and refusals by reproductive scientists to undertake such projects, the NCMH could not place its sponsored spermicide research in American universities. It therefore contracted with F. A. E. Crew's Department of Research in Animal Breeding at the University of Edinburgh (Borell 1987a; Reed 1983:242). The Bureau of Social Hygiene, supported by Rockefeller monies, funded the research.

By the 1930s, both the legitimacy and the legality of birth control expanded. Professional medicine responded. With pressure from Dickinson and the NCMH, the American Medical Association created a Committee on Contraception in 1935, in part as a response to the dangers of the totally unregulated contraceptive products industry. This was about a $250-million per year business, specializing in condoms and other means carefully billed as "disease prevention" devices.[16] In 1937, thanks to considerable effort by the NCMH, this committee recommended an AMA-sponsored study of techniques and standards, promotion of birth control instruction in medical schools, and physician advice on contraception based "largely on the judgment and wishes of individual patients" (Reed 1983:122–24).

By this time, in the middle of the Great Depression, medical contraceptive advocacy was also changing. Many physicians formerly opposed to birth control, such as Kosmak of the AMA, now asserted that birth control did not reach those who needed it most—the indigent. Echoing eugenicists, physicians now asserted that the poor lacked clinic access and in any case were deemed incapable of learning "the birth control habit" required for effective diaphragm use. Other methods were therefore needed, and medical debate centered on what kinds of contraception these should be: "simple" or "scientific." Many physician advocates of birth control, like Dickinson, believed that "major progress would have to wait for breakthroughs in basic science that would provide methods requiring less motivation or skill from the user" (Reed 1983:190, 212–14).

At the core of these objections lay the culture of scientific medicine revealed in physicians' dislike of available simple methods of contraception. A medical journal editor spoke for a good part of the general public as well as his profession when he declared in 1943: "Caustic self-analysis leads to only one honest conclusion: candid physicians are ashamed of these messy makeshifts. . . . [T]here is a sense of relative inadequacy . . . nourished by the contemplation of these disreputable paraphernalia. The messy little gadgets, the pastes and creams and jellies [were simply] an embarrassment to the scientific mind" (Reed 1979:132). Yet other NCMH physicians, notably Robert Latou Dickinson and Clarence Gamble, argued for expanded research and application of such "simpler" methods. Reproductive scientist F. A. E. Crew agreed, noting that for a country like China, contraceptives should be based on materials available in coolies' pantries.[17] Gamble, a physician and philanthropist, sought doctor-free contraception.

In 1934, Gamble's offer to fund a "Standards Program" for testing contraceptive product effectiveness through the NCMH was accepted. This became the NCMH's second spermicide research project, including the establishment of state and federal product regulations. Gamble established the R. L. Dickinson Research Fellowship in Chemistry at New York University in 1935, which was held by Leo Shedlovsky, Ph.D. Research focused on measuring the physical and chemical properties of the more than forty contraceptives then on the market (mostly spermicides). This was the first laboratory study of contraceptives in the United States, notable here because it was done in a chemistry department rather than a biology or medicine department. Reprints of Shedlovsky's work were sent to fifteen hundred teaching physicians throughout the United States as part of the NCMH effort to get the AMA Council on Pharmacy and Chemistry to issue reports on contraceptives as it already did on other drugs; the effort succeeded, and a major report was published in 1943 (Reed 1983:245–46).

As birth control became more legitimate and "scientific," both suited to medical *science* and increasingly under its professional control, hostility within the medical profession ebbed. Moreover, medical efforts to take over the birth control movement could certainly be said to have succeeded by 1950.

Social/Academic Movements: Eugenics and Neo-Malthusianism

Other social worlds concerned with birth control were eugenics and neo-Malthusian movements. Within and beyond the academy, across multiple disciplines and professions but probably most deeply based within biology, these two social movements were confronting birth control issues. Eugenics was a social and intellectual movement, begun in Great Britain in the nineteenth century, that sought to apply hereditarian principles of improved agricultural breeding to humans. Eugenicists hoped to breed "better" people through positive eugenic activities (increasing the reproduction of persons deemed "fit," or aristogenic) and negative eugenic activities (decreasing the reproduction of persons deemed "unfit," or cacogenic). Eugenic conceptions of fitness were deeply class- and race-based, focusing on increased reproduction among the Anglo-Saxon upper classes and decreased reproduction among the lower classes, both white (especially in England) and of color (especially in the United States and in British colonial regimes).[18]

Most eugenicists initially opposed birth control for popular use during the early decades of this century, fearing that upper-class women would use it more effectively than would people of other classes, thereby reducing the numbers of the "fit" while the "unfit" multiplied unchecked. They viewed birth control solely as a technique for negative eugenics.[19] Eugenicists' contraceptive advocacy had focused on negative eugenics since the turn of the century. Eugenicists advocated involuntary surgical sterilization of the "unfit" with institutionalized criminal, insane, and "feebleminded" people as targets of special legislation. But by the mid-1930s, such laws met with considerable opposition, especially after the Nazis copied and used them. Many eugenicists had also regarded such sterilizations as an ineffective strategy.[20]

Demonstrating the diversities *within* these movements, several eugenicist strategists were also early birth control advocates. E. M. East, a Harvard biologist and member of the Advisory Board of Sanger's Clinical Research Bureau, was one. In 1925, he persuaded Sanger not to publish an attack on eugenicists in the *Birth Control Review* for failing to support contraception, arguing that she needed their support and that they, in time, would need her. East warned: "No matter what you say, birth control is only part of a eugenical program. It is a secondary aspect of a larger whole, but it is the key. The mere fact that so many eugenicists have not been able to think straight does not make the abstract subject itself any less valued" (Reed 1983:135). During the 1920s, other eugenicists sought evaluation of the eugenic value of contraception, including Simon Flexner, C. C. Little, and Adolph Meyer of the Committee on Eugenic Birth Control.[21]

During the Great Depression era 1930s, more eugenicists and other social conservatives began to find contraception attractive, especially as birth control advocates exploited the issue of skyrocketing welfare costs. They talked much less of women controlling their bodies and much more of the need to "democratize" contraceptive practice—to spread it "down" from the upper and middle classes to the lower classes.[22] Since the middle classes clearly would not stop practicing contraception, eugenicists concerned about differential fertility between classes believed that their best hope for altering "dysgenic" population trends was promoting birth control for the poor. How much this was also racialized varied among individuals and regionally (e.g., McCann 1994; Larson 1995).

Some eugenicists were swayed by Raymond Pearl's studies at Johns Hopkins of populations and reproduction by economic sector or class. In studies supported by the Milbank Fund and drawing on sophisticated Pearsonian statistics, Pearl demonstrated that the differences in fertility by class and race correlated with differences in access to and use of contraceptive information and technologies. Pearl's conclusions ran counter to current biological explanations and other social/cultural explanations (including Pearl's own beliefs) of the incapacity of the lower classes to practice contraception. The studies were therefore significant in convincing eugenicists of the need for broad-based access to contraceptives (Allen 1991; Notestein 1982). In Pearl's words, "Hitherto, everybody excepting the scientist had a chance at directing the course of human evolution. In the eugenics movement an earnest attempt is being made to show that science is the only safe guide in respect to the most fundamental social problems." Pearl then sought changes in policy among the "agencies under social control that may improve or impair the racial qualities of future generations" toward providing contraceptive information (Allen 1991:235; Cooke 1997).

Under the influence of Fredrick Osborn, men who placed less stress on heredity and more on environment replaced the old leadership of the American Eugenics Society in the 1930s. Osborn said in 1937: "The question I want light on is how the spread of contraception can be carried on in such a way that it will give opportunities for contraceptive practice to those families who shouldn't have children without indoctrinating too much those families who should have more children?" Ideally, eugenicists would decide who should and who should not practice contraception. Osborn was anxious to cooperate with birth control advocates in spreading contraception among the poor, but he insisted that greater emphasis be placed on "positive" eugenics: "birth control" should be replaced by "family planning" and encouragement of large families for those who could afford them (Reed 1983:213, 136). Policing yet another boundary, Osborn also convinced Margaret Sanger to withdraw as a candidate for vice president of the Population Association of America, arguing that it should be a "scientific" organization (Notestein 1982:660).

In accepting voluntary birth control as a eugenic strategy, eugenicists themselves then ceded ground on both negative and positive eugenics. At that time sterilization was the only method by which to address directly the inheritance of dysgenic qualities. Moreover, eugenicists had to acknowledge the failure of "positive" eugenics. In short, eugenicists accepted birth control and population control because they had no other activist choices.[23] Voluntarism rather than state compulsion seemed more likely to succeed in reducing the numbers of the "unfit." There was even talk of combining the ABC League and the American Eugenics Society (McCann 1994:181).

Neo-Malthusianism was the name used early in the twentieth century for the social and academic movement of those concerned with overpopulation, both numerically and proportionally by social class, who also supported birth control. As noted earlier, the term *Malthusian* was also used synonymously with what we now call birth control (as in Foucault's Malthusian couple). By 1940, neo-Malthusians had moved successfully into the scientific study of population phenomena as a means of promoting social policy, developing an elaborate institutional infrastructure for their new discipline of demography. The list on page 57 contains some of the key organizations and events in the movement's development. Its rhetoric shifted from neo-Malthusianism to population research to population control and demography.[24]

At the organizing meeting for the Population Association for the United

States in 1930, Dr. Henry Pratt Fairchild summed up its mission: "We are all convinced of the importance of having an association to consolidate the population interests of this country. . . . [W]e are in a position to take up the phenomenon of population as one of the great factors of human welfare to be rationally manipulated, just as we manipulate the other factors in human relations."[25] However, neo-Malthusian population scientists were not in accord on contraceptive advocacy. They debated effectiveness, costs, and accessibility. Many population scientists asserted a direct correlation between socioeconomic status and the ability to nurture children in ways that remain too familiar. Many advocates of population control through contraception were also deeply racist, targeting lower-class and poor people and racial/ethnic groups of color both in the United States and abroad.[26]

The period from 1920 to 1940 constituted the "emergence" era of the population enterprise, which coalesced between about 1940 and 1965.[27] The British movement, which was larger and stronger than the American during the 1920s, focused primarily on colonial populations. British-ruled India had the first government-sponsored birth control clinic in the world, opened in 1930 (Hartmann 1987/1995). In the United States, organizing efforts focused on the academy and the philanthropic foundations. United States possessions were also the focus of birth control/population control programs; in the 1930s, a major program was established in Puerto Rico focusing on diaphragms, spermicides, and surgical sterilization (Ramirez de Arellano and Seipp 1983). This network was later enrolled to serve as the home base for testing the birth control pill prior to its approval for U.S. distribution (Oudshoorn 1994:122–37).

A number of reproductive and related scientists actively participated in the population establishment. For example, participants in the World Population Conference of 1927 included Leon Cole, C. C. Little, Adolph Meyer, Raymond Pearl, and J. Whitridge Williams (Hopkins gynecologist). Fellows and members of the Population Association of America included Little, Pearl, Dickinson (NCMH), L. B. Dunham (BSH), E. B. Wilson, Clark Wissler, and Robert Yerkes.[28] Population concerns were raised in various media by these and a host of related organizations and demographers, generating wide cultural interest in population, and hence in reproductive issues more broadly.[29] One of the key organizations in the present story is the Population Council, through which modern scientific IUDs (along with implantable hormonal contraceptives) were developed (Segal 1987), discussed next as a Rockefeller organization.

Rockefeller Philanthropy and Contraception

In addition to social movement groups committed to birth control and enhanced control over family size and composition, one of the major philanthropic families of the twentieth century also manifested sustained commitments and a wide range of efforts in such directions. In some ways, Rockefeller involvement has been so powerful that it can easily be seen as on a par with social movement organizations as an actor in the arena. The Rockefeller-sponsored Bureau of Social Hygiene initiated such Rockefeller involvement in the birth control and population causes. In the 1920s, its commitment to birth control and population studies was thus not a wholly new direction. Like many other eugenics groups, Rockefeller interests shifted from contraception to population control (Allen 1981:253). The Laura Spellman Rockefeller Memorial Fund was supporting population research at the Scripps Institute in the 1920s (Notestein 1982:654). And as early as 1924, Raymond B. Fosdick, president of the Rockefeller Foundation, had written to J. D. Rockefeller Jr.: "I believe that the problem of population constitutes one of the great perils of the future. . . . Scientists are pointing hopefully to such methods as Mrs. Sanger and her associates are advocating" (Borell 1987a:66). Fosdick himself had served briefly as the general counsel of Sanger's ABC League (Harr and Johnson 1988:191). Such philanthropists' commitments were significant for reproductive scientists because these same funding sources were often simultaneously sponsoring their basic research. Some sponsors attempted to recruit reproductive scientists for research on specific contraceptive projects, while other sponsors provided liaisons between birth control advocates and reproductive scientists. Reproductive scientists were obliged by their reliance on such sponsors to respond, often awkwardly.

The Bureau of Social Hygiene (BSH), funder of both the NRC/CRPS and the NCMH, was active in both liaison efforts and direct funding of contraceptive research. During her tenure as director of the BSH, Katherine Davis made numerous attempts to further such research.[30] When she retired and L. B. Dunham took over as director in 1928, he was unsure about continued Rockefeller commitment to the birth control cause: "It seems to me that the project on spermatocides . . . would lead to an extremely controversial field and one that is surcharged with theological politics. It seems to me that, necessary as that work is, it ought to be carried out as part and parcel of a larger research project by some medical center. Another course, it seems to me, might expose the Bureau to a lot of publicity of a nature that would lessen its general effectiveness."[31] Dunham was quickly put in his new and "proper" place as a Rockefeller-funded birth control advocate by Raymond Fosdick of the Rockefeller Foundation, who vividly reasserted the Rockefeller commitment to contraception: "I do not share your feeling of [not] getting the Bureau into the controversial field of birth control. I think the Bureau ought to get into this field, and as a matter of fact it is in, and so is Mr. Rockefeller. Surveys of the type proposed by Dr. Dickinson [on spermatocides] are enormously important and *the Bureau exists for just that purpose.*"[32] Dunham then became a promoter of contraceptive research among reproductive scientists. For example, he set up a Conference on Birth Control in 1931. Guests included reproductive scientists Walter Cannon (Harvard Medical School and member of the NRC/CRPS) and Charles Stockard (Cornell Medical School researcher supported by the NRC/CRPS), as well as Henry Pratt Fairchild (demographer and president of the American Eugenics Society).[33]

The BSH also sought to expand its funding of contraceptive research to include fresh efforts by reproductive scientists. Ruth Topping of the BSH talked about this goal at length on several occasions with Carl Hartman, who made numerous arguments for basic reproductive research as leading ultimately to contraceptive research (discussed in detail later in the chapter). Topping wrote to Dunham in 1931: "Might it not be possible to stimulate . . . observation and experimentation [leading to contraception] among workers who are studying the reproductive cycle under grants from the [NRC/CRPS]? If some of these scientists became especially interested in the search for a contraceptive, the Bureau might later make supplemental grants."[34] As we shall see, the NRC/CRPS refused such overtures. But the importance of such efforts by the BSH and the Rockefeller Foundation is that they added the voices of a major philanthropy and a major reproductive sciences funding source to the chorus of advocates attempting to engage American reproductive scientists in contraceptive research during the 1920s, 1930s, and 1940s.

In the 1950s, Rockefeller changed the form of its support for birth control. A key Rockefeller organization is the Population Council, through which modern scientific IUDs were developed. This organization was founded in 1952, and was funded through the direct commitments of John D. Rockefeller III, who despite being a board member, could not convince the Rockefeller Foundation of the importance of population control. At the time, the foundation was deeply involved in international agricultural reform and improvement, which, it was hoped, might eliminate the problem of "overpopulation" through production of adequate food. Moreover, the foundation per se had avoided directly supporting contraception and population projects for many years by funneling them through the BSH. After the BSH was terminated in 1933, the foundation had carefully avoided such responsibilities and had explicitly eschewed them during the McCarthy era, when it was under considerable scrutiny as a "liberal" organization. Instead, Rockefeller Foundation executives were pleased that other groups were shouldering this burden.[35] The Population Council became, in fact, one of the sites of the implemented merger among birth control, eugenic, and population control groups.

A Synthesized Movement: Family Planning and Population Control

Family planning/population control became the banner or umbrella framework for an amalgam of birth control, eugenics, neo-Malthusian, and population/demographic movements and interests by about 1940, and by about 1950 it formed a fully articulated ideology (Gordon 1976:391). This banner provided excellent symbolic rhetoric for all of these groups. First, like the reproductive sciences, population control had developed a considerable scholarly scientific reputation, along with a well-organized institutional infrastructure (Allen 1991). Second, the terms *family planning* and *population control* omitted the words *sex* and *birth control,* sounded objective and scientific, and allowed racism to be expressed apparently neutrally concerning whole populations.[36]

Population control organizers had considered the merger since the early 1930s. As Henry Pratt Fairchild said at the founding of the Population Association: "When this idea [for a Population Association] first came into my mind I was thinking about a possible merger of the Eugenics and Birth Control interests in the country, but now it is seen as a much bigger thing. . . . It is feared by some that anything approaching consolidation may lose us support. There are some people who believe in eugenics, but not in birth control, and vice versa. We might lose some support on both sides, but would get it back from the united front we would present."[37] And they did.

By 1934, greater coordination of effort among the constituent segments was already apparent: "There is clear evidence [of] greater coordination in the work of the [ABC] League, a sharper definition of program, and greater cooperation with such organizations as the National Committee on Maternal Health, the eugenics-focused Human Betterment Foundation in California, the National Committee on Federal Legislation [for Birth Control], the Population Association of America, and the American Eugenics Society."[38] Further evidence of coordination and integration lies in the interlocking memberships and directorates of the multiple population, birth control, neo-Malthusian, and eugenics organizations, and in the new mission statements issued by these organizations. For example, the first Board of Directors of the Planned Parenthood Federation of America included former presidents of both the American Eugenics Society and the Race Betterment Conference.[39] By 1953, American foundations had contributed over $3 million to the field of population study (Osborn 1967:368), and this was *before* the era of extensive government and foundation involvement and sponsorship (Greep, Koblinsky, and Jaffe 1976). The scale of private funding for population control was immeasurably greater in the 1930s, and especially after World War II, than it had been for orthodox eugenics (Allen 1991:254).

Fairchild made another statement about the merger to the annual meeting of the Birth Control Federation (successor to the ABC League) in 1940: "One of the outstanding features of the present conference is the practically universal acceptance of the fact that these two great movements have now come to such a thorough understanding and have drawn so close together as to be almost indistinguishable" (Gordon 1975:273). Within the birth control movement, those segments most supportive of eugenics and population control then became active around the International Planned Parenthood Federation, housed in the Eugenics Society building in London. Those in the middle of the road were active in the Planned Parenthood Federation of America, focused on the incorporation of reproductive control into state programs as a form of social planning and ultimately population control (Gordon 1976:342–47). Feminists and other progressives seem to have left the birth control/population control movement entirely at this time, or to have worked very locally in clinics providing direct access to birth control for women.

By the late 1930s, the birth control, eugenics, and neo-Malthusian movements had synthesized into a new "family planning and population control" movement. Sanger herself (1937:3–4) best captured the contraceptive advocacy of the newly synthesized movement in the quote that began this book. Sanger further argued: "We should place the scientists not only at the helm but on the bridge [of the movement] as captains to guide humanity." As we shall see, scientists were, by the end of World War II, almost ready to comply. Putting scientists at the helm transformed the nature of modern contraception.

REPRODUCTIVE SCIENTISTS AND
CONTRACEPTIVE TECHNOLOGIES

Responding to the loud and determined chorus of voices urging reproductive scientists into contraceptive research between 1925 and 1945, the scientists used three key strategies. They distinguished reproductive from contraceptive research; they argued with birth control advocates for basic research on reproduction from which applications such as contraception would flow; and they redirected contraceptive research from simple to scientific methods. It was eugenic arguments that first captured reproductive scientists' interest in birth control as a scientific problem (Borell 1987a), as many of them had both intellectual and organizational commitments to that movement. However, all of the initial voices seeking research on simple contraceptives were from the lay and medical birth control movements. The *initial* strategic response of reproductive scientists to these demanding yet illegitimate audiences was to turn a deaf ear.

First Strategy: Distinguishing Reproductive from Contraceptive Research

Reproductive scientists initially focused on distancing their enterprise from that of birth control advocates and establishing a clear set of distinctions between them. This strategy reflected both the general illegitimacy of the birth control movement (with its tattered but still present feminist garb in the 1920s) and reproductive scientists' own designation of contraceptive research as unattractive applied work. In 1920, reproductive scientists had strong hopes that their research area would become as prestigious as any other area of basic biology, a hope gradually abandoned over the next decades, especially after World War II.

Reproductive scientists worked hard to demarcate the boundaries of their work to exclude explicitly contraceptive research. Robert Latou Dickinson of the NCMH approached the NRC/CRPS on several occasions with a request to undertake contraceptive research. In 1924, he recounted one response he received:

> A year ago we [the NCMH] tried to get some of our borderline sex problems, like sterility and information bearing on sex life in our histories, taken up by [the NRC/CRPS] and received a written answer that their Committee was only interested in animal research. Several months later when sex life of human beings was included in their studies we again tried to delimit our respective fields and suggested the whole subject be a matter of [joint] conference and allotment. Their meeting considered the matter and decided they need not coordinate the work as the Committee on Maternal Health had only to do with birth control.[40]

At this point reproductive scientists in the NRC/CRPS rebuffed birth control research *and* any other research that the NCMH might have sought. While there was, in fact, considerable overlap in investigations sponsored by the two organizations, association with a birth control organization, even a medical one, was clearly not on their agenda.

Both the NRC/CRPS and the NCMH received support from Rockefeller philanthropies. A dozen years later, in 1936, the NCMH sought Rockefeller funding for sterilization and other research, including projects on both simple and scientific means of contraception, which the NRC/CRPS had refused to address.[41] Warren Weaver, recently of the Rockefeller Foundation, then wrote to Robert Yerkes, chairman of NRC/CRPS since its inception in 1921. Weaver felt these projects "would appear to fall within the scope of the NRC/CRPS . . . [yet] . . . It is not clear to me whether such topics would be [so] viewed by your committee." Weaver even implied that if the NRC/CRPS would address the topics, its budget might be expanded accordingly.[42] Here Yerkes's response to Weaver was the third rebuff of the

NCMH and such "human side" problems. Yerkes strongly reasserted the NRC/CRPS's clearly bounded research policy to Weaver:

> Reference to [the NRC/CRPS] . . . is not clearly indicated. The committee in question [the NCMH] is, like my own, composed of reputable specialists whose judgments are trustworthy. In my opinion, neither committee should be asked to advise concerning or endorse the program of the other. Inasmuch as the Committee on Maternal Health is concerned primarily with applied aspects of research on sex and reproduction, whereas the N.R.C. Committee has dealt almost exclusively with so-called fundamental problems in the biology of these subjects, I doubt that the N.R.C. Committee would favor support of such studies as are listed in your letter.[43]

Finally, in 1939, the Rockefeller Foundation gave the NCMH funds for research that the NRC/CRPS refused to undertake, including studies of sperm morphology, spermatoxins, reproductive endocrinology, and sex cells (Reed 1983:269; see chapter 7).

The second element of the strategy of distinguishing reproductive from contraceptive research was refusing to participate in research on simple means of contraception such as spermicides and condemning any reproductive scientists who did so. The first two major studies of spermicides were undertaken in Great Britain because of the refusal of American scientists to undertake the work, combined with the restrictions of the Comstock Act. British scientists were also generally unenthusiastic about applied research on simple contraceptives (Soloway 1995). The outcomes of both studies demonstrate my point.

Cecil Voge conducted one study under the direction of F. A. E. Crew of the Animal Breeding Research Department of the University of Edinburgh. Voge's work focused on tests of extant spermicides to determine if there was a safe, highly effective one that would also work as a prophylactic against venereal diseases (a search that continues to this day; see Clarke 1997). Voge's project was sponsored by the NCMH and funded by the Rockefeller-supported BSH. Crew's department at Edinburgh was transformed between 1927 and 1930 into the Institute of Animal Genetics by a matching grant from the Rockefeller International Education Board that provided an endowed chair, buildings, and equipment (Hogben 1974:139). Apparently, Crew's approval of Voge's contraceptive research project was grudging, and his approval may well have been "induced" by his other Rockefeller grant. The NCMH's contraceptive advocacy here was for an "easily available chemical in a form that should keep in good condition over a long period of time and in all climates, and be so easy to use that the most ignorant woman in the Orient, the tropics, the rural outposts or the city slums might be protected."[44] The Voge study, published in 1933, did not produce such a "magic bullet" or miracle contraceptive, but sponsors considered it a great success in terms of establishing standards of safety and effectiveness.[45]

Crew, however, had a very different reaction, calling Voge "a traitor to science."[46] Despite having a doctorate in immunology, Voge (1933:11) had somehow crossed the invisible and shifting border into "applied" research. Crew then recommended that the NCMH cease to support Voge's work because his future as a research chemist was being jeopardized. Voge ultimately "fulfilled the worst fears of his colleagues" when he went into business as a consulting industrial chemist (Reed 1983:243). There was also some controversy about Voge's use of Baker's early research (Soloway 1995), discussed next.

The second spermicides study in Britain was sponsored by the Birth Control Investigation Committee, part of the British activist clinic movement, along with the British Eugenics Society and the American BSH and NCMH. Initially, reproductive scientist F. H. A. Marshall, then president of the Cambridge birth control clinic, tried to place the project in a lab at Cambridge University, but he was unsuccessful (Soloway 1995). Instead, in the late 1920s, John R. Baker, an ardent eugenicist of the Department of Zoology at Oxford, began examining the spermicidal value of pure chemicals, as well as testing extant means and vehicles used to deliver them vaginally (Baker 1930a,b, 1931a,b). According to one source, Baker assembled at Oxford a "team" of scientists in zoology, chemistry, physiology, and bacteriology and related both clinical and laboratory findings.[47] Baker specified that the ideal contraceptive should be inexpensive and small; require no special appliance for insertion into the vagina; be unaffected by the ordinary range of climates; leave no trace on skin nor stain fabrics; contain no volatile or odorous substance; be nonirritating to the vagina, cervix, and penis; be without pharmaceutical effect if absorbed into the bloodstream; contain a substance reducing surface tension to ensure that the smallest crevices of the folds of the vagina are reached; be able to kill sperm at five-eighths or lower concentration in the alkaline and acid test to avoid harm to mucous membranes; and be able to diffuse rapidly into the semen (Robertson 1989:84–85). These remain the key requirements for this common and simple contraceptive.

During the late 1930s, this work led to the development of a popular and highly effective spermicide called Volpar for *vo*luntary *par*enthood (Borell 1987a). Baker, however, was forced to leave the Department of Zoology at Oxford when the director discovered the purpose of his experiments. (He was allowed to relocate to the Department of Pathology.) In Baker's own assessment, his contraceptive research was "rather prejudicial to his career" (Porter and Hall 1995:176). It was "permanently symbolized in his recollection of assembling his apparatus and reagents on a handcart and trundling this from department to department," although he did remain in academic chemistry. Clarence Gamble then funded a research fellowship in chemistry at New York University to "complete the work done by Voge and Baker," focusing on spermicides available in the United States (Reed 1983:243–45).

In the United States, the NCMH made at least one attempt to "piggy-back" applied spermicide research to ride on the back of "basic" sperm survival research. In 1938, the NCMH offered a grant to the Carnegie Department of Embryology to study the transport and viability of spermatozoa in the genital tracts of female dogs and monkeys.[48] The department agreed, "provided work is designed specifically for study of the reproductive cycle and not for collateral problems of a social type."[49] But in a personal letter to Carl Hartman of the Department of Embryology, Raymond Squier, then executive secretary of the NCMH, tried to remind Hartman that another reproductive scientist member of the NCMH (Earl Engle of Columbia) had discussed this matter privately with Hartman. The NCMH thought they had come to an understanding that spermicidal testing would be incorporated into the research. Squier said he was sure that Hartman understood that the NCMH could not afford to spend "$3000 simply on further study of the estrous cycle of dogs or other work on monkeys having no relation at all to possible practical applications for the control of human reproduction."[50]

Despite his own long-term commitments to the birth control movement, Hartman's response fell fully within the strategy of reproductive scientists regarding their birth control audiences: he refused to incorporate the contraceptive research. He wrote to the head of the Carnegie Department of Embryology: "I assured Squier that we could work on any phase of pure science that we wished, leaving propaganda and 'applications or social implications' for organizations like his. As to effect of chemical or physical agents on sperms—we don't propose to touch that subject unless we get a new 'lead' that justifies [it]. . . . What we shall do is study sperm survival under normal conditions—there will be little time for anything else."[51] Even Hartman, a former chairman for research of the NCMH (from 1934 to 1937), would not bend the rules or cross the boundaries of the Carnegie Department of Embryology specifically or of the basic reproductive research enterprise generally.[52]

Reproductive scientists' overall strategy of distinguishing reproductive research from contraceptive research was successful for them, especially in highlighting distinctions between applied and basic research and in clarifying their basic research identity. The career trajectories of reproductive scientists who did undertake research on simple contraceptives vividly demonstrated that there was an applied/basic boundary that could not be crossed without negative consequences. Not only was birth control research socially illegitimate; it was also scientifically marginal or illegitimate—especially when it focused on simple methods.

Second Strategy: Arguing for Basic Reproductive Research

A corollary second strategy reproductive scientists used in response to birth control advocates was arguing for basic research as both the prerequisite for and the ultimate source of improved means of contraception. Here reproductive scientists turned the tables and attempted to recruit birth control advocates into providing financial and other support for basic reproductive research. Again, they were successful in the long run.

Carl Hartman at Hopkins, a major reproductive scientist active in birth control worlds, articulated this strategy very clearly when queried by Ruth Topping, a staff member of the Bureau of Social Hygiene:

> When I asked Dr. Hartman in what directions research for a better contraceptive might most profitably be conducted, he recommended an indirect rather than a direct approach to the problem. After pointing out the vast amount of research being done in this country in the physiology of reproduction, particularly in relation to glandular activity, he expressed the opinion that if some of the outstanding workers in this field could be persuaded to keep contraceptive possibilities in mind in connection with their observation of the reproductive process, some of them might discover ways and means of interrupting the process at given points or under given conditions. These observations might narrow the lines along which specific research might then be carried on.

Here Hartman was speculating on the possibility of hormonal contraception emerging from reproductive endocrinological investigations. He further suggested that such work might well be carried on at or in connection with agricultural experiment stations, attempting to place it in supposedly intrinsically "applied" settings rather than "basic" reproductive biology labs.[53]

Similar arguments were made by Lillie of Chicago and Crew of Edinburgh.[54] In case Topping and other birth control advocates did not understand the distinction between basic and applied research, Crew clarified it: "It is impossible, in Dr. Crew's opinion, to make definite programs in scientific research. 'The real scientist is not an employee,' he said. 'He starts out to find something but may discover something on the way that changes the whole course of his investigations. He can't have someone pulling strings and keeping him to a course.'"[55] This is a classic argument for both basic research and the autonomy of the scientific enterprise.[56] Medical reproductive scientists made similar arguments for basic research, including Earl Engle, who bluntly exclaimed, "We don't give a damn about contraception. We want a study of basic factors in human reproduction," and Howard Taylor, who complained that "birth control was a banal topic for the first-class clinician." Even a physician birth control advocate such as Dickinson believed that "major progress would have to wait for breakthroughs in basic science" (Reed 1983:243, 129, 214).

An integral part of reproductive scientists' strategy here was to provide birth control advocates with token offerings from basic research. Many reproductive scientists in the United States undertook basic research that had clear potential for contraceptive development, while eschewing the simple-method spermicide studies of their British brethren. The classic basic investigations focused on the timing of fertility in women, which allowed more precise determination of "the safe period" during which unprotected intercourse would not result in pregnancy, generally known as the rhythm method. This research involved a wide range of basic problems intriguing to reproductive scientists, including the timing and occurrence of ovulation in relation to menstruation, egg transport through the fallopian tube, fertilization, implantation, and sperm vitality and motility.

In 1922, participants in the International Neo-Malthusian and Birth Control Conference lamented the lack of clarity about the timing of fertility (Pierpoint 1922:270), and the next decade saw numerous efforts in this direction. The leading researcher on this problem in the United States was Carl Hartman,[57] who conducted numerous nonhuman primate studies (e.g., 1939) and also worked with Raymond Pearl (1932) on human studies. The major difficulties encountered by scientists pursuing this topic was the range of variation in women's cycles, both among women as a group and within individual women over time (Hartman 1962:vii). As Hartman put it, "There are almost no regularly menstruating women, any more than there are regularly menstruating monkeys" (Sanger 1934:53). Hartman published "Catholic Advice on the 'Safe Period'" (1933) in a birth control journal. His summary work was *Time of Ovulation in Women: A Study on the Fertile Period in the Menstrual Cycle* (1936), part of the Medical Aspects of Fertility Series sponsored by the NCMH.[58]

George Papanicolaou of the Cornell Medical Center was also engaged in work sponsored by the NCMH on the "safe period," attempting to discover a means of determining the day of ovulation in women through vaginal smears (Papanicolaou 1933), excellent indicators in laboratory animals (Stockard and Papanicolaou 1917). Edgar Allen and his colleagues (Allen et al. 1928) also engaged in studies focused on the timing of ovulation and surgically recovered live human ova from the fallopian tubes, charting their place in the cycle. These researches offered some immediate contraceptive payoffs but were far from direct responses to birth control advocates' explicit requests for investigations of simple contraceptive technologies.

Third Strategy: Redirecting Contraceptive Research

The third strategy of reproductive scientists regarding birth control advocates was to continue with their own basic research agendas and claim that new means of contraception would eventually flow from this work. Here reproductive scientists essentially redirected contraceptive research along new basic "scientific" research lines and away from the "simple" means initially sought by birth control advocates. They did so by promoting four major research directions for modern "scientific" contraception: endocrinological, immunological, intrauterine, and radiation—most only in women. Each of these was attractive to a different subset of reproductive scientists, as we shall see.

Promoting Endocrinological Intervention.   Promoting endocrinological intervention in the female cycle can be analyzed as precursor research to the Pill, which operates through this mechanism. Such possibilities were attractive to both funding sources and some scientists by the 1920s. The basic principle was suggested by Haberlandt in 1921 (National Science Foundation 1973:10–12), though it seems to have been ignored. By the mid-1930s, however, Max Mason of the Rockefeller Foundation thought that "the ultimate solution of the problem [of birth control] may well lie in the studies of endocrinology, particularly antihormones" (which would counter routine cycling).[59] The overall strategy was to use hormones to intervene in the monthly cycle of women to prevent conception, or, as Hartman put it, "to interrupt the process at given points or under given conditions" (Borell 1987a:fn76). Crew suggested experimental work with hormone injections for the object of developing a chemical combination that would prevent the ovum from entering the uterus.[60]

Wary discussion of the possibilities of hormonal contraception began in the birth control literature in about 1928.[61] The fundamental requirements for such methods were a clear understanding of the reproductive endocrinological cycle (e.g., Aberle 1934; Allen 1932) and chemical isolation and production of pure hormones (Djerassi 1981). These were precisely the tasks that many reproductive scientists had set for themselves during the "heroic age of reproductive endocrinology" between 1925 and 1940 (Parkes 1966a). Moreover, American reproductive scientists had sustained fiscal support in these endeavors through the NRC/CRPS, and by about 1940 hormones were widely used for medical treatment (Bell 1986, 1994b), though not for contraception.

In 1937, a summary of these endocrinological strategies was published by Ralph Kurzrok, a Columbia University endocrinologist, as "The Prospects for Hormonal Sterilization." He discussed six alternative interventions in the female hormonal cycle that would likely prevent conception, including estrogen injections to inhibit ovulation (the subsequent basis of the Pill). He concluded, "The potentialities of hormonal sterilization are tremendous. The problem is important enough to warrant extensive work on the human." All of Kurzrok's fourteen citations were to basic reproductive scientists, most of whom were working with rats and rabbits at the time. But reproductive scientists did not answer his call to work on humans for many years, nor did he pursue such efforts himself. Serious work on the Pill itself did not begin until about 1951.

Movement toward scientific contraception was not always smooth, and there were debates about particular lines of research. In 1938, for example, Nicholas Eastman, a gynecologist at Johns Hopkins, was studying spermatoxins with NCMH sponsorship. He wanted to change "the direction of his work . . . to hormonal means for avoiding pregnancy." However, Earl Engle, research director for the NCMH, decided that "the hormonal field is not very promising" and refused to sanction the change because the drug company that provided Eastman's funds through the NCMH was interested in spermatoxins and might withdraw its support. By 1945, Fuller Albright of Harvard was arguing in support of Kurzrok's hormonal method for women (Reed 1983:270, 315).

But talk about developing hormonal means of contraception was cheap. Reproductive scientists did not have to engage in applied research to make claims of future contraceptive payoffs from their work. As one historian has noted (Johnson 1977:77fn10), Sanger knew what she wanted from the scientists, knew what their scientific research on contraception would likely produce, and was still unable to induce any scientist who could make a contribution to engage in such work until the 1950s. In fact, scientists did not undertake this work in explicit basic research settings until as late as the 1960s.

Ultimately, development of the Pill was initiated and fiscally supported by Sanger, her ally Katherine McCormick, and the lay birth control movement. It was developed through the efforts of several scientists, all of whom, at the time, were operating from institutional sites on the fringes of academia or in industry. Specifically, Gregory Pincus and M. C. Chang were at the private Worcester Institute of Experimental Biology, which in 1950 was fiscally dependent on contract pharmaceutical industry research. Pincus had a strong background in the agricultural end of the reproductive sciences from his personal experiences, his undergraduate studies in biology from Cornell, and a year spent at Cambridge University in one of the major British centers of agricultural reproductive science with John Hammond, F. H. A. Marshall's primary student then working on artificial insemination (Pauly 1987:187). Like Walter Heape and Jacques Loeb, Pincus had worked on artificial parthenogenesis and other reproductive problems in the 1930s and 1940s (Biggers 1991). When he began explicit work on the Pill, Pincus was already "a refugee from academic biology" (Reed 1983:316), after being denied tenure at Harvard during the era when "proper" biology departments were getting out of the reproductive science business and expressing anti-Semitism.[62]

Pincus had received $14,500 from the PPFA in 1948 and 1949 for work on the mammalian egg. In 1951, he conferred with Sanger regarding hormonal contraception and then reapplied to the PPFA for support of this line of research, receiving $3,100 in 1951 and $3,400 in 1952. Pincus then sent in a most promising report of this work, which was ignored by William Vogt (then directing Planned Parenthood), who wanted organizational expansion to be focused on his administrative functions rather than animal testing of the Pill. Sanger, in one of the preemptory moves for which she was famous, simply bypassed him. In 1953, she convinced Katherine McCormick, heir to the International Harvester fortune and longtime suffragist and birth control advocate, to accompany her on the now-famous visit to Pincus at the WFEB. At the end of their conversation, McCormick promised Pincus $10,000 per year on the spot; this increased to $150,000 per year and more during her life (totaling about $2 million), and she left the Worcester Foundation $1 million in her will (Reed 1983:340; Chesler 1992:432).

The strategy of endocrinological contraception was also appealing to biochemists, and developments in steroid chemistry were key to the Pill. Russell Marker's and Carl Djerassi's chemical efforts were based at different times in Syntex, the industrial pharmaceutical company Marker had helped to form in Mexico. When Marker analyzed plant steroids for the first time he realized that hormones could be produced synthetically using a Mexican yam. Frustrated by his inability to locate support, he left academia and went to Mexico to pursue this line of research. Djerassi joined Syntex after Marker's departure, and with colleagues produced an orally active estrogen, which he then sent to Pincus and others for testing. Both Searle (with whom Pincus was already working) and Syntex eventually produced birth control pills.[63]

Not all reproductive scientists were thrilled with the Pill, and the clinical trials proved problematic.[64] Carl Hartman, then chairman of the medical committee of Planned Parenthood, expressed reservations about the Pill's systemic properties and predicted a fifteen- to twenty-year period before its safety could be assessed (about the same amount of time women's health activists also estimated as necessary). But Sanger and McCormick were "so confident . . . of the Pill's revolutionary consequences that they seemed positively immune to any objections to it whatsoever, and interpreted reasonable concerns about the liabilities of experimenting with so potent a drug as just one more round in the arsenal of opposition that birth control advocates had confronted for years" (Chesler 1992:434, 445). This passage also reminds us that women and feminists have held multiple positions about the Pill.

Pincus, Chang, Marker, and Djerassi all left academia under different conditions to pursue their work on their own terms in industrial or semi-industrial venues. They may have laughed at scholars' rejection all the way to the bank, but academic reproductive scientists were still refusing to do explicitly contraceptive research. These four in fact, had gone beyond the scholarly pale of their era—more or less commercial.[65] It was not until well into the 1960s that "population" funding from foundations and the federal government filtered into academia on a scale massive enough to involve basic reproductive scientists in research related, both directly and indirectly, to endocrinological contraception (Greep, Koblinsky, and Jaffe 1976). By then, such research was undertaken almost exclusively in medical settings. By 1970, there were 9 million American women using the Pill. Currently about 60 million women around the world do so.[66] Women Pill users are configured as active participants in contraception because the Pill must be taken daily.

Promoting Intrauterine Intervention.   Intrauterine devices (IUDs) are made of various substances (silk coils, rubber, metal, and after about 1958, plastic) and are placed into the uterus through the cervix. It is surmised that they prevent conception by creating a hostile uterine environment (one too irritated to allow implantation). Traditionally, the devices have been inserted by physicians (Langley 1973:336–37). IUDs are obviously directed at women actors—women as implicated users.

By the nineteenth century, IUDs had been patented and were in use for contraceptive purposes; Robert Latou Dickinson began promoting such devices in the United States in 1916 (Southam 1965:3). IUDs were also discussed at the Fifth International Conference on Birth Control in 1922 (Pierpoint 1922:275–77). The first modern developer was Ernest Grafenberg, a German gynecologist, who began experimenting with various types of devices in 1909 and began publishing on IUDs in 1928 (Langley 1973:336).[67] Grafenberg reported great success with the method in 1930 at the Seventh International Birth Control Congress, and considerable experimentation followed with what were then called "Grafenberg rings" (Reed 1983:275). But IUDs also generated considerable debate *within* the medical community in the 1930s and later, with many physicians vehemently opposed to their use, largely on grounds of risk of infection.[68] Physician opposition to it was strongest in the United States, where it was difficult even to publish on this method.[69] "No physician who himself had used IUCDs published a report in any medical journal of the Western countries between 1934 and 1959" (Tietze 1965b:1148).

The increased availability of antibiotics after World War II helped to overcome both the fears and the infections (Bullough 1994:186). Drawing on work done in Israel and Japan (Tietze 1965b), Lazar Margulies of the Department of Obstetrics of Mt. Sinai Hospital in New York and Jack Lippes of the University of Buffalo resurrected IUDs in the United States. Between 1958 and 1960, they pioneered a plastic product as a new, modern means of "scientific" contraception. The Population Council provided grants covering about 95 percent of development costs (Notestein 1982:678). Christopher Tietze of the Population Council candidly stated: "It was a very exciting period. . . . [W]e were working with something that had been absolutely rejected by the profession. . . . There was such a feeling of urgency among professional people, not among the masses, but something had to be done. And this was something that you could do to the people rather than something people could do for themselves. So it made it very attractive to the doers" (Reed 1983:307). It is this controlling approach—seeking something "you could do to the people"—that has guided much subsequent research within the population control framework.

As predicted by physicians in the 1930s, problems did appear with all IUDs, especially infection and "traveling." But one device in particular, the Dalkon Shield, was a transnational disaster, associated with an estimated seventeen deaths and extensive morbidity, including permanent infertility.[70] Such disasters have certainly sustained the controversial status of the reproductive sciences. Currently only a few IUDs are marketed in the United States because of steep product liability costs following the Dalkon Shield case (Mastroianni, Donaldson, and Kane 1990).

The configured users of the IUD are women who do not want to or cannot practice a method of contraception that requires active involvement, such as taking the Pill daily or using condoms. Those who developed techniques of contraception such as the IUD (and later injectables and implantables) to be "done to the people," in Tietze's terms, have taken an array of approaches that draw on different professional skills and knowledges within different and often competitive organizations.[71] But not all such efforts were as successful as the Pill and the IUD, as we shall see next.

Technological Intervention: Radiation for Sterilization. Voluntary (instead of involuntary, state-ordered) sterilization began to be seen as a viable means of contraception by birth control advocates in the 1920s (e.g., Dickinson and Gamble 1950; Sanger 1934:71). Although the usual means of sterilization were surgical (Langley 1973:272–336), a "simpler" and less invasive method of achieving permanent sterility was seen as desirable, and research was undertaken on sterilization by irradiation of the ovaries and testes. Radiation technology was the current "magic bullet" for new approaches to old problems. Whether the sterilizing potential of x-rays was discovered inadvertently is not clear. An early text on fertility and sterility notes, "A few years ago before the nature of the Roentgen rays [was] understood, practically all x-ray workers were sterile" (Reynolds and Macomber 1924:128). This method was therefore directed at both women and men as implicated actors/users. Both would be configured as passive users once radiation had been done.

In 1922, Donald Hooker of Hopkins reported on his preliminary investigations of sterilization by x-rays in the rat (Pierpoint 1922:236–39).[72] Hooker's research then generated further funding from the NRC/CRPS for the years 1922 to 1925; the committee also briefly funded clinical research on the effects of x-rays on sterility and fertility from 1924 to 1927 (Aberle and Corner 1953:93, 120). In 1925, Robert Latou Dickinson wrote to Katherine Davis of the BSH that in order to get away from mechanical appliances and "to suspend temporarily or to arrest ovulation permanently, irradiation of the ovaries must be studied in animals, especially in monkeys."[73] The BSH then offered Dickinson and the NCMH a matching grant for such research.[74] After consulting with Hooker at Hopkins, Corner at Rochester, and Stockard at Cornell Medical School, the NCMH granted aid to Halsey J. Bagg and Harold Bailey for a project using monkeys, to be co-sponsored by the Carnegie Institution of Washington.[75] Dickinson's project was challenged by C. C. Little, president of the University of Michigan, and member of the board of Sanger's Clinical Research Bureau, who wrote to Sanger in 1925 that physicians were reckless in attempting x-ray-induced infertility (McCann 1994:85). Again, multiple positions were held within the scientific community.

By about 1930, investigations of radiation as a means of contraceptive sterilization began to disappear from the literature. One German physician opposed x-ray sterilization because she regarded the maintenance of the endocrine organs (ovaries) as essential for prevention of premature menopause (Sanger and Stone 1931:118).[76] In Germany, one physician attempting to avoid the use of genocide as "the final solution" of "the Jewish problem" proposed covertly radiating all Jews and thereby sterilizing them (Proctor 1995). When the AMA's Council on Pharmacy and Chemistry began reporting on contraceptives in the late 1930s, it found that the use of x-rays for contraception was "of no value" (Reed 1983:245)—and highly carcinogenic and unreliable to boot.

Radiation sterilization initially offered a promising line of investigation to predominantly medical reproductive scientists, suitable both on scientific research grounds and as fundable work. Medical scientists thus found *scientific* contraception appropriate, regardless of the ultimate demise of this method. Investigating the consequences of radiation was also not viewed as, or at least was not transparent as, contraceptive research.

Promoting Immunologic Intervention: Spermatoxins.   In the search for scientific biological contraception, as opposed to simple and local chemical or mechanical means, reproductive scientists viewed immunology as a logical and exciting research path and sought means of immunizing women against pregnancy. The means of effecting immunity at that time was subcutaneous injection of the female with a serum or spermatoxin derived from fresh sperm of the same or different species. Mention was made of the possibilities of contraceptive autoimmunity in the male, but as in the lay and medical birth control movements, the focus was on female means of contraception (Sanger and Stone 1931:112–13). Biologists also found sperm research problems of classic physiological and morphological interest. Animal agricultural scientists were also interested in sperm studies, especially in relation to artificial insemination (Brackett, Seidel, and Seidel 1981). Both basic and clinical medical scientists found spermatoxin research problems attractive especially in relation to "classic" problems in immunology.

Initial work done in Germany at the turn of the century was continued in Germany (e.g., Ardelt 1931), and in the United States new work was begun by W. F. Guyer of the Department of Zoology at Wisconsin, who worked with rabbits and guinea pigs (Cooper 1928:115). The NCMH funded Guyer's endeavor,[77] and he was soon joined by others such as J. L. McCartney (Cooper 1928:268) and M. J. Baskin (1934), who performed clinical trials calling the method "temporary sterilization." Biologist investigators were quickly followed into this line of work by medical scientists.[78]

Because animal sperm were more available and hence more desirable for serum preparation, international debate focused on whether same-species sperm were requisite.[79] Guyer, for example, worked with whale testes and sperm, plentiful if properly preserved. In 1929, Stewart Mudd, a microbiologist of the Phipps Institute at the University of Pennsylvania and an active birth control advocate, in research with Emily Mudd, a sociologist on the medical school faculty, found both species and tissue specificity in mammals. There was also debate about how and where in the reproductive system spermatoxins operated and concern about possible "side-effects."[80]

As with some other methods of contraception, Soviet scientists were pioneers because of the legitimacy of birth control and hence of contraceptive research there: "To them it is a problem of scientific interest, worthy of the same amount of study as any other problem of scientific research, such as control of tuberculosis or cancer" (Daniels in Sanger and Stone 1931:109). By the mid-1920s, research on humans had begun: "The Russians feel that the use of spermatoxins has come out of the stage of pure theoretical research and has entered into the field of practical experimentation" (Stone in Sanger 1934:105–8). The Russians were certainly faster in moving from pure to applied contraceptive research, and American birth control advo-

cates were most interested. Marie Kopp, an American clinical and epidemiological birth control researcher, went to the Soviet Union in 1932 to
gather information on birth control methods and report back to American
colleagues (Kopp 1933).[81]

Two aspects of spermatoxin contraception became especially attractive
during the Great Depression: its simplicity and its low cost. "Think of how
wonderful it would be if one could immunize a patient by *simple hypodermic
injection* once every six months, just as we today immunize children against
diphtheria. It will indeed be a new and wonderful era in the practice of
preventive gynecology" (Daniels in Sanger and Stone 1931:111, emphasis
added). The appeal of injectable hormonal means is clear here as well. Dr.
McCartney commented: "Devices are all very nice for those who can afford
them. The poor people with whom we are really concerned in this [Depres-
sion] recovery program cannot afford them. . . . [I]t is quite necessary to be
concerned with something that can be applied very much more cheaply.
Spermatoxins . . . are one of the methods" (Sanger 1934:111). Whether
they actually would have been cheaper is debatable; they certainly would
have been more easily controlled by physicians. Women here were configured as semiactive users because they would need to receive injections
at regular intervals.

In the late 1930s, the NCMH again supported spermatoxin research
through grants from Squibb and Sons. The scientists' conclusions were
the (temporary) death knell of spermatoxin research: "When one com-
pares . . . the fertility of the injected animals with the controls, it appears
that paraenteral injection of live sperm reduces slightly the fertility of the
recipients, but the reduction is neither of significant degree nor of practical importance" (Eastman, Guttmacher, and Stewart 1939:151). While contraceptive application seemed futile, spermatoxin research had instigated
considerable sperm research in humans. One product at the time was a
much greater understanding of male infertility and sterility, issues of concern to the NCMH and other birth control organizations as they shifted
from woman-controlled birth control to "family planning" approaches and
included infertility research and treatment in their array of services (e.g.,
Reynolds and Macomber 1924; Weisman 1941).

Further, spermatoxin research had proved to be of considerable interest to biomedical scientists regardless of its association with birth control.
Again, the appeal of research on *scientific* means of contraception to reproductive scientists was clearly demonstrated to birth control advocates during the 1930s. Since about 1967, there has been a renaissance of interest
in what is now called "immunoreproduction," with considerable focus on
finding a male means of spermatoxic contraception. This research initiative
was led by Bulgarian scientists, echoing the Russian initiatives of half a century earlier.[82] But it has also been sustained in the United States and else-

where (Mastroianni, Donaldson, and Kane 1990:33). However, national and transnational women's health groups have raised serious questions about the safety and efficacy of immunocontraception (e.g., Richter 1993). Their concerns center on the consequences of contraceptive-caused immunosuppression or immune system compromise, both because of the AIDS epidemic and for many women who are already malnourished. Other lines of current immunological contraceptive research continue to seek what, during the 1930s, Max Mason of the Rockefeller Foundation called "anti-hormones": vaccines to block hormones needed for very early pregnancy and a vaccine to block the hormone needed for the surface of the egg to function properly (Mastroianni, Donaldson, and Kane 1990:33; Alexander 1995).

Each of the four methods of contraception examined here involved different key actors and reproductive sciences worlds. Each addressed birth control advocates' goals in some way. Most were directed exclusively at women users, who were not included in the design stage but instead were positioned as implicated actors. None of these methods met the original desires of the early feminist lay birth control movement for safe and effective, simple means of contraception that would enhance women's autonomy. All met the goals of reproductive scientists to make contraception scientific.

THE QUID PRO QUO

Through ongoing negotiations, heterogeneous birth control advocates and reproductive scientists arrived, between 1925 and 1945, at a congruence of interests that adequately met the changed needs of the major participants in the birth control arena. The quid pro quo achieved was based on changes, compromises, and trade-offs both within and among participating social worlds. Reproductive scientists had demonstrated that they would do "basic" research on problems related to "scientific" means of contraception and publishable in their "basic science" journals. In some such instances, they would even accept fiscal support from the birth control/population control movements, as some already did from pharmaceutical companies. In turn, birth control advocates had learned to cease demanding reproductive scientists' involvement in research on simple chemical and mechanical means of contraception (such as spermicides and diaphragms) and found other avenues through which such research could be pursued (such as academic chemistry and the pharmaceutical industry). This quid pro quo has been the fundamental basis for all subsequent relations over half a century.

But this accommodation and quid pro quo could only have been achieved given the shifts *within* the lay, medical, and academic birth control movements between 1925 and 1945. The most pronounced shifts were from commitments to birth control as a means of enhancing reproductive and sexual autonomy for women to contraception within an economic ethic of childbearing—economic planning, eugenics, and population control, often with racialized agendas (e.g., McCann 1994). These shifts led many birth control advocates to seek modern "scientific" means of contraception that are "done to the people," relying for effectiveness more on biological and medical research and expert control than on the users' own motivation.

Reproductive scientists also underwent transformatory experiences during this period. In the development of this quid pro quo, reproductive scientists' struggles for professional legitimacy, autonomy, and cultural authority for their enterprise were central. That is, the driving force behind the development of "scientific" means of contraception was and remains reproductive scientists' desires for professional autonomy as "basic" scientists. As Borell put it, reproductive scientists continued to do their "pure" or "basic" research, but they also provided a social product—the technology of scientific biomedical contraception—that gave them greater social authority.[83] In so doing, they both drew upon and further contributed to the cultural authority of science. Final development of means of contraception using that technology was to be left to the pharmaceutical industry and clinical practitioners (e.g., Segal 1987; Mastroianni, Donaldson, and Kane 1990).

The contraceptive Pill, based on decades of reproductive endocrinological and physiological research, and developed in marginal academic and commercial institutions, is the strongest demonstration of this process. Academic reproductive scientists did the bulk of the "basic" work, leaving it to lapsed scholars in quasi-industrial settings to push and polish it into a final product, with support from only two pharmaceutical companies from the established industry and a couple of new companies founded by other renegade scholars. The fiscal support provided by the birth control and population control movements from the 1930s to the 1950s was still too low to stimulate deeper involvement of reproductive scientists (Greep, Koblinsky, and Jaffe 1976). Moreover, contraceptive research still bore the stigma of illegitimacy. The clinical trials of the Pill, done almost exclusively on women of color in the Third World/Southern Hemisphere countries, were also problematic.[84]

The problem of the illegitimacy of birth control was alleviated by the coalescence of the various birth control movements into a legitimate, middle-class, professional, international family planning and population control establishment between about 1940 and 1965. This establishment was deeply linked with the reproductive sciences, sharing quite porous boundaries. As late as 1959, the *Ladies' Home Journal* would not address modern birth control in its regular medical column (Meldrum 1996). But by the 1960s, the publicity achieved by the population establishment claiming a "population explosion" in the Third World was sufficient to trigger the federal government's involvement in both contraceptive development and distribution. As Reed (1983:373) observed, "Social order everywhere suddenly seemed threatened by human fertility."[85] The National Academy of Sciences Committee on Science and Public Policy selected population problems as its focus in 1961 (National Academy of Sciences 1979:v). Most reproductive scientists agreed with these arguments (e.g., Pincus 1965; Djerassi 1981), including proposals for more integrated approaches such as Shelesnyak's (1963a,b) call for "biodynamics" as a new interdisciplinary frame for the study of reproductive phenomena and fertility control in all their complexity. During these years and after, reproductive scientists were drawn ever more deeply into public- and foundation-funded research that addressed "population problems"—basic research yielding clear and high contraceptive payoffs. But their involvement was very much on the terms of the quid pro quo negotiated with birth control advocates before World War II.[86] The arguments for basic research made by reproductive scientists enhanced the legitimacy, autonomy, and social and scientific authority of the enterprise. The culture of science predominated, and women were by far the most commonly configured users.

Both federal policy and public opinion on contraception also changed dramatically between 1945 and 1970. In 1942, after over a quarter century of agitation by the lay birth control movements and their establishment of 803 birth control clinics throughout the country as their major form of activism, the U.S. Public Health Service ruled that federal funds allocated for local health services could be used for family planning in the states (Ray and Gosling 1984–85:404). By 1963, however, only fifteen state health departments offered such services (Reed 1983:268). In 1959, President Dwight Eisenhower responded to a question about foreign aid for contraception by stating: "I cannot imagine anything more emphatically a subject that is not a proper political or governmental activity or function or responsibility. . . . This government will not, as long as I am here, have a positive political doctrine in its program that has to do with the problem of birth control. That's not our business." Four years later, during the administration of the first Catholic president, Democrat John F. Kennedy, Republican Eisenhower dramatically changed his mind. He then wrote in the *Saturday Evening Post* that population growth posed a threat to world peace and that birth control was a legitimate concern of government (Reed 1984–85:383).

After Kennedy's assassination, the Johnson administration provided an array of family planning services nationally and transnationally through many legislative acts. The Fulbright amendment to the foreign aid bill, signed in December 1963, authorized programs in population research and technical assistance. Special recognition of American family planning needs began in 1967, and in 1969 the National Center for Family Planning Services was established in the Department of Health, Education, and Welfare. The Family Planning Act of 1970, under President Nixon, expanded services and federal funding, which totaled over $68 million in 1971 and $336 million in 1987 (Davis 1991:386–87, 398). Extensive research, transnational distribution, and technical support for family planning services has been provided by the U.S. Agency for International Development and other organizations. In short, the United States became the dominant transnational distributor of the means of control over reproduction. By the late 1960s, thirteen pharmaceutical companies were involved in contraceptive research and development (Djerassi 1992:119). The "Contraceptive Revolution" (Westoff and Ryder 1977) took place in the 1960s and 1970s as the direct result of the negotiation of the quid pro quo between birth control advocates and reproductive scientists. Its impacts have been and continue to be global.

Feminist voices, so strong at the beginning of the century in the formation of lay birth control movements, were co-opted and silenced in the shift from birth control to family planning and population control by the end of the Great Depression (McCann 1994:chapters 5–6). Ironically, they reappeared in new forms in the 1970s at the height of population control efforts. National and transnational women's health movements have formulated multiple, divergent critiques of the contraceptive revolution, and such groups are now participating in many of the venues where family planning and population concerns are translated into health care policy and foreign policy.[87] Further, over eighty years since Margaret Sanger's first appeal, demands for more and better *simple* means of contraception are still heard, along with detailed explication of concerns with safety, such as the following, derived from the 1994 Cairo Conference Organizing Committee (Organizing Committee 1994:6):

> Item 13. In the area of contraceptive technology, resources should be redirected from provider-controlled and potentially high-risk methods, like the vaccine, to barrier methods. A significant proportion of the participants also felt strongly that Norplant or other long-term hormonal contraceptives should be explicitly mentioned as high-risk methods from which resources should be redirected. Female controlled methods that provide both contraception and protection from sexually transmitted diseases, including HIV, as well as male methods, should receive highest priority in contraceptive research and development. Women's organizations are entitled to indepen-

dently monitor contraceptive trials and ensure women's free, informed
consent to enter the trial. Trial results must be available for women's organizations at the different stages of such trials, including the very early stages.

Equally significant, in the United States and abroad, women have voted with
their feet, resisting and rejecting means of contraception that do not meet
their needs. Many feminists tacitly or explicitly draw on the "three contraceptive axioms" specified by Dr. Mary Calderone (1964:153) when she was
medical director of Planned Parenthood–World Population:

1. *Any* method of birth control is more effective than no method.
2. The most effective method is the one the couple will use with
   the greatest consistency.
3. Acceptability is the most critical factor in the effectiveness of a
   contraceptive method.

Partly because of such feminist interventions, there has been a shift away
from the modernist, standardized "one-size-fits-all" approach so deeply embedded in the search for scientific contraception described in this chapter. The shift is to a more postmodern, economic, and individualized niche-
oriented "cafeteria approach" offering an array of means of contraception,
ideally suited to the highly varied health care and living situations of prospective users—men as well as women—and accommodating changing reproductive needs and goals across the life course. However, the modernist
"one-size-fits-all" pattern remains dominant in many Southern Hemisphere
countries, while the postmodern "cafeteria" is available primarily in the
Northern Hemisphere (Oudshoorn 1995, 1996a).

CONCLUSIONS

The arenas concerned with human reproduction changed between 1925
and 1945 in ways that ultimately allowed the quid pro quo to develop. One
shift was from progressive reform to conservative control—from birth control as a means of individual self-determination, especially for women, to
family planning and population control. There was also a shift from an
individual choice to a social control agenda, and shifts of focus from concerns about qualities of individuals to quantities of populations, and from
user control of simple means of contraception to professional control over
scientific means of contraception, from means "people do for themselves"
to means "done to the people." The rationalized family could be achieved
via modernist control over reproduction, biologically based social engineering that allowed scientific management and planning to be applied in
the supposedly private domain of reproduction—the bedroom.[88]
This chapter illustrates the utility of a social worlds and arenas approach

in technoscience studies. Scientific enterprises such as the reproductive sciences are especially in need of individual case studies and comparative analyses that examine their embeddedness in specific market and resource networks. Multiple nonmonolithic social worlds were engaged in the birth control arena at the turn of the century, and others were reluctantly enrolled. That is, reproductive scientists who by and large did not want to do contraceptive research could not avoid participating directly or indirectly in the birth control arena. We can see them as reluctant actors, coerced or seduced by funding and their own dreams for the larger enterprise.

I examined the earliest moments in the making of two successful technologies of modern scientific contraception—the Pill and the IUD—analyzing the interests and commitments built into the actual design of these technologies by examining the engaged social worlds, their perspectives and commitments. Failed approaches, specifically immunotoxins and sterilization by radiation, were also discussed. Women were the targeted/ implicated users (Clarke and Montini 1993) but were excluded from direct participation, then as now. Most users were configured (Woolgar 1991) as women, and they were reconfigured from Sanger's goal of women as autonomous sexual beings to people something should "be done to." Both the Pill and the IUD were intended as what Oudshoorn (1995, 1996a) has called universal, "one-size-fits-all" technologies. Latour's (1987, 1991) notions that technology is society made durable and that scientists should be seen as in the driver's seat are clearly upheld in the case of the reproductive sciences and contraceptive technologies.

Contraceptives are what Foucault termed "disciplinary technologies" (Rabinow 1984:17), part of the "socialization of reproductive behavior" that can discipline such behavior in multiple ways. But, simultaneously, contraceptives can be means of liberation, offering strategies of resistance against related disciplines of gender as well as race, class, and global position. Many contradictions are carried on the n-way webs of relations along which both simple and scientific means of contraception travel. As feminist women's health advocates have learned, especially but not only through the transnationalization of their movements, the heterogeneity of women's situations must be of paramount concern. This heterogeneity requires that women and men have access to a diversity of means of control over reproduction. Current feminist goals call for active user participation in design and in all subsequent stages. Further, the calculus of risks and benefits for each method must take diversities of women's health care, cultural, and economic situations into account. This would, of course, change the reproductive arena considerably.

Hard (1993) has argued for a more explicitly and vividly conflictful social constructionism as not only possible but also likely to be found in empirical research, along with issues of power, stratification, and hierarchy.

Drawing upon social worlds analysis, the story of the emergence of modern scientific contraception told here meets these criteria. The reproductive arena was conflictful when it emerged, it remains conflictful today, and closure is not in sight. It is a modernist technoscience story of hierarchies, gender, and power that has now segued into the postmodern era and is still unfolding. But the quid pro quo constructed between reproductive scientists and birth control advocates of multiple kinds remains the foundational moment that still must be addressed.

CHAPTER SEVEN

Funding the Reproductive Sciences

Money matters, in science as elsewhere. The modern adage that "he who pays the piper calls the tune" also echoes strongly in social studies of science and technology. This is especially the case in studies of disciplinary formation because new knowledge production is usually expensive (e.g., Jasanoff et al. 1995; Shapin 1992). The deeply controversial nature of the reproductive sciences qua sciences makes the analysis of their funding even more salient than for more conventionally accepted research areas. I have therefore devoted a full chapter to an overview of the funding sources of the reproductive sciences since about 1910. Both the stature and the extent of the funding of reproductive research during its formation and coalescence periods were unique and significant in enabling this controversial line of research work to establish itself as a "going concern," a recognized, viable scientific enterprise.

The history of funding for research in science and technology, between 1910 and 1963, is fascinating. This was the era of the key shift from funding by private individuals (usually scientists or personal benefactors) to university departmental research budgets to corporate foundation support and, finally, to governmental support. This shift ultimately transformed the world.

Sociologically, funding is a key basis for linking heterogeneous social worlds and for building new infrastructure across socioeconomic sectors (such as the academy, philanthropy, and corporations). Funding is usually pivotal to legitimacy as well—sometimes more important than the science itself. The modernist era of "Big Science" and external research support began in the decades after World War I (Price 1963; Kohler 1991; Kleinman 1994). "Big Science" funding hit the reproductive sciences immediately via the National Research Council Committee for Research in Problems of Sex, which is examined in detail in chapter 4. Here I emphasize other sources, including industrial support.

There has been only minimal documentation of reproductive sciences funding.[1] The only such analysis for the period prior to World War II is that of Roy Greep and his associates, sponsored by the Ford Foundation. They argue that, due to the general illegitimacy of sex and reproduction as both social issues and scientific research foci, "to initiate and sustain serious research in the reproductive sciences has required for more than half a century concerted effort by interested individuals and private organizations, mainly from outside the mainstream of the biomedical research community" (Greep, Koblinsky, and Jaffe 1976:367–71). My analysis both sustains and challenges their views. I attempt to portray the breadth of funding sources, the extent of funding, and types of research funded where possible, along with a historical orientation to each of the major funding sources.[2]

More specifically, Greep and his associates (1976:370) argued that funding for the reproductive sciences before World War II was both slight and far from the mainstream of the biomedical research community. They also asserted that reproductive research, especially as related to the development of contraception, was relatively underfunded as compared with other biomedical research fields during this period. In contrast, I conclude that considerable funding was provided through prestigious organizations by the major biomedical research–oriented foundations to the "basic" reproductive sciences. However, as Greep and his colleagues asserted, there was little funding of explicitly contraceptive research until the 1950s and 1960s.[3] The key difference in our analyses is that I have carefully distinguished between loosely "basic" research in the reproductive sciences (in biology, medicine, and agriculture) and explicitly contraceptive research. I make this distinction because American reproductive scientists largely eschewed explicitly contraceptive research and punished those who pursued it at least until the 1950s or 1960s. It was the quid pro quo constructed among reproductive scientists and birth control advocates in the 1940s and 1950s that fused the previously distinctive reproductive and contraceptive research traditions. That quid pro quo also fused the funding patterns and identities of the reproductive sciences more generally. Old boundaries were dissolved, and the applications of the reproductive sciences were more fully acknowledged. For a host of likely reasons, Greep and his colleagues, writing in the 1970s, seem to have blurred reproductive and contraceptive research and funding in their analyses, reflecting the more contemporary intimate relations of these two endeavors following World War II.

This chapter documents the successes of reproductive scientists in gaining prestigious, sustained, and significant support for their work prior to World War II. I examine the major funding sources beginning with the National Research Council (sponsor of reproductive research through several subagencies), the National Committee on Maternal Health, direct foundation support, and industrial support. Last, I offer a brief synopsis of funding since 1940 to demonstrate changes in the fiscal "career" of the reproductive sciences enterprise.

OVERVIEW OF REPRODUCTIVE SCIENCES FUNDING, 1910–40

Between about 1910 and 1940, most reproductive research was undertaken in university departments. Funding was both internal (from routine departmental research budgets) and external (from sources outside the local institution). While external funding sources (analyzed later in this chapter) were diverse and fairly extensive, I believe a precise fiscal analysis of reproductive research would reveal that routine departmental research budgets were the major source of reproductive sciences funding before World War II. At some institutions, such budgets were supplemented with revenue from patents secured by faculty reproductive scientists for reproductive hormonal extraction, isolation, and production procedures.[4] Because research costs were comparatively low, reliance on local funding sources was likely typical in many other areas of scientific research as well.

Until after World War I, the primary external research funding sources, although not strong, were major foundations and industry. I suspect that industry played a particularly significant role for the reproductive sciences both initially and more recently because of both the illegitimacy of those sciences and the simultaneous demand for their technoscientific products for clinical and agricultural work. This certainly was the case in Europe (Oudshoorn 1994). After World War I, direct funding of American reproductive research was often provided by private nonprofit agencies committed to science or social change of some kind, but the actual funds such agencies dispersed derived primarily from foundations. Individual benefactors also funded the reproductive sciences. Table 8 presents Greep and his associates' (1976:371) summary of private agency reproductive research expenditures from 1922 to 1940.

Included here are expenditures of the National Research Council Committee for Research in Problems of Sex and Committee on Research in Endocrinology, and the private National Committee on Maternal Health. Startlingly, this total constitutes over 10 percent of foundation contributions to the entire NRC during this era.[5] This is a very significant proportion and, moreover, was not the only funding the reproductive sciences received.

The United States government did not provide extensive fiscal support to any kind of biomedical research until after World War II. The Hygienic Laboratory, which had been founded in 1897, was enlarged as the National

TABLE 8   Private Agency Expenditures on Reproductive
Science in the United States, 1922–1940 (in 1976 dollars)

Year	Expenditure
1922–1925	99,600
1926–1930	323,500
1931–1935	352,700
1936–1940	520,100
Total	1,295,900

SOURCE: Greep, Koblinsky, and Jaffe 1976:371.

Institute of Health (NIH) in 1930. But in 1935 the science budget of the
Public Health Service, including the NIH research budget and representing almost the total federal health research investment, was only $508,000
for all research (Strickland and Strickland 1976:5). Support was focused
on research on acute infectious diseases (Rosen 1965; Swain 1962). The
major exception was government funding of agricultural research, which
began during the late nineteenth century (Rosenberg 1976). Some proportion of these funds was certainly used to support reproductive research
under agricultural auspices by scientists trained in a wide variety of settings.[6] Amounts are unclear, but the physiology of reproduction in farm/
meat animals was not a focus until after 1925 and the area was still relatively
minor until after World War II, when it intensified considerably (Byerly
1986).

NATIONAL RESEARCH COUNCIL SPONSORSHIP

The National Research Council (NRC) is a suborganization of the National
Academy of Science (NAS). The NRC itself was founded in 1916 as an
agency to inventory research toward enhanced military preparedness; it focused primarily on the natural and physical sciences. After World War I, it
was quickly transformed into a science sponsorship forum with a variety
of committees and subcommittees funded (along with the Academy) by a
grant of $5 million from the Carnegie Corporation (Tobey 1971:35, 53).
The Rockefeller Foundation was also an early and extensive supporter of
the NRC.[7] Nearly $12 million of foundation support was provided to the
NRC from 1916 to 1940; 98 percent of these funds came from Rockefeller
and Carnegie boards (Kohler 1991:104).

The NRC was a prestigious organization from its inception, thanks to its
early association with the NAS, the Carnegie Corporation, and the Rockefeller Foundation. Kohler (1991:109) has argued that the NRC essentially
served as an intermediary between the foundations and scientists in the

interwar years: "Biology, which was a congeries of competing and contentious subspecialties or subcultures, with varied relations with medicine, agriculture, psychology, natural resource management, all of which offered attractive but competing opportunities for discipline," posed particular problems for funders. The proto–peer review mechanisms offered through the NRC provided useful insulation for the foundations as they moved into what Kohler has called "partnerships" with the sciences qua research institutions. Even if one takes a more critical perspective and views the foundations as shaping or engineering the future by shaping the directions of sciences toward their own interests, the peer review mechanisms were useful in improving foundation understanding and access to information.

Committees of the NRC could be initiated from within or without the agency, but they required agency approval. Before World War II, two such committees sponsored reproductive research: the Committee for Research in Problems of Sex and the Committee on Endocrinology. The reproductive sciences were also funded through the NRC Grants-in-Aid Program. Two other post–World War II NRC committees, the Committee on Human Reproduction and the Committee on Contraceptive Technology, also became involved later.

The NRC Committee for Research in Problems of Sex

My commentary on the NRC Committee for Research in Problems of Sex (NRC/CRPS) here is brief; its founding and the redirection of its mission from sexology to basic research in reproductive biology is analyzed in considerable depth in chapter 4. The NRC/CRPS, which existed from 1921 to 1962 (National Academy of Sciences 1979:v) in the Medical Sciences Division of the NRC, was the major external funding source for reproductive research prior to World War II. One historian has asserted: "The committee virtually paid for the development in American universities of [reproductive] endocrinology" (Reed 1983:283). From 1921 to 1940, the NRC/CRPS sponsored reproductive research by means of grants totaling $1,087,322; from 1940 to 1947, an additional $368,934 was expended (Aberle and Corner 1953:113).

The NRC/CRPS itself was funded almost exclusively by Rockefeller monies, initially through the Bureau of Social Hygiene and, after 1931, through the Rockefeller Foundation (Aberle and Corner 1953). In later years it also received funding from the Ford Foundation (National Academy of Sciences 1979:v). Rather than provide grants to individuals at many institutions, the NRC/CRPS primarily funded established and emerging centers of reproductive sciences staffed by multiple investigators under the leadership of a prominent scientist. From 1921 to 1947, "104 cooperating investigators received approximately 470 grants, under which 585 individu-

als took part in the researches" (Aberle and Corner 1953:70). Directing
investigators thus received an average of 4.5 grants. This innovative means
of organizing scientific research sponsorship promoted what would today
be termed "project-oriented" research, drawing together investigators from
several salient disciplines to address a related set of problems.[8]

As Table 10 demonstrates, research sponsored through the NRC/CRPS
was largely, though far from exclusively, endocrinological in nature. During
the years before World War II, most sponsored research utilized animal
rather than human materials. The status and prestige of the NRC affiliation
lent stature to the CRPS specifically and to the reproductive sciences enterprise generally. It seems unlikely that well over $1 million would have
been provided to the committee by Rockefeller philanthropies had it not
found an institutional "home" with the NRC.

The NRC Committee on Endocrinology

The NRC Committee on Endocrinology was founded in 1936 and remained
active until 1950 (Greep, Koblinsky, and Jaffe 1976:370). I have argued in
chapter 5 that the reproductive sciences coalesced around the core activity
of reproductive endocrinology as a means of gaining legitimacy for the
enterprise by riding on the coattails of general endocrinology. It is thus
both ironic and anomalous, as I will attempt to explain, that the major NRC
committee addressing the reproductive sciences (the NRC/CRPS) existed
for fifteen years prior to the establishment of the NRC Committee on Endocrinology.

By 1933, there was extensive discussion of the need for an NRC committee on endocrinology both within the Rockefeller Foundation and with
NRC representatives. As one report noted, "The other [non-sex] hormones are not of lesser importance."[9] Meanwhile, the Markle Foundation
(founded in 1927), which was undergoing a major program review in 1934
and 1935, decided to focus its sponsorship afresh on medical research, as
many other foundations were doing at the time (Strickland and Strickland
1976:6). Officers of the Markle Foundation then approached Robert Yerkes
(chairman of the NRC/CRPS and a former NRC officer) for advice. Yerkes
arranged a conference with Frank Lillie, who suggested that research in
endocrinology needed assistance. A report assessing the field was supplied
by Roy Hoskins, editor of *Endocrinology* (Cannon 1942:844). The NRC/
CRPS could not support nonreproductive endocrinological research, as it
was increasingly being asked to do. The Markle Foundation offered funds
for such a committee.[10]

During its fourteen years of existence, the NRC Committee on Endocrinology expended $561,000 on grants in aid of research. According to
Greep and his associates (1976:370), $71,000 of this amount was devoted

directly or indirectly to reproductive endocrinological research. Walter Cannon, a professor of physiology at Harvard, was the first chairman of the committee.[11] There was concern from the outset regarding the boundaries between these two NRC committees, as Yerkes wrote to Warren Weaver of the Rockefeller Foundation: "The rumor is abroad that support of endocrinological studies is being lessened [by the NRC/CRPS]. Actually there is every reason to suppose the [NRC/CRPS] will continue to support such studies. . . . Obviously it is essential that the overlap of interest between [the two committees] . . . be carefully scrutinized, and the two committees so conducted with reference to promotion of endocrinological studies of sex that maximal assistance shall be rendered without undesirable duplication . . . or oversight."[12]

L. H. Weed, chairman of the Medical Sciences Division of the NRC, sought to facilitate the cooperation of the two committees structurally, arranging for their chairs to sit ex officio on the other committee with planned successive meetings. Weed reported to the Rockefeller Foundation that the NRC/CRPS was "allowing most of the proposals in the endocrine field to be taken by the Endocrine Committee."[13] This freed NRC/CRPS funds for other purposes, largely human sexuality studies after 1940. By the late 1940s, the glamour of nonreproductive endocrinology had apparently worn thin as well. As Maienschein (1994) puts it, "Cutting edges cut both ways." The Markle Foundation, with a new president, refocused its giving on the Markle Scholars program to enable medical schools to retain promising graduates and prepare them for careers in academic medicine and research, a program it then supported for over twenty years (Strickland and Strickland 1976:18).

The anomaly of the NRC/CRPS preceding the NRC Committee on Endocrinology by fifteen years, despite the greater legitimacy of general endocrinology and its consequently greater apparent "fundability," cannot be overlooked. The main explanation is that the original mission of the NRC/CRPS was not, in fact, support of reproductive biological or endocrinological research but support for research on sexual problems in humans to prevent and alleviate social problems. The Bureau of Social Hygiene was its original institutional sponsor. However, this mission was redirected by the members of the NRC/CRPS toward reproductive biological research, especially reproductive endocrinology, from its earliest days, a contingency that could not have been anticipated by its founders.

Second, despite its redirected mission, the research sponsored by the NRC/CRPS included endocrinological problems that were not solely reproductive. Both physiologically and in funding practice, the boundaries between reproductive and general endocrinology were blurred, as were the boundaries among enzymes, vitamins, and hormones.[14] This blurring was well recognized in a 1933 Rockefeller Foundation report, which proposed "three separate committees dealing with the fields of enzymes, vitamins and hormones. . . . The three committee point of view is suggested for, . . . in general, there are three rather distinct groups of workers. . . . A Committee on endocrinology . . . seems almost certain . . . to shed much light on the chemical aspect of life and the control of certain diseases; with also some probability of leading into the fields of psychobiology and personality problems."[15]

The NRC Committee on Infectious Abortion

The NRC Committee on Infectious Abortion was jointly sponsored by the Division of Medical Sciences and the Division of Biology and Agriculture of the NRC. Infectious abortion in animals, especially beef cattle and dairy cows, was of considerable concern to agricultural breeders and scientists. It is caused by the genus *Brucella*, which also causes undulant fever in humans. The Committee on Infectious Abortion established a research station at Lansing, Michigan (supported by the Commonwealth Fund of New York), and sponsored a variety of researches, including studies of reproductive problems, in aid of furthering understanding of the physiological processes of infectious abortion. These researches were jointly funded by the American Medical Association, the Certified Milk Producers' Association, the U.S. Department of Agriculture's Bureau of Animal Husbandry, and the Michigan State College of Agriculture through the NRC.[16] This group, then, was another minor sponsor of mammalian reproductive research.

The NRC Grants-in-Aid Program

In addition to its standing committees, during the 1930s the NRC also administered an individual Grants-in-Aid Program, which served as another, if relatively minor, funding source for reproductive scientists. Funded by the Rockefeller Foundation, from 1929 to 1935 it made 267 grants in the medical and biological sciences for a total of $132,511; the average grant in all fields was $532 (Bowman 1935:339). Kohler (1991:105–13) provides a vivid account of the entrepreneurship and stewardship of Frank Lillie in developing these grants. Lillie drew strongly on his successes in the early 1920s with the NRC/CRPS. A review of archival materials demonstrates that a number of reproductive scientists, including Doisy, Backman, Bissonette, Lillie, Turner, Allee, Long, Guthrie, Geiling, and Rasmussen, received funds from the Grants-in-Aid Program for work on a wide variety of reproductive research problems. Their studies addressed the histology of lactation, the effects of x-rays on ovarian and uterine tissue, ovarian hormones, vertebrate oocytes, reproductive endocrinology in the whale, and comparative histology of the human hypophysis in pregnant and nonpregnant women.[17] These data confirm my contention that funding was not at all minor, and certainly came from reputable, mainstream sources.

The NRC Committee on Human Reproduction

The NRC Committee on Human Reproduction was established in 1947 and existed only until 1951 (National Academy of Sciences 1979:v). Originated through efforts of activists in the lay and medical birth control movements, an agreement was constructed whereby the NRC would sponsor this committee while the Planned Parenthood Federation of America and the National Committee on Maternal Health (another reproductive and contraceptive research funding source discussed later in this chapter) would raise the funds to support it. However, only $40,000 was raised by these groups for this committee, despite the direct involvement of John D. Rockefeller III, who was instead committing himself to the Population Council (discussed later).[18]

Howard Taylor Jr., a physician on the faculty of the Columbia University medical school and a longtime activist in the National Committee on Maternal Health, served as chairman of the Committee on Human Reproduction (Reed 1983:271). Plans were laid for funding a wide range of reproductive researches within a budget of about $220,000 per year. A fourteen-member committee was recruited that strongly represented both reproductive biology and medicine, with other members from public health, psychology, and sociology (Taylor 1948:3). During its four-year existence, this committee funded only nine projects and held four conferences, expending a total of $112,000 (Greep, Koblinsky, and Jaffe 1976:374). Of this amount, $7,500 went to Gregory Pincus of the Worcester Foundation for Experimental Biology for studies of the fertilization and development of the mammalian egg; $5,400 went to John Rock of the Free Hospital for Women in Boston for infertility research. Both studies were concerned with the hormonal control of ovulation and later contributed to the development of the birth control pill. Margaret Sanger had also attempted to gain the ear and support of Katherine McCormick to fund the NRC Committee on Human Reproduction, but McCormick's funds were tied up at the time and the committee died for lack of support. McCormick later put nearly $2 million into Pincus's work on the birth control pill at the Worcester Foundation.[19]

The NRC Committee on Contraceptive Technology

Almost a quarter century elapsed between the failure of the first NRC Committee on Human Reproduction, which was interested in both reproductive and contraceptive research, and the establishment of a second such effort. The Assembly of the Life Sciences of the NRC established the Committee on Contraceptive Technology in 1977 within the Division of Medical Sciences (National Academy of Sciences 1979:vii). Such a committee was sought on the basis of population issues raised by the Committee on Science and Public Policy since 1963. The goal of the group, which continues today, is to serve as an intersectional organization among the reproductive sciences, population/demography research and fertility control research worlds, to assess current research status and needs, and to plan coordinated efforts. The full integration of the reproductive sciences enterprise with those of population and contraceptive research worlds in the years after World War II is reflected in the existence, structure, and mission of this NRC committee.

In 1990, the renamed Committee on Contraceptive Development published the results of the latest major assessment of the international reproductive biology and contraceptive research situation (Mastroianni, Donaldson, and Kane 1990), the first since that of Greep and his colleagues (1976, 1977) sponsored by the Ford Foundation. It focuses on the present status and future of contraceptive research in the United States and internationally, arguing that funding for such endeavors has been deemed inadequate; specific problems are examined in detail. This book project as a whole was sponsored by the Andrew W. Mellon Foundation. The committee is now jointly staffed and administered by the NRC Committee on Population and the Institute of Medicine's Division of International Health.

THE NATIONAL COMMITTEE ON MATERNAL HEALTH

The private National Committee on Maternal Health (NCMH) was founded in 1925 as a birth control advocacy and research organization and lasted until 1967. It was intended by and for practicing physicians, but eventually it included both medical and biological reproductive scientists.[20] The NCMH developed out of gynecologist Robert Latou Dickinson's work with the Bureau of Social Hygiene and was supported by the Bureau and major foundations.[21] The NCMH had several major programs during its forty-four-year history, and it was the site of a number of internal struggles regarding the direction and sponsorship of different activities.

The initial focus of the NCMH, from about 1923 to 1928, was on both "clinical" contraceptive and some "basic" reproductive research. The basic scientists who received support undertook the following projects:

1. "Ovarian Function in Rabbits and Rats," Dr. D. Macomber, Boston
2. "Vaginal Scrapes in Relation to Ovulation," Dr. G. Papanicolaou, Cornell Medical School

3. "Effect of Irradiation on the Ovaries and Progeny of Monkeys," Drs. Bailey and Bagg, Memorial Hospital
4. "Effect of Lead on Fertility," Dr. Emerson, Columbia College of Physicians and Surgeons
5. "Spermatoxins," Prof. W. F. Guyer, Department of Zoology, University of Wisconsin
6. "Physiology of Sperms" [*sic*], Dr. Max Mayer, Mt. Sinai Hospital
7. "Bacteriology of the Normal Vagina and Cervix," Drs. J. W. Harris and J. H. Brown, Johns Hopkins
8. "The Cytology of Sperm," Dr. G. Moench, Post Graduate Medical School and Hospital[22]

The last study, Moench's work on the cytology of sperm, was considered the most successful. It resulted in a monograph in German and a wide variety of English publications.[23] Robert T. Frank, Robert Latou Dickinson, and Herbert McLean Evans reviewed the manuscript. "Dr. Frank, our Chairman of Research, considers Moench's study the best in its field, and we see constant references to it in medical articles."[24]

The major NCMH goals during this early period were establishing and raising standards for clinical contraceptive research.[25] By 1928, however, it became clear to Dickinson and others involved that the basic scientists they had supported in hopes of generating new and/or improved means of contraception were not responding as desired. Several of the reproductive scientists would not even send reports of their progress.[26] Reed's (1983:181–84) analysis here is that "the committee lacked both the personnel to supervise such projects and the money required to back research from which no immediate results could be demonstrated to donors." I would argue further that reproductive scientists were likely asserting their autonomy over their work in response to unwanted demands from birth control advocates. Even if they happily took money from this agency, basic reproductive scientists were unlikely to pursue contraceptive research at this historical moment, although "raiding the larder" of the NCMH seems to have been acceptable. Further, there was an increasing array of potential sponsors for noncontraceptive research. Regardless, the NCMH temporarily left the field of basic research sponsorship to the NRC/CRPS and other groups around 1928.

Dickinson next guided the NCMH into a new role as medical birth control publicist (ca.1928–35). Some of the rationales for this organizational strategy emerged through both legal decisions and birth control movement strategies promoting medical control over the practice of many kinds of contraception through medicine's exclusive authority to prescribe drugs and certain devices (Chesler 1992; McCann 1994). To both expand

and consolidate medical authority in the birth control arena, during the NCMH's medical publicist era, several NCMH-sponsored monographs were produced to serve as contraceptive handbooks for doctors. These works provided information used to justify shifts in their clinical and personal opinions on contraception for which many medical men were ready—as long as the information came from physicians. Dr. Dickinson's strategy for the publications noted that "contraception alone will carry less difficulty if bracketed with sterility when it comes to enlisting professional interest." The NCMH-sponsored monographs included Dickinson and Louise Bryant's book *Control of Conception* (1931), his *Human Sex Anatomy* (1933), Norman Himes's *Medical History of Contraception* (1936), Cecil Voge's *Chemistry and Physics of Contraception* (1933), Carl Hartman's *The Time of Ovulation in Women* (1936), several studies of human sexuality, and works on abortion and sterility. Dickinson and the NCMH were much more successful as professors to the medical guild than as organizers of basic research (Reed 1983:182–85, 409).

Internal organizational struggles occurred in the NCMH in the years after 1929 between Dickinson and Clarence Gamble, a member of the NCMH, a philanthropist, and a physician who advocated simple means of contraception with nonmedical delivery. Gamble wanted the NCMH to invest in simple contraceptive research and delivery, including clinics. With some concessions to Gamble, Dickinson prevailed and further pushed the NCMH to broaden its audience to include nonmedical scientific and professional societies, both to raise money and to provide information to lay groups. Apparently, there was also some debate about whether the NCMH should focus on birth control or population control (Reed 1983:185).

Yet another shift in direction of the NCMH occurred ca. 1935 with a new generation of leadership. Carl Hartman at Johns Hopkins had been the long-distance research director. Now Earl Engle of Columbia University's medical school, handily in New York City, took that position.[27] Engle also had considered becoming executive director of the NCMH but instead remained in teaching and reproductive research.[28] The NCMH now became less interested in legal aspects of sex and contraception and eugenics,[29] and its program again became increasingly biological and "fundamental" over the years 1935–42.[30] This shift may well have been an attempt by basic scientists active within the NCMH to "redirect" the mission of the NCMH as other scientists had succeeded in doing within the NRC/CRPS. The goals of the NCMH were explicitly framed afresh in 1939 along such lines: "The function of the Committee is to select, plan, and supervise research projects conducted by qualified experts in hospitals and university departments where their status makes the prosecution of research effective. The Committee furthermore solicits funds for such research projects and acts as a coordinating, educative and critical agency in the planning of research work and human sex phenomena."[31] Probably because of these new goals, in 1939 the Rockefeller Foundation gave the NCMH $12,000 for research in aspects of human fertility that were not being covered by the NRC/CRPS. The NCMH then sponsored research in sperm morphology, spermatoxins, and other studies of sex cells at Yale, Cornell, Johns Hopkins, Rochester, and the University of Pennsylvania (Reed 1983:269). Also in 1939, there was a "Conference of Investigators Working on Various Problems Relating to Sperm Biology Under the Auspices of the NCMH." And, in 1940, the NCMH considered changing its name to the Research Council on Human Reproduction.[32]

This infusion of Rockefeller Foundation funds strengthened the hand of those in the NCMH who wanted to leave actual contraceptive testing— the major early activity of the NCMH—to other organizations. In 1940, Kenneth Rose of the Birth Control Federation (the predecessor of Planned Parenthood) worked out an arrangement with the NCMH by which the federation would be responsible for all laboratory and field trials of contraceptives except where special technical problems were involved. In turn, the federation was to raise $25,000 per year to support the NCMH in its role as sponsor of basic reproductive research. In early 1941, Dickinson's dream of hiring a medical scientist to head the NCMH came true. Clair E. Folsome, an assistant professor at the University of Michigan School of Medicine, became executive secretary of the NCMH. However, research funds dried up during World War II, and Folsome left the NCMH to become research director for Ortho Pharmaceuticals (Reed 1983:270).

In 1948, there was an attempt to revitalize the NCMH as a fund-raising organization for the newly established NRC Committee on Human Reproduction, but the effort failed (Reed 1983:271). Instead of Gamble being forced out of a revitalized basic reproductive research organization, the NCMH became a paper corporation, leaving Gamble free to use it as a sponsor for his mostly "applied" contraceptive research projects from 1949 to 1957. His projects consisted primarily of contraceptive standards research and delivery work, with the assistance for some years of Christopher Tietze, a medical statistician and evaluator of family planning programs (Reed 1983:272). In 1957, Gamble and his family established the Pathfinder Fund, a population control research organization, and he turned the NCMH over to Tietze. At this point, Teitze's work under NCMH auspices became wholly sponsored by the Population Council as its "favorite child," in Tietze's words. Ten years later, the NCMH was wholly absorbed into the Population Council's Bio-Medical Division.[33] Thus the NCMH ended up in an appropriately modern home within the reproductive/contraceptive/ population research establishment of the late twentieth century. Its early history, reflecting these heterogeneous commitments, made the NCMH an exemplary funding organization of the American reproductive sciences.

DIRECT FOUNDATION SUPPORT OF REPRODUCTIVE SCIENCES

In addition to large grants to scientific and social action agencies for dis-tribution as reproductive sciences research grants, several major American foundations also directly funded reproductive scientists and centers during the years before World War II. Full documentation of such funding remains to be undertaken. My intent here is merely to sketch the range and extent of such direct funding.[34]

The longest-lived example of direct foundation funding of a center of reproductive research is the Carnegie Institution of Washington's Depart-ment of Embryology, established at the Johns Hopkins Medical School in 1913 (Sabin 1934:303). Before 1940, this department had varied reproduc-tive research foci, but after about 1923 it was an institution at the heart of reproductive physiological and endocrinological research. It also published a major journal in the field, *Carnegie Contributions to Embryology*, which was not limited in content by its title. The following description is found in a report by James Ebert (1975–76:7): "The Department was for five decades the world's leading center for the study of the human embryo. It pioneered in the development of primates for research, having the earliest successful American monkey breeding colony. Using these animals, large strides were made toward understanding menstruation and cyclic changes in the ovaries and uterus, laying much of the groundwork for recent advances in fam-ily planning." Many of the medically oriented reproductive scientists work-ing in the decades up to 1955 spent some parts of their careers there or worked closely with the department's faculty (e.g., Corner 1981). In 1955, the department's focus shifted away from reproductive to molecular topics.

In 1932, the Josiah Macy, Jr., Foundation began to make a series of grants in reproductive science (Osborn 1967:367), including, for example, a grant to Gregory Pincus at Harvard for studies of ovulation (published as *The Eggs of Mammals* in 1936) and a grant to George E. Coghill of the Wistar Institute in Philadelphia for investigations in embryonic development and behavior correlations (Josiah Macy, Jr., Foundation 1950:26). In 1936, the Macy Foundation funded Dr. Ephraim Schorr's research at Cornell Medical School for studies on the correlation of the menstrual cycle with changes in the vaginal epithelium. Schorr was also working with George Papanicolaou at the time. Additional grants were made to C. C. Little at the Jackson Me-morial Laboratory for investigations of the relations between the adrenal cortex and the gonads (Josiah Macy, Jr., Foundation 1955:118–22).

The Markle Foundation, in addition to supporting the NRC Committee on Endocrinology, also provided some direct grants to reproductive scien-tists, among others (Strickland and Strickland 1976). In 1938, for example, it granted $9,000 over three years to Dr. George W. Corner of the Depart-ment of Anatomy of the University of Rochester.[35] (Although Corner was a major reproductive scientist of the interwar years, he was not a recipient of NRC/CRPS support.)

The Milbank Memorial Fund, which was then broadly focused on population research, provided partial support of Raymond Pearl's (e.g., 1932) studies of actual contraceptive practices in Baltimore, studies that were especially significant for their statistical innovations. Pearl was a biologist, initially based in agriculture and later moving to public health, who pursued an array of reproductive investigations that demonstrated the shift from eugenics to population control as eugenics in its own name waned during the 1930s (Allen 1991). Pearl's previous population research studies had been funded by the Rockefeller Foundation as part of the Biological Institute at Johns Hopkins ca. 1925–1930 (Allen 1991:252). After this project, Pearl shifted from a biological interpretation of class differences in fertility to a contraceptive usage interpretation, an important shift in the development of population research with clear implications for contraceptive research and development (Osborn 1967:366).

The most extensive direct foundation support of reproductive scientists and centers prior to World War II seems to have come from the Rockefeller Foundation.[36] There were two main avenues to direct Rockefeller Foundation funding: direct application or recommendation by foundation staff; and direct foundation sponsorship offered to centers of reproductive research initially supported by the NRC/CRPS for some years. The Rockefeller Foundation operated its own programs of support for life sciences research and recruited investigators for such support. Reproductive scientists who were directly funded as individuals by the Rockefeller Foundation included the following.

L. J. Cole, Department of Animal Genetics, University of Wisconsin. Physiology and endocrinology of reproduction in farm animals. Funded for about $6,800 for 1934–36.[37]

George W. Corner, Department of Anatomy, University of Rochester Medical School. Physiology of reproduction in rhesus monkeys. Funded for a total of $13,200 between 1935 and 1938.[38]

William W. Greulich, Department of Anatomy, Yale University School of Medicine. Endocrinological changes in human adolescence. Funded for $36,000 from 1939 to 1941.[39]

Ross G. Harrison, Department of Zoology, Yale University. Experimental embryological investigations. Funded for $22,000 from 1936 to 1938.[40]

Charles B. Stockard, Department of Anatomy, Cornell Medical School (Peekskill Farm). Heredity and development interactions in mammals (dogs). Funded 1925–40 at $25,000 per year, for a total of about $375,000.[41]

As noted previously, the NRC/CRPS had a policy of supporting major centers of reproductive research with key researchers as leaders. After about a decade, the NRC/CRPS membership realized that its ongoing commitments to a limited number of centers were preventing the agency from branching out in new directions. However, the committee did not want to abandon those centers that had more than fulfilled their goals. Negotiations between NRC/CRPS members, Rockefeller Foundation staff, and reproductive scientists resulted in several such centers being transferred from NRC/CRPS sponsorship to direct Rockefeller Foundation sponsorship (discussed in chapter 4), including the following.

Herbert M. Evans, Institute of Experimental Biology, University of California, Berkeley. Reproductive endocrinology and nutritional aspects of reproduction. Transferred from NRC/CRPS to the Rockefeller Foundation in 1929; initial direct grant of $10,000 per year for five years, renewable for five years.[42]

F. L. Hisaw, Biological Laboratories, Harvard University. Reproductive endocrinology. Received NRC/CRPS funds while at the University of Wisconsin; transferred to the Rockefeller Foundation in 1937, with a grant of $18,000 for 1937–41.[43]

Frank L. Lillie/Carl R. Moore, Department of Zoology, University of Chicago. Reproductive endocrinology and physiology. Joint sponsorship by both the Rockefeller Foundation and the NRC/CRPS for 1929–34 through a blanket grant to the University of Chicago for biological sciences research. Complete transfer to direct Rockefeller Foundation support in 1934.[44]

P. E. Smith and E. E. Engle, Department of Anatomy, Columbia University. Reproductive endocrinology. Joint Rockefeller Foundation and NRC/CRPS sponsorship for 1934–38; fully transferred to the Rockefeller Foundation in 1938; annual funding in 1938 was $21,000. From 1934 to 1940, a total of $52,950 was provided to this center.[45]

The Rockefeller Foundation also provided a grant of $2 million to Robert Yerkes and the Yale Laboratory of Primate Biology in Orange Park, Florida, in 1929; some of these funds supported reproductive research (Yerkes 1935; Haraway 1989). There was also a prolonged but ultimately unsuccessful effort on the part of Edwin Embree of the Rockefeller Foundation to start a program in human biology from around 1925 to 1928 (Kohler 1991:125–28). In 1928 Embree himself became president of the Rosenwald Foundation, where he supported the reproduction-related work of E. E. Just on fertilization (Manning 1983). To my knowledge, Just was the only African-American reproductive scientist until after World War II. Rockefeller Foundation patronage during these decades shows a shift from support from wealthy individual patrons to a more bureaucratic and corporate management of funding and programs by scientifically trained experts.[46]

Direct foundation funding of reproductive research prior to World War II was considerable, definitely exceeding $1 million and probably approaching $2 million. The foundations providing such support were certainly in the mainstream of the biomedical research community. Despite the illegitimacy of the reproductive sciences and contraception, research funding was clearly and powerfully forthcoming.

INDUSTRIAL SPONSORSHIP OF REPRODUCTIVE RESEARCH

The most elusive funding source and sponsor of the reproductive sciences is industry. These sources are both historically and contemporarily difficult to ferret out of the historical record, due in some part to the proprietary interests of the companies but also to the controversies attached to sex hormones and other technoscience products of reproductive research.[47] Yet a wide variety of industries contributed funds and materials to university-based reproductive research efforts. The pharmaceutical industry in the United States and Europe also sponsored some reproductive research.

Industry funding and contributions of materials were generally arranged directly with universities or with reproductive scientists themselves, making systematic documentation scant, if not impossible to unearth. For example, Swift and Company, the Chicago meatpacking company, contributed a considerable amount of fresh materials to Frank Lillie's reproductive sciences center at the University of Chicago (Lillie 1917a,b). Mr. Swift himself was a member of the board of directors of the university.[48] Similarly, George Corner's autobiography contains multiple accounts of obtaining sow uteri and ovaries from slaughterhouses, but payment is not mentioned unless the entire sow was purchased. Corner also returned some of his grant funds to the Rockefeller Foundation because "the contribution by various industries of materials" made purchase unnecessary.[49]

The American Meat Packers Association (founded in 1906) transformed itself into the Institute of American Meat Packers (IAMP) in 1919, with a focus on industrial research and the development of new products and by-products. Interestingly, this led to the establishment of a research laboratory by the IAMP at the University of Chicago, not usually a very applied research site.[50] The by-products of mutual interest to the packing industry, pharmaceutical companies, and reproductive scientists were, of course, glandular materials for hormone extraction. The meatpacking industry became the major supplier of such materials both to pharmaceutical houses for use in making organotherapeutic products and to reproductive and other scientists for research purposes (School of Commerce and IAMP

1924:285–88). IAMP research laboratory workers were in contact with reproductive scientists on campus, and members of the IAMP research staff held appointments in university departments, including F. C. Koch's Department of Biochemistry, enabling graduate students to work in the IAMP laboratory. Koch's department worked regularly with Lillie and Moore's center (Clarke 1993). Upon his retirement from the university, Koch himself became director of biochemical research for Armour and Company (American Foundation 1955:1:310–13).

In sharp contrast to the case in the Netherlands, where Organon was founded in 1923 to pursue intensive endocrinological research (Oudshoorn 1994:69), the pharmaceutical industry in the United States seems not to have sponsored much reproductive research prior to World War II, despite the fact that by the 1920s forty-six drug companies had established their own research laboratories (Shryock 1947:132). Moreover, beginning in World War I and continuing in the 1920s and 1930s, the NRC actively fostered cooperative research between universities and industry (Swann 1988:18). In contrast, Shering AG of Berlin, Germany, spent approximately $5 million on endocrinological research during the 1930s, and CIBA of Basel, Switzerland, committed a total of about $1 million (Greep, Koblinsky, and Jaffe 1976:371), though how much of this was for reproductive endocrinology is unclear.

American pharmaceutical companies began to jump on the endocrinological bandwagon in the mid-1930s. For example, by 1940 Abbott Laboratories offered as specialty drugs "the increasingly important gland products, topped by the synthetic hormones Estrone, Estiol, and Progestin," which were marketed directly to physicians by "detail men." In 1940, about five hundred gallons of urine from pregnant mares were used to obtain one ounce of Estrone (Abbott Laboratories 1940:104, 62). Abbott Laboratories, located near Chicago, was the employer of choice for many life sciences graduates of the University of Chicago. Merck, too, entered the fray, instigating research at Rahway, New Jersey, and linking up with chemists at Princeton (Swann 1988:84). Their focus was on the production of "female" hormones for medical treatment of menopause and menstrual problems, Foucault's (1978) "hysterical woman."

Indirectly, however, pharmaceutical companies did contribute to the research budgets of university scientists, often providing research materials. For example, the Wisconsin group, including Hisaw and Fevold, acknowledged that Parke, Davis and Company, E. R. Squibb and Sons, and the Wilson Laboratories had provided dessicated anterior lobe powder for use in research (Long 1990:458). Another practice was the sale of a reproductive scientist's patent by a university to a pharmaceutical company. Such patents were generally secured for development of hormonal isolation, purification, and production procedures. Funds so generated were sometimes returned to the campus research budgets of the scientists who had obtained the patents.[51] The third major pattern of industrial support of university-based scientists was through consultancies. Finally, reproductive scientists often headed up pharmaceutical research departments late in their careers, as was true of Carl Hartman at Ortho and Fred Koch at Armour.

Beginning in 1939, funds for awards with honoraria were provided by pharmaceutical companies to honor outstanding reproductive and other scientists selected by the Endocrine Society. Lisser (1967:24–26) notes that recipients of the thousand-dollar E. R. Squibb and Sons Award (given 1940–53) included George Corner, Phillip Smith, Fred Koch, Edward Doisy, Carl Hartman, Herbert Evans, and C. N. Long. The Ciba Award was established in 1942 to recognize exceptional junior scientists. The Ayerst, McKenna, and Harrison Fellowship began in 1947, the Squibb Fellowship in 1956, the Schering Scholarship began in 1949, and the Upjohn Scholarship in 1955. Postgraduate Assemblies in Endocrinology, also sponsored by the Endocrine Society starting in 1948, held parties using a fund jointly created for the purpose by E. R. Squibb and Sons, Ciba Pharmaceutical Products, Schering Corporation, and Ayerst, McKenna and Harrison (Lisser 1967:20–26).

Standing in direct contrast to such sponsorship was the reluctance of several major American pharmaceutical companies as late as 1950 to become involved in contraceptive research, a reluctance widely noted in the literature. Companies typically feared that negative opinion among Roman Catholics might affect sales or lead to boycotts of all products. The illegitimacy of reproductive and contraceptive research thus extended to the marketplace.[52]

The total value of industrial contributions and payments toward the reproductive research effort is probably indeterminable. But it clearly was significant and must be acknowledged in analyzing funding of the reproductive sciences.

REPRODUCTIVE SCIENCES FUNDING SINCE WORLD WAR II

With the increasing social legitimacy of reproductive and contraceptive research after World War II, funding increased. With the creation of overpopulation as a social problem in the mid-1950s, increases skyrocketed. Greep and his associates (1976:378, 383, 402–3) provided the estimates in Table 9, which include contraceptive research and development as well as reproductive sciences.[53]

There were also some major changes in private sponsorship of the reproductive sciences after World War II. The decline of Rockefeller Foundation support continued as the foundation's investments in molecular biol-

TABLE 9   Private Agency Expenditures on Reproductive
Science in the United States, 1946–74 (in 1976 dollars)

Year	Expenditure
1946–50	1,413,300
1951–55	855,500
1956–60	2,603,000
1961–65	18,600,000
1966–69	unavailable
1970–74	83,080,000
Total	106,551,800

SOURCE: Greep, Koblinsky, and Jaffe 1976:378, 383, 402–3.

ogy expanded and as other private resources appeared on the horizon.
The Rockefeller Foundation seemed to be investing less in earlier hopes for
rational control over human behavior (Morawski 1986:239–40), to which
Weaver wrote his mid-1930s paean that began this book, and more in genetic control over "life itself." Two important new funding entities entered
the reproductive arena during the 1940s and 1950s, both of which were
key to the realignment of the reproductive sciences with (rather than in
opposition to) contraceptive research.

Instead of sponsoring another NRC committee as his father had done,
John D. Rockefeller III founded the Population Council in 1952. He apparently was frustrated in his efforts to lead the Rockefeller Foundation into
more extensive, programmatic, and applied effort in reproduction, population, and contraception. The "philanthropoid" managers of the foundation were loath to have it directly involved in anything as controversial as
birth control—particularly during the McCarthy era, when the foundation
was already under scrutiny by conservatives. A new autonomous organization, the Population Council, was funded initially for about $500,000 per
year (Reed 1983:271, 287). Most of its subsequent funding has come from
Rockefeller sources and the Ford Foundation. The internationally oriented
Population Council became the locus of development of contraceptives requiring medical rather than user initiative such as the IUD and long-acting
hormonal implants such as Norplant. It has emphasized the cultivation of
elite international connections and "quietly identified itself as a neutral,
scientific organization" as part of its strategy to avoid controversy (Onorato
1991:1). By 1957, it had established a research laboratory at the Rockefeller
Institute for Medical Research, where studies focused on stopping sperm
development, immunological methods of fertility control, implants, and
IUDs. The Population Council has become one of a handful of major actors
in the international reproduction/population domain. Rockefeller "lent

the weight of his family's name to give credibility to a cause which could engender considerable controversy."[54]

A second new actor on the scene was the Ford Foundation, which funded reproductive studies extensively from 1959 to 1983 (Hertz 1984). The Ford Foundation's program, situated in its International Division, included both basic reproductive sciences and contraceptive development. Since World War II, this new combination of basic and applied interests has been characteristic of most funding sources. Ford funding ranged from $1.5 million in its first year to a high of about $15 million for 1969, leveling off at about $3 million per year toward the end of its commitment. In addition to research support, the Ford Foundation funded the ambitious Greep reports (1976, 1977) and a series of Karolinska Symposia on Methods in Reproductive Endocrinology in collaboration with the Karolinska Institute of Stockholm and the World Health Organization. Like the NRC/CRPS, the Ford Foundation tended to support major centers of research rather than individual scientists. Its centers have included many that are recognizable from earlier eras of the reproductive sciences, along with new ones.

University of Wisconsin, 1963–82, $2,843,000. Funded in part explicitly because of its intersectional collaborations. Focus was on fertility control through use of ovarian hormones. Directed by R. K. Meyer, Department of Zoology.

Marshall Laboratory, Department of Physiology, Cambridge University, 1963–81, $928,000. Directed initially by Sir Alan Parkes and then by C. R. Austin, with a special readership held by R. G. Edwards. Focus on in vitro fertilization leading to the birth of the world's first "test-tube baby," Louise Brown, in 1978.

Karolinska Institute of Stockholm, 1962–82, $2,277,000. Directed by Egon Diczfalusy, focus was on the physiological role of the fetoplacental unit, and on means for monitoring the course of pregnancy. Became the first Research and Training Center of the World Health Organization Programme in Human Reproduction.

Laboratory of Human Reproduction and Reproductive Biology, Harvard Medical School, 1965–83, initial grant of $3 million for a new building. Directed (in sequence) by Roy Greep, Kenneth Ryan, and John Biggers. Focus on hormonal factors controlling ovulation, implantation, tubal transport, spermatogenesis, and male contraception.

Weitzman Institute, Israel, 1962–83. $3,442,500. Directed by M. C. Shelesnyak and H. R. Lindner. Focus was on the role of histamines in nidation, radioimmunoassays of steroids and other hormones, and ovulation processes.

International Institute for the Study of Human Reproduction, Columbia

University, 1962–83. Initial funding of $6,738,000. This became
the Center for Reproductive Sciences, the Center for Human Male
Infertility, and the Center for Population and Family Health. Directed by Howard C. Taylor.

The Ford Foundation also ran regional and nationwide programs, such as
one in India that focused on primate research and one in Egypt that focused on contraception. One in Chile and Brazil became the Latin American Association for Research in Human Reproduction. The foundation
supported the research and training efforts of the World Health Organization and also sponsored an extensive fellowship program and an array of
international programmatic efforts (Hertz 1984:107–26).

After 1960, the U.S. federal government also became a major funder of
the reproductive sciences. Federal expenditures on reproductive and contraceptive research skyrocketed from a 1961–65 total of about $19 mil-
lion to a 1970–74 total of over $183 million (Greep, Koblinsky, and Jaffe
1976:402–3). Within the National Institutes of Health, funding was provided especially through the National Institute of Child Health and Human
Development (NICHHD), founded in 1963, the year after the NRC/CRPS
was terminated. A Center for Population Research was then developed
within NICHHD in 1968. Federal funding for contraceptive research was
also channeled through the Office of Population of the U.S. Agency for
International Development (USAID) (Mastroianni, Donaldson, and Kane
1990:75).

Mastroianni and his associates (1990:80) provide an update on funding
from 1973 to 1987, helpfully distinguishing between reproductive biology
and contraceptive research in Table 10.[55] This is essentially a continuation
of the earlier chart by Greep and his colleagues, starting just after World
War II. It shows a trend of expanding support both for basic reproductive
sciences and for contraceptive research: "In current dollars, spending for
reproductive biology research more than quadrupled, from $30 million
in 1973 to $135 million in 1987; spending for contraceptive develop-
ment grew from $7 million in 1973 to $36 million in 1987" (Mastroianni,
Donaldson, and Kane 1990:79).

After about 1960, once it was clear that it was both relatively safe and
profitable for pharmaceutical companies to produce contraceptives, industry expenditures on research grew dramatically. Between 1965 and 1974,
the annual industry expenditure on reproductive and contraceptive research was about $12 million. Interestingly, over these same years, the in-
dustry proportion dropped from about 39 percent of the funding to 19
percent, while the government proportion rose from 38 to 61 percent
(Greep, Koblinsky, and Jaffe 1976:402–3). Around 1970, at least half a
dozen major American pharmaceutical companies were each spending sev-

Table 10   Federal and Foundation Funding for Basic
Research in Reproductive Biology and Contraceptive
Development, 1973–87 (in constant 1973 millions of dollars)

Year	Reproductive Biology				Contraceptive Development			
	Total[a]	HHS	AID	Foundations[b]	Total	AID	HHS	Foundations[b]
1973	30.2	22.8		6.7	7.4	2.9	3.2	1.3
1974	33.7	27.6		5.6	9.6	2.1	3.9	3.6
1975	29.7	24.5		4.7	10.3	2.8	5.1	2.3
1976	32.6	27.9		3.4	10.9	3.6	5.3	2.1
1977	29.9	25.6		3.3	14.1	5.3	5.4	3.3
1978	35.6	30.4		3.6	11.8	4.5	4.9	2.4
1979	38.5	33.1		3.6	11.2	4.8	4.5	1.8
1980	39.4	35.4		1.9	10.8	4.3	4.9	1.5
1981	43.1	39.0		2.0	10.6	3.5	4.8	2.3
1982	42.6	38.0		1.9	9.8	3.6	4.4	1.7
1983	44.5	40.8		1.3	9.5	3.4	4.4	1.7
1984	43.0	40.2		.8	9.0	4.5	3.1	1.4
1985	43.4	39.4		1.1	11.6	6.8	3.8	1.0
1986	43.6	38.4		1.5	12.3	7.3	3.6	1.4
1987	49.5	44.4		1.7	13.2	8.1	3.8	1.3

[a]Total includes other federal sources not shown separately in table.
[b]Population council plus Ford, Rockefeller, and Mellon foundations.
SOURCE: Mastroianni, Donaldson, and Kane 1990:80, using unpublished data from the National Institute of Child Health and Human Development (NICHHD), National Institutes of Health, Bethesda, Maryland.

eral million dollars per year on contraceptive research and development. Since that time, however, most have dropped out of research and development participation, others have ceased or been forced to cease distribution of their contraceptive products because of safety problems (discussed in chapter 8), and only one major company (Ortho Pharmaceutical Corporation) still has an active research and development program.[56] Thus the post–World War II era has seen a shift in sponsorship of reproductive and contraceptive research from almost solely private and corporate philanthropy to include both governmental and industrial sponsorship. These new sources were then and remain problematic and unstable.

CONCLUSIONS

Contra Greep and his colleagues (1976), I found that a variety of funding sources were available for the reproductive sciences, most of them highly prestigious and well within the mainstream of the biomedical research community. Given that most external support for *all* types of research was obtained through private philanthropic organizations during this era, the reproductive sciences enterprise was fairly typically funded. It was the stature of such private organizations (including three NRC committees), as well as the stature of the ultimate donors (the Rockefeller, Macy, and Markle Foundations, and the Carnegie Institution of Washington), that were particularly significant. This can perhaps be better appreciated if one recalls that even mainstream feminist organizations were not mentioning, much less supporting, birth control as an issue during the 1920s. Yet during these same years the Rockefeller-funded NRC/CRPS gleaned about 10 percent of all the funding of the NRC itself.[57] Both the funds and the prestige lent crucial legitimacy to the enterprise in the decades before World War II.[58] While the reproductive sciences did not share in initial federal largesse in terms of research support immediately following World War II, by the 1960s federal support had begun expanding to impressive levels. In addition, powerful new foundation support was forthcoming, which helped to consolidate the new alliance among the reproductive sciences, birth control, and population control worlds.

How such funding sources helped to shape research agendas on reproductive topics was addressed in more detail in chapters 4 and 6. We can also take note here of what was, by and large, either not funded or else funded less generously: simple means of contraception (which Margaret Sanger and other feminists had begun requesting from reproductive scientists in 1915); other women's health issues articulated through organizations concerned with women's health (such as the American Medical Women's Association and the Children's Bureau); and more physiological and comparative studies of reproductive phenomena. Instead, focus was on scientific means of contraception to be directed at what Foucault (1978:105) called "the Malthusian couple," with women as the configured users, and on reproductive endocrinological research for hormonal interventions directed almost exclusively at "the hysterical woman."

This entire chapter raises the broader issue of *why* such extensive funding was provided to the reproductive sciences by such prestigious sources despite the illegitimacy of this research. Clearly there were deep commitments among the major foundations to the development of improved means of control over reproduction—including birth control, population control, eugenics, and family planning. Interestingly, explicit discussion of *why* these commitments are important is rare in the archival materials, which tend to focus instead on *how* funding should be spent. The discussion of the illegitimacy of the reproductive sciences to which we next turn should heighten amazement at the existence of any such funding, much less funding of this scale and scope.

PART FOUR

Disciplining Reproduction
in Modernity

CHAPTER EIGHT

Illegitimate Science

Reproducing Controversy

·Addressing controversial science, Norbert Wiener asked (1964:49–50): "I have said that the reprobation attaching in former ages to the sin of sorcery attaches now in many minds to the speculations of modern cybernetics. . . . [But what] is sorcery, and why is it condemned as a sin?" In this chapter, I examine what happens if you replace the word *cybernetics* with *reproductive sciences*. Throughout this book, I have made reference to the multiple ways in which the reproductive sciences have been and continue to be viewed as illegitimate by various sectors of American society.[1] To some social worlds, the reproductive sciences are improper, even sinful, science. The illegitimacy of this work has made the arena of reproduction controversial for all the social worlds and actors involved—human and nonhuman alike. All must confront and cope with its controversial status in some ways.

An appreciation of the extent of the illegitimacy of the reproductive sciences is fundamental to a nuanced and complicated understanding of the formation and development of the American reproductive sciences through the present moment. This chapter, therefore, cuts back through the history of the reproductive sciences across the twentieth century at a different angle. The rest of the book has focused directly or indirectly on efforts to create, cohere, and stabilize this line of scientific work. Here I focus instead on a breathtaking array of efforts to destabilize, resist, and/or reconfigure the work of the reproductive sciences to meet others' agendas. I touch on a wide range of popular cultural, religious, mass media, social movement, and other critical social and cultural interpretations of the reproductive sciences and their technoscientific products—interpretations that have been consequential for that work from the outset. Multiple alternative and critical positions are taken, ranging from those who prefer a more biological rather than endocrinological emphasis to those who see any science of reproduction as blasphemy. Learning to distinguish among such positions is part of the work of reproductive scientists, and hence is important to the present project as well.

Most scientific controversies occur *within* a particular discipline and focus on the validity of findings, substantive issues, methods, theories, or shifting disciplinary boundaries. The problematics in the reproductive sciences are rather different. What makes an entire scientific discipline morally controversial? Latour (1987) has ably argued that science is politics by other means. Schneider (1984:181) points out that "the construction, maintenance and change of morality is profoundly political." Here these two politics intersect: the politics of doing the science confront the politics of changing moralities. The result is a line of scientific work that succeeded in becoming a discipline despite its controversial status for well over a century.

The reproductive sciences intervene in "natural reproduction," which in Western culture had been the moral and ethical norm (Jordanova 1989:51–116). Today, for kinship—family—"If nature has not disappeared, then, *its grounding function has*" (Strathern 1992:195, emphasis in original). And almost everyone knows this. Here the very doing of the science can be construed as demonstrating controversial moral commitments of some kind. Every act of research can be viewed as an immoral and corrupting intervention. Other classic modern examples of controversial disciplines/ immoral science include nuclear physics, environmental studies, and sociobiology. Research in particular areas such as race, gender, or class has often also been morally and politically charged.

My argument is that the reproductive sciences lie at the most extreme end of a continuum of controversy in terms of provoking claims of the illegitimacy of doing the science and developing the technologies at all. They also are at the extreme in provoking other kinds of seriously sustained controversies. Popular media coverage of cloning, infertility treatments, the ongoing American abortion rights and terrorism stories, and the 1994 United Nations International Conference on Population and Development in Cairo has featured the interventions of the reproductive sciences. It is, therefore, much easier in the mid-1990s for me to make this claim about the controversial nature of the reproductive sciences and have it be widely understood than it was when I began making it in the mid-1980s. The day I originally drafted this paragraph, Shannon Lowney and Lee Ann Nichols, receptionists at abortion clinics in Massachusetts, were murdered, shot to death simply because of where they worked.

Two key conditions of social structure place the reproductive sciences at the top of the public agenda. First, reproductive phenomena are at the heart, core, and "soul" of social life for many people. Family and biological kinship matter across an array of social differences that is truly quite stunning. I suspect many of us as modernists and postmodernists lose sight of this nonuniversal but fundamental "social fact." Ruptures in the fabric of familial existence—unwanted pregnancy, abortion, infertility, sexual problems, genetic screening and/or disease, birth, illness, and death—bring reproductive issues into sharp focus. Reproductive issues are simultaneously and inextricably social and individual in ways that deeply problematize them and can create profound conflicts (Petchesky 1984/1990). Reproduction is also deeply culturally, economically, and politically organized in ways that typically remain invisible to us; it is simultaneously very private and highly public; and it is understudied as a social and cultural phenomenon outside the family context (Robertson 1991; Strathern 1992).

Second, like other sciences, the reproductive sciences must be "sold" to various audiences in order to obtain the resources requisite for doing scientific work and for making technoscientific products (e.g., Gieryn 1983; Nelkin 1987). It is fundamentally because of and through these marketing processes that sciences become vulnerable to controversy, for it is through selling a science that nonscientific audiences learn about it. Scientists must claim "that particular scientific findings are useful, that is, relevant to the concerns of the particular audience addressed" and that their science is "socially necessary" (Aronson 1984:13). Such claims became routine after World War I as "extramural" funding was increasingly sought from foundations and government agencies and a rhetoric of usefulness became the basis for justification of spending (Abir-Am 1982). Such sales issues have permeated the development of the reproductive sciences (e.g., Lincoln and Kaeser 1988). The transparency to the public of how basic reproductive sciences could be applied immediately politicizes such claims. The authority of Western sciences has rested to some degree on assumptions about scientific neutrality (Proctor 1988; Longino 1990). However, in the reproductive arena, there is no neutral position, and most people are aware of this. Alternatively, in science studies terms, we might state that in the case of reproduction there is no boundary between science and society (Gieryn 1995). In fact, the reproductive sciences have been built upon the transparencies of both social life and their own technoscientific products. Political challenges and moral crusades abound and will continue.

The fates of all the reproductive sciences have been intertwined, but they are not identical. While a particular controversy may affect reproductive scientists in biology or medicine more than in agriculture, or vice versa, all are implicated. In fact, unlike many other lines of scientific work where the relationship of basic research to applied and clinical potentials is opaque, for the reproductive sciences in all three professional contexts, the applications of each are transparent to many if not most public constituencies. This has created a sustained sense of vulnerability among reproductive scientists.[2]

Situating illegitimate/controversial science and technology more broadly, Nelkin (1995) points out that, over the past few decades, science has increasingly become an arena in which to battle out deeply contested values in American society. The broader critique of technoscience has moved from superficial and dichotomous framings such as "modern magicians" and "science as miracle" versus Drs. Frankenstein and Strangelove to include discourses on risks, benefits, and trade-offs. Many social movements have become exceptionally sophisticated about relevant lines of scientific work, including AIDS, breast cancer, and feminist women's health movements.[3] Some critics are not only questioning research practices but also challenging the values undergirding research and asking whether certain kinds of research should be done at all. Such assertions can be made on both structural and moral grounds.

Moreover, growing public awareness of conflicts within science, and of scientists' enrollment as advocates by heterogeneous social actors (from cigarette companies to space agencies), have led to demands for more democratic participation in the direction and regulation of science and technology. Ezrahi has stated: "In the closing decades of the twentieth century, the intellectual and technical advances of science coincide with its visible decline as a force in the rhetoric of liberal democratic politics" (Nelkin 1995:447). I would argue that what is in decline is science as an *autonomous* force, and that it is science's autonomy and its lack of social accountability that are being and will continue to be challenged by different constituencies to allow broader democratic participation. This theme echoes throughout the chapter.

My definition of controversy is based in an interactionist arena model. An arena is composed of interested social worlds—groups or constituencies that care enough about some issues to do something about them. Controversy derives from the collision of these constituencies' different perspectives on what should happen, when, how, where, and how much. Constituencies typically back up their political/moral commitments by allocating resources, organizing, and generating public voices to advance their perspectives over and against others. Controversies thus occur where different social worlds meet in arenas of some sort.[4]

To understand controversy on a sociological level, it is important to grasp the perspectives of all arena participants. In the reproductive arena, constituencies include the reproductive sciences, family planning and population control worlds, religious groups, new eugenicists and geneticists, feminist and other consumer groups focused on health, investigators, technologies themselves and the means of their production, pharmaceutical companies and associations, research funding sources (foundations and governments), regulatory entities, professional associations, and so on. None of these sets of actors is monolithic or uniform. All actors who have participated in the development of the American reproductive sciences are somehow involved and implicated in controversies that affect the arena. All of the humans seek legitimacy, authority, and power to further their causes.[5]

In the next section I lay out the illegitimacy argument more fully. Then I address the four major realms in which controversies around the reproductive sciences have taken place over the past century: their association with sexuality and reproduction, with controversial social movements, with clinical quackery, and with the ability to create "brave new worlds." I then turn to a discussion of reproductive scientists' strategies for managing the illegitimacy of their identities and their work. Finally I examine some of the consequences of illegitimacy for the reproductive sciences as an enterprise and for scientists' careers.

THE ILLEGITIMACY ARGUMENT

One of the striking features of reproductive physiology as a line of scientific work was the lateness of its development in comparison with the physiology of other major organ systems. The most common explanation for this lateness emphasizes the illegitimacy of the topic of reproduction: largely because of its association with sexuality, reproduction was not considered a dignified scientific subject and therefore was eschewed by most serious scientists. Countervailing forces were requisite for the reproductive sciences to be worth legitimacy risks for scientists and their institutions. These forces were composed of emergent markets for scientific knowledge about reproduction, including academic departments of biology, medicine, and agriculture, along with birth control, eugenics, and neo-Malthusian movements and philanthropic organizations. These social movements aided reproductive researchers initially by placing reproductive topics at the center of public discussion—bringing them "out of the closet" through the development of a public forum on human reproductive issues between 1900 and 1920. The stature of many advocates—elite groups of scientists, physicians, philanthropists, and other professionals—also enhanced legitimacy. Subsequently, these movements became powerful and well-funded consumer markets and sponsors of the reproductive sciences. Other major markets were animal production industries and the medical specialties of obstetrics and gynecology, as illustrated in Figure 4. Both animal production industries and birth control movements were at the forefront in articulating goals of control over reproduction throughout the "Chain of Being." The "laws of nature" could now be replaced by the scientific ingenuity of humans as the means and mechanisms of rationalization passed from the factory to agricultural and social life.

"New reproductive technologies" for humans have been refined and applied since about 1970. Often initiated in earlier eras in agricultural reproductive sciences, these technologies include artificial insemination, sex preselection by means of sperm filtration, superovulation, embryo recovery and transfer, synchronized estrus, and genetic cloning.[6] Over the past decades, most of these technologies have been applied as infertility treatments in humans, adding considerably to current controversies in the reproductive arena.

Controversy can cut at least two ways. On one hand it can thrust a field into disrepute; on the other it can be the basis of organizing both supporters and opponents, with varied consequences (cf. Maienschein 1994). For example, it was, ironically, the organization of British *anti*vivisectionists and their legislative agenda in late-nineteenth-century Britain that led to the founding of the Physiological Society to oppose them (Sharpey-Shafer 1927)! Similar ironies abound in the following analysis.

Association with Sexuality and Reproduction

The first realm of controversy concerns the explicit focus on sexuality and reproduction, which is considered improper and illegitimate by at least some constituencies in most human societies. M. C. Chang (Chang et al. 1977:434), along with Gregory Pincus one of the developers of the Pill, said: "The connection between reproduction and sex has always evoked a degree of emotional inhibition in both Western and Eastern countries. In early times, except for a few embryologists, the study of reproduction was in the hands of animal breeders and gynecologists interested in the improvement of fertility or the cure of sterility." Consequently, the reproductive sciences, and reproductive scientists, have often been stigmatized (Goffman 1963). The very doing of reproductive research was, to some, "dirty work" in Hughes's (1971) sense of work that somehow impugns, sullies, and discredits the identities of those who do it.

This impugning of identity may have very early origins. It has long been known that the renowned English surgeon and anatomist John Hunter (1728–93) had successfully transplanted cock testes into hens. Though he reported this only briefly, specimens remain preserved in London. Money (1983:391–92) suggests that Hunter may have "refrained from reporting to avoid publicity and the possible accusation of witchcraft. Fallout from the gruesome centuries of the Inquisition had still to be reckoned with . . . and crowing hens and sexually denatured men and beasts were signs of witchcraft."

The interests of the Roman Catholic Church in sex and reproduction have been extensive (e.g., Horn 1994; Kertzer 1994). Such religious concerns were a constant backdrop, and were sometimes foregrounded, during the formation of the reproductive sciences. Some of the major debates in the history of modern science took up related controversial issues, such as that between Geoffroy and Cuvier (Appel 1987) and between Pasteur and Pouchet (Farley and Geison 1974; Geison 1995). Both of these nineteenth-century debates raised the specter of science as blasphemy and had what we would now refer to as "chilling effects" on certain lines of scientific work. But it should be clear that not only the Catholic Church but also many other religious bodies have proscribed public elaboration of the facts of sexuality and reproduction. Such prohibitions also seep deeply into popular culture.

An early-twentieth-century example concerns the founding of the National Research Council Committee for Research in Problems of Sex (NRC/CRPS) in 1921, which almost foundered around issues of impropriety. According to Aberle and Corner (1953:1), "There had been in the United States no coordinated effort to bring all the available knowledge to a useful focus or to encourage intensive research in the field. It was in fact first necessary to establish and defend the dignity of such studies." The first barrier confronted by the committee's sponsors was finding an administrative home within the NRC. After the Division of Anthropology and Psychology refused to sponsor the committee, the proposal was then greeted coolly by the Division of Medical Sciences, despite promised external support through Rockefeller funds. Only when a physician familiar with venereal disease became chairman of the medical division did the proposal succeed. In ways that foretold the future, the linkage to clinical work carried the day.

The NRC/CRPS sponsored publication of *Sex and Internal Secretions* (Allen, ed., 1932) which, as described in chapter 5, was the bible of the American reproductive sciences for fifty years. In his foreword to the third edition, George Corner (1961:x–xi, emphasis added) observed:

> The younger readers of this book will hardly be able to appreciate the full significance of such an alliance between biologists, psychologists, and physicians on one hand, and social philanthropists on the other. It represented a major break from the so-called Victorian attitude which in the English-speaking countries had long impeded scientific and sociologic investigations of sexual matters and placed taboos on open consideration of human mating and childbearing as if these essential activities were intrinsically indecent. *To investigate such matters, even in the laboratory with rats and rabbits, required of American scientists . . . a certain degree of moral stamina. A member of the . . . Committee once heard himself introduced by a fellow scientist to a new acquaintance as one of the men who had "made sex respectable."*

Many early investigators who did select reproductive problems felt they were placing themselves beyond the pale of propriety by doing so. They repeatedly stated to the NRC/CRPS that reluctant administrators in their universities had finally approved their proposed investigations only because they had the backing of an NRC grant (Aberle and Corner 1953:89). Frank Lillie (1938:68–69) wrote: "We are accustomed in our free society to hold that the development of all science is good; in certain countries less free it is ruled that only those aspects of science that contribute to their special national ideologies are good. But there is agreement that in science is power. . . . [Yet science] has often had to fight its way . . . [and] restrictions are placed on the teaching of the facts concerning human reproduction."

On a more humorous note (and humor is a key strategy used by reproductive scientists to manage controversy), Carl Hartman reported that his paper "How Large Is the Human Egg?" was rejected by the *Ladies' Home Journal* as too close to the pornographic! It ended up in *Scientific American.* Further, when George Streeter, the head of the Carnegie Department of Embryology, was asked to give a public talk about human developmental anomalies, he was cautioned not to use the word *uterus.* For Solly Zuckerman's lecture before the Royal Society, "he was told he must not use the term menstrual cycle as laymen would be present and even women!" (Hartman 1967:6).

The uproar in the 1950s over Alfred Kinsey's research demonstrates the continuity of opprobrium adhering to sex-related topics (Pomeroy 1982). It cost Kinsey some of his research funding. George Corner (1981:316), then chair of the NRC/CRPS, reported that when the Rockefeller Foundation was under attack as a left liberal organization by "rabid anti-Communists of the McCarthy type" during the early 1950s, Dean Rusk, the head of the foundation, surreptitiously called him. Rockefeller Foundation support of Kinsey through the NRC was soon terminated.

The association of the reproductive sciences with issues of sexuality and sex education remains highly problematic today (e.g., Booth 1989; Holden 1989). In 1991, a major study of human sexuality, led by sociologist Edward Laumann of the University of Chicago, was defunded by the National Institute on Child Health and Human Development (NICHHD) of the National Institutes of Health (NIH). Intended to update Kinsey's research, now over forty years old, the research was also intended to improve AIDS prevention education. Laumann responded that it "challenges the integrity of the whole system of peer review. It represents a chilling of the scientific discipline" (Moffat 1991:1483). A much abridged study has been completed (Laumann et al. 1994). On the lighter side, a recent joke does illustrate change: A man goes into a drugstore and says to the druggist, "I'll have a dozen condoms, please." Then he leans forward and says, under his breath, "And a pack of Marlboros" (Treichler 1993).

The stigmatization of the reproductive sciences because of associations with sexuality could be viewed as a self-constructed and self-serving myth used rhetorically by scientists to improve their status. However, the historical record supports scientists' claims to being hobbled in the competition for respect and resources.[7] Of course, this does not mean that their stigmatization did not also help their cause in some situations, especially with certain funding sources. Scientists' appeals for support assuredly drew upon this aspect in constructing "progressive" research programs (e.g., Aberle and Corner 1953).

Association with Controversial Social Movements

The reproductive sciences have long been associated with the birth control, eugenics, and population control movements, and thus both directly and indirectly with national and international imperialism. All three social movements share the goal of enhanced control over human reproduction, although their emphases differ considerably. Separating sexuality from reproduction is controversial, and all three of these science-based social movements have sought to do so for over a century. During the first half of this century, American reproductive scientists valiantly attempted to distinguish their work from these quite controversial movements. But after World War II, this became increasingly difficult and, for many reproductive scientists, an undesirable strategy. The association of the reproductive sciences with these controversial social movements has been complicated, producing both positive and negative consequences for those sciences. Initially, these movements generated much support, funding, and legitimacy for the scientific study of reproductive phenomena. But they have also served to mobilize oppositional and/or critical movements focused on five major issues related to the reproductive sciences: contraception, abortion, sterilization, infertility services, and reproductive (especially fetal) research.

Historically, Roman Catholic and other religious groups have opposed the reproductive sciences as enhancing the capacity for intervention in natural processes, viewed by them as sinful. There have been papal encyclicals against abortion (Mohr 1978:186–87), against sterilization for contraceptive eugenic purposes (Editor 1931:73), against "unnatural" methods of contraception, and against infertility treatments (E. Moore 1931; Dienes 1972). Birth control advocates were highly sensitive to Catholic objections, and a significant impetus in the 1940s to rename the movement "family planning" and/or "planned parenthood" and to begin offering infertility services was intended to address Roman Catholics and gain legitimacy (Gordon 1976; Reed 1983). "Morality is first and foremost a matter of how things are named" (Schneider 1984:182).

The fight for legal abortion, like that for legal contraception in the United States, was long, is ongoing, and has become violent to the point of full-blown terrorism and multiple murders.[8] The antiabortion movement has increasingly extended its objections to contraceptive research and to federal and state distribution of contraception through family planning programs (e.g., Rosoff 1988). There has clearly been a chilling environment in the United States for RU486, the "French abortion pill," also used as a morning-after pill, although it is now being tested here.[9] Moreover, antiabortionists' increased use of fetal imagery in popular appeals has had negative consequences for fetal research on reproductive and other problems (CIBA Foundation 1986; Petchesky 1987), although reproductive and other scientists have developed new guidelines for such research (Gerrity 1993; Annas and Elias 1989).

Sterilization abuse—terminating the reproductive capacity of women and men without their full knowledge, understanding, or consent—has a long history in the United States that has done little to advance the reproductive sciences. Eugenic sterilization laws of the first half of the twentieth century, aimed largely at institutionalized retarded and mentally ill people, fell into disrepute with the rise of the Nazis. Further controversies related to sterilization without consent have erupted, concerning "Mississippi appendectomies" in the American South during the civil rights movement, several cases of abuse of Black, Mexican, and Native American women during the 1970s, and cases involving poor women in Puerto Rico and Central America. Then and now these controversies are reinvoked via "temporary sterilization" threats to welfare mothers, including requiring use of implanted contraceptives such as Norplant. To many communities, especially communities of color in the United States and elsewhere, the reproductive sciences and their technoscientific products are viewed as tools of racist repression and coercion.[10] It was no accident that *The Bell Curve* took up the fertility of African-American and Latina women along with IQ (Herrnstein and Murray 1994), despite scientists' repudiation of any biological "meaning" of race.

Over time, the association of the reproductive sciences with controversial social movements has both benefited the reproductive sciences and entrenched them ever more deeply in highly controversial arenas. In the eyes of some constituencies, it has made reproductive scientists "moral entrepreneurs" (Becker 1963) by the very nature of their work.

Association with Clinical Quackery

The third realm of controversy is the historical and contemporary association of the reproductive sciences with clinical quackery and problematic or hotly debated treatments. The modern form of this association began with one of the "founding fathers" of the modern scientific study of reproduction, Charles-Edouard Brown-Séquard (1817–94). This renowned French neurologist and physiologist taught in the United States, did major work on the adrenal glands, and assumed famed physiologist Claude Bernard's chair at the Collège de France upon Bernard's death in 1878 (Olmstead 1946). In 1889, he made the following announcement: "I sent to the Society of Biology a communication, which was followed by several others, showing the remarkable effects produced on myself by subcutaneous injection of a liquid obtained by the maceration on a mortar of the testicle of a dog or of a guinea pig to which one has added a little water" (Medvei 1982:289). Many people thought this could be the start of something big. As documented by Borell (1976a:309): "Within weeks, testicular extract was being given to patients with every kind of illness. Within two years, many physicians thought that not only the testes but every organ of the body possessed some active principle which might be of immediate therapeutic value. Organotherapy, or the method of Brown-Séquard, as it was often called, came to be the therapeutic hope of physicians from Cleveland to Bucharest." Brown-Séquard had considerable scientific stature—he was a fellow of the Royal College of Physicians, a Fellow of the Royal Society, and recipient of an honorary degree from Cambridge University (Medvei 1982:291). Three weeks after his announced use of testicular extract, the *British Medical Journal* snidely reported it in an article titled "The Pentacle of Rejuvenescence," referring to a symbol used in magic (Borell 1976b). Reflecting on these events some years later, the reproductive endocrinologist Herbert Evans said, "Endocrinology suffered obstetric deformity in its very birth" (Borell 1978:283).

Shortly after Brown-Séquard's work, the discovery that extracts of thyroid alleviated myxedema (1891) and the identification of adrenaline (1894) and secretin (1902) added fuel to the organotherapy fire between clinicians and laboratory scientists. The "use of organ extracts by practitioners . . . quickly outstripped study of these same preparations by experimentalists" (Borell 1985:3). Both were viewed as new miracles of scientific medicine. Sensationalism endured. Well into the 1920s, Harvey Cushing of Harvard was still concerned about practitioners' prescription of dubious substances to "credulous people" (Medvei 1982:504). Another endocrinologist wrote: "Certain therapeutic products are particularly suited to the game of racketeers. . . . The products of the endocrine glands are also particularly adapted to exploitation" (Pottenger 1942:846). The resulting "tension between the clinic and the laboratory became a major feature of the early years of endocrinological research"; this was especially true with regard to the evaluation of extracts of the testes and ovaries, where "particularly controversial therapeutic claims were made" (Borell 1985:4).

Two other ultimately hormonal interventions to achieve rejuvenation— also both for men—were popular. One was a surgery that internally opened the vas deferens so that sperm were resorbed rather than exiting the body. Perfected by Eugen Steinach in Vienna, the technique was informally called the "Steinachschnitt" (Steinach-cut) in a play on words echoing

"Caesarschnitt" for Caesarian section in women. (Later, Hitler's forced sterilizations were called "Hitlerschnitts.") A number of well-known men underwent this surgery, including Freud (Sengoopta 1993). American reproductive scientist Carl Moore at the University of Chicago engaged in
prolonged debate with Steinach about his claims of hormonal antagonism
on which this surgery was based.

The most outrageous therapeutic claims were made in what came to
be called "the monkey gland affair" (Hamilton 1986). Several practitioners
transplanted monkey and other testes into men, sheep, prize bulls, horses,
and dogs for purposes of sexual and geriatric rejuvenation. The most renowned practitioner was Serge-Samuel Voronoff, Russian émigré to France,
a surgeon who held an appointment in physiology at the Collège de France.
Voronoff began his testicular transplantation practice in 1917, operating on
hundreds of men and animals in Europe and the Middle East through 1930,
when the surgery began to lose credibility. Another major practitioner was
the American John R. Brinkley, who advertised his goat gland transplants
on his own radio station in rural Kansas and ran for governor. Despite his
dubious medical credentials, Brinkley became a millionaire. Other practitioners used similar approaches. Interestingly, it was agricultural scientists
who first seriously criticized Voronoff's lack of scientific method in his efforts to create "supersheep." They especially criticized the omission of random selection for treatment and the lack of control groups. Scientific developments also contributed to the gradual abandonment of the surgery,
notably animal studies of the actual effects of testosterone and Mayo clinic
research on graft rejection that essentially repudiated the effectiveness
of glandular grafting (Hamilton 1986:136–37). But the popular press was
riveted and created an intense public discourse (Rechter 1997). That discourse echoes even today in connection with DHEA, the new candidate for
"the hormone of youth." Samuel Yen and Etienne E. Baulieu, the latter
famous for his work on the development of the abortifacient RU486, are
pursuing trials of DHEA (Perlman 1995). In 1997, the National Institute
on Aging began distributing public service announcements for TV and radio warning men of the potential dangers of hormones such as DHEA and
melatonin (Rosenblatt 1997).

Why did these extracts and surgeries seem so reasonable to so many—
scientists, physicians, and lay people alike? The promise of clinical endocrinology was at its height. Organotherapy had achieved signal successes with
insulin and thyroid extracts. And transplantation techniques had been pioneered by Nobelist Alexis Carrel of the Rockefeller Institute. Glandular
transplantation linked these cutting-edge sciences in *clinical* practice, for it
made both common and medical sense that transplanting a gland would
have beneficial effects. Moreover, specific testicular therapy to aid rejuvenescence and sexual capacity built upon John Hunter's eighteenth-century

transplantations and Brown-Séquard's technique of ingesting testicular extracts for these purposes. Medical miracles were becoming commonplace.
Last, and very far from least, as Sengoopta notes (1993:55), "Much of this
research was conceived along accepted scientific doctrine of the time."

In its effects on the legitimacy of the sciences, organotherapeutic sensationalism cut two ways. On the one hand, according to laboratory scientists,
it cast an illegitimate pall over endocrinology through continued association with quackery. On the other hand, it brought publicity to the science
of hormone study as offering great clinical promise. When more biologically controlled substances were found specifically effective, prestige was
heightened. Sensational or not, endocrinology was cutting-edge research,
and the reproductive sciences benefited from the association, especially
between the two world wars.[11]

Subsequently a wide array of drugs and clinical treatments, developed
through the reproductive sciences and built upon principles of organotherapy, have caused serious and extended controversies of several types.
In the late 1930s, diethylstilbestrol (DES), a synthetic estrogenic substance,
began to be used for numerous "female problems" associated with reproduction. Its carcinogenic risks were ignored by clinicians despite researchers' repeated publication of evidence.[12] One use was in estrogen replacement therapy (ERT) for menopausal women, the sequelae of which
have included cancer and other serious problems, generating heated debate
about its necessity and the means used to convince patients of its worth.
Prescription of ERT is much higher in the United States, with its for-profit
health system, than, for example, in the British National Health Service.[13]

ERT was specially promoted from the outset, as the following excerpt
from an article in *Fortune Magazine* on "Abbott Laboratories" (1940:62) illustrates. The article describes a (seemingly fictitious) meeting between
"Mr. Miller," the Abbott traveling sales representative (or "detail man"),
and "Dr. Brush":

> The subjects of vitamins and sex hormones came up without any effort; ev-
> erybody was talking about them these days. . . . Mr. Miller felt encouraged to
> chat with assurance about epithelial stimulation, the work of Doisy, and the
> definition of the International Units; wisely ducked all discussion of dosage
> (because of the trickiness of the substance), and offered to have the medical
> director in Abbott's home office write to Dr. Brush. Estrone was too expensive
> for routine sampling, but Miller resolved to wangle a half-dozen 1-mg. am-
> poules ($4.89 wholesale) for Dr. Brush if he could.

Thus was Brown-Séquard's organotherapeutic tradition sustained in *Fortune
Magazine* a half century later, as was the controversy.

Even more provocative of controversy were the sequelae of the use of
DES by pregnant women to prevent miscarriage, begun during World War

II and approved by the FDA in 1947. Because DES had not been patented, it could be distributed for profit by any pharmaceutical company. Again, warnings of serious problems were ignored, only to resurface in 1971 with diagnoses of adenocarcinoma of the cervix in daughters of women who took DES in pregnancy, various congenital sexual abnormalities in their sons, and higher rates of infertility in both. Probably about 20,000 to 100,000 DES-exposed babies were born every year between 1960 and 1970 (Bell 1980:6). More than sixty-seven different brand-name preparations containing DES and related substances may have been prescribed to pregnant women.[14] A strong "victims" movement for education, research, and improved clinical treatment has extended the controversy.[15]

DES had major consequences in agriculture as well. It was widely used in feedlots during the 1950s and 1960s to accelerate weight gain in cattle. The original research for this had been undertaken at Iowa State College and, in 1954, "according to [Wise] Burroughs, placing 11 milligrams of the hormone in the daily ration . . . 'resulted in 37 percent faster gains, 15 percent greater corn consumption, 20 per cent less feed required per pound of gain, and 1/6 less costs per pound' . . . [with] no side effects during the feeding period. . . . Word leaked out that something big was afoot at Iowa State," and promotion of DES was extensive (Marcus 1993:81–82; 1995). As late as 1978, over thirty tons of DES were used annually as an animal feed additive because it dramatically reduced the costs of meat production. In 1979 the FDA withdrew its approval for feedlot use when DES was detected in edible tissue as long as seven days after administration. DES implants, however, were used illegally after that date, causing further controversy. Some breast cancer activists attribute the recent rise in breast cancer rates in the United States to consumption of additives such as DES in meats and other foods. "Natural" beef, guaranteed to be unexposed to additives, has been one industry response, a particular market niche.[16]

Contraceptives such as the Pill, IUDs, and injectables like Depo-Provera have also generated many public, heated, and prolonged controversies since the 1930s. Contested issues have included the general morality of contraception, the ethics of contraceptive testing and distribution in Third World countries and other areas with limited medical follow-up, coercion into use, medical risks to users, and fears of "medicalization" of women's health.[17] Women's health movements in the United States and transnationally have mounted powerful campaigns against the birth control pill (Seaman 1969/ 1980; Ruzek 1978); against FDA approval of Depo-Provera as a contraceptive (Rakusen 1981; National Women's Health Network 1985); and in support of women maimed and killed by the Dalkon Shield IUD (Mintz 1985; Grant 1992; Hicks 1994). Seemingly all IUDs are capable of causing infections that can lead to infertility, a risk vehemently noted by more cautious clinicians in the 1930s. Only a very few IUDs are currently on the U.S.

market. One company planning to manufacture and distribute another kind will not carry product liability insurance and will be fiscally structured so that it can quickly go into bankruptcy while protecting its assets should consumer product liability grow too costly (Klitsch 1988).

The most recent controversies surrounding contraception center on hormonal implants (notably Norplant) and on vaccines. Norplant, which is effective for about five years, consists of six Silastic rods containing the progestin levonorgestrel. The rods are implanted in the upper arm during outpatient surgery. Developed by the Population Council and produced since 1983, the implants had been used by about half a million women by 1990. In poorer countries, the major medical risks are anemia and liver problems; many women may also be coerced into using the implants (a problem also common in the West). Difficulties in removal are common (usually because of extensive scar tissue buildup at the implant sites). There have been claims as well that clinical trials did not obtain adequately informed consent from participants.

In addition to implants, several vaccines focused on intervening in the action of sperm, eggs, and (especially) hormones are coming into use. The risks here are autoimmune diseases, compromised immunity adding to AIDS risks, unwanted permanent sterility, and risks to fetuses of unknown or subsequent pregnancy. Both implants and vaccines require more elaborate health care systems than are available in much of the world. Provider refusal to remove Norplant during clinical trials in Egypt despite repeated requests was documented. Some women's health groups have called for research on vaccines to be stopped completely, especially because of the associated increased risk of AIDS and other sexually transmitted diseases. Numerous suits involving problematic removal of Norplant have been filed in the United States, with considerable national media coverage, even though the implant has only been available for a short time.[18]

Today, American pharmaceutical companies consider federal regulation of contraceptive research and development so stringent, and the risks of product safety liability so high, that few are willing to undertake such work (e.g., Mastroianni, Donaldson, and Kane 1990). A movement for federal sponsorship of private pharmaceutical contraceptive research and development has been growing.[19] The days of birth control as a modern medical miracle are over.

Thus not only those who oppose the use of birth control but also health care consumers seeking safe and reliable modern scientific contraception and other reproduction-related medications and treatments have objected to the reproductive sciences.[20] Many feminists consider it no accident that no hormonal or implantable contraceptives have been developed for men (Lissner 1992) in the thirty-five years since the start of the "Contraceptive Revolution." Many believe the exclusive focus on women reflects a sustained intentionality on the part of developers that women should bear the burden of contraception as well as of pregnancy and birth. Certainly the many agencies sponsoring contraceptive research during these decades have not strongly promoted development of male methods (Oudshoorn 1995, 1996b, 1997a). An ambitious national and transnational infrastructure of women's health groups has emerged, consisting largely of nongovernmental organizations committed to improving the situations of women concerning contraception and health broadly conceived. Part of their task is technology assessment and organizing resistance as appropriate. Despite over twenty-five years of such efforts, feminist women's health activists in interaction with reproductive scientists do not feel heard or understood. A recent paper was titled "Are We Speaking the Same Language? Women's Health Advocates and Scientists Talk about Contraceptive Technology" (Germain 1993). In these spheres of activity, controversy is quite unlikely to abate. Instead it could intensify.[21]

Other reproduction-related treatments, such as infertility treatments, have been extensively scrutinized over the past decade. One study placed the average cost of in vitro deliveries at $72,000 (Associated Press 1995). Misrepresentation of conception and delivery rates has been a grave charge against some facilities, leading to new legislative efforts at regulation of a range of laboratory practices (Gerrity 1993). Laboratory registration, certification, inspection, and participation in proficiency testing are all now (varyingly) mandated by law, affecting reproductive endocrinology, andrology, and embryology. Several professional societies collaborated in developing the new regulations. Still, public and media opinion are mixed at best. While in 1996 the *New York Times* ran a front-page series on the miracles of infertility treatments (Gabriel 1996), the *Ladies Home Journal* ran a critical piece focused on the high costs for patients and high profits for service providers (Fessenden 1996).

The reproductive sciences have long been associated with an array of practices that can be described as quackery and with medical interventions that have been disastrous for patients/consumers. Some of these disasters were scientifically unnecessary. The lack of accountability, other than through product liability (itself now threatened by federally imposed limitations in the United States), seems to place the reproductive sciences quite visibly outside the social order—at risk of a continuing reputation as "outlaw science."

Association with "Brave New Worlds"

Since the turn of the twentieth century, the reproductive sciences have been associated by some constituencies with creating "brave new worlds," evoking Huxley's (1932) dystopia. Here the reproductive sciences are viewed as rupturing the situatedness of human reproduction in "nature," as "natural" and properly inviolate phenomena. The reproductive sciences thereby challenge or threaten the "natural order" of life. They substitute a technological order, usually with scientists "at the helm," as Sanger put it. Such accusations have taken many forms over the years.

The first dramatic events in this realm were Jacques Loeb's experiments in artificial parthenogenesis. In 1899, Loeb succeeded in artificially producing normal larvae from the unfertilized eggs of the sea urchin by altering the inorganic salt solutions in which the urchins lived. This process had formerly required the sperm of the male urchin. Suddenly the physical chemistry that Loeb believed should be the basis of modern biology "could be a tool for altering the basic process of reproduction" (Pauly 1987:93). Loeb was a major public figure in turn-of-the-century biology who held a number of prestigious university positions at Chicago, Berkeley, and the Rockefeller Institute. He has come to symbolize both the pioneering and the ultimate success of reductionist approaches in the life sciences, such as molecular biology. Loeb served as the model for the modern research scientist in Sinclair Lewis's *Arrowsmith*. His work brought him both scientific fame and popular notoriety as a modern Faust through popular accounts of his work in newspapers and magazines. Loeb believed that control over both heredity and reproduction could and should be achieved. Moreover, as Pauly notes (1987:94): "The invention of artificial parthenogenesis represented an attack on the privileged status of natural reproduction. . . . The possibility of human parthenogenesis, the sort of basic social reformation to which science could provide the key, was evident from the start. Artificial parthenogenesis was a vindication of Loeb's hopes and a model for science to come, in which biologists would constantly work to reconstruct the natural order to make it more rational, efficient and responsive to the ongoing development of engineering science." Such programs for "man remaking the world in his own image" have not always been well received.

Gregory Pincus was one of the next generation of biologists to carry Loeb's mantle. Unlike Loeb, Pincus became a full-fledged reproductive scientist. Born into a family of agricultural scientists, he brought practical as well as theoretical concerns to bear upon his work. Pincus's early efforts focused on artificial insemination, in vitro fertilization, and artificial parthenogenesis. In 1934, his work on in vitro fertilization became a hot media item. The story on the science page of the *New York Times* contained the headline "Rabbits Born in Glass: Haldane-Huxley Fantasy Made Real by Harvard Biologists." This referred directly to Huxley's (1932) work *Brave New World,* which itself was based on a book by British geneticist J. B. S. Haldane.[22] In 1936, Pincus declared that he had succeeded in producing artificial parthenogenesis in the rabbit. The media renamed the process "Pincogenesis," which may well have been a form of red-baiting given

Pincus's progressive politics. Whether Pincus had actually succeeded has been hotly debated.[23] Regardless, reception of this work by the media was dubious and sometimes highly negative, making it important for our understanding of the illegitimacy of the reproductive sciences. This was in sharp contrast to the neutral to miraculous portrayals that had greeted Loeb's similar efforts in an earlier era when the miracles of modern science were unquestioned. An article on Pincus's work in *Collier's* in 1937, titled "No Father to Guide Them," combined antifeminism, anti-Semitism, and criticism of the "tricks" that biologists were playing on nature in what historian Reed (1983:323) termed a "subtle but vicious report." The article caused a sensation in Cambridge. Pincus was soon denied tenure at Harvard and eventually ended up at the Worcester Foundation for Experimental Biology (Pauly 1987). It was there Margaret Sanger and Katharine McCormick went in 1953 to get him to continue his work on reproduction that led to the Pill (as described in chapter 6). Pincus was thus connected with two realms of reproductive scientific controversy—problematic treatments and brave new worlds. Squier (1995) characterized such early twentieth-century visions as "babies in bottles."

More recent reproductive science applications such as artificial insemination, in vitro fertilization, embryo transfer, superovulation, sex preselection, and related technologies in humans, including their use in surrogacy arrangements, have received constant media coverage over the past decade. On the one hand, consumers both recognize and express appreciation of the daring of reproductive scientists. For example, an unsolicited letter to a developer of sex preselection techniques said, "Thank you for being brave enough to develop your sperm separation technique. I'm sure you get threatening mail saying you are tampering with a divine process." Another consumer wrote, "It must take much bravery to even enter such 'sacred ground' as sex selection" (Chico 1989:224). In the United States, sex selection is generally sought for a third or later child of the other sex than those already produced by the couple. In India and China, on the other hand, sex ratios have already changed because of the wide application of sex preselection to detect and abort female fetuses (Luthra 1994; Greenhalgh and Li 1995).

Tampering with fetuses in fetal tissue research, surgery, and/or treatment is also controversial. To date, fetal tissue research has yielded treatments for Parkinson's disease and certain cancers; it is also being pursued for wound healing interventions, since fetuses themselves heal without scarring. Regulation of this research has been a key concern in the West; there have been prohibitions against such research in the United States and elsewhere. While still rare, fetal treatment and in vivo surgery also raise ethical, political, and financial issues—concerning not only the fetuses but also the women in whom they are embedded. These issues are likely to expand in the future, and the fetus will become even more a site of controversy.[24]

Genetic screening, testing, and therapies are widely recognized as controversial for moral, political, economic, and many other reasons—including the problematics of screening accurately. New approaches to screening are routinely sought; in the United States, state organizations proliferate, offering increasingly elaborate testing to more and more pregnant women while not having any "treatment" to offer other than abortion for fetuses with many serious hereditary conditions.[25]

But human cloning and related genetic manipulations stand out as the most radical and controversial interventions made possible by the reproductive sciences to date—long anticipated by science fiction (Bann 1994). They offer not only the modern potential to control life but also the postmodern potential to transform life itself. Brave new worlds indeed were heralded by the media fanfare given to Dolly, the Scottish sheep cloned in 1997. *Time Magazine* led off its primary coverage: "One doesn't expect Dr. Frankenstein to show up in a wool sweater, baggy parka, soft British accent and the face of a bank clerk. But there in all banal benignity he was: Dr. Ian Wilmut, the first man to create fully formed life from adult body parts since Mary Shelly's mad scientist" (Krauthammer 1997:60–61).

What is scientifically special is that this sheep was made by cloning from adult cells, not embryonic cells. She was named after Dolly Parton because she was cloned from mammary gland cells. Cloning by splitting embryo cells has been done for years and is routine in the cattle industry. This process creates identical twin or multiple embryos from the sperm and eggs of known parents. Figure 6 shows this process in cattle. Human cloning through embryo splitting received an "amber light" in 1994 in the United States from the National Advisory Board on Ethics in Reproduction (1994). This kind of cloning is viewed as highly desirable by most infertility physicians and their patients/consumers, since fewer surgical and hormonal procedures on women are needed to produce multiple embryos, while still increasing chances for successful conception, implantation, and birth.

In contrast, the capacity to clone from adult cells means one can know in advance many aspects of the outcome by knowing the living organism itself. As explained in *Time,* "With adult-cell cloning, you can wait to see how well an individual turns out before deciding whether to clone it" (Nash 1997:64). If embryo cloning has offered an array of economic advantages, adult-cell cloning is even more promising. A *Wall Street Journal* headline asked, "Who Will Cash In on Breakthrough in Cloning?" The article answered that a tiny company could emerge a big winner (Krauthammer 1997:60). Wilmut did patent his process before announcing it to the world.

In addition to "simple cloning," genes in sperm can now be altered, "passing the changes to the animal's progeny . . . [and] bring[ing] the brave new world of gene manipulation hurtling ever closer" (Kolata 1996). The means of accomplishing genetic selection have recently been termed "trait-selection technologies" and justified in a legal journal on the grounds of man-made evolution (Jones 1993). What Hartouni (1997) calls "replicating the singular self" profoundly violates assumed "natural" features of familial and individual identity. The social body is deeply threatened if not torn asunder. Yet "in vitro man" has already been to some degree domesticated if not displaced by media images of "the desperately infertile." "The border over which cloning intensifies reflection, in other words, is hardly untrafficked territory" (Hartouni 1997:130). Regardless, cloning and genetic manipulation are quite likely to be the most controversial of all reproductive technologies, exceeding in the twenty-first century the controversy surrounding birth control and abortion in the twentieth.

But it is not only manipulations of humans which have been highly controversial in terms of creating "Brave New Worlds" where life itself is transformed. Agricultural reproductive scientists have also been the focus of controversies posed by animal rights movements, by ecological groups concerned about the costs and safety of protein derived from meat and dairy products, and by groups concerned about the "pharmaceutical farm," biotechnologies, the survival of small farmers, and related issues. Scientists' biotechnological creation of a "leaner" pig that could not stand up and was also otherwise deformed did little to reduce such controversy. Genetically engineered calves have been more successfully reproduced with embryo-splitting techniques.[26] Interspecies pregnancy by means of in vitro fertilization is another focus of recent research (Fields 1992) that is likely to engender even greater controversy. Tensions here are likely to be generated in part by the reproduction programs in zoos for endangered species by in vitro fertilization with gestation in other species. Nonhuman primates are likely to be further colonized for transplantation purposes rather than as surrogates for human mothers.

Growth hormone controversies have also been especially heated. Growth hormone, "discovered" by reproductive scientist Herbert Evans, who regularly traversed the boundaries among reproductive, endocrinological, and nutrition research, has recently found new applications. Bovine growth hormone (recombinant bovine somatotropin) can dramatically increase milk production in cows. Although it has been approved for use in American dairy cattle, the possibility of complications both in the cows and in people who eat their products has aroused criticism.[27] Human growth hormone has also come under attack (Cassidy 1991). Currently Genentech is being sued for racketeering because of its methods of promoting sales (Bloomberg Business News 1994).

While not causally attributable to the reproductive sciences, the recent and ongoing controversy about the human sperm count implicates those sciences. A book called *Our Stolen Future: Are We Threatening Our Fertility, Intelligence and Survival? A Scientific Detective Story* (Colborn, Dumanoski, and Myers 1996), with a foreword by Vice President Al Gore, has been widely reviewed. The news has been full of related coverage (e.g., Kolata 1996). The gist of this issue is whether and/or how severely the human sperm count has been reduced by environmental toxins of various kinds. The sperm counts of different countries have been pitted against one another in newly nationalized measurements of masculinity. The reproductive sciences have responded with proposals to implant frozen human sperm in an animal host such as a rat or mouse that would then produce the donor's sperm. Researchers have already successfully transplanted testicular stem cells across the species barrier (Avarbock, Brinster, and Brinster 1996). Such manipulations are guaranteed to deepen the controversial status of the reproductive sciences.

The reproductive sciences in biology, medicine, and agriculture are each and all quite controversial and illegitimate. Almost every moment in the reproductive process offers an opportunity for contested intervention. Different constituencies are distraught for different reasons. Conservative leaders, along with Catholic and fundamentalist theologians, object to interventions in "natural" processes (e.g., Dienes 1972). Some feminists view these technologies as rendering women as breeders on the one hand, while potentially denying them motherhood on the other by developing artificial wombs, and as raising a host of both medical and ethical problems.[28] Others are concerned about the high costs of these technologies, which typically are not covered by insurance, both as they compare with costs of health care in general and because poorer people are less likely to have access to them.[29] Disabled communities have found much to object to in terms of both their access to and applications of reproductive technologies. Disabled people have often been the focus of eugenic efforts to prevent and/or dissuade them from reproducing. Some disabled people also view genetic screening for certain disabilities, with abortion as the preferred or only treatment, as direct attacks on disabled fetuses—people-to-be. Lawyers and ethicists are also kept rather busy addressing these issues.[30]

Of all the controversial realms in which the reproductive sciences have been embedded, their association with "brave new worlds," the capacity to radically manipulate and even create new forms of life, from nude mice to "designer" humans, is the most significant. The capacity to manipulate both human and animal capital and liabilities is truly revolutionary (Austin and Short 1972/1986). While the first three realms of controversy are distinctively modern, the capacity to create "brave new worlds" bridges modern and postmodern approaches to reproduction. It is characteristic not only of the past but even more so of the future. The illegitimacy of the reproductive sciences is thus not likely to abate.

MANAGING ILLEGITIMACY

Reproductive scientists have used a variety of strategies to manage their illegitimate and/or controversial status and to obtain funding across these highly varying historical conditions. First, and on a continuing basis, they drew upon the cultural authority of science. Biologists such as Frank Lillie of Chicago, Emil Witschi at Iowa, Frederick Hisaw at Wisconsin and Harvard, and many others provided this counter to illegitimacy challenges. The membership of key reproductive scientists in social elites was also important (Borell 1987a). This phenomenon can be viewed as to some degree parallel to the ways in which physicists are said to have lent social, scientific, and cultural authority to molecular biology (Keller 1993). In Hall's (1974:92) words: "Men ambitious for a scientifically respectable study of sex recognized that its basis must be broadly biological and independent of human interest or subjective experience. . . . [T]his was a liberal position, and liberated biology as an autonomous science . . . the biological scientists of the twenties did not create social policy, but, driven by internal pressures for a respectable science, they created an increasingly biochemical science whose voice spoke with . . . the 'magic' of esoteric authority."

Using another management strategy, reproductive scientists have assumed positions of cultural and moral authority and brought voices of calm moderation, as the "hallmark of science," to bear upon controversial issues of reproduction and sexuality. They have addressed both popular and highly educated audiences through their writing. The moral propriety of some early reproductive scientists, such as Lillie and Corner, was also unquestionable. They quite intentionally turned these personal advantages to the advantage of the wider enterprise.[31]

Some early reproductive scientists pursued another strategy, protecting their personal careers by simultaneously doing other less controversial but related research. This research often involved the anterior pituitary gland, which produces both reproductive and other hormones. This discovery linked reproductive endocrinology with general endocrinology in endocrinology's heyday in the 1920s and 1930s (as discussed in chapter 5). For example, Bernardo Houssay worked on the anterior pituitary and sugar metabolism; Herbert Evans worked on growth hormone from the anterior pituitary and on vitamins; and Oscar Riddle worked on problems in genetics (Medvei 1982).

Considerable emphasis on understanding infertility and its treatment during the 1940s and 1950s simultaneously aided legitimacy and countered criticisms of the reproductive sciences for their development of contraceptives. For some, the view of infertility as disease has been inadequate (e.g., Pfeffer 1993; Gabriel 1996). Since about 1980, distinctive new centers for infertility services, often separate from all other reproductive services, have highlighted this aspect of reproductive science. Such centers typically combine both clinical and basic research with clinical services and are aimed at particular market niches. In some, fees for clinical services partially cover research costs. Focusing on infertility since the 1980s has again provided American reproductive scientists with funding and has enhanced legitimacy among some constituencies, as it did in the 1940s and 1950s. Certainly this focus has "regrounded nature" in the heterosexual nuclear family, enabling biological children and families to be made where otherwise none would exist. However, access to such services has usually been limited to heterosexual married couples by state regulation and/or insurance coverage. New gay, lesbian, and other family forms have not been supported (Franklin 1995). Ironically, scientists have also recently confronted extensive controversy over such "new reproductive technologies."

Like many other scientists, reproductive scientists have claimed that their science will solve social problems. Aronson (1984) terms this the "scientization" of social problems, a process similar to the "medicalization" of social problems. Of course, the key social problems reproductive scientists in medicine and biology claim to address are those concerned with population and reproduction. In consequence, biomedical reproductive sciences are now inextricably linked to those realms, and their standing fluctuates with the rise and fall of these as social problems (Hilgartner and Bosk 1988). For example, some analysts have recently argued that concern about "overpopulation" has abated, decreasing commitments to reproductive research that would help to solve such problems (e.g., Djerassi 1992). The American controversy over abortion led to prohibitions against funding research into any method that may be used to induce abortion or improve abortion techniques (Lincoln and Kaeser 1988). It also isolated the reproductive sciences more generally. The now-routine headlines about developments in one reproductive technology or another serve as a series of dramatic public events, keeping the arena "hot."

For over a century, reproductive scientists managed their controversial status, developing strategies and tactics to handle their divergent audiences and constituencies and at times suffering the painful consequences. Problems are moved from the front to the back burner and vice versa, depending in part on the pragmatics of the current situation.[32] Meanwhile, the mantles of Loeb and Pincus have been appropriated by colleagues in Britain, Australia, Sweden, India, and elsewhere as American preeminence in the reproductive sciences dims and the global scientific economy rises in more "hospitable" environments (Atkinson, Lincoln, and Forrest 1985). The crisis of scientific authority is intersecting with the fiscal crisis of the state, and a radical restructuring of the international scientific economy is in process.

CONSEQUENCES OF CONTROVERSY AND ILLEGITIMACY

The controversial and illegitimate status of the reproductive sciences has been consequential for those sciences in terms of both scientific recognition and access to research funding. Recognition of the achievements of reproductive scientists has been limited, possibly because of the problematic status of the field. Despite the momentous nature of their "discoveries," there were fewer Nobel Prizes and a seemingly lower rate of election to honorific societies than might be expected. For example, between 1926 and 1940, the years Guy Marrian called the "heroic age of reproductive endocrinology" (Parkes 1966a:xx), there was no Nobel Prize in medicine or physiology for explicitly reproductive research.

Instead, there seems to have been a pattern of awarding the Nobel Prize to reproductive endocrinologists for work only tangentially related to reproductive endocrinology. In 1939, for example, Adolf Butenant in Germany, who had done considerable reproductive endocrinological research, won the Nobel Prize in chemistry with Leopold Ruzicka for changing cholesterol into a synthetic duplicate of natural testosterone (Reed 1983:314; Maisel 1965:37). And in 1947, Bernardo Houssay, another investigator who had worked on reproductive problems, was awarded a Nobel Prize for studies demonstrating the importance of the anterior pituitary in sugar metabolism (Medvei 1982:505). And many investigators have argued, on behalf of others if not themselves, that the Nobel Prize was deserved by several reproductive scientists who did not receive it, including George Corner and Herbert Evans.[33] In addition, fewer American investigators in the reproductive sciences were elected to the National Academy of Science than might have been expected (Long 1987:266). And despite many honors, the British "father" of the reproductive sciences, F. H. A. Marshall, was never promoted to professor (Medvei 1982:776; Biggers 1991).

Nor was Margaret Sanger ever honored by her own country. She was a candidate for the Presidential Medal of Freedom in 1965, but President Johnson declined to make the award because of "certain difficulties." The Johnson administration policy on birth control and population control was to move ahead with a variety of programs but without publicity to avoid confrontation with Catholic and other opposition. An award to Sanger would have focused unwanted attention on these efforts. A letter from Lady Bird Johnson wishing her well was the closest Sanger came to national recognition. A testimonial dinner by Planned Parenthood advocates named her "The Woman of the Century," which was closer to the mark regardless.[34] As an example of the shift to the national legitimacy of population control and the authority of science, within a decade of Sanger's death, Carl Djerassi received the National Medal of Science from President Richard M. Nixon in 1973, "In recognition of his major contributions to . . . steroid hormones and to their application to medicinal chemistry and population control by means of oral contraceptives" (Djerassi 1992:72).

Funding the reproductive sciences has been highly contingent on legitimacy issues. As I argued in chapter 7, the American reproductive sciences have received serious, solid, and prestigious funding from a variety of sources since 1921. Different kinds of projects were typically funded by different sources, and this is where legitimacy issues seem to have entered the calculus. Until the 1960s, NRC funding and some minimal federal funds focused on *basic* reproductive research. Contraceptive and other explicitly applied research was typically funded by private foundations and individuals. After World War II, the burden of funding basic science in the United States began shifting to the federal government, especially medical research, which was supported by the NIH. But not all sciences benefited equally or immediately. The reproductive sciences remained pariahs—excluded from the missions of both the NIH and the National Science Foundation. Moreover, the NIH was forbidden from funding birth control research prior to 1959 (Greep, Koblinsky, and Jaffe 1976:367). Instead, from 1945 to 1960 the U.S. Department of Agriculture was the major source of federal funds for reproductive research, which focused on quick and sensitive assays for hormones, including development of the radioimmunoassay technique in 1960.

After 1965, support from both federal and industry (largely pharmaceutical) sources rose dramatically. The National Academy of Sciences Committee on Science and Public Policy selected population problems as its focus in 1961 (National Academy of Sciences 1979:v). In 1963, the National Institute on Child Health and Human Development was established in the NIH; in the view of the Kennedy administration, its mission included sponsorship of both the reproductive sciences and fertility control research. The Rockefeller Foundation and the Ford Foundation designated population a major area of concern, and the World Health Organization began supporting the reproductive sciences as well. Funding jumped from under $38 million for 1960–65 to $332 million for 1969–74 (Greep, Koblinsky, and Jaffe 1976:382).

However, fiscal austerity hit federal research support by the mid-1970s. During the 1980s, the Reagan and Bush administrations, probably because of strong alliances with antiabortion movements, proved extremely hostile to almost all aspects of the reproductive sciences, from basic research to contraceptive research to infertility research and certainly to fetal research. It has been claimed that "in real dollars, worldwide spending for contraceptive development by both governments and the pharmaceutical industry has declined by nearly one-quarter since its peak in 1972" (Lincoln and Kaeser 1988:20–21). Whole university-based programs vaunted in the 1960s as signaling a new age are being dismantled.[35] The federal regulatory environment has become increasingly restrictive as agencies such as the FDA respond to an array of consumer groups on the one hand and anxious clinicians fearing malpractice claims on the other. Many assert that the United States is losing its preeminence in the field for the first time since World War I (Lincoln and Kaeser 1988; Rosoff 1988; Mastroianni, Donaldson, and Kane 1990). Without a doubt, the funding of the reproductive sciences remains politically contingent.

CONCLUSIONS

It seems clear that the reproductive sciences are seen as illegitimate and hence controversial as science.[36] However, controversy does not mean there is a consensus about the illegitimacy of a particular line of scientific work. Nor does it mean that that work is doomed to failure. Rather, it means that an analysis of power within the contested arena is requisite for participants (as well as for sociologists and historians). Such analyses must be ongoing to perceive the shifts and alternative strategies that might lead to survival and/or success *despite* controversy (Star 1986; Fujimura 1987). For there is no final consensus in any field, merely successful or unsuccessful negotiations among those involved at a given historical moment (Strauss 1979). In fact, the robustness of the closure of some controversies can be grounded not in consensus but in the mobilization of effective social networks and/or the construction of "black boxes" around controversial phenomena that render them (temporarily) invisible (Rip 1986).

The "golden age" for scientists, when anything scientific was hallowed, has passed. Today esoteric authority has, to varying degrees and for varied audiences, lost some of its power. I have focused here on a striking array of efforts to destabilize, stop, resist, and reconfigure the work of the reproductive sciences. The reproductive sciences in biology, medicine, and agriculture are being held increasingly accountable to the demands of conflicting social worlds, and the Sisyphean aspects of doing reproductive science include continual battles for legitimacy. In this respect, their situation is similar to that of an increasing number of other sciences—the reproductive sciences themselves have been disciplined by controversy.

CHAPTER NINE

Disciplining Reproduction
in Modernity

This book has analyzed the formation and coalescence of the reproductive sciences as a disciplinary enterprise in the United States between 1910 and 1963. It has examined the reproductive sciences as social worlds situated in a much broader reproductive arena that included other salient worlds such as social movements and funding sources, offering a historical and sociological "big picture" of the development of the reproductive sciences through an ecology of knowledge and the conditions of its production. In concluding, I provide a synopsis of the argument and then revisit the themes of the book: disciplinary formation and the social worlds/arenas approach; illegitimacy, controversy, and the construction of boundaries; concerns with gender and the technosciences of reproduction; and, last, the goal of controlling life by disciplining reproduction in modernity.

SYNOPSIS OF THE ARGUMENT

I began these stories at the turn of the twentieth century with a portrait of the life sciences and the related institutions in which the American reproductive sciences would soon emerge. The social processes characteristic of this period were those of industrialization—rationalization, professionalization, and specialization in terms of market value and effectiveness. The sciences were professionalizing and the professions were consolidating as market-based occupations. Universities were transforming themselves into corporations for the production and distribution of knowledge. Science qua institution was becoming more akin to industries with specialized markets. Economic conditions in this period were also becoming increasingly supportive of research that would improve food production both for growing urban America and for export.

The major professional social worlds that would soon participate in the formation and coalescence of the reproductive sciences—biology, medicine, and agriculture—all offered academic homes. Social movements focused on birth control, eugenics, and neo-Malthusianism, along with developing animal production industries were becoming new markets for such knowledge. All were at the forefront of articulation of goals of control over reproduction throughout the "Great Chain of Being" in the new world order of the early twentieth century. The laws of nature were to be supplanted by the scientific ingenuity of humans as the means and mechanisms of rationalization and industrialization passed from the factory to agricultural and social life. Fundamental to this transformation was the shift in the locus of control over the means of biological reproduction from nature to human through the reproductive sciences and their technoscientific products.

Major reform movements in the life sciences were also occurring. At the turn of the century, these sciences were shifting from predominantly morphological to experimental modes of working. They were also undergoing a major conceptual and practical redivision of labor as newly framed disciplines of genetics, developmental embryology, and evolutionary theory were teased out of what in retrospect was once a densely tangled nexus of concerns. In the expanding academy, a new, overarching domain of "biology" served to hold all these new and older life science disciplines together. Largely beyond the boundaries of the academy, the discipline of sexology was developing, nursed along by scientific and clinical men in private institutions and organizations.

The comparative "lateness" of the development of the physiology of reproduction was a key feature of its emergence and disciplinary formation. The illegitimacy of the scientific pursuit of reproductive problems, "problems of sex," was apparent from the outset. Interestingly, the autonomy of reproductive problems as a discipline was first articulated in 1910 through the work of F. H. A. Marshall. His pioneering book, *The Physiology of Reproduction,* carefully distinguished the study of reproduction from that of genetics and cytology. Unconcerned with evolutionary theory and developmental embryology, Marshall instead deemed the problems of reproduction sufficient unto themselves for a new discipline. Disciplinary formation began at about the same time in the United States. By 1920, blood-borne hormones of reproduction and the vaginal smear, the two major nonhuman actors in the saga, along with many research materials, especially the hypophysectomized rat, were all on the scene. And most had come from the embryological investigations so dear to the hearts of American (as compared with British) life scientists.

The problem structures of the American reproductive sciences across the three professions varied. Biologists tended to focus on analytic problems such as sex determination, sex differentiation, and fertilization, with the species as their basic unit of analysis. Medical reproductive scientists tended to focus on the reproductive system as a system, as medical research tends to reflect the organization of service delivery. And agricultural scientists tended to focus on the reproductive system in particularly profitable and manipulable domestic organisms. Across all three professional domains, the major problems addressed during the 1910–25 era were fertilization, sex differentiation, the estrus and menstrual cycles in females, ovarian function, and the corpus luteum. In agriculture, chicken reproduction was successfully industrialized by means of technological solutions to natural limitations, including incubators. There were also some nascent developments in reproductive endocrinology as well, including the discovery of estrogens by the mid-1920s.

At about this time, Frank Lillie of the University of Chicago, already a statesman of American science, framed reproductive research as "the biology of sex," including some of his own group's work. Lillie was clear that these problems were ripe for investigation—reproductive research was doable. But doability includes affording the costs of research, and the new experimental approaches were considerably more costly and increasingly difficult to squeeze out of departmental budgets. External support became tremendously appealing. Lillie's potent framing of "the biology of sex" had been done at the suggestion of Robert Yerkes, chairman of the new National Research Council Committee for Research in Problems of Sex (NRC/CRPS), of which Lillie was a charter member. Yerkes had asked all members to help frame an agenda for research to be funded by this committee, founded in 1921 for the express purpose of supporting human sexuality research to solve social problems. Lillie's was, however, the *only* agenda developed.

Most of the biological problems Lillie framed were funded, creating a number of major new American centers of research on "problems of sex" and reproduction in biological and medical contexts. The biologists thus succeeded in seizing the means of studying reproduction—over twenty years of funding and the considerable prestige of sponsorship by major American scientific institutions, the NRC and the Rockefeller Foundation's Division of Natural Sciences. "Human side" proposals to investigate sexuality were largely put on hold until about 1940. Then the committee, repositioned in the Medical Division of the Rockefeller Foundation, shifted its emphasis in that direction, providing extensive and sustained support to Alfred Kinsey's sex research for well over a decade. By the 1940s, the reproductive sciences had also developed alternative funding sources.

During the coalescence of the reproductive sciences around endocrinology between 1925 and 1940, concern with nonhuman research materials heightened as the collection of sows' ovaries, bulls' testes, mares' blood, and stallions' urine, along with colonies of rats, opossums, and nonhuman primates, became requisite. Reproductive scientists also made the right (glandular) connections by carefully exploiting the linkages between reproductive endocrinology and general endocrinology. The NRC/CRPS published Allen's *Sex and Internal Secretions* in 1932 (Allen, ed., 1932), which fast became the American bible of the reproductive sciences. Study of the internal secretions, reproductive endocrinology, became the "model work" and core activity of the reproductive sciences during the years between 1925 and 1940. The chief naturally occurring estrogens, androgens, and progesterone were isolated and characterized, and the anterior pituitary, placental, and endometrial gonadotropins were also discovered.

At this juncture, the main goal of reproductive scientists regarding their discipline and professions was to put reproductive research "on the map" as a fully scientific, appropriately experimental, appropriately physiological and later biochemical endeavor. Reigning paradigms and standards of scientific research had to be applied in full, systematically and routinely. Coalescence thus also included the usual activities of professionalization of a new discipline: publishing new journals, forming new associations, and holding national and international meetings. Between 1925 and 1940, however, reproductive scientists tended to professionalize *within* their usual venues in biology, medicine, and agriculture, publishing in their own professional journals. There was one key transprofessional journal, *Endocrinology*, and almost all reproductive scientists published there. The journal was published by the Association for the Study of Internal Secretions, the key organization of the intersection, now the Endocrine Society. Only after World War II did reproductive scientists form additional transprofessional societies; the Society for the Study of Reproduction was not formed until 1967, with its journal, *Biology of Reproduction,* first published in 1969.

While there were tensions in the field, both before and after World War II, the new discipline of the reproductive sciences did much in the service of each profession. It provided biologists with a new line of research as they sought to expand their discipline. It provided medicine with a wide array of nonsurgical diagnostics and therapeutics for functional reproductive problems in gynecology and urology/andrology. And it provided agriculture with revolutionary reproductive technologies that dramatically improved animal production. Last but not least, it provided a fundable set of research problems for all, furthering each profession's place in the sun.

A key story of the disciplining of reproduction in modernity relates how, between roughly 1915 and 1945, the very nature of what *modern* contraception would be was negotiated between reproductive scientists and several varieties of birth control advocates—lay feminists, physicians, eugenicists, and neo-Malthusians. To recruit reproductive scientists into the birth control arena, the means of contraception had to be made scientific. This ran counter to the explicit desires of birth control advocates, such as Margaret Sanger, for improved simple means such as diaphragms and spermicides. These could be controlled by women to enhance their own sexual and reproductive autonomy. Reproductive scientists ultimately captured definitional authority as physicians, eugenicists, and neo-Malthusians conservatized the birth control movement into one for family planning and population control, displacing feminists from key organizational positions.

Reproductive scientists used several strategies in relation to their often insistent market audience of birth control advocates to assert their legitimacy, autonomy, and cultural authority. First, they carefully distinguished reproductive research from contraceptive research, refusing to participate in studies of *simple* contraceptives and making marginal within the profession any reproductive scientists who did so. Second, they argued with birth control advocates for basic research as the ultimate source of modern contraception and made token offerings from their "basic" research work (such as accurate information on the timing of ovulation). Third, they redirected contraceptive research toward new *scientific* methods: hormonal contraception, spermatoxins, IUDs, and sterilization by radiation.

Ultimately, by about 1945, a quid pro quo was established between the reproductive sciences and birth control worlds. Through negotiations among birth control advocates, reproductive scientists, hormones, foundations, laboratories, the National Research Council, primates, and others, a congruence of interests was reached that adequately "fit" the changing needs of the various arena participants. This quid pro quo could only have been achieved given shifts *within* the various birth control movements themselves between 1915 and 1940. The contraceptive advocacy of these movements shifted from commitments to individual choice to social control over reproduction, from a focus on qualities of individuals to quantities of populations, and from user control to professional medical control over the means of contraception. It was these shifts that had led lay birth control advocates themselves to seek "scientific" rather than "simple" means of contraception. In the 1950s and 1960s, the quid pro quo was consolidated as reproductive scientists largely outside the academy finally produced the major modern scientific means of contraception—birth control pills, IUDs, injectable hormones, and improved means of surgical sterilization. All of these modern scientific methods have become part of the "socialization of reproductive behavior" of "the Malthusian couple," in Foucault's (1978) terms. Thus was reproduction disciplined for lay people as well as scientists.

The American reproductive sciences have had an unusual funding career. Despite serious legitimacy problems, they were quite successful prior to World War II in obtaining external funding from highly prestigious sources well within the mainstream of the biomedical research community. The stature of these sources was particularly impressive and significant, including three NRC committees, the Rockefeller, Macy, and Markle foundations, and the Carnegie Institution of Washington. Remarkably, during the 1920s, the Rockefeller-funded NRC/CRPS gleaned about 10 percent of *all* the funding of the entire NRC. Both the funds and their provenance lent sorely needed legitimacy and support to the development of reproductive research as a viable scientific enterprise in the decades before World War II. A wide variety of industries also contributed funds and materials to university-based reproductive research efforts, and the American and European pharmaceutical industries also directly sponsored some investigations. External expenditures on reproductive research in the United States between 1922 and 1940 (in 1976 dollars) have been estimated at $1,295,900 (Greep, Koblinsky, and Jaffe 1976:371).[1] Actual external support figures are undeterminable, but my estimates are nearly twice this figure.

The reproductive sciences have been and continue to be viewed as illegitimate. For some groups, this reputation is due to their association with sexuality and reproduction; for others it results from their association with clinical quackery and problematic treatments (from rejuvenescence to DES to contraceptives' negative side effects). For yet others their association with controversial social movements (eugenics, birth control, abortion, population control) make them anathema. But it is their association with the construction of "brave new worlds," in which nature itself is manipulated, transforming and reconfiguring human and animal bodies and reproductive capacities—producing cyborgs or clones—that has drawn the most opposition to date. In consequence, reproductive scientists have received no Nobel Prizes for their work; they have received fewer awards and, many would assert, lesser rewards. Moreover, they must routinely devote time and energy to coping with and managing the illegitimacy of their pursuits to some constituencies. Paradoxically, their success has been made possible not only by their own efforts but also by the sustained support of highly prestigious scientific organizations, philanthropies, and individuals who have provided funding, legitimacy, and many other kinds of support for the better part of a century.

While the reproductive sciences did not share in initial federal largesse in terms of research support immediately after World War II, by the 1960s federal support began expanding to impressive levels. In addition, powerful new foundation support (especially from the Ford Foundation) came forth, promoting the consolidation of new alliances among the reproductive sciences, birth control, and population control worlds. Significantly, it was not until population issues and scientific contraception were matters of public policy and federal support that scientific organizations broadly focused on reproduction come into being.

THEMES REVISITED
Disciplinary Formation and Social Worlds/Arenas

Most studies of disciplinary formation are case studies. Within social studies of science and technology, there have been ongoing debates about the definitions and usefulness of different units of analysis such as discipline, research school, research center, field, specialty area, and/or profession.[2] Typically, these debates get lost in a morass of finely tuned definitions. I chose instead to focus here on examination of the broader situation— the reproductive arena—in which the reproductive sciences successfully emerged and coalesced. Like American nuclear physics, the formation of the American reproductive sciences was very "field-dependent," and the social worlds/arenas approach captures the field in a complex fashion. I have examined particular research centers of the American reproductive sciences elsewhere.[3]

Social worlds and arenas analysis offers a number of analytic advantages to studies of disciplinary formation. First, and of special import in historical research, social worlds analysis bridges internal and external concerns by encompassing the involvement and contributions of all the salient social worlds. Both internal and external topics may be relevant. Social worlds are genuinely social units of analysis, elastic and plastic enough to allow very diverse applications. One can avoid misrepresenting collective social actors as monolithic by examining diversities within worlds, while still tracking and tracing their overall collective perspectives, ideologies, thrusts, and goals. One can comfortably analyze the work of particular individuals as important to the arena, without being limited to an individual approach. Perhaps most important, in the very framing of an arena, one is analytically led to examine the negotiations within and between worlds that are most consequential for the development of the arena over time.

This study speaks to a few issues raised in the recent literature on disciplinary formation. First, some recent technoscience studies have drawn on, if not centered on, the implications of the actual practices of science for disciplinary formation, standing the traditional theory-driven notion of disciplinary formation on its head.[4] Similarly, I have discussed such techniques as the vaginal smear and the hypophysectomized rat as key experimental technologies in disciplinary formation and coalescence. Given the very slow pace of most mammalian reproductive processes in vivo—a matter of some comment in my interviews with reproductive and related scientists—the vaginal smear was a key technical resource facilitating the doability of research in the emergent discipline. Hormone extracts, hypophysectomized rats, and vaginal smears together made a wonderful theory/methods package (Fujimura 1996). They composed the "right tools for the job" (Clarke and Fujimura 1992) of reproductive endocrinology.

Second, several recent studies, also countertraditionally, have taken up the effects of medical practices—clinical work—on the historical organization of biomedical sciences. Lowy (1987, 1993), for example, offers an elegant analysis of how scientific and clinical lines of work in medicine can move closer together to jointly establish a new specialty area and yet hold on to and later retreat back into more usual autonomous styles of interaction. The reproductive sciences followed a parallel pattern. Like Lowy, Baszanger's (1992, 1995, 1998a,b) study of disciplinary formation found much movement across time but found local contingency more consequential: different models of the "new" discipline of "pain medicine" emerged in different places depending upon both the local formations of the "original" disciplines and the commitments of the major actors at specific sites. Similarly, the cross-professional intersections among biological, medical, and agricultural reproductive scientists examined here were shaped by patterns of both production and market consumption. Moreover, given the distinctive institutional and professional independence of participants, collaboration posed few risks of loss of professional autonomy. As Baszanger also found, there was much local variation in the kinds and degrees of cross-professional intersectionality and in the general shape of local centers of the reproductive sciences.

Rue Bucher's (1988) work on the organization of medicine over time argues that we can usefully view disciplines, specialties, and segments thereof as social movements. Similarly, Halpern's (1988) study of the formation of pediatrics as a medical specialty specified that changes in work patterns can promote and provoke new organizational forms. New occupational segments can become specialties that (re)structure markets for service delivery. In the case of the reproductive sciences examined here, the desires of gynecologists for functional rather than surgical interventions to sustain their specialty in the earlier decades of this century certainly provided legitimacy for medical reproductive scientists for many years—indeed, through the present. The division of labor in animal agriculture by type of domestic animal similarly created "specialty" sites for the application of reproductive interventions to improve production. The potential for immediate market payoffs added impetus.

New specialties may also form in conjunction with social movements and social problems. At the beginning of the twentieth century, this pattern characterized pediatrics in relation to child and family reform (Halpern 1988), and nutrition science in relation to labor/management conflict

(Aronson 1979, 1982). The notion of social movements invoking and perhaps even inscribing new sciences has also been brought home to roost in this volume regarding transformations in the birth control, neo-Malthusian, and eugenics movements, which had multiple relations with the study of reproductive phenomena. Crucially, all these movements were present at the outset, creating and sustaining a public reproductive arena and a technoscientific marketplace in which the reproductive sciences were able to become key actors.

Disciplines must often be constructed and maintained against other disciplinary enemies in a very conflictful field of strategic action (Bourdieu 1975; Cambrosio and Keating 1983). Here the ability to exercise "collegiate" control of the production and reproduction of knowledge is fundamental. I find the metaphor of a conflictful field compelling, but the case presented here both exemplifies it and offers a counterexample. The reproductive sciences exemplify conflict in terms of ongoing competition for scientific legitimacy and in terms of seizing or stealing the means of knowledge production from sexology in its takeover of the NRC/CRPS. But the reproductive sciences also provide a counterexample, a discipline that emerged "late," one might even say reluctantly, only when fed, nurtured, and legitimated by extrascientific interests and social worlds. The case of the formation and coalescence of demography offers a similar counterexample (Demeny 1988; Greenhalgh 1996). I suspect Bourdieu's agonistic field approach may be more salient where the science in question is not itself controversial, or when there is intense competition over scarce resources.

Actor network theory, developed by Latour, Callon, and Law, treats the network as the unit of analysis rather than a discipline or specialty per se.[5] I view actor networks as an "allied" and useful perspective in the fullest sense. I especially value its inclusion of nonhumans, which I have focused upon here and in other stories about the reproductive sciences (Clarke 1987, 1993, 1995a). Yet networks and worlds are analytically different. Network analysis emphasizes the recruitment and enrollment of allies instead of the mutuality of negotiations or the trade-offs often featured in social worlds analyses. Further, implicated actors—those silent or not present but affected by the action—are invisible in network analyses and are *structurally* rendered invisible, just as the silent or silenced are invisible in conversational analysis. They can easily be taken into account in a social worlds approach. In actor networks, differences among actors are also submerged, while in social worlds approaches they are highlighted and can be examined in ongoing negotiations. Many actor network studies feature an "executive" node that somehow is in charge of the action. In social worlds studies, the distribution of power is more an empirical question to be addressed.

Accounts of disciplinary formation can, inadvertently or not, merely provide second-order legitimations of dominant "insider histories," or of other insider accounts that already serve as the first-order legitimations of a field, as Abir-Am (1985) notes. All histories may well be hagiographic in that they selectively attend to some aspects of the past over others, a phenomenon akin to the adage "There's no such thing as bad advertising." Abir-Am (1985:106, 75) objects to "a view [of science] which projects its products, scientific discoveries and facts—as a simplistic derivation of natural reality," and to an approach that is "systematically evasive on the questions of conceptual dissent in both the past and present." To counteract such tendencies, she calls for attention to power as fluid across situations, to hierarchies, to differences and conflicts of perspective within the science, and to resistances.

A social worlds/arenas analysis attends to all these issues. It can take the deconstructive process further, going beyond the confines of the scientific work itself into the wider social sites of action and interaction where that science "matters." Arenas are the places where the "differences" a (techno)science makes are recognized and monitored.[6] Here differences among scientists were featured not only in terms of professional background and concerns (biology, medicine, and agriculture) but also in terms of ongoing tensions in the discipline (largely between more organismic and more reductionist endocrinological commitments). I have addressed not only sociopolitical and other differences within the discipline but also relations with kindred social movements and funding sources. Admittedly, the formation of the reproductive sciences does lend itself to such deconstruction because the illegitimacy of the science and the controversial nature of the arena clarify such differences and conflicts, which are often unarticulated in the historical record. But I would argue that the social worlds and arenas framework draws these elements into the analytic foreground regardless. The range of variation of participants' interests and perspectives is to be specified and not papered over in favor of a more consensual, monolithic, or universalizing narrative of development. Differences and conflict are key analytic moments to be highlighted rather than obscured.

In analyzing disciplinary formation, Shapin (1992) made a strong case for not wholly abandoning notions of internal and external aspects of scientific work (in favor of networks, for example) as categories of analysis. The social worlds/arenas framework allows such distinctions to serve as an analytic resource and provides a reliable way in which to represent the perspectives of the actors under study. Further, the arena model provokes more refined analytic attention to specifying the "external," rather than leaving it unspecified and undifferentiated—as in some mythic "society." The other social worlds in the arena also must be understood on their own terms.

Related to these concerns with the problematics of disciplinary formation are recent approaches in technology studies.[7] The key salient arguments from the "social construction of technology" approach are, first, that the analysis should focus on the design stage rather than on the down-stream "social impacts" of technologies, for technologies are constructed by particular actors who have particular interests and perspectives at particular moments of history. Second, the "engineering" required to build technologies and their delivery systems includes social and political elements, as well as technical and economic elements more traditionally placed at the center of analysis. Third, the delivery systems should actually be conceived as integral elements of the technology per se because in practice they are inseparable. Such works have emphasized the "seamless web" of relations and, especially relevant here, configuring the users of technologies to accept them. I have found these approaches both very useful and largely congruent with social worlds/arenas analysis. We can certainly see in the sustained illegitimacy of the reproductive sciences, and the impossibility of closure regarding contraceptive technologies, how delivery systems are consequential in terms of attempting to configure users and engendering resistance. Webs are not necessarily seamless.

The social worlds/arenas approach also, of course, has limitations. First, in seeking so seriously to (re)present the perspectives of the actors in its gaze, it risks displacing others' perspectives, including my own. I had to be especially reflexive to avoid getting lost in reproductive scientists' stories and losing sight of the wider arena. Had a major overview of disciplinary formation of the reproductive sciences existed when I began, I would have focused much more on the negotiations among the social worlds within the arena, concerns here largely restricted to the chapters on the NRC/CRPS and on the construction of the contraceptive quid pro quo. Further, I would have investigated more deeply feminist perspectives on women's health articulated in negotiations with reproductive scientists between 1920 and 1965. Second, social worlds/arenas approaches to date articulate awkwardly with discursive approaches, although both are constructionist. For example, Foucault's approach to the ways in which disciplinary discourses (re)constitute and (re)constellate actors such as the Malthusian couple and the hysterical woman would be valuable to pursue in relation to the reproductive sciences. A coherent integration of such approaches awaits further effort.

Boundaries, Controversy, and Illegitimacy

Boundary work (Gieryn 1995) is central to the disciplinary formation stories told here. All boundaries are about difference claims of some sort. I have discussed six types of boundaries that have been salient to the disciplining of reproduction across the twentieth century. First, the boundary between science and society usually claimed by science was rarely solid but rather opaque or transparent to almost everyone in terms of the visibility of applications. This is a fundamental feature of the reproductive sciences. Moreover, as in molecular biology (Kay 1993a), the intended applications of the reproductive sciences were inscribed on that work from the outset, especially but not only by the social movements supporting it.

Second, boundaries between sciences, delimiting one discipline from another, typically very important during disciplinary formation, were important here. The segmentation of genetics, developmental embryology, and evolutionary theory also framed a clear set of "problems of sex" for pursuit. While there were some blurred edges to the boundaries of these emergent disciplines, relative coherence within each was quickly achieved. In several cases, the coherence was distinctively American.

Third, boundaries constructed *within* a discipline, which define what is to count as "basic" versus "applied" knowledge and research, were extremely important to reproductive scientists. Initially attempting to construct a fully basic research discipline, reproductive scientists undertook more "applied" work inside the academy only when acting in the capacity of agricultural scientists or when external philanthropic and federal research support was available for it, largely after World War II. Fourth, boundaries between the "normal" and the "pathological" largely paralleled those between "basic" and "applied." However, I would also argue strongly that both of these boundaries (basic/applied and normal/pathological) were and remain open to renegotiation. Like the color line in the United States (Park 1952), they move. Such negotiations were intense during the period I examine.

The introduction of biochemistry into biological, medical, and agricultural sites of reproductive science further destabilized these boundaries.[8] In the 1940s and 1950s, the boundaries between the normal and the pathological were deeply challenged. Diethylstilbestrol and other estrogenic hormones were used in medicine in ways that reconstructed what was to count as normal and as pathological. For example, menopause was recast from a natural or normal process to a pathological one. (Thus was Foucault's hysterical woman addressed.) In agriculture, providing estrogenic supplements to normal animals to intensify feedlot weight gain was similarly "naturalized." Perhaps most radically, the birth control pill, a medication to be taken daily by otherwise healthy women, in some ways reconfigured the face of biomedicine. The Pill even recast the "technoscience frames" of pharmaceutical companies, which at that time were quite shocked by the willingness of healthy women to take such potent drugs on a regular basis. The women's willingness demonstrates how assiduously control over reproduction was sought by multiple and heterogeneous actors to whom such boundaries could become essentially irrelevant.

Fifth, boundaries of hierarchy, prestige, and cultural authority *within* a discipline in this case study also by and large paralleled those between "basic" and "applied." That is, within each profession (biology, medicine, and agriculture), the more basic investigators typically had greater prestige *within* the scientific world. However, beyond the walls of academe, prestige has often accrued to applied researchers whose contributions were known and valued more widely and lucratively. Last, in the rank orderings of the sciences themselves, the reproductive sciences have been placed quite low on the totem pole. The sustained illegitimacy of these sciences and the intensity of controversies surrounding them have continued to assure their relatively deprivileged status.

Yet the reproductive sciences were also founded on an erasure, or at least a dimming, of boundaries—both professional and religious. These sciences began as an intersectional effort with disciplinary formation and contributors in biology, medicine, and agriculture, along with deep linkages to philanthropy and to birth control, eugenics, and neo-Malthusian movements. This dense "web of group affiliations" (Simmel 1904/1971) has protected the reproductive sciences for many decades. However, to some constituencies and science observers, the carefully stitched seams that hold this web together are much less reminiscent of a cozy quilt than they are of Frankenstein—a monster composed of soiled, unnatural, and obscene parts cobbled together in violation of all that is holy, natural, or uniquely human. To some, the reproductive sciences were deformed at their very birth, but not, as Herbert Evans has argued, by their initial association with quackery. Instead these sciences are inherently deformed. They dare to represent and intervene in one of the most sacred domains of human life—reproduction. They are Frankenstein's monster himself as a scientist (Bann 1994)!

Thus some boundaries seem clear and salient precisely because of the illegitimacy of the work of reproductive sciences and the controversies surrounding it. These boundaries are important not only to the reproductive sciences but also to other sciences and nonscientific worlds. For example, the boundary between the reproductive sciences and genetics is publicly construed by most geneticists as absolute and never to be crossed. While prenatal genetic screening and diagnostics, gene therapies, and fetal surgery are all predicated on the availability of abortion and other reproductive science interventions, these necessities must not be mentioned. Instead, lay people and reproductive scientists alike are to focus on the miracles of the "new reproductive technologies," creating a new discourse of scientific promise. These technologies of conception promise no less than the resurrection, by technoscientific means, of the heterosexual nuclear family (Franklin 1995; Casper 1998). Today, demand for and appreciation of these technologies protect the reproductive sciences from even further controversy.

Gender and the Technosciences of Reproduction

If one attends to who or what is present in an arena but silenced, not present but targeted or otherwise involved either at the moment or downstream, conflicts are foregrounded and so are the fluidities of power, very much as Abir-Am (1985) desires. In this saga of the development of the reproductive sciences, women were mostly implicated actors. A few were scientists, but they moved into regular academic positions only after World War II deci-mated the male academic ranks.[9] Others were birth control activists and feminist physicians in the birth control movement and its clinics (see references in chapter 6). But overall, women were mostly the targeted con-sumers of technoscientific products. I originally generated the concept of implicated actors by trying to account for women in this saga of the forma-tion of the reproductive sciences. I wanted to strengthen social worlds and arenas theory by representing the implicit as well as the explicit, the quiet or silenced along with the loud and predominant. I was, of course, familiar with the ways in which medicine and science have constructed certain social actors, often but certainly not always women, "for their own good."

Assuming that culture operates through representations and that "the biomedical sciences deploy, and are themselves, systems of representation," Jordanova (1989:23) has argued that scientific frames permeate lay frames, and that the power to define has been, and remains, largely masculine. Certainly this book has demonstrated that the power to define the science of reproduction and to shape its technoscientific products between 1910 and 1963 was largely masculine. A number of scholars have argued that there was a fundamental shift in the ways in which sex and gender were represented beginning after about 1650, from a predominant biomedical rhetoric of gender hierarchy, with women viewed as "lesser" or "weaker" men, to one of categorical difference that pervades the entire gendered body.[10] The reproductive scientists examined here certainly acted to main-tain the theory of categorical difference. In so doing, they violated common assumptions of scientific method about clarity of naming by preserving a hormonal nomenclature of difference that was not evident in their own scientific work. In fact, Lillie's (1932, 1939) explicit and self-conscious re-tention of the terminology of "male" and "female" hormones, despite con-trary evidence that would have required much more complicated and ten-tative representations of "nature," has been retained through the present moment. This constitutes part of what Long (1997) terms the definitive "controlled vocabulary" of sex and gender difference in biomedicine.

Another gender-related concern is the continued insistence by many re-productive scientists and the largely male leadership of what became the family planning and population control institutional matrix that women be viewed as objects rather than subjects. The persistence and intensity of efforts in these worlds to exclude or marginalize women and women's concerns and desires regarding contraception is, today, almost shocking. The science I found was peculiarly (however normatively) disengaged from its objects as agentic subjects. This disengagement was peculiar because of the very transparency of reproductive science to most people as supposedly seeking to understand and control reproductive phenomena. Its subjects, female and male, are all too aware of its inadequacies.

Currently there are moves to democratize science and science policy to include what I have called "implicated actors," those who will be directly affected. Such attempts are being made in the reproductive arena as well. For the present, however, serious inclusion seems a remote possibility. Yet the strength of "weak" actors, like "the strength of weak ties" (Granovetter 1973), can be telling. A national and transnational matrix of feminist women's health organizations has developed out of heterogeneous resistances. In the United States, product liability cases can also be read as an index of resistance. New markets might emerge from attending to what technoscientific products women themselves want. The latest move in both contraceptive development and reproductive medicine is to focus on the male; new birth control methods and the medical specialty of andrology are likely to alter the face(s) of implicated actors. It will be interesting to see if men as patients of reproductive medicine continue to be treated like women patients as Pfeffer (1985) found.

DISCIPLINING REPRODUCTION/CONTROLLING LIFE

The sociological tradition in which I was trained asks a simple yet pivotal analytic question about a given research project: What is this a story of?[11] There are many genres of story in this book. There are once-upon-a-time narratives of the making of the reproductive sciences, of "discoveries" and an emerging discipline. There are many tales of contestation among the multiple and heterogeneous social worlds concerned with reproduction in twentieth-century America, with each world trying to shape the reproductive sciences in its own interests. There are tales of money flowing, ebbing, and flowing again. There are sagas of coercion, disease, resistance, and acceptance of the technoscientific products of the reproductive sciences with glee or resignation as they have been distributed across the planet. But the story of disciplining reproduction has most to do with the modernist project of controlling life itself.

Controlling life was and is to be achieved in part by rationalizing and industrializing reproductive processes. Multiple heterogeneous and contradictory groups have had an interest in achieving such control—from elites seeking to control others to individuals, especially women, trying to get a grip on their own lives through controlling their reproduction; from eugenicists ultimately trying to control evolution to neo-Malthusians trying to control national and global population size; from philanthropists and foundation executives trying to shape the future of science and human life in varied directions to reproductive scientists trying to do their research. I emphasize heterogeneity again here specifically to disrupt in advance a simplistic reading of the next paragraphs, where I take up questions of control, specifically: Whose control over whose reproduction? And under what conditions? I want to end by offering the beginnings of an answer to a haunting question: Why did the reproductive sciences receive the extensive and prestigious institutional and financial support they did when they were and remain so deeply illegitimate and controversial?

The social movements and philanthropies that put the reproductive sciences on the map were all solidly established by the time those sciences emerged. Each—eugenics, birth control, and neo-Malthusianism—sought some means of (social) control over reproduction. Clearly there were also deep and long-lived commitments among major philanthropists and foundations, especially Rockefeller interests, to the development of improved means of control over reproduction—birth control, population control, eugenics, and family planning. Interestingly, explicit discussion of "why" these commitments are important is almost invisible in the archival materials, which instead focus on "how" funding should be spent.[12]

The Rockefeller Foundation, throughout its early years, as a number of scholars have argued (Kay 1993a,b; Kohler 1991), sought to invest in sciences that had clear social applications, useful in improving the human condition *as they construed it.* An advisory group stated clearly in 1934, "Indeed we would strongly advocate a shift of emphasis in favor not only of the dissemination of knowledge, but of the practical application of knowledge in fields where human need is great and opportunity is real."[13] The foundation sought to "rationalize human behavior" with the aim of achieving "control through understanding" so that knowledge could "rapidly pass . . . from the laboratory to the hospital and home."[14] There were in these materials what Hall (1978:14) termed "implicit models of human society managed by scientists in the interests of human fulfillment." Investments in biomedical sciences, including psychiatry, were to produce applications and interventions toward building such models into society. These expectations characterized the NRC/CRPS and the reproductive science it sponsored from the outset. But among some of the men in leadership elites in the early twentieth century, "rather than an end, social control was regarded as a means of enhancing the inevitable progress toward the ideal of democracy" (Fisher 1990:111). Mitman's (1992) and Cross and Albury's (1987) concerns with social control strategies frame these as responses to the "crisis of civilization of the times." During the first decades of the century, the possibilities for natural social spontaneity were read by leadership elites as having come to an end. There was a tremendous need, some believed, for newly engineered mechanisms of scientific social control.[15]

Control over reproduction was commonly viewed as a key part of that need. In 1933, Warren Weaver wrote to Frank Lillie about his new program in vital processes: "To indicate inclusion rather than exclusion, we will interest ourselves particularly in work in genetics; in hormones, vitamins and enzymes; in cell physiology; in nerve physiology; in psychobiology; and in the whole range of problems specifically and fundamentally involved in the biology of reproduction."[16] In a related statement on the Program in Experimental Biology two years later, Weaver went on: "Of all the recognized interests in the program, none stands closer to practical application than the field of endocrinology and the interrelated field of sex research. Moreover, these fields of research are fundamental to the broad common program of the foundation which seeks a rational understanding of human behavior."[17] The reproductive sciences could and did provide the kinds of interventions of control the Rockefeller Foundation sought.

In social movement worlds, too, control was the order of the day. Margaret Sanger and her colleagues named their movement the "birth *control* movement" specifically to embrace the values of rational, scientific management. Sanger noted: "Nothing better expresses the idea of purposive, responsible and self-directed guidance of the reproductive powers. . . . The verb 'control' means to exercise a directing, guiding, or restraining influence. . . . It implies intelligence, forethought and responsibility" (McCann 1994:11). It also was a necessary part of progress.

But for the reproductive sciences or molecular biology or birth control to be part of a wider framework of social control, they need to be translated into biomedical applications. The biomedicalization of life itself (human, plant, and animal) is the key overarching and usually taken-for-granted *social* process here.[18] Biomedicalization means the ongoing extension of biomedicine and technology into new and previously unmedicalized aspects of life, often imaged as a juggernaut of technological imperatives (Koenig 1988). Applications that could effect the kinds of biological engineering control discussed at the turn of the century were not generally available until after its midpoint. At that juncture, state-supported institutions such as the National Institutes of Health "pushed to integrate science, therapy and policy," becoming over the remainder of the century almost "the only research game in town" (Pauly 1993:137). Such integration over the past half century, as recent efforts to change health care organization have revealed, constitutes a robust biomedicalization of life indeed.

Many recent works on the body are concerned with these issues. Duden (1990:1, 4) has argued, "To study the making of the modern body is to study the gradual unfolding of something that is now self-evident. . . . [T]he genesis of the modern body is consistent with other aspects of the modern image of man, the *homo oeconomicus*."[19] Further, the modern reproductive body should be governed by what McCann (1994:13–14) terms *the economic ethic of fertility*, which emerged at the turn of the century and was foundational to the birth control movement. Derived from Thomas Malthus, this ethic asserts that families should not have more children than they can afford to support, constituting a "'moral prescription' against large families . . . [which] assumes a market society in which children, like property, are counted as assets or liabilities. . . . If society would permit women to follow this ethic, families would not be driven to destitution by the effort to nurture and educate their children. Thus, social efficiency would be enhanced."[20]

To follow the economic ethic of fertility, the modern body required and still requires the reproductive sciences and their technoscientific products both to have and to avoid having children. While I agree in part with Latour (1994) that we have never actually been modern, I would argue that this has not been due to lack of effort on the parts of many people. Folbre (1994) has recently deconstructed and reconceptualized "Rational Economic Man" into "Imperfectly Rational Somewhat Economic Persons," reminding us of the messy and erratic ways in which cultures are practiced. Translating, then, we are at the end of the millennium "sort of modern" in terms of both individual psyches and social philosophies and "somewhat modern" in terms of exercising control over reproduction.

Many of us who study the life sciences and biomedicine have noted that in the future, if not the present, "nature will be 'operationalized' for the good of society" (Lock 1993:148). Reproduction is being "enterprised up" (Strathern 1992). In the emergent industry of biotechnology, "the politics of fertility [now] extend from the soil to star wars" (Franklin 1995:326). Our task is to continue to examine these processes. Much scholarly energy has recently been focused on the Human Genome Initiative funded for $3 billion through the NIH and the Department of Energy to map genes and redesign life.[21] However, it has been and continues to be the reproductive sciences that have to date facilitated not only control over reproduction but also control over heredity, and hence over life itself. Warren Weaver well understood the interdependencies of genetics, molecular biology, and the reproductive sciences and the need for all to control life through the "new science of man." Ironically, the reproductive sciences have themselves been marginalized, and their centrality to the overall project of controlling life has thereby been comparatively ignored—by other scientists and historians and sociologists of science if not by the media and the public. This book, then, has pulled back the veil not from nature but from the reproductive sciences as a discipline that has had considerable success in disciplining reproduction, but has been rendered invisible perhaps as much as it has been applied in modernity and beyond.

APPENDIX ONE
HISTORIOGRAPHIC AND
METHODOLOGICAL NOTE

The formation and organization of the modern reproductive sciences as a discipline in the twentieth century have barely been examined. Data sources for this research were heterogeneous. I routinely used the small secondary literature on reproductive sciences both in the United States and Great Britain, which aided in developing some key comparisons. The "insider" histories—accounts of events and discoveries, biographies and autobiographies, status reports and so on written by reproductive researchers themselves, which I considered primary data, were invaluable (see citations in Chapter 1 and passim). In addition, many researchers began review articles with historical overviews of research on given topics (e.g., Allen 1932), which were also useful. All insider histories were considered primary data.

I also drew heavily on published journal reports and monographs of reproductive research (cited in the bibliography). Symposia, prefaces to texts, and introductions by senior researchers were all especially useful in providing scientists' own talk *about* their work rather than the results *of* the work. I also interviewed several reproductive scientists (some of whom had been students before World War II) and other individuals concerned with the reproductive sciences. Here my focus was especially on their assessments of how the reproductive sciences had been built as a disciplinary enterprise. I was pursuing, in the interviews, what qualitative researchers call "respondent validation," confirmation and refutation of aspects of my own broader analysis of the formation of the discipline.

In addition, I conducted extensive archival research, first examining the relevant papers held by the key funding source of the reproductive sciences during the period examined, the Rockefeller Foundation and its subsidiaries. I received a generous grant from the Rockefeller Archives to undertake this segment of the research. Second, I pursued archival materials at the sites of three of the major reproductive research centers in existence prior to World War II. Given the nature of the reproductive scientific enterprise as an intersection of efforts in biology, medicine and agriculture, I selected one center from each field. The Departments of Zoology, Anatomy and Physiological Chemistry at the University of Chicago served as the exemplar of a biological center (Clarke 1993; Mitman, Maienschein and Clarke 1993). The Carnegie Institution of Washington's Department of Embryology at Johns Hopkins Medical School served as the medical center (Clarke 1987/1995). And the Department of Animal Science at the University of California at Davis served as the agricultural center. I also examined the Frank R. Lillie papers held at the Woods Hole Marine Biological Laboratory which include all of the Annual Reports of the Chicago center to their major funding source, the NRC/CRPS.

The qualitative research method utilized was "grounded theory" as developed by Glaser and Strauss (1967; Glaser 1978; Strauss 1987; and Strauss and Corbin 1990). This is especially amenable to historical sociological research, especially using the social worlds approach discussed in chapters 1 and 9. In this method, the data are coded, and codes are densified and ultimately integrated into an analysis of the substantive area. Analysis is on-going throughout the research; data gathering is guided by sampling for highest ranges of variation and pursuit of specific analytic issues (Clarke 1990b, 1991b).

INTERVIEWS

A number of reproductive scientists and people associated with such work were kind enough to grant me interviews. Respondents willing to be cited for the record included: Andrew Nalbandov (University of Illinois, Urbana/Champaign), Neena Schwartz (Northwestern University), Larry Ewing (Johns Hopkins Medical Institutions), George Stabenfelt (University of California, Davis), Reuben Albaugh (University of California, Davis), Perry T. Cupps (University of California, Davis), Hubert Heitman (University of California, Davis), John Biggers (Harvard University Medical School), Roy Greep (Harvard University Medical School), and M. C. Shelesnyak (the Weizmann Institute). Their assistance was invaluable.

APPENDIX TWO

ON THE NATIONAL RESEARCH COUNCIL COMMITTEE FOR RESEARCH IN PROBLEMS OF SEX

FRANK LILLIE'S 1922 "A CLASSIFICATION OF SUBJECTS IN THE BIOLOGY OF SEX" (ABERLE AND CORNER 1953:102–4)

I. The Genetics of Sex.
   A. *The inheritance of sex and of sex-linked characters.*
   B. *Cytological (sex chromosomes).*
II. Determination of Sex.
   A. *Genetic or zygotic factors in the determination of sex.* The literature in this field has been more thoroughly explored, probably, than any other in the biology of sex. Presumably, therefore, not so much in need of support as other parts of the subject.
   Problem for investigation: If sex is determined by two kinds of spermatozoa, is any process of selection possible by which one or the other kind may predominate?
   B. *Environmental factors in the determination of sex.* There is a large literature dating from early times on this subject, mostly outlived. In addition, there are some still vital problems, e.g., (1) Does the time of conception in the oestrous cycle of the female influence the sex ratio? How? (2) May zygotic factors be overbalanced by environmental conditions? e.g., Are females ever transformed into males? At what time in the life cycle, etc.? (Evidence from some invertebrates, fish, etc.) (3) Do conditions of nutrition play any part in the determination of the sex ratio?
   C. *The interpretation of sex ratios with reference to sex determining factors.*
III. Sex Development; Differentiation of Sex.
   A. *Descriptive, normal (including hermaphroditism).*
      1. Embryonic—Fairly well known.

279

2. Juvenile   ⎧ We need here especially a complete
3. Adult   ⎨ histological picture of gonads, etc.,
4. Senescent   ⎩ at all ages. The knowledge on this
                 subject is singularly incomplete.

B. *The problem of sex hormones.* The influence of the homologous and heterologous hormones at all stages of the life history on anatomy, physiology, psyche and physiological age.
  1. Histological.
     (a) The embryonic history of interstitial cells. Important for understanding embryonic sex differentiation.
     (b) The interstitial cells of the normal and experimentally modified ovary and testis—the data for the ovary are especially obscure and conflicting.
     (c) The seasonal cycle of interstitial cells in various vertebrates.
  2. Experimental.
     (a) The influence of the homologous and heterologous hormones in embryonic life. To what extent are sex characters reversible?
     (b) Sex modifications *in utero* by other hormones or by antibodies.
     (c) Sexual modification after birth by hormones; and development: Castration, homologous and heterologous grafting, sex gland extracts, etc., including structure, function, psyche.
     (d) Effect of similar experiments (as in c) on age and rejuvenation.
     (e) To what extent are sex hormones *species*-specific?
  3. Chemical. It will be the work of the biologist to test the nature and limits of hormone action, as in 1 and 2 above, and to discover proper criteria and indicators. It will be the province of the chemist to endeavor to identify, isolate and ultimately synthesize the sex hormones. The possibility of an ultimate ready control of sex characters and behavior within the limits discovered to be possible by the biologist must depend on the chemist working in close cooperation with the biologist.

C. *The study of other factors*, e.g., other internal secretions on the development of sex.

IV. The Problem of Sex Inter-relations.
So far as these problems are human, they will be included in the physiological, psychological and sociological division of the work of the Committee. But the biological aspect of this subject, so extensive and so controllable, offers a field of great promise.

V. Sex Functions.
This heading trespasses on the physiological division of the work of the Committee, but no line can be drawn between the biological and the physiological. It is impossible to carry out the program under III without attacking certain parts of this field. The subjects closest to the biological field are the following:

A. *Variation of sex glands under experimental conditions:*
  1. Transplantation
  2. Vasectomy

3. X-rays and other radiations
4. Antibody injections
5. Vital staining
6. General physiology of the sex glands
B. *Sterility:*
   1. Incompatibility of gametes
   2. Other causes
   3. Experimentally produced sterility
VI. Systematics of Sex in Animals and Plants.

The comparative anatomy, neurology, physiology and pathology of primary and secondary sex organs and sex characters in animals and plants. The evolution of sex, hermaphroditism, normal and accidental, in its various forms, sex dimorphism, organs of sex recognition, stimulation and realization (special sense organs, songs, ornamental characters, sex odors, organs of attack, etc.), brooding and placental structures, adaptations and habits, etc.

LIST OF MEMBERS OF THE NATIONAL RESEARCH COUNCIL COMMITTEE FOR RESEARCH IN PROBLEMS OF SEX, 1921–53

List notes members' initial year and range of appointment (accurate through 1953), their position at the time they were appointed and subsequently. 19** indicates still serving as a member in 1953.

Allen, Willard	1945–19**	Professor of Obstetrics and Gynecology, Washington University
Cannon, Walter B.	1921–1945	Professor of Physiology, Harvard Medical School
Conklin, E. G.	1921–1922	Professor of Zoology, Princeton University
Corner, George W.	1934–19**	Professor of Anatomy, U. of Rochester School of Medicine Director, Department of Embryology, Carnegie Institution of Washington
Davis, Katherine Bement	1922–1928	General Secretary, Bureau of Social Hygiene
Fenn, Wallace O.	1945–1948	Professor of Physiology, U. of Rochester School of Medicine
Kluckhohn, Clyde K.	1949–19**	Professor of Anthropology, Harvard University
Lashley, Karl S.	1934–19**	Professor of Psychology, University of Chicago > Professor of Psychology, Harvard University > Director, Yerkes Laboratory of Primate Biology
Lillie, Frank R.	1922–1937	Professor of Zoology, University of Chicago

Long, C. N. Hugh	1945–19**	Professor of Physiological Chemistry, Yale University
Meyer, Adolph	1928–1945	Professor of Psychiatry, Johns Hopkins U. School of Medicine
Moore, Carl R.	1938–19**	Professor of Zoology, University of Chicago
Neel, James V.	1949–19**	Associate Geneticist > Associate Professor of Medical Genetics Laboratory of Vertebrate Biology, University of Michigan
Ogburn, William F.	1925–1928	Professor of Sociology, Columbia University Professor of Sociology, University of Chicago
Romano, John	1945–1948	Professor of Psychiatry, Cincinnati Medical School> Professor of Psychiatry, U. of Rochester Medical School
Salmon, Thomas W.	1922–1927	Professor of Psychiatry, Columbia University
Taylor, Howard C.	1947–1951	Professor of Gynecology and Obstetrics, College of Physicians and Surgeons, Columbia University
Wissler, Clark	1925–1936	Curator, Anthropology, American Museum of Natural History> Professor, Institute for Human Relations, Yale University
Yerkes, Robert M.	1921–1947	Chairman of the Committee Chairman, Research Information Service, NRC Professor of Psychology, Yale University Professor of Psychobiology, Yale University Director, Yale Laboratories of Primate Biology
Zinn, Earl F.	1921–1929	Executive Secretary of the Committee

(Aberle and Corner 1953:105–7)

TABLE 11 Centers of Reproductive Research Sponsored by the National Research
Council's Committee for Research on Problems of Sex, 1922–1940 by Number of Publications

Investigator	University	# Pubs.	Years Supported		Problem Focus
Lillie, FR	Chicago	222	1922	1934	biology of sex hormones
Evans, HM	Berkeley	153	1922	1934	nutrition & endocrine relations
Witschi, E	Iowa	126	1929	1947	physiology of reproduction
Smith, PE	Stanford, Columbia	115	1926	1938	pituitary hormones, cytology of sex
Hisaw, FL	Wisconsin, Harvard	70	1926	1936	physiology of corpus luteum
Allen, E	Washington, Missouri, Yale	69	1923	1943	follicular hormones
Bisonette, TH	Trinity	48	1929	1938	light & periodicity
Stone, CP	Stanford	48	1922	1941	sexual behavior
Stockard, CR	Cornell	39	1922	1939	physiology & morphology of estrus cycle
Cunningham, RS	Vanderbilt	30	1930	1933	reproduction physiology
Yerkes, RM	Yale	30	1925	1934	psychobiology of sex in monkeys
Gustavson, RG	Chicago, Denver, Colorado	27	1929	1938	assay for female sex hormones
Slonaker,JR	Stanford	27	1923	1935	influences on sexual behavior
Metz, CW	Carnegie Institute	24	1926	1935	sex determination
Reynolds, SRM	LI College of Medicine	24	1934	1941	uterus & acetylcholine & estrogen
Young, WC	Brown, Yale	24	1935	1941	structure & behavior of reproduction
Markee, JE	Stanford	20	1930	1941	physiology of the uterus, ovogenesis
Swingle, WW	Iowa	19	1927	1929	biology of sex
Bard, P	Johns Hopkins	17	1933	1944	neural bases of sexual behavior
Cannon, WB	Harvard	15	1936	1939	neural influence of sex functions
Painter, T	Texas	14	1922	1926	mammalian spermatogenesis
Terman, LM	Stanford	14	1925	1945	sex differences, psychobiology
Koch, FC	Chicago	13	1930	1942	biochemistry & metabolism of sex hormones
Humphrey, RR	Buffalo	12	1929	1933	biology of sex & sex reversal

(continued)

TABLE 11 (continued)

Investigator	University	# Pubs.	Years Supported		Problem Focus
Noble, GK	American Museum of Natural History	13	1935	1940	sexual dimorphism & neurobehavior
Cole, LJ	Wisconsin	12	1930	1935	physiology of reproduction in pigeons
Aberle, SB	Yale	11	1930	1934	cyclic changes in humans
Blakeslee AF	Carnegie Institution	10	1924	1925	measures of sex differences
Hartman, CG & Meyer, A	Carnegie Institution	10	1935	1941	reproductive physiology in mammals
Pincus, G	Harvard, Clark	10	1933	1943	tissue culture fertilization & metabolism of ovarian hormone
Wells, LJ	Missouri	10	1935	1937	prolonged gestation in rats
Britton, SW	Virginia	9	1932	1935	adrenal physiology & sex
Friedman, MH	Penn.	9	1930	1932	ovulation in the rabbit
Kelly, GL	Georgia	8	1927	1931	physiology & endocrinology of pregnancy
Smith, GVS	Free Hospital for Women, MA	7	1938	1942	estrogen metabolism in pregnant women
Marker, RE	Penn. State	6	1939	1940	sex homones in urine
Papanicolaou, G	Cornell	6	1939	1940	physiology & morphology of sex in mammals
Peck, MW	Harvard	6	1924	1925	sex & homosexuality in adolescents
Whiting, PW	Harvard	6	1926	1927	genetics & cytology of sex determination
Parker, GF	Harvard	5	1928	1931	cilia of oviducts
Fluhman, CF	Stanford	4	1937	1938	bioassay for blood progesterone
Frank, RT & Gustavson, RG	Denver	4	1936	1929	bioassay for female hormone
Blandau, RJ	Brown, Hawaii, Rochester	3	1939	1947	reproductive cycle & embryo development
Hartman, CG	Texas, Illinois	3	1925	1947	expedition; assays of hormones

TABLE 11 *(continued)*

Investigator	University	# Pubs.	Years Supported		Problem Focus
Huggins, C	Chicago	3	1939	1947	physiology & cancer of the prostate
Kelly, EL	Conn. State	3	1934	1939	psychobiology & sexual compatibility
Landis, C	NYS Psychiatric Hospital	3	1934	1943	psychosexual development
Lashley, KS	Minnesota, Harvard	3	1922	1938	glandular function in rats
Wissler, C	Yale	3	1926	1931	human sex behavior
Albright, F	Mass General Hospital	2	1938	1942	FSH production
Atwell, WJ	Buffalo	2	1932	1933	pituitary/adrenal/ gonadal relations
Cole, LJ & Painter, T	Wisconsin	2	1928	1930	avian spermatogenesis
Okey, R	California	2	1927	1928	menstrual variance in blood contents
Oslund, RM	Vanderbilt	2	1924	1925	effects of x-rays on rat testes
Ransom, SW	Northwestern	2	1939	1943	hypothalmus & estrus & pregnancy
Rock, J	Free Hospital for Women, MA	2	1938	1941	bioelectrical aspects of ovulation
Snyder, FF	Hopkins	2	1936	1937	control of parturition
Wislocki, GB	Harvard	2	1936	1937	twinning in marmosets
Amer. Roentgen Ray Society	New York	1	1924	1927	x-rays & fertility and sterility
Baldwin, BT	Iowa	1	1922	1922	sperm cells in boys
Corner GW	Rochester	1	1926	1929	cyclic changes in the uterus
Howard, E	Venezuela	1	1927	1928	adrenal cortex & gonadal relations.
Leonard, SL	Union C.	1	1934	1935	physiology of sex hormones
Meyer, A.	Hopkins, Carnegie	1	1922	1942	psychophysiology of human sex behavior
Moore, CR	Chicago	1	1930	1947	reproduction in high altitudes
Potter, HW	Letchworth Village	1	1924	1925	sex behavior of mentally retarded
Severinghaus, A	Wisc. General Hospital	1	1934	1935	anterior pituitary hormone in blood & urine

(continued)

TABLE 11 *(continued)*

Investigator	University	# Pubs.	Years Supported		Problem Focus
Hilario, A	Philippines	0	1926	1927	biology of sex
Selle, RM	Occidental	0	1927	1928	endocrinology & development of white rat
Spaeth, RA	Bangkok	0	1924	1924	ovulation & menstruation in apes

NOTE: This chart reflects problems considered worthy of pursuit by the NRC/CRPS to 1940. Based on Appendices 7 and 8 of Aberle and Corner (1953). Years Supported are first and last years, and do *not* imply continuous support.

NOTES

CHAPTER ONE

1. Lillie went on to be a leading reproductive scientist and a senior statesman of American science, the only individual ever to serve simultaneously as the president of both the National Academy of Sciences (1935–39) and the National Research Council (1935–36) (Willier 1957). I take this story up in more detail in chapter 3 and elsewhere (Clarke 1991a, 1996).

2. Although the initial work was solely Papanicolaou's, by convention the head of the laboratory was listed as first author on all publications. Papanicolaou later objected, and Stockard agreed to end this practice (Carmichael 1973:49–50). Despite evidence that the vaginal smear, now known as the Pap smear in his honor, could provide indications of cancer or precancerous conditions in the vagina or uterus, Papanicolaou received no serious support for this research until 1939. Since then, the Pap smear has become one of the major cancer screening technologies in the world, used both diagnostically and for epidemiological purposes. See Carmichael (1973), Casper and Clarke (1997), and Clarke and Casper (1996).

3. "His organization and maintenance of his monkey colony set the standard for such work in primate research centers to the present day, including his insistence upon daily observation," without which his key findings might well have been missed (Ramsay 1994:66–67). It is most appropriate to start this book with a story from George Corner's work since his wonderful autobiography was the first thing I read in my research. He was both reflective and reflexive, himself a historian of medicine and chronicler of the reproductive sciences (e.g., Corner 1965, 1960, 1951; Aberle and Corner 1953). I suspect he well knew that his autobiography would someday serve as data for others. A major recent review of reproductive research from antiquity to the late twentieth century (Gruhn and Kazer 1989) frames all the work reviewed as either "Before Corner" or "After Corner," making his con-

tributions the turning point into modernity. In his spare time Corner wrote books for young people on sex: *Attaining Manhood: A Doctor Talks to Boys about Sex* (1938) and a girls' version (similarly titled) the following year (1939).

4. See RAC, RG3, 915, Box 1.7. Weaver's Report, February 14, 1934, pp. 2–3.

5. On Pincus's family background, see Stellhorn (1978). More generally and for this story, see Pauly (1987:186–94), Ingle (1971), and Reed (1983:319–33).

6. On the human/nonhuman distinction, see Haraway (1992), Callon (1985), and Latour (1987).

7. See Farber (1982a:132) and Gerson (1983) on disciplinary necessities and scientific social worlds.

8. I draw here on recent studies of knowledge production discussed below, which, in turn, draw generously on Foucault and others.

9. Farley (1982) ambitiously examined the study of reproduction in both flora and fauna up to ca. 1915. Greep and his colleagues (1976, 1977) thoroughly examined the mammalian reproductive sciences after about 1960, including elaborate conceptual mappings of earlier work; Hertz (1984) and Mastroianni, Donaldson, and Kane (1990) flesh out this account almost to the present.

10. See also Gasking (1967) and Bodemer (1976); on reproduction as creation and the creation of monsters by science, see Bann (1994).

11. For recent work on the indeterminacy of sex and sex hormones, see, for example, Fausto-Sterling (1993, 1998) and Oudshoorn (1994). There also is considerable debate regarding the sex-gender distinction (e.g., Barrett and Phillips 1992; Gatens 1996). My goal here is to be systematic and clear in my narrative, sometimes in contrast with the framings of the reproductive scientists themselves, who may have had other agendas. At the same time, I recognize the contradictions between my seemingly realist linguistic "definitions" and my own constructionist approach.

12. The terms *modern, premodern,* and *postmodern* are highly loaded and problematic. I use them advisedly, especially to mark historical eras. For premodern and early modern studies of reproduction, see Farley (1982), Gasking (1967), and Riddle (1992).

13. The premodern, modern, and postmodern are mutually constitutive. See Clarke (1995a) for my extended argument on this distinction. On the simultaneity of the premodern with the modern and with the postmodern, see also Riddle (1992) and Pickstone (1993a,b). Martin (1990, 1994) seems to argue for a less traversed boundary. In the modern mode, the lived body is to be controlled, and changes planned across the life course. The social goal is achieving the traditional heterosexual nuclear family ideal (biological mother, father, and two children, one of each sex) in a managed fashion. The reproductive body politic is centered on population control. Lives are "Taylored," reframed following the scientific management ethos of Frederick Taylor (Banta 1993). In contrast, in the postmodern mode, the lived body is manipulated, transformed, and customized with what Martin (1990) has called "tailor-made specificities," flexibly accumulating desired capacities. The social body is transformed with new and diverse social meanings for mother, father, and most especially for "family" (biological/social/surrogate/donor/other). Sexual preferences and/or identities become increasingly irrelevant

to reproduction. Families—both traditional and nontraditional—become a new industry/market and policy niche.

14. See, for example, Robinson (1976), Foucault (1978), Birken (1988), Irvine (1990), and Bullough (1994).

15. During the era examined, contraceptives were used widely only on and by humans, who were viewed as the end users. Uses in animals in the "wild" and in zoos to regulate populations and reproduction are actually part of the postmodern era, transforming nature and animal bodies in the very ways discussed earlier.

16. Key studies that fall loosely in this vein include Edge and Mulkay (1976), Farber (1982a), Fye (1987), Kohler (1982), Law (1980), Mullins (1972), and Pickering (1984). Reviews of this "generation" of work are provided by Chubin (1976), Graham, Lepenies, and Weingart (1983), Lemaine et al. (1976), and Zuckerman (1989). See also Kohler (1981), and Whitley (1984).

17. Geison (1981) raised the issue of the relationships of parts (specialties, research schools, centers) to wholes (disciplines), asserting that in such ecologies, local centers of activity must be taken into account. Centers of research were crucial actors in my analysis. I was particularly sensitized to these historical and historiographic issues by the teaching of Dan Todes and Gert Brieger at the University of California, San Francisco, in the early 1980s, and the work and counsel of Gerald Geison, Charles Rosenberg, and Jane Maienschein in early phases of this project.

18. See, for example, Abir-Am (1982, 1985, 1993), Kohler (1976, 1978, 1991), Arnove (1980), Cueto, ed. (1994), Fisher (1990), Kay (1993a,b), Morawski (1986), and Fisher (1993).

19. Those who work in this vein also deprivilege certain knowledges, such as that of the sciences, asserting instead that valued knowledge, even if "unofficial," can be produced in any number of places. On this point see also Watson-Verran and Turnbull (1995).

20. Key interactionists here include Park (1952), Hughes (1971), and Blumer (1969/1993). For the ecological vision, see Rosenberg (1979b) and Star (1995).

21. See Mead (1938/1972:518) for this interesting early use of discourse. For explicit social worlds theory, see Strauss (1978, 1979, 1982, 1991, 1993) and Clarke (1990b, 1991b).

22. More specifically, in Strauss's words (1978:122, emphasis in original): "In each social world, at least one primary *activity* (along with related activities) is strikingly evident, i.e., . . . researching, collecting. There are *sites* where activities occur: hence space and a shaped landscape are relevant. *Technology* (inherited or innovative means of carrying out the social world's activities) is always involved. . . . In social worlds at their outset, there may be only a temporary division of labor, but once underway, *organizations* inevitably evolve to further one aspect or another of the world's activities."

23. For studies of different arenas in the arts, sciences, and computing, see Becker (1982), Wiener (1981), Clarke (1990a,b), Clarke and Montini (1993), Fujimura (1988), Kling and Gerson (1978), Star (1986, 1989), and Star and Griesemer (1989).

24. This, of course, creates the "problem of insider histories." See Clarke (1985:468–71) and Woolgar (1976) on the use of discovery accounts.

25. Of course the entire arena analysis is not necessarily presented in publications but is used in the research phase. I have told other stories about the reproductive sciences elsewhere (Clarke 1987, 1990a,b, 1991a, 1993, 1995a,b).

26. Greenhalgh (1996) argues that demography has had similar problems of illegitimacy and that it has dwelled at the margins, if not outside, of the academy for decades, with deleterious effects for its theoretical and methodological development.

27. See Aronson (1984) and Gieryn (1983, 1995).

28. On classical anatomy see, for example, Tuana (1993), Laqueur (1990), Jordanova (1989), Schiebinger (1989, 1993), and Moore and Clarke (1995). On physiology, see Shuttleworth (1990); on gynecology, see Moscucci (1990) and Dally (1992); on neuroendocrinology, see van den Wijngaard (1991); on neurology, see Fausto-Sterling (1992); on genetics, see Rapp (1990), and Hubbard (1990); and on space biology, see Casper and Moore (1995). On the rhetorical and other practices of many sciences there are a number of important works (e.g., Stepan 1986; Schiebinger 1989, 1993; Martin 1987/1992, 1994; Keller 1992; Harding 1991; and Treichler 1993).

29. See Borell (1976a,b,c, 1978, 1985, 1987a), (Long) Hall (1974, 1976, 1978, 1979), Long (1987, 1990), Oudshoorn (1994, 1995, 1996a,b), and Rechter (1997). For other recent science studies works on reproductive topics see van den Wijngaard (1994), Pfeffer (1993), Courey (1994), Casper (1994a,b, 1995, 1998), and Dugdale (1995).

30. See, for example, Fausto-Sterling (1993, 1998), Terry (1990), Hirschauer (1991), Chase (1997), and Balsamo (1996).

31. See, for example, on the women's health movements, Ruzek (1978), Lewin and Olesen (1985), Dixon-Mueller (1993a,b), Boston Women's Health Book Collective (1992), and Fee and Krieger (1994).

32. See Farley (1982), Star (1986, 1989), and Russett (1989) for discussion of triangulation of robustness.

33. See, for example, Churchill (1979), Farley (1982), Fausto-Sterling (1989, 1998), and Longino and Doell (1983).

34. The recent intersections of feminist, technoscience, and cultural studies provide provocative directions in which to seek answers (e.g., McNeil and Franklin 1991). On feminist theory, see, for example, Haraway (1989, 1991), Collins (1990), Butler (1993), and Barrett and Phillips (1992).

35. See Clarke (1995a) for a detailed definition of industrialization. See, for example, Aronson (1979) on the industrialization of food and Fitzgerald (in progress) on the industrialization of agriculture in the early to mid–twentieth century.

36. See, for example, Haraway (1992, 1995), Lock (1993), Rabinow (1992), Latour (1993), and Cronon (1995).

37. See, for example, Maier (1984) and Banta (1993) on ideologies of industrial management; Cohen and Skull (1983) and Mayer (1983) on social control and the state in the early twentieth century; and Burnham (1972) on medical specialties and social control ideologies in the Progressive Era.

38. Haraway's (1995) discussion and charts of biological projects across the twentieth century are riveting. Controlling race (ca. 1900–1930s) and population

(ca.1940–1970s) were part of what I have termed the modernist frame (Clarke 1995a). Controlling evolution (1975–1990s) goes far beyond that. Haraway (1995:349) notes that "biotechnology in the service of corporate profit is a revolutionary force for remaking the inhabitants of planet earth, from viruses and bacteria right up the now repudiated chain of being to Homo sapiens and beyond."

39. Kay finds parallel developments in the social sciences, which also gleaned Rockefeller Foundation support during this era, focusing on behaviorist approaches, personality, and socialization. Allan Gregg's emphasis on the development of psychiatry through the Medical Division of the Rockefeller Foundation, which he headed as the "golden age" of the reproductive sciences was ending in the 1930s and 1940s, raises the important point of the continuities of foundation investments in terms of goals of actually applying scientific knowledge, not merely producing it (Pressman 1997). Morawski (1986:219–20) fleshes this out with the story of Yale's Institute of Human Relations, which received $4.5 million from the Rockefeller Foundation during its first decade 1929–39 to help solve "problems of man's individual and group conduct . . . to achieve the rational control of human behavior."

40. See Riddle (1992), Riessman (1983), and Folbre (1994).

CHAPTER TWO

1. See, for example, DeVane (1965), Kohlstedt (1985), Jarausch (1983), Larson (1977), Light (1983), Vesey (1965), Abbott (1988), and Geiger (1986).

2. On the historical development of professionalized sciences in the United States, see, for example, Kohlstedt (1976, 1985), Kohlstedt and Rossiter (1986), and Rothblatt (1983). On the question of what constitutes a profession, Freidson (1970:4, xvii) observes that it is "folly to be dogmatic about any definition"; at its most basic level, a profession is "an occupation which has assumed a dominant position in a division of labor, so that it gains control over the determination of the substance of its own work." Unlike most occupations, professions have strong (though never completely) autonomous and self-directing attributes (e.g., Hirsch 1974; Restivo 1974). Professionals have both social/cultural and scientific authority as experts over their jurisdictional domains; strength and stability characterize their preeminence, once achieved (Freidson 1970, 1994; Strauss 1971). For further discussion of professionalization processes as more analytically useful than lists of attributes of professions, see Bucher and Strauss (1961), Strauss (1971), and Abbott (1988).

3. Though there is general accord that the sciences were professionalized by the early twentieth century, there has been debate over whether the sciences as disciplines and scientific research as an occupation were/are professions per se. Contributors to this debate include Beer and Lewis (1974), Farber (1982a,b), Freidson (1968), Geison (1981 1983), Gerson (1983), Hughes (1971), Larson (1977), Rosenberg (1979b), and Strauss (1971).

4. See Strauss (1971). Herbst (1983:201) also stresses the impacts of extrauniversity organizations such as private industry and government on the profession,

such as influencing pay scales within the university. Abbott (1988) and Freidson (1994) provide important comparative work.

5. Such lay "demand" for services has recently been addressed. See Geison on professions (1983) and Riessman (1983) on women's activities in the medicalization of women's bodily processes.

6. See, for example, Freidson (1970), Geison (1983), Gieryn (1983), Herbst (1983), Light (1983), Rosenberg (1976), and Strauss (1971).

7. For discussion of the origins and development of the term biology, see, for example, Coleman (1971:1–3) and Pauly (1984:370).

8. Research on the institutionalization of professional biology in the late nineteenth century has been ambitious over the past decade or so. See Allen (1981), Churchill (1981), Maienschein (1985a,b,c,d), Pauly (1984), Mitman (1992), Kay (1993b), and the collections edited by Rainger, Benson, and Maienschein (1988), Benson, Maienschein, and Rainger (1991), and Mitman, Clarke, and Maienschein (1993).

9. See Pauly (1984:371), Rainger, Benson, and Maienschein (1988:3–10), and Pauly (1987).

10. Corner (1960:181) notes similar processes on the medical side in anatomy. These students were exposed to a unique combination of faculty at Johns Hopkins: H. Newell Martin offering physiology in a medical framework (prior to the development of a medical school) and W. K. Brooks offering evolutionary morphology and comparative anatomy (Benson 1981, 1985, 1989; Gilbert 1978:308). As Pauly (1984:381) put it, "Their students began to take seriously their pursuit of biology—seen as an intermingling of animal (largely invertebrate) physiology and morphology."

11. On Whitman, see especially Maienschein (1988) and Pauly (1994).

12. Handwritten on University of Chicago Stationery (emphasis in original); undated (ca. 1891 or 1892). UChiA PP1:B18, F6.

13. For accounts of some of these departments, see Pauly (1984), Benson (1981,1985), and Mitman, Clarke, and Maienschein (1993).

14. See Churchill (1981:189), Cravens (1978:25), Rosenberg (1967:38–40), Pauly (1984:371), Rainger, Benson, and Maienschein (1988:3–11), and Kimmelman (1987, 1992).

15. See, for Woods Hole, Cravens (1978), Lillie (1944), Maienschein (1985a,b,c, 1991b), Werdinger (1980), and Pauly (1988). On Cold Spring Harbor, see Allen (1986) and Cravens (1978).

16. See Churchill (1981:188), Cravens (1978:28–29), Kohlstedt (1976, 1985), Kiger (1963:265), and Appel (1987).

17. There is a vast historical and sociological literature on the development of a medical monopoly through professionalization and specialization processes (e.g., Berlant 1975; Brown 1979; Conrad and Kern 1981; Freidson 1970, 1975, 1994; Larson 1977; Starr 1982; Stevens 1971; Markowitz and Rosner 1979; Numbers 1980; Cangi 1982; Harvey 1981; Sabin 1934; Oakley 1984; Stevens 1971; Sturdy 1993; Halpern 1988; and Digby 1994).

18. See Harvey (1981:104–26) and Kiger (1963).

19. See Harvey (1981:78), Numbers (1980), Shryock (1947), and (Sabin 1934:303).

20. See Marks (1983) and Meldrum (1996).

21. See Lilienfeld (1980) and Brieger (1980).

22. The classic references include Brown (1979), Shryock (1947), Starr (1982), and Stevens (1971). Sabin (1934:251–80) provides an excellent insider history of the development of medicine as science in an elite institution in her biography of Franklin Paine Mall. Sabin (1934:255–58) chronicles earlier efforts in this direction by anatomy faculty at Chicago and Johns Hopkins. Such faculty in numerous instances led the way by seeing themselves as equally close to zoologists involved in the new experimental biology as they were to medicine (Blake 1980:41).

23. See Cangi (1982), Numbers (1980), and Sabin (1934). For accounts of the shift toward scientific medicine in each of the major medical disciplines, see Numbers (1980) and Vogel and Rosenberg (1979). Whether this was originally a two-track or a three-track segmentation is unclear. Certainly three distinctive lines of work developed in medical institutions over this century, with tensions among them: basic research, clinical research, and clinical teaching and practice (Geison 1979; Harvey 1981; Numbers 1980; Shryock 1947:183; Vogel and Rosenberg 1979; Warner 1980:70). There is not a single reference to a reproductive problem addressed by clinical research from ca. 1905 to 1945 in Harvey's (1981) classic work.

24. When he was young, he had wanted to become a zoologist, but this was not seen as an acceptable career in his family (Corner 1958a, 1981).

25. Unquestionably, links to the experimental sciences also gave medicine a new "culturally compelling basis for consolidating its status as an autonomous 'learned profession,' with all of the corporate and material advantages that such status implies" (Geison 1979:85). But whether the science was part of actual practice, "window-dressing," good training in the logics of the body, another terminology for bureaucratization, and/or something else are open questions, subject to multiple readings. Major contributors to this debate include Geison (1979, 1987), Warner (1985), Lawrence (1985), Pauly (1987), Sturdy (1993), and others. Cooter and Sturdy (1992) argue that the increasing emphasis on scientific medicine was part of a growing interest in scientific management more generally, what I have subsumed as industrialization.

26. The literature is ambitious (e.g., Antler and Fox 1978; Apfel and Fisher 1984; Bell 1986, Hiddinga 1987; Corea 1977; Dreifus 1978; Ehrenreich and English 1979; Gordon 1976; Leavitt 1986; Mohr 1978; Oakley 1984; Reed 1983; Scully 1980; Wertz and Wertz 1977; Dally 1992; Moscucci 1990; Riessman 1983; Apple 1990; and Digby 1994).

27. Due to a "jurisdictional battle over the abdomen with the general surgeons," the AMA section was renamed Obstetrics, Gynecology and Abdominal Surgery in 1912, reverting to Obstetrics and Gynecology alone in 1938. On early gynecologic surgery, see also McGregor (1989).

28. The emphasis on surgical solutions to reproductive problems during nineteenth-century gynecology is clear in the insider histories (e.g., Leonardo 1944; Speert 1980:37–71) and in recent secondary works (e.g., Moscucci 1990; and Dally

1992). See also the debate regarding J. Marion Sims's gynecologic surgery (Barker-Benfield 1976; McGregor 1989; Scully 1980), and accounts of early gynecologic surgery in Brieger (1980).

29. See Ludmerer (1983) on teaching hospitals, and see Leavitt (1986) and Miller (1979) on anesthesia. There is now an extensive literature on the elimination of midwives (e.g., Declercq and Lacroix 1985; Haller 1981; Leavitt 1986; Wertz and Wertz 1977, 1981; Wertz 1983; Oakley 1984; Apple 1990).

30. See Oakley (1984), Speert (1980:142–49), Stevens (1971:200), and Fildes, Marks, and Marland (1992).

31. On maternal health, see, for example, Antler and Fox (1978), Lansing, Penman, and Davis (1983), Wertz and Wertz (1977), and Stevens (1971:199–204).

32. See also Riessman (1983), and Edwards and Waldorf (1984).

33. A specialists' text of the era was Hamblen's *Endocrine Gynecology* (1939). Medical researchers focused largely on the female cycle up to ca. 1940 and then added phenomena of pregnancy to their problems; they did not particularly attend to male reproductive phenomena until long after 1940, though biological and agricultural reproductive researchers did (American Foundation 1955 2:139–40).

34. See Longo (1980:218–19, 1981) and Hahn (1987).

35. See Reed (1983:164); Williams also noted the characteristic lack of clinical opportunities for obstetrics students during the late nineteenth century (Reed 1983:163; Ludmerer 1983). See also Longo (1980, 1981).

36. See Geison (1979) for specific contrasts between the earnings of physician researchers and practitioners.

37. See Corner (1958a:27) and Ramsay (1994:63). See also Sabin (1934:254) for another version of Mall's views on basic research. Mall subsequently became head of the Carnegie Institution of Washington's Department of Embryology at Johns Hopkins.

38. See Apfel and Fisher (1984), Bell (1986), and Borell (1985). J. B. Collip (Hamblen 1939:ix, emphasis added) stated, for example: "Quite irrespective, then, of the degree of clarity that has been obtained in the elucidation of the physiological or pharmacologic properties of chemically pure hormones or extracts of hormones, the clinical value—if any—of such work must be determined by clinical experiment *by clinicians* working alone or with their colleagues of the laboratory." This text included clinical studies of endocrine therapies; the commercial preparations used were provided by major American pharmaceutical companies (Hamblen 1939:xiii).

39. There is a superb if small secondary literature on the history of American agriculture and agricultural research. See Busch (1981, 1982), Busch and Lacey (1983), Kimmelman (1983, 1987, 1992), Rosenberg (1976), Rossiter (1975, 1976, 1979), Marcus (1985, 1988), and Volberg (1983). Indeed, Rosenberg's (1976) analysis of the situation of agricultural experiment stations and their scientists in relation to the conflicting demands of their audiences, consumers, and professions informs my own. Regrettably, with some exceptions, little has been done on the early development of animal (especially mammalian) agricultural research (Asdell 1977; Byerly 1976; Rossiter 1979). See also Brown (1979), Randolph and Sachs (1981:96), and Lewontin (1982). Randolph and Sachs (1981:96–97) emphasize a

contrast between physicians, who were trained in science, and farmers, who were not, creating a need for agricultural science to be "translated" for farmers, largely by agricultural extension workers. I would argue, in contrast, that these were and remain differences in degree rather than in kind. Certainly during the pre–World War II era, many practicing physicians also needed lay translations of developments in medical science. See Harrower (1917) and Robinson (1934) for examples. Moreover, as more and more farmers were educated in agricultural schools and the sciences became specialized, differences likely diminished further. Specialization may not have been as extensive as supposed, however (Gregson 1993).

40. See Rosenberg (1976:135–52), Rossiter (1975), Krohn and Schafer (1976), Fitzgerald (in progress), and Marcus (1985).

41. See Rosenberg (1976:148). True and Clark (1900) offer a full report on the status of the experiment stations to date; see Dupree (1957) for analyses of the origins of the USDA and experiment stations, and Knoblauch, Law, and Meyer (1962) for the centennial insider history of agricultural experiment stations. See also Willham (1986).

42. See Rosenberg (1976:148), Marcus (1985), and Dupree (1957:170).

43. Pursell (1968) provides an intriguing analysis of innovation and rearticulation of goals under duress in agricultural research.

44. See Rosenberg (1976:151). Several efforts in the late nineteenth century failed to establish engineering research stations modeled on those developed in agriculture (Busch and Lacey 1983:14). Busch and Lacey (1983:8) attribute the success of agriculturalists to their pragmatic, problem-focused, Baconian model of corporate research for the public weal, a new and different model of science than had formerly been promoted.

45. See Kohler (1979:50), Rossiter (1975), and Marcus (1985, 1988).

46. See Busch and Lacey (1983), Kimmelman (1983, 1987), and Rosenberg (1976, 1979a). See especially the graphic presentation by Busch and Lacey (1983:12).

47. In many agricultural institutions today these divisions remain lively, reflecting continued commercial interest in their viability. Interviews conducted at the University of California, Davis, and H. H. Cole's (1977) oral history.

48. Where two association names are connected by >, the name was changed to the latter in the year noted after the latter name. See Busch and Lacey (1983), Rossiter (1979), and True and Clark (1900).

49. In 1905, there were 7 zoologists and biologists employed, compared with 143 animal husbandmen, poultrymen, dairymen, and veterinarians (Rossiter 1979:217).

50. On breeding, see Allen (1991), Byerly (1976), Lush (1951), Reingold (1982), Kimmelman (1987:chapter 5), Provine (1986:98–160, 317–26), and Chapman (1987). Bugos (1992) discusses unique intellectual property issues in the history of chicken breeding. Cooke (1997) discusses innovations in chicken breeding linked to statistics.

51. See Powell (1927:19), and also Wiser (1987), Wiser, Mark, and Purchase (1987), and Byerly (1986). On contagious abortion, see Wilkinson (1992).

52. For example, agricultural breeding specialist Jay Lush wrote his 1925 doc-

toral dissertation on "sex control by artificial insemination with centrifuged spermatozoa," under L. J. Cole of the University of Wisconsin's Department of Experimental Breeding (Chapman 1987:280).

53. Interview with A. V. Nalbandov, April 7, 1984, Urbana, Illinois. See Herman (1981) for a history of artificial insemination in farm animals.

54. Specialization was not the refined process it is today. This does not mean that there was no competition between groups with different emphases. See, for example, Dodds (1941) and Parkes (1963).

55. Charles Otis Whitman's report on "The Hull Zoological Laboratory" in The President's Report, University of Chicago, 1898–99:182.

56. Debate focused on whether the shift was revolutionary or evolutionary, whether there was a revolt from the morphological approaches that characterized nineteenth-century life sciences (Allen 1978, 1979, 1981; Coleman 1971:162; 1985) or a more gradual shift to incorporate the new approaches (Benson 1981, 1985, 1989; Farber 1982a,b; Maienschein 1981, 1983, 1985a,b,d; Maienschein, Rainger, and Benson 1981). Churchill (1981) offers an excellent summary of debate to that date. More recent work (Rainger, Benson, and Maienschein 1988; and Benson, Maienschein, and Rainger 1991) argues for diversity and multiplicity of approaches to the shift.

57. See Allen (1978), Churchill (1970, 1973), Oppenheimer (1967:188–205), Gilbert (1987, 1991), Clarke (1991a), and Maienschein (1991a).

58. See, for example, Maienschein (1991b), and Mayr and Provine (1980). That is, for example, while histology and cytology in medicine were generally "part of" anatomy, anatomy was itself becoming increasingly physiological and biochemical in its approaches to research; many anatomists saw themselves as experimental zoologists in medical institutions (Blake 1980; Corner 1958a,b, 1960), discussed further below. Workers from varying perspectives also had differing definitions of the scope of cytology (cf. Allen 1978; Bourne and Danielli 1952; Corner 1958a,b, 1960; and Farley 1982).

59. See Kohler (1979, 1982), Rossiter (1975), and Cranefield (1959:264).

60. See Beer and Lewis (1974), Jarausch (1983), Kohlstedt (1985), Vesey (1965), and Geiger (1986).

61. University of Chicago President's Reports, 1892–1902:53.

62. See DeVane (1965), Jarausch (1983), Light (1983), Vesey (1965), and Geiger (1986). Both Geiger and the monograph edited by Jarausch (1983) engage many of Vesey's (1965) analyses in fresh debate, beyond the present scope.

63. See Jarausch (1983:13). A reliable estimate of the proportion in relation to population enrolled in colleges and graduate schools is 5 percent in 1900, 5.6 percent in 1910, 9 percent in 1920, and 15 percent in 1930. These are based on age-appropriate cohorts by Burke (in Jarausch 1983:14–16). Coben (1979:229) notes 4.0 percent in 1900 to 12.42 percent in 1930.

64. See DeVane (1965:81) and Machlup (1962:77–78, 91). In 1900, there were 5,688 students; in 1910, there were more than 6,000; in 1930, there were 47,225; and in 1950, there were 233,786 (DeVane 1965:51).

65. See DeVane (1965:42) and Barrow (1990:60–95). Vesey (1965:267–68) notes the paucity of data on the origins of these organizational schema. Only the

details, he found, appear in the record, with no discussion of the larger issues and assumptions about the nature of organizational changes that were so similar across divergent institutions that they could not be local variations. Vesey (1965) and DeVane (1965) largely attribute the shift in approach to a corporate model of organization to the replacement of clergymen on university boards of trustees with businessmen.

66. Borell (1989) points to the similar physical organization of university laboratories and factories in photos of the era.

67. In 1920, there were about three hundred industrial research laboratories, growing to over one thousand in 1927 (Coben 1979:229). By 1940, more than two thousand corporations reported laboratories employing about seventy thousand people (Birr 1979:199).

68. See, for example, DuPree (1957), Shryock (1947), Geiger (1986:2), and Clarke (1993).

69. See Clarke (1987, 1995b), Shapin (1988), and Gossel (1992).

70. See, for example, Aberle and Corner (1953), Nagi and Corwin (1972:15), Abir-Am (1982), Haraway (1989), Kohler (1976, 1978, 1991), and Geiger (1993). Clarke (1993) provides a case study in the reproductive sciences.

71. Program in Experimental Biology, April 17, 1935. RAC RF RG1.1 S216 B8 F103.

72. To Frank R. Lillie from Warren Weaver, October 6, 1933. RAC RF RG1.1 S216d B8 F105.

73. Regrettably, Gregg does not provide Cannon's response. To Dr. Yerkes, November 23, 1942. RAC RF RG1.1 S200 B39 F443.

74. There is general accord on this point in the secondary literature and in "insider histories." See Asdell (1977), Borell (1985), Corner (1981), Evans (1959), Medvei (1982), and Parkes (1966a,b). Pressman (1991, 1997) takes up the timing of the development of psychiatry in America in similar ways.

75. To Col. A. Woods, Rockefeller Foundation, April 12, 1928. RAC RF RG1.1 S200 B40 F453.

76. See especially Aberle and Corner (1953) and Corner (1981) for this perspective.

77. Asdell's (1977:8, emphasis added) second argument is most intriguing. Here he addresses the problem structure that life scientists had constructed and themselves confronted around the turn of the twentieth century: "In fact, the physiology of reproduction was investigated very slowly. After the initial discoveries [of ova and sperm], the attention of biologists seems to have been diverted in the direction of working out the changes that take place in the cell nucleus during division, and in the study of embryological development. Eventually, both of these led back to reproduction, in the case of embryology because of the demand for more accurately aged material." Asdell's description of what scientists did attend to is certainly accurate: heredity and evolution were central. Moreover, researchers' demands for more accurately aged embryonic material did lead back to reproductive research problems in ironic ways. The irony is that a key piece of research in the United States that promoted the development of reproductive research as a major line of work was not in pursuit of a reproductive problem. Charles R. Stockard and

George Papanicolaou (1917a) published on the estrus cycle of the guinea pig as a scientific by-product of their attempt to date guinea pig embryos (Oppenheimer 1984); see also Pauly (1996). This research was followed by parallel work dating the estrus cycle via vaginal smears by Joseph A. Long and Herbert M. Evans's work on the rat (1922), Edgar Allen's on the mouse (1922), George W. Corner's on the monkey (1923), and Evans and Cole's (1931) on the dog (which did not work well), all projects central to the reproductive sciences (discussed in chapter 4). I discuss these researches in some detail in chapter 4. Studer and Chubin (1976:12) offer interesting citation analyses on these key articles.

78. There is an ambitious literature on eugenics. See especially Bajema (1976), Haller (1963), Kevles (1981, 1985), Ludmerer (1972), Pickens (1968), Searle (1981), Soloway (1982, 1990), and Pauly (1993). For intensive analysis of the relations between the eugenics and birth control movements, see Gordon (1975, 1976/1990) and Chesler (1992).

79. See, for example, Kevles (1985), Ludmerer (1983), Soloway (1995) and Pauly (1984:395, 1996).

80. For an explicit articulation of criteria, see H. Laughlin's Model Eugenical Sterilization Law, first published in 1922, in Bajema (1976:139–45).

81. See, for example, Pickens (1968), Reed (1983), Sanger (1971), Chesler (1992), and McCann (1994).

82. See MacKenzie (1981a), and Haraway (1995). There had, of course, been earlier forms of population-based science centered on census data and other similar approaches (MacKenzie 1981a,b; Provine 1986).

83. See Kevles (1981, 1985), MacKenzie (1981a), Allen (1991), and Porter (1995).

84. See Borell (1987a), Ledbetter (1976), Maas, (1974), Marks (1982), Osborn (1967), Reed (1983:202–6, 301, 337), and Harr and Johnson (1988:452–67). On the history of demography, see Hodgson (1983, 1988, 1991) and Greenhalgh (1996).

85. Minutes of the Preliminary Conference on a Population Association for the United States. New York University, December 15, 1930, with the cooperation of the Milbank Memorial Fund. RAC BSH SIII-2 B9 F191.

CHAPTER THREE

1. These are addressed in detail by the "insider histories" of reproductive research written by many of the researchers themselves. See Asdell (1977), Corner (1951, 1958a, 1963, 1965, 1981), Dodds (1941), Gruhn and Kazer (1989), Hamblen (1939), McCance (1977), Medvei (1982), Parkes (1962b,c, 1963, 1966a,b), Short (1977), Zondek (1941), and Zuckerman (1970, 1978).

2. Certainly there had been considerable earlier consideration of some kind of blood-borne messengers. See Medvei (1982).

3. Borell (1985) argues that it was from physiology and endocrinology that the British reproductive research enterprise emerged. In contrast, I have found that in the U.S. reproductive research enterprise had its origins in embryology, though

clarifications of hormone actions were central to its development. These points are discussed more fully in chapter 4.

4. Although agricultural scientists have contributed, no such histories have been undertaken with the exception of Cole (1977) and Asdell (1977). General histories and those of reproductive research include Bliss (1982), Borell (1976a,b,c 1978, 1985), Corner (1951, 1963, 1965, 1981), Dodds (1941), Fulton and Wilson (1966), Glick (1976), Hall (1974, 1976, 1978, 1979), Hall and Glick (1976), Hamblen (1939), Lisser (1967), Maisel (1965), McCance (1977), Medvei (1982), Parkes (1962b, 1963, 1966a,b), Rosenberg (1976), Short (1977), Shryock (1947:212–15), Studer and Chubin (1976), Thorne (1976), Young (1970), and Zondek (1941). Regarding "insider" histories of early reproductive endocrinological research as data, see Appendix 1. Curiously, Maienschein's (1985d) review of the history of biology omits the history of endocrinology.

5. Based on Borell (1985) and Medvei (1982). For more elaborate chronologies, see also Greep and Koblinsky (1977), Hamblen (1939), and Studer and Chubin (1976). On French and German contributions, see also Simmer (1978) and Jorgensen (1971).

6. See Borell (1976a,b,c; 1985:4). For examples of popular and medical literature on endocrinology in the United States, see Harrower (1917) and Robinson (1934). For the Netherlands, see Oudshoorn (1994).

7. See Borell (1985:6, 11; 1978:286). In Britain, the term *hormone* was used for chemicals with demonstrable physiological effects and was more in the domain of laboratory scientists; the term *internal secretions* was used to suggest a hypothetical entity whose absence resulted in disease and was more in the domain of clinicians (Borell 1985:4–5). In the United States, usage of these terms does not seem so clear-cut.

8. Borell (1976c:xii) analyzes this segmentation as parallel to that of genetics. There was, as with Mendelian genetics, rediscovery of a significant earlier researcher—A. A. Berthold. In 1849, Berthold published a paper demonstrating that transplantation of fowl cock's testes prevented atrophy of the comb, the usual result of castration; Berthold's work was "rediscovered" early this century (Medvei 1982:217) and pursued by an array of investigators at Chicago (Clarke 1993).

9. For an analysis of the situation of endocrinology in Britain around 1920, see Hall (1976); for Germany, see Zondek (1941); for the Netherlands, see Oudshoorn (1994); for the United States, see Aberle and Corner (1953); more generally, see Medvei (1982).

10. It includes, for example, Allen (e.g., 1978, 1979), Benson (1981), Brush (1978), Burkhardt (1979), Churchill (1979, 1985a,b), Coleman (1980), Farley (1982), Gerson (1983), Gilbert (1978), Hamburger (1980), Ludmerer (1972), Maienschein (1984, 1985d), Mayr and Provine (1980), Rosenberg (1967, 1976), Sapp (1983), Stubbe (1972), and Sturtevant (1965). For a wonderful commentary on the "borderland" between genetics and embryology made shortly after Morgan won the Nobel Prize in 1933, see Streeter (1935).

11. On some of the consequences, see Keller (1987, 1992), Lloyd (1993a,b), and Griesemer (1994, forthcoming).

12. Gilbert (1978:346) considers the sex-determination problem so central to

the development of the gene theory to have been a "fundamental controversy in embryology." Farley (1982) devotes a chapter to efforts of cytologists who were not necessarily embryologists. The porousness of the boundaries between "disciplines" makes specific disciplinary attribution highly problematic.

13. See Coleman (1971), Allen (1978), Churchill (1969, 1970, 1973, 1979, 1981, 1985a,b), Hamburger (1980), Maienschein (1984), Mayr and Provine (1980), and Farley (1982).

14. See Sturtevant (1965), Farley (1982), Maienschein (1984, 1991a), Rosenberg (1967), and Stubbe (1972).

15. See Allen (1991), Kay (1993a), Haraway (1995), and Provine (1986).

16. Oppenheimer (1967:35–38) notes that certain geneticists lobbied against such restrictiveness, notably E. B. Wilson and Sewall Wright, and that Wilson's work led to cytogenetics and cytochemistry, which subsequently merged into molecular biological approaches to similar problems.

17. Many of these "geneticists" were themselves embryologically trained (Gilbert 1978, 1987, 1991).

18. See Lillie (1919:129, emphasis added). Garland Publishing has reprinted this book in its series Great Books in Experimental Biology (1988).

19. Problems of sex determination versus sex differentiation are classic examples of such ambiguous problems. See Maienschein (1984, 1985d:161). Lillie (1932:5) argued years later that "we must make a radical distinction between" the two, with the former being chromosomal (genetic) and the latter, in higher animals, being hormonal. Aspects of this problem have yet to be clarified. See Farley (1982:259–63), Price (1972), and Gorbman (1979). Farley (1982:259–63) harshly criticizes contemporary biology and genetics texts for limiting their discussions of sex determination to X and Y chromosomes. He attributes this narrowness of vision to "modern biology's preoccupation with evolutionary theory" (1982:260) and its ignoring of the problem "What exactly does the sperm do to the egg to stimulate its development?"

20. For an ambitious analysis of British endeavors, see Borell (1976a,b,c, 1978, and especially 1985 and 1987a) and Parkes (1962b,c, 1966a,b). For analysis of Dutch work, see Oudshoorn (1994); for German contributions, see Zondek (1941), and especially for those of German/Viennese gynecologists, see Corner (1965) and Simmer (1978); for French contributions, see (Medvei 1982); and for Brazilian contributions, see Corgi et al. (1963).

21. There was a growing general physiological research emphasis in British life sciences at this time. See Borell (1976a,b,c, 1978, 1985), Geison (1978), Hall (1974, 1976), and Long (1987).

22. Heape came to Cambridge in 1879 to work with F. M. Balfour on embryological problems. Upon Balfour's death in 1882, Heape and Adam Sedgwick published on embryology under the names of Foster and Balfour. After several academic positions, Heape was elected to the Balfour studentship (fellowship) in zoology in 1890 (Marshall 1929:588).

23. Heape's (1894, 1897, 1898) cyclicity work is well known (Marshall 1929:588; Biggers 1991). American reproductive scientist George Corner also published

such popular works. See Corner (1981) for discussion. In both instances, the then blurred boundaries between sexology and the reproductive sciences are quite visible.

24. See Parkes (1962c) and, for an ambitious analysis and bibliography of Heape's work, Biggers (1991).

25. See Heape (1899, 1905), Marshall (1930:xvi), and Biggers (1991).

26. See Porter and Hall (1995:170–73) for context.

27. Costs of this research were covered through a gift of two hundred pounds from Lord Carmichael of Skirling (Parkes 1952:ix), an early example of external funding of reproductive research. This was the famous case of interspecies mating of Lord Morton's mare. Burkhardt's (1979) article provides an illuminating discussion. Lord Morton had reported to the Royal Society in 1820 that an earlier mating of a purebred mare with a quagga (a striped zebra/horse–type animal, extinct by the turn of the century) had resulted in the foal from a later mating with a purebred stallion being striped like the quagga (Burkhardt 1979). This anomaly "inspired the most extensive work in experimental animal breeding conducted in Britain between Darwin's death in 1882 and the rediscovery of Mendel's laws in 1900" (Burkhardt 1979:2). Ewart and Marshall's efforts bred zebras and horses, experiments that took about one year each, with multiple breedings required, and ultimately proved negative.

28. This demonstrates again, along with Lord Carmichael's financial assistance, the early philanthropic interest in reproductive problems. Marshall did a brief stint as director of the Institute of Animal Nutrition and studied the most economic age and condition at which to slaughter cattle. Subsequent researches focused on environmental factors in the reproductive processes, including light and climate. Marshall served on the Council of Management of the *Journal of Endocrinology* and was an honorary member of the Society for Endocrinology (Parkes 1952:x–xi).

29. I sought reviews in the major salient American journals, finding none between 1910 and 1915 in the *Journal of Anatomy,* the *American Journal of Physiology,* the *Anatomical Record,* the *American Journal of Anatomy,* the *Journal of Morphology,* the *Journal of the American Medical Association,* the *Journal of Biology,* the *Biological Bulletin,* the *Journal of Experimental Zoology,* the *Journal of Biological Chemistry,* or the *Journal of Experimental Medicine. Physiological Reviews,* a likely review source, began after this time (1921). The absence of reviews may reflect the illegitimacy of reproductive science at the time. For a description of Marshall's work from the point of view of sexology, see Porter and Hall (1995:169–71).

30. The major changes between the first edition (1910) and the second (1922) were (1) revision and expansion of the section on the biochemistry of the sexual organs (by William Cramer) and (2) revision and expansion of the section on changes in the maternal organism during pregnancy (by James Lochhead). Marshall (1922:vii) notes that almost no changes were made in the chapter on fetal nutrition and the physiology of the placenta, "since the quantity of original work done in this field during the last decade has been relatively small."

31. Parkes further notes that by 1935 it was clear that a third edition should be prepared as soon as possible. Because of World War II and other problems, this edition was not issued until 1952–66, and it appeared in installments.

32. This perspective strongly paralleled that of Frank Lillie in the United States. See Lillie (1919), Oppenheimer (1967:39–55), and Farley (1982:237–51). Lillie and Crew's groups were also in direct contact (e.g., Crew to Lillie, 4 April 1928; FRLP BII F20).

33. In the 1920s, Crew was director of the Animal Breeding Research Department and a lecturer in genetics at the University of Edinburgh (1927), continuing the reproductive focus of Ewart and Marshall. Through his many students, Crew ultimately sustained Edinburgh as a center for reproductive research well into the twentieth century, including some forays into Rockefeller-sponsored contraceptive research, discussed in chapter 6.

34. For further information on Hammond, see Russell (1966:336–37) and Parkes (1962c).

35. In 1960, Parkes became Mary Marshall Chair of the Physiology of Reproduction, a chair endowed by Marshall in memory of his mother (Parkes 1966b:33–35). For a more general view of British physiology of the day, see Butler (1988).

36. See American Foundation (1955:2:139–40). Many of these efforts and a full representation of the intersection in British reproductive sciences appear in Parkes's *Marshall's Physiology of Reproduction* (1952–66).

37. That is, once biology was established on the graduate level in the United States, early graduates found academic positions not only in biology departments but also in agriculture-based, land-grant institutions (Cravens 1978; Rosenberg 1967; Rossiter 1986). Yet these men were and remain claimed by later agricultural scientists as agricultural scientists (e.g., Nalbandov interview 1984). Major contributions of agriculturally trained scientists to reproductive research came later during the coalescence around reproductive endocrinology, the "endocrinological gold rush" (Parkes 1966a) during the years after ca. 1925. They are addressed more fully in chapter 5.

38. See Willier and Oppenheimer (1964:118), Manning (1983), and Gilbert (1987).

39. See Appendix 2 for the complete version (Aberle and Corner 1953).

40. Neither the researchers cited nor the problems listed are meant to be exhaustive. Such a chronicle is beyond the scope of this book. Major listings of research on reproduction are found in Greep and Koblinsky (1977), Studer and Chubin (1976), and Gruhn and Kazer (1989).

41. Individual animals were of minimal concern to most agricultural scientists because improved production of animals and their consumable products was the goal; less productive or nonproductive individuals could simply be culled and used for meat or other products. Hence the contrast with medicine is extensive, given the major medical goal of preserving individuals.

42. There was a crisis of sorts in Britain among those working in endocrinology in the 1920s. See Hall (1976).

43. See, for example, Allen (1970), Loeb (1958), and Parker (1973).

44. Newman (1948:231) dates this as 1916 but most likely was mistaken. Willier (1957:216) dates the onset of Lillie's freemartin work as the autumn of 1914. And Leon J. Cole, who specialized in experimental breeding at Wisconsin, was already

in correspondence with Lillie on freemartins in late 1915 (Cole to Lillie, 17 November 1915, and passim, FRLP BII F15 UChiA). This was, of course, not the first research on freemartins, since the sterility of such a cow was important to farmers. For a description of earlier work, see Forbes (1946).

45. He had a collection of postembryonic freemartin gonadal material for study, complementing Lillie's embryos and fetuses. Lillie responded that cooperation would be valuable, and that he had already amassed twenty-five pairs of embryonic twins. Lillie to Cole, 22 November 1915. FRLP BII F15 UChiA.

46. Cole to Lillie, 21 February 1917. FRLP BII F15 UChiA.

47. See Willier (1957:215) and Lillie (1916b:612). However, this was not always smooth. In 1918 Lillie noted, "I am having no success in securing new material from the stockyards. New federal regulations and reduction in the amount of business done there combined to make the embryonic material very scarce." Lillie to Cole, 13 January 1918. FRLP BII F15 UChiA.

48. Lillie to Cole, 3 December 1915. FRLP BII F15 UChiA.

49. Focus was upon collecting specimens of different sizes and ages for comparative purposes (including adult freemartins), and seeking a range of anatomic and physiological variation in freemartins (including fertility). T. H. Bissonette to Lillie, 4 August 1922. FRLP BII F3 UChiA.

50. Lillie to Bissonette, 21 May 1928. FRLP BII F3 UChiA.

51. Lillie to Dr. C. J. Elmore, 26 October 1928. FRLP BIII F6 UChiA.

52. See "The Mystery of Sterile Twin Heifer Solved," by Science Service, hand dated 17 July 1922. FRLP BVI F3 UChiA.

53. Crew to Lillie, 4 April 1928. FRLP BII F20 UChiA; Bissonette to Lillie, 1 January 1929. BII F3. On Crew and his work, see Hogben (1974).

54. Edwin E. Slosson to Lillie, 28 June 1922. FRLP BVI F3 UChiA.

55. Elsewhere (Clarke 1993) I argue that while Lillie seems to initially have simply fallen into what would become the reproductive sciences from his "usual" embryological investigations, he and his colleagues then pursued such problems enthusiastically. They did so in part because of the generous external funding they were able to obtain from the NRC/CRPS in what those scientists saw as desperate times for the life sciences at the University of Chicago.

56. See Gorbman (1979), Moore (1932), and Price (1967, 1975).

57. See, for example, Willier (1957:219), Willier and Oppenheimer (1964:136–43, esp. pp. 137–38), Jorgensen (1971), Farley (1982:259–63), Price (1967, 1972, 1975), Biggers and McFeeley (1966), Watterson (1985), Gorbman (1979), and Lyet et al. (1995). For a description of "the borderland between genetics and embryology" and how geneticists do not go far enough, see Streeter (1935).

58. The historiographical conflict is between the accounts of Oppenheimer (1968, 1984) and Carmichael (1973:44–53). Oppenheimer, like more general sources, attributes the work to both Stockard and Papanicolaou, as published. She further argues that the smear was undertaken in relation to improving "controls" for the alcohol studies. In sharp contrast, Carmichael's biography of Papanicolaou quotes him as saying these cytological efforts were part of his own personal sex determination research but was initially published under both names because that

was the department's custom. Papanicolaou then became distraught when Stockard was given the bulk of the credit by his colleagues at Woods Hole (where Papanicolaou did not spend time); he raised the matter with Stockard, who said that his name need no longer be added to Papanicolaou's own work. Obviously, intellectual property issues were important then as now. See also Fulton and Wilson (1966:395–98).

59. Colonies were not very well established, and improvements were constantly being sought. The smear permitted prompt and effective mating. See Young (1961:xiv) and Clarke (1987, 1995b).

60. See Cole (1930), Hammond (1927), Cole and Miller (1931), McKenzie and Terrill (1937), and Wilson (1926).

61. In clinical work of this era, pathologists greatly preferred to diagnose problems from biopsied materials removed with surrounding tissue from specific sites (in situ). In sharp contrast, cytological smears from the vagina can contain cells shed from throughout the reproductive tract as they gradually drift out of the body through the vagina. For extended discussion, see Papanicolaou (1933), Casper and Clarke (1998), and Clarke and Casper (1996).

62. Because of both world wars, there were problems in getting out later editions of Marshall's (British) text, leaving the field more open to the Americans. See Marshall (1922) and Parkes (1952–66).

63. See Allen (1978), Kohler (1993a,b), Fitzgerald (1986), Paul and Kimmelman (1988), and Kimmelman (1992) on different tools, and Clarke and Fujimura (1992) on the construction of "rightness."

64. The same was true in Britain. See, for example, Marrian (1967:v–xvi).

65. On Koch, see Clarke (1993). For other specific individuals, see Corner (1981), Allen (1970), Fevold, Hisaw, and Leonard (1931), Fulton and Wilson (1966:403), and Li, Simpson, and Evans (1940). Koch and his associates developed separation and distillation methods for hormones, especially in urine, and began synthesis of androsterone. Report for 1934–35 on the Grant for Biological Research made by the Rockefeller Foundation, 8 November 1935, pp. 3–5. Rockefeller Archives Center, RF RG1.1 S216d B8 F107. See also Koch (1932, 1937) and Corner, Danforth, and Stone (1943).

CHAPTER FOUR

1. There is now a fairly substantial literature on the history of sexology, a topic much more delimited than the history of sexuality and becoming more sophisticated in terms of historiography. See Robinson (1976), Brecher (1969), Foucault (1978), Pomeroy (1982), Birken (1988), Irvine (1990), Bullough (1994), Porter and Teich (1994), and Porter and Hall (1995). Irvine makes an important argument that sexology mimicked biomedical methodology in its quest for professional legitimacy. Bullough emphasizes the marginality of sexuality studies and how individuals and groups with different agendas often directed the fate of sexology for their own purposes. Porter and Hall (1995:183) argue that "sexology as a science

was being increasingly co-opted into the more scientifically neutral field of reproductive biology and investigation focused on non-human animals." Foucault (1978) argued for the underdevelopment of sexology as compared to the reproductive sciences.

2. I was alerted to the import of the NRC/CRPS by Aberle and Corner's (1953) key "insider history," which is both borne out and contradicted by the archival materials. This chapter is based largely on analysis of archival materials on the NRC/CRPS in the Rockefeller Archives Center to which my access was much enhanced by a fellowship from the Rockefeller University.

3. See Hall (1974, 1978), Longino and Doell (1983), Long (1990, 1997), Oudshoorn (1994), Rechter (1997). The handbooks of the reproductive sciences produced by the committee, three editions of *Sex and Internal Secretions* (Allen, ed., 1932, 1939; Young 1961), are ripe for further textual analysis.

4. Diana Long Hall (1978) prepared an important unpublished paper on the committee, to which I gained access after writing the version presented here. Hall's work confirmed several of my own assessments, for example those concerning the primacy of natural over social sciences within the committee. For another account of the formation of the committee and its work, from the point of view of sexology, see Bullough (1994:chapter 5).

5. The proposals I am referring to concern the actions of the committee itself. The NRC/CRPS discarded its declination files, so who and what kinds of projects were not funded cannot be determined or studied (Long 1990:456).

6. RAC, "The BSH Collection," Introductory Remarks, 1 August 1969.

7. On Rockefeller and Davis, see also Reed (1983:283–85) and Bullough (1994:112–22).

8. See RAC, "The BSH Collection," Introductory Remarks, 1 August 1969.

9. Howe (1982) analyzes the investigation of the Rockefeller Foundation by the United States Commission on Industrial Relations in 1913–14 concerning strike activities in Colorado. After that, the foundation shied away from economic and social research, especially of a controversial nature (Kohler 1978, 1991).

10. See BSH, Inc. A Report to the Trustees Covering the Years 1928, 1929, 1930. RAC BSH SI B1 F1.

11. On Katherine Davis see, for example, Rosenberg (1982) and Lewis (1971); on her relationship to John D. Rockefeller Jr., see Bullough (1994:112–18). Lawrence B. Dunham succeeded her as director until 1934, when new programming ceased. See RAC, "The BSH Collection," Introductory Remarks, 1 August 1969. On the BSH, see also Burnham (1972).

12. In 1922, Yerkes also became chairman of the NRC's Committee on Scientific Problems of Human Migration (Marks 1982:104).

13. On Yerkes, see Haraway (1989:59–83).

14. First Annual Report, NRC/CRPS. For period July 1, 1921–Dec. 31, 1922. Dated March 1, 1923, p. 1. Prepared by Earl F. Zinn, Executive Secretary. RAC BSH SIII-2 B8 F189.

15. From MM's [Max Mason] diary: [Meeting with] Dr. F. R. Lillie and Dr. E. G., Conklin, 2 September 1929. RAC RF RG1.1 S216 B8 F103.

16. See BSH, Inc. A Report to the Trustees Covering the Years 1928, 1929, 1930, pp. 54–55. RAC BSH SI B1 F1. Vaughn was also active in the development of the NRC Committee on Drug Addiction, which was key to the disciplinary formation of pharmacology (Acker 1995).

17. See Aberle and Corner (1953:12). A full list of conference attendees is found in Aberle and Corner (1953:12). See also Zinn (1924:95–96).

18. See BSH, Inc. A Report to the Trustees Covering the Years 1928, 1929, 1930, pp. 54–55. RAC BSH SI B1 F1. Walter Cannon, a subsequent member of the NRC/CRPS, claims to have written this resolution. To Ruth Topping, Secy., BSH, from W. B. Cannon, Dept. of Physiology, Harvard Medical School. 25 October 1930. RAC BSH SIII-2 B8 F186. On Cannon, see Benison, Barger, and Wolfe (1987).

19. Additional members and the year of their initial appointment or duration of tenure were Willard Allen (obstetrics and gynecology, Washington University School of Medicine, 1945); George W. Corner (University of Rochester School of Medicine, 1947); Wallace O. Fenn (University of Rochester School of Medicine 1945–48); Karl S. Lashley (psychology, University of Chicago, then Harvard University, then Director, Yerkes Laboratory of Primate Biology, 1934); C. N. Hugh Long (physiological chemistry, Yale University, 1945); Adolph Meyer (psychiatry, Johns Hopkins University School of Medicine, 1928–45); Carl R. Moore (zoology, University of Chicago, 1938); William F. Ogburn (sociology, Columbia University, 1925–28); John Romano (psychiatry, Cincinnati Medical School, then University of Rochester Medical School, 1945–48); Clark Wissler (anthropology, American Museum of Natural History, 1925–36); Clyde K. Kluckhohn (anthropology, Harvard University, 1949); James V. Neel (genetics, University of Michigan, 1949); and Howard C. Taylor (gynecology and obstetrics, College of Physicians and Surgeons, Columbia University, 1947–51) (Aberle and Corner 1953:105–7).

20. Quoted at length above. See First Annual Report NRC/CRPS, Division of Medical Sciences. For period July 1, 1921–December 31, 1922. 1 March 1923, p. 1. Prepared by Earl F. Zinn, Executive Secretary. RAC BSH SIII-2 B8 F189.

21. See Aberle and Corner (1953:17). In 1925, when anthropologist Clark Wissler later joined the NRC/CRPS, he drew up a plan of studies of sexuality among primitive peoples; this was not extensively funded by the NRC/CRPS (Ibid.: 93–96). Zinn was also to have drawn up a "personal program of sex research" but apparently did not (Ibid.:14).

22. Aberle and Corner (1953:102–4) reprinted Lillie's complete plan in their history of the NRC/CRPS; Lashley's plan is neither reprinted nor mentioned again, although his research was funded. On Lillie as a scientist-entrepreneur, see Kohler (1991:e.g., 111–12) and Clarke (1993).

23. A number of small conferences were held with prospective scientists (Aberle and Corner 1953:16–17, 109–10).

24. First Annual Report, NRC/CRPS. For period July 1, 1921–December 31, 1922. Dated March 1, 1923, p. 6. Prepared by Earl F. Zinn, Executive Secretary. RAC BSH SIII-2 B8 F189.

25. "Suggestions for Organization and Conduct of Research in Problems of

Sex" (from the First Annual Report of the Committee, January 1 to December 31, 1922. Exhibit A by Robert M. Yerkes, p. 1. RAC RF RG1.1 S200 B40 F453).

26. See Appendix 2 for a partial listing of major centers and directions of research sponsored by the NRC/CRPS. See Aberle and Corner (1953:chapters 3–4) for a complete account to that date.

27. Sixth Annual Report, NRC/CRPS. Dated ca. June 30, 1928. Prepared by Earl F. Zinn. RAC BSH SIII-2 B8 F189.

28. First Annual Report, NRC/CRPS. For period July 1, 1921–Dec. 31, 1922. Dated March 1, 1923, p. 7. Prepared by Earl F. Zinn. RAC BSH SIII-2 B8 F189.

29. "Suggestions for Organization and Conduct of Research in Problems of Sex" (from the First Annual Report, NRC/CRPS, January 1 to December 31, 1922. Exhibit A by Robert M. Yerkes, p. 4. RAC RF RG1.1 S200 B40 F453).

30. First Annual Report, NRC/CRPS. For period July 1, 1921–Dec. 31, 1922. Dated March 1, 1923, p. 8. Prepared by Earl F. Zinn. RAC BSH SIII-2 B8 F189.

31. Ibid.

32. "Suggestions for Organization and Conduct of Research in Problems of Sex" (from the First Annual Report, NRC/CRPS, January 1 to December 31, 1922. Exhibit A by Robert M. Yerkes, pp. 2–4, 6). Yerkes's plan for nonhuman primate research is on pp. 6–9. RAC RF RG1.1 S200 B40 F453. See also Clarke (1987, 1995b) and Haraway (1989:59–83).

33. First Annual Report, NRC/CRPS. For period July 1, 1921–Dec. 31, 1922. Dated March 1, 1923, p. 7; emphasis in original. Prepared by Earl F. Zinn. RAC BSH SIII-2 B8 F189.

34. Ibid.:7–8.

35. Eleventh Annual Report, NRC/CRPS. For the year July 1, 1931–June 30, 1932. Prepared by Robert M. Yerkes, Chairman. Exhibit A: Research on Biological Problems of Sex. Recommendation that the work of the NRC/CRPS be continued. May 20, 1932, pp. 25–26 (emphasis added). RAC BSH SIII-2 B8 F189.

36. The SSRC was established through the efforts of Beardsley Ruml of the Laura Spellman Rockefeller Foundation, which was its primary initial funding source (Faris 1965:54).

37. Laurence B. Dunham, BSH File Memorandum. 16 March 1928. RAC BSH SIII-2 B9 F200.

38. To Mr. Dunham from Earl F. Zinn, 2 March 1928. RAC BSH SIII-2 B9 F200.

39. Whether members of the NRC/CRPS later regretted this after Hamilton's work was presented in a sensational manner in the popular press is not known. But this coverage of sex research, which included the BSH and Rockefeller names, created quite a brouhaha for the committee. See Aberle and Corner (1953:47, 78) and RAC BSH SIII-2 B9 F200. See also Bullough (1994:117–21).

40. See Bullough (1994:118–19), Hall (1978), Haraway (1989:59–83). Despite Hamilton's primate studies and psychobiological interests, this research seems to me to be clearly on the "human side" both methodologically and substantively. Bugos (1989) offers a more organizational and NRC-oriented perspective on some of these issues.

41. Proposed Plan for the Continuation of the Sex Research Project, Exhibit A.

Sixth Annual Report, NRC/CRPS. Dated ca. June 30, 1928; emphasis added. Prepared by Earl F. Zinn. RAC BSH SIII-2 B8 F189. This plan seems to link up with earlier discussions of local centers of psychobiological work, including one proposed for Boston/Cambridge (Hall 1978:17). See also Bugos (1989).

42. Sixth Annual Report, NRC/CRPS. Dated ca. June 30, 1928, p. 13; emphasis added. Prepared by Earl F. Zinn. RAC BSH SIII-2 B8 F189.

43. See Proposed Plan for the Continuation of the Sex Research Project, Exhibit A. Sixth Annual Report, NRC/CRPS. Dated ca. June 30, 1928. Prepared by Earl F. Zinn. RAC BSH SIII-2 B8 F189.

44. See Kohler (1976, 1978, 1991), Harr and Johnson (1988:192–96), and Jonas (1989).

45. L. B. Dunham to Mr. Fosdick [RF], 12 March 1928. RAC BSH SIII-2 B9 F200.

46. To L. B. Dunham (BSH) from R. B. Fosdick (President of the RF), 26 March 1928. BSH SIII-2 B8 F185.

47. Arthur Woods of the Rockefeller Foundation wrote in a memorandum for Mr. Rockefeller, "We have not been convinced that his work is valuable" (1 May 1928. BSH SIII-2 B8 F185). According to BSH files, Zinn went on to direct a project in the field of psychoanalysis (BSH, Inc. A Report to the Trustees Covering the Years 1928, 1929, 1930. RAC BSH SI B1 F1).

48. Aberle and Corner (1953:21, 76, 82–84) note that the NRC/CRPS initially considered establishing an administrative subcommittee to generate lay-oriented publications and to distribute information on sex research. Because of the decision to focus on "basic research," this did not occur; publication was left to the initiative of funded scientists through scientific journals.

49. See Eighth Annual Report, NRC/CRPS. For the year July 1, 1929–June 30, 1930. Prepared by Robert M. Yerkes, Chairman. RAC BSH SIII-2 B8 F189. And see L. B. Dunham to Dr. E. V. Cowdry, Chairman, Division of Medical Sciences, NRC, 17 December 1930, and response 18 December 1930. RAC BSH SIII-2 B8 F186.

50. "NRC/CRPS Progress Report," 1929. Ludwig Hectoen, Chairman, Division of Medical Sciences, NRC, 27 November 1929. RAC BSH SIII-2 B8 F186.

51. NRC/CRPS, Committee for Research Program and Budget 1928–29. RAC RF RG1.1 S200 B40 F453.

52. From MM's diary: Dr. F. R. Lillie and Dr. E. G., Conklin, 2 September 1929. RAC RF RG1.1 S216 B8 F103.

53. Eleventh Annual Report, NRC/CRPS. For the year July 1, 1931–June 30, 1932, pp. 28–30. Prepared by Robert M. Yerkes. RAC BSH SIII-2 B8 F189.

54. To Colonel Woods and Mr. Fosdick, from L. B. Dunham, Subject: Sex Cmte. 12 March 1928. BSH SIII-2 B8 F185.

55. Ibid.

56. LBD File Memorandum, BSH, March 16, 1928. BSH SIII-2 B8 F185.

57. To Col. Woods and Mr. Fosdick, from L. B. Dunham, 28 March 1928. BSH SIII-2 B8 F185.

58. To R. B. Fosdick from Arthur Woods, memorandum, 29 March 1928. BSH SIII-2 B8 F185.

59. Max Mason of the Rockefeller Foundation was interested because of the

biochemistry research of the NRC/CRPS. BSH, Inc. A Report to the Trustees Covering the Years 1928, 1929, 1930. RAC BSH SI B1 F1.

60. To Mr. Fosdick (RF) from L. B. Dunham (BSH), Subject: NRC/CRPS, 6 February 1931. RAC BSH SIII-2 B8 F186.

61. RF Resolution 31195, Research Work in Sex Problems, 28 April 1931. RAC BSH SIII-2 B8 F187.

62. Eleventh Annual Report, NRC/CRPS. For the year July 1, 1931–June 30, 1932, p. 30. Prepared by Robert M. Yerkes. RAC BSH SIII-2 B8 F189.

63. Status of CRPS NRC. Statement supplementary to report and request, by Robert M. Yerkes, July 8, 1933. RAC RF RG1.1 S200 B40 F453. These issues are discussed further later in this chapter and in chapter 7.

64. Recommendation for funding, NRC/CRPS 14 December 1932. RAC RF RG1.1 S200 B38 F436.

65. Status of CRPS NRC. Statement supplementary to report and request, by Robert M. Yerkes, July 8, 1933. RAC RF RG1.1 S200 B40 F453.

66. See Aberle and Corner (1953) and Pomeroy (1982). See also Hall (1974, 1978), Haraway (1989), Bugos (1989), and Bullough (1994).

67. These supposed group differences paralleled the individual differences being established in quantitative psychology at the time. On gender differences, see especially Hall (1974, 1978) and Fausto-Sterling (1998). On race, see Aberle and Corner (1953:49–50). See Marks (1982). Haraway (1995) discusses the shift from individuals to populations as the unit of analysis and it implications.

68. See, for example, Aberle and Corner (1953:49) and FBH diary, Brown University, Prof. W. C. Young, 6 May 1937. RAC RF RG1.1 S200 B39 F441. This was parallel to Weaver's goals for biology (Abir-Am 1982:350).

69. To Yerkes from Gregg, 7 September 1943. RAC RF RG1.1 S200 B39 F443.

70. For an account of problems Kinsey confronted with the NRC/CRPS and the Rockefeller Foundation in the 1950s, see Corner (1981:314–17) and Pomeroy (1982).

71. There is some confusion in the record. See Aberle and Corner (1953:20, 66, 74), Greep, Koblinsky, and Jaffe (1976:365–92), and the Weaver/Yerkes correspondence (RAC RF RG1.1 S200 B38 F437).

72. An NRC Committee on Human Reproduction was begun in 1947, but it administered few funds (Greep, Koblinsky, and Jaffe 1976:374).

73. RF Resolution 41011, 17 January 1941. RAC RF RG1.1 S200 B38 F436.

74. Recommendation for funding, NRC/CRPS 14 December 1932. RAC RF RG1.1 S200 B38 F436.

75. Abir-Am (1982), Kohler (1976), and I concur with this general analysis of the materials examined at the RAC.

76. The NRC/CRPS had always routinely sent copies of its minutes and annual reports to the BSH and the Rockefeller Foundation (Aberle and Corner 1953:64).

77. WW memo, Dr. F. R. Lillie, 8–11 September 1933, Woods Hole. RAC RF RG1.1 S216D B8 F105.

78. Unsigned, during Lillie's chairmanship. ZDP BII F3 UChiA.

79. See C. E. McClung to Lillie, Jan. 7, 1920, and Minutes of the Committee, Mar. 20, 1920. FRLP BIII F8 UChiA. Lillie sent out fliers for the congress, writing

that "this meeting will . . . be one of the greatest events in the history of this subject, which has hardly reached the dignity of either an art or science so far." Lillie to Dr. Anna Blount, Jan. 31, 1921. FRLP BIII F8 UChiA.

80. Lillie to C. C. Little, April 13, 1921. FRLP BIII F8 UChiA.

81. See Lillie to Irving Fisher, May 18, 1922. FRLP BIII F8 UChiA. Document of the International Committee on Eugenics, Eugenics Committee of the U.S.A., Irving Fisher, Chair. Oct. 10, 1923. FRLP BIII F8 UChiA.

82. The President's Report, 1924–25:6, UChiA.

83. Lillie to Wycliffe Rose, June 17, 1924. RF RG1.1 S216D B8 F104 RA. See also Mitman's (1992:96–109) account of the plans for this institute.

84. Ibid.

85. Lillie to Mason, June 5, 1931. RF RG1.1 S216D B8 F104 RA.

86. Lillie submitted preliminary organizational plans to Max Mason of the Rockefeller Foundation in 1932, which basically included all of the faculty working on reproductive research problems, and discussion of both a new laboratory and animal quarters (Lillie to Mason, Feb. 20, 1932. RF RG1.1 S216D B8 F104 RA). Consideration of the proposal was delayed, however, because of a planned review of NRC/CRPS work (Weaver to Lillie, April 1, 1932. RF RG1.1 S216D B8 F104 RA). In late 1933, Weaver wrote at length to Lillie, saying that it was not at present within the financial possibilities of the foundation, "nor consonant with the spirit of the times," to contemplate being sole donor of such an institute; but, a step-by-step program building toward it might be viewed favorably, especially if planned with other programs such as the NRC/CRPS in mind (Weaver to Lillie, Nov. 6, 1933. RF RG1.1 S216D B8 F105 RA).

87. Weaver, Univ. of Chicago visit, Jan. 18–19, 1934. RF RG1.1 S216D B8 F106 RA.

88. Ibid.:2–3.

89. Lillie here articulated the posture of the "transition generation" of eugenists, who eschewed the old, simplistic eugenics in favor of a modern genetics-based, scientific eugenics (Clarke 1981:120–22; Osborn 1966:158). See also Allen (1991) on eugenics and Mitman (1992:96–109) on the significance of Lillie's proposal for recasting population as the fundamental unit of ecological, evolutionary, and social change.

90. Hutchins to Mason, with attached twelve-page proposal by Lillie, Feb. 1, 1934. RF RG1.1 S216D B8 F106 RA.

91. Ibid., pp. 5–7.

92. See file RF RG1.1 S216D B8 F106 RA.

93. The papers available at the Rockefeller Archives have been edited. Whether concluding correspondence, giving reasons for terminating consideration of this proposal, ever existed cannot be determined. Discussions may well have been in person.

94. See Haller (1963), Ludmerer (1972), and Kevles (1985).

95. Laughlin's model law (Bajema 1976:138–45) was used in many of the states of the United States as such legislation was formulated. See Robitscher (1973).

96. See Committee of the American Neurological Association (1936). Ironically, this study was funded by the Carnegie Foundation and may reflect its disen-

gagement from prior eugenic commitments (Haller 1963:179). See also Allen (1991).

97. See Rosenberg (1961:272), Ludmerer (1972:46), and L. C. Dunn in Chase (1975:372).

98. Nor did it include much experimental embryology, which Weaver saw as a small but healthy field needing no stimulation or long-term development funds. He thought that there would be important advances in biochemical and x-ray analysis of developing embryos, but that the field would not reach this stage for some time to come. Hence he was content to let the field remain small (Kohler 1976:302). Moreover, the Carnegie Institution was a primary funder in this area.

99. RF Staff Conference, 24 January 1935. RAC RF RG1.1 S200 B38 F439.

100. For a sociological framing of fashion, see Simmel (1904/1971).

101. RF Resolution 41011, 17 January 1941. RAC RF RG1.1 S200 B38 F436.

102. See, for example, Harrower (1917), Robinson (1934), and Frank (1929, 1931, 1935).

103. There is an ambitious literature (e.g., Bell 1986, 1995; Hall 1974; Kohler 1976:295; Borell 1976a,b, 1985).

104. See, for example, entry from AG's [Alan Gregg] diary, Dr. Yerkes, 16 December 1940 (RAC RF RG1.1 S200 B39 F442), and letter to Yerkes from Alan Gregg, 17 January 1941 (RAC RF RG1.1 S200 B39 F442).

105. From AG's [Alan Gregg] diary, Dr. Yerkes, 16 December 1940. RAC RF RG1.1 S200 B39 F442. See also Aberle and Corner (1953).

106. RF Resolution 44002, NRC/CRPS, 21 January 1944. RAC RF RG1.1 S200 B39 F444.

107. RF Resolution 41011, 17 January 1941. RAC RF RG1.1 S200 B38 F436.

CHAPTER FIVE

1. There are a number of "insider histories," which provide accounts of these researches that are not recounted here. See Amoroso (1963), Asdell (1977), Corner (1951, 1958a, 1963, 1965, 1981), Dodds (1941), Everett and Sawyer (1987), Gruhn and Kazer (1989), Hamblen (1939), Klein (1963), Lisser (1967), McCance (1977), Medvei (1982), Parkes (1962b,c, 1963, 1966a,b), Price (1975), Short (1977), Zondek (1941), and Zuckerman (1970, 1978).

2. Bartelmez (1937), Ehrenfest (1937), and Corner (1951) provide major reviews.

3. On the Pill's development, see, for example, McLaughlin (1982), Djerassi (1981), and Pincus (1965). The rhetoric of "fertility and sterility" research was the segue between "birth control and sex" rhetorics of the earlier years of the century and the "population control" rhetorics developing in the 1950s. See chapter 8.

4. Sengoopta (1993:60–61) details the surgery. On Steinach's scientific position, see also Sengoopta (1995), Rechter (1997), Lipschutz (1925), Steinach (1940), and Benjamin (1945).

5. For their challenges to Steinach's argument, see Moore (1931a, 1938), Price (1972, 1975), and Fausto-Sterling (1998).

6. The 1932 version of Lillie's "Biological Introduction" simply asserts that the "male hormone" originates in the testis and the "female hormone" in the ovary. Lillie goes to some length to counter Steinach's theory of sex hormone antagonism, asserting that "each operates independently with its own field" (Lillie 1932:8).

7. For entrée into the sex differences literatures, see, for example, Parsons (1980), Longino (1990), Harding and O'Barr (1987), and Oudshoorn (1994).

8. Feminists here include Hall (1974), Longino and Doell (1983), Oudshoorn and van den Wijngaard (1991), Oudshoorn (1994), van den Wijngaard (1991), Rechter (1997), and, perhaps most ambitiously, Fausto-Sterling (1998).

9. Sociologists Studer and Chubin (1976) also take issue with the patent retrospective sequencing of the development of the reproductive sciences.

10. Doisy later shared the 1943 Nobel Prize for his work on the isolation of vitamin K (Medvei 1982:727).

11. His work was supported by the NRC/CRPS directly from 1930 to 1934 (Aberle and Corner 1953:121), and subsequently through assistance from the Rockefeller grant for research in the Biological Sciences Division. Report for 1934–35 on the Grant for Biological Research Made by the Rockefeller Foundation," Nov. 8, 1935:3–5. RAC RF RG1.1 S216d B8 F107. See also Clarke (1993).

12. See Figure 5.1. See also the disciplinary and professional mix of authors in the journal *Endocrinology* during this period.

13. Chapter 8, which focuses on the relations of reproductive scientists to birth control advocates during this period, demonstrates American scientists' refusal to participate in explicitly contraceptive research, despite considerable demands and offers of support. Of course, some reproductive scientists, notably Carl Hartman (1931, 1933, 1936, 1937), published popular, practical works with contraceptive implications.

14. Of course, many other investigators pursued it prior to and at the same time as Smith. See Medvei (1982) and Greep and Koblinsky (1977). Like that of many other reproductive scientists, Smith's background included extensive work in embryology, including the development of the pituitary gland (Agate 1975:473).

15. Agate (1975:472–75) notes that Bennett M. Allen at the University of Kansas was conducting "almost identical research," and that he and Smith had met and discussed their work and developed some kind of understanding regarding publication of this groundbreaking research. See also Medvei (1982:323). See Agate (1975), Amoroso and Corner (1975), and Corner (1981) for Smith's relations with Herbert M. Evans, who pursued research in hypophyseal hormones after working with Smith at the University of California, Berkeley.

16. Greep, personal communication.

17. Such scientists included Herbert M. Evans at the University of California, Berkeley (Amoroso and Corner 1975; Corner 1981) and Frederick L. Hisaw, Harry L. Fevold, and Roy Greep at Wisconsin (Greep 1967, 1973). The involvement of the adrenal cortex in these phenomena was not clarified until after 1940 (Klein 1963:301.

18. This was part of a progress report from Frederick L. Hisaw, E. L. Severinghaus, and L. J. Cole of the University of Wisconsin, titled "Physiology and Chemistry of Endocrines Concerned with the Physiology of Reproduction and Application to

Clinical Medicine and Agriculture," dated 1934, located in the Rockefeller Foundation Archives (RF RG1.1 S200D B162 F1996). It was probably also submitted to the NRC/CRPS, which provided extensive support of their work (Aberle and Corner 1953).

19. Focused as these scientists were on reproduction, they omitted other hormone-producing organs from the sketch (e.g., the thyroid, adrenal cortex). The authors assumed, I believe, that the biological sciences were the heart of the research effort, making explicit reference to "cooperating laboratories" in agriculture, medicine, and social sciences.

20. It was not noted whether anterior pituitary gonadotropic hormones were counted as gonadal or pituitary.

21. In 1931, sponsorship had been shifted from the Rockefeller-funded social action agency, the Bureau of Social Hygiene, directly to the Natural Sciences Division of the Rockefeller Foundation as a full-fledged biomedical research endeavor. See chapter 4.

22. The second edition (Allen, ed., 1939) had one British contributor. See Aberle and Corner (1953:27–28). For careful analyses of the contributions of Europeans, other than British workers, see Klein (1963), Medvei (1982), and Short (1977). For examples of French contributions, see Brouha (1938).

23. Weaver attended the NRC/CRPS Conference on the Biology of Sex at Woods Hole in 1934, based on the work drawn together in *Sex and Internal Secretions*. See W. W. Memo on this conference, ca. 10 Sept. 1934. RAC RF RG1.1 S200 B38 F438.

24. See, for example, Cole (1930) and Cole and Hart (1930). But here we also see identification by biologists of zoologists working in agricultural settings as still biologists, while agricultural scientists viewed them as agricultural scientists.

25. Beach (1981) wrote an ambitious paper on the historical origins of the study of hormones and behavior. The paper has inaccuracies, however, including misdating the first and second editions of *Sex and Internal Secretions*.

26. Beginning in 1959, the Ford Foundation became a major private sponsor of the reproductive sciences. Hertz (1984) provides an excellent overview of their activities from then to 1983.

27. See Cravens (1978), Evans and Cowles (1940), Gregory (1935), Kiger (1963), Lisser (1967), Mengert (1934), Sabin (1934), and Stevens (1971).

28. Mengert (1934) was attempting to determine which were the major journals of the field that scientists should follow to keep up-to-date.

29. See, for example, Borell (1985, 1987a), Hall (1974, 1976), and Medvei (1982).

30. There was an NRC Committee for Research in Problems of Sex fifteen years before the NRC Committee on Endocrinology was established. See chapter 7 for discussion.

31. Eighth Annual Report of Committee for Research on Sex Problems of the Division of Medical Sciences, National Research Council. For the year 1 July 1929 to 30 June 1930. Prepared for the Committee by Robert M. Yerkes, Chairman. RAC BSH SIII-2 B8 F189.

32. The 1932 conference was attended by Doisy, Butenandt, Laqueur, Marrian,

Dodds, Parkes, and Dale, who chaired. Doisy was the only American—and a chemist. The 1935 conference, also chaired by Dale, added American chemists F. C. Koch from Chicago and Willard Allen, who worked with Corner at Rochester, along with K. Meischer from CIBA Basel, adding further industrial connections. See Parkes (1985:130–33).

33. Attending from the United States were J. B. Collip, Herbert M. Evans, P. E. Smith, Frank Young, and Bernardo A. Houssay. See Parkes (1985:130–33).

34. The (American) Endocrine Society was formed in 1917; the (British) Society for Endocrinology was not founded until 1946, although the *Journal of Endocrinology* of the Royal Society of Medicine began in 1938 (Medvei 1982:502). The (British) Society for the Study of Fertility started in 1944 (Cook 1994). Prior to 1960, the organization published the proceedings of its annual meetings in book form (Parkes 1966a).

35. Lowy cites a 1991 talk Galison gave as stimulating her. This discussion appears in his *Image and Logic* (1997). See also Galison and Stump (1996).

36. See Borell (1985, 1987a), Hall (1974, 1976), and Oudshoorn (1994).

37. See Schwartz et al. (1977). This was also confirmed in interviews with both Neena Schwartz and Andrew Nalbandov. See also Clarke (1998).

38. See the Frank R. Lillie Papers, UChiA.

39. Hisaw later went to Harvard as Fisher Professor of Natural History, and Fevold and Greep accompanied him (Fulton and Wilson 1966:403). Severinghaus went to Columbia's College of Physicians and Surgeons, where he worked with P. E. Smith and Earl T. Engle (Allen, ed., 1932). Cole remained at Wisconsin. Roy Greep and his associates (1976, 1977) offer useful histories of reproductive research, especially as related to contraception.

40. Medical scientists who developed such colonies include Edgar Allen (at Washington University and Yale), George Corner (at Hopkins and Rochester), Philip Smith (at Columbia), and George Bartelmez (at Chicago) (Clarke 1987, 1995b).

41. Letter from Warren Weaver of the Rockefeller Foundation to Frank R. Lillie, Oct. 6, 1933. RAC RG1.1 S216D B8 F105.

42. Interviews at the University of California, Davis, 1985.

43. Interview with Nalbandov in Urbana, Illinois, April 7, 1984. Radioimmunoassay, developed around 1960 (Medvei 1982:556–57), transformed such processes because vast quantities of urine no longer needed to be distilled to obtain small amounts of active hormone. On materials access in the Netherlands, see Oudshoorn (1994).

44. Of course, unlike the vaginal smear, examination of these organs required surgery, making them more costly indicators in terms of time, effort, and risk to materials.

45. Cf. Benson (1981). Farley (1982:209–59) provides a lovely overview of the salience of cytology to turn-of-the-century problems in sexual reproduction, prior to and during the three-way split.

46. See Fulton and Wilson (1966:399). Smith's work further demonstrated that transplants of the anterior pituitary were capable of restoring the functions that had been atrophied by hypophysectomy. Smith also showed that anterior pituitary

transplants into immature female rats produced a rapid and precocious development of the genital system. This work linked the reproductive endocrinological system to the general bodily endocrinological system through the functions of the anterior pituitary gland.

47. I thank Studer and Chubin (1976) for pointing out this source.

48. For recent discussion of this work, including the concepts of threshold and tissue sensitivity, see Sinding (1990:205–10); for original descriptions, see Domm, Juhn, and Gustavson (1932). See also Price (1974, 1975).

49. Evidence is limited but highly suggestive. The roots of these tensions most likely lie, of course, in the turn-of-the-century shifts of emphasis in biological and medical research from morphology and anatomy to experimental and physiological approaches. See Benson (1989) for a general discussion. Werdinger (1980:338–39) notes significant tensions within embryology along these lines.

50. See Nalbandov (1958, 1970, 1973, 1976, 1978). He carefully notes (1976:1) that this diversity is largely restricted to females: "reproduction in males is remarkably uniform across species."

51. Interview with Andrew Nalbandov, April 7, 1984. See also Schwartz et al. (1977).

52. See Farley (1982:235–51) for a superb account of the dialogue between Lillie and Loeb. See Oppenheimer (1967:29–44) for further development of Lillie's broad biological view. See also Clarke (1993).

53. The review appeared in a new journal, *Animal Reproduction Science* (1978), an international publication with an animal agricultural science focus.

54. See also Frank (1929, 1935), Pratt and Allen (1926), and Doisy (1941a,b).

55. See Carmichael (1973:68–97), Clarke and Casper (1996), and Casper and Clarke (1997).

56. In medicine, the germ theory of disease and control over contagious diseases had paved the way to some degree for acceptance of scientific innovations.

57. The oral history of Harold H. Cole, professor of animal science at the University of California, Davis, provides a superb saga of the tensions confronted by the first generation of serious animal scientists and how they managed them through understanding their own "double mission" as scientists and as "animal men" (Cole 1977).

58. Considerable pioneering work in this field was done by Russian investigators (Herman 1981:3).

59. See Provine (1986), Chapman (1987), and Lush (1951).

60. See Reingold (1982:146), Randle (1993), Fechheimer (1986), and Kunkle and Hagevoort (1994:251).

61. The image is from Reingold (1982:152). Valuable summaries of the impacts of reproductive technologies on agriculture in this century are found in Byerly (1976), Biggers (1991), Corea (1985), Wiser, Mark, and Purchase (1987), Brackett, Seidel, and Seidel (1981), and Herman (1981). The Research and Education Association (Reingold 1982) provides an excellent overview that is marred by its lack of attention to and recognition of developments in scientific animal agriculture prior to 1950. This source also addresses the problems of the need to "trade off" among various technological improvements because not all can be implemented simulta-

neously, and some have unwanted side effects. On this point, see also Nalbandov (1978). In some animals, such as sheep, the reproductive patterns are not amenable to scientific intervention. Corea (1985) attends to the transfer of these agricultural technologies to humans with histories of their development in agriculture.

CHAPTER SIX

1. In 1914, only three articles on birth control appeared in the *New York Times*, and in 1915 only fourteen. But in 1916–17 ninety appeared, and news magazines had similar coverage. See Chesler (1992:129–30).

2. Certainly some reproductive scientists were also active in birth control organizations (described in detail later in this chapter). But by and large, the positions these activists themselves articulated regarding contraceptive research were closer to those of other reproductive scientists than of birth control advocates.

3. See Bijker, Hughes, and Pinch (1987), Bijker and Law (1992), and Pinch (1997); cf. Clarke (1985).

4. On the concept of implicated actors, see Clarke and Montini (1993).

5. I am not addressing infanticide here, although it obviously was and continues to be a means of fertility control, if not birth control, whether practiced intentionally or tacitly by neglect. For example, Kertzer (1994) recently documented Italian Catholic practices requiring infant abandonment by unwed mothers, which led to extremely high rates of infant death. Such practices are certainly open to being termed infanticide and, as he reveals, ended barely a century ago. Zelizer's (1994) historical analysis of the price and value of children, the high infant mortality of baby farms, and baby-selling practices in the United States, (which extended well into the twentieth century and in fact continue underground) also deserve examination. On infanticide in contemporary China, see Greenhalgh and Li (1995).

6. There is a strong and expanding literature on the history of contraception. For pre-nineteenth-century modes, see Himes (1936), Bodemer (1976), Robertson (1991), and Riddle (1992). An excellent new work on the nineteenth-century United States is Brodie (1994); on the social constructions of the condom—"rubber wars"—see Gamson (1990).

7. However, this is generally limited to applied industrial chemistry and rubber technology, with animal testing. While *using* "safe period" techniques does not require scientifically based products, *determining* the safe period with precision depended on basic research. Information on these techniques was notoriously erroneous until well into the 1920s and 1930s. See Hartman (1933, 1936, 1937, 1962), Knaus (1934a,b), Langley (1973:96–132), and Ogino (1924, 1930, 1934).

8. Diaphragms and cervical caps require "fitting" by trained personnel, not necessarily physicians, and there is debate over the extent of training required (e.g., Holmes, Hoskins, and Gross 1980).

9. Some argue that the birth control pill could safely be distributed "over the counter" like condoms. See, for example, Dixon-Mueller (1993a).

10. For nineteenth-century predecessors, see especially Brodie (1994), Gordon (1976), Chandrasekhar (1981), Himes (1936), and Reed (1983).

11. The NBCL changed its name to the Voluntary Parenthood League in 1919. On Dennett, see Chesler (1992:143–44, 167–70). See also McCann (1994).

12. Four prominent American biologists served on the Advisory Board: C. C. Little; geneticist Edward M. East of Harvard; Raymond Pearl; and Leon J. Cole. Both Little and East were very active in American eugenics organizations (Borell 1987a). Of these, only Cole could be considered a prominent reproductive scientist.

13. On birth control conferences, see Borell (1987a), Gordon (1976), Kennedy (1970), Pierpoint (1922), Reed (1983), Sanger (1934, 1938/1971), and Sanger and Stone (1931). On the international conference, see Carl Moore's statement on the meeting, included in the Eighth Annual Report of the NRC/CRPS, prepared by R. M. Yerkes 1930. RAC BSH SIII-2 B8 F189.

14. See chapter 7 for a discussion of funding of the NCMH and of reproductive research by the NCMH. Both Carl Hartman and Earl Engle were on the board of the NCMH in the 1930s in charge of research. See RAC RF RG1.1 S200A B99 F1199. See also RAC RF RG1.1 S200A B99 F1199 and RAC BSH SIII-2 B7 F172.

15. See McCann (1994:chapter 3) for a recent and very rich account of relations between the lay birth control movement and medicine in the United States. C. C. Little even wanted to include sociologists on the advisory board of the research organization! Soloway (1995) focuses on the integration of birth control research within the agendas of eugenics societies in Britain and the United States in the interwar years; developments were quite parallel.

16. That is, most of the business involved means and mechanisms of contraception marketed as other things. See Riddle (1992) and McCann (1994).

17. See File Memorandum RT (Ruth Topping), "Crew Study and Interview with Dr. Crew." 12 September 1932. RAC BSH SIII-2 B7 F174.

18. On eugenics in the United States, see especially Bajema (1976), Duster (1990), Haller (1963), Kevles (1985), Ludmerer (1972), Pickens (1968), Searle (1981), and Soloway (1982, 1990, 1995). For intensive analysis of the relations between the eugenics and birth control movements, see Gordon (1975, 1976, 1990), Petchesky (1984/1990), McCann (1994:chapter 4), and Larson (1995).

19. Birth control advocates of all political stripes also advocated contraception on negative eugenic grounds from the late nineteenth century on (Gordon 1976; Sanger 1920, 1971). The NCMH had even approached eugenicists for joint sponsorship of birth control research in the early 1920s, was initially rebuffed, and then received: Committee on Maternal Health [C.M.H.], March 1924. Researches. RAC BSH SIII-2 B7 F175.

20. Harry Laughlin's "Model Eugenical Sterilization Law" (Bajema 1976:138–45) was almost directly translated as the Nazi law of 1933. On eugenic sterilization and other sterilization abuse in the United States, see Kevles (1985), Landman (1932), Pickens (1968), Robitscher (1973), Shapiro (1985), Reilly (1991), and Clarke (1984).

21. See enclosure with materials from the Eugenics Committee of the U.S.A., dated 10 October 1923, FRLP BIII F8 UChiA.

22. On this use of the term, see Himes (1936), Pierpoint (1922), and Sanger (1920).

23. Recently there has been a renaissance of eugenics in its own name and again focused on the quality of individuals (e.g., Bajema 1976; Carter 1983; Duster 1990).

24. Key cites include Ledbetter (1976), Gordon (1990), Courey (1994), Sharpless (1993), Hodgson (1983, 1988, 1991), and Greenhalgh (1995, 1996).

25. Minutes of the Preliminary Conference on a Population Association for the United States. New York University, 5 December 1930, with the cooperation of the Milbank Memorial Fund. RAC BSH SIII-2 B9 F191.

26. See, for example, Gordon (1976/1990), Maas (1974), and Reed (1983).

27. For an excellent insider's account of the development of population studies, see Notestein (1982), who spent his professional life at the Milbank Memorial Fund, Princeton University, and the Population Council.

28. See RAC BSH SIII-2 B9 F190–91 and B10 F218; and First Annual Meeting roster, April 22–23, 1932 (RAC BSH SIII-2 B9 F190). Most were also members of the Population Association of America, founded in 1931 (Notestein 1982).

29. See Wilmoth and Ball (1992) and Courey (1994) on American media. For a contrasting situation where underpopulation became a matter of state concern—Fascist Italy—see Horn (1994).

30. See RAC BSH SIII-2 B7.

31. To Mr. Fosdick from L. B. Dunham 14 December 1927. RAC BSH SIII-2 B7 F173.

32. Response from Fosdick to Dunham, 22 December 1927. RAC BSH SIII-2 B7 F173; emphasis added.

33. To Mr. Fosdick from L. B. Dunham, Subject: NRC/CRPS. 6 February 1931. RAC BSH SIII-2 B8 F186. To Mr. Fosdick from Mr. Dunham, Subject: Conference on Birth Control. 19 March 1931, pp. 1–3. RAC BSH SIII-2 B7 F166.

34. Memo to Mr. Dunham, 15 October 1931; and see other documents in this folder (RAC BSH SIII-2 B7 F166). Topping, a key BSH staff person, became executive secretary of the ABC League in 1933, when the BSH ceased functioning. See Topping to J. Kingsbury, Milbank Memorial Fund. 21 January 1933. RAC BSH SIII-2 B8 F187.

35. See Sharpless (1993), and chapters 4 and 7 here.

36. See Haraway (1995) on the shift from race to population to the genome across the twentieth century.

37. Minutes of the Preliminary Conference on a Population Association for the United States. New York University, 15 December 1930, with the cooperation of the Milbank Memorial Fund. RAC BSH SIII-2 B9 F191.

38. These were noted by Rockefeller philanthropies. See E.C. 5 and 9 January 1934. American Birth Control League (p. 92). RAC BSH SIII-2 B7 F163.

39. See Maas (1974:656); see also Borell (1987a), Gordon (1976), Kevles (1985); Marks (1982), Reed (1983), and Shapiro (1985). For the mission statements, see, on eugenics, Osborn (1951); for birth control excerpts in Gordon (1976:349–53); for neo-Malthusianism, see Ledbetter (1976) and Chase (1975).

40. See Bureau, 26 July 1923. RAC BSH SIII-2 B7 F172, and Committee on Maternal Health [NCMH], March 1924. Researches. RAC BSH SIII-2 B7 F175.

41. The NCMH was sponsoring a book on sterilization with Dr. Howard C. Taylor of Columbia as primary author; other methods to be researched included the IUD, clinical research on the safe period, sperm antigens (inoculations or spermatoxins), and contraceptive jellies. See to Weaver from Raymond Squier, NCMH. 21 January 1936. RAC RF RG1.1 S200A B99 F1199.

42. Weaver to Yerkes. 28 February 1936. RAC RF RG1.1 S200A B99 F1199.

43. 6 March 1936. RAC RF RG1.1 S200A B99 F1199.

44. From the foreword to Voge's book (1933:12) by Robert Latou Dickinson of the NCMH. Robert T. Frank was the director of research for the NCMH at this time, and the manuscript was also reviewed by Carl Hartman of Hopkins.

45. See File Memoranda: Crew Spermaticide Study. RAC BSH SIII-2 B7 F174.

46. As reported by Ruth Topping of the BSH staff: File Memorandum RT. Subject: Crew Study and Interview with Dr. Crew. 12 September 1932. RAC BSH SIII-2 B7 F174.

47. Memo to Mr. Dunham from Ruth Topping, Subject: Contraceptive Research, 30 September 1931. RAC BSH SIII-2 B7 F166. See also Soloway (1995). Porter and Hall (1995:176) assert that Solly Zuckerman received some American funding with Baker. Subsequently, they also report, Baker relied on funding from the (British) Eugenics Society and from the pharmaceutical company British Drug Houses, Ltd.

48. The NCMH would locate and fund a scientist, cover some expenses, and use the department's primate colony. See to Dr. Merriam from G. Streeter, 12 March 1938. JHA CDoE SP (then unsorted; now likely filed under NCMH).

49. To George Streeter, Director of the Department of Embryology, from President Merriam of the Carnegie Institution. 4 June 1938. JHA CDoE SP (then unsorted; now likely filed under NCMH).

50. To Hartman from Dr. Raymond Squier. 7 July 1938. JHA CDoE SP (then unsorted; now likely filed under NCMH).

51. 13 July 1938. JHA CDoE SP (then unsorted; now likely filed under NCMH).

52. See to Alan Gregg, RF, from Dr. Louise F. Bryant, NCMH, 21 December 1934. Letter from Hartman to Bryant as attachment 5 December 1934. RAC RF RG1.1 S200A B99 F1199.

53. See Borell (1987a:fn76) and to Mr. Dunham from Ruth Topping, Subject: Contraceptive Research. 15 October 1931. RAC BSH SIII-2 B7 F166. The only pre-1940 example of agricultural institution-based research on contraception I located was Cole and Bunde (1937). Later artificial insemination research began to include immunological problems (e.g., Menge et al. 1962).

54. Ruth Topping wrote, "It is interesting to note that Dr. Crew's apparent belief that a narrowly restricted search for a better contraceptive is less apt to yield the desired results than a broadly exploratory process is in general line with a suggestion made by Dr. Carl G. Hartman of Carnegie Corporation [*sic*] some time ago when he recommended having several of the many students of physiology of reproduction keep in mind the significance of their observations in relation to the pos-

sibility of the control of fertility. Dr. Lillie of Chicago suggested in addition that the problem was one to be worked out jointly by a laboratory man and a clinician." File Memorandum RT. Subject: Crew Study and Interview with Dr. Crew. 12 September 1932. RAC BSH SIII-2 B7 F174.

55. Topping reported: File Memorandum RT. Subject: Crew Study and Interview with Dr. Crew (punctuated as original). 12 September 1932. RAC BSH SIII-2 B7 F174.

56. Despite such rhetoric, Crew's institute later sponsored a wide range of "applied" undertakings, including Voge's work noted earlier, the first Pregnancy Diagnosis Laboratory in the United Kingdom, and investigations of artificial insemination. Ironically, according to one biographer, Crew's own involvement in basic research ended prematurely with his acceptance of applied administrative research positions (Hogben 1974)!

57. Ogino (1924, 1930, 1934) was the leading Japanese contributor, writing in German and Japanese. The leading German worker was Knaus (1934a,b), who had worked with British reproductive scientists.

58. See Borell (1987a:fn77); see also Hartman (1937, 1939, 1962). The NCMH book series is discussed in chapter 7.

59. MM's diary, interview with Arthur W. Packard. 12 June 1934. RAC RF RG1.1 S200A B99 F1199. See also Sinding (1990).

60. File Memorandum RT. Subject: Crew Study and Interview with Dr. Crew. 12 September 1932. RAC BSH SIII-2 B7 F174.

61. See Cooper (1928:120), and several articles on the interruption of pregnancy through administration of estrogens (Smith 1926; Makepeace, Weinstein, and Freidman 1937; Parkes and Noble 1938). H. Taylor reported on hormonal contraceptive research at Edinburgh in 1930 (in Sanger and Stone 1931:98–104). See also Dickinson and Bryant (1931), Sanger (1934), and Sanger and Stone (1931). Studer and Chubin (1976) and Gunn (1987) also take up some of these points.

62. Another major American reproductive scientist of the first generation, Frederick Hisaw, was recruited to Harvard in the mid-1930s from Wisconsin and then did little reproductive research. While at Harvard, Pincus had done research on mammalian sexual physiology supported by both the NRC/CRPS and the Macy Foundation (Reed 1983:319–20). See Reed (1983:chapters 25–27) for a fuller account of Pincus's career and his work with Chang on Pill development. See Pincus (1965) for his summary work on control of fertility. Pincus did his undergraduate work at Cornell's School of Agriculture, focusing on biochemistry and animal breeding (Johnson 1977:68). For Pincus as a disciple of Jacques Loeb's biological engineering ideology, see Pauly (1987:182–98). See also Djerassi (1992) and Robertson (1989).

63. See Pramik (1978), Djerassi (1981, 1992), Applezweig (1975), Marker (1986), Goldzieher (1993), and Perone (1993). Perone describes how difficult progesterone was to obtain, and all discuss the controversy which surrounded Syntex for years.

64. See Ramirez de Arellano and Seipp (1983), Oudshoorn (1994), and Meldrum (1996).

65. This analysis differs radically from those of Pill development done for the National Science Foundation (1968) by TRACES and Batelle (National Science Foundation 1973), which offered an individualist "technical scientific entrepreneur" account focused on Pincus. Such accounts ignore 120 years of activity by birth control advocates, including their recruitment of scientists, and the crucial structural positions of the major developers outside of the academy. For a more fully developed analysis that takes all of the significant actors into account, see Courey (1994:chapter 1).

66. See Djerassi (1992:121) and Chesler (1992). It has also been argued that the role of physicians in family planning was transformed by the Pill from incidental participants to essential players, while patients also had to become more active to obtain and calibrate the Pill or other modern scientific means of contraception, changing the overall balance of power between physicians and patients as well (Watkins 1995).

67. For a good example of Grafenberg's work, see his 1931 article reprinted in Langley (1973:340–356). For an historical actor network approach to the development of IUDs, see Dugdale (1995).

68. For examples and accounts of these debates especially in the 1930s, see Langley (1973:336–339, 357), Sanger and Stone (1931:33–71), Sanger (1934:86–93) and Tietze (1962, 1965b).

69. Dr. Mary Halton, Margaret Sanger's gynecologist, showed Dickinson over one thousand case histories in 1924. Dickinson wanted a full investigation of the method, but not until 1947 was there a serious effort to publish Halton's results; then her "Contraception with an Intrauterine Silk Coil" was rejected by the *American Journal of Obstetrics and Gynecology*. The NCMH refused to sponsor the paper; Earl Engle and Howard Taylor Jr. said that "this was too hot to be [easily] cleared." The article was finally published in *Human Fertility* in 1948, the journal of Sanger's Clinical Research Bureau, with editorial warnings. Ironically, in 1964 Taylor hailed the IUD as a "contribution to . . . the freedom of mankind" (Reed 1983:275–76).

70. On the Dalkon Shield controversy, see Mintz (1985), Grant (1992), and Hicks (1994). On IUDs more broadly, see Dugdale (1995).

71. In the development sagas of the Pill and the IUD, there seems to have been competition between sponsoring organizations, and between physician-developers of the IUD versus the biologist-developers of hormonal contraception. For example, Gregory Pincus was "profoundly uninterested" in participating in evaluation of conventional barrier methods, and Reed (1983:375) also found that: "the IUD remains the butt of jokes at the Worcester Foundation, while representatives of the Population Council make vague references to the 'commercial interests' that control distribution of the Pill." Onorato (1991) compared the organizational styles and successes of the Population Council and the Planned Parenthood Federation of America in terms of contraceptive research.

72. This research may have been supported by the NCMH (see CMH "Research Problems." March 1924. RAC BSH SIII-2 B7 F175).

73. See RLD 17 June 1925. RAC BSH SIII-2 B7 F172.

74. To Katherine Davis from R. L. Dickinson. 14 January 1925. RAC BSH SIII-2

B7 F172. Radiation sterilization research was part of the NCMH's initial laboratory research program, from about 1923 to 1928, as discussed in chapter 7.

75. To Mr. C. Heydt, Treas. BSH, Inc. from R. L. Dickinson. 10 June 1925. RAC BSH SIII-2 B7 F172.

76. In 1935, the NCMH program statement notes, "Sterilization by *radiation* has still to be evaluated as a measure for extended use." See RAC RF RG1.1 S200A B99 F1207.

77. Summary of "Cooperative Laboratory Researches," NCMH, Sub-Committee on Research, Robert T. Frank, M. D., Chairman. 23 November 1928. RAC BSH SIII-2 B7 F173.

78. American biological scientists included Guyer, S. Mudd, and W. T. Pommerenke; physician scientists included McCartney, S. J. Fogelson, M. J. Baskin, W. Henle, J. Jarcho, and N. Hyde; reproductive scientists such as Leon Cole of Wisconsin, Ralph Kurzrok of Columbia, and Carl Hartman of Carnegie/Hopkins were involved in discussions. For a summary of efforts, see Baskin's report in Sanger (1934:94–112) and Henle (1937).

79. Oudshoorn (1994) argues that already organized obstetrical and gynecological clinics served as a source of research materials—female urine—for the development of female hormones to be used in treatment. These organized clinics gave impetus to the primacy of female hormonal interventions and both sustained and metamorphosed gender bias in science. Bull testes, a common source for male hormones, were gathered in slaughterhouses but were much less productive and difficult to obtain in sufficient quantity (Clarke 1987). Given the absence of a medical specialty in male reproductive health at the time (Alexander 1980), there was no parallel organizational means of obtaining sperm unless urology was used. Moreover, the likelihood of infection in the woman was great after injection.

80. See Sanger and Stone (1931:111–15), Henle (1937), and Reed (1983:127, 231).

81. See RAC BSH SIII-2 B8 F183.

82. See, for example, Edwards (1969), Edwards and Johnson (1976), and Metz (1979).

83. Personal communication, May 1985.

84. See Oudshoorn (1994, 1995) for a recent feminist science and technology studies analyses. See also Johnson (1977), Hartmann (1987/1995), McLaughlin (1982), Pincus (1965), Seaman (1969/1980), Seaman and Seaman (1977), and Meldrum (1996).

85. See Reed (1983:373). For analysis of popular culture discussions of population, see Wilmoth and Ball (1992) and Courey (1994).

86. For bibliographies on contraception, see Hartman (1959) for clinical trials prior to 1950, and Tietze (1965a) for 1950–65, and Freedman (1962) for major trends. For major prospective and retrospective assessments, see Shelesnyak (1963a,b), Greep and associates (1976, 1977), Atkinson (1979), Clark (1982), Notestein (1982), Hertz (1984), Segal (1987), and Mastroianni, Donaldson, and Kane (1990). For recent comparative assessments of contraceptive effectiveness for new and established users, see Trussell and Kost (1987) and Steiner, Trussell, and Hertzpiccioto (1996).

87. See Boston Women's Health Book Collective (1992), Sen, Germain, and Chen (1994), Dixon-Mueller (1993a,b), Holmes (1992), Hartmann (1987/1995), and Sen and Snow (1994).

88. See Pauly (1987).

CHAPTER SEVEN

1. See Aberle and Corner (1953), Greep, Koblinsky, and Jaffe (1976), and Mastroianni, Donaldson, and Kane (1990).

2. A fine-grained fiscal analysis remains to be researched. Such an analysis should include careful examination of foundation contributions to individual scientists, as well as to organizations sponsoring reproductive research generally, and some examination of departmental research budgets in the major reproductive research centers. Both of these efforts are beyond the scope of the present work. Explicit comparisons remain to be made with other specialty biomedical research fields during this era.

3. Courey (1994:31–51) also found a more extensive network of funding sources than Greep and his colleagues had noted. Particularly for contraceptive research pursued at the Worcester Foundation for Experimental Biology led by Gregory Pincus there were many industrial and foundation supporters that have not received adequate attention in the historical record, likely intentionally "hidden" from historians' gaze because of the controversial nature of contraception.

4. This was certainly the case at the University of California, Davis. (Interview data; see Appendix 1.)

5. My calculations are based on Kohler (1991:104), who states that almost $12 million came to the NRC from foundations, primarily Rockefeller and Carnegie, and on Aberle and Corner's (1953) figures.

6. Much of this research was "basic" investigation of reproductive phenomena in farm animals. Considerable focus was placed during these years on studies in aid of improved means of artificial insemination for animal breeding (Greep, Koblinsky, and Jaffe 1976:370), which included studies of the timing of fertility, pregnancy diagnosis, and sperm production, activity, and preservation. See also Brackett, Seidel, and Seidel (1981).

7. By 1920, the foundation had given $540,000, and other Rockefeller agencies were also fiscally supportive. See letter to George Vincent from James R. Angell, 3 June 1920. RAC RF RG1.1 S200 B36 F416. See also Harr and Johnson (1988).

8. This aspect of the work of the NRC/CRPS deserves further attention, especially in relation to the larger sponsorship philosophies of the Rockefeller and other philanthropies and their changes during this period (e.g., Abir-Am 1982; Arnove 1980; Kohler 1978, 1991; Harr and Johnson 1988).

9. RF Inter-Office Memorandum by F. Blair Hanson of the RF, 26 December 1933. RAC RF RG1.1 200 B70 F589.

10. Aberle and Corner (1953:24–25) provided the bulk of this account of the committee's actual inception. In essence, during this period different foundations

seem to have been primary sponsors of different NRC committees. The Markle Foundation appears to have been the sole supporter of this committee (Strickland and Strickland 1976:7).

11. On Cannon, see Benison, Barger, and Wolfe (1987).

12. Yerkes to Weaver, 9 November 1937. RAC RF RG1.1 S200 B39 F441.

13. From Alan Gregg's diary, meeting with L. H. Weed, 9 May 1940. RAC RF RG1.1 S200 B39 F442.

14. See Appendix 2 for NRC/CRPS research foci, and Aberle and Corner (1953).

15. RF Inter-Office Memorandum by FBH, 26 December 1933. RA RF RG1.1 200 B70 F589.

16. See the Report of the National Research Council for 1929–30; and NRC Division of Medical Sciences 1930–31, Circular Letter, 4 February 1931. RAC RF RG1.1 S200 B38 F433.

17. These are selected examples only; a more systematic examination of those records should be undertaken to clarify the extent of support of reproductive research prior to World War II. See, for example, "NRC Research Aid Fund, July–December 1932," attachment to letter to Norma Thompson, Secretary, RF, from Herbert J. Yule, Bursar, NRC, 13 July 1932. RAC RG1.1 S200 B37 F422. NRC Committee on Grants-in-Aid, 1 March 1930. Report of the Committee. RAC RF RG1.1 S200 B38 F432. NRC Research Aid Fund, Reports 1931. RAC RF RG1.1 S200 B38 F433. NRC Check-List of Grants-in-Aid for the period May 1929 to December 1937. 8 June 1938. RAC RF RG1.1 S200 B38 F435.

18. It seems likely that the Rockefeller Foundation chose not to sponsor this committee because of its long-term commitments to the NRC/CRPS, the tensions around the NRC/CRPS's funding of Alfred Kinsey's research, and broad questioning of the foundation's activities during the cold war/McCarthy era (personal communication with archivists, RAC; Pomeroy [1982:10, 298, 361]; Reed [1983:286]; and Harr and Johnson [1988:462]).

19. See Reed (1983:271, 334–45), and Chesler (1992:430–32).

20. Both Carl Hartman of Carnegie/Hopkins and Earl Engle of Columbia were on the board of the NCMH during the 1930s, guiding research efforts. See RAC RF RG1.1 S200A B99 F1199.

21. Between 1923 and 1936, Rockefeller sources provided $103,900 and other sources (including the Milbank, Carnegie, Macy, and Markle foundations and the Commonwealth Fund) provided $165,262. See RAC RF RG1.1 S200A B99 F1199.

22. See to Dunham, BSH, from Bryant, NCMH, 8 December 1928 with attached report. RAC BSH SIII-2 B7 F173. Summary of these "Cooperative Laboratory Researches," NCMH, Sub-Committee on Research, Robert T. Frank, M.D., Chairman. 23 November 1928. RAC BSH SIII-2 B7 F173. Both Stockard and Papanicolaou of Cornell Medical School were supported. RAC BSH SIII-2 B7 F172. See also Reed (1983).

23. Dr. Moench's work was published in the *Biological Bulletin* (November 1929), the *Medical Herald* and *Physical Therapy* (California, January 1930), the *American Journal of Obstetrics and Gynecology* (April 1930), and the *Journal of the American Medical Association* (April 19, 1930). The full report was published under the title "Stu-

dien zur Fertilität," in Germany. See File Memorandum JBW, Subject: NCMH—Information in Files on Prof. G. L. Moench's "Studien Zur Fertilitat," 15 September 1932, RAC BSH SIII-2 B7 F174. For a long list of Moench's publications out of this research, see attachment to this document.

24. See to Dunham from Bryant, 2 June 1932. RAC BSH SIII-2 B7 F173.

25. See to Katherine B. Davis from R. L. Dickinson, July 26 1923. RAC BSH SIII-2 B7 F172. And to KBD from RLD, 18 February 1925, with attachments, including a discussion of clinical research standards. RAC BSH SIII-2 B7 F172.

26. See to Dunham from Bryant, 8 December 1928, with attached report. RAC BSH SIII-2 B7 F173.

27. For program changes after 1935 and a major program statement, see Warren Weaver memo, 18 March 1937, and to Weaver from Squier, 26 March 1937. RAC RF RG1.1 S200A B99 F1200.

28. From AG's Diary, 3 May 1939: Lunch with Dr. Engle. RAC RF RG1.1 S200A B99 F1202.

29. Memo of Interview of AG with Drs. Squier and Engle, May 19 1937. RAC RF RG1.1 S200A B99 F1200.

30. See RAC RF RG1.1 S200A B99 F1201. And From AG's Diary, 16 March 1939. RAC RF RG1.1 S200A B99 F1202. There are also data here on the shift in research away from "compilation and interpretation of personal history" to "experimental work."

31. See RF Resolution 39066 6/9/39. RAC RF RG1.1 S200A B99 F1199.

32. See RAC RF RG1.1 S200A B99 F1199 and F1203.

33. See Reed (1983:305), McCann (1994), and Dugdale (1995). On Tietze, see Landy and Ratnam (1986).

34. I have undertaken a thorough analysis of materials at the Rockefeller Archive Center, including the funding of reproductive science under several programs. I have not examined parallel archival materials of the other major foundations interested in reproductive research problems (such as the Macy and Markle, foundations and the Milbank Memorial Fund).

35. See "University of Rochester-Physiology of Reproduction." Appraisal by W.W. RAC RF RG1.1 S200D B162 F1988. Given ambiguous language, there is some remote chance that this grant was through the NRC Committee on Endocrinology rather than direct foundation support.

36. Precise comparison of funding by the major foundations has not been done. See Kohler (1976, 1978, 1991) for general background on Rockefeller Foundation support of the life sciences. See Hinsey (1967) for general background on foundation support of biomedical research.

37. See RAC RF RG1.1 S200D B162 F1994. F. L. Hisaw was funded at Wisconsin by the NRC/CRPS and later at Harvard directly by the RF (see later discussion).

38. Corner also received earlier support from the Rockefeller-provided Fluid Research Fund for the University of Rochester School of Medicine and Dentistry. See RAC RF RG1.1 S200D B162 F1988.

39. These studies had been begun under an earlier grant by the General Education Board of $15,000 per year for three years. See RAC RF RG1.1 S200A B119 F1463.

40. Harrison had received $8,000 from the Rockefeller General Education Board for European studies, ca. 1927–28. See RAC RF RG1.1 S200D B169 F2055.

41. This work can be construed more as breeding/genetics research. An additional special grant was given of $20,000 for purchase of a farm and buildings for this work. The first five years of funding were provided through the Rockefeller General Education Board, while the last years were covered by the Rockefeller Foundation. See RAC RF RG1.1 S200A B81 F975.

42. See RF Resolution, 16 March 1934. RAC RF RG1.1 S205 B4 F57.

43. See RAC RF RG1.1 S200D B140 F1726.

44. Because of the blanket nature of the Rockefeller Foundation grants to Chicago, precise allocations to the Lillie/Moore center of reproductive research are unclear; the funding was at $30,000 per year for the five years 1929–34, $50,000 per year for the four years 1934–38, and $60,000 per year for the three years 1938–41. An endowment of $1.5 million (which required matching funds) was provided in 1941. See RAC RF RG1.1 S216 B8 F103 and F108. For a very detailed assessment of the financial situation at Chicago, see Clarke (1993).

45. See RF Resolution 37233, 21 May 1937. RAC RF RG1.1 S200D B134 F1656.

46. See Weindling (1988). On the Rockefeller Foundation, see also Arnove (1980), Brown (1979), Harr and Johnson (1988), Jonas (1989), Kohler (1991), and Wheatley (1989).

47. Historians of the American pharmaceutical industry note these difficulties routinely (Liebenau 1987; Swann 1988; Parascandola 1992). But such difficulties are more often confronted at the early dissertation stage of research, when access to archives is initially denied and research cannot be pursued. The exception to this rule to date is the company Organon in the Netherlands, whose records on sex hormones were made available to Oudshoorn (1994). Certainly historical and sociological research on sex hormone products in the United States, given the extensive legal entanglements and medical debates associated with their application in meat animals and humans, has not been facilitated by access to pharmaceutical industry records (e.g., Marcus 1995; Bell 1994b).

48. No mention of the Department of Zoology's paying for such materials appears in the archival materials examined at Chicago, although there is documentation of the department's purchase of a car to be used to pick up the fresh materials at the slaughterhouse.

49. See Corner (1981) and "Appraisal (August 1939)":3. RAC RF RG1.1 S200D B162 F1988.

50. In 1940, its name was changed yet again to the American Meat Institute.

51. Interview materials, University of California, Davis.

52. For pharmaceutical company reluctance, see Reed (1983), Greep and his colleagues (1976, 1977), and Mastroianni and his colleagues (1990:esp. 59–61). Charo (1991) provides a contemporary view of reluctance regarding the abortifacient RU486. A similar pattern in AIDS drug research has been documented (Epstein 1996). Clarke and Montini (1993) analyze the perspectives different participants in the reproductive arena bring to RU486.

53. Figure 7.4 includes expenditures made by the National Research Council

Committee for Research in Problems of Sex, the Committee on Growth and the Committee on Research in Endocrinology, the private National Committee on Maternal Health, the Rockefeller Foundation, Planned Parenthood Federation of America, the Sunnen Foundation, the Ford Foundation, the Population Council, and others (Greep, Koblinsky, and Jaffe 1976:378, 383, 402–3).

54. See Sharpless (1993:8), and Grant (1992), Segal (1987), and Dugdale (1995).

55. Mastroianni and his associates (1990:78–79) note that these figures, provided largely by the NICHHD and its cooperating agency the Interagency Council on Population Research, are in substantial disagreement with the study by the Alan Guttmacher Institute (Atkinson, Lincoln, and Forrest 1985), which had estimates about one-third lower. They believe these differences are the result of different classification of projects as basic reproductive research or applied contraceptive development. Mastroianni and his colleagues used the NICHHD definitions. Basic reproductive research includes development and function of the reproductive system, male and female fertility, fertilization including immediate prefertilization processes, preimplantation development, implantation, and reproductive endocrinology. Contraceptive development includes research on (extant and new) drug syntheses and testing, drug delivery systems and oral formulations testing, vaginal and uterine contraceptive devices and drugs, and sterilization including reversal.

56. See Mastroianni, Donaldson, and Kane (1990:76), Grant (1992), and, on pharmaceutical investment issues, Charo (1991).

57. See note 3.

58. Not included in this chapter is an account of the funding of distinctively *contraceptive* research support prior to about 1950 because the history of that movement and funding is quite complex and, at least to some extent, has been addressed by others. See Greep, Koblinsky, and Jaffe (1976), Reed (1983), Chesler (1992), McCann (1994), Courey (1994), and Gordon (1990). Hartman (1959) offers an annotated list of published clinical trials.

CHAPTER EIGHT

1. This chapter draws and expands on an earlier paper (Clarke 1990a).

2. All of the interviews undertaken for this project and many other conversations with reproductive scientists have confirmed this.

3. See, for example, Ruzek (1978), Lewin and Olesen (1985), Epstein (1996), Martin (1990, 1994), Dixon-Mueller (1993b), Montini (1996), Barroso and Corea (1995), and Annandale and Clark (1996).

4. On sites where social worlds meet, see, for example, Park (1952), Hughes (1971), Fujimura (1988), and Bucher (1988).

5. There are obvious links between analyzing something as controversial and analyzing its emergence as a social problem (e.g., Hilgartner and Bosk 1988). Some important conceptual links are delineated by Aronson (1984).

6. See Institute of Medicine (1989) for human applications and research is-

328   NOTES TO PAGES 241-249

sues. On prior agricultural development and applications, see Brackett, Seidel, and Seidel (1981), Biggers (1981, 1984, 1987, 1991), Betteridge (1986), Schaffir (1991), and Schneider (1988a,b).

7. See also the works of Borell, Hall, Long, and Oudshoorn.

8. See Petchesky (1984/1990, 1985), Kort (1987), and Rimer (1995).

9. Baulieu was a protégé of Gregory Pincus and part of the third generation of twentieth-century reproductive scientists. See Clarke and Montini (1993), Baulieu (1991), and Chonir (1994).

10. See Robitscher (1973), Ramirez de Arellano and Seipp (1983), Clarke (1984), Shapiro (1985), Reilly (1991), Coliver (1995), Finley (1996), Moskowitz and Jennings (1996), Pies (1997).

11. On how "cutting edges" cut both ways, see also Maienschein (1994).

12. On DES in humans, see Bell (1980, 1986, 1987, 1989a, 1994b, 1995), Apfel and Fisher (1984), Gillam and Bernstein (1987), Dutton (1988), and Bell and Apfel (1995).

13. There is an extensive critical literature across many years. See, for example, McKinlay and McKinlay (1973); Olesen (1982); Riessman (1983); Kaufert and McKinlay (1985); and Angier (1997). For a superb paper comparing the British and American prescription and usage patterns under differently financed health systems, see McCrea and Markle (1984).

14. See Apfel and Fisher (1984:132) for a complete listing.

15. See note 12.

16. See Marcus (1993, 1995) for a full account of Burroughs's experiments and the wider linkages between nutrition and endocrinology. See Zuckerman (1987:91) on natural and lean beef.

17. See, for example, Dienes (1972), Johnson (1977), McLaughlin (1982), Pincus (1965), Pramik (1978), Riessman (1983), Reed (1983), Ward (1986), Gunn (1987), Vaughn (1970), Hartmann (1987/1995), Dixon-Mueller (1993a,b), and Watkins (1995). On coercion, see note 10.

18. On implants and vaccines, see Hardon (1992), Schrater (1992), Morsy (1991, 1995), Ravindran and Berer (1994), Aldhous (1994), and Pies (1997).

19. See Greep, Koblinsky, and Jaffe (1976), Djerassi (1981, 1989), Rosoff (1988), Lincoln and Kaeser (1988), and Segal (1987).

20. See Ruzek (1978), Scully (1980), Holmes, Hoskins, and Gross (1980), Arditti, Klein, and Minden (1984), Fisher (1986), and Holmes (1992).

21. See, for example, Dixon-Mueller and Germain (1993), the new journal *Reproductive Health Matters,* no.3 (1994), Dixon-Mueller (1993a,b), Sen, Germain, and Chen (1994), and Holmes (1992). Transmission of AIDS through heterosexual intercourse has become a central concern to feminists, especially outside the United States. See, for example, Treichler (1993). On resistance, see Bloom and Parsons (1994).

22. Haldane's book, *Daedalus, or Science and the Future,* described techniques for in vitro development of human embryos, hormonal prevention of aging, and pharmacological control of behavior. The article on Pincus explained the implications of his work for the future of eugenic improvements, the emancipation of women,

and the freeing of love from the requirements of reproduction (Pauly 1987:189–91). Pincus had transferred the fertilized eggs to living hosts, so the rabbits were not born in a test tube. Moreover, the hosts were sacrificed before the embryos grew to term, so they were not actually "born" either (Reed 1983:321).

23. See Ingle (1971), Werthessen and Johnson (1974), and Reed (1983:317–33).

24. On fetal tissue research, see Annas and Elias (1989), Casper (1994b), Childress (1991), and Mulkay (1993). On fetal surgery as well, see Casper (1994a, 1995, 1998).

25. See Rapp (1990, 1995), Ginsberg and Rapp (1995), Duster (1990), Cook-Deegan (1991), Nelkin and Tancredi (1994), Rothenberg and Thompson (1994), and Hartouni (1997).

26. On agricultural development and applications, see Brackett, Seidel, and Seidel (1981), Biggers (1981, 1984, 1987), Herman (1981), Betteridge (1986), Schaffir (1991), Schneider (1988a,b), Schell (1984); Petters (1986), and Marcus (1995).

27. See Gibbons (1990) and Schneider (1988a,b).

28. See, for example, Arditti, Klein, and Minden (1984), Corea (1985), Holmes (1992), Lasker and Borg (1987), Overall (1987), Raymond (1989), Rothman (1984, 1986), Rose (1987), Rowland (1987), Spallone and Steinberg (1987), and Stanworth (1987).

29. See Nsiah-Jefferson (1989), Doyal (1987), and Muller (1988).

30. On disability, see, for example, Asch (1989), Deegan and Brooks (1985), and Finger (1985). On legal issues, see, for example, Cohen and Taub (1989), Elias and Annas (1987), and Shultz (1994).

31. Thanks to Diana Long (once Hall) for clarifying this point. For popular works see, for example, Corner (1938, 1939) and Hartman (1933); for works for more highly educated audiences, see, for example, Corner (1944) and Maisel (1965). On scientists' propriety, see Corner (1981), Ramsay (1994), and Clarke (1993).

32. Interview with Dr. M. C. Shelesnyak, June 1989.

33. This issue was often raised in my interviews with senior reproductive scientists; see also Corner (1981).

34. Sanger had received the Third Order of the Sacred Crown from Japan in 1965. See Chesler (1992:464–67). Ironically, the birth control pill that she helped to pioneer is still not approved for distribution there.

35. Interview with Dr. John Biggers, Harvard Medical School, 1987; see also Hertz (1984) and Lincoln and Kaeser (1988).

36. See, for example, Nelkin (1984, 1995), Mazur (1981), Engelhardt and Caplan (1987), Chubin and Chu (1989), and Petersen and Markle (1989).

CHAPTER NINE

1. Included here are expenditures made by the NRC/CRPS and the Committee on Research in Endocrinology, and the private National Committee on Mater-

nal Health. The Carnegie Institution's Department of Embryology is not included, nor is U.S. Department of Agriculture funding for reproductive research. See chapter 7.

2. On what constitutes a case, see Ragin and Becker (1992). See, for example, Becher (1989), Bechtel (1986), Bourdieu (1975), Chubin (1976), Farber (1982a,b), Geison (1978, 1981, 1983), Geison and Holmes (1993), Graham, Lepenies, and Weingart (1983), Hall and Glick (1976), Kohler (1982), Lemaine et al. (1976), Rosenberg (1979b), and Whitley (1976). Many (but not all) of these earlier works have an underlying if not explicit assumption that there is *one single explanation* that is necessary and sufficient to account for the phenomena of disciplines despite their diversity. Such categorical explanations include economic, sociopolitical, technical/instrumental, or intellectual/theoretical reasons. That is, the need for historical accounts of specific disciplines or areas of study as specific entities goes relatively unquestioned—in some kind of tacit recognition of diversity and the value of case studies. Yet, ironically, some fantasy of generalizability across disciplines simultaneously obtains. The risks, in Pauly's (1993:135) terms, are that "practitioners of systematic comparison are liable either to drown in details or to produce generalizations that are empty." There are, then, limits to the utility of generalization that, however, do not undercut the value of empirical case studies.

3. Clarke (1993) focuses on research on reproduction undertaken at the University of Chicago from about 1910 to 1950. Clarke (1987) discusses the early organization of access to a range of human and nonhuman research materials at the Carnegie Institution of Washington's Department of Embryology at Johns Hopkins Medical School.

4. See, for example, Gossel (1992), Keating, Cambrosio, and Mackenzie (1992), and Fujimura (1996).

5. See Latour and Woolgar (1979/1986), Latour (1983, 1987, 1988), Callon (1985, 1995), and Law (1980, 1991). For critical comment on actor network theory, see Shapin (1988), Amsterdamska (1990), Fujimura (1992), Star (1991), Sturdy (1993), and Collins and Yearley (1992).

6. On "mattering," see Butler (1993) and Rabinow (1992). Attributed meanings and consequentialities make a difference.

7. See Bijker, Hughes, and Pinch (1987), Woolgar (1991), and Bijker and Law (1992).

8. Sturdy (1993:372) has a distinctive view of the British case and the general processes: "From the beginning, medical chemists ignored established boundaries, not just between scientific disciplines, but also between pure and applied science, and above all between laboratory science and the practice of medicine. . . . Medical chemistry thus represented, in effect, a new scientific formation which broke with older forms of disciplinary organization . . . which begs explanation." Cf. Kohler (1982).

9. On women as reproductive scientists, see Price (1967, 1972, 1975), Hyman (1957), Hyman and Hutchinson (1991), the oral history of ecologist Thomas Park in the Special Collections of the Regenstein Library, University of Chicago, and Hall (1974). After World War II, many more women went into the reproductive sciences. See, for example, Schwartz (1984) and Greep and associates (1976, 1977).

10. See Schiebinger (1987, 1989, 1993), Laqueur (1987, 1990), Oudshoorn (1994), and Long (1997). However, both rhetorics have been simultaneously available for deployment.

11. Thanks again to the late Anselm Strauss, whom I will always picture in our qualitative analysis seminar staring over the tops of his glasses and gently saying, "So, tell me, what is this a story of?" A dozen years later I begin to grasp the subtleties of this intervention.

12. See Kohler (1976, 1978, 1991) on "partnerships." Cf. Abir-Am (1982, 1985, 1993), Arnove (1980), Cueto (1994), Fisher (1990), Kay (1993a,b), and Morawski (1986).

13. Exerpted from the Report of the (Foundation) Committee on Appraisal and Plan, Dec. 11, 1934, pp. 42–43, quoted by Kay (1993b:48).

14. See Pressman (1991:14–15, 20) and Morawski (1986).

15. Much of the work on historical and contemporary eugenics movements centers on control over heredity. See, for example, Allen (1986), Kevles (1985), Ludmerer (1972), Haller (1963), and Reilly (1991). Certainly control over reproduction is implicated in concerns with heredity in evolutionary theory, although it is often rendered invisible (Lloyd 1993; Keller 1987; Griesemer forthcoming).

16. See letter to Frank R. Lillie from Warren Weaver, 6 October 1933. RAC RF RG1.1 S216d B8 F105.

17. See Program in Experimental Biology, 17 April 1935, RAC RF RG1.1 S216 B8 F103.

18. On biomedicalization, see Zola (1976), Conrad and Schneider (1980), Riessman (1983), Estes and Binney (1989), and Clarke and Olesen (1998).

19. See Martin (1987/1992:37), who discusses Frederick T. Gates's metaphors of the body as model of industrial society. Gates was a key adviser on medical philanthropy of John D. Rockefeller. On psychiatry, see Pressman (1991, 1997).

20. Folbre's (1994) recent book addresses problems in economic theory, which does not take reproduction into account. There are multiple possible sites and modes of intervention to control life: educational, environmental, hereditary, biological, psychological, social, and so on. Some are meliorist, and others, such as gene therapy (e.g., Culver 1994), are transformative of life itself.

21. Rabinow (1992:241) argues that eugenics projects were not directly within scientific practices: "They were never *dans le vrai* to use George Canguilhem's telling phrase." Perhaps not entirely, although I can see them as such. But the reproductive sciences were, and therein lie the concrete practices of eugenics. On the Human Genome Initiative, see Hilgartner (1995).

BIBLIOGRAPHY

ARCHIVAL MATERIALS

Archival research was conducted at the following institutions:

The Regenstein Library: University of Chicago

Papers consulted are as follows. Abbreviations used in the text are noted.

PP1 UChiA	President's Papers I Collection: 1889–1925
PP2 UChiA	President's Papers II Collection: 1925–45
COWP UChiA	Charles Otis Whitman Papers
FRLP UChiA	Frank Ratray Lillie Papers
ZDP UChiA	Zoology Department Papers
BTM UChiA	Board of Trustees Minutes

The Chesney Archives: Johns Hopkins Medical Institutions

At the time of my research, the Chesney Archives had just obtained the Mall and Streeter Papers, which were thus only partially catalogued when I examined them. Textual references give the names of the correspondents and/or other likely future file names. Papers consulted are as follows. Abbreviations used in the text are noted.

HLP JHMI	Hunterian Laboratory Papers
JHH JHMI	Johns Hopkins Hospital Department of Gynecology Women's Clinic
LFB JHMI	Lewellys F. Barker Papers

HAK JHMI	Howard A. Kelly Papers
JWW JHMI	J. Whitridge Williams Papers
TSC JHMI	Thomas S. Cullen Papers
AM JHMI	Adolph Meyer Papers
CIW DoE EC JHMI	Carnegie Institution of Washington, Department of Embryology at Hopkins Papers on the Embryo Collection
CIW DoE JHMI	Carnegie Institution of Washington, Papers at Hopkins Department of Embryology Franklin P. Mall Papers George Streeter Papers

The Rockefeller Archives Center

Thanks to a research grant from the Rockefeller University, I had access to the papers listed below. In the text, I refer to these papers by their archival source data, followed by RAC, denoting Rockefeller Archives Center.

BUREAU OF SOCIAL HYGIENE PAPERS:

Birth Control
Committee for Research in Problems of Sex
Department of Venereal Disease at Johns Hopkins
Eugenics and Sterilization
Carl Hartman Correspondence
National Committee on Maternal Health
Population Organizations and Conferences
Marie Kopp Correspondence

ROCKEFELLER FOUNDATION PAPERS:

National Committee on Maternal Health
National Research Council Papers on the Committee for Research in Problems of Sex
University of California, Sex Research
Carnegie Institution of Washington, Department of Embryology at Johns Hopkins Medical School
University of Chicago, Biological Sciences
University of Iowa, Emil Witschi
University of Rochester, Sex Research
University of Wisconsin, Endocrinology
Columbia University, Sex Research
Columbia University, Embryology
University of Missouri, Lactation Studies

University of Missouri, Zoology
Johns Hopkins University, Obstetrical Records
Harvard University, Endocrinology
Veterinary Survey, 1930–39
Yale University, Endocrinology
Yale University, Experimental Embryology
Yale University, Anthropoid Research
Cornell University, Anatomy
National Research Council, Genetics Stocks

Special Collections: University of California, Davis

At Davis, my archival research was confined to the recently gathered Papers
of the Animal Sciences Department, which were as yet uncatalogued. References to them therefore simply state the date and nature of the document, followed by ASDP UCD, denoting Animal Sciences Department Pa-
persat UC Davis. In addition, the Davis campus has actively participated in
a Regional Oral History Project, based at the Bancroft Library of the University of California, Berkeley. I reviewed the following oral histories available in Special Collections at Davis, referred to in the text by author:
Albaugh, Reuben: "The College Cowboy." 1977.
Cole, Harold H.: "Adventurer in Animal Science." 1977.
Erdman, Henry E.: "Agricultural Economics: Teaching, Research and Writing, Uni-
    versity of California, Berkeley, 1922–1969." 1971.
Hutchinson, Claude B.: "The College of Agriculture, University of California,
    1922–1952." 1961.
Kleiber, Max: "An Old Professor Ruminates." 1976.
Mrak, Emil: "A Journey Through Three Epochs." 1974.
Storer, Tracy I.: "From Observation to Experimentation." 1975.

PUBLISHED SOURCES

Abbot, Andrew. 1988. The System of Professions: An Essay on the Division of Ex-
    pert Labor. Chicago: University of Chicago Press.
Abbot Laboratories. 1940. Fortune, August, 62–69, 102, 104, 107–10.
Aberle, Sophie D. 1934. The Endocrine Control of the Uterus. In Margaret Sanger
    (Ed.), Biological and Medical Aspects of Contraception, 41–45. [American Con-
    ference on Birth Control and National Recovery.] Washington, D.C.: National
    Committee on Federal Legislation for Birth Control.
Aberle, Sophie D., and George W. Corner. 1953. Twenty-five Years of Sex Research:
    History of the National Research Council Committee for Research in Problems
    of Sex, 1922–1947. Philadelphia: Saunders.
Abir-Am, Pnina G. 1982. The Discourse of Physical Power and Biological Knowl-

edge in the 1930s: A Reappraisal of the Rockefeller Foundation's "Policy" in Molecular Biology. Social Studies of Science 12:341–82.

———. 1985. Themes, Genres and Orders of Legitimation in the Consolidation of New Disciplines: Deconstructing the Historiography of Molecular Biology. History of Science 23:73–117.

———. 1988. The Assessment of Interdisciplinary Research in the 1930s: The Rockefeller Foundation and Physico-chemical Morphology. Minerva: A Review of Science, Learning and Policy 26(2):153–76.

———. 1993. From Multidisciplinary Collaboration to Transnational Objectivity: International Spaces as Constitutive of Molecular Biology, 1930–1970. In Elizabeth Crawford, Terry Shin, and Tverker Shaford (Eds.), Denationalizing Science: The Contexts of International Scientific Practice, 153–86. Dordrecht: Kluwer Academic.

Abrams, Sarah E. 1993. Brilliance and Bureaucracy: Nursing and Changes in the Rockefeller Foundation, 1915–1930. Nursing History Review 1:119–37.

Acai, J. 1920. Follicular Growth in the Ovary. American Journal of Anatomy 28:59–72.

Acker, Carolyn Jean. 1995. Addiction and the Laboratory: The Work of the National Research Council's Committee on Drug Addiction, 1928–1939. Isis 86:167–93.

Ackernecht, Erwin H. 1982. A Short History of Medicine. Rev. ed. Baltimore, Md.: Johns Hopkins University Press.

Agate, Frederick J. 1975. Philip Edward Smith. In Charles Coulston Gillispie (Ed.), Dictionary of Scientific Biography. Vol. 12. New York: Scribner.

Aldhous, Peter. 1994. A Booster for Contraceptive Vaccines. Science 266:1484–86.

Alexander, Nancy J. 1980. Andrology in the Year 2000 (Presidential Address of the American Society of Andrology). Journal of Andrology 1:149–57.

———. 1995. Future Contraceptives. Scientific American, September, 136–41.

———. (Ed.). 1978. Animal Models for Research on Contraception and Fertility. Hagerstown, Md.: Harper and Row.

Allen, Edgar. 1922. The Oestrus Cycle in the Mouse. American Journal of Anatomy 30:297–372.

———. 1926. The Time of Ovulation in the Menstrual Cycle of the Monkey, *M. Rhesus*. Proceedings of the Society for Experimental Biology and Medicine 23:281–383.

———. 1928. Reactions of Immature Monkeys (M. Rhesus) to Injections of Ovarian Hormone. Journal of Morphology and Physiology 46:479–519.

———. 1932. Ovarian Follicular Hormone, Theelin: Animal Reactions. In Edgar Allen (Ed.), Sex and Internal Secretions, 392–480. Baltimore, Md.: Williams and Wilkins.

———. 1933. The Irregularity of the Menstrual Function. American Journal of Obstetrics and Gynecology 25:705–9.

———. 1943. Publications. Yale Journal of Biology and Medicine 17:1–12.

——— (Ed.). 1932. Sex and Internal Secretions: A Survey of Recent Research. Baltimore, Md.: Williams and Wilkins.

——— (Ed.). 1939. Sex and Internal Secretions: A Survey of Recent Research. 2d ed. Baltimore, Md.: Williams and Wilkins.

Allen, Edgar, and Edward Doisy. 1923. An Ovarian Hormone: Preliminary Report on Its Localization, Extraction and Partial Purification, and Action. Journal of the American Medical Association 81:819–21.

Allen, Edgar, J. P. Pratt, Q. U. Newell, and L. Bland. 1928. Recovery of Human Ova from the Uterine Tubes: Time of Ovulation in the Menstrual Cycle. Journal of the American Medical Association 91:1018–20.

Allen, Garland E. 1975. The Introduction of *Drosophila* into the Study of Heredity and Evolution, 1900–1910. Isis 66:322–33.

———. 1978. Life Sciences in the Twentieth Century. New York: Cambridge University Press.

———. 1979. The Transformation of a Science: T. H. Morgan and the Emergence of a New American Biology. In Alexandra Oleson and John Voss (Eds.), The Organization of Knowledge in Modern America, 1860–1920. Baltimore, Md.: Johns Hopkins University Press.

———. 1981. Morphology and Twentieth-Century Biology: A Response. Journal of the History of Biology 14:159–76.

———. 1986a. Eugenics Record Office at Cold Spring Harbor, 1910–1940: An Essay in Institutional History. Osiris, 2d ser., 2:225–64.

———. 1986b. T. H. Morgan and the Split between Embryology and Genetics, 1910–1935. In T. J. Horder, J. A. Witkowski, and C. C. Wylie (Eds.), A History of Embryology: The Eighth Symposium of the British Society for Developmental Biology, 113–46. Cambridge: Cambridge University Press.

———. 1991. Old Wine in New Bottles: From Eugenics to Population Control in the Work of Raymond Pearl. In Keith Benson, Jane Maienschein, and Ronald Rainger (Eds.), The American Expansion of Biology, 231–61. New Brunswick, N.J.: Rutgers University Press.

Allen, Willard M. 1970. Progesterone: How Did the Name Originate? Southern Medical Journal 63:1151–55.

Altherr, Thomas L. 1983. Procreation or Pleasure? Sexual Attitudes in American History. Malabar, Fla.: Robert E. Krieger.

American Foundation, The. 1955. Medical Research: A Midcentury Survey. Vol. 1, American Medical Research in Principle and Practice. Vol. 2, Unsolved Clinical Problems in Biological Perspective. Boston: Little, Brown for the American Foundation.

Aminoff, Michael J. 1993. Brown-Sequard: A Visionary of Science. New York: Raven Press.

Amoroso, E. C. 1963. Inaugural Lecture on Present Perspectives in Endocrinology. In Peter Eckstein and Francis Knowles (Eds.), Techniques in Endocrine Research, 1–14. London: Academic.

Amoroso, E. C., and G. W. Corner. 1975. Herbert McLean Evans, 1882–1971. Biographical Memoirs of Fellows of the Royal Society 21:83–186.

Amsterdamska, Olga. 1990. Review of Bruno Latour's *Science in Action*. Science, Technology and Human Values 15:495–505.

Angier, Natalie. 1997. New Respect for Estrogen's Influence. New York Times, June 24, B9, B12.

Annandale, Ellen, and Judith Clark. 1996. What Is Gender? Feminist Theory and the Sociology of Human Reproduction. Sociology of Health and Illness 18:17–44.

Annas, George J., and Sherman Elias. 1989. The Politics of Transplantation of Human Fetal Tissue. New England Journal of Medicine 320:1079–82.

Annas, George J., and Sherman Elias (Eds.). 1992. Gene Mapping: Using Law and Ethics as Guides. New York: Oxford University Press.

Antler, Joyce, and Daniel M. Fox. 1978. The Movement toward a Safe Maternity: Physician Accountability in New York City, 1915–1940. In Judith Waltzer Leavitt and Ronald L. Numbers (Eds.), Sickness and Health in America, 375–92. Madison: University of Wisconsin Press.

Apfel, Roberta J., and Susan M. Fisher. 1984. To Do No Harm: DES and the Dilemmas of Modern Medicine. New Haven, Conn.: Yale University Press.

Appel, Toby A. 1987. The Cuvier-Geoffroy Debate: French Biology in the Decades before Darwin. New York: Oxford University Press.

Apple, Rima (Ed.). 1990. The History of Women, Health and Medicine in America: An Encyclopedic Handbook. New York: Garland.

Applezweig, Norman. 1975. Russel Marker to Gregory Pincus: The Mexican Steroid Industry and the Development of Modern Contraceptive Technology. Based on a lecture given at the Symposium on the Historical Development of Anticonceptive Methods, First Chemical Congress of the North American Continent, Mexico. Center for the History of Chemistry News, Fall, 1–3.

Arai, Hayato. 1920. On the Cause of the Hypertrophy of the Surviving Ovary after Semi-spaying (Albino Rat) and on the Number of Ova in It. American Journal of Anatomy 28:59–79.

Ardelt, F. 1931. Production of Temporary Sterility in Female Rabbits by Means of Sperm Toxins. Archiv fur Gynakologie 145:474–94.

Arditti, Rita, Renate Duelli Klein, and Shelley Minden (Eds.). 1984. Test Tube Women: What Future for Motherhood? Boston: Pandora/Routledge Kegan Paul.

Arey, Leslie B. 1939. The Degree of Normal Menstrual Irregularity. American Journal of Obstetrics and Gynecology 37:12–29.

Arnove, Robert F. (Ed.). 1980. Philanthropy and Cultural Imperialism: The Foundations at Home and Abroad. Bloomington: Indiana University Press.

Aronson, Naomi. 1979. Fuel for the Human Machine: The Industrialization of Eating in America. Ann Arbor, Mich.: University Microfilms.

———. 1982. Nutrition as a Social Problem: A Case Study of Entrepreneurial Strategy in Science. Social Problems 29:474–87.

———. 1984. Science as Claimsmaking: Implications for Social Problems Research. In Joseph Schneider and John Kitsuse (Eds.), Studies in the Sociology of Social Problems, 1–30. Norwood, N.J.:Ablex.

Asch, Adrienne. 1989. Reproductive Technology and Disability. In Sherrill Cohen and Nadine Taub (Eds.), Reproductive Laws for the 1990s, 69–117. Clifton, N.J.: Humana Press.

Aschheim, S., and B. Zondek. 1927. Hypophsenvorderlappenhormon und Ovarialhormon in Harn von Schwangeren. Klinische Wochenschrift 6:1322.

Asdell, S. A. 1946. Patterns of Mammalian Reproduction. Ithaca, N.Y.: Comstock.

———. 1977. Historical Introduction. In H. H. Cole and P. T. Cupps (Eds.), Reproduction in Domestic Animals, x–xxi. 3d ed. New York: Academic Press.

Associated Press. 1995. Test Tube Babies Expensive—$60,000 to $110,000 per Child. San Francisco Chronicle, July 28, A4.

Atkinson, Linda E. 1979. Status of Funding and Costs of Reproductive Science Research and Contraceptive Development. In National Academy of Sciences (Ed.), Contraception: Science, Technology and Application, 292–305. Washington, D.C.: National Academy of Sciences.

Atkinson, Linda E., R. Lincoln, and J. D. Forrest. 1985. Worldwide Trends in Funding for Contraceptive Research and Evaluation. Family Planning Perspectives 17:260–62.

Austin, C. R., and R. V. Short (Eds.). 1972. Artificial Control of Reproduction. 1st ed. Cambridge: Cambridge University Press.

Austin, C. R., and R. V. Short (Eds.). 1986. Manipulating Reproduction. 2d edition. New York: Cambridge University Press.

Avarbock, M. R., R. L. Brinster, and G. T. Brinster. 1996. Reconstitution of Spermatogenesis from Frozen Spermatogonial Stem Cells. Nature Medicine 2:693–96.

Backman, Carl Bennett. 1983a. Resource Utilization in Biomedical Science: An Institutional History. Unpublished manuscript used with permission.

———. 1983b. Resource Utilization in Biomedical Science: Patterns of Research on Nonhuman Primate Reproductive Physiology. Ph.D. diss., Cornell University.

Bajema, Carl J. (Ed.). 1976. Eugenics Then and Now. Benchmark Papers in Genetics/ 5. Stroudsburg, Pa.: Dowden, Hutchinson and Ross.

Baker, J. R. 1930a. The Spermicidal Power of Chemical Contraception. I. Introduction: Experiments on Guinea Pig Sperm. Journal of Hygiene 29:323–29.

———. 1930b. The Spermicidal Power of Chemical Contraception. II. Pure Substances. Journal of Hygiene 30:273–94.

———. 1931a. Chemical Contraceptives. In A. W. Greenwood (Ed.), Proceedings of the Second International Congress for Sex Research, 1930, 179–87. Edinburgh/ London: Oliver and Boyd.

———. 1931b. The Spermicidal Power of Chemical Contraception. III. Pessaries. Journal of Hygiene 31:309–20.

———. 1935. The Chemical Control of Conception. London: Chapman and Hall.

Balsamo, Anne. 1996. Technologies of the Gendered Body: Reading Cyborg Women. Durham, N.C.: Duke University Press.

Bang, Frederick B. 1977. History of Tissue Culture at Johns Hopkins. Bulletin of the History of Medicine 51:516–37.

Banks, J. A., and Olive Banks. 1964. Feminism and Family Planning in Victorian England. New York: Schocken.

Bann, Stephen (Ed.). 1994. Frankenstein, Creation and Monstrosity. London: Reaktion Books.

Banta, Martha. 1993. Taylored Lives: Narrative Productions in the Age of Taylor, Veblen and Ford. Chicago: University of Chicago Press.

Barker, Lewellys F. 1917. The Study of the Internal Secretions: An Introduction. Endocrinology 1:1–4.

———. 1922. The Principles Underlying Organotherapy and Hormonotherapy. Endocrinology 6:592–97.

Barker-Benfield, G. J. 1976. The Horrors of the Half-Known Life: Male Attitudes toward Women and Sexuality in Nineteenth-Century America. New York: Harper and Row.

Barrett, Michele, and Anne Phillips (Eds.). 1992. Destabilizing Theory: Contemporary Feminist Debates. Stanford, Calif.: Stanford University Press.

Barroso, Carmen, and Sonia Corea. 1995. Public Servants, Professionals and Feminists: The Politics of Contraceptive Research in Brazil. In Faye D. Ginsberg and Rayna Rapp (Eds.), Conceiving the New World Order: The Global Stratification of Reproduction, 292–306. Berkeley: University of California Press.

Barrow, Clyde W. 1990. Universities and the Capitalist State: Corporate Liberalism and the Reconstruction of American Higher Education, 1894–1928. Madison: University of Wisconsin Press.

Bartelmez, George W. 1933. (With C. Cuthbertson.) Histologic Studies of Menstruating Mucus Membrane of the Human Uterus. Carnegie Contributions to Embryology, no. 142:141–86.

———. 1935. The Circulation in the Intervillous Space of the Macaque Placenta. Anatomical Record 61 (suppl. A):4–27.

———. 1937. Menstruation. Physiological Reviews 17:28–72.

Bartelmez, George W., George W. Corner, and Carl G. Hartman. 1951. Cyclic Changes in the Endometrium of the Rhesus Monkey. Carnegie Contributions to Embryology 34:99–144.

Baskin, Morris J. 1934. Immunity as a Method of Birth Control. In Margaret Sanger (Ed.), Biological and Medical Aspects of Contraception, 94–101. [American Conference on Birth Control and National Recovery.] Washington, D.C.: National Committee on Federal Legislation for Birth Control.

Baszanger, Isabelle. 1992. Deciphering Chronic Pain. Sociology of Health and Illness 14:181–215.

———. 1995. Douleur et Medicine, La Fin d'un Oubli. Paris: Seuil.

———. 1998a. Pain and Medicine: The End of Neglect. New Brunswick, N.J.: Rutgers University Press.

———. 1998b. Pain Physicians: All Alike, All Different. In Marc Berg and Annamarie Mol (Eds.), Differences in Medicine: Unraveling Practices, Techniques and Bodies. Durham, N.C.: Duke University Press.

Baulieu, Etienne-Emile, with Mort Rosenblum. 1991. The "Abortion Pill" RU486: A Woman's Choice. New York: Simon and Schuster.

Beach, Frank A. 1948. Hormones and Behavior. New York: Paul B. Hoeber.

———. 1974. Behavioral Endocrinology and the Study of Reproduction. Fifth Hartman Lecture. Biology of Reproduction 10:2–18.

———. 1981. Historical Origins of Modern Research on Hormones and Behavior. Hormones and Behavior 15:325–76.

Becher, Tony. 1989. Academic Tribes and Territories: Intellectual Enquiry and the Cultures of Disciplining. Bristol, Pa.: Society for Research into Higher Education and Open University Press.

Bechtel, William (Ed.). 1986. Integrating Scientific Disciplines. Dordrecht: Nijhoff.

Becker, Howard S. 1960. Notes on the Concept of Commitment. American Journal of Sociology 66:32–40.

——. 1963. Outsiders: Studies in the Sociology of Deviance. New York: Free Press.

——. 1967. Whose Side Are We On? Social Problems 14:239–47. Reprinted in his Sociological Work: Method and Substance, 123–35 (New Brunswick, N.J.: Transaction Books, 1970).

——. 1970. Sociological Work: Method and Substance. New Brunswick, N.J.: Transaction Books.

——. 1982. Art Worlds. Berkeley: University of California Press.

Becker, Howard S., Blanche Geer, Everett C. Hughes, and Anselm L. Strauss. 1961. Boys in White: Student Culture in Medical School. New Brunswick, N.J.: Transaction Books.

Beer, John B., and W. Daniel Lewis. 1974. Aspects of the Professionalization of Science. In Sal P. Restivo and Christopher K. Vanderpool (Eds.), Comparative Studies in Science and Society. Columbus, Ohio: Merrill.

Bell, Susan E. 1980. The Synthetic Compound Diethylstilbestrol (DES) 1938–1941: The Social Construction of a Medical Treatment. Ph.D. diss., Brandeis University.

——. 1984. Birth Control. In Boston Women's Health Book Collective (Eds.), The New Our Bodies, Ourselves, 220–62. New York: Simon and Schuster. Update in 1994, pp. 259–307, with the assistance of S. Cooper-Doyle, J. Norsigian, and F. Stewart.

——. 1986. A New Model of Medical Technology Development: A Case Study of DES. In Julius Roth and Sheryl Ruzek (Eds.), Research in the Sociology of Health Care, vol. 4:1–32. Greenwich, Conn.: Jai Press.

——. 1987. Changing Ideas: The Medicalization of Menopause. Social Science and Medicine 24:535–42. Reprinted in R. Formanek (Ed.), Menopause. Hillsdale, N.J.: Analytic Press, 1990.

——. 1989a. The Meaning of Risk, Choice, and Responsibility for a DES Daughter. In K. S. Ratcliff, Myra Marx Ferree, Gail O. Mellow, Barbara Drygulski Wright, Glenda D. Price, Kim Yonoshik, and Margie S. Freston (Eds.), Healing Technology: Feminist Perspectives, 245–61. Ann Arbor: University of Michigan Press.

——. 1989b. Technology in Medicine: Development, Diffusion, and Health Policy. In H. E. Freeman and S. Levin (Eds.), Handbook of Medical Sociology, 185–204. 4th ed. New York: Prentice-Hall.

——. 1994a. Birth Control for Women in Midlife: Update. In Paula Doress-Worters and Diana Siegel (Eds.), The New Ourselves Growing Older, 101–7. New York: Simon and Schuster.

——. 1994b. From Local to Global: Resolving Uncertainty about the Safety of DES in Menopause. Research in the Sociology of Health Care 11:41–56.

——. 1994c. Translating Science to the People: Updating The New Our Bodies, Ourselves. Women's Studies International Forum 17:9–18.

——. 1995. Gendered Medical Science: Producing a Drug for Women. Feminist Studies 21:469–500.

Bell, Susan E., and Robert J. Apfel. 1995. Looking at Bodies: Insights and Inquiries about DES-Related Cancer. Qualitative Sociology 18(1):3–19.

Bell, Susan E. Paula Garbarino, Jeanne Hubbich, Adrienne Ingram, Lyn Koehnline, and Jill Wolhandler. 1980. Reclaiming Reproductive Control: A Feminist Approach to Fertility Consciousness. Science for the People January/February:6–9, 30–35.

Bell, W. Blair. 1916. The Sex Complex: A Study of the Relationship of the Internal Secretions of the Female Characteristics and Functions in Health and Disease. London: Balliere, Tidall, Cox.

Benedict, Francis G. 1910. Suggestions Regarding Research Work in Animal Nutrition. American Society of Animal Nutrition, Record of Proceedings of the Annual Meeting of 1909:20–27.

Benison, Saul, Clifford Barger, and Ellen L. Wolfe. 1987. Walter B. Cannon: The Life and Times of a Young Scientist. Cambridge, Mass.: Belknap Press of Harvard University Press.

Benjamin, H. 1945. Eugen Steinach, 1861–1944: A Life of Research. Scientific Monthly 61:427–42.

Benson, Keith R. 1981. Problems of Individual Development: Descriptive Embryological Morphology in America at the Turn of the Century. Journal of the History of Biology 14:115–28.

———. 1985. American Morphology in the Late Nineteenth Century: The Biology Department at Johns Hopkins University. Journal of the History of Biology 18:163–205.

———. 1989. Biology's Phoenix: Historical Perspectives on the Importance of the Organism. American Zoologist 29:1067–74.

Benson, Keith R., Jane Maienschein, and Ronald Rainger (Eds.). 1991. The American Expansion of Biology: New Brunswick, N.J.: Rutgers University Press.

Berkman, Joyce Avrech. 1980. Historical Styles of Contraceptive Advocacy. In Helen B. Holmes, Betty B. Hoskins, and Michael Gross (Eds.), Birth Control and Controlling Birth: Women-Centered Perspectives, 23–26. Clifton, N.J.: Humana Press.

Berlant, Jeffrey Lionel. 1975. Profession and Monopoly: A Study of Medicine in the United States and Great Britain. Berkeley: University of California Press.

Berliner, Howard. 1982. Medical Modes of Production. In Peter Wright and Andrew Treacher (Eds.), The Problem of Medical Knowledge: Examining the Social Construction of Medicine, 162–73. Edinburgh: Edinburgh University Press.

Bernard, Claude. 1957. An Introduction to the Study of Experimental Medicine. 1865. Reprint, New York: Dover.

Betteridge, K. J. 1986. Increasing Productivity in Farm Animals. In C. R. Austin and R. V. Short (Eds.), Manipulating Reproduction, 1–47. 2d ed. Cambridge: Cambridge University Press.

Biggers, John D. 1970. Introduction of the First Carl G. Hartman Lecturer. Biology of Reproduction 2:1–4.

———. 1981. In Vitro Fertilization and Embryo Transfer in Human Beings. New England Journal of Medicine 304:336–42.

———. 1984. In Vitro Fertilization and Embryo Transfer in Historical Perspective. In Alan Trouson and Carl Wood (Eds.), In Vitro Fertilization and Embryo Transfer, 3–15. London: Churchill Livingstone.

———. 1987. Pioneering Mammalian Embryo Culture. In Barry Bavister (Ed.), The Mammalian Preimplantation Embryo, 1–22. New York: Plenum Press.

———. 1991. Walter Heape, FRS: A Pioneer in Reproductive Biology. Centenary of

His Embryo Transfer Experiments. Journal of Reproduction and Fertility 93:173–86.

Biggers, John D., and R. A. McFeely. 1966. Intersexuality in Domestic Mammals. In Anne McLaren (Ed.), Advances in Reproductive Physiology, 29–61. London: Logos Press/Academic Press.

Bijker, Wiebe E. 1987. The Social Construction of Bakelite: Towards a Theory of Invention. In Wiebe E. Bijker, Thomas P. Hughes, and Trevor Pinch (Eds.), The Social Construction of Technological Systems, 159–87. Cambridge, Mass.: MIT Press.

———. 1995. Socio-Historical Technology Studies. In Sheila Jasanoff, Gerald E. Markle, James Petersen, and Trevor Pinch (Eds.), Handbook of Science and Technology Studies, 229–55. Thousand Oaks, Calif.: Sage.

Bijker, Wiebe E., Thomas P. Hughes, and Trevor Pinch (Eds.). 1987. The Social Construction of Technological Systems. Cambridge, Mass.: MIT Press.

Bijker, Wiebe E., and John Law (Eds.). 1992. Shaping Technology/Building Society. Cambridge, Mass.: MIT Press.

Billingham, Rupert E., and Alan E. Beer. 1984. Reproductive Immunology: Past, Present and Future. Perspectives in Biology and Medicine 27:259–75.

Billings, E. I., J. B. Brown, J. J. Billings, and H. G. Burger. 1972. Symptoms and Hormonal Changes Accompanying Ovulation. Lancet 1:282–84.

Billings, F. 1924. Glandular Therapy. Journal of the American Medical Association 83:1000.

Birken, Lawrence. 1988. Consuming Desire: Sexual Science and the Emergence of a Culture of Abundance, 1871–1914. Ithaca, N.Y.: Cornell University Press.

Birr, Kendall. 1979. Industrial Research Laboratories. In Nathan Reingold (Ed.), The Sciences in the American Content: New Perspectives, 193–208. Washington, D.C.: Smithsonian Institution.

Blacker, C. P. 1961. Voluntary Sterilization. Eugenics Review 53:145–47.

Blake, John B. 1980. Anatomy. In Ronald L. Numbers (Ed.), The Education of American Physicians, 29–47. Berkeley: University of California Press.

Bliss, Michael. 1982. The Discovery of Insulin. Chicago: University of Chicago Press.

Bloom, Amy S., and P. Ellen Parsons. 1994. 25th Anniversary of "The Doctor's Case against the Pill." National Women's Health Network News, November–December, 1, 3.

Bloomberg Business News. 1994. Teenager Sues Genentech for Racketeering. San Francisco Chronicle, August 23, B1, B3.

Blumer, Herbert. 1969/1993. Symbolic Interactionism: Perspective and Method. Berkeley: University of California Press.

Bodemer, Charles W. 1973. The Biology of the Blastocyst in Historical Perspective. In R. J. Blandau (Ed.), The Biology of the Blastocyst, 1–25. Chicago: University of Chicago Press.

———. 1975. The Microscope in Early Embryological Investigation. Gynecological Investigations 4:188–209.

———. 1976. Concepts of Reproduction and Its Regulation in the History of Western Civilization. Contraception 13:427–46.

Bodian, David. 1973. George William Bartelmez, 1885–1967. Biographical Memoirs of the National Academy of Science 43:1–26.

Bonner, Thomas Neville. 1957. Medicine in Chicago: 1850–1950. Madison, Wis.: American History Research Center.

Booth, William. 1989. WHO Seeks Global Data on Sexual Practices. Science 244:418–19.

Borell, Merriley. 1976a. Brown-Sequard's Organotherapy and Its Appearance in America at the End of the Nineteenth Century. Bulletin of the History of Medicine 50:309–20.

——. 1976b. Organotherapy, British Physiology and Discovery of the Internal Secretions. Journal of the History of Biology 9:235–68.

——. 1976c. Origins of the Hormone Concept: Internal Secretions and Physiological Research, 1889–1905. Ph.D. diss., Yale University.

——. 1978. Setting the Standards for a New Science: Edward Schafer and Endocrinology. Medical History 22:282–90.

——. 1985. Organotherapy and the Emergence of Reproductive Endocrinology. Journal of the History of Biology 18:1–30.

——. 1987a. Biologists and the Promotion of Birth Control Research, 1918–1938. Journal of the History of Biology 19:51–87.

——. 1987b. Instrumentation and the Rise of Physiology. Science and Technology Studies 5(2):53–62.

——. 1989. Album of Science: The Biological Sciences in the Twentieth Century. New York: Scribner.

Boston Women's Health Book Collective. 1971. Our Bodies, Our Selves. 1st ed. Boston: South End Press.

Boston Women's Health Book Collective. 1984/1992. The New Our Bodies, Our Selves. 2d and 3d editions. New York: Simon and Schuster.

Bourdieu, Pierre. 1975. The Specificity of the Scientific Field and the Social Conditions of the Progress of Reason. Social Science Information 14:19–47.

Bourdieu, Pierre, Jean-Claude Passeron, and Monique de Saint Martin, with contributions by Christian Baudelot and Guy Vincent. 1994. Academic Discourse: Linguistic Misunderstanding and Professorial Power. Cambridge: Polity Press.

Bourne, Geoffrey H. (Ed.). 1973. Nonhuman Primates and Medical Research. New York: Academic Press.

——. 1977. Progress in Ape Research. New York: Academic Press.

Bourne, Geoffrey H., and J. F. Danielli (Eds.). 1952. International Review of Cytology. Vol. 1. New York: Academic Press.

Bowman, Isaiah. 1935. Summary Statement of the Work of the National Research Council—1934–1935. Science 82:337–42.

Brackett, Benjamin G., George E. Seidel, and Sarah M. Seidel (Eds.). 1981. New Technologies in Animal Breeding. New York: Academic Press.

Bradfield, Richard. 1962. The Sciences, Pure and Applied, in the First Century of the Land-Grant Institutions. Science Education 46:240–47.

Brecher, Edward M. 1969. The Sex Researchers. Boston: Little, Brown.

Brieger, Gert H. 1980. Surgery. In Ronald L. Numbers (Ed.), The Education of American Physicians, 175–204. Berkeley: University of California Press.

Brobeck, John R., Orr E. Reynolds, and Toby A. Appel (Eds.). 1987. History of the American Physiological Society: The First Century, 1887–1987. Bethesda, Md.: American Physiological Society.

Brodie, Janet Farrell. 1994. Contraception and Abortion in Nineteenth-Century America. Ithaca, N.Y.: Cornell University Press.

Brody, S., C. W. Turner, and A. C. Ragsdale. 1924. The Relation between the Initial Rise and Subsequent Decline of Milk Secretion following Parturition. Journal of General Physiology 6:541.

Brooks, Chandler McC. 1959. The Development of Physiology in the Last Fifty Years. Bulletin of the History of Medicine 33:249–62.

Brouha, L. (Ed.). 1938. Les Hormones Sexuelles. Colloque International/Conferences du College de France/Fondation Singer-Polignac. Paris: Hermann et Cie.

Brown, E. Richard. 1979. Rockefeller Medicine Men: Medicine and Capitalism in America. Berkeley: University of California Press.

Bruce, Judith. 1987. Users' Perspectives on Contraceptive Technology and Delivery Systems: Highlighting Some Feminist Issues. Technology in Society 9:359–83.

———. 1990. Fundamental Elements of the Quality of Care: A Simple Framework. Studies in Family Planning 21:61–91.

Brush, Stephen G. 1978. Nettie M. Stevens and the Discovery of Sex Determination by Chromosomes. Isis 69:163–72.

Bucher, Rue. 1962. Pathology: A Study of Social Movements within a Profession. Social Problems 10:40–51.

———. 1988. On the Natural History of Health Care Occupations. Work and Occupations 15(2):131–47.

Bucher, Rue, and Anselm L. Strauss. 1961. Professions in Process. American Journal of Sociology 66:325–34.

Bugos, Glenn E. 1989. Managing Cooperative Research and Borderland Science in the National Research Council, 1922–1942. Historical Studies in the Physical Sciences 20(1):1–32.

Bugos, Glen E. 1992. Intellectual Property Issues in the American Chicken Breeding Industry. Business History Review 66:127–68.

Bullough, Vern. L. 1976. Sexual Variance in Society and History. Chicago: University of Chicago Press.

———. 1980. Technology and Female Sexuality. Journal of Sex Research 16:59–71.

———. 1981. A Brief Note on Rubber Technology. Technology and Culture 22:104–6.

———. 1985. The Rockefellers and Sex Research. Journal of Sex Research 21:113–25.

———. 1988. Katherine Bement Davis, Sex Research and the Rockefeller Foundation. Bulletin of the History of Medicine 62:74–89.

———. 1989. The Physician and Sex Research in Nineteenth-Century Germany. Bulletin of the History of Medicine 63:247–67.

———. 1994. Science in the Bedroom: A History of Sex Research. New York: Basic Books.

Bullough, Vern L., and Marshal Voughy. 1973. Women, Menstruation and Nineteenth-Century Medicine. Bulletin of the History of Medicine 47:66–82.

Burkhardt, Richard W. 1979. Closing the Door on Lord Morton's Mare: The Rise and Fall of Telegony. In William Coleman and Camille Limoges (Eds.), Studies in the History of Biology 3, 1–21. Baltimore, Md.: Johns Hopkins University Press.

Burnham, John C. 1972. Medical Specialists and the Movements toward Social Control in the Progressive Era: Three Examples. In Jerry Israel (Ed.), Building the Organizational Society: Essays on Associational Activists in Modern America, 19–30. New York: Free Press.

———. 1996. How the Concept of Profession Evolved in the Work of Historians of Medicine. Bulletin of the History of Medicine 70:1–24.

Burroughs, Wise., C. C. Culbertson, R. M. McWilliams, Joseph Kastelic, and William Hald. 1954. Hormone Feeding (Diethylstilbestrol) to Fatten Cattle I. Iowa State College Animal Husbandry Leaflet No. 188.

Busch, Lawrence. 1982. History, Negotiation and Structure in Agricultural Research. Urban Life 11:368–84.

——— (Ed.). 1981. Science and Agricultural Development. Totowa, N.J.: Allanheld, Osmun.

Busch, Lawrence, and William B. Lacey. 1983. Science, Agriculture and the Politics of Research. Boulder, Colo.: Westview.

Butler, Judith. 1993. Bodies That Matter: On the Discursive Limits of "Sex." New York: Routledge.

Butler, Stella V. 1988. Centers and Peripheries: The Development of British Physiology, 1870–1914. Journal of the History of Biology 21:473–500.

Byerly, T. C. 1976. Changes in Animal Science. Agricultural History 50:258–74.

———. 1986. Animal Husbandry—Animal Science. In Vivian Wiser, Larry Mark, and H. Graham Purchase (Eds.), One Hundred Years of Animal Health, 65–111. Journal of National Agricultural Library Associates 11 (1–4) [A Centennial Special Volume].

Calderone, Mary Steichen. 1964. Manual of Contraceptive Practice. Baltimore, Md.: Williams and Wilkins.

Callon, Michel. 1985. Some Elements of a Sociology of Translation: Domestication of the Scallops and the Fishermen of St. Brieuc Bay. In John Law (Ed.), Power, Action and Belief: A New Sociology of Knowledge?, 196–233. Sociological Review Monograph 32. London: Routledge and Kegan Paul.

———. 1991. Techno-economic Networks and Irreversibility. In John Law (Ed.), A Sociology of Monsters: Essays on Power, Technology and Domination, 132–64. New York: Routledge.

———. 1995. Four Models for the Dynamics of Science. In Sheila Jasanoff, Gerald E. Markle, James Petersen, and Trevor Pinch (Eds.), Handbook of Science and Technology Studies, 29–63. Thousand Oaks, Calif.: Sage.

Callon, Michel, John Law, and Ari Rip (Eds.). 1986. Mapping the Dynamics of Science and Technology: Sociology of Science in the Real World. London: Macmillan.

Cambrosio, Alberto, and Peter Keating. 1983. The Disciplinary Stake: The Case of Chronobiology. Social Studies of Science 13:323–53.

Cangi, Ellen Corwin. 1982. Abraham Flexner's Philanthropy: The Full-Time System in the Department of Surgery at the University of Cincinnati College of Medicine, 1910–1930. Bulletin of the History of Medicine 56:160–74.

Canguilhem, George. 1978. On the Normal and the Pathological. Translated by Carolyn R. Fawcett. Dordrecht: Reidel.

Cannon, Walter Bradford. 1942. Roy Graham Hoskins: An Appreciation. Endocrinology 30:839–45.

Carlson, A. J. 1956–57. Carl Richard Moore, 1892–1955. Institute of Medicine of Chicago, Proceedings 21:82–83.

Carmichael, D. Erskine. 1973. The Pap Smear: Life of George N. Papanicolaou. Springfield, Ill.: Charles C. Thomas.

Carson, G. 1960. The Roguish World of Doctor Brinkley. New York: Holt, Rinehart, and Winston.

Carter, C. O. (Ed.). 1983. Developments in Human Reproduction and Their Eugenic, Ethical Implications: Proceedings of the Nineteenth Annual Symposium of the Eugenics Society. London: Academic Press.

Casida, Lester E. 1935. Prepuberal Development of the Pig Ovary and Its Relation to Stimulation with Gonadotropic Hormones. Anatomical Record 61:389–96.

———. 1938. The Endocrine System. American Society of Animal Production, Record of Proceedings of the Thirty-first Annual Meeting:13–17.

———. 1976. Ovulation Studies with Particular Reference to the Pig. Seventh Hartman Lecture. Biology of Reproduction 14:95–106.

Casper, Monica. 1994a. At the Margins of Humanity: Fetal Positions in Science and Medicine. Science, Technology and Human Values 19:307–23.

———. 1994b. Reframing and Grounding Nonhuman Agency: What Makes a Fetus an Agent? American Behavioral Scientist 37:839–56.

———. 1995. Fetal Cyborgs and Technomoms on the Reproductive Frontier: Or, Which Way to the Carnival? In Chris Hables Gray (Ed.), with Heidi J. Figueroa-Sarriera and Steven Mentor, The Cyborg Handbook, 183–201. New York: Routledge.

———. 1998. Working on and around Fetuses: The Contested Domain of Fetal Surgery. In Marc Berg and Annemarie Mol (Eds.), Differences in Medicine: Unraveling Practices, Techniques and Bodies. Durham, N.C.: Duke University Press.

Casper, Monica, and Adele Clarke. 1998. Making the Pap Smear into the Right Tool for the Job: Cervical Cancer Screening in the U.S., c1940–1995. Social Studies of Science 28:forthcoming.

Casper, Monica, and Lisa Jean Moore. 1995. Inscribing Bodies, Inscribing the Future: Gender, Sex and Reproduction in Outer Space. Sociological Perspectives 38:311–33.

Cassidy, Claire M. 1991. The Good Body: When Big Is Better. Medical Anthropology 13:181–213.

Chandrasekhar, S. 1981. A Dirty, Filthy Book: The Writings of Charles Knowlton and Annie Besant on Reproductive Physiology and Birth Control and an Account of the Bradlaugh-Besant Trial. Berkeley: University of California Press.

Chang, M. C., C. R. Austin, J. M. Bedford, B. G. Brackett, R. H. F. Hunter, and R. Yanagimachi. 1977. Capacitation of Spermatozoa and Fertilization in Mammals. In Roy O. Greep and Marjorie A. Koblinsky (Eds.), Frontiers in Reproduction and Fertility Control: A Review of the Reproductive Sciences and Contraceptive Development, 434–51. Boston: MIT (Ford Foundation).

Chang, M. C., and G. Pincus. 1931. Physiology of Fertilization in Mammals. Physiological Reviews 31:1.

Chapman, Arthur B. 1987. Jay Laurence Lush, January 3, 1896–May 1, 1982. Biographical Memoirs of the National Academy of Science 57:277–305.

Charo, R. Alta. 1991. A Political History of RU486. In Kathi E. Hanna (Ed.) for the Institute of Medicine, Biomedical Politics, 43–93. Washington, D.C.: National Academy Press.

Chase, Allan. 1975. The Legacy of Malthus: The Social Costs of the New Scientific Racism. New York: Alfred A. Knopf.

Chase, Cheryl. 1997. Hermaphrodites with Attitude: Mapping the Emergence of Intersex Political Activism. Unpublished manuscript. Available from Intersex Society of America, P.O. Box 31791, San Francisco, CA, 94131. Website: www.isna.org

Chesler, Ellen. 1992. Woman of Valor: Margaret Sanger and the Birth Control Movement in America. New York: Simon and Schuster.

Chico, Nan Paulsen. 1984. Sterilization Regrets: Who Seeks Reversals? Mobius 4:87–92.

———. 1989. Confronting the Dilemmas of Reproductive Choice: The Process of Sex Preselection. Ph.D. diss., University of California, San Francisco.

Childress, James F. 1991. Deliberations of the Human Fetal Tissue Transplantation Research Panel. In Kathi E. Hanna (Ed.) for the Institute of Medicine, Biomedical Politics, 215–48. Washington, D.C: National Academy Press.

Chonir, Neva. 1994. Morning-After Politics. San Francisco Bay Guardian, August 24, 19.

Christy, Nicholas P. 1972. Philip Edward Smith, Ph.D. (1884–1970). Endocrinology 90:1415–16.

Chubin, Daryl. 1976. The Conceptualization of Scientific Specialties. Sociological Quarterly 17:448–76.

Chubin, Daryl, and Ellen Chu (Eds.). 1989. Science Off the Pedestal: Social Perspectives on Science and Technology. Belmont, Calif.: Wadsworth.

Churchill, Frederick B. 1968. August Weisman and a Break from Tradition. Journal of the History of Biology 1:91–112.

———. 1969. From Machine Theory to Entelechy: Two Studies in Developmental Teleology. Journal of the History of Biology 2:165–85.

———. 1970. Hertwig, Weismann, and the Meaning of Reduction Division circa 1890. Isis 61:429–57.

———. 1973. Chabry, Roux and the Experimental Method in Nineteenth-Century Embryology. In R. N. Giere and R. S. Westfall (Eds.), Foundations of Scientific Method. Bloomington: Indiana University Press.

———. 1974. William Johannsen and the Genotype Concept. Journal of the History of Biology 7:5–30.

———. 1979. Sex and the Single Organism: Biological Theories of Sexuality in Mid–Nineteenth Century. In William Coleman and Camille Limoges (Eds.), Studies in the History of Biology 3, 139–78. Baltimore, Md.: Johns Hopkins University Press.

——. 1981. In Search of the New Biology: An Epilogue. Journal of the History of Biology 14:177–91.

——. 1985a. Weismann, Hydromedusae, and the Biogenetic Imperative: A Reconsideration. New York: Cambridge University Press.

——. 1985b. Weismann's Continuity of the Germ Plasm in Historical Perspective. Freiburg: University of Freiburg Press.

CIBA Foundation. 1986. Human Embryo Research: Yes or No? London: Tavistock.

Clark, Anne Harrison. 1982. Funding Support for Population Research. Women and Health 7(1):73–81.

Clarke, Adele E. 1981. Eugenic Sterilization in the United States, 1889–1945. Unpublished manuscript, University of California, San Francisco.

——. 1984. Subtle Sterilization Abuse: A Reproductive Rights Perspective. In Rita Arditti, Renata Duelli Klein, and Shelly Minden (Eds.), Test Tube Women: What Future for Motherhood?, 188–212. Boston: Pandora/Routledge and Kegan Paul.

——. 1985. Emergence of the Reproductive Research Enterprise: A Sociology of Biological, Medical, and Agricultural Science in the United States, 1910–1940. Ph.D. diss., University of California, San Francisco.

——. 1987. Research Materials and Reproductive Science in the United States, 1910–1940. In Gerald L. Geison (Ed.), Physiology in the American Context, 1850–1940, 323–50. Bethesda, Md.: American Physiological Society/Waverly.

——. 1988. Controversy and the Development of American Reproductive Science. MBL [Marine Biological Laboratory, Woods Hole] Science 3(1):36–39.

——. 1990a. Controversy and the Development of Reproductive Sciences. Social Problems 37:18–37.

——. 1990b. A Social Worlds Research Adventure: The Case of Reproductive Science. In Susan E. Cozzens and Thomas F. Gieryn (Eds.), Theories of Science in Society, 15–42. Bloomington: Indiana University Press.

——. 1990c. Women's Health over the Life Cycle. In Rima Apple (Ed.), The History of Women, Health and Medicine in America: An Encyclopedic Handbook, 3–39. New York: Garland.

——. 1991a. Embryology and the Development of American Reproductive Sciences, 1910–1945. In Keith Benson, Jane Maienschein, and Ronald Rainger (Eds.), The American Expansion of Biology, 107–32. New Brunswick, N.J.: Rutgers University Press.

——. 1991b. Social Worlds Theory as Organization Theory. In David Maines (Ed.), Social Organization and Social Process: Essays in Honor of Anselm Strauss, 119–58. Hawthorne, N.Y.: Aldine de Gruyter.

——. 1993. Money, Sex and Legitimacy at Chicago, 1900–1940: Lillie's Center of Reproductive Biology. Special Issue on Biology at the University of Chicago, Perspectives on Science 1:367–415.

——. 1995a. Modernity, Postmodernity and Human Reproductive Processes c1890–1990, or "Mommy, Where Do Cyborgs Come from Anyway?" In Chris Hables Gray (Ed.), with Heidi J. Figueroa-Sarriera and Steven Mentor, The Cyborg Handbook, 139–55. New York: Routledge.

——. 1995b. Research Materials and Reproductive Science in the United States, 1910–1940 with Epilogue: Research Materials (Re)Visited. In Susan Leigh Star (Ed.), Ecologies of Knowledge: New Directions in Sociology of Science and Technology, 183–225. Albany: State University of New York Press.

——. 1996. Frank Rattray Lillie. American National Biography. New York: American Council of Learned Societies and Oxford University Press.

——. 1997. Maverick Reproductive Scientists and the Production of Contraceptives. Paper presented at meetings of the Society for Social Studies of Science. Bielefeld, Germany, October.

——. 1998. Humans as Research Materials: Problematics of Subjects Who Speak.

Clarke, Adele E., and Monica Casper. 1996. From Simple Technique to Complex System: Classification of Pap Smears, 1917–1990. Medical Anthropology Quarterly 11:601–23.

Clarke, Adele E., and Joan Fujimura (Eds.). 1992. The Right Tools for the Job: At Work in Twentieth-Century Life Sciences. Princeton, N.J.: Princeton University Press. French translation, Paris: Sythelabo Press, 1996.

Clarke, Adele E., and Elihu M. Gerson. 1990. Symbolic Interactionism in Science Studies. In Howard S. Becker and Michal McCall (Eds.), Symbolic Interaction and Cultural Studies, 179–214. Chicago: University of Chicago Press.

Clarke, Adele E., and Theresa Montini. 1993. The Many Faces of RU486: Tales of Situated Knowledges and Technological Contestations. Science, Technology and Human Values 18:42–78.

Clarke, Adele E., and Virginia Olesen (Eds.). 1998. Revisioning Women, Health and Healing: Feminist, Cultural and Technoscience Perspectives. New York and London: Routledge.

Clermont, Y. 1991. Four Decades of Research on the Biology of the Male Reproductive System: A Few Landmarks. Annals of the New York Academy of Sciences 637:17–25.

Cobb, Ivo Geikie. 1927. The Glands of Destiny: A Study of the Personality. London: W. Heinemann.

Coben, Stanley. 1979. American Foundations as Patrons of Science: The Commitment to Individual Research. In Nathan Reingold (Ed.), The Sciences in the American Context: New Perspectives, 229–48. Washington, D.C.: Smithsonian Institution.

Cochran, William G., Frederick Mosteller, John W. Tukey, and W. O. Jenkins. 1954. Statistical Problems of the Kinsey Report on Sexual Behavior in the Human Male. Washington, D.C.: American Statistical Association.

Cockburn, Cynthia. 1985. Machinery of Dominance: Women, Men, and Technical Know-How. Boston: Northeastern University Press.

Cohen, Sherrill, and Nadine Taub (Eds.). 1989. Reproductive Laws for the 1990s. Clifton, N.J.: Humana.

Cohen, Stanley, and Andrew Scull. 1983. Introduction: Social Control in History and Sociology. In Stanley Cohen and Andrew Scull (Eds.), Social Control and the State, 1–16. New York: St. Martin's Press.

Colborn, Theo, Dianne Dumanoski, and John Petersen Meyers. 1996. Our Stolen

Future: Are We Threatening Our Fertility, Intelligence and Survival? A Scientific Detective Story. New York: Dutton.

Cole, Harold H. 1930. A Study of the Mucosa of the Genital Tract of the Cow, with Special Reference to Cyclic Changes. American Journal of Anatomy 46:261–301.

———. 1937. Superfecundity in Rats Treated with Mare Gonadotropic Hormone. American Journal of Physiology 109:704–12.

———. 1938. The Endocrine Control of Growth. American Society of Animal Production, Record of Proceedings of Thirty-first Annual Meeting:20–25.

———. 1953. Problems in the Field of Physiology of Reproduction of Farm Animals. Iowa State College Journal of Science 28:133–38.

———. 1977. Adventurer in Animal Science: Harold H. Cole. The Oral History Center, Shields Library, University of California, Davis.

Cole, Harold H., and P. T. Cupps. 1959. Reproduction in Domestic Animals. New York and London: Academic Press.

Cole, Harold H., and H. Goss. 1943. The Source of Equine Gonadotropin. In Essays in Biology in Honor of Herbert Evans, 105–120. Berkeley: University of California Press.

Cole, Harold H., H. R. Guilbert, and H. Goss. 1932. Further Considerations of the Properties of the Gonad-Stimulating Principle of Mare Serum. American Journal of Physiology 102:237–40.

Cole, Harold H., and G. H. Hart. 1930. The Potency of Blood Serum of Mares in Progressive Stages of Pregnancy in Effecting the Sexual Maturity of the Immature Rat. American Journal of Physiology 94:57–68.

Cole, Harold H., and R. F. Miller. 1931. The Vaginal Smear of the Ewe. Proceedings of the Society for Experimental Biology and Medicine 28:841–43.

Cole, Harold H., and M. Ronning (Eds.). 1974. Animal Agriculture. San Francisco: Freeman.

Cole, Leon J. 1916. Twinning in Cattle with Special Reference to the Freemartin. Science 43:177–81.

Cole, Leon J., and Carl A. Bunde. 1937. Animal Experiments with Foam Powder. Journal of Contraception 3:127–30.

Coleman, William B. 1971. Biology in the Nineteenth Century: Problems of Form, Function and Transformation. New York: Cambridge University Press.

———. 1980. Morphology in the Evolutionary Synthesis. In Ernst Mayr and William B. Provine (Eds.), The Evolutionary Synthesis: Perspectives on the Unification of Biology, 274–301. Cambridge, Mass.: Harvard University Press.

———. 1985. The Cognitive Basis of the Discipline: Claude Bernard on Physiology. Isis 76:49–70.

Coleman, William B., and Frederic L. Holmes (Eds.). 1988. The Investigative Enterprise: Experimental Physiology in Nineteenth-Century Medicine. Berkeley: University of California Press.

Coliver, Sandra (Ed.), for Article 19. 1995. The Right to Know: Human Rights and Access to Reproductive Health Information. Philadelphia: Article 19 and University of Pennsylvania Press.

Collat, G. 1994. Genes in Sperm Can Be Altered. San Francisco Chronicle, November 23, A6.

Collins, Harry H., and Steven Yearley. 1992. Epistemological Chicken. In Andrew Pickering (Ed.), Science as Practice and Culture, 301–26. Chicago: University of Chicago Press.

Collins, Patricia Hill. 1990. Black Feminist Thought: Knowledge, Consciousness and the Politics of Empowerment. Boston: Unwin Hyman.

Collins, Randall, and Sal Restivo. 1983. Development, Diversity and Conflict in the Sociology of Science. Sociological Quarterly 24:185–200.

Committee of the American Neurological Association for the Investigation of Eugenical Sterilization. 1936. Eugenical Sterilization: A Reorientation of the Problem. New York: Macmillan.

Cone, Richard A., and Kevin J. Whalley. 1994. Review Article: Monoclonal Antibodies for Reproductive Health: Part I. Preventing Sexual Transmission of Disease and Pregnancy with Topically Applied Antibodies. American Journal of Reproductive Immunology 32:114–31.

Conrad, Peter. 1992. Medicalization and Social Control. Annual Review of Sociology 18:209–32.

Conrad, Peter, and Rochelle Kern (Eds.). 1981. The Sociology of Health and Illness: Critical Perspectives. New York: St. Martin's Press.

Conrad, Peter, and Joseph Schneider. 1980. Deviance and Medicalization: From Badness to Sickness. St. Louis, Mo.: C. V. Mosby.

Cook, Brian. 1994. JRF: The First 100 Issues. Journal of Reproduction and Fertility 100:2–4.

Cook-Degan, Robert Mullan. 1991. The Human Genome Project: The Formation of Federal Policies in the US: 1986–1990. In Kathi E. Hanna (Ed.) for the Institute of Medicine, Biomedical Politics, 99–168. Washington, D.C: National Academy Press.

Cooke, Kathy J. 1997. From Science to Practice, or Practice to Science? Chickens and Eggs in Raymond Pearl's Agricultural Breeding Research, 1907–1916. Isis 88:62–86.

Cooper, James F. 1928. Technique of Contraception. New York: [American Birth Control League].

Cooter, Roger, and Steve Sturdy. 1992. Scientific Management and the Structure of the Medical Revolution in Britain 1900–1939. Paper presented at the Joint Meeting of the History of Science Society and the British Society for the History of Science. Toronto, 25–28 July.

Corea, Gena. 1977. The Hidden Malpractice. New York: Harcourt, Brace Jovanovich.

——. 1985. The Mother Machine: Reproductive Technologies from Artificial Insemination to Artificial Wombs. New York: Harper and Row.

Corgi, C. F., V. G. Foglia, L. F. Leloir, and S. Ocha (Eds.). 1963. Perspectives in Biology: A Collection of Papers Dedicated to Bernardo A. Houssay. New York: Elsevier.

Corner, George W. 1915. The Corpus Luteum of Pregnancy As It Is in Swine. Carnegie Contributions to Embryology, no. 5:69–94.

———. 1921a. Abnormalities of the Mammalian Embryo Occurring before Implantation. Carnegie Contributions to Embryology, no. 60:61–66.

———. 1921b. Cyclic Changes in the Ovaries and Uterus of the Sow, and Their Relation to the Mechanism of Implantation. Carnegie Contributions to Embryology, no. 64:117–46.

———. 1923. Ovulation and Menstruation in *Macacus rhesus*. Carnegie Contributions to Embryology, no. 75:73–110.

———. 1927. The Relation between Menstruation and Ovulation in the Monkey: Its Possible Significance for Man. Journal of the American Medical Association 89:1838–40.

———. 1930. The Hormonal Control of Lactation. 1. Non-effect of the Corpus Luteum. 2. Positive Action of Extracts of the Hypophysis. American Journal of Physiology 95:43–55.

———. 1933. The Nature of the Menstrual Cycle. Medicine 12:61–82.

———. 1938. Attaining Manhood: A Doctor Talks to Boys about Sex. New York: Harper.

———. 1939. Attaining Womanhood: A Doctor Talks to Girls about Sex. New York: Harper.

———. 1944. Ourselves Unborn: An Embryologist's Essay on Man. New Haven, Conn.: Yale University Press.

———. 1951. Our Knowledge of the Menstrual Cycle, 1910–1950. Fourth Annual Addison Lecture Delivered at Guy's Hospital, London, July 13, 1950. Lancet 1:919–23.

———. 1958a. Anatomist at Large: An Autobiography and Selected Essays. New York: Basic Books.

———. 1958b. The Role of Anatomy in Medical Education. Journal of Medical Education 33:1–8.

———. 1960. The Past of Anatomy in the United States. Anatomical Record 137:179–82.

———. 1961. Foreword. In William C. Young (Ed.), Sex and Internal Secretions, ix–xii. 3d ed. Baltimore, Md.: Williams and Wilkins.

———. 1963. The Hormones in Human Reproduction. 1942. Reprint, New York: Atheneum.

———. 1965. The Early History of the Estrogenic Hormones. Journal of Endocrinology (Proceedings of the Society) 31:iii–xvii.

———. 1967. The Generality and Particularity of Man. [Exerpt from Ourselves Unborn, 1944.] In Caryl B. Haskins (Ed.), The Search for Understanding: Selected Writings of the Carnegie Institution. Cambridge: Massachusetts Institute of Technology.

———. 1981. Seven Ages of a Medical Scientist: An Autobiography. Philadelphia: University of Pennsylvania Press.

Corner, George W., and Willard M. Allen. 1929a. Physiology of the Corpus Luteum. 2. Production of a Special Uterine Reaction (Progestational Proliferation) by Extracts of the Corpus Luteum. American Journal of Physiology 88:326–29.

———. 1929b. Physiology of the Corpus Luteum. 3. Normal Growth and Implantation of Embryos after Very Early Ablation of the Ovaries, Under the Influence of Extracts of the Corpus Luteum. American Journal of Physiology 88:340–46.

Corner, George W., Charles H. Danforth, and L. S. Stone. 1943. Edgar Allen, 1892–1943. Anatomical Record 86:595–97.

Corvie, A. T. 1948. Pregnancy Diagnosis Tests: A Review. Edinburgh: Commonwealth Bureau of Animal Breeding.

Cott, Nancy F. 1987. The Grounding of Modern Feminism. New Haven, Conn.: Yale University Press.

Council of the Chicago Medical Society. 1922. History of Medicine and Surgery and Physicians and Surgeons of Chicago. Chicago: Biographical Publications.

Courey, Renee. 1994. The Virgin, the Dynamo and the Improper Arts: American Industry and the Development of the Oral Contraceptive, 1930–1970. Ph.D. diss., University of California, Berkeley.

Cowan, Ruth Schwartz. 1970. Edgar Allen. In Charles Coulston Gillispie (Ed.), Dictionary of Scientific Biography. Vol. 1. New York: Scribner.

Cozzens, Susan E., and Edward J. Woodhouse. 1995. Science, Government and the Politics of Knowledge. In Sheila Jasanoff, Gerald E. Markle, James Petersen, and Trevor Pinch (Eds.), Handbook of Science and Technology Studies, 533–53. Thousand Oaks, Calif.: Sage.

Cranefield, Paul F. 1959. Microscopic Physiology since 1908. Bulletin of the History of Medicine 33:263–75.

Cravens, Hamilton. 1978. The Triumph of Evolution: American Scientists and the Heredity-Environment Controversy, 1900–1941. Philadelphia: University of Pennsylvania Press.

Cronin, Helena. 1992. Sexual Selection: Historical Perspectives. In Evelyn Fox Keller and Elisabeth A. Lloyd (Eds.), Keywords in Evolutionary Biology, 120–21. Cambridge, Mass.: Harvard University Press.

Cronon, William (Ed.). 1995. Uncommon Ground: Toward Reinventing Nature. New York: Norton.

Cross, Stephen J., and William R. Albury. 1987. Walter B. Cannon, L. J. Henderson and the Organic Analogy. Osiris, 2d ser., 3:165–92.

Cueto, Marcos. 1994. Laboratory Styles in Argentine Physiology. Isis 85:228–46.

—— (Ed.). 1994. Missionaries of Science: The Rockefeller Foundation and Latin America. Philanthropic Studies May 1994. Bloomington: Indiana University Press.

Culver, Kenneth W., M.D. 1994. Gene Therapy: A Handbook for Physicians. New York: Mary Anne Liebert.

Dale, Henry H. 1963. Some Endocrinological Memories. In C. F. Corgi, V. G. Foglia, L. F. Leloir, and S. Ocha (Eds.), Perspectives in Biology: A Collection of Papers Dedicated to Bernardo A. Houssay, 19–23. New York: Elsevier.

Dally, Ann G. 1992. Women under the Knife: A History of Surgery. New York: Routledge.

Danbom, David B. 1989. The North Dakota Agricultural Experiment Station and the Struggle to Create a Dairy State. Agricultural History 63:174–86.

Danforth, C. H. 1932. Interrelation of Genetic and Endocrine Factors in Sex. In

Edgar Allen (Ed.), Sex and Internal Secretions, 12–54. Baltimore, Md.: Williams and Wilkins.

David, Paul A., and Warren C. Sanderson. 1987. The Emergence of a Two-Child Norm among American Birth-Controllers. Population and Development Review 13:1–41.

Davis, Katherine Bement. 1929. Factors in the Sex Life of Twenty-two Hundred Women. New York: Harper and Brothers.

Davis, William L. 1991. Family Planning Services: A History of U.S. Federal Legislation. Journal of Family History 16:381–400.

Davis-Floyd, Robbie E. 1992. Birth as an American Rite of Passage. Berkeley: University of California Press.

Declercq, Eugene, and Richard Lacroix. 1985. Immigrant Midwives of Lawrence: Conflict between Law and Culture in Early Twentieth-Century Massachusetts. Bulletin of the History of Medicine 59:232–46.

Deegan, Mary Jo, and Nancy A. Brooks (Eds.). 1985. Women and Disability: The Double Handicap. New Brunswick, N.J.: Transaction Books.

de Kruif, Paul. 1945. The Male Hormone. New York: Harcourt, Brace.

Demeny, Paul. 1988. Social Science and Population Policy. Population and Development Review 14:451–79.

Dempsey, Edward W. 1968. William Caldwell Young, An Appreciation. In Milton Diamond (Ed.), Perspectives in Reproduction and Sexual Behavior, 453–58. Bloomington: Indiana University Press.

DeVane, William Clyde. 1965. Higher Education in Twentieth-Century America. Cambridge, Mass.: Harvard University Press.

Dickinson, Robert Latou. 1933. Human Sex Anatomy. Baltimore, Md.: Williams and Wilkins.

Dickinson, Robert Latou, and L. Beam. 1931. A Thousand Marriages: A Medical Study of Sex Adjustment. Baltimore, Md.: Williams and Wilkins.

Dickinson, Robert Latou, and Louise S. Bryant. 1931. Control of Conception. New York: National Committee on Maternal Health.

Dickinson, Robert Latou, and Clarence James Gamble. 1950. Human Sterilization: Techniques of Permanent Conception Control. New York: National Committee on Maternal Health.

Dickinson, Robert Latou, and Woodbridge Edwards Morris. 1941a. Techniques of Conception Control: A Practical Manual Issued by the Birth Control Federation of America, Inc. Baltimore, Md.: Williams and Wilkins.

———. 1941b. Techniques of Contraception. New York: Day-Nichols.

Dienes, C. Thomas. 1972. Law, Politics and Birth Control. Urbana: University of Illinois Press.

Digby, Anne. 1994. Making a Medical Market: Doctors and Their Patients in English Society 1720–1911. New York: Cambridge University Press.

Dixon-Mueller, Ruth. 1993a. Population Policy and Women's Rights: Transforming Reproductive Choice. New York: Praeger.

———. 1993b. The Sexuality Connection in Reproductive Health. Studies in Family Planning 24:269–82.

Dixon-Mueller, Ruth, and Adrienne Germain. 1993. Four Essays on Birth Control Needs and Risks. New York: International Women's Health Coalition.

Djerassi, Carl. 1966. Steroid Oral Contraceptive. Science 151:1055–61.

———. 1981. The Politics of Contraception: Birth Control in the Year 2001. San Francisco: Freeman.

———. 1989. The Bitter Pill. Science 245:356–61.

———. 1990. Steroids Made It Possible: An Autobiography. Washington, D.C.: American Chemical Society.

———. 1992. The Pill, Pygmy Chimps, and Degas' Horse: The Autobiography of Carl Djerassi. New York: Basic Books.

Dodds, E. C. 1941. The New Oestrogens. Edinburgh Medical Journal 48:1–13.

Doisy, Edward A. 1932. Biochemistry of the Follicular Hormone Theelin. In Edgar Allen (Ed.), Sex and Internal Secretions, 481–98. Baltimore, Md.: Williams and Wilkins.

———. 1941a. Glandular Physiology and Therapy: The Estrogenic Substances. Journal of the American Medical Association 116:501–505.

———. 1941b. The Ovarian Follicular Hormone. In Edward A. Doisy, Philip E. Smith, Robert T. Frank, and Elmer L. Severinghaus (Eds.), Female Sex Hormones, 1–17. Philadelphia: University of Pennsylvania Press.

Doisy, Edward A., Philip E. Smith, Robert T. Frank, and Elmer L. Severinghaus (Eds.). 1941. Female Sex Hormones. Philadelphia: University of Pennsylvania Press.

Domm, L. V., Mary Juhn, and R. G. Gustavson. 1932. Plumage Tests in Birds. In Edgar Allen (Ed.), Sex and Internal Secretions, 584–646. Baltimore, Md.: Williams and Wilkins.

Douglas, Mary. 1966. Purity and Danger: An Analysis of the Concepts of Pollution and Taboo. New York: Praeger.

Doyal, Lesley. 1987. Infertility—A Life Sentence? Women and the National Health Service. In Michelle Stanworth (Ed.), Reproductive Technologies: Gender, Motherhood and Medicine, 174–90. Minneapolis: University of Minnesota Press.

Dreifus, Claudia. 1978. Seizing Our Bodies: The Politics of Women's Health. New York: Vintage/Random House.

Dreyfus, Hubert L., and Paul Rabinow. 1982. Michel Foucault: Beyond Structuralism and Hermeneutics. 2d ed. Chicago: University of Chicago Press.

Duden, Barbara. 1991. The Woman beneath the Skin: A Doctor's Patients in Eighteenth-Century Germany. Translated by Thomas Dunlap. Cambridge, Mass.: Harvard University Press.

Dugdale, Ann. 1995. Devices and Desires: Constructing the Intrauterine Device, 1908–1988. Ph.D. diss., University of Wollongong, Australia.

Dunn, L. C. 1965. A Short History of Genetics. New York: Academic Press.

Dupree, A. Hunter (Ed.). 1957. Science in the Federal Government: A History of Policies and Activities to 1940. Cambridge, Mass.: Belknap Press of Harvard University Press.

———. 1963. Science and the Emergence of Modern America, 1865–1916. Chicago: Rand McNally.

Duster, Troy. 1990. Eugenics through the Back Door. Berkeley: University of California Press.

Dutton, Diana B. 1988. Worse than the Disease: Pitfalls of Medical Progress. Cambridge: Cambridge University Press.

Eastman, N. J., A. F. Guttmacher, and E. H. Stewart. 1939. Experimental Observations on Sperm Immunity in the Rat. Journal of Contraception 4(7):147–51.

Ebert, James D. 1975–76. Department of Embryology Report—Introduction. Carnegie Institute of Washington Yearbook 75. Washington, D.C.: Carnegie Institute of Washington.

Edge, David, and Michael Mulkay. 1976. Astronomy Transformed: The Emergence of Radio Astronomy in Britain. New York: Wiley.

Editor. 1921a. Disappointments of Endocrinology. Journal of the American Medical Association 76:1685–86.

———. 1921b. The Endocrine Glands: A Caution. Journal of the American Medical Association 76:1500–1501.

———. 1931. The Papal Encyclical. Eugenics: Journal of Race Betterment 4(2):73.

———. 1939. Estrogen Therapy: A Warning. Journal of the American Medical Association 1113:2323–24.

Edwards, Margot, and Mary Waldorf. 1984. Reclaiming Birth: History and Heroines of American Childbirth Reform. Trumansburg, N.Y.: Crossing Press.

Edwards, Robert G. 1989. Life before Birth: Reflections on the Embryo Debate. New York: Basic Books.

——— (Ed.). 1969. Immunology and Reproduction: Proceedings of the First Symposium of the International Coordination Committee for the Immunology of Reproduction. London: International Planned Parenthood Federation.

Edwards, Robert G., and M. H. Johnson (Eds.). 1976. Physiological Effects of Immunity against Reproductive Hormones. Cambridge: Cambridge University Press.

Ehrenfest, Hugo. 1937. Menstruation and Its Disorders: A Critical Review of the Literature from 1933–1936 Inclusive. American Journal of Obstetrics and Gynecology 34:530–47, 699–729, 1051–76.

Ehrenreich, Barbara, and Deirdre English. 1979. For Her Own Good: 150 Years of the Experts' Advice to Women. Garden City, N.Y.: Anchor/Doubleday.

Elias, Sherman, and George J. Annas. 1987. Reproductive Genetics and the Law. Chicago: Yearbook Medical Publishers.

Ellinger, Tage. 1921. The Influence of Age on Fertility in Swine. Proceedings of the National Academy of Sciences 7:134–38.

Engelhardt, Tristram, and Arthur L. Caplan (Eds.). 1987. Scientific Controversies: Case Studies in the Resolution and Closure of Disputes in Science and Technology. Cambridge: Cambridge University Press.

Engle, Earl T. 1932. Effects of Extracts of the Anterior Pituitary and Similar Active Principles of Blood and Urine. In Edgar Allen (Ed.), Sex and Internal Secretions, 765–804. Baltimore, Md.: Williams and Wilkins.

———. 1958. Obituary. Journal of Clinical Endocrinology and Metabolism 18:670–73.

Engle, Earl T., and Roger C. Crafts. 1939. Uterine Effects from Single Treatments of Stilboestrol and Ethinyl-Estradiol in Monkeys. Proceedings of the Society for Experimental Biology and Medicine 42:293–96.

Epstein, Steven. 1996. Impure Science: AIDS, Activism, and the Politics of Knowledge. Berkeley: University of California Press.

Estes, Carroll L. 1979. The Aging Enterprise. San Francisco: Jossey-Bass.

Estes, Carroll L., and Elizabeth A. Binney. 1989. The Biomedicalization of Aging: Dangers and Dilemmas. Gerontologist 29:587–96.

Evans, Herbert M. 1939. Endocrine Glands: Gonads, Pituitary and Adrenals. Annual Review of Physiology 1:577–651.

———. 1959. Foreword to H. H. Cole and P. T. Cupps, Reproduction in Domestic Animals. New York: Academic Press.

Evans, Herbert M., and H. H. Cole. 1931. An Introduction to the Study of the Oestrous Cycle in the Dog. Memoirs of the University of California 9(2):65–118.

Evans, Herbert M., and Barbara Cowles. 1940. The Endocrine Literature of 1939. Endocrinology 26:906–12.

Evans, Herbert M., and Marian Simpson. 1928. Antagonism of Growth and Sex Hormones of the Anterior Hypophysis. Journal of the American Medical Association 91:1337–38.

Evans, Mary Alice, and Howard Ensign Evans. 1970. William Morton Wheeler, Biologist. Cambridge, Mass.: Harvard University Press.

Everett, John W., and Charles H. Sawyer. 1987. Endocrinology and Reproductive Biology. In John E. Pauly (Ed.), The American Association of Anatomists, 1888–1897, 183–97. Baltimore, Md.: Williams and Wilkins.

Farber, Paul L. 1982a. The Emergence of Ornithology as a Scientific Discipline. Boston: D. Reidel.

———. 1982b. The Transformation of Natural History in the Nineteenth Century. Journal of the History of Biology 15:145–52.

Farberman, Harvey A. 1979. A Review Symposium: Anselm L. Strauss—Negotiations: Varieties, Contexts, Processes and Social Order. Symbolic Interaction 2:153–68.

Faris, Robert E. L. 1965. Chicago Sociology, 1920–1932. Chicago: University of Chicago Press.

Farley, John. 1982. Gametes and Spores: Ideas about Sexual Reproduction, 1750–1914. Baltimore, Md.: Johns Hopkins University Press.

Farley, John, and Gerald L. Geison. 1974. Science, Politics and Spontaneous Generation in Nineteenth-Century France: The Pasteur-Pouchet Debate. Bulletin of the History of Medicine 48:161–98.

Fausto-Sterling, Anne. 1989. Life in the XY Corral. Women's Studies International Forum 12:319–31.

———. 1990. Personal statement. Course syllabus, The Biology of Gender, Brown University.

———. 1992. Myths of Gender: Biological Theories about Women and Men. 2d ed. New York: Basic Books.

———. 1993. The Five Sexes. The Sciences, March–April, 20–25.

———. 1998. Body-Building: How Biologists Construct Sexuality. New York: Basic Books.

Fechheimer, N. S. 1986. Interrelationships between Recent Developments in Molecular Genetics and Cytogenetics and Animal Breeding. Journal of Dairy Science 69:1743–51.

Fee, Elizabeth, and Nancy Krieger (Eds.). 1994. Women's Health, Politics, and Power: Essays on Sex/Gender, Medicine and Public Health. Amityville, N.Y.: Baywood.

Fee, Elizabeth, and Michael Wallace. 1979. The History and Politics of Birth Control: A Review Essay. Feminist Studies 5:201–15.

Ferguson, Russell, Martha Gever, Trinh T. Minh-ha, and Cornel West (Eds.). 1990. Out There: Marginalization and Contemporary Cultures. New York, and Cambridge, Mass.: New Museum of Contemporary Art and MIT Press.

Fessenden, Ford. 1996. Infertility, Inc. Ladies' Home Journal, April, 66–70.

Fevold, H. L., F. L. Hisaw, and Roy O. Greep. 1936. Effect of Estrin on Activity of the Anterior Lobe of the Pituitary. American Journal of Physiology 114:508.

Fevold, H. L., F. L. Hisaw, and S. L. Leonard. 1931. The Gonad-Stimulating and the Leutinizing Hormones of the Anterior Lobe of the Hypophysis. American Journal of Physiology 97:291–301.

Fields, Rita Ann Schlumpberger. 1992. Micromanipulation of Sheep and Goat Embryos to Facilitate Interspecies Pregnancy. Ph.D. diss., University of California, Davis.

Fiennes, R. N. (Ed.). 1966. Some Recent Developments in Comparative Medicine. Symposium of the Zoological Society of London No. 17. London: Academic Press for the Zoological Society.

Fildes, Valerie, Lara Marks, and Hilary Marland (Eds.). 1992. Women and Children First: International Maternal and Infant Welfare, 1870–1945. New York: Routledge.

Finger, Anne. 1984. Claiming All of Our Bodies: Reproductive Rights and Disabilities. In Rita Arditti, Renate Duelli Klein, and Shelly Minden (Eds.), Test Tube Women: What Future for Motherhood?, 281–97. Boston: Pandora/Routledge.

———. 1985. Reproductive Rights and Disability. In Susan E. Browne, Debra Connors, and Nanci Stern (Eds.), With the Power of Each Breath: A Disabled Women's Anthology, 292–307. Pittsburgh: Cleis.

Finkelstein, Michael. 1966. Professor Bernhard Zondek: An Interview. Journal of Reproduction and Fertility 12:3–19.

Finlay, Mark R. 1988. The German Agricultural Experiment Stations and the Beginnings of American Agricultural Research. Agricultural History 62(2):174–99.

———. 1990. The Industrial Utilization of Farm Products and By-products: The USDA Regional Research Laboratories. Agricultural History 64(2):41–52.

Finley, Lucinda. 1996. The Pharmaceutical Industry and Women's Reproductive Health. In Elizabeth Szockyj and James G. Fox (Eds.), Corporate Victimization of Women, 59–110. Boston: Northeastern University Press.

Fisher, Donald. 1990. Boundary Work and Science: The Relation between Power and Knowledge. In Susan E. Cozzens and Thomas F. Gieryn (Eds.), Theories of Science in Society, 98–119. Bloomington: Indiana University Press.

——. 1993. Fundamental Development of the Social Sciences: Rockefeller Philanthropy and the United States Social Science Research Council. Ann Arbor: University of Michigan Press.

Fisher, Sue. 1986. In the Patient's Best Interest: Women and the Politics of Medical Decisions. New Brunswick, N.J.: Rutgers University Press.

Fitzgerald, Deborah. Yeoman No More: The Industrialization of American Agriculture. Manuscript in progress.

Fleck, Ludwick. 1935/1979. Genesis and Development of a Scientific Fact. Chicago: University of Chicago Press.

Fletcher, Suzanne W., Robert H. Fletcher, and M. Andrew Greganti. 1981. Clinical Research Trends in General Medical Journals, 1946–1976. In Edward B. Roberts, Robert I. Levy, Stan N. Finkelstein, Jay Moscowitz, and Edward J. Sondik (Eds.), Biomedical Innovation, 284–300. Cambridge, Mass.: MIT Press.

Flood, Dom Peter (Ed.). 1955. Medical Experimentation on Man. Translated by M. G. Carroll. Chicago: Henry Regnery.

Folbre, Nancy. 1994. Who Pays for the Kids? Gender and the Structures of Constraint. New York: Routledge.

Foote, Robert H. 1981. The Artificial Insemination Industry. In Benjamin G. Brachett, George E. Seidel Jr., and Sarah M. Seidel (Eds.), New Technologies in Animal Biology, 203–59. New York: Academic Press.

Forbes, Thomas R. 1946. The Origin of the Freemartin. Bulletin of the History of Medicine 20:461–66.

Foucault, Michel. 1975. The Birth of the Clinic. New York: Vintage.

——. 1977. Discipline and Punish. Harmondsworth, England: Penguin.

——. 1978. The History of Sexuality. Volume 1: An Introduction. New York: Vintage.

Fox, Renee C., and Judith P. Swazey. 1973. The Courage to Fail: A Social View of Organ Transplants and Dialysis. 2d rev. ed. Chicago: University of Chicago Press.

Frank, A. H. 1942. The Endocrine Glands in Health and Disease: Keeping Livestock Healthy. USDA Yearbook of Agriculture 1942:155–78.

Frank, Robert T. 1929. The Female Sex Hormone: Part I. Biology Pharmacology and Chemistry. Part II. Clinical Investigations Based on the Female Sex Hormone Blood Test. Springfield, Ill.: Charles C. Thomas.

——. 1931. The Hormonal Causes of Premenstrual Tension. Archives of Neurology and Psychiatry 7:6.

——. 1935. The Endocrine Aspects of Gynecology. New York: T. Nelson and Sons.

Frank, Robert T., R. G. Gustavson, J. Holloway, D. Hyndman, H. Krueger, and J. White. 1926. The Occurrence and Present Chemical Status of the Female Sex Hormone. Endocrinology 10:260.

Franklin, Sarah. 1993. Essentialism, Which Essentialism? Some Implications of Reproductive and Genetic Techno-science. Journal of Homosexuality 24(3/4):27–39.

——. 1995. Postmodern Procreation: A Cultural Account of Assisted Reproduction. In Faye D. Ginsberg and Rayna Rapp (Eds.), Conceiving the New World Order: The Global Stratification of Reproduction, 323–45. Berkeley: University of California Press.

Freedman, Ronald. 1962. American Studies of Family Planning and Fertility: A

Review of Major Trends and Issues. In Clyde V. Kiser (Ed.), Conference on Research in Family Planning, 1–43. Princeton, N.J.: Princeton University Press.

Freid, Marlene Gerber (Ed.). 1990. From Abortion to Reproductive Freedom: Transforming a Movement. Boston: South End Press.

Freidson, Eliot. 1968. The Impurity of Professional Authority. In Howard S. Becker, Blanche Geer, David Reisman, and Robert Weiss (Eds.), Institutional Office and the Person: Essays Presented to Everett C. Hughes, 47–73. Chicago: Aldine.

———. 1970. Profession of Medicine: A Study of the Sociology of Applied Knowledge. New York: Harper and Row.

———. 1975. Doctoring Together: A Study of Professional Social Control. Chicago: University of Chicago Press.

———. 1981. Professional Dominance and the Ordering of Health Services: Some Consequences. In Peter Conrad and Rochelle Kern (Eds.), The Sociology of Health and Illness: Critical Perspectives. New York: St. Martin's Press.

———. 1994. Professionalism Reborn: Theory, Prophecy and Policy. Chicago: University of Chicago Press.

French, Richard D. 1975. Antivivisection and Medical Science in Victorian Society. Princeton, N.J.: Princeton University Press.

Fuerst, John A. 1982. The Role of Reductionism in the Development of Molecular Biology: Peripheral or Central? Social Studies of Science 12:241–78.

Fujimura, Joan H. 1987. Constructing Doable Problems in Cancer Research: Articulating Alignment. Social Studies of Science 17:257–93.

———. 1988. The Molecular Biological Bandwagon in Cancer Research: Where Social Worlds Meet. Social Problems 35:261–83.

———. 1992. Crafting Science: Standardized Packages, Boundary Objects and "Translation." In Andrew Pickering (Ed.), Science as Practice and Culture, 168–214. Chicago: University of Chicago Press.

———. 1995. Ecologies of Action: Recombining Genes, Molecularizing Cancer and Transforming Biology. In Susan Leigh Star (Ed.), Ecologies of Knowledge: New Directions in the Sociology of Science and Technology, 302–45. Albany: State University of New York Press.

———. 1996. Crafting Science: A Socio-history of the Quest for the Genetics of Cancer. Cambridge, Mass.: Harvard University Press.

Fukui, N. 1923. On a Hitherto Unknown Action of Heat Ray on Testicles. Japanese Medical World 3 (January–December):27–28.

Fulton, John F., and Leonard G. Wilson (Eds.). 1966. Selected Readings in the History of Physiology. 2d ed. Springfield, Ill.: Charles C. Thomas.

Funk, Casimir, and Benjamin Harrow. 1929. The Male Hormone. Proceedings of the Society for Experimental Biology 26:325–26.

Fye, W. Bruce. 1987. The Development of American Physiology: Scientific Medicine in the Nineteenth Century. Baltimore, Md.: Johns Hopkins University Press.

Gabriel, Trip. 1996. The Fertility Market [series of 4 articles]. New York Times, January 7–10.

Gaines, Walter Lee. 1915. A Contribution to the Physiology of Lactation. American Journal of Physiology 38:285–312.

Galison, Peter. 1997. Image and Logic: The Material Culture of Modern Physics. Cambridge, Mass.: Harvard University Press.

Galison, Peter, and David J. Stump (Eds.). 1996. The Disunity of Science: Boundaries, Contexts, and Power. Stanford, Calif.: Stanford University Press.

Gamson, Joshua. 1990. Rubber Wars: Struggles over the Condom in the United States. Journal of the History of Sexuality 1:262–82.

Gapen, P. 1987. Don't Expect New Abortion Drugs in U.S. Wall Street Journal, September 11.

Gardner, Eldon J. 1972. History of Biology. Minneapolis, Minn.: Burgess.

Gasking, Elizabeth. 1967. Investigations into Generation 1651–1828. Baltimore, Md.: Johns Hopkins University Press.

Gatens, Moira. 1996. Imaginary Bodies: Ethics, Power and Corporeality. London: Routledge.

Geddes, Donald Porter (Ed.). 1954. An Analysis of the Kinsey Reports on Sexual Behavior in the Human Male and Female. New York: Dutton.

Geddes, Patrick, and J. Arthur Thompson. 1889. The Evolution of Sex. London: W. Scott.

Geiger, Roger L. 1993. Research and Relevant Knowledge: American Research Universities since World War II. New York: Oxford University Press.

Geiger, Roger L. 1986. To Advance Knowledge: The Growth of American Research Universities. New York: Oxford University Press.

Geison, Gerald L. 1978. Michael Foster and the Cambridge School of Physiology: The Scientific Enterprise in Late Victorian Society. Princeton, N.J.: Princeton University Press.

———. 1979. Divided We Stand: Physiologists and Clinicians in the American Context. In Morris J. Vogel and Charles E. Rosenberg (Eds.), The Therapeutic Revolution: Essays in the Social History of American Medicine, 67–90. Philadelphia: University of Pennsylvania Press.

———. 1981. Scientific Change, Emerging Specialties and Research Schools. History of Science 19:20–40.

———. 1995. The Private Science of Louis Pasteur. Princeton, N.J.: Princeton University Press.

——— (Ed). 1983. Professions and Professional Ideology in America. Chapel Hill: University of North Carolina Press.

———. 1987. Physiology in the American Context, 1850–1940. Bethesda, Md.: American Physiological Society.

Geison, Gerald L., and Frederic L. Holmes (Eds.). 1993. Research Schools: Historical Reappraisals. Osiris 8:vii–238.

Gelb, Steven A. 1990. Degeneracy Theory, Eugenics and Family Studies. Journal of the History of Behavioral Sciences 26:242–46.

Gelijns, Annetine C., and C. Ok Pannenborg. 1993. The Development of Contraceptive Technology: Case Studies of Incentives and Disincentives to Innovation. International Journal of Technology Assessment in Health Care 9:210–32.

Germain, Adrienne. 1993. Are We Speaking the Same Language? Women's Health Advocates and Scientists Talk about Contraceptive Technology. Four Essays on

Birth Control Needs and Risks. New York: International Women's Health Coalition.

Germain, Adrienne, and Ruth Dixon-Mueller. 1993. Whose Life Is It, Anyway? Assessing the Relative Risks of Contraception and Pregnancy. Four Essays on Birth Control Needs and Risks. New York: International Women's Health Coalition.

Gerrity, Marybeth. 1993. Legislative Efforts Affecting the Reproductive Biology Laboratory. Current Opinion in Obstetrics and Gynecology 5:623–29.

Gerson, Elihu M. 1983. Scientific Work and Social Worlds. Knowledge 4:357–77.

Gerstman, G., T. Gross, D. Kennedy, R. Bennett, D. Tomita, and B. Stadel. 1991. Trends in the Content and Use of Oral Contraceptives in the United States, 1964–1988. American Journal of Public Health 81:90–96.

Gibbons, Ann. 1990. NIH Panel: Bovine Hormone Gets the Nod. Science 250:1506.

Gieryn, Thomas F. 1983. Boundary-work and the Demarcation of Science from Non-science: Strains and Interests in Professional Ideologies of Scientists. American Sociological Review 48:781–95.

———. 1995. Boundaries of Science. In Sheila Jasanoff, Gerald E. Markle, James Petersen, and Trevor Pinch (Eds.), Handbook of Science and Technology Studies, 393–445. Thousand Oaks, Calif.: Sage.

Gilbert, Scott F. 1978. The Embryological Origins of the Gene Theory. Journal of the History of Biology 11:307–51.

——— 1987. In Friendly Disagreement: Wilson, Morgan, and the Embryological Origins of the Gene Theory. American Zoologist 27:797–806.

———. (Ed.). 1991. A Conceptual History of Modern Embryology. Developmental Biology: A Comprehensive Synthesis, 7. New York: Plenum Press.

Gillam, Richard, and Barton Bernstein. 1987. Doing Harm: The DES Tragedy and Modern American Medicine. Public Historian 9(1):57–82.

Gillis, John R., Louise A. Tilly, and David Levine (Eds.). 1992. The European Experience of Declining Fertility: A Quiet Revolution, 1850–1970. Cambridge, Mass.: Blackwell Publishers.

Ginsberg, Faye D., and Rayna Rapp (Eds.). 1995. Conceiving the New World Order: The Global Stratification of Reproduction. Berkeley: University of California Press.

Gittins, Diana. 1982. Fair Sex: Family Size and Structure in Britain, 1900–39. New York: St. Martin's Press.

Glaser, Barney G. 1978. Theoretical Sensitivity: Advances in the Methodology of Grounded Theory. Mill Valley, Calif.: Sociology Press.

Glaser, Barney G., and Anselm L. Strauss. 1968. The Discovery of Grounded Theory: Strategies for Qualitative Research. New York: Aldine.

Glick, Thomas F. 1976. On the Diffusion of a New Specialty: Maranon and the Crisis of Endocrinology in Spain. Journal of the History of Biology 9:287–300.

Goffman, Erving. 1963. Stigma: The Management of Spoiled Identity. Harmondsworth, England: Penguin.

Goldstein, Jan. 1984. Foucault among the Sociologists: Discipline and History. History and Theory 23:172–92.

Goldzieher, Joseph W. 1993. The History of Steroidal Contraceptive Development: The Estrogens. Perspectives in Biology and Medicine 36:363–68.

Goodfield, June. 1960. The Growth of Scientific Physiology. New York: Harper Colophon.

Gorbman, Aubrey. 1979. Emil Witschi and the Problem of Vertebrate Sexual Differentiation. American Zoologist 19:1261–70.

Gordon, Linda. 1975. The Politics of Birth Control, 1920–1940: The Impact of Professionals. International Journal of Health Services 5:253–77.

———. 1976/1990. Woman's Body, Woman's Right: A Social History of Birth Control in America. First and second editions. New York: Viking.

Gossel, Patricia. 1992. A Need for Standard Methods: The Case of American Bacteriology. In Adele Clarke and Joan Fujimura (Eds.), The Right Tools for the Job: At Work in Twentieth-Century Life Sciences, 287–311. Princeton, N.J.: Princeton University Press.

Gould, Stephen J. 1984. Just in the Middle: A Solution to the Mechanist-Vitalist Controversy. Natural History 97 (January):24–33.

Graefenberg, E. 1931. Intrauterine Methods: An Intrauterine Contraceptive Method. In Margaret Sanger and Hannah M. Stone (Eds.), The Practice of Contraception: Proceedings of the Seventh International Birth Control Conference, 33–47. Baltimore, Md.: Williams and Wilkens.

Graham, Loren, Wolf Lepenies, and Peter Weingart (Eds.). 1983. Functions and Uses of Disciplinary History. Dordrecht and Boston: D. Reidel/Kluwer.

Granovetter, Marc S. 1973. The Strength of Weak Ties. American Journal of Sociology 78:1360–80.

Grant, Nicole J. 1992. The Selling of Contraception: The Dalkon Shield Case, Sexuality and Women's Autonomy. Columbus: Ohio State University Press.

Green, W. W., and L. M. Winters. 1935. Studies on the Physiology of Reproduction in the Sheep. III. The Time of Ovulation and the Rate of Sperm Travel. Anatomical Record 61:457–67.

Greenhalgh, Susan. 1996. The Social Construction of Population Science: An Intellectual, Institutional and Political History of Twentieth-Century Demography. Comparative Studies in Society and History 38:26–66.

——— (Ed.). 1995. Situating Fertility: Anthropology and Demographic Inquiry. Cambridge: Cambridge University Press.

Greenhalgh, Susan, and Jiali Li. 1995. Engendering Reproductive Policy and Practice in Peasant China: For a Feminist Demography of Reproduction. Signs 20:601–40.

Greenwood, A. W. (Ed.). 1931. Proceedings of the Second International Congress for Sex Research, London, 1930. London: Oliver and Boyd.

Greep, Roy O. 1967. The Saga and the Science of the Gonadotrophins. The Dale Lecture. Journal of Endocrinology (Proceedings of the Society) 39:ii–ix.

———. 1972. In Honor of Emil Witschi. American Zoologist 12:175–77.

———. 1973. A Vista of Research on the Gonadotrophins. Fourth Hartman Lecture. Biology of Reproduction 8:2–10.

———. 1985. Edwin Bennet Astwood, December 29, 1909–February 17, 1976. Biographical Memoirs of the National Academy of Science 55:3–42.

Greep, Roy O., and Marjorie A. Koblinsky. 1977. Frontiers in Reproduction and

Fertility Control: A Review of the Reproductive Sciences and Contraceptive Development. Boston: MIT Press (Ford Foundation).

Greep, Roy O., Marjorie A. Koblinsky, and F. S. Jaffe. 1976. Reproduction and Human Welfare: A Challenge to Research. Boston: MIT Press (Ford Foundation).

Gregg, Alan. 1955. A Medical Aspect of the Population Problem. Science 121:681–82. Reprinted in Garrett Hardin (Ed.), 1964. Population, Evolution and Birth Control: A Collage of Controversial Readings. San Francisco: Freeman.

Gregory, Jennie. 1935. An Evaluation of Periodical Literature from the Standpoint of Endocrinology. Endocrinology 19:213–15.

Gregson, Mary Eschelbach. 1993. Specialization in Late-Nineteenth-Century Agriculture: Missouri as a Test Case. Agricultural History 67:16–35.

Griesemer, James. 1994. Tools for Talking: Human Nature, Weismannism and the Interpretation of Genetic Information. In Carl Cranor (Ed.), Are Genes Us? The Social Consequences of the New Genetics, 69–88. New Brunswick, N.J.: Rutgers University Press.

———. Forthcoming. The Informational Gene and the Substantial Body: On the Generalization of Evolutionary Theory by Abstraction. In Nancy Cartwright and M. Jones (Eds.), Varieties of Idealization. Poznan Studies Series. Amsterdam: Rodopi Publishers.

Griffiths, W. F. B., and E. C. Amoroso. 1939. Proestrus, Oestrus, Ovulation and Mating in the Greyhound Bitch. Veterinary Record 51:1279–84.

Gruhn, John G., and Ralph R. Kazer. 1989. Hormonal Regulation of the Menstrual Cycle: The Evolution of Concepts. New York: Plenum Medical Book Company.

Gunn, A. D. G. 1987. Oral Contraception in Perspective: Thirty Years of Clinical Experience with the Pill. Park Ridge, N.J.: Parthenon.

Gustavson, R. G. 1939. Bioassay of Androgens and Estrogens. In Edgar Allen (Ed.), Sex and Internal Secretions, 877–900. 2d ed. Baltimore, Md.: Williams and Wilkins.

Guttmacher, Alan Frank. 1933. Life in the Making. Garden City, N.Y.: Garden City Publishers.

Guttmacher, Alan Frank. 1938. Practical Experience with Artificial Insemination. Journal of Contraception 3(4):75–77.

Hacking, Ian. 1983. Representing and Intervening. Cambridge: Cambridge University Press.

Hahn, R. 1987. Division of Labor: Obstetricians, Women, and Society in *Williams' Obstetrics*, 1903–1985. Medical Anthropology Quarterly, n.s., 1(3):256–82.

Hall, Diana Long. 1974. Biology, Sex Hormones and Sexism in the 1920s. Philosophical Forum 5:81–96.

———. 1976. The Critic and the Advocate: Contrasting British Views on the State of Endocrinology in the 1920s. Journal of the History of Biology 9:269–85.

———. 1978. Sex, Fertility and Taboo: The Committee for Research on Problems of Sex, 1920–1940. Unpublished paper, presented at Workshop on Historical Perspectives on the Scientific Study of Fertility in the United States, American Academy of Arts and Sciences, Boston.

———. 1979. Academics, Bluestockings and Biologists: Women at the University of Chicago, 1892–1932. Annals of the New York Academy of Sciences 42:300–320.

Hall, Diana Long, and Thomas F. Glick. 1976. Endocrinology: A Brief Introduction. Journal of the History of Biology 9:229–33. [See also Diana Long.]

Haller, John S. 971. Outcasts from Evolution: Scientific Attitudes of Racial Inferiority, 1859–1900. New York: McGraw-Hill.

———. 1981. American Medicine in Transition. Urbana: University of Illinois Press.

Haller, John S., and Robin M. Haller. 1974. The Physician and Sexuality in Victorian America. Urbana: University of Illinois Press.

Haller, Mark. 1963. Eugenics: Hereditarian Attitudes in American Thought. New Brunswick, N.J.: Rutgers University Press.

Halpern, Sydney A. 1988. American Pediatrics: The Social Dynamics of Professionalism, 1880–1980. Berkeley: University of California Press.

Hamblen, E. C. 1939. Endocrine Gynecology. Springfield, Ill.: Charles C.Thomas.

Hamburger, Viktor. 1980. Embryology and the Modern Synthesis in Evolutionary Theory. In Ernst Mayr and William B. Provine (Eds.), The Evolutionary Synthesis: Perspectives on the Unification of Biology, 97–111. Cambridge, Mass.: Harvard University Press.

Hamilton, David. 1986. The Monkey Gland Affair. London: Chatto and Windus.

Hammond, John. 1925. Reproduction in the Rabbit. Edinburgh: Oliver and Boyd.

———. 1927. The Physiology of Reproduction in the Cow. New York: Cambridge University Press.

Hammonds, Evelynn. 1994. Black (W)holes and the Geometry of Black Female Sexuality. Differences 6(2–3):126–45.

Haraway, Donna. 1976. Crystals, Fabrics and Fields: Metaphors of Organicism in Twentieth-Century Developmental Biology. New Haven, Conn.: Yale University Press.

———. 1989. Primate Visions: Gender, Race and Nature in the World of Modern Science. New York: Routledge.

———. 1991. Simians, Cyborgs and Women: The Reinvention of Nature. New York: Routledge.

———. 1992. The Promises of Monsters: A Regenerative Politics for Inappropriate/d Others. In Lawrence Grossberg, Cary Nelson, and Paula Treichler (Eds.), Cultural Studies, 295–337. New York: Routledge.

———. 1995. Universal Donors in a Vampire Culture: It's All in the Family: Biological Kinship Categories in the Twentieth-Century United States. In William Cronon (Ed.), Uncommon Ground: Toward Reinventing Nature, 321–78. New York: Norton.

Hard, Mikael. 1993. Beyond Harmony and Consensus: A Social Conflict Approach to Technology. Science, Technology and Human Values 18:408–32.

Hardin, Garrett. 1993. Living within the Limits: Ecology, Economics, and Population Taboos. New York: Oxford University Press.

Harding, Sandra. 1991. Whose Science? Whose Knowledge? Thinking from Women's Lives. Ithaca, N.Y.: Cornell University Press.

Harding, Sandra, and Jean F. O'Barr (Eds.). 1987. Sex and Scientific Inquiry. Chicago: University of Chicago Press.

Hardon, Anita. 1992. Norplant: Conflicting Views on Its Safety and Acceptability. In Helen Bequaert Holmes (Ed.), Issues in Reproductive Technology I: An Anthology, 11–30. New York. Garland.

Harr, John Ensor, and Peter J. Johnson. 1988. The Rockefeller Century. New York: Scribner's.

Harrison, Brian. 1981. Women's Health and the Women's Movement in Britain, 1840–1940. In Charles Webster (Ed.), Biology, Medicine and Society, 1840–1940, 15–71. Cambridge: Cambridge University Press.

Harrison, Ross Granville. 1937. Embryology and Its Relations. Science 85:369–74.

——. 1969. The Organization and Development of the Embryo. Sally Willens (Ed.). New Haven, Conn.: Yale University Press.

Harrower, Henry R. 1913. Anatomy: Its Scope, Methods, and Relations to Other Biological Sciences. Anatomical Record 7:401–10.

——. 1917. The Internal Secretions in Practical Medicine. 2d ed. Chicago: Chicago Medical Book Company.

Hart, G. H., and H. H. Cole. 1934. The Source of Oestrin in the Pregnant Mare. American Journal of Physiology 109:320–23.

Hartman, Carl G. 1920. Studies in the Development of the Opossum V. The Phenomena of Parturition. Anatomical Record 18:251–61.

——. 1921. Dioestrus Changes in the Mammary Gland of the Opossum and the Diagnosis of Pregnancy. American Journal of Physiology 55:308–9.

——. 1923. The Oestrus Cycle in the Opossum. American Journal of Anatomy 32:353–421.

——. 1924. Observation on the Viability of the Mammalian Ovum. American Journal of Obstetrics and Gynecology 7:40–43.

——. 1930. Bimanual Rectal Palpation as Applied to the Female Rhesus Monkey. Anatomical Record 45:263.

——. 1931. On the Relative Sterility of the Adolescent Organism. Science 74:226–27.

——. 1932a. Ovulation and the Transport and Viability of Ova and Sperm in the Female Genital Tract. In Edgar Allen (Ed.), Sex and Internal Secretions, 647–732. Baltimore, Md.: Williams and Wilkins.

——. 1932b. Studies in the Reproduction of the Monkey Macacus rhesus, with Special Reference to Menstruation and Pregnancy. Carnegie Contributions to Embryology, no. 134:1–161.

——. 1933. Catholic Advice on the Safe Period. Birth Control Review 17 (May):117–19.

——. 1936. Time of Ovulation in Women: A Study on the Fertile Period in the Menstrual Cycle. Baltimore, Md.: Williams and Wilkins.

——. 1937. Facts and Fallacies of the Safe Period. Journal of Contraception 2:51–61.

——. 1939. Studies on Reproduction in the Monkey and Their Bearing in Gynecology and Anthropology. Endocrinology 25:670–82.

——. 1945. The Mating of Mammals. In E. J. Farris (Ed.), Special Issue on Animal Colony Maintenance. Annals of the New York Academy of Science 46 (June 15):23–44.

——. 1956. The Scientific Achievements of George W. Corner. American Journal of Anatomy 98:5–19.

———. 1959. Annotated List of Published Reports on Clinical Trials with Contraceptives. Fertility and Sterility 10(2):177–89.

———. 1962. Science and the Safe Period: A Compendium of Human Reproduction. Baltimore, Md.: Williams and Wilkins.

———. 1967. Research Should Spell FUN. In G. W. Duncan, R. J. Ericsson, and R. G. Zimbelman (Eds.), Capacitation of Spermatozoa and Endocrine Control of Spermatogenesis, 1–10. Oxford: Blackwell Scientific.

Hartman, Carl G., and George W. Corner. 1941. The First Maturation Division of the Macaque Ovum. Carnegie Contributions to Embryology, no. 179:1–14.

Hartman, Carl G., and W. M. Firor. 1937. Is There a Hormone of Menstruation? Quarterly Review of Biology 12:85–88.

Hartman, Carl G., and W. L. Strauss, Jr. 1961. The Anatomy of the Rhesus Monkey. New York: Hafner.

Hartman, Carl G., and W. L. Strauss, Jr. (Eds.). 1933. The Anatomy of the Rhesus Monkey. Baltimore, Md.: Williams and Wilkins.

Hartmann, Betsy. 1987/1995. Reproductive Rights and Wrongs: The Global Politics of Population Control and Contraceptive Choice. 1st and 2d editions. New York: Harper and Row.

Hartmann, Betsy. 1992. Contraceptives: A Multitude of Meanings. In Helen Bequaert Holmes (Ed.), Issues in Reproductive Technology I: An Anthology, 3–10. New York. Garland.

Hartouni, Valerie. 1997. Cultural Conceptions: On Reproductive Technologies and the Remaking of Life. Minneapolis: University of Minnesota Press.

Harvey, A. McGehee. 1976. Adventures in Medical Research: A Century of Discovery at Johns Hopkins. Baltimore, Md.: Johns Hopkins University Press.

———. 1981. Science at the Bedside: Clinical Research in American Medicine, 1905–1945. Baltimore, Md.: Johns Hopkins University Press.

Harvey, David. 1989. The Condition of Postmodernity: An Enquiry into the Origins of Cultural Change. Cambridge: Basil Blackwell.

Hawkins, Hugh. 1960. Pioneer: A History of the Johns Hopkins University, 1874–1889. Ithaca, N.Y.: Cornell University Press.

Hays, Samuel P. 1972. Introduction: The New Organizational Society. In Jerry Israel (Ed.), Building the Organizational Society: Essays on Associational Activists in Modern America, 1–15. New York: Free Press.

Heape, Walter. 1894. The Menstruation of *Semnopithecus entellus*. Philosophical Transactions of the Royal Society of London. Proceedings of the Royal Society of London. Series B: Biological Sciences 185:411–71.

———. 1897. The Artificial Insemination of Mammals and Subsequent Possible Fretilization or Impregnation of their Ova. Proceedings of the Royal Society of London. Series B: Biological Sciences 65:99–111.

———. 1898. On Menstruation of Monkeys and the Human Female. Transactions of the Obstetrical Society 40:161–74.

———. 1899. Abortion, Barrenness and Fertility in Sheep. Journal of the Royal Agricultural Society, 3d ser., 10:1–32.

———. 1900. On the "Sexual Season" of Mammals and the Relation of the Pro-Oestrum to Menstruation. Quarterly Journal of Microscopic Science 44:1–70.

———. 1905. Ovulation and Degeneration of Ova in the Rabbit. Proceedings of the Royal Society of London. Series B: Biological Sciences 76:260–68.

———. 1906. The Breeding Industry: Its Value to the Country and Its Needs. Cambridge: Cambridge University Press.

———. 1913. Sex Antagonism. New York: Putnam.

———. 1914. Preparation for Marriage. London: Cassell.

Henle, Werner. 1937. The Relation of Spermatoxic Immunity to Fertility. Journal of Contraception 3:30–33.

Henriksen, E. 1941. Pregnancy Tests of the Past and Present. Western Journal of Surgical Obstetric Gynecology 85:610–18.

Herbst, Jurgen. 1983. Diversification in American Education. In Konrad H. Jarausch (Ed.), The Transformation of Higher Learning 1860–1930, 198–224. Chicago: University of Chicago Press.

Herman, Harry A. 1981. Improving Cattle by the Millions: NAAB and the Development and Worldwide Application of Artificial Insemination. Columbia: University of Missouri Press.

Herrnstein, Richard J., and Charles Murray. 1994. The Bell Curve: Intelligence and Class Structure in American Life. New York: Free Press.

Hertz, Roy. 1984. A Quest for Better Contraception: The Ford Foundation's Contribution to Reproductive Science and Contraceptive Development, 1959–1983. Contraception 29:287–319.

Heuser, Chester H., and George L. Streeter. 1941. Development of the Macaque Embryo. Carnegie Contributions to Embryology, no. 181:15–55.

Hicks, Karen. 1994. Surviving the Dalkon Shield IUD: Women vs. the Pharmaceutical Industry. New York. Teacher's College Press.

Hiddinga, Anja. 1987 Obstetrical Research in the Netherlands in the Nineteenth Century. Medical History 31: 281–305.

Higham, John. 1978. Strangers in the Land: Patterns of American Nativism 1860–1925. New York: Atheneum.

Hilgard, Ernest R. 1965. Robert Means Yerkes, 1876–1956. Biographical Memoirs of the National Academy of Sciences 38:384–411.

Hilgartner, Stephen, and Charles Bosk. 1988. The Rise and Fall of Social Problems: A Public Arenas Model. American Journal of Sociology 94:53–78.

Himes, Norman E. 1936. Medical History of Contraception. Baltimore, Md.: Williams and Wilkins.

Hinsey, Joseph C. 1967. The Role of Private Foundations in the Development of Modern Medicine. In Warren Weaver (Ed.), U.S. Philanthropic Foundations, 74–92. New York: Harper and Row.

Hirsch, Walter. 1974. The Autonomy of Science. In Sal P. Restivo and Christopher K. Vanderpool (Eds.), Comparative Studies in Science and Society, 194–221. Columbus, Ohio: Merrill.

Hirschauer, Stefan. 1991. The Manufacture of Bodies in Surgery. Social Studies of Science 21:279–320.

———. 1992. The Meanings of Transsexuality. In J. Lachmundt and G. Stollberg (Eds.), The Social Construction of Illness, 174–99. Stuttgart/New York: Steiner.

———. 1998. Shifting Contradictions: Doing Sex and Doing Gender in Medical Disciplines. To appear in Annemarie Mol and Marc Berg (Eds.), Differences in Medicine. Durham, N.C.: Duke University Press.

Hisaw, Frederick L. 1932. Physiology of the Corpus Luteum. In Edgar Allen (Ed.), Sex and Internal Secretions, 499–543. Baltimore, Md.: Williams and Wilkins.

———. 1956. Award of the Medal of the Endocrine Society. Journal of Clinical Endocrinology and Metabolism 16(2):992–93.

Hisaw, Frederick L., and R. K. Meyer. 1929. The Oestrus Hormone in the Urine of Pregnant Cows. Proceedings of the Society of Experimental Biology and Medicine 26:586.

Hisaw, Frederick L., R. K. Meyer, and H. L. Fevold. 1930. Production of a Premenstrual Endometrium in Castrated Monkeys by Ovarian Hormones. Proceedings of the Society of Experimental Biology and Medicine 27:400.

Hodgson, Dennis. 1983. Demography as Social Science and Policy Science. Population and Development Review 9:1–34.

———. 1988. Orthodoxy and Revisionism in American Demography. Population and Development Review 14:541–69.

———. 1991. The Ideological Origins of the Population Association of America. Population and Development Review 17:1–34.

Hofmann, Fredrick G. 1967. Editorial: The Fiftieth Anniversary. Endocrinology 80:1–4.

Hogben, Lancelot. 1974. Francis Albert Eley Crew, 1886–1973. Biographical Memoirs of Fellows of the Royal Society 20:134–53.

Holden, Constance. 1989. Briefings: Sex Secrets Safe. Science 245:599.

Hollender, Marc H. 1970. The Medical Profession and Sex in 1900. American Journal of Obstetrics and Gynecology 108:139–48.

Holmes, Helen Bequaert (Ed.). 1992. Issues in Reproductive Technology. New York: Garland.

Holmes, Helen, Betty B. Hoskins, and Michael Gross (Eds.). 1980. Birth Control and Controlling Birth: Women-Centered Perspectives. Clifton, N.J.: Humana Press.

Horder, T. J. 1986. Origins of the Embryological Tradition in the United States. In T. J. Horder, J. A. Witkowski, and C. C. Wylie (Eds.), A History of Embryology: The Eighth Symposium of the British Society for Developmental Biology, 109–12. Cambridge: Cambridge University Press.

Horder, T. J., J. A. Witkowski, and C. C. Wylie (Eds.). 1986. A History of Embryology: The Eighth Symposium of the British Society for Developmental Biology. Cambridge: Cambridge University Press.

Horn, David G. 1994. Social Bodies: Science, Reproduction and Italian Modernity. Princeton, N.J.: Princeton University Press.

Horowitz, Maryanne Cline. 1987. The Science of Embryology before the Discovery of the Ovum. In M. Boxer, J. H. Quataert, and J. W. Scott (Eds.), Connecting Spheres: Women in the Western World, 1500 to the Present, 238–54. New York: Oxford University Press.

Houck, Ulysses Grant. 1924. The Bureau of Animal Industry of the United States Department of Agriculture: Its Establishment, Achievements, and Current Activities. Washington, D.C.: Hayworth Printing Company.

Howard-Jones, Norman. 1982. Human Experimentation in Historical and Ethical Perspectives. Social Science and Medicine 16:1429–48.

Howe, Barbara. 1982. The Emergence of Scientific Philanthropy, 1900–1920: Origins, Issues and Outcomes. 25 Robert F. Arnove (Ed.), Philanthropy and Cultural Imperialism: The Foundations at Home and Abroad, 25–54. Bloomington: Indiana University Press.

Hubbard, Ruth. 1990. The Politics of Women's Biology. New Brunswick, N.J.: Rutgers University Press.

Hughes, Everett C. 1962. Good People and Dirty Work. Social Problems 10:3–10.

———. 1971. The Sociological Eye. Chicago: Aldine Atherton.

Hughes, Thomas P. 1989. American Genesis: A Century of Invention and Technological Enthusiasm. New York: Penguin.

Hurt, R. Douglas, and Mary Ellen Hurt. 1994. The History of Agricultural Science and Technology: An International Annotated Bibliography. New York: Garland.

Huxley, Aldous. 1932. Brave New World. London: Chatto and Windus.

Hyman, Libbie H. 1957. Charles Manning Child, 1869–1954. Biographical Memoirs of the National Academy of Sciences 30:73–103.

Hyman, Libbie H., and G. Evelyn Hutchinson. 1991. Libbie Henrietta Hyman, December 6, 1888–August 3, 1969. Biographical Memoirs of the National Academy of Sciences 60:102–14.

Hynes, H. Patricia. 1989. The Recurring Silent Spring. New York: Pergamon Press.

———. 1991. Biotechnology in Agriculture and Reproduction: The Parallels in Public Policy. In Patricia Hynes (Ed.), Reconstructing Babylon: Essays on Women and Technology, 103–30. Bloomington: Indiana University Press.

Ingle, Dwight J. 1971. Gregory Goodwin Pincus, 1903–1967. Biographical Memoirs of the National Academy of Sciences 42:228–47.

Institute of Medicine. 1989. Division of Health Sciences Policy and National Research Council (Board on Agriculture). Medically Assisted Conception: An Agenda for Research. Washington, D.C.: National Academy Press.

Irvine, Janice M. 1990. Disorders of Desire: Sex and Gender in Modern American Sexology. Philadelphia: Temple University Press.

ISNA (Intersex Society of North America). 1995–96. Hermaphrodites with Attitude: A Quarterly Journal. info@isna.org P.O. Box 31791 San Francisco, CA 94131.

Jacobson, Jodi L. 1991. Women's Reproductive Health: The Silent Emergency. Worldwatch Paper 102. Washington, D.C.: Worldwatch Institute.

Janko, Jan. 1977. From Physiological Chemistry to Biochemistry. Acta Historiae Rerum Naturalium nec non Technicarum 9:223–79.

Jarausch, Konrad H. (Ed.). 1983. The Transformation of Higher Learning 1860–1930. Chicago: University of Chicago Press.

Jasanoff, Sheila, Gerald E. Markle, James Petersen, and Trevor Pinch (Eds.). 1995. Handbook of Science and Technology Studies. Thousand Oaks, Calif.: Sage.

Jensen, Joan M. 1981. The Evolution of Margaret Sanger's Family Limitation Pamphlet, 1914–1921. Signs 6:548–67.

Joffe, Carole. 1986. The Regulation of Sexuality: Experiences of Family Planning Workers. Philadelphia: Temple University Press.

———. 1995. Doctors of Conscience: The Struggle to Provide Abortion before and after *Roe v. Wade*. Boston: Beacon Press.

Johnson, R. Christian. 1977. Feminism, Philanthropy and Science in the Development of the Oral Contraceptive Pill. Pharmacy in History 19(2):63–78.

Jonas, Gerald. 1989. The Circuit Riders: Rockefeller Money and the Rise of Modern Science. New York: Norton.

Jones, James, H. 1981. Bad Blood: The Tuskeegee Experiments. New York: Free Press.

Jones, Owen D. 1993. Reproductive Autonomy and Evolutionary Biology: A Regulatory Framework for Trait-Selection Technologies. American Journal of Law and Medicine 19:187–231.

Jordan, Brigitte. 1983. Birth in Four Cultures. Montreal: Eden Press.

Jordanova, Ludmilla. 1989. Sexual Visions: Images of Gender in Science and Medicine between the Eighteenth and Twentieth Centuries. Madison: University of Wisconsin Press.

———. 1993. Gender and the Historiography of Science. British Journal of the History of Science 26:469–83.

———. 1995. Interrogating the Concept of Reproduction in the Eighteenth Century. In Faye D. Ginsberg and Rayna Rapp (Eds.), Conceiving the New World Order: The Global Stratification of Reproduction, 369–86. Berkeley: University of California Press.

Jorgensen, C. Barker. 1971. John Hunter, A. A. Berthold, and the Origins of Endocrinology. Odense, Denmark: Odense University Press.

Josiah Macy, Jr., Foundation. 1950. Twentieth Anniversary Review of the Josiah Macy, Jr., Foundation. New York: Josiah Macy, Jr., Foundation.

———. 1955. The Josiah Macy, Jr., Foundation, 1930–1955: A Review of Activities. New York: Josiah Macy, Jr., Foundation.

Just, Ernest Everett. 1919. The Fertilization Reaction in *Echinarachnius parma*. I–III. Biological Bulletin 36:1–53.

———. 1939. The Biology of the Cell Surface. Philadelphia: Blakiston's.

Kargon, Robert, and Elizabeth Hodes. 1985. Karl Compton, Isaiah Bowman, and the Politics of Science in the Great Depression. Isis 76:301–18.

Kaufert, Patricia A., and Sonja M. McKinlay. 1985. Estrogen Replacement Therapy: The Production of Medical Knowledge and the Emergence of Policy. In Ellen Lewin and Virginia Olesen (Eds.), Women, Health, and Healing: Toward a New Perspective, 113–38. New York: Tavistock.

Kay, Lily E. 1993a. Life as Technology: Representing, Intervening and Molecularizing. Rivista di Storia Scienza, n.s., 1(2):85–103.

———. 1993b. The Molecular Vision of Life: Caltech, the Rockefeller Foundation and the New Biology. New York: Oxford University Press.

Keating, Peter, Alberto Cambrosio, and Michael Mackenzie. 1992. The Tools of the Discipline: Standards, Models, and Measures in the Affinity/Avidity Controversy in Immunology. In Adele Clarke and Joan Fujimura (Eds.), The Right Tools for the Job: At Work in Twentieth-Century Life Sciences, 312–54. Princeton, N.J.: Princeton University Press.

Keibel, Franz, and Franklin P. Mall. 1910. Manual of Human Embryology. Philadelphia: Lippincott.

Keller, Evelyn Fox. 1987. Reproduction and the Central Project of Evolutionary Theory. Biology and Philosophy 2:73–86.

———. 1990. Physics and the Emergence of Molecular Biology: A History of Cognitive and Political Synergy. Journal of the History of Biology 23:389–409.

———. 1992a. The Paradox of Scientific Subjectivity. Annals of Scholarship 9:135–53.

———. 1992b. Secrets of Life, Secrets of Death. New York: Routledge.

———. 1993. Fractured Images of Science, Language and Power: A Postmodern Optic or Just Bad Eyesight? In Ellen Messer-Davidow, David R. Shumway, and David J. Sylvan (Eds.), Knowledges: Historical and Critical Studies in Disciplinarity, 54–69. Charlottesville: University Press of Virginia.

———. 1995. Gender and Science: Origin, History and Politics. Osiris 10:27–38.

Keller, Evelyn Fox, and Elizabeth Lloyd. 1992. Keywords in Evolutionary Biology. Cambridge, Mass.: Harvard University Press.

Kennedy, David M. 1970. Birth Control in America: The Career of Margaret Sanger. New Haven, Conn.: Yale University Press.

Kennedy, W. 1933. The Menarche and Menstrual Type: Notes on Ten Thousand Case Records. Journal of Obstetrics and Gynecology of the British Empire 40:792.

Kentenich, H. 1993. [The Man in Reproductive Medicine: An Invisible Being.] In German. Archives of Gynecology and Obstetrics 254(1–4):1178–84.

Kertzer, David I. 1994. Sacrificed for Honor: Italian Infant Abandonment and the Politics of Reproductive Control. Boston: Beacon Press.

Kessler, Suzanne J. 1990. The Medical Construction of Gender: Case Management of Intersexed Infants. Signs 16:3–26.

Kevles, Daniel J. 1981. Genetics in the United States and Great Britain, 1890–1930: A Review with Speculations. In Charles Webster (Ed.), Biology, Medicine and Society, 1840–1940, 193–215. Cambridge: Cambridge University Press.

———. 1985. In the Name of Eugenics: Genetics and the Uses of Human Heredity. New York: Alfred A. Knopf.

Kevles, Daniel J., and Gerald L. Geison. 1995. The Experimental Life Sciences in the Twentieth Century. Osiris 10:97–121.

Kiger, Joseph C. 1963. American Learned Societies. Washington, D.C.: Public Affairs Press.

Kimmelman, Barbara A. 1983. The American Breeders' Association: Genetics and Eugenics in an Agricultural Context, 1903–1913. Social Studies of Science 13:163–204.

———. 1987. A Progressive Era Discipline: Genetics at American Agricultural Colleges and Experiment Stations, 1890–1920. Ph.D. diss., University of Pennsylvania.

———. 1992. Organisms and Interests in Scientific Research: R. A. Emerson's Claims for the Unique Contribution of Agricultural Genetics. In Adele Clarke and Joan Fujimura (Eds.), The Right Tools for the Job: At Work in Twentieth-Century Life Sciences, 172–97. Princeton, N.J.: Princeton University Press.

King, Jessie L. 1926. Menstrual Records and Vaginal Smears in a Selected Group of Normal Women. Carnegie Contributions to Embryology, no. 95:79–93.

Kingsland, Sharon E. 1991. Toward a Natural History of the Human Psyche: Charles Manning Child, Charles Judson Herrick, and the Dynamic View of the Individual at the University of Chicago. In Keith Benson, Jane Maienschein, and Ronald Rainger (Eds.), The Expansion of American Biology, 195–230. New Brunswick, N.J.: Rutgers University Press.

Kinsey, A., W. Pomeroy, and C. Martin. 1948. Sexual Behavior in the Human Male. Philadelphia: Saunders.

Kinsey, A., W. Pomeroy, C. Martin, and P. Gebhard. 1953. Sexual Behavior in the Human Female. Philadelphia: Saunders.

Klein, Julie Thompson. 1996. Crossing Boundaries: Knowledge, Disciplinarity and Interdisciplinarity. Charlottesville: University Press of Virginia.

Klein, Marc. 1963. Trends in the Methodology of Endocrinological Techniques. In Peter Eckstein and Francis Knowles (Eds.), Techniques in Endocrine Research, 289–302. London: Academic Press.

Kleinman, Daniel L. 1994. Layers of Interests, Layers of Influence: Business and the Genesis of the National Science Foundation. Science, Technology and Human Values 19:259–82.

Kline, Ronald. 1995. Construing "Technology" as "Applied Science": Public Rhetoric of Scientists and Engineers in the United States, 1880–1945. Isis 86:194–221.

Kling, Rob, and Elihu M. Gerson. 1978. Patterns of Segmentation and Intersection in the Computing World. Symbolic Interaction 2:25–43.

Klitsch, M. 1988. The Return of the IUD. Family Planning Perspectives 20:19.

Knaus, Hermann. 1934a. Periodic Fertility and Sterility in Woman: A Natural Method of Birth Control. Chicago: Chicago Medical Book Company.

———. 1934b. Periodic Fertility and Sterility in Women. Vienna: Wm. Maudrich.

Knoblauch, H. C., E. M. Law, and W. P. Meyer. 1962. State Agricultural Experiment Stations: A History of Research Policy and Procedure. Washington, D.C.: USDA Miscellaneous Publication No. 904.

Knorr-Cetina, Karin. 1995. Laboratory Studies: The Cultural Approach to the Study of Science. In Sheila Jasanoff, Gerald E. Markle, James Petersen, and Trevor Pinch (Eds.), Handbook of Science and Technology Studies, 140–66. Thousand Oaks, Calif.: Sage.

Knorr-Cetina, Karin, and Michael Mulkay. 1983. Science Observed: Perspectives on the Social Study of Science. Beverly Hills, Calif.: Sage.

Kobrin, Frances E. 1966. The American Midwife Controversy: A Crisis of Professionalization. Bulletin of the History of Medicine 40:350–63.

Koch, Fred C. 1932. Biochemistry and Assay of the Testis Hormones. In Edgar Allen (Ed.), Sex and Internal Secretions, 372–91. Baltimore, Md.: Williams and Wilkins.

———. 1937. The Male Sex Hormones. Physiological Reviews 17(2):153.

Koenig, Barbara. 1988. The Technological Imperative in Medical Practice: The Social Creation of a Routine Treatment. In Margaret Lock and Deborah R. Gordon (Eds.), Biomedicine Examined, 465–96. Boston and Dordrecht: Kluwer.

Kohler, Robert E. 1976. The Management of Science: The Experience of Warren

Weaver and the Rockefeller Foundation Programme in Molecular Biology. Minerva 14:279–306.

———. 1978. A Policy for the Advancement of Science: The Rockefeller Foundation, 1924–1929. Minerva 16:480–515.

———. 1979. Medical Reform and Biomedical Science: Biochemistry: A Case Study. In Morris J. Vogel and Charles E. Rosenberg (Eds.), The Therapeutic Revolution, 27–66. Philadelphia: University of Pennsylvania Press.

———. 1981. Discipline History. In W. F. Bynum, E. J. Brown, and Ray Parks (Eds)., The Dictionary of the History of Science. Princeton, N.J.: Princeton University Press.

———. 1982. From Medical Chemistry to Biochemistry: The Making of a Biomedical Discipline. Cambridge: Cambridge University Press.

———. 1987. Science, Foundations and American Universities in the 1920s. Osiris, 2d ser., 3:135–64.

———. 1991. Partners in Science: Foundations and Natural Scientists, 1900–1945. Chicago: University of Chicago Press.

———. 1993a. *Drosophila:* A Life in the Laboratory. Journal of the History of Biology 26:281–310.

———. 1993b. Lords of the Fly: *Drosophila* and the Experimental Life. Chicago: University of Chicago Press.

Kohlstedt, Sally Gregory. 1976. The Formation of the American Scientific Community. Urbana: University of Illinois Press.

———. 1985. Institutional History. Osiris, n.s., 1:17–36.

Kohlstedt, Sally Gregory, and Margaret Rossiter (Eds.). 1986. Historical Writings on American Science: Perspectives and Prospects. Baltimore, Md.: Johns Hopkins University Press.

Kolata, Gina. 1994. Genes in Sperm Can Be Altered. San Francisco Chronicle, November 23, A6.

———. 1996. Measuring Men Up, Sperm by Sperm. New York Times, May 5, A4.

Kopp, Marie E. 1933. Birth Control in Practice: Analysis of Ten Thousand Case Histories of the Birth Control Clinical Research Bureau. New York: Robert M. McBride.

Kort, Michelle. 1987. Domestic Terrorism: On the Front Line at an Abortion Clinic. Ms. Magazine, May, 48–53.

Koya, Yoshio. 1958. Seven Years of a Family Planning Program in Three Typical Japanese Villages. Milbank Memorial Fund Quarterly 36:363–72.

Krauthammer, Charles. 1997. A Special Report on Cloning. Time Magazine, March 10, 60–61.

Krohn, Wolfgang, and Wolf Schafer. 1976. The Origins and Structure of Agricultural Chemistry. In Gerard Lemaine, Roy Macleod, Michael Mulkay, and Peter Weingart (Eds.), Perspectives on the Emergence of Scientific Disciplines, 27–52. Chicago: Aldine.

Kunkel, H. O., Hagevoort G. R. 1994. Construction of Science for Animal Agriculture. Journal of Animal Science 72:247–53.

Kurzrok, Raphael. 1937. The Prospects for Hormonal Sterilization. Journal of Contraception 2 (February):27–29.

Lachenbruch, Jerome. 1923. The Fight to Conquer Old Age, the Rejuvenation Theory and the Results Achieved from it by Steinach. Scientific American 128:397–400.

Landman, J. H. 1932. Human Sterilization: The History of the Sexual Sterilization Movement. New York: Macmillan.

Landy, Uta, and S. S. Ratnam (Eds.). 1986. Prevention and Treatment of Contraceptive Failure: In Honor of Christopher Tietze. New York: Plenum Press.

Langley, L. L. (Ed.). 1973. Contraception. Benchmark Papers in Human Physiology. Stroudsburg, Pa.: Dowden, Hutchinson and Ross.

Lansing, Dorothy I., W. Robert Penman, and Dorland J. Davis. 1983. Puerperal Fever and the Group B Beta Hemolytic Streptococcus. Bulletin of the History of Medicine 57:70–80.

Laqueur, Ernst, and S. E. De Jongh. 1925. A Female (Sexual) Hormone Menformon and Standardized Ovarian Preparations. Journal of the American Medical Association 91:1169–72.

Laqueur, Thomas W. 1987. Orgasm, Generation and the Politics of Reproductive Biology. In Catherine Gallagher and Thomas Laqueur (Eds.), The Making of the Modern Body: Sexuality and Society in the Nineteenth Century, 1–41. Berkeley: University of California Press.

———. 1990. Making Sex: Body and Gender from the Greeks to Freud. Cambridge, Mass.: Harvard University Press.

Larson, Edward J. 1995. Sex, Race, and Science: Eugenics in the Deep South. Baltimore, Md.: Johns Hopkins University Press.

Larson, Magali Sarfatti. 1977. The Rise of Professionalism: A Sociological Analysis. Berkeley: University of California Press.

Lasker, Judith, and Susan Borg. 1987. In Search of Parenthood: Coping with Infertility and High-Tech Conception. Boston: Beacon Press.

Latour, Bruno. 1983. Give Me a Laboratory and I Will Raise the World. In Karin Knorr-Cetina and Michael Mulkay (Eds.), Science Observed, 141–70. Beverly Hills, Calif.: Sage.

———. 1987. Science in Action. Cambridge, Mass.: Harvard University Press.

———. 1988. The Pasteurization of France. Translated by Alan Sheridan and John Law. Cambridge, Mass.: Harvard University Press.

———. 1991. Materials of Power: Technology Is Society Made Durable. In John Law (Ed.), A Sociology of Monsters: Essays on Power, Technology and Domination, 103–31. New York: Routledge.

———. 1993. We Have Never Been Modern. Translated by Catherine Porter. Cambridge, Mass.: Harvard University Press.

Latour, Bruno, and Steve Woolgar. 1979/1986. Laboratory Life: The Social Construction of Scientific Facts. Beverly Hills, Calif.: Sage.

Laughlin, Harry. 1922. Model Eugenical Sterilization Law. In Carl Bajema (Ed.), Eugenics Then and Now. Benchmark Papers in Genetics/5. Stroudsburg, Pa.: Dowden, Hutchinson and Ross, 1976.

Laumann, Edward O., John H. Gagnon, Robert T. Michael, and Stuart Michaels. 1994. The Social Organization of Sexual Practices in the United States. Chicago: University of Chicago Press.

Law, John. 1976a. The Development of Specialties in Science: The Case of X-ray Protein Crystallography. In Gerard Lemaine, Roy MacLeod, Michael Mulkay, and Peter Weingart (Eds.), Perspectives on the Emergence of Scientific Disciplines, 123–52. The Hague and Chicago: Mouton/Aldine.
———. 1976b. Theories and Methods in the Sociology of Science: An Interpretative Approach. In Gerard Lemaine, Roy MacLeod, Michael Mulkay, and Peter Weingart (Eds.), Perspectives on the Emergence of Scientific Disciplines, 221–32. The Hague and Chicago: Mouton/Aldine.
———. 1980. Fragmentation and Investment in Sedimentology. Social Studies of Science 10:1–22.
——— (Ed). 1991. Introduction: Monsters, Machines and Sociotechnical Relations, and Power, Discretion, and Strategy. In John Law (Ed.), A Sociology of Monsters: Essays on Power, Technology and Domination, 1–25 and 165–91. New York: Routledge.
Lawrence, Christopher. 1985. Incommunicable Knowledge: Science, Technology, and the Clinical Art in Britain, 1850–1914. Journal of Contemporary History 20:503–20.
Leavitt, Judith Walzer. 1986. Brought to Bed: Childbearing in America 1750–1950. New York: Oxford University Press.
Leavitt, Judith Waltzer, and Ronald L. Numbers (Eds.). 1978. Sickness and Health in America: Readings in the History of Medicine and Public Health. Madison: University of Wisconsin Press.
Ledbetter, Rosanna. 1976. A History of the Malthusian League, 1877–1927. Columbus: Ohio State University Press.
Lederer, Susan Eyrich. 1984. The Right and Wrong of Making Experiments on Human Beings: Udo J. Wile and Syphilis. Bulletin of the History of Medicine 58:380–97.
———. 1985. Hedeyo Noguchi's Luentin Experiment and the Antivivisectionists. Isis 76:31–48.
Lederman, Muriel, and Richard M. Burian. 1993. The Right Organism for the Job: Introduction. Journal of the History of Biology 26:235–38.
Lemaine, Gerard, Roy MacLeod, Michael Mulkay, and Peter Weingart (Eds.). 1976. Perspectives on the Emergence of Scientific Disciplines. The Hague and Chicago: Mouton/Aldine.
Leonardo, Richard A. 1944. History of Gynecology. New York: Froben.
Lesch, John E. 1984. Science and Medicine in France: The Emergence of Experimental Physiology, 1790–1855. Cambridge, Mass.: Harvard University Press.
Levin, L., P. A. Katzman, and E. A. Doisy. 1931. Effects of Estrogenic Substances and the Leutinizing Factor on Pregnancy in the Albino Rat. Endocrinology 15:207.
Levins, Richard. 1973. Fundamental and Applied Research in Agriculture. Science 181:523–24.
Lewin, Ellen, and Virginia Olesen (Eds.). 1985. Women, Health and Healing: Toward a New Perspective. New York: Methuen/Tavistock.

Lewis, W. David. 1971. Katherine Bement Davis. In Edward T. James (Ed.), Notable American Women 1607–1950, vol. 1:439–41. Cambridge, Mass.: Belknap Press of Harvard University Press.

Lewontin, R. C. 1982. Agricultural Research and the Penetration of Capital. Science for the People, January/February, 12–17.

———. 1983. The Corpse in the Elevator. New York Review of Books, January 20, 34–37.

Li, Choh Hao, Miriam Simpson, and Herbert M. Evans. 1940. Purification of the Pituitary Interstitial Cell Stimulating Hormone. Science 92:355–56.

Liebenau, Jonathan. 1987. Medical Science and Medical Industry: The Formation of the American Pharmaceutical Industry. Baltimore, Md.: Johns Hopkins University Press.

Light, Donald W. 1983. The Development of Professional Schools in America. In Konrad Jarausch (Ed.), The Transformation of Higher Learning 1860–1930. Chicago: University of Chicago Press.

Lilienfeld, Abraham M. (Ed.). 1980. Times, Places and Persons: Aspects of the History of Epidemiology. Baltimore, Md.: Johns Hopkins University Press.

Lillie, Frank R. 1908. The Development of the Chick. Chicago: University of Chicago Press.

———. 1911. Charles O. Whitman. Journal of Morphology 22:xv–lxxvii.

———. 1916a. The History of the Fertilization Problem. Science 42:39–53.

———. 1916b. The Theory of the Free-Martin. Science 43:611–13.

———. 1917a. The Free-Martin; A Study of the Action of Sex Hormones in the Foetal Life of Cattle. Journal of Experimental Zoology 23:371–452.

———. 1917b. Sex-Determination and Sex-Differentiation in Mammals. Proceedings of National Academy of Science 3:464–70.

———. 1919. Problems of Fertilization. Chicago: University of Chicago Press. Reprinted, New York: Garland, 1988.

———. 1932. General Biological Introduction. In Edgar Allen (Ed.), Sex and Internal Secretions: A Survey of Recent Research, 1–11. Baltimore, Md.: Williams and Wilkins.

———. 1938. Zoological Sciences in the Future. Science 88:65–72.

———. 1939. General Biological Introduction. In Edgar Allen (Ed.), Sex and Internal Secretions: A Survey of Recent Research, 3–14. 2d ed. Baltimore, Md.: Williams and Wilkins.

———. 1944. The Woods Hole Marine Biological Laboratory. Chicago: University of Chicago Press.

Lincoln, Richard, and Lisa Kaeser. 1988. Whatever Happened to the Contraceptive Revolution? Family Planning Perspectives 20(1):20–24.

Lipschutz, Alexander. 1925. Is There an Antagonism between the Male and the Female Sex-Endocrine Gland? Endocrinology (March–April): 109–16.

Lisser, Hans. 1967. The Endocrine Society: The First Forty Years. Endocrinology 80:5–28.

Lissner, Elaine A. 1992. Frontiers in Nonhormone Male Contraceptive Research. In Helen Bequaert Holmes (Ed.), Issues in Reproductive Technology I: An Anthology, 53–70. New York: Garland.

Lloyd, Elizabeth. 1993. All about Eve: Evolutionary Explanations of Women's Sexuality. Princeton, N.J.: Princeton University Press.

Lock, Margaret. 1993. Cultivating the Body: Anthropology and Epistemologies of Bodily Practices and Knowledge. Annual Review of Anthropology 22:133–55.

Loeb, Leo. 1911. The Cyclic Changes in the Ovary of the Guinea Pig. Journal of Morphology 23:37–70.

———. 1923. The Mechanism of the Sexual Cycle with Special Reference to the Corpus Luteum. American Journal of Anatomy 32:305.

———. 1958. Autobiographical Notes. Perspectives in Biology and Medicine 2:1–23.

Long, Diana E. 1987. Physiological Identity of American Sex Researchers between the Two World Wars. In Gerald L. Geison (Ed.), Physiology in the American Context, 1850–1940, 263–78. Bethesda, Md.: American Physiological Society.

———. 1990. Moving Reprints: A Historian Looks at Sex Research Publications of the 1930s. Journal of the History of Medicine and Allied Sciences 45:452–68.

———. 1997. Hidden Persuaders: Medical Indexing and the Gendered Professionalism of American Medicine, 1880–1932. Osiris 12:100–120. [See also Diana Long Hall.]

Long, J. A., and H. M. Evans. 1920. The Oestrus Cycle in the Rat. Anatomical Record 18:241–48.

———. 1922. The Oestrus Cycle in the Rat and Its Associated Phenomena. Memoirs of the University of California 6(2):1–148.

Long, P. H., E. A. Bliss, and H. M. Carpenter. 1931. Etiology of Influenza: Transmission Experiments in Chimpanzees with Filtered Material Derived from Human Influenza. Journal of the American Medical Association 97:1122–27.

Longino, Helen. 1990. Science as Social Knowledge: Values and Objectivity in Scientific Inquiry. Princeton, N.J.: Princeton University Press.

Longino, Helen, and Ruth Doell. 1983. Body, Bias and Behavior: A Comparative Analysis of Reasoning in Two Areas of Science. Signs 9:206–27.

Longo, Lawrence D. 1980. Obstetrics and Gynecology. In Ronald L. Numbers (Ed.), The Education of American Physicians, 205–25. Berkeley: University of California Press.

———. 1981. John Whittridge Williams and Academic Obstetrics in America. Transactions and Studies of the College of Physicians of Philadelphia, 5th ser., 3(4):221–54.

Loosli, J. K. 1992. The Journal of Animal Science 1949–1960. Journal of Animal Science 70:329–49.

Lowy, Ilana. 1987. The Impact of Medical Practice on Biomedical Research: The Case of Human Leukocyte Antigens Studies. Minerva 25:171–200.

———. 1992. The Strength of Loose Concepts: Boundary Concepts, Federative Experimental Strategies, and Disciplinary Growth: The Case of Immunology. History of Science 30(90):371–96.

———. 1993. Introduction: Medicine and Change. In Ilana Lowy (Ed.), Medicine and Change: Historical and Sociological Studies of Medical Innovation, 1–20. Montrouge, France: John Libbey Eurotext (Les edition INSERM).

Ludmerer, Kenneth M. 1972. Genetics and American Society: A Historical Appraisal. Baltimore, Md.: Johns Hopkins University Press.

———. 1983. The Plight of Clinical Teaching in America. Bulletin of the History of Medicine 57:218–29.

Lush, Jay L. 1951. Genetics and Animal Breeding. In L. C. Dunn (Ed.), Genetics in the Twentieth Century, 197–233. New York: Macmillan.

Luthra, Rashmi. 1994. A Case of Problematic Diffusion: The Use of Sex Determination Techniques in India. Knowledge: Creation, Diffusion, Utilization 15:259–72.

Lyet, L., F. Louis, M. G. Forest, N. Josso, R. R. Behringer, and B. Vigier. 1995. Ontogeny of Reproductive Abnormalities Induced by Deregulation of Anti-Mullerian Hormone Expression in Transgenic Mice. Biology of Reproduction 52:444–54.

M., E. 1911. Review of *The Physiology of Reproduction* by F. H. A. Marshall. American Journal of Obstetrics and Diseases of Women and Children 63:690.

Maas, Bonnie. 1974. An Historical Sketch of the American Population Control Movement. International Journal of Health Services 4:651–676.

———. 1977. Population Target: The Political Economy of Population Control in Latin America. Toronto: Canadian Women's Educational Press.

Machlup, Fritz. 1962. The Production and Distribution of Knowledge in the United States. Princeton, N.J.: Princeton University Press.

MacKenzie, Donald. 1981a. Sociobiologies in Competition: The Biometrician-Mendelian Debate. In Charles Webster (Ed.), Biology, Medicine and Society, 1840–1940, 243–88. Cambridge: Cambridge University Press.

———. 1981b. Statistics in Britain, 1865–1930. Edinburgh: University of Edinburgh Press.

Mackinnon, Alison. 1995. Were Women Present at the Demographic Transition? Questions from a Feminist Historian to Historical Demographers. Gender and History 7:222–40.

MacLeod, Roy. 1977. Changing Perspectives in the Social History of Science. In Ina Spiegel-Rosing and Derek de Solla Price (Eds.), Science, Technology and Society: A Cross-Disciplinary Perspective, 43–71. Beverly Hills, Calif.: Sage.

MacNicol, John. 1992. The Campaign for Voluntary Sterilization in Britain, 1918–1939. Journal of the History of Sexuality 2(3)422–38.

Maienschein, Jane. 1978. Cell Lineage, Ancestral Reminiscence, and Biogenetic Law. Journal of the History of Biology 11:129–58.

———. 1981. Shifting Assumptions in American Biology: Embryology, 1890–1910. Journal of the History of Biology 14:89–113.

———. 1983. Experimental Biology in Transition: Harrison's Embryology, 1895–1910. In William Coleman and Camille Limoges (Eds.), Studies in the History of Biology 6, 107–27. Baltimore, Md.: Johns Hopkins University Press.

———. 1984. What Determines Sex? A Study of Converging Approaches, 1880–1916. Isis 75:457–80.

———. 1985a. Agassiz, Hyatt, Whitman, and the Birth of the Marine Biological Laboratory. Biological Bulletin 168 (suppl.):26–34.

———. 1985b. Early Struggles at the Marine Biological Laboratory over Mission and Money. Biological Bulletin 168 (suppl.):192–96.

————. 1985c. First Impressions: American Biologists at Naples. Biological Bulletin 168 (suppl.):187–91.

————. 1985d. History of Biology. Osiris, 2d ser., 1:147–62.

————. 1988. Whitman at Chicago: Establishing a Chicago Style of Biology. In Ronald Rainger, Keith Benson, and Jane Maienschein (Eds.), The American Development of Biology, 151–84. Philadelphia: University of Pennsylvania Press.

————. 1991a. Cytology in 1924: Expansion and Collaboration. In Keith Benson, Jane Maienschein, and Ronald Rainger (Eds.), The American Expansion of Biology, 23–52. New Brunswick, N.J.: Rutgers University Press.

————. 1991b. Epistemic Styles in German and American Embryology. Science in Context 4:407–27.

————. 1994. Cutting Edges Cut Both Ways. Biology and Philosopy 9:1–24.

Maienschein, Jane, Ronald Rainger, and Keith R. Benson. 1981. Introduction: Were American Morphologists in Revolt? Journal of the History of Biology 14:83–87.

Maier, Charles S. 1984. The Factory as Society: Ideologies of Industrial Management in the Twentieth Century. In R. J. Bullen, H. P. Strandmann, and A. B. Polonsky (Eds.), Ideas into Politics: Aspects of European History 1880–1950, 147–63. Totowa, N.J.: Barnes and Noble Books.

Maisel, Albert Q. 1965. The Hormone Quest. New York: Random House.

Makepeace, A. W., C. L. Weinstein, and M. H. Freidman. 1937. The Effects of Progestin and Progesterone in Ovulation in the Rabbit. American Journal of Physiology 119:512–16.

Mann, Thaddeus. 1967. Capacitation for Reproductive Research. Journal of Reproduction and Fertility 2 (suppl.):149–55

Manning, Kenneth R. 1983. Black Apollo of Science: The Life of Ernest Everett Just. New York: Oxford University Press.

Marcus, Alan I. 1985. Agricultural Science and the Quest for Legitimacy: Farmers, Agricultural Colleges, and Experiment Stations, 1870–1890. Ames: Iowa State University Press.

————. 1988. The Wisdom of the Body Politic: The Changing Nature of Publically Sponsored American Agricultural Research since the 1830s. Agricultural History 62(2):4–26.

————. 1993. The Newest Knowledge of Nutrition: Wise Burroughs, DES, and Modern Meat. Agricultural History 67(3): 66–85.

————. 1995. Cancer from Beef: DES, Federal Food Regulation, and Consumer Confidence. Baltimore, Md.: Johns Hopkins University Press.

Marcuse, Max. 1928. Verhandlungen des I. Internationalen Kongresses fur Sexualforschung, Berlin, 1926. Berlin: A. Marcus and E. Weber.

Markee, J. Eldridge. 1940. Menstruation in Intraocular Endometrial Transplants in the Rhesus Monkey. Carnegie Contributions to Embryology, no. 177:232–308.

Marker, Russel E. [1970?]1986. The Early Production of Steroidal Hormones. Center for the History of Chemistry News, Spring, 3–6.

Markowitz, Gerald E., and David Rosner. 1979. Doctors in Crisis: Medical Education and Medical Reform during the Progressive Era, 1985–1915. In Susan Reverby and David Rosner (Eds.), Health Care in America: Essays in Social History, 185–205. Philadephia: Temple University Press.

Marks, Harry M. 1983. Ideas as Social Reforms: The Legacies of Randomized Clinical Trials. Unpublished manuscript.

———. 1988. Notes from the Underground: The Social Organization of Therapeutic Research In Diana E. Long and Russell Maulitz (Eds.), Grand Rounds: One Hundred Years of Internal Medicine, 297–336. Philadelphia: University of Pennsylvania Press.

Marks, Russell. 1982. Legitimating Industrial Capitalism: Philanthropy and Individual Differences. In Robert F. Arnove (Ed.), Philanthropy and Cultural Imperialism: The Foundations at Home and Abroad, 87–122. Bloomington: Indiana University Press.

Marrian, Guy F. 1967. Early Work on the Chemistry of Pregnanediol and the Oestrogenic Hormones: The Sir Henry Dale Lecture for 1966. Journal of Endocrinology (Proceedings of the Society) 35(4):v–xvi.

Marshall, F. H. A. 1910. The Physiology of Reproduction. London: Longmans, Green.

———. 1922. The Physiology of Reproduction. 2d ed. London: Longmans, Green.

———. 1929. Walter Heape, F.R.S.: Obituary. Nature 124:588–89.

———. 1930. Walter Heape, 1855–1929. Proceedings of the Royal Society of London. Series B: Biological Sciences 106: xv–xviii.

———. 1936. Sexual Periodicity and the Causes Which Determine It. Eleventh Croonian Lecture. Philosophical Transactions of the Royal Society of London. Series B: Biological Sciences 226:423–56.

Marshall, F. H. A., and W. A. Jolly. 1905. Ovarian Hormones in the Dog and the Rat. Philosophical Transactions of the Royal Society of London. Series B: Biological Sciences 198:99.

Martin, Brian, and Evelleen Richards. 1995. Scientific Knowledge, Controversy and Public Decision-Making. In Sheila Jasanoff, Gerald E. Markle, James Petersen, and Trevor Pinch (Eds.), Handbook of Science and Technology Studies, 506–26. Thousand Oaks, Calif.: Sage.

Martin, Emily. 1987/1992. The Woman in the Body: A Cultural Analysis of Reproduction. Boston: Beacon Press.

———. 1988. Medical Metaphors of Women's Bodies: Menstruation and Menopause. International Journal of Health Services 18:237–54.

———. 1989. The Cultural Construction of Gendered Bodies: Biology and Metaphors of Production and Destruction. Ethnos 54(3–4):143–60.

———. 1990. Science and Women's Bodies: Forms of Anthropological Knowledge. In Mary Jacobus, Evelyn Fox Keller, and Sally Shuttleworth (Eds.), Body/Politics: Women and the Discourse of Science, 69–82. New York: Methuen.

———. 1994. Flexible Bodies: Tracking Immunity in American Culture from the Days of Polio to the Age of AIDS. Boston. Beacon Press.

Mastroianni, Luigi, Jr., Peter J. Donaldson, and Thomas T. Kane (Eds.). 1990. Developing New Contraceptives: Obstacles and Opportunities. Washington, D.C.: National Academy Press.

Mayer, John A. 1983. Notes toward a Working Definition of Social Control in Historical Analysis. In Stanley Cohen and Andrew Scull (Eds.), Social Control and the State, 17–38. New York: St. Martin's Press.

Mayr, Ernst, and William B. Provine (Eds.). 1980. The Evolutionary Synthesis: Perspectives on the Unification of Biology. Cambridge, Mass.: Harvard University Press.

Mazur, Allen. 1981. The Dynamics of Technical Controversies. Washington, D.C.: Communications Press.

McCance, R. A. 1977. Perinatal Physiology. In A. L. Hodgkin, A. F. Huxley, W. Feldberg, W. A. H. Rushton, R. A. Gregory, and R. A. McCance. The Pursuit of Nature: Informal Essays on the History of Physiology. Cambridge: Cambridge University Press.

McCann, Carole R. 1994. Birth Control Politics in the United States, 1916–1945. Ithaca, N.Y.: Cornell University Press.

McCrea, Frances B. 1983. The Politics of Menopause: The Discovery of a Deficiency Disease. Social Problems 31:111–23.

McCrea, Frances B., and Gerald E. Markle. 1984. The Estrogen Replacement Controversy in the USA and the UK: Different Answers to the Same Question? Social Studies of Science 14:1–26.

McGee, L. C. 1927. The Effect of the Injection of a Lipoid Fraction of Bull Testicle in Capons. Proceedings of the Institute of Medicine of Chicago 6:242.

McGregor, Deborah Kuhn. 1989. Sexual Surgery and the Origins of Gynecology: J. Marion Sims, His Hospital, and His Patients. New York: Garland

McKenzie, F. F. 1926. The Estrus Cycle in the Pig. Missouri University Agricultural Experiment Station Research Bulletin 86.

McKenzie, F. F., and C. E. Terrill. 1937. The Estrus Cycle in the Ewe. Missouri University Agricultural Experiment Station Research Bulletin 264.

McKinlay, John B. 1981. From Promising Report to Standard Procedure: Seven Stages in the Career of a Medical Innovation. Health and Society 59:374–411.

McKinlay, Sonja M., and John B. McKinlay. 1973. Selected Studies of the Menopause: An Annotated Bibliography. Biosocial Science 5:533–55.

McLaren, Angus. 1978. Birth Control in Nineteenth-Century England. London: Croom Helm.

———. 1983. Sexuality and Social Order: The Debate over the Fertility of Women and Workers in France, 1770–1920. New York: Holmes and Meier.

McLaughlin, Loretta. 1982. The Pill, John Rock and the Church: The Biography of a Revolution. Boston: Little, Brown.

McNeil, Maureen, and Sarah Franklin. 1991. Science and Technology: Questions for Cultural Studies and Feminism. In Sarah Franklin, Celia Lury, and Jackie Stacey (Eds.), Off-Centre: Feminism and Cultural Studies, 129–46. London: Harper Collins Academic.

McNeil, Maureen, Ian Varcoe, and Steven Yearley (Eds.). 1990. The New Reproductive Technologies. London: Macmillan.

Mead, George Herbert. 1917. Scientific Method and the Individual Thinker. In John Dewey (Ed.), Creative Intelligence: Essays in the Pragmatic Attitude, 176–227. New York: Henry Holt.

———. 1927/1964. The Objective Reality of Perspectives. In A. J. Reck (Ed.), Selected Writings of George Herbert Mead, 306–19. Chicago: University of Chicago Press.

———. 1938/1972. The Philosophy of the Act. Chicago: University of Chicago Press.

Medvei, Victor C. 1982. A History of Endocrinology. Lancaster, Pa.: MTP. 1992.

Meites, Joseph, Bernard T. Donovan, and Samuel M. McCann (Eds.). 1975. Pioneers in Neuroendocrinology. Vol. 1. New York: Plenum Press.

———. 1978. Pioneers in Neuroendocrinology. Vol. 2. New York: Plenum Press.

Meldrum, Marcia. 1996. "Simple Methods" and "Determined Contraceptors": The Statistical Evaluation of Fertility Control, 1957–1968. Bulletin of the History of Medicine 70:266–95.

Menge, A. C., W. H. Stone, W. J. Tyler, and L. E. Casida. 1962. Immunological Studies on Fertility and Sterility IV: Fertility of Cattle and Rabbits Inseminated with Semen Treated with Antibodies Produced against Semen, Spermatozoa and Erythrocytes. Journal of Reproduction and Fertility 3:331–41.

Mengert, William F. 1934. Periodicals on Endocrinology of Sex. Endocrinology 18:421–22.

Merkin, Donald H. 1976. Pregnancy as a Disease: The Pill in Society. Port Washington, N.Y.: Kennikat Press/National University Press.

Messer-Davidow, Ellen, David R. Shumway, and David J. Sylvan (Eds.). 1993. Knowledges: Historical and Critical Studies in Disciplinarity. Charlottesville: University Press of Virginia.

Metz, Charles B. 1979. Immunological Inhibition of Sperm and Egg Function: Prospects for an Antifertility Vaccine from Gametes. In National Academy of Sciences (Ed.), Contraception: Science, Technology and Application, 180–220. Washington, D.C.: National Academy of Sciences.

Meyers, J. A. 1917. Studies on the Mammary Gland III. Anatomical Record 13:205–47.

Michaelson, Karen L. (Ed.). 1981. And the Poor Get Children: Radical Perspectives on Population Dynamics. New York: Monthly Review.

Miller, Howard S. 1971. Dollars for Research: Science and Its Patrons in Nineteenth-Century America. Seattle: University of Washington Press.

Miller, Lawrence G. 1979. Pain, Parturition and the Profession: Twilight Sleep in America. In Susan Reverby and David Rosner (Eds.), Health Care in America: Essays in Social History, 19–44. Philadephia: Temple University Press.

Mintz, Morton. 1985. At Any Cost: Corporate Greed, Women and the Dalcon Shield. New York: Pantheon/Random House.

Mitman, Gregg. 1992. Of a Social Nature: Animal Ecology and Community at Chicago, 1900–1950. Chicago: University of Chicago Press.

Mitman, Gregg, and Richard W. Burkhardt. 1991. Struggling for Identity: The Study of Animal Behavior in America. In Keith Benson, Jane Maienschein, and Ronald Rainger (Eds.), The American Expansion of Biology, 164–94. New Brunswick, N.J.: Rutgers University Press.

Mitman, Gregg, Adele Clarke, and Jane Maienschein (Guest Eds.). 1993. Introduction to Special Issue on Biology at the University of Chicago, c1891–1950. Perspectives on Science 1:359–66.

Moffat, Anne Simon. 1991. Another Sex Survey Bites the Dust. Science 253:1483.

Mohr, James C. 1978. Abortion in America: The Origins and Evolution of a National Policy, 1800–1900. New York: Oxford Unversity Press.

Money, John. 1983. The Genealogical Descent of Sexual Psychoneuroendocrinology from Sex and Health Theory: The Eighteenth to the Twentieth Centuries. Psychoneuroendocrinology 8:391–400.

Money, John, and Anke A. Ehrhardt. 1972. Man and Woman, Boy and Girl: The Differentiation and Dimorphism of Gender Identity from Conception to Maturity. Baltimore, Md.: Johns Hopkins University Press.

Montini, Theresa. 1996. Gender, Emotion and the Presentation of Self in a Political Arena: The Case of Breast Cancer Informed Consent. Gender and Society 10:9–23.

Moore, Carl R. 1919. On the Properties of the Gonads as the Controllers of Somatic and Physical Characteristics I. The Rat. Journal of Experimental Zoology 28:137–60.

———. 1926. The Biology of the Mammalian Testis and Scrotum. Quarterly Review of Biology 1:4–28.

———. 1931a. A Critique of Sex Hormone Antagonism. In A. W. Greenwood (Ed.), Proceedings of the Second International Congress for Sex Research, London, 1930, 293–95. London: Oliver and Boyd.

———. 1931b. The Regulation of Production of the Male Sex Hormone. Journal of the American Medical Association 97:518–23.

———. 1932. Biology of the Testis. In Edgar Allen (Ed.), Sex and Internal Secretions, 281–371. Baltimore, Md.: Williams and Wilkins.

———. 1938. Endocrines and Male Reproductive Behavior. American Society of Animal Production, Record of Proceedings of Thirty-first Annual Meeting:26–29.

———. 1947. Embryonic Sex Hormones and Sexual Differentiation. Springfield, Ill.: C. C. Thomas.

———. 1948. Frank Rattray Lillie. Science 107:33–35.

Moore, Carl R., T. F. Gallagher, and F. C. Koch. 1929. The Effects of Extracts of Testis in Correcting the Castrated Condition in the Fowl and in the Mammal. Endocrinology 13:367–74.

Moore, Carl R., and Dorothy Price. 1932. Gonad Hormone Functions and the Reciprocal Influence between Gonads and Hypophysis with Its Bearing on the Problem of Sex Hormone Antagonism. American Journal of Anatomy 50:13.

Moore, Carl R., and W. J. Quick. 1923. The Scrotum as a Temperature Regulator for the Testes. American Journal of Physiology 68:70–79.

Moore, E. Roberts. 1931. The Case against Birth Control. Introduction by Patrick Cardinal Hayes. New York: Century.

Moore, Lisa Jean, and Adele E. Clarke. 1995. Genital Conventions and Transgressions: Graphic Representations in Anatomy Texts, c1900–1991. Feminist Studies 22:255–301.

Moore, Lisa Jean, and Matt Schmidt. 1997. The Spermatic Enterprise: Marketing Technosemen and the Construction of Male Difference. masculinities 4(1):forthcoming.

Morales, A. J., J. Nolan, and S. C. Yen. 1995. Effects of Replacement Dose of DHEA in Men and Women of Advancing Age. Journal of Clinical Endocrinology and Metabolism 80(9):2799.

Morantz, Regina M. 1977. The Scientist as Sex Crusader: Alfred C. Kinsey and American Culture. American Quarterly 29:563–89.

Morawski, J. G. 1986. Organizing Knowledge and Behavior at Yale's Institute of Human Relations. Isis 77:219–42.

Morsy, Soheir. 1991. Safeguarding Women's Bodies: The White Man's Burden Medicalized. Medical Anthropology Quarterly 5:19–24.

———. 1995. Maternal Mortality in Egypt: Selective Health Strategy and the Medicalization of Population Control. In Faye D. Ginsberg and Rayna Rapp (Eds.), Conceiving the New World Order: The Global Stratification of Reproduction, 162–76. Berkeley: University of California Press.

Moscucci, Ornella. 1990. The Science of Woman: Gynaecology and Gender in England, 1880–1929. Cambridge: Cambridge University Press.

Moskowitz, Ellen H., and Bruce Jennings (Eds.). 1996. Coerced Contraception? Moral and Policy Challenges of Long-Acting Birth Control. Washington, D.C.: Georgetown University Press.

Mulkay, M. J. 1977. Sociology of the Scientific Research Community. In Ina Spiegel-Rosing and Derek de Solla Price (Eds.), Science, Technology and Society: A Cross-Disciplinary Perspective, 93–148. Beverly Hills, Calif.: Sage.

———. 1993. Rhetorics of Hope and Fear in the Great Embryo Debate. Social Studies of Science 23:721–42.

Muller, Charlotte. 1988. Medicaid: The Lower Tier of Health Care for Women. Women and Health 14(2):81–103.

Mullins, Nicholas. 1972. The Development of a Scientific Specialty. Minerva 10:51–82.

Mumby, Dennis K. (Ed.). 1993. Narrative and Social Control: Critical Perspectives. Sage Annual Reviews of Communication Research. Vol. 21. Beverley Hills, Calif.: Sage.

Nagi, Saad Z., and Ronald Corwin (Eds.). 1972. The Social Contexts of Research. London and New York: Wiley-Interscience.

Nalbandov, Andrew V. 1958. Reproductive Physiology: Comparative Reproductive Physiology of Domestic Animals, Laboratory Animals and Man. San Francisco: Freeman.

———. 1970. Comparative Aspects of Corpus Luteum Function. First Hartman Lecture. Biology of Reproduction 2:7–13.

———. 1973. Puzzles of Reproductive Physiology: The Fourth Hammond Memorial Lecture. Journal of Reproduction and Fertility 34:1–8.

———. 1976. Reproductive Physiology of Mammals and Birds: A Comparative Physiology of Domestic and Laboratory Animals and Man. 3d ed. San Francisco: Freeman.

———. 1978. Retrospects and Prospects in Reproductive Physiology. In Charles H. Spelman and John W. Wilks (Eds.), Novel Aspects of Reproductive Physiology, 1–10. New York: Halsted/Wiley.

Nalbandov, Andrew V., and L. E. Casida. 1942. Ovulation and Its Relation to Estrus in Cows. Journal of Animal Science 1:189–98.

Nash, Madeleine. 1997. The Age of Cloning. Time Magazine, March 10, 62–65.

National Academy of Sciences. 1979. Contraception: Science, Technology and Application. Proceedings of a Symposium, Division of Medical Sciences, Assembly of Life Sciences, National Research Council. Washington, D.C.: National Academy of Sciences.

National Advisory Board on Ethics in Reproduction. 1994 Report on Human Cloning through Embryo Splitting. Kennedy Institute of Ethics Journal 4:251–82.

National Science Foundation [Batelle Institute] 1968/69. Technology in Retrospect and Critical Events in Science [TRACES]. Vol. 1 (Dec. 15, 1968) and Vol. 2 (Jan. 30, 1969).

———. 1973. Interactions of Science and Technology in the Innovative Process: Some Case Studies. Final Report/NSF-6667.

National Women's Health Network (NWHN). 1985. The Depo-Provera Debate: A Report by the National Women's Health Network. Washington, D.C.: NWHN.

Nelkin, Dorothy. 1987. Selling Science: How the Press Covers Science and Technology. New York: Freeman.

———. 1995. Science Controversies: The Dynamics of Public Disputes in the United States. In Sheila Jasanoff, Gerald E. Markle, James Petersen, and Trevor Pinch (Eds.), Handbook of Science and Technology Studies, 444–56. Thousand Oaks, Calif.: Sage.

——— (Ed.). 1984. Controversy: Politics of Technical Decisions. 2d ed. Beverly Hills, Calif.: Sage.

Nelkin, Dorothy, and Laurence Tancredi. 1994. Dangerous Diagnostics: The Social Power of Biological Information. 2d ed. Chicago: University of Chicago Press.

Newman, H. H. 1948. History of the Department of Zoology in the University of Chicago. Bios 19(4):215–39.

Nicholas, J. S. 1961. Ross Granville Harrison, 1870–1959. Biographical Memoirs of the National Academy of Sciences 35:131–62.

Niemi, Mikko. 1987. Andrology as a Specialty: Its Origin. Journal of Andrology 8:201–2.

Niwa, T. 1961. Researches and Practices in the Artificial Insemination of Pigs. Proceedings of the Fourth International Congress on Animal Reproduction, The Hague, vol. 1:83–115.

Noakes, Jeremy. 1984. Nazism and Eugenics: The Background to the Nazi Sterilization Law of 14 July 1933. In R. J. Bullen, H. Pogge von Strandmann, and A. B. Polonsky (Eds.), Ideas into Politics: Aspects of European History, 1880–1950, 75–94. London: Croom Helm.

Notestein, Frank W. 1982. Demography in the United States: A Partial Account of the Development of the Field. Population and Development Review 8:651–87.

Novak, Emil. 1920. The Role of the Endocrine Glands in Certain Menstrual Disorders. Endocrinology 8:219–33.

Nsiah-Jefferson, Laurie. 1989. Reproductive Laws, Women of Color and Low-Income Women. In Sherrill Cohen and Nadine Taub (Eds.), Reproductive Laws for the 1990s, 23–68. Clifton, N.J.: Humana.

Numbers, Ronald L. (Ed.). 1980. The Education of American Physicians: Historical Essays. Berkeley: University of California Press.

Oakley, Ann. 1984. The Captured Womb: A History of the Medical Care of Pregnant Women. New York: Basil Blackwell.

Ogino, Kyusaku. 1924. Ovulationstermin. Nippon Fruzinka Gakkei Zassli.

———. 1930. Ovulationstermin und Konzeptionstermin. Zentralblatt für Gynäkologie 54:464–79.

———. 1934. Conception Period of Women. Harrisburg, Pa.: Medical Arts Press.

Olby, Robert. 1991. Social Imperialism and State Support for Agricultural Research in Edwardian Britain. Annals of Science 48:509–26.

Olesen, Virginia. 1982. Sociological Observations on Ethical Issues Implicated in Estrogen Replacement Therapy at Menopause. In Ann M. Voda, Myra Dinnerstein, and Sheryl R. O'Donnell (Eds.), Changing Perspectives on Menopause, 346–60. Austin: University of Texas Press.

Oleson, Alexandra, and Sanborn C. Brown (Eds.). 1976. The Pursuit of Knowledge in the Early American Republic: American Scientific and Learned Societies from Colonial Times to the Civil War. Baltimore, Md.: Johns Hopkins University Press.

Oleson, Alexandra, and John Voss (Eds.). 1979. The Organization of Knowledge in Modern America, 1860–1920. Baltimore, Md.: Johns Hopkins University Press.

Olmstead, J. D. M. 1946. Charles Edouard Brown-Sequard: Neurophysiologist and Endocrinologist. Baltimore, Md.: Johns Hopkins University Press.

Onorato, Suzanne. 1991. The Population Council and the Development of Contraceptive Technologies. Research Reports from the Rockefeller Archive Center 1 (Spring):6–7.

Oppenheimer, Jane M. 1967. Essays in the History of Embryology and Biology. Cambridge, Mass.: MIT Press.

———. 1968. Some Historical Relationships between Teratology and Experimental Embryology. Bulletin of the History of Medicine 42:145–59.

———. 1984. Basic Embryology and Clinical Medicine: A Case History in Serendipity. Bulletin of the History of Medicine 58:236–40.

Organizing Committee. 1994. Reproductive Health and Justice: International Women's Health Conference for Cairo '94, January 24–28, 1994, Rio De Janeiro. New York: International Women's Health Coalition.

Osborn, Frederick. 1951. Preface to Eugenics. New York: Harper and Row.

———. 1966. Eugenics *(Encyclopaedia Britannica)*. Eugenics Quarterly 13:155–64.

———. 1967. American Foundations and Population Problems. In Warren Weaver (Ed.), U.S. Philanthropic Foundations: Their History, Structure, Management and Record, 365–74.New York: Harper and Row.

Oudshoorn, Nelly. 1994. Beyond the Natural Body: An Archeology of Sex Hormones. London: Routledge.

———. 1995. Discourse Coalitions in Contraceptive Technologies: The Case of Male Contraceptives. Paper presented at meetings of the Society for Social Studies of Science. Charlottesville, Virginia, October.

———. 1996a. The Decline of the One-Size-Fits-All Paradigm, or How Reproductive Scientists Try to Cope with Postmodernity. In Nina Lyke and Rosi Braidotti (Eds.), Between Monsters, Goddesses and Cyborgs: Feminist Confrontations with Science, Medicine and Cyberspace, 153–72. London: ZED Books.

———. 1996b. From Population Control Politics to Chemicals: The WHO as an Intermediary Organization in Contraceptive Development. Social Studies of Science 27:41–72.

———. 1996c. A Natural Order of Things? Reproductive Sciences and the Politics of Othering. In George Robertson, Melinda Mash, Lisa Tichner, John Bird, Barry Curtis, and Tim Putnam (Eds.), Future Natural: Nature, Science, Culture, 122–33. London and New York: Routledge.

———. 1997a. On Masculinities, Technologies and Pain: The Testing of Male Contraceptive Technologies in the Clinic and the Media. Paper presented at the workshop Gender, Science and Technology, Trondheim, Norway, May.

———. 1997b. Shifting Boundaries between Industry and Science: The Role of the WHO in Contraceptive Development. Forthcoming in Jean-Paul Gaudiliere, Ilana Lowy, and D. Pestre (Eds.), The Invisible Industrialist: Manufacturers and the Construction of Scientific Knowledge. London: Macmillan.

Oudshoorn, Nelly, and Marianne van den Wijngaard. 1991. Dualism in Biology: The Case of Sex Hormones. Women's Studies International Forum 14: 459–71.

Overall, Christine. 1987. Ethics and Human Reproduction: A Feminist Analysis. Boston: Allen and Unwin.

Painter, T. S. 1922. Studies in Mammalian Spermatogenesis I. The Spermatogenesis of the Opossum. Journal of Experimental Zoology 35:13.

———. 1923. Studies in Mammalian Spermatogenesis II. The Spermatogenesis of Man. Journal of Experimental Zoology 37:291.

Papanicolaou, George N. 1933. The Sexual Cycle in the Human Female as Revealed by Vaginal Smear. American Journal of Anatomy 52:519–637.

Papanicolaou, George N., and C. R. Stockard. 1920. Effect of Underfeeding on Ovulation and Oestrus Rhythm in Guinea Pigs. Proceedings of the Society for Experimental Biology and Medicine 17:143.

Parascandola, John. 1992. The Development of American Pharmacology: John J. Abel and the Shaping of a Discipline. Baltimore, Md.: Johns Hopkins University Press.

Park, Robert Ezra. 1952. Human Communities. Glencoe, Ill.: Free Press.

Parker, Franklin. 1973. Leo Loeb. In Charles Coulston Gillispie (Ed.), Dictionary of Scientific Biography. Vol. 8. New York: Scribner.

Parkes, A. S. 1952–66. Marshall's Physiology of Reproduction. 3d ed. New York: Longmans Green.

———. 1962a. Biological Control of Conception: The Fifth Oliver Bird Lecture. Journal of Reproduction and Fertility 3:159–72.

———. 1962b. Prospect and Retrospect in the Physiology of Reproduction. British Medical Journal 2:71–75.

———. 1962c. Sir John Hammond: An Interview. Journal of Reproduction and Fertility 3:2–13.

———. 1963. The Exocrinology of Reproduction. In C. F. Cori, V. G. Foglia, L. F. Leloir, and S. Ochoa (Eds.), Perspectives in Biology, Dedicated to B. A. Houssay, 33–38. New York: Elsevier.

——. 1966a. The Rise of Reproductive Endocrinology, 1926–1940. The Dale Lecture for 1965. Journal of Endocrinology (Proceedings of the Society) 34(3):xx–xxxii.

——. 1966b. Sex, Science and Society: Addresses, Lectures and Articles. London: Oriel Press.

——. 1985. Off-Beat Biologist: The Autobiography of Alan S. Parkes. Cambridge: Galton Foundation.

Parkes, A. S., and R. L. Noble. 1938. Interruption of Early Pregnancy by Means of Orally Active Oestrogens. British Medical Journal 2:557–9.

Parsons, Jacquelynne E. (Ed.). 1980. The Psychobiology of Sex Differences and Sex Roles. New York: Hemisphere/McGraw-Hill.

Paul, Diane B. 1991. The Rockefeller Foundation and the Origins of Behavior Genetics. In Keith Benson, Jane Maienschein, and Ronald Rainger (Eds.), The American Expansion of Biology, 262–83. New Brunswick, N.J.: Rutgers University Press.

Paul, Diane, and Barbara Kimmelman. 1988. Mendel in America: Theory and Practice, 1900–1919. In Ronald Rainger, Keith Benson, and Jane Maienschein (Eds.), The American Development of Biology, 281–310. Philadelphia: University of Pennsylvania Press.

Pauly, Philip J. 1984. The Appearance of Academic Biology in Late Nineteenth-Century America. Journal of the History of Biology 17:369–97.

——. 1987. Controlling Life: Jacques Loeb and the Engineering Ideal in Biology. New York: Oxford University Press.

——. 1988. Summer Resort and Scientific Discipline: Woods Hole and the Structure of American Biology, 1882–1925. In Ronald Rainger, Keith Benson, and Jane Maienschein (Eds.), The American Development of Biology, 121–50. Philadelphia: University of Pennsylvania Press.

——. 1990. The Struggle for Ignorance about Alcohol: American Physiologists, Wilbur Olin Atwater and the Women's Christian Temperance Union. Bulletin of the History of Medicine 64:366–92.

——. 1993. Essay Review: The Eugenics Industry—Growth or Restructuring? Journal of the History of Biology 27:131–45.

——. 1994. Modernist Practice in American Biology. In Dorothy Ross (Ed.), Modernist Impulses in the Human Sciences, 272–89. Baltimore, Md.: Johns Hopkins University Press.

——. 1996. From Adventism to Biology: The Development of Charles Otis Whitman. Perspectives in Biology and Medicine 37:395–408.

Pearl, Raymond. 1932. Contraception and Fertility in 2,000 Women. Human Biology 4:363–407.

Perlman, David. 1995. Researchers Test "Hormone of Youth." San Francisco Chronicle, January 13, A7.

Perone, Nicola. 1993. The History of Steroidal Contraceptive Development: The Progestins. Perspectives in Biology and Medicine 36:347–62.

Perry, Enos J. 1945. The Artificial Insemination of Farm Animals. New Brunswick, N.J.: Rutgers University Press.

Petchesky, Rosalind Pollack. 1984/1990. Abortion and Woman's Choice: The State, Sexuality and Reproductive Freedom. 1st and 2nd eds. New York: Longman.

———. 1985. Abortion in the 1980s: Feminist Morality and Women's Health. In Ellen Lewin and Virginia Olesen (Eds.), Women, Health and Healing: Toward a New Perspective, 139–73. New York: Tavistock.

———. 1987. Fetal Images: The Power of Visual Culture in the Politics of Reproduction. Feminist Studies 13:263–92.

———. 1995. Commentary: From Population Control to Reproductive Rights: Feminist Fault Lines. Reproductive Health Matters 6 (November):152–61.

Petersen, James C., and Gerald E. Markle. 1989. Controversies in Science and Technology. In Daryl Chubin and Ellen Chu (Eds.), Science Off the Pedestal: Social Perspectives on Science and Technology, 5–18. Belmont, Calif.: Wadsworth.

Petters, Robert M. 1986. Recombinant DNA, Gene Transfer and the Future of Animal Agriculture. Journal of Animal Science 62:1759–68.

Pfeffer, Naomi. 1985. The Hidden Pathology of the Male Reproductive System. In Hilary Homans (Ed.), The Sexual Politics of Reproduction, 30–44. Aldershot, UK: Gower.

———. 1993. The Stork and the Syringe: A Political History of Reproductive Medicine. Cambridge: Polity Press/Blackwell.

Phillips, Ralph W. 1947. Artificial Breeding. Science in Farming Section. USDA Yearbook in Agriculture, 1943–1947:113–32.

———. 1994. The Journal of Animal Science: Its Beginnings—1942–1949. Journal of Animal Science 70:1–3.

Pickens, Donald K. 1968. Eugenics and the Progressives. Nashville, Tenn.: Vanderbilt University Press.

Pickering, Andrew. 1984. Constructing Quarks: A Sociological History of Particle Physics. Chicago: University of Chicago Press.

Pickstone, John V. 1993a. The Biographical and the Analytical: Towards a Historical Model of Science and Practice in Modern Medicine. In Ilana Lowy (Ed.), Medicine and Change: Historical and Sociological Studies of Medical Innovation, 23–47. Montrouge, France: John Libbey Eurotext (Les edition INSERM).

———. 1993b. Ways of Knowing: Towards a Historical Sociology of Science, Technology and Medicine. British Journal of the History of Science 26:433–58.

Pierpoint, Raymond. 1922. Report of the Fifth International Neo-Malthusian and Birth Control Conference, London. London: William Heinemann.

Pies, Cheri. 1997. The Ongoing Politics of Contraception: Norplant and Other Emerging Technologies. In Sheryl B. Ruzek, Virginia Olesen, and Adele E. Clarke (Eds.), Women's Health: Complexities and Differences, 520–46. Columbus: Ohio State University Press.

Pinch, Trevor. 1991. The Role of Scientific Communities in the Development of Science: A Historical and Sociological Perspective. Impact of Science on Society 159:219–25.

———. 1996. The Social Construction of Technology: A Review. In Robert Fox (Ed.), Technological Change, 1–36. Australia/United States: Harwood Academic Press.

Pincus, Gregory. 1933. History of the Society. American Society of Animal Production, Record of Proceedings of Twenty-fifth Annual Meeting:377–79.

——. 1936. The Eggs of Mammals. New York: Macmillan.

——. 1965. The Control of Fertility. New York: Academic Press.

Pincus, Gregory, and K. V. Thimann. 1948. The Hormones: Physiology, Chemistry and Applications. Vol. 1. New York: Academic Press.

——. 1950. The Hormones: Physiology, Chemistry and Applications. Vol. 2. New York: Academic Press.

Piotrow, Phyllis Tilson. 1973. World Population Crisis: The United States' Response. New York: Praeger.

Pocock, R. I. 1906. Notes upon Menstruation, Gestation and Parturition of Some Monkeys That Have Lived in the Society Gardens. Proceedings of the Zoological Society of London 46:558–70.

Polge, Chris. 1994. Sir Alan Parkes, CBE, SCD, FRS, 1900–1990. Journal of Reproduction and Fertility 100:1–8.

Pomeroy, Wardell B. 1982. Dr. Kinsey and the Institute for Sex Research. New Haven, Conn.: Yale University Press.

Pope, L. S. 1980. Animal Science in the Twentieth Century. Agricultural History 54:64–70.

Porter, Roy, and Lesley Hall. 1995. The Facts of Life: The Creation of Sexual Knowledge in Britain, 1650–1950. New Haven, Conn.: Yale University Press.

Porter, Roy, and Mikulas Teich (Eds.). 1994. Sexual Knowledge, Sexual Science: The History of Attitudes to Sexuality. Cambridge: Cambridge University Press.

Porter, Theodore M. 1995. Trust in Numbers: The Pursuit of Objectivity in Science and Public Life. Princeton, N.J.: Princeton University Press.

Pottenger, F. M. 1942. The Association for the Study of Internal Secretions. Its Past: Its Future. Endocrinology 30:846–52.

Powell, Fred Wilbur. 1927. The Bureau of Animal Industry: Its History, Activities, and Organization. Baltimore, Md.: Johns Hopkins University Press.

Pramik, Mary Jean (Ed.). 1978. Norethindrone: The First Three Decades. Palo Alto, Calif.: Syntex Laboratories.

Pratt, Jean Paul. 1932. Endocrine Disorders in Sex Function in Man. In Edgar Allen (Ed.), Sex and Internal Secretions, 880–912. Baltimore, Md.: Williams and Wilkins.

——. 1937. Endocrinology and Reproduction. Journal of Contraception 2(4):75–78.

Pratt, Jean Paul, and Edgar Allen. 1926. Clinical Tests of the Ovarian Follicular Hormone. Journal of the American Medical Association 86:1964–69.

Pressman, Jack. 1991. Human Understanding: The Rockefeller Foundation's Attempt to Construct a Scientific Psychiatry in America, 1930–1950. Paper presented at Melon Conference, MIT, Cambridge, Mass.

——. 1997. Last Resort: Psychosurgery and the Problem of Mental Disorder, 1935–1955. New York: Cambridge University Press.

Price, Derek J. de Solla. 1963. Little Science, Big Science. New York: Columbia University Press.

Price, Dorothy. 1956. Carl R. Moore, 1892–1955. Endocrinology 58:529–30.

———. 1967. A Historical Review of Embryology and Intersexuality: Fact and Fancy. Leiden: E. J. Brill.

———. 1972. Mammalian Conception, Sex Differentiation, and Hermaphroditism as Viewed in Historical Perspective. American Zoologist 12:179–91.

———. 1974. Carl Richard Moore, Dec. 5, 1892–Oct. 16 1935. Biographical Memoirs of the National Academy of Sciences 45:385–412.

———. 1975. Feedback Control of Gonadal and Hypophyseal Hormones: Evolution of the Concept. In Joseph Meired, Bernard T. Donovan, and Samuel M. Mc Cann (Eds.), Pioneers in Neuro-Endocrinology, 219–38. New York: Plenum Press.

Proctor, Robert N. 1988. Racial Hygiene: Medicine under the Nazis. Cambridge, Mass.: Harvard University Press.

———. 1995. The Destruction of "Lives Not Worth Living." In Jennifer Terry and Jacqueline Urla (Eds.), Deviant Bodies: Critical Perspectives on Difference in Science and Popular Culture, 170–96. Bloomington: Indiana University Press.

Provine, William B. 1980. Epilogue. In Ernst Mayr and William B. Provine (Eds.), The Evolutionary Synthesis: Perspectives on the Unification of Biology. Cambridge, Mass.: Harvard University Press.

———. 1986. Sewell Wright and Evolutionary Biology. Chicago: University of Chicago Press.

Pursell, Carroll W. 1968. The Administration of Science in the Department of Agriculture, 1933–1940. Agricultural History 42:231–40.

Quinn, Brother C. Edward. 1982. Ancestry and Beginnings: The Early History of the American Society of Zoologists. American Zoologist 22:735–48.

Raacke, I. D. 1983. Herbert McLean Evans (1882–1971): A Biographical Sketch. Journal of Nutrition 113:928–43.

Rabinow, Paul. 1992. Artificiality and Enlightenment: From Sociobiology to Biosociality. In Jonathan Crary and Stanford Kwinter (Eds.), Incorporations, 234–52. New York: Zone.

——— (Ed.). 1984. The Foucault Reader. New York: Pantheon.

Ragin, Charles C., and Howard S. Becker (Eds.). 1992. What Is a Case? Exploring the Foundations of Social Inquiry. New York: Cambridge University Press.

Rainger, Ronald, Keith Benson, and Jane Maienschein (Eds.). 1988. The American Development of Biology. Philadelphia: University of Pennsylvania Press.

Rakusen, Jill. 1981. Depo-Provera: The Extent of the Problem. In Helen Roberts (Ed.), Women, Health and Reproduction, 75–108. Boston: Routledge and Kegan Paul.

Ramirez de Arellano, Annette B., and Conrad Seipp. 1983. Colonialism, Catholicism and Contraception: A History of Birth Control in Puerto Rico. Chapel Hill: University of North Carolina Press.

Ramsay, Elizabeth M. 1994. George Washington Corner. Biographical Memoirs, National Academy of Sciences 65:57–93.

Randle, Richard F. 1993. Production Medicine Considerations for Enhanced Reproductive Performance in Beef Herds. Veterinary Clinics of North America: Food Animal Practice 9:405–15.

Randolph, S. Randi, and Carolyn Sachs. 1981. The Establishment of Applied Sciences: Medicine and Agriculture Compared. In Lawrence Busch (Ed.), Science and Agricultural Development, 83–112. Totowa, N.J.: Allanheld, Osmun.

Rapp, Rayna. 1990. Constructing Amniocentesis: Maternal and Medical Discourses. In Faye Ginsburg and Anna Lowenhaupt Tsing (Eds.), Uncertain Terms: Negotiating Gender in American Culture, 28–42. Boston: Beacon Press.

Rasmussen, Wayne D. (Ed.). 1960. Readings in the History of American Agriculture. Urbana: University of Illinois Press.

———. (Ed.). 1989. Taking the University to the People: Seventy-five Years of Cooperative Extension. Ames: Iowa State University Press.

Ratcliff, Kathryn Strother (Ed.). 1989. Healing Technology: Feminist Perspectives. Ann Arbor: University of Michigan Press.

Ravindran, T. K. Sundari, and Marge Berer. 1994. Contraceptive Safety and Effectiveness: Re-evaluating Women's Needs and Professional Criteria. Reproductive Health Matters 3:6–12.

Ray, Joyce M., and F. G. Gosling. 1984–85. American Physicians and Birth Control, 1936–1947. Journal of Social History 18:399–409.

Raymond, Janice G. 1989. At Issue: Reproductive Technologies, Radical Feminism and Socialist Liberalism. Reproductive and Genetic Engineering 2:133–42.

Rechter, Julia. 1997. "The Glands of Destiny": The Development and Popularization of Sex Hormones in 1920s America. Ph.D. diss., University of California, Berkeley.

Redfield, Robert (Ed.). 1942. Levels of Integration in Biological and Social Systems. Biological Symposia. Vol. 8. Lancaster, Pa.: Jacques Cattell Press.

Reed, James. 1979. Doctors, Birth Control and Social Values, 1830–1970. In Morris J. Vogel and Charles E. Rosenberg (Eds.), The Therapeutic Revolution: Essays in the Social History of American Medicine. 109–34. Philadelphia: University of Pennsylvania Press.

———. 1983. The Birth Control Movement and American Society: From Private Vice to Public Virtue. 2d ed. Princeton, N.J.: Princeton University Press.

———. 1984–85. Public Policy on Human Reproduction and the Historian. Journal of Social History 18:383–98.

Reilly, Philip R. 1991. The Surgical Solution: A History of Involuntary Sterilization in the United States. Baltimore, Md.: Johns Hopkins University Press.

Reingold, Nathan. 1976. Definitions and Speculations: The Professionalization of Science in America in the Nineteenth Century. In Alexandra Oleson and Sanborn C. Brown (Eds.), The Pursuit of Knowledge in the Early American Republic: American Scientific and Learned Societies from Colonial Times to the Civil War, 33–69. Baltimore, Md.: Johns Hopkins University Press.

———. 1979. National Science Policy in a Private Foundation: The Carnegie Institution of Washington. In Alexandra Oleson and John Voss (Eds.), The Organization of Knowledge in Modern America, 1860–1920, 313–41.Baltimore, Md.: Johns Hopkins University Press.

———. 1982. Genetic Engineering. New York: Research and Education Association (REA).

——— (Ed.). 1964. Science in Nineteenth-Century America: A Documentary History. New York: Hill and Wang.

—— (Ed.). 1979. The Sciences in the American Content: New Perspectives. Washington, D.C.: Smithsonian Institution.

Restivo, Sal P. 1974. The Ideology of Basic Science. In Sal P. Restivo and Christopher K. Vanderpool (Eds.), Comparative Studies in Science and Society, 25–49. Columbus, Ohio: Merrill.

——. 1988. Modern Science as a Social Problem. Social Problems 35:206–25.

Restivo, Sal P., and Christopher K. Vanderpool (Eds.). 1974. Comparative Studies in Science and Society. Columbus, Ohio: Merrill.

Reverby, Susan, and David Rosner (Eds.). 1979. Health Care in America: Essays in Social History. Philadephia: Temple University Press.

Reynolds, Edward, and Donald Macomber. 1924. Fertility and Sterility in Human Marriages. Philadelphia: Saunders.

Reynolds, Samuel R. M. 1937. The Nature of Uterine Contractility: A Survey of Recent Trends. Physiological Review 17:304–34.

——. 1939. Physiology of the Uterus with Clinical Correlations. New York: P. B. Hoeber.

Richter, Judith. 1993. Vaccination against Pregnancy: Miracle or Menace? Amsterdam: Health Action International [HAI—Europe].

Riddle, John M. 1992. Contraception and Abortion from the Ancient World to the Renaissance. Cambridge, Mass.: Harvard University Press.

Riddle, Oscar. 1933. The Preparation, Identification and Assay of Prolactin—A Hormone of the Anterior Pituitary. American Journal of Physiology 105:191–213.

Riddle, Oscar, Robert Wesley Bates, and Simon W. Dykshorn. 1932. Prolactin. Proceedings of the Society for Experimental Biology and Medicine 29:1211.

Riessman, Cathrine Kohler. 1983. Women and Medicalization: A New Perspective. Social Policy 17 (Summer):3–18.

Rimer, Sara. 1995. Abortion Rights Are Called Threatened by Violence. New York Times, January 22, 10.

Rip, Arie. 1986. Controversies as Informal Technology Assessment. Knowledge 8:349–71.

Robertson, A. F. 1991. Beyond the Family: The Social Organization of Human Reproduction. Berkeley: University of California Press.

Robertson, William H. 1989. An Illustrated History of Contraception: A Concise Account of the Quest for Fertility Control. Park Ridge, N.J.: Parthenon.

Robinson, Paul. 1976. The Modernization of Sex: Havelock Ellis, Alfred Kinsey, William Masters and Virginia Johnson. Ithaca, N.Y.: Cornell University Press.

Robinson, T. J. 1978. Book Review: Reproduction by Jack Cohen. Animal Reproduction Science 1:189–91.

Robinson, William J. 1934. Our Mysterious Life Glands and How They Affect Us. New York: Eugenics Publishing.

Robitscher, Jonas. 1973. Eugenic Sterilization. Springfield, Ill.: Charles C. Thomas.

Rock, John, and M. K. Bartlett. 1937. Biopsy Studies of the Human Endometrium. Journal of the American Medical Association 108:2022.

Roofe, Paul G. 1968. William Caldwell Young. In Milton Diamond (Ed.), Perspectives in Reproduction and Sexual Behavior, 449–52. Bloomington: Indiana University Press.

Rose, Hilary. 1987. Victorian Values in the Test-Tube: The Politics of Reproductive Science and Technology. In Michelle Stanworth (Ed.), Reproductive Technologies: Gender, Motherhood and Medicine, 151–73. Minneapolis: University of Minnesota Press.

Rosen, George. 1965. Patterns of Health Research in the United States, 1900–1960. Bulletin of the History of Medicine 34:201–21.

Rosenberg, Charles E. 1961. Charles Benedict Davenport and the Beginning of Human Genetics. Bulletin of the History of Medicine 35:266–76.

———. 1964. On the Study of American Biology and Medicine: Some Justifications. Bulletin of the History of Medicine 38:364–76.

———. 1967. Factors in the Development of Genetics in the United States: Some Suggestions. Journal of the History of Medicine and Allied Sciences 22:27–46.

———. 1976. No Other Gods: On Science and American Social Thought. Baltimore, Md.: Johns Hopkins University Press.

———. 1979a. Rationalization and Reality in Shaping American Agricultural Research, 1875–1914. In Nathan Reingold (Ed.), The Sciences in the American Context: New Perspectives, 143–64. Washington, D.C.: Smithsonian Institution.

———. 1979b. Toward an Ecology of Knowledge: On Discipline, Contexts and History. In Alexandra Oleson and John Voss (Eds.), The Organization of Knowledge in Modern America. Baltimore, Md.: Johns Hopkins University Press.

Rosenberg, Rosalind. 1982. Beyond Separate Spheres: Intellectual Roots of Modern Feminism. New Haven, Conn.: Yale University Press.

Rosenblatt, Robert A. 1997. Ad Push against Using Hormone Pills. San Francisco Chronicle, April 28, A8.

Rosencrantz, Barbara Gutmann. 1985. The Trouble with Bovine Tuberculosis. Bulletin of the History of Medicine 59:155–75.

Rosenfeld, Louis. 1982. Origins of Clinical Chemistry: The Evolution of Protein Analysis. New York: Academic Press.

Rosoff, Jeannie I. 1988. The Politics of Birth Control. Family Planning Perspectives 20:312–20.

Ross, Dorothy. 1991. The Origins of American Social Science. New York: Cambridge University Press.

Rossiter, Margaret W. 1975. The Emergence of Agricultural Science: Justus Leibig and the Americans, 1840–1880. New Haven, Conn.: Yale University Press.

———. 1976. The Organization of Agricultural Improvement in the United States, 1785–1865. In Alexandra Oleson and Sanborn C. Brown (Eds.), The Pursuit of Knowledge in the Early American Republic: American Scientific and Learned Societies from Colonial Times to the Civil War, 279–98. Baltimore, Md.: Johns Hopkins University Press.

———. 1979. The Organization of the Agricultural Sciences. In A. Oleson and J. Voss (Eds.), The Organization of Knowledge in Modern America, 1860–1920, 211–48. Baltimore, Md.: Johns Hopkins University Press.

———. 1986. Graduate Work in the Agricultural Sciences, 1900–1970. Agricultural History 60(2):37–57.

Rothblatt, Sheldon. 1983. The Diversification of Higher Education in England. In Konrad Jarausch (Ed.), The Transformation of Higher Learning 1860–1930, 147–84. Chicago: University of Chicago Press.

Rothenberg, Karen H., and Elizabeth J. Thompson (Eds.). 1994. Women and Prenatal Testing: Facing the Challenges of Genetic Technology. Columbus: Ohio State University Press.

Rothman, Barbara Katz. 1984. The Meanings of Choice in Reproductive Technology. In Rita Arditti, Renate Klein, and Shelley Minden (Eds.), Test-Tube Women: What Future for Mother hood?, 23–33. Boston: Pandora Press/Routledge and Kegan Paul.

———. 1986. The Tentative Pregnancy: Prenatal Diagnosis and the Future of Motherhood. New York: Penguin.

Rothman, Shiela. 1978. Woman's Proper Place: A History of Changing Ideals and Practices, 1870 to the Present. New York: Basic Books.

Rowland, Robyn. 1987. Technology and Motherhood: Reproductive Choice Reconsidered. Signs 12:512–28.

———. 1992. Living Laboratories: Women and Reproductive Technologies. Bloomington: Indiana University Press.

Rupp, Leila J., and Verta Taylor. 1987. Survival in the Doldrums: The American Women's Rights Movement, 1945 to the 1960s. New York: Oxford University Press.

Russell, Sir E. John. 1966. A History of Agricultural Science in Great Britain, 1620–1954. London: Allen and Unwin.

Russett, Cynthia E. 1989. Sexual Science: The Victorian Construction of Womanhood. Cambridge, Mass.: Harvard University Press.

Ruzek, Sheryl Burt. 1978. The Women's Health Movement: Feminist Alternatives to Medical Control. New York: Praeger.

———. 1980. Medical Response to Women's Health Activities: Conflict, Cooptation and Accommodation. Research in the Sociology of Health Care 1:335–54.

Ryan, Mary P. 1979. Reproduction in American History. Journal of Interdisciplinary History 10:319–32.

Sabin, Florence Rena. 1934. Franklin Paine Mall: The Story of a Mind. Baltimore, Md.: Johns Hopkins University Press.

Sandelowski, Margarete. 1991. Compelled to Try: The Never-Enough Quality of Conceptive Technology. Medical Anthropology Quarterly 5:29–47.

Sanger, Margaret. 1919. Birth Control and Racial Betterment. Birth Control Review 3 (February):11–12

———. 1920. Woman and the New Race. New York: Brentano's.

———. 1937. The Future of Contraception. Journal of Contraception 2:3–4.

———. 1938/1971. An Autobiography. Reprint, New York: Dover.

——— (Ed). 1934. Biological and Medical Aspects of Contraception. [American Conference on Birth Control and National Recovery.] Washington, D.C.: National Committee on Federal Legislation for Birth Control.

Sanger, Margaret, and Hannah M. Stone. 1931. The Practice of Contraception: An International Symposium and Survey. Proceedings of the Seventh International Birth Control Conference, Zurich, 1930. Baltimore, Md.: Williams and Wilkins.

Sapp, Jan. 1983. The Struggle for Authority in the Field of Heredity, 1900–1932: New Perspectives on the Rise of Genetics. Journal of the History of Biology 16:311–42.

———. 1987. Beyond the Gene: Cytoplasmic Inheritance and the Struggle for Authority in Genetics. New York: Oxford University Press.

Saunders, F. J., and H. H. Cole. 1935. Two Gonadotropic Substances in Mare Serum. Proceedings of the Society for Experimental Biology and Medicine 32:1476–78.

Schaffir, Jonathan. 1991. What Are Little Boys Made Of? The Never-Ending Search for Sex Selection Techniques. Perspectives in Biology and Medicine 34:517–25.

Schell, Orville. 1984. Modern Meat: Antibiotics, Hormones and the Pharmaceutical Farm. New York: Random House.

Schenk, Faith, and A. S. Parkes. 1968. The Activities of the Eugenics Society. Eugenics Review 60:142–61.

Schiebinger, Londa. 1987. Skeletons in the Closet: The First Illustrations of the Female Skeleton in Eighteenth-Century Anatomy. In Catherine Gallagher and Thomas Laqueur (Eds.), The Making of the Modern Body: Sexuality and Society in the Nineteenth Century, 42–82. Berkeley: University of California Press.

———. 1989. The Mind Has No Sex? Women in the Origins of Modern Science. Cambridge, Mass.: Harvard University Press.

———. 1993. Nature's Body: Gender in the Making of Modern Science. Boston: Beacon Press.

Schmidt, Karl Patterson. 1957. Walter Clyde Allee, 1885–1955. Biographical Memoirs of the National Academy of Science 30:3–40.

Schmidt, L. H. 1972. Problems and Opportunities of Breeding Primates. In W. I. B. Beveridge (Ed.), Breeding Primates: Proceedings of the International Symposium on Breeding Non-Human Primates for Laboratory Use, Bern, 1971, 1–22. New York and Basel: S. Karger.

Schmidt, Matt, and Lisa Jean Moore. 1998. Constructing a Good Catch, Picking a Winner: The Development of Technosemen and the Deconstruction of the Monolithic Male. Forthcoming in Robbie Davis-Floyd and Joseph Dumit (Eds.), Cyborg Babies: From Techno-Sex to Techno-Tots. New York: Routledge.

Schneider, Joseph. 1984. Morality, Social Problems and Everyday Life. In Joseph Schneider and John Kitsuse (Eds.), Studies in the Sociology of Social Problems, 180–205. Norwood, N.J.: Ablex.

Schneider, Keith. 1988a. Better Farm Animals Duplicated by Cloning. New York Times, February 17, 1, 38.

———. 1988b. Biotechnology's Cash Cow. New York Times Magazine, June 12, 44–53.

School of Commerce and Administration and the Institute of American Meat Packers. 1924. The Packing Industry: A Series of Lectures. Chicago: University of Chicago Press.

Schrater, Angeline Faye. 1992. Contraceptive Vaccines: Promises and Problems. In
Helen Bequaert Holmes (Ed.), Issues in Reproductive Technology I: An Anthology, 31–52. New York. Garland.
Schultz. A. H. 1940. Growth and Development of the Chimpanzee. Carnegie Contributions to Embryology, no. 170:1–63.
———. 1941. Growth and Development of the Orang-Utan. Carnegie Contributions to Embryology, no. 182:57–62.
———. 1971. The Rise of Primatology in the Twentieth Century. In J. Biegert and
W. Leutenegger (Eds.), Proceedings of the Third International Congress of Primatology, Zurich, 1970. Vol. 1, Taxonomy, Anatomy, Reproduction. New York
and Basel: S. Karger.
Schwabe, Calvin W. 1984. Veterinary Medicine and Human Health. 3d ed. Baltimore, Md.: Williams and Wilkins.
Schwartz, Neena B. 1984. Endocrinology as Paradigm, Endocrinology as Authority.
Presidential Address of the Endocrine Society Sixty-fifth Annual Meeting. En-
docrinology 114:308–13.
Schwartz, Neena B., Donald J. Dierschke, Charles E. McCormack, and Paul W.
Waltz. 1977. Feedback Regulation of Reproductive Cycles in Rats, Sheep, Mon-
keys, and Humans with Particular Attention to Computer Modeling. In Roy O.
Greep and Marjorie A. Koblinsky (Eds.), Frontiers in Reproduction and Fertility
Control: A Review of the Reproductive Sciences and Contraceptive Develop-
ment, 55–89. Cambridge, Mass.: MIT Press.
Scott, Pam, Eveleen Richards, and Brian Martin. 1990. Captives of Controversy:
The Myth of the Neutral Social Researcher in Contemporary Scientific Contro-
versies. Science, Technology and Human Values 15:474–94.
Scully, Diana. 1980. Men Who Control Women's Health: The Miseducation of Ob-
stetrician-Gynecologists. New York: Houghton Mifflin.
Seaman, Barbara. 1969/1980. The Doctors' Case against the Pill. 1st and 2d edi-
tions. New York: Doubleday.
Seaman, Barbara, and Gideon Seaman, M.D. 1977. Women and the Crisis in Sex
Hormones. New York: Bantam.
Searle, G. R. 1976. Eugenics and Politics in Britain, 1900–1914. Leyden: Noordhoff
International.
———. 1981. Eugenics and Class. In Charles Webster (Ed.), Biology, Medicine and
Society 1840–1940, 217–42. Cambridge: Cambridge University Press.
Sechzer, Jeri A. 1981. Historical Issues Concerning Animal Experimentation in the
United States. Social Science and Medicine 15(F):13–17.
——— (Ed.). 1983. The Role of Animals in Biomedical Research. Annals of the
New York Academy of Sciences 406. New York: New York Academy of Sciences.
Segal, Sheldon J. 1987. The Development of Modern Contraceptive Technology.
Technology in Society 9:277–82.
Seibel, Michelle. 1988. A New Era in Reproductive Technology: In Vitro Fertiliza-
tion, Gamete Intrafallopian Transfer, and Donated Gametes and Embryos. New
England Journal of Medicine 318:828–34.
Sen, Gita, Adrienne Germain, and Lincoln C. Chen (Eds.). 1994. Population Poli-

cies Reconsidered: Health, Empowerment, and Rights. Cambridge, Mass.: Harvard University Press.

Sen, Gita, and Rachel C. Snow (Eds.). 1994. Power and Decision: The Social Control of Reproduction. Harvard Series on Population and International Health. Boston: Harvard School of Public Health/Harvard University Press.

Sengoopta, Chandak. 1993. Rejuvenation and the Prolongation of Life: Science or Quackery? Perspectives in Biology and Medicine 37:55–66.

———. 1995. Glandular Politics: Endocrinology, Sexual Orientation, and Emancipation in Early Twentieth-Century Eastern Europe. Paper presented at meeting of the American Association for the History of Medicine. Pittsburgh.

Service, Robert F. 1994. Barriers Hold Back New Contraception Strategies. Science 266:1489.

Servos, John. 1976. The Knowledge Corporation: A. A. Noyes and Chemistry at Cal-Tech, 1915–1930. Ambix 23(3):175–86.

Setchell, Brian P. (Ed.). 1984. Male Reproduction. Benchmark Papers in Human Physiology 17. New York: Van Nostrand Reinhold.

Severinghaus, Aura Edward. 1971. A Memorial Resolution for Philip Edward Smith. American Journal of Anatomy 135:159–64.

Severinghaus, Aura Edward, E. T. Engle, and P. E. Smith. 1932. Anterior Pituitary Changes Referable to the Reproductive Hormones, and the Influence of the Thyroid and the Adrenals on Genital Function. In Edgar Allen (Ed.), Sex and Internal Secretions, 805–27. Baltimore, Md.: Williams and Wilkins.

Severinghaus, Elmer L. 1942. Commercial Endocrine Preparations. Endocrinology 30:912–21.

Shapin, Steven. 1988. Following Scientists Around: Review of Latour 1987. Social Studies of Science 18:533–50.

———. 1992. Discipline and Bounding: The History and Sociology of Science as Seen through the Externalism-Internalism Debate. History of Science 30:333–69.

Shapiro, Thomas M. 1985. Population Control Politics: Women, Sterilization and Reproductive Choice. Philadelphia: Temple University Press.

Sharpey-Shafer, Sir Edward. 1926. The Endocrine Organs. 2d ed. London: Cambridge University Press.

———. 1927. History of the Physiological Society during Its First Fifty Years, 1876–1926. London: Cambridge University Press.

Sharpless, John B. 1993. The Rockefeller Foundation, the Population Council and the Groundwork for New Population Policies. In Erwin Levold and Ken Rose (Eds.), Rockefeller Archive Center Newsletter 1:7–8. Tarrytown, N.Y.: Rockefeller Archive Center.

Shelesnyak, M. C. 1963a. Biodynamics and the Population Explosion. Ariel 13:21–33.

———. 1963b. Interdisciplinary Approaches to the Endocrinology of Reproduction. In Peter Eckstein and Frances Knowles (Eds.), Techniques in Endocrine Research, 231–43. New York: Academic Press.

———. 1964. Exploration of Biological Bases for Fertility Control. Proceedings of the Second International Congress of Endocrinology, London, August. Excerpta Medica International Congress Series No. 83, 1365–72. Amsterdam: Excerpta Medica Foundation.

———. 1975. Comments. In Joseph Meites, Bernard T. Donovan, and Samuel McCann (Eds.), Pioneers in Neuroendocrinology, vol. 1:269–78. New York: Plenum Press.

Sherman, J. K. 1979. Historical Synopsis of Human Semen Cryobanking. In George David and Wendel Price (Eds), Human Artificial Insemination and Semen Preservation, 95–105. Paris: International Symposium on Artificial Insemination and Semen Preservation.

Short, R. V. 1977. The Discovery of the Ovaries. In Professor Lord Zuckerman and Barbara J. Weir (Eds.), The Ovary. Vol. 1, General Aspects, 1–39. 2d ed. New York: Academic Press.

Short, S. E. D. 1983. Physicians, Science and Status: Issues in the Professionalization of Anglo-American Medicine in the Ninteenth Century. Medical History 27:51–68.

Shryock, Richard H. 1936. The Development of Modern Medicine: An Interpretation of the Social and Scientific Factors Involved. Madison: University of Wisconsin Press.

———. 1947. American Medical Research. New York: Commonwealth Fund.

Shultz, Marjorie M. 1994. Reproductive Technology and Infant-Based Parenthood: An Opportunity for Gender Neutrality. Wisconsin Law Review 1990:297–398.

Shuttleworth, Sally. 1990. Female Circulation: Medical Discourse and Popular Advertising in the Mid-Victorian Era. In Mary Jacobus, Evelyn Fox Keller, and Sally Shuttleworth (Eds.), Body/Politics: Women and the Discourses of Science, 47–68. New York: Routledge.

Simmel, Georg. 1904/1971. Fashion. In Donald L. Levine (Ed.), Georg Simmel: On Individuality and Social Forms, 294–323. Chicago: University of Chicago Press.

Simmer, Hans H. 1978. Die Auffindung eines Zyklus im desquamierten menschlichen Vaginakepthel. In Christa Habrich et al. (Eds.), Medizinische Diagnostik in Geshichte und Gegenwart, 341–56. Munich: Fritsch.

Sinding, Christiane. 1990. Clinical Research and Basic Science: The Development of the Concept of End-Organ Resistance to a Hormone. Journal of the History of Medicine and Allied Sciences 45:198–232.

Smith, David C. 1980. The Maine Agricultural Experiment Station: A Bountiful Alliance of Science and Husbandry. Orono: University of Maine Press.

Smith, M. G. 1926. On Interruption of Pregnancy by Injection of Ovarian Follicular Extract. Bulletin of Johns Hopkins Hospital 39:203–14.

Smith, Philip E. 1916. Experimental Ablation of the Hypophysis in the Frog Embryo. Science 44:280–82.

———. 1927. The Disabilities Caused by Hypophysectomy and Their Repair. Journal of the American Medical Association 88:158–61.

———. 1930. Hypophysectomy and a Replacement Therapy in the Rat. American Journal of Anatomy 45:205–73.

———. 1932. Effect on the Reproductive System of Ablation and Implantation of the Anterior Hypophysis. In Edgar Allen (Ed.), Sex and Internal Secretions, 734–64. Baltimore, Md.: Williams and Wilkins.

Smithcors, J. F. 1963. The American Veterinary Profession: Its Background and Development. Ames: Iowa State University Press.

Soloway, Richard A. 1982. Birth Control and the Population Question in England, 1877–1930. Chapel Hill: University of North Carolina Press.

———. 1990. Demography and Degeneration: Eugenics and the Declining Birthrate in Twentieth-Century Britain. Chapel Hill: University of North Carolina Press.

———. 1995. The "Perfect Contraceptive": Eugenics and Birth Control Research in Britain and America in the Interwar Years. Journal of Contemporary History 30:637–64.

Southam, Anna L. 1965. Historical Review of Intra-Uterine Devices. In S. J. Segal, A. Southam, and K. D. Shafer (Eds.), Intra-Uterine Contraception: Proceedings of the Second International Conference. International Congress Series No. 86, 3–5. Amsterdam: Exerpta Medica Foundation.

Spallone, Patricia, and Deborah Lynn Steinberg (Eds.). 1987. Made to Order: The Myth of Reproductive and Genetic Progress. New York: Pergamon.

Speert, Harold. 1980. Obstetrics and Gynecology in America: A History. Chicago: American College of Obstetricians and Gynecologists.

Spilman, C. H., T. J. Lobl, and K. T. Kirton (Eds.). 1976. Regulatory Mechanisms of Male Reproductive Physiology: Sixth Brook Lodge Workshop on Problems of Reproductive Biology. New York: American Elsevier.

Squier, Susan. 1995. Babies in Bottles: Twentieth-Century Visions of Reproductive Technology. New Brunswick, N.J.: Rutgers University Press.

Stalheim, Ole H. V. 1988. The Hog Cholera Battle and Veterinary Professionalism. Agricultural History 62:116–21.

Stanworth, Michelle. 1990. Birth Pangs: Conceptive Technologies and the Threat to Motherhood. In Marianne Hirsch and Evelyn Fox Keller (Eds.), Conflicts in Feminism, 174–98. New York: Routledge.

——— (Ed.). 1987. Reproductive Technologies: Gender, Motherhood and Medicine. Minneapolis: University of Minnesota Press.

Star, S. Leigh. 1983. Simplification in Scientific Work: An Example from Neuroscience Research. Social Studies of Science 13:208–26.

———. 1985. Scientific Work and Uncertainty. Social Studies of Science 15:391–427.

———. 1986. Triangulating Clinical and Basic Research: British Localizationists, 1870–1906. History of Science 24:29–48.

———. 1989. Regions of the Mind: Brain Research and the Quest for Scientific Certainty. Stanford, Calif.: Stanford University Press.

———. 1991. Power, Technologies and the Phenomenology of Conventions: On Being Allergic to Onions. In John Law (Ed.), A Sociology of Monsters: Essays on Power, Technology and Domination, 26–56. New York: Routledge.

——— (Ed.). 1995. Ecologies of Knowledge: New Directions in the Sociology of Science and Technology. Albany: State University of New York Press.

Star, S. Leigh, and James Griesemer. 1989. Institutional Ecology, "Translations" and Boundary Objects: Amateurs and Professionals in Berkeley's Museum of Vertebrate Zoology, 1907–1939. Social Studies of Science 19:387–420.

Starr, Paul. 1982. The Social Transformation of American Medicine. New York: Basic Books.

Stefferud, Alfred. (Ed.). 1962. After a Hundred Years. The Yearbook of Agriculture, 1962. Washington, D.C.: U.S. Government Printing Office.

Steinach, Eugen. 1940. Sex and Life: Forty Years of Biological and Medical Experiments. New York: Viking Press.

Steiner, M., R. Dominik, J. Trussell, and I. Hertzpiccioto. 1996. Measuring Contraceptive Effectiveness: A Conceptual Framework. Obstetrics and Gynecology 88:524–30.

Stellhorn, Paul A. 1978. Planned and Utopian Experiments: Four New Jersey Towns. Tenth New Jersey Historical Symposium. Trenton: New Jersey Historical Commission.

Stepan, Nancy. 1986. Race and Gender: The Role of Analogy in Science. Isis 77:261–77.

Stevens, Rosemary. 1971. American Medicine and the Public Interest. New Haven, Conn.: Yale University Press.

Stewart, T. Dale. 1983. Adolph Hans Schultz. Biographical Memoirs of the National Academy of Sciences, U.S.A. 54:325–49.

Stockard, Charles R., and George Papanicolaou. 1917a. The Existence of a Typical Oestrous Cycle in the Guinea-Pig, with a Study of Its Histological and Physiological Changes. American Journal of Anatomy 22:225–83.

———. 1917b. A Rhythmical "Heat Period" in the Guinea-Pig. Science 46:42–44.

Strathern, Marilyn. 1992. Reproducing the Future: Essays on Anthropology, Kinship and the New Reproductive Technologies. New York: Routledge.

Strauss, Anselm L. 1971. Professions, Work and Careers. San Francisco: Sociology Press.

———. 1978. A Social Worlds Perspective. Studies in Symbolic Interaction 1:119–28.

———. 1979. Negotiations: Varieties, Contexts, Processes and Social Order. San Francisco: Jossey-Bass.

———. 1982. Social Worlds and Legitimation Processes. In Norman Denzin (Ed.), Studies in Symbolic Interaction 4:171–90.

———. 1987. Qualitative Analysis for Social Scientists. Cambridge: Cambridge University Press.

———. 1991. Creating Sociological Awareness: Collective Images and Symbolic Representation. New Brunswick, N.J.: Transaction Books.

———. 1993. Continual Permutation of Action. New York: Aldine de Gruyter.

Strauss, Anselm L., and Lee Rainwater. 1962. The Professional Scientist: A Study of American Chemists. Chicago: Aldine.

Streeter, George L. 1935. The Significance of Morbid Processes in the Fetus. The Harvey Lectures (1933–1934) Series 29:204–16. Baltimore, Md.: Williams and Wilkins.

Strickland, Tamara G., and Stephen P. Strickland. 1976. The Markle Scholars: A Brief History. New York: Prodist for the John and Mary R. Markle Foundation.

Strong, Bryan. 1972. The Ideas of the Early Sex Education Movement in America, 1890–1920. History of Education Quarterly 12 (Summer):129–61.

Stubbe, Hans. 1972. History of Genetics from Prehistoric Times to the Rediscovery of Mendel's Laws. Cambridge, Mass.: MIT Press.

Studer, Kenneth E., and Daryl Chubin. 1976. The Heroic Age of Reproductive Endocrinology: Its Development and Structure. Unpublished manuscript, Research Program on Social Analyses of Science Systems, Cornell University, used with permission.

———. 1980. The Cancer Mission: Social Contexts of Biomedical Research. Beverly Hills, Calif.: Sage.

Sturdy, Steve. 1993. Medical Chemistry and Clinical Medicine's Academics and Scientization of Medical Practice in Britain, 1900–1925. In Ilana Lowy (Ed.), Medicine and Change: Historical and Sociological Studies of Medical Innovation, 371–94. Montrouge, France: John Libbey Eurotext (Les editions INSERM).

Sturtevant, A. H. 1965. A History of Genetics. New York: Harper and Row.

Suplee, Curt. 1996. Sperm-Producing Cells Transplanted across Species Barrier. San Francisco Chronicle, May 30, A3.

Swain, Donald C. 1962. The Rise of a Research Empire: NIH, 1930 to 1950. Science 138:1233–37.

Swann, John P. 1988. Academic Scientists and the Pharmaceutical Industry: Cooperative Research in Twentieth-Century America. Baltimore, Md.: Johns Hopkins University Press.

Symonds, Richard, and Michael Carder. 1973. The United Nations and the Population Question, 1945–1970. New York: McGraw-Hill.

Taylor, Howard C., Jr. 1948. Research in Human Reproduction: Medical Aspects. Human Fertility 13(1):1–5.

Terry, Jennifer. 1990. Lesbians under the Medical Gaze: Scientists Search for Remarkable Differences. Journal of Sex Research 27:317–39.

Thomas, W. I. 1914. The Polish-Prussian Situation: An Experiment in Assimilation. American Journal of Sociology 19:624–39.

Thorne, George W. 1976. Metabolism and Endocrinology. In John Z. Bowers and Elizabeth Purcell (Eds.), Advances in American Medicine: Essays at the Bicentennial, vol. 1:159–209. New York: Josiah Macy, Jr., Foundation and the National Library of Medicine.

Tietze, Christopher. 1962. Intra-Uterine Contraceptive Rings: History and Statistical Appraisal. In C. Tietze and S. Lewis (Eds.), Intra-Uterine Contraceptive Devices: Proceedings of the Conference, 1–34. New York: Excerpta Medica.

———. 1965a. Bibliography of Fertility Control: 1950–1965. Publication No. 23. New York: National Committee on Maternal Health.

———. 1965b. History and Statistical Evaluation of Intrauterine Contraceptive Devices. Journal of Chronic Disease 18:1147–59.

Timme, Walter. 1924. Relation between Clinical and Experimental Endocrinology. Endocrinology 12:719–29.

Tobey, Ronald C. 1971. The American Ideology of National Science, 1919–1930. Pittsburgh: University of Pittsburgh Press.

Treichler, Paula A. 1990. Feminism, Medicine, and the Meaning of Childbirth. In

Mary Jacobus, Evelyn Fox Keller, and Sally Shuttleworth (Eds.), Body Politics: Women and the Discourses of Science, 113–38. New York: Routledge.

———. 1993. How to Use a Condom: Some Serious Lessons from Contemporary AIDS Discourses. Paper presented at the Conference on Postdisciplinary Approaches to the Technosciences. University of California, Los Angeles, April.

True, A. C. 1937. A History of Agricultural Experimentation and Research in the United States, 1607–1925. Miscellaneous Publication No. 251. Washington, D.C.: U.S. Department of Agriculture.

True, A. C., and V. A. Clark. 1900. The Agricultural Experiment Stations in the United States. Bulletin No. 80. Washington, D.C.: U.S. Department of Agriculture.

Trussell, James, and Kathryn Kost. 1987. Contraceptive Failure in the United States: A Critical Review of the Literature. Studies in Family Planning 18:237–83.

Tsing, Anna Lowenhaupt. 1993. In the Realm of the Diamond Queen: Marginalities in Out of the Way Places. Princeton, N.J.: Princeton University Press.

Tuana, Nancy. 1993. The Less Noble Sex: Scientific, Religious, and Philosophical Conceptions of Woman's Nature. Bloomington: University of Indiana Press.

Turner, C. W. 1932. The Mammary Glands. In Edgar Allen (Ed.), Sex and Internal Secretions, 544–83. Baltimore, Md.: Williams and Wilkins.

Turner, James. 1980. Reckoning with the Beast: Animals, Pain and Humanity in the Victorian Mind. Baltimore, Md.: Johns Hopkins University Press.

van den Wijngaard, Marianne. 1991. The Acceptance of Scientific Theories and Images of Masculinity and Femininity: 1959–c1985. Journal of the History of Biology 24:19–49.

———. 1994. Feminism and the Biological Construction of Female and Male Behavior. Journal of the History of Biology 27:61–90.

van Wagenen, Gertrude. 1924. Degeneration of the Germinal Epithelium in the Testis of the Rat as a Result of Efferent Duct Ligation. Anatomical Record 27:189.

van Wagenen, Gertrude, and Miriam E. Simpson. 1973. Postnatal Development of the Ovary in *Homo sapiens* and *Macaca mulatta*. New Haven, Conn.: Yale University Press.

Vance, Carole S. (Ed.). 1984. Pleasure and Danger: Exploring Female Sexuality. Boston: Routledge and Kegan Paul.

Vaughn, Paul. 1970. The Pill on Trial. New York: Coward-McCann.

Veith, Ilza, and Franklin C. McLean. 1952. The University of Chicago Clinics and Clinical Departments, 1927–1952. Chicago: University of Chicago Press.

Velardo, Joseph Thomas, and Barbara A. Kasprow (Eds.). 1972. Biology of Reproduction: Basic and Clinical Studies. New Orleans: Third Pan American Congress of Anatomy.

Vesey, Lawrence. 1965. The Emergence of the American University. Chicago: University of Chicago Press.

Vines, Gail. 1993. Raging Hormones: Do They Rule Our Lives? Berkeley: University of California Press.

Voda, Ann M., Myra Dinnerstein, and Sheryl R. O'Donnell (Eds.). 1982. Changing Perspectives on Menopause. Austin: University of Texas Press.

Voge, Cecil I. B. 1933. The Chemistry and Physics of Contraception. London: Jonathan Cape.

Vogel, Morris J., and Charles E. Rosenberg (Eds.). 1979. The Therapeutic Revolution: Essays in the Social History of American Medicine. Philadelphia: University of Pennsylvania Press.

Volberg, Rachel A. 1983. Constraints and Commitments in the Development of American Botany, 1880–1920. Ph.D. diss., University of California, San Francisco.

Vollman, Rudolph P. 1965. Fifty Years of Research on Mammalian Reproduction: Carl G. Hartman. USDHEW Public Health Service Publication No. 1281. Washington, D.C.: U.S. Government Printing Office.

Wade, Nicholas. 1981. The Nobel Duel. Garden City, N.Y.: Anchor/Doubleday.

Wajcman, Judy. 1991. Feminism Confronts Technology. University Park: Pennsylvania State University Press.

———. 1995. Feminist Theories of Technology. In Sheila Jasanoff, Gerald E. Markle, James Peterson, and Trevor Pinch (Eds.), Handbook of Science and Technology Studies, 189–204. Thousand Oaks, Calif.: Sage.

Ward, Martha C. 1986. Poor Women, Powerful Men: America's Great Experiment in Family Planning. Boulder, Colo.: Westview.

Warner, John Harley. 1980. Physiology. In Ronald L. Numbers (Ed.), The Education of American Physicians, 48–71. Berkeley: University of California Press.

———. 1985. Science in Medicine. Osiris 1:37–58.

———. 1995. The History of Science and the Sciences of Medicine. Osiris 10:164–93.

Watkins, Elizabeth. 1995. "Perils of the Pill": Medical Controversy and Public Concern over the Health Effects of Oral Contraceptives in the Late 1960s. Paper presented at meeting of the American Association for the History of Medicine. Pittsburgh.

Watson-Verran, Helen, and David Turnbull. 1995. Science and Other Indigenous Knowledge Systems. In Sheila Jasanoff, Gerald E. Markle, James Petersen, and Trevor Pinch (Eds.), Handbook of Science and Technology Studies, 115–39. Thousand Oaks, Calif.: Sage.

Watterson, Ray L. 1973. Frank Ratray Lillie. In Charles Coulston Gillispie (Ed.), Dictionary of Scientific Biography. Vol. 8. New York: Scribner.

———. 1985. Benjamin Harrison Willier, November 2, 1890–Decemeber 3, 1972. Biographical Memoirs of the National Academy of Science 55:539–628.

Weindling, Paul. 1988. The Rockefeller Foundation and German Biomedical Sciences, 1920–40: From Educational Philanthropy to International Science Policy. In Nicolaas A. Rupke (Ed.), Science, Politics and the Public Good: Essays in Honor of Margaret Gowing, 197–231. Oxford: Macmillan Press.

Weiner, Charles. 1989. Patents and Academic Research. In Vivian Weil and John W. Snapper (Eds.), Owning Scientific and Technical Information: Value and Ethical Issues, 87–109. New Brunswick, N.J.: Rutgers University Press.

Weisman, Abner I. 1941. Spermatozoa and Sterility: A Clinical Manual. New York: Paul B. Hoeber.

Welbourn, Richard B. 1990. The History of Endocrine Surgery. New York: Praeger.

Werdinger, Jeffrey. 1980. Embryology at Woods Hole: The Emergence of a New American Biology. Ph.D. diss., Indiana University.

Werthessen, N. T., with R. C. Johnson. 1974. Pincogenesis: Parthenogenesis in Rabbits by Gregory Pincus. Perspectives in Biology and Medicine 18:86–93.

Wertz, Dorothy C. 1983. What Birth Has Done for Doctors: A Historical View. Women and Health 8(1):7–24.

Wertz, Dorothy C., and John C. Fletcher (Eds.). 1989. Ethics and Human Genetics: A Cross-Cultural Perspective. New York: Springer-Verlag.

Wertz, Richard W., and Dorothy C. Wertz 1977. Lying-In: A History of Childbirth in America. New York: Free Press.

——. 1981. Notes on the Decline of Midwives and the Rise of Medical Obstetricians. In Peter Conrad and Rochelle Kern (Eds.), The Sociology of Health and Illness: Critical Perspectives, 165–83. New York: St. Martin's Press.

Westoff, Charles F., and Norman B. Ryder. 1977. The Contraceptive Revolution. Princeton, N.J.: Princeton University Press.

Whalen, Richard E. 1984. Multiple Actions of Steroids and Their Antagonists. Archives of Sexual Behavior 13:497–502.

Wheatley, Steven C. 1989. The Politics of Philanthropy: Abraham Flexner and Medical Education. Madison: University of Wisconsin Press.

Whitley, Richard. 1976. Umbrella and Polytheistic Scientific Disciplines and Their Elites. Social Studies of Science 6:471–97.

——. 1984. The Intellectual and Social Organization of the Sciences. New York: Oxford University Press.

Whitman, Charles O. 1902. A Biological Farm for the Experimental Investigation of Heredity, Variation and Evolution and for the Study of Life Histories, Habits, Instincts and Intelligence. Science 16:504–10.

Whorton, James. 1980. Chemistry. In Ronald L. Numbers (Ed.), The Education of American Physicians, 72–94. Berkeley: University of California Press.

Wiener, Carolyn. 1981. The Politics of Alcoholism: A Social Worlds Analysis. New Brunswick, N.J.: Transaction Books.

Wiener, Norbert. 1964. God and Golem, Inc. Cambridge, Mass.: MIT Press.

Wilkinson, Lise. 1992. Animals and Disease: An Introduction to the History of Comparative Medicine. New York: Cambridge University Press.

Willham, R. L. 1986. From Husbandry to Science: A Highly Significant Facet of Our Livestock Heritage. Journal of Animal Science 62:1742–58.

Williams, Doone, and Greer Williams. 1978. Every Child a Wanted Child: Clarence James Gamble, M.D., and His Work in the Birth Control Movement. Emily Flint (Ed.). Boston: Harvard University Press.

Williams, Raymond. 1976. Key Words: A Vocabulary of Culture and Society. New York: Oxford University Press.

Willier, Benjamin H. 1932. Embryological Foundations of Sex in Vertebrates. In Edgar Allen (Ed.), Sex and Internal Secretions, 94–159. Baltimore, Md.: Williams and Wilkins.

——. 1957. Frank Ratray Lillie, 1870–1947. Biographical Memoirs of the National Academy of Science, U.S.A. 30:179–236.

Willier, Benjamin H., and Jane M. Oppenheimer (Eds.). 1964. Foundations of Experimental Embryology. Englewood Cliffs, N.J.: Prentice-Hall.

Wilmoth, John R., and Patrick Ball. 1992. The Population Debate in American Popular Magazines, 1946–90. Population Development Review 18:631–68.

Wilson, Karl M. 1926. Histological Changes in the Vaginal Mucosa of the Sow in Relation to the Oestrus Cycle. American Journal of Anatomy 37:417–31.

Wiser, Vivian. 1987. Healthy Livestock: Wholesale Meat. In Vivian Wiser, Larry Mark, and H. Graham Purchase (Eds.), One Hundred Years of Animal Health, 1–18. Beltsville, Md.: Associates of the National Agricultural Library.

Wiser, Vivian, Larry Mark, and H. Graham Purchase (Eds.). 1987. One Hundred Years of Animal Health. Beltsville, Md.: Associates of the National Agricultural Library.

Witschi, Emil. 1932. Sex Deviations, Inversions and Parabiosis. In Edgar Allen (Ed.), Sex and Internal Secretions, 160–245. Baltimore, Md.: Williams and Wilkins.

Wood, Clive, and Beryl Suitters. 1970. The Fight for Acceptance: A History of Contraception. Aylesbury, England: Medical and Technical Publishing.

Woolgar, Steve. 1976. The Identification and Definition of Scientific Collectivities. In Gerard Lemaine, Roy MacLeod, Michael Mulkay, and Peter Weingart (Eds.), Perspectives on the Emergence of Scientific Disciplines, 233–46. The Hague and Chicago: Mouton/Aldine.

———. 1981. Interests and Explanation in the Social Study of Science. Social Studies of Science 11:365–94.

———. 1991. Configuring the User: The Case of Usability Trials. In John Law (Ed.), A Sociology of Monsters: Essays on Power, Technology and Domination, 57–102. New York: Routledge.

Worthman, Carol M. 1995. Hormones, Sex and Gender. Annual Review of Anthropology 24:593–616.

Wright, Robert. 1997. Can Souls Be Cloned? Time Magazine, March 10, 73.

Wright, Sewall. 1921. Systems of Mating. Genetics 6:111–78.

———. 1922. Coefficients of Inbreeding and Relationship. American Naturalist 56:330–38.

———. 1931. Evolution in Mendelian Populations. Chicago: University of Chicago Press.

Wymelenberg, Suzanne, for the Institute of Medicine (Ed.), Science and Babies: Private Decisions: Public Dilemmas. Washington, D.C.: National Academy Press.

Yerkes, Robert M. 1916. Provision for the Study of Monkeys and Apes. Science 43:231–34.

———. 1919. Report of the Psychology Committee of the National Research Council. Psychological Review 26:83–149.

———. 1925. Almost Human. New York and London: Century.

———. 1932. Psychobiologist: A History of Psychology in Autobiography, vol. 2:381–407. Worcester, Mass.: Clark University Press.

———. 1935. Yale Laboratories of Primate Biology, Inc. Science 82:618–20.

———. 1935/36. The Significance of Chimpanzee-Culture for Biological Research. Harvey Society Lectures 31:57–73.

——. 1943. Chimpanzees: A Laboratory Colony. New Haven, Conn.: Yale University and Oxford University Presses.

——. 1963. Creating a Chimpanzee Community. [Edited from archival materials by Roberta W. Yerkes.] Yale Journal of Biology and Medicine 36:205–23.

Yerkes, Robert M., and Ada W. Yerkes. 1929. The Great Apes. New Haven, Conn.: Yale University Press.

Young, F. G. 1970. The Evolution of Ideas about Animal Hormones. In Joseph Needham (Ed.), The Chemistry of Life: Lectures on the History of Biochemistry, 125–55. Cambridge: Cambridge University Press.

Young, William C. 1927. The Influence of High Temperature on the Guinea-Pig Testis. Journal of Experimental Zoology 49:459–62, 489–99.

——. 1929. The Influence of High Temperature on the Reproductive Capacity of Guinea Pig Spermatozoa Determined by Means of Artificial Insemination. Physiological Zoology 2:1.

——. 1931. A Study of the Function of the Epididemis. British Journal of Experimental Biology 8:151.

——. 1961. Edgar Allen, 1892–1943. In William C. Young (Ed.), Sex and Internal Secretions, vol. 1:xiii–xix. 3d ed. Baltimore, Md.: Williams and Wilkins.

—— (Ed.). 1961. Sex and Internal Secretions. 2 vols. 3d ed. Baltimore, Md.: Williams and Wilkins.

Yoxen, E. 1982. Giving Life a New Meaning: The Rise of the Molecular Biology Establishment. In Norbert Elias, Herminio Martins, and Richard Whitley (Eds.), The Rise of the Molecular Biology Establishment, 123–44. Boston: D. Reidel.

Zelizer, Viviana. 1994. Pricing the Priceless Child: The Changing Social Value of Children. Princeton, N.J.: Princeton University Press.

Zinn, Earl F. 1923. National Research Council Committee for Research on Sex Problems. Journal of the American Medical Association 81:1811–12.

——. 1924. History, Purpose and Policy of the National Research Council's Committee for Research on Sex Problems. Mental Hygiene 8:94–105.

Zola, Irving Kenneth. 1976. Medicine as an Institution of Social Control. Sociological Review 20:487–504.

Zondek, Bernhard. 1934a. Mass Excretion of Oestrogenic Hormone in the Urine of the Stallion. Nature 133:209.

——. 1934b. Oestrogenic Hormone in the Urine of the Stallion. Nature 133:494.

——. 1941. Clinical and Experimental Investigations on the Genital Functions and Their Hormonal Regulation. Baltimore, Md.: Williams and Wilkins.

——. 1956. Functional Significance of the Cervical Mucus. International Journal of Fertility 1:225.

Zondek, Bernhard, with S. Rozin. 1954a. Cervical Mucus Arborization: Its Use in Determination of Corpus Luteum Function. Obstetrics and Gynecology 3:463.

Zondek, Bernhard, with K. Cooper. 1954b. Cervical Mucus in Pregnancy. Obstetrics and Gynecology 4:484.

Zuckerman, Edward. 1987. How Now to Sell a Cow? New York Times Magazine, November 29, 68–69, 76, 78, 91.

Zuckerman, Harriet. 1989. The Sociology of Science. In Neil Smelser (Ed.), Handbook of Sociology, 511–74. Newbury Park, Calif.: Sage.

Zuckerman, Sir Solly. 1930. The Menstrual Cycle of the Primates. Part I: General Nature and Homology. Proceedings of the Zoological Society of London, October 22, 691–754.

———. 1959. Mechanisms Involved in Contraception. Science 30:1260–64.

———. 1970. Beyond the Ivory Tower: The Frontiers of Public and Private Science. New York: Taplinger.

———. 1978. From Apes to Warlords. New York: Harper and Row.

INDEX

Physiological Reviews, 140
Physiology, 32–33; chemistry and, 33; development of, 88, 260; reproduction and, 5, 11, 27, 64, 68, 70–72, 74, 137, 152, 260; sex and, 102
Physiology of Reproduction in the Cow (Hammond), 74
Physiology of Reproduction (Marshall), 5, 11, 27, 64, 68, 70–72, 137, 152, 260
Pidgin zones, 146
Pierpoint, R., 195, 197
"Pill." *See* Birth Control and contraception, oral contraceptives
Pincus, G., 5, 24, 79, 123, 144, 150–51, 174, 193–95, 220, 238, 249, 284
PL. *See* Prolactin
Planned Parenthood Federation of America (PPFA), 141, 173, 184–85, 194, 257
PMSG. *See* Pregnant male serum gonadotropin
Pomeroy, W., 53, 93
Population Association of America, 57, 180–81, 184
Population control, 6, 54–59. *See also* Birth control
Population Council, 58, 226, 247
Population Reference Bureau, 57
Postmodern reproduction, 10–11
Pottenger, F. M., 243
Potter, H., 285
Poultry Science, 42
Pregnancy diagnosis, 45
Pregnant male serum gonadotropin (PMSG), 4, 148
Preparation for Marriage (Heape), 70, 125
Price, D., 81, 124–26, 150
Problems of Fertilization (Lillie), 69
Problems of sex, 12, 90–118
Professionalization, 32, 41; and reproductive sciences, 139–45
Prolactin (PL), 133
Psychobiology, 33, 102, 104
Public Health Service, 210

Quackery, 242–48
Quarterly Journal of Experimental Physiology, 66

Race Betterment Conference, 184
Race Betterment Foundation, 57
Race suicide, 54

Radiation sterilization, 196–97
Ransom, S., 285
Rasmussen, W., 214
"Rational economic man," 276
Reagan, R., 257
Recent Progress in Hormone Research, 144
Rechter, J., 22, 65, 244
Reed, J., 54–55, 175, 177–80, 187–89, 191, 193–96, 217, 219, 226, 241, 250, 256
Reingold, N., 159–60
Reproduction, 8–9; gender and, 21–24, 272–73; heredity and, 71–72; modernism and, 9–12, 259; "natural," 234–35; postmodernism and, 10–12; production and, 9
Reproduction (Cohen), 156
Reproduction in the Rabbit (Hammond), 74, 153
Reproductive and Human Welfare: A Challenge to Research, 139
Reproductive research: aging for, 190–91; British, 69–74; birth control and, 200–206
Reproductive sciences, 9, 12, 91; Americans, 75–78; birth control and, 263; contraceptive technologies and, 185–200; controversy and, 233–58; development of, 18; developmental embryology and, 66–69; doability of, 85–88; foundation support for, 220–23; funding and, 207–30; illegitimacy and, 52–54, 264; intersectional structure of, 145–51; lateness and, 52–54; medical science and, 157; organizational development of, 145; professionalizing, 139–45; Roman Catholic and, 241; tensions and, 152–57
Reproductive scientists: controversies, 252; endocrinology and, 129; Rockefeller Foundation and, 221
Research, 224; biology and, 108; contraceptive, 186–90; endocrinology and, 108; fetal tissue research and, 250; major centers of, 227; pill and, 201; reproductive, 186–90; sexology and, 100; technosciences and, 12–13
Research in Reproduction, 141
Reynolds, S., 197, 199, 283
Riddle, O., 124, 143, 150, 167, 254
Robinson, T. J., 156
Rock, J., 125, 285
Rockefeller Foundation, 51, 90, 92, 106–8,

Compositor: J. Jarrett Engineering, Inc.
Text: 10/12 Baskerville
Display: Baskerville
Printer and Binder: Thomson-Shore, Inc.